GREEK FEDERAL STATES

GREEK FEDERAL STATES

Their Institutions and History

BY

J. A. O LARSEN

CLARENDON PRESS · OXFORD
1968

Oxford University Press, Ely House, London W. 1

GLASGOW NEW YORK TORONTO MELBOURNE WELLINGTON
CAPE TOWN SALISBURY IBADAN NAIROBI LUSAKA ADDIS ABABA
BOMBAY CALCUTTA MADRAS KARACHI LAHORE DACCA
KUALA LUMPUR HONG KONG TOKYO

PRINTED IN GREAT BRITAIN BY
SPOTTISWOODE, BALLANTYNE AND CO. LTD
LONDON AND COLCHESTER

PREFACE

The present work attempts to fill a real need. The last general account of the subject was E. A. Freeman's *History of Federal Government in Greece and Italy*, of which the first edition was published in 1863, and the second, edited by J. B. Bury, in 1893. Since then the field, except for special studies on individual states, has been left largely to the handbooks on constitutional history, notably those of Heinrich Swoboda and Georg Busolt. These muster a mass of material much of which was not yet accessible to Freeman. Yet even they did not include everything. Nor did they attempt the same broad treatment of the history of federal states that Freeman had given.

Meanwhile our knowledge of federalism has been increased particularly in three ways: through the discovery of papyrus manuscripts, through the publication of numerous inscriptions, and through the analysis of ancient writers, especially Polybius. The *Hellenica Oxyrhynchia*, fragments of a Greek history by an unknown author, has furnished a description of the governments of Boeotian cities and the Boeotian Confederacy, while there is hardly a confederacy which has not had one or more facets of its institutions or history illuminated by the discovery of inscriptions. As for Polybius, the chief literary source for Hellenistic federalism and the Roman wars in Greece, the past generation has witnessed a considerable advance in Polybian studies. This began with the articles and two books on the Achaean Confederacy published by the late André Aymard in 1938 and with the work of F. W. Walbank, starting with *Aratos of Sicyon* (1933), largely based on Polybius, and culminating in his *A Historical Commentary on Polybius*, still in progress (vol. i, 1957; ii, 1967). It is also gratifying to note that there is a new generation of scholars devoted to the study of Polybius. Prominent among them is Paul Pédech with *La Méthode historique de Polybe* (1964).

My own involvement with Greek federalism began in 1921. In spite of considerable work on a variety of details, the result is far from perfect, but it is to be hoped that it will prove helpful to future students and investigators. I owe a great deal of thanks to a host of friends and scholars, of whom only a very few have been mentioned above. To the Delegates of the Clarendon Press I owe warm thanks for the acceptance of the manuscript and to members of the staff and the compositors for considerate and careful work.

J. A. O. LARSEN

Columbia, Missouri
June, 1967

CONTENTS

ABBREVIATIONS

(Shortened titles of modern books, when easily recognized, are not included. Neither are the normal abbreviations for ancient authors and their works.)

ACA	A. Aymard, *Les Assemblées de la confédération achaienne*, 1938.
Acme	*Annali della Facoltà di Lettere e Filosofia dell' Università di Milano.*
AJA	*American Journal of Archaeology.*
AJP	*American Journal of Philology.*
ATL	B. D. Meritt, H. T. Wade-Gery, and M. F. McGregor, *The Athenian Tribute Lists*, 1939–53.
BCH	*Bulletin de correspondance hellénique.*
BSA	*Annual of the British School at Athens.*
Bull. ép.	J. and L. Robert, *Bulletin épigraphique* in *REG.*
CAH	*Cambridge Ancient History.*
CP	*Classical Philogy.*
FGrH	F. Jacoby, *Fragmente der griechischen Historiker.*
GdA	*Geschichte des Altertums.*
GrG	*Griechische Geschichte.*
IG	*Inscriptiones graecae.*
IGR	R. Cagnat and others, *Inscriptiones graecae ad res romanas pertinentes*, i, iii, and iv, 1906–27.
PIR²	*Prosopographia Imperii Romani*, 2 ed.
MRR	T. R. S. Broughton, *The Magistrates of the Roman Republic.*
OCD	*Oxford Classical Dictionary.*
OG	Dittenberger, *Orientis graeci inscriptiones selectae*, 1903–05.
RE	Pauly, Wissowa, and others, *Realenzyklopädie der klassischen Altertumswissenschaft.*
Riv. fil.	*Rivista di filologia e di istruzione classica.*
REA	*Revue des études anciennes.*
REG	*Revue des études grecques.*
SIG³	Dittenberger, *Sylloge inscriptionum graecarum*, 3 ed., 1915–24.
SEG	*Supplementum epigraphicum graecum.*
SGDI	H. Collitz and others, *Sammlung der griechischen Dialektinschriften*, 1884–1915.
TAM	*Tituli Asiae Minoris.*
TAPA	*Transactions and Proceedings of the American Philological Association.*

INTRODUCTION: THE NATURE OF
A GREEK FEDERAL STATE

THE statement which follows would be almost equally appropriate as a part of the conclusion of the book, but it is impossible to follow an account of the history and accomplishments of Greek federal states without some knowledge of the nature of such a state. For that reason it is placed first, but it is based on material culled from the accounts concerning various states given below. Possibly it contains enough to satisfy the curiosity of readers who take no special interest in ancient history. Scholars in other fields of social studies should be warned that there are questions that cannot be answered because the evidence is lacking, and other questions for which the evidence is so scattered and difficult that it may take a lifetime to discover it. Here 'discover' is used intentionally instead of 'muster', for the more difficult problems are often such that one cannot muster the evidence but must wait until it is discovered as a result of long and varied investigations or, equally often, of accident when some evidence almost forces itself upon the attention of the investigator.

It is hardly necessary to say that the reason for the shortage of information concerning the federal states is the extent to which ancient political thought was dominated by the city-state. There is reason to believe that Aristotle or his pupils wrote descriptions of the governments of a number of federal states[1] and understood the nature of such states.[2] If one of these descriptions had been preserved, we should probably have had for one Greek federal state something corresponding to Aristotle's *Constitution of the Athenians*, though it is unlikely that other constitutions were described at as great length as that of Athens. As things are, the best description we have of the government of a Greek federal state is the short description of the government of the Boeotian Confederacy given in the *Hellenica Oxyrhynchia*. Moreover, if Aristotle studied and described the governments of federal states, this has scarcely left any mark on his *Politics*. Yet Aristotle's failure to give adequate attention to the federal state is much less surprising than the failure of Polybius to do so.

If there was any Greek writer from whom an account of federalism could be expected, it was precisely Polybius. His father, Lycortas, was a prominent Achaean statesman who served as general or president of the Confederacy more than once. In addition, he was the right hand

---

[1] *CP* xl (1945), 74 and n. 55.   [2] Ibid. 78, n. 72.

man of Philopoemen, who, after the death of Aratus in 213 B.C., became the leading statesman of the Confederacy. Polybius was early associated with his father in Achaean politics. The relation of the two to Philopoemen is indicated by the facts that, when the latter was killed in Messenia in 182, Lycortas was elected general to fill out the rest of his term of office, and, when Lycortas arranged to have the ashes of Philopoemen brought home in state, Polybius carried the urn. For the early period of the history of the Confederacy after its revival in 280, Polybius relied on the recollections of older Achaeans and above all on the memoirs of Aratus. Nor does it seem that his relation to Aratus entirely lacked the personal touch. The Aratus, son of Aratus of Sicyon, who in 181 was selected ambassador to go to Egypt with Lycortas and Polybius—an embassy which did not materialize— was in all likelihood the grandson of the great Aratus. At the time Polybius probably was selected ambassador as his father's son, but later he became prominent in his own right and in 170–169 served as hipparch or, we might say, vice-president of the Confederacy. Nor did the fact that he later developed a great admiration for Rome prevent him from remaining an Achaean first, last, and all the time. This statement may be challenged on the grounds that Polybius was first and foremost a citizen of Megalopolis and by descent an Arcadian, and that he often passed judgement on men and events from the point of view of an Arcadian or a Megalopolitan. True enough, but to Polybius the Arcadians were citizens of the new Achaean nation and Megalopolis a member of the Achaean Confederacy.

The extent to which the history of Polybius is coloured by his Achaean point of view is easily overlooked by those who use it chiefly as a source for Roman history. It is easy to concentrate on Rome and to consider the information about Achaean and other Greek affairs merely as troublesome details connected with the Roman expansion in the Balkans. Yet all that should be needed to bring out the Achaean point of view is a rather rapid reading of the first two books. It is not necessary to say that this will reveal that the main topic is a success story, the success of Rome, but second place is given to another success story, that of the Achaean Confederacy, which succeeded far beyond any predecessor in uniting the Peloponnesus. This statement must have been written before the dismemberment of the Achaean Confederacy in 145 and at a time when Polybius intended to carry his narrative only through the Third Macedonian War.[1]

His Achaean point of view is shown in another way. The rise of the Achaeans and their unification of the Peloponnesus inspires the first

---

[1] Pol. ii. 37, especially sections 8–11; cf. Walbank, *Commentary* on 37. 8.

important disquisition on causation. Otherwise the first two books emphasize more the play of fate and reversals of fortune, and it must be admitted that the First Punic War is exceptionally well suited to such an approach. Another incident which accords with this treatment is the siege of Medeon, during which the Aetolians, the very day before the siege was raised by the Illyrians, debated about the inscription to be placed on the spoils they expected to take. On the other hand, when Polybius came to the rise of the Achaeans, he remarked that it would not be proper but rather cheap to attribute this to chance; it was better to seek the cause. This he found in the excellence of the 'democratic' institutions and particularly in the practice of giving equal rights to new members and reserving no special privileges for the original members. Thus, as in the case of Rome, the cause is to be found in the excellency of the polity, the form of government or constitution.

On the basis of such cases as these it seems natural to ask whether there is anything more mysterious behind Polybius' habit of sometimes emphasizing the play of chance and sometimes the utility of the study of causation than a tendency to be dominated by the material on hand. When there are startling reversals of fortune, Tyche is given a curtain call; when the situation lends itself to an analysis of causes, there follows a disquisition about the utility of the study of causation. Except for the outbreak of major wars, the chief occasions for such studies seem to be furnished by long-range developments such as the rise of Rome, the rise of the Achaeans, and the evolution of forms of government.

Polybius, while aware that the Achaean Confederacy was a federal state, tends to apply to it terms which could equally well be applied to city-states and to characterize the unification of the Peloponnesus by the Achaeans—undoubtedly inaccurately—as being almost as complete as that of a city-state. Yet he recognizes that what resulted from the adoption of the Achaean government and name by Arcadians, Laconians, and others was not a city-state but a nation (*ethnos*), which practically means that it was a federal state. Otherwise he too, like all ancient political theorists, was dominated by the idea of the city-state. He gives no analysis of federalism, gives very little information about the differences between the governments of various confederacies, and does not mention federalism in his account of forms of government in his sixth book. He does give considerable information about the government of the Achaean Confederacy and a little about that of the Aetolians, but this comes in incidental remarks and has often proved difficult to interpret. He does not seem to have written any general description of the Achaean government aside from what little is contained in his account of the early history of the Confederacy. This is probably because he wrote primarily for those who did not need such information. He did somewhat better for the Macedonian republics established in 167, but this compensates only to a slight degree for his failure to give more information concerning the leading Greek federal states. Whatever the reason, the fact remains that the ancient writer best qualified to give an analysis of Greek federalism has failed to do so.

This in turn means that our knowledge of Greek federalism is built up of odds and ends in literary sources and inscriptions. It is somewhat fuller for the narrative history than for the institutions; for the latter indeed its extent depends pretty much on chance. The statements given in this chapter will be based on the accounts given below in greater detail. Therefore, it will not be documented except for points that receive their chief treatment in it. It is to be hoped that this pre-liminary survey will make what follows easier to understand and that, in some cases, it may help to make conclusions drawn from scanty evi-dence more readily accepted when the reader knows in advance that there is evidence for similar usages in other federal states.

Before proceeding to the description of Greek federal states, it may be well to say a word about terminology.[1] The reader may have noticed that the term 'Achaean Confederacy' has been used instead of the more common 'Achaean League'. This form has been adopted in order to have a term which will distinguish a true federal state from a looser organization. Throughout the present work 'confederacy' will be applied to federal states and 'league' to looser organizations. From our point of view the most important of the latter are the symmachies, the permanent alliances of the type of the Peloponnesian and Delian leagues and the Hellenic League, commonly called the Corinthian League, presided over by the Macedonian kings. Then there are also the amphictionies, in which the emphasis is more on religion and the maintenance of cults. The choice of terms, of course, is purely arbit-rary. In Greek any of these organizations could be called a *koinon*, a word which could be used about almost any kind of association. It goes without saying that it is sometimes difficult to know just how to classify an organization and, therefore, whether to call it a league or a con-federacy. When applied to a federal state, *koinon* means the common-wealth, or the federal state or government, often in opposition to the local community or government. Another word frequently used is *ethnos*, a word which is commonly translated 'tribe' but which, when applied to a federal state, can best be rendered by 'nation'. On the superficial reading of documents, the two words often seem inter-changeable, and they are interchangeable in the sense that a statement

[1] Cf. the discussion in Larsen, *Representative Government in Greek and Roman History* (1955), 23–25.

about the Achaean or the Lycian Confederacy is equally true whether the confederacy is called *koinon* or *ethnos*, but close reading will reveal that the two words have different connotations or overtones. The one indicates the state, commonwealth, or federal government; the other, the nation or people of the state. A third word applied to a federal state or its citizenship, *sympoliteia*, refers to the sharing of citizenship and thus is the most technical of the three terms. True, it can be applied also to the merging of two cities into one with a single citizenship. However, when it is applied to an organization in which there are several cities and a joint central government, it is enough to indicate that we are dealing with a federal state.[1]

In defining a federal state it is scarcely necessary to go farther than to say that it is a state in which there is a local citizenship in the smaller communities as well as a joint or federal citizenship and in which the citizens are under the jurisdiction both of federal and local authorities. Since there existed in early Greece tribal groupings too loose to be called federal states, probably the clearest proof to be found for the existence of a sympolity consists of records of grants of citizenship simultaneously by local and federal authorities. Almost equally convincing is the application of the word *sympoliteia* to an organization embracing a number of cities. There may also be cases in which the existence of both local and federal citizenship is proved more indirectly simply by the functioning of the two sets of authorities.

The local units of federal states could be either cities or tribes, but cities were the more common for the simple reason that the city-state was the most widely prevalent political unit among the ancient Greeks. These city-states were so small that only a few of the largest, such as Athens and later Rhodes, could hope to have an independent foreign policy, and these tended to impose their leadership on lesser states. The stories of Corcyra and Corinth just before and during the early part of the Peloponnesian War as told by Thucydides illustrate the situation.[2] Corinth tried to exercise leadership over a group of allies mainly consisting of colonies she had founded, but she was wordly wise enough to retain membership in the Peloponnesian League. Within the latter she was not always the subservient ally but at times adopted a balance of power policy to prevent Sparta from becoming too strong. Thus she claimed to have opposed intervention by the Peloponnesian League against Athens at the time of the revolt of Samos. How she later practically threatened Sparta with secession from the League if the

---

[1] One of the best sources for a study of the use of the three terms is an inscription from Araxa in Lycia (*SEG* xviii. 570). For a discussion cf. *CP* li (1956), 151–69.

[2] Some of the details concerning Corinth are discussed in *CP* xliv (1949), 259 f. in a review of A. W. Gomme, *Commentary on Thucydides*, vol. i.

latter would not intervene against Athens at a time when Corinth desired the intervention is known to all readers of Thucydides. One of the cities over which Corinth wished to exercise leadership was Corcyra. The latter for some time tried to have an independent foreign policy, that is, she opposed the leadership of Corinth and, in addition, remained outside the Peloponnesian and Delian leagues. Only when involved in war did Corcyra approach Athens and even then in the spirit of a state strong enough to bargain and to accompany the offer of an alliance with threats concerning what might follow if the offer were rejected. The results of the alliance which followed were disastrous and particularly so for Corcyra. Her experiences at the time undoubtedly explain the fact that the city is never known to have had a really independent policy thereafter and later became a subservient free city under Roman protection. Most small cities did not need such an experience. They knew that they could not live alone but had to co-operate with others and, when they broke with one organization, it was in order to join another. Yet, while they knew that they must have connexions with others, they also wished to retain their own independence. For that reason, it seems, they preferred to join symmachies, alliances which were formed for co-operation in war and foreign policy and in theory recognized the independence of their members. Such organizations were not but might have developed into federal states.

Thus the tendency towards union did not necessarily produce federal states, though the latter may trace their beginnings far back. The federal states developed from tribal units or groups, such as the Boeotians, Achaeans, Aetolians, and Arcadians. Where there was a feeling of tribal kinship, some tradition of co-operation in war, or a special religious cult kept up by the group, it was natural enough, when cities grew up, for a federal state to develop. Such states were usually small and apparently did not normally go beyond the boundary of the tribal unit, though exceptions to this rule began earlier and were more numerous than we used to believe. The Achaeans went beyond the ethnic boundary early in the fourth century, the Chalcidians of Thrace probably already in the fifth century, and it is not certain that all cities that belonged to the Boeotian Confederacy in the same century considered themselves Boeotians. Naturally the members of such widely scattered tribes as the Ionians and the Dorians were never all united in a single federal state. The Ionian League, which was probably an incipient federal state,[1] included only cities on the coast of Asia Minor and adjoining islands. Thus prerequisites for the formation of federal states were both a feeling of kinship and geographical

[1] Larsen, *Rep. Govt.* 27–30; C. A. Roebuck, *CP* l (1955), 26–40; *Ionian Trade and Colonization* (1959), 28–31.

propinquity. States might make alliances with more distant cities of another tribe but did not readily combine with them in the closer bonds of federalism. Nevertheless, to create federal states of any considerable size and power, it was necessary to overstep the ethnic boundary and admit members of other tribes. This was done most successfully by the Achaeans, but even so the Achaean Confederacy at its greatest extent was a petty state compared with the great empires of antiquity. Thus all that can be said is that Greek federalism proved reasonably successful on a small scale. Probably the largest federal state of antiquity was the short-lived organization of Rome's revolting allies during the Marsic War. There were large organizations also in the Roman Empire, notably the Commonality of the Three Gauls with headquarters at the altar area near Lugdunum, but such organizations were not federal states and we do not possess enough information to know whether there were intelligent discussions in the assembly of problems which concerned the entire Commonality.[1] The poor means of communications in antiquity would have been a great obstacle to the successful functioning of federal government on a large scale.

To bring out more clearly the nature of federal institutions, it may be well to sketch briefly the institutions of the quasi-federal permanent alliances.[2] By seeing to what extent the federal states went beyond the institutions of these symmachies, it will be easier to estimate their progress. In the symmachies the executive department was at first in the hands of the state wielding the hegemony or leadership of the league, for instance Sparta in the Peloponnesian and Athens in the Delian and Second Athenian League. Any administrative officials needed were supplied by this city. This was true even of the *Hellenotamiai*, the treasurers of the Delian League, at least after the removal of the treasury to Athens.[3] A change came with the Hellenic League of Philip II and his successors in that the king held the hegemony. Another change seen clearly in the Hellenic League was probably first adopted in the Second Athenian League organized in 378. In the Hellenic League a committee of five presiding officers called *proëdroi* served as chairmen of the assembly, had a part in determining when and where extraordinary meetings were to be called, and issued the summons to all meetings both regular and irregular. The *proëdroi*

---

[1] On these organizations see *Rep. Govt.*, ch. vii.

[2] A somewhat fuller sketch is given in *Rep. Govt.*, ch. iii. For a detailed argument attempting to prove that the Hellenic League of 338 was not a symmachy, see T. T. B. Ryder, *Koine Eirene* (1965), 150–62. In spite of Ryder (p. 158) I still find the argument from *SIG*³ 665 convincing.

[3] A. G. Woodhead, *JHS* lxxix (1959), 149–53, argues convincingly that at first the assembly had a voice in the selection of both the *Hellenotamiai* and the particular Athenian generals who were to command the allied fleet.

b

further had the task of preparing the material to be presented to the assembly. Others who had matters to lay before the assembly were to present the material in written form to the *proëdroi*. Thus their activities began before the meetings. They also continued after the meetings, for it was the duty of the *proëdroi* to see to it that the secretaries correctly recorded the measures adopted. All this implies that they were the heads of a small permanent bureaucracy.[1] This at least was the plan. Whether it functioned continuously for any length of time is another question. The seat of the bureaucracy and the capital of the League must have been Corinth, though the meetings of the assembly were not always held there.

To return to the federal states, the great question is whether they went so far beyond the symmachies as really to deserve the name. Did the cities actually co-operate much except in war? Or did they otherwise go their own way? Did the citizens in one community of the confederacy possess civil rights within the others or did the cities treat each other as foreign countries? In general it can be said that institutions were not uniform in all Greek federal states but that they were unified and centralized far more than the symmachies. Thus, while in the normal city-state outsiders could not acquire land unless they had been given the special right to do so known as *enktesis*, in a normal federal state citizens possessed this right in all the cities of the confederacy. In some of the federal states organized under Roman patronage there were restrictions, but this was the exception and not the rule.[2]

[1] Information about the *proëdroi* is derived mainly from *IG* iv². 1. 68, an inscription found at Epidaurus which gives the constitution of the Hellenic League as refounded in 302 B.C. by Demetrius Poliorcetes. At the time the *proëdroi* were delegates of the king and were to continue to be so as long as the current war lasted. What is given above is a description of their position in time of peace. This is done on the theory that this was the original system of Philip II later modified by Demetrius for the duration of the war in which he was engaged. Of course, under Demetrius the permanent or peace-time system was never used. The publication by E. Schweigert in *Hesperia* ix (1940), 348, no. 45 of an Athenian decree honouring Adeimantus of Lampsacus has given rise to a group of articles discussing the *proëdroi*. The evidence of this inscription has shown that it is necessary to abandon a theory once defended by myself (*CP* xx (1925), 328) that the *proëdroi* appointed by the king were chosen from among the representatives of the member states. They were rather the delegates of the king. See especially L. Robert, 'Adeimantos et la Ligue de Corinthe', *Hellenica*, ii (1946), 15–33 and G. Daux, 'Adeimantos de Lampsaque et le renouvelement de la Ligue de Corinthe par Demetrios Poliorcète', *Arch. ephem.* (1953–4), 245–54.

[2] For the study of problems connected with Greek citizenship, E. Szanto, *Das griechische Bürgerrecht* (1892) remains important. He maintains (p. 150) that federal citizenship included the civil rights of citizenship in all states within a confederacy. So also H. Francotte, *La Polis grecque* (1907), 151; Beloch, *GrG²* iv. i (1925), 604; H. Swoboda, *Staatsaltertümer* (1913), 209. The latter, however, changed his mind and expressed the opposite view in 'Zwei Kapitel aus dem griechischen Bundesrecht', *Sitzungsberichte*, Vienna, 199, 2 (1924). Such an act by so keen and candid a scholar was very impressive, and his detailed argumentation at first sight convincing. This time, however, he was wrong, and two refutations written independently soon appeared, namely, W. Kolbe, 'Das griechische Bundesbürgerrecht der hellenistischen

Thus there was an economic advantage in belonging to a federal state which there was not in a symmachy. In a symmachy, the members might receive protection and possibly some preferential treatment from other members. On the whole, however, there were no greater privileges for citizens of a member state than for other foreigners, and any special privileges had to be arranged by negotiations and treaties. In a federal state, on the other hand, citizens of one city could own land in any state within the confederacy and conduct business there on the same terms as its own citizens. With this went also the right of intermarriage, though it must be admitted that direct evidence is very scarce before the Roman period, when intermarriages became common not only within federal states but also beyond their boundaries.[1]

The political rights of local citizenship, voting and holding office, naturally could be exercised by a citizen only in one of the cities of a federal state, normally his native city. Likewise political rights of federal citizens were exercised by them as citizens of the same community, just as the citizenship within a city was exercised through membership in one of the subdivisions of the citizen body. Thus a citizen of a federal state could vote for representatives of his home community in the federal council, and it stands to reason that normally he was not allowed to do this in more than one city. If he attended a federal council or assembly, he did so as a representative or citizen of a particular community. This is obvious for representative assemblies, but holds good also for primary assemblies. When such assemblies

---

Zeit', *Zeitschrift der Savigny-Stiftung*, il (1929), 129–54 and W. Schwahn, 'Das Bürgerrecht der sympolitischen Bundesstaaten bei den Griechen', *Hermes*, lxvi (1931), 97–118. See further Larsen, 'Lycia and Greek Federal Citizenship', *Symbolae Osloenses*, xxxiii (1957), 5–26, adding to the evidence used by other scholars the evidence from Lycia. Cf. also Bengtson, *GrG*² 442 and n. 2; Ehrenberg, *Staat*, 155 (*Gk. State*, 127). The latter, and apparently also Bengtson, goes too far in including political rights throughout all cities.

[1] There is some interesting evidence for the Lycian Confederacy in Roman times, particularly in the genealogical inscription from Oenoanda (*IGR* iii. 500; references are given below by sections and lines). Licinnius Thoas of Oenoanda married as his second wife Flavia Platonis of Cibyra (ii. 34–38); Iulia Lysimache, daughter of Iulius Antoninus of Oenoanda was married to Claudius Dryantianus of Patara (ii. 60–65); Licinnia Ge, daughter of Licinnius Longus of Oenoanda, was married twice, first to Titus Flavius Claudius Capito of Pinara and next to Marcus Claudius Flavianus of Cadyanda (iii. 70–79); her son by her first marriage, Titus Flavius Titianus Capito of Pinara, took as his wife Baebia Anassa of Patara; their daughter, Flavia Lycia, was married to Simonides of Oenoanda (iv. 1–11), thus returning to the city of her great-grandfather; Licinnia Ge's son by her second marriage, Claudius Longus of Cadyanda, married Mettia Cleonis of Xanthus (v. 3–6). Except for Cibyra, all cities mentioned were members of the Lycian Confederacy, and, except for Simonides, all individuals mentioned were also Roman citizens. Within circles such as this, apparently, wives were often taken from other cities, and one would think that there was little local patriotism. Yet, if one of these men were to speak of his *patris*, the chances are that he would refer to the city to which his family belonged; cf. p. xxi, n. 1 below. Some evidence of intermarriages in a still wider field in Roman times is given in 'A Thessalian Family under the Principate', *CP* xlviii (1953), 86–95 at 90 and 93 f.

existed in federal states, it became common to take the vote by cities, though this practice was not universal. Thus the Aetolians seem to have retained the old democratic system of counting the votes in their primary assembly by heads. Where the vote was taken by cities, the citizens of the various cities must have been grouped together and undoubtedly had their right to be present and vote checked by officials from their home community. Hence at the meeting of the Achaean *ekklesia* at Sicyon in 198 at which the Achaeans decided to break with Macedonia and go over to Rome, we learn that the contingents from certain cities withdrew from the meeting before the vote was taken. Therefore, if, for instance, an Achaean citizen moved from one city to another within the Confederacy and retained his registration in his former city, he could not be registered as a voter and could not exercise political rights in his new community. Thus a casualty list from Epidaurus for 146 B.C. shows that there were many Achaeans resident there who were not members of the local tribes (*phylai*). Since membership in these was necessary for voting, the Achaeans in question could not vote at Epidaurus and were not citizens of Epidaurus.[1] For military service, however, they were apparently brigaded with the citizens of the city in which they lived rather than of the city in which they exercised their citizenship. It is impossible, however, to say whether this was the normal practice or an emergency measure adopted, at the time.

It is possible, though not likely, that in some federal states a citizen possessed potential citizenship in all cities of the confederacy so that, if he wished, he could by registering transfer his active citizenship to any of them that he wished. When the federal government granted citizenship to an outsider, the new citizen undoubtedly had the right to assume local citizenship in one of the cities of the confederacy. There actually were cases in which citizenship was granted in all cities of the confederacy. For practical purposes this must have meant that the new citizen could pick whatever community he wished. When such a community had been selected, the new citizen remained a citizen of it permanently. Likewise, old citizens normally were expected to retain the local citizenship which they had inherited. Hence, for instance, if Achaeans moved from other cities to Epidaurus to go into business there, they could buy a home in their new community and would have the same civil rights as the local citizens. They might even serve in the local contingent in the Achaean army, but they remained voters and

---

[1] This fact, pretty much neglected in the literature on federal citizenship, was pointed out by K. Latte in *Gnomon*, vii (1931), 125 in a review of *IG* iv². 1. The casualty list is no. 28 in this volume.

citizens of the city of their fathers and could fill the normal political and administrative offices only there, though they undoubtedly could act as benefactors in other cities if they so wished.

Evidence from the Lycian Confederacy seems to confirm this interpretation, though the issue is somewhat confused by grants of honorary citizenship and by the local terminology. From the time of independence and into the second century of the Christian era it was common for prominent citizens to be honoured for having performed public services in all the cities of Lycia. They were also frequently honoured by grants of citizenship by cities belonging to the Confederacy. Nevertheless, they exercised active local citizenship only in their ancestral city. This city was what was meant when a citizen of a federal state spoke of his *patris*, as is attested both for Lycia and Achaea. The other citizenships were purely honorary. At the same time there is ample evidence to show that they possessed civil rights in all cities within the Confederacy.[1]

When we turn to the machinery of government, it is seen that the federal states possessed a more highly developed executive and offered more opportunities for quick action than the symmachies. There was, in the first place, a federal executive department which could be approached at any time of the year. The head of the state was usually a single official, though sometimes a larger group of officials filled the place. Thus, the Achaean Confederacy from 280 to 255 B.C. had two generals at its head, but thereafter one. The commonest title for the head was *strategos* or general, but here too there are exceptions. The Thessalians in the fourth century adopted a title with less warlike implications, namely, *archon*. In the Boeotian Confederacy the real leadership certainly belonged to the board of Boeotarchs. Nevertheless, in the fourth century a single *archon* is mentioned in the documents, though he appears to be little more than a figurehead. Yet the most common form of leadership was by a single official with the title of *strategos*. Alongside him there was some kind of group or board of magistrates which he could consult on decisions which could be made or had to be made without referring the question to an assembly. In the Achaean Confederacy the group contained the general himself, the hipparch or vice-president, and the ten *damiourgoi*; in Boeotia, the Boeotarchs served the purpose; in the Aetolian Confederacy apparently the larger secret council known as the *apokletoi*. Whether the secretary or secretaries were regular members it is difficult to say. Probably they had charge of the records and the government bureaux but did not have a voice in formulating executive decrees. For Lycia

---

[1] Cf. Larsen, 'Lycia and Greek Federal Citizenship', *Symbolae Osloenses*, xxxiii (1957), 5–26. It seems that Lycians often had close relations also with the city of their mothers.

we have evidence for the functioning of a cabinet of this kind—if we may call it that—but little information about its composition.

'Cabinet' actually seems to be the best name to apply to such bodies or committees. This institution is one of the chief contributions of Greek federalism to the development of Government. The reason is easy to see. In the city-state magistrates were responsible directly to the council and assembly, and, when necessary, could call a meeting even of the assembly on short notice. In federal states, the federal assembly met only a few times a year—two regular meetings a year in the Aetolian Confederacy, four in the Achaean—and extraordinary meetings were serious affairs and not to be thoughtlessly called. Even meetings of the council (*boule, synedrion*) were ponderous and involved attendance by men living at some distance. Therefore it became necessary to have some organ which could make decisions on actions that had to be taken without waiting for a meeting of one of these bodies. The earliest cabinet of the kind known to us is that of the Boeotarchs of the period 447–386 B.C., who, at the same time, were also the chief magistrates and the commanders of the army. Thus there was less specialization than, for instance, in the later Achaean Confederacy, in which the *damiourgoi* were distinct from the generals.

There is not a great deal known about the functioning of these cabinets, probably the best known being the *apokletoi* of the Aetolians, a body which was particularly active during wars. They, as a matter of fact, seem to have been a committee of the council (*boule, synedrion*), but this did not prevent them from acting as a federal executive committee. The smaller Achaean committee of *damiourgoi* and chief magistrates undoubtedly constituted the group which from time to time conferred with visiting Romans. Then when we hear, for instance, of a city within the Confederacy sending 'ambassadors' to 'the Achaeans' requesting exemption from the embargo on wheat, it is reasonably clear that this must have been granted by executive decree and not submitted to the assembly. Unfortunately we have little information concerning transactions of the kind, but there must have been numerous details settled by federal officials and boards. Larger questions were submitted to the federal council and/or assembly. Probably most federal states had possessed a council and an assembly, which frequently bore the same names as those of the city-states, namely, *boule* and *ekklesia*. The Boeotian Confederacy of 447–386 had no federal *ekklesia* but only a *boule* and thus possessed outright representative government. Later federal states returned to the use of primary assemblies, but they met infrequently, and consequently the *boule* and the magistrates had to decide much on their own authority. In the Aetolian Confederacy the primary assembly had two regular meetings a year; in the Achaean, apparently four. In addition extraordinary meetings could be summoned. When representative government was reintroduced shortly before 200 B.C., the Achaeans brought it into effect by ruling that the *ekklesia* was not to be summoned to the four regular meetings of the year but only to extraordinary meetings for major decisions on questions of foreign policy. The Lycians retained both *boule* and *ekklesia* but transformed the latter as well into a representative assembly. We know less about changes in other places. After 200 B.C. several new federal governments organized had no *ekklesia* but only a council. Examples are the Thessalian Confederacy organized after the Second Macedonian War and the four Macedonian republics set up in 167 B.C.

It has already been noted that the head of a federal state commonly bore the title of *strategos* or general, while the next highest official was the *hipparchos* or cavalry commander. In the frequent wars of the times these officials usually took the field themselves as commanders of the troops. Yet, where we have records, it is clear that there was a purely administrative official who ranked almost as high at least as the hipparch. This was the secretary of the confederacy. It seems significant that Polybius, when he describes the government of the Achaeans after the revival of their Confederacy in 280, states that they elected for a fixed term a federal secretary and two generals. Here the secretary comes first, and no hipparch is mentioned. Later the importance of the secretary is indicated by the fact that at times he was listed in documents as an eponymous magistrate. In Aetolia too the secretary—and later sometimes two secretaries—appears as eponymous magistrate either alone or with the general or with the general and hipparch. The so-called public secretary was important enough to be exempted, as well as the general and hipparch, in the treaty of 189 from service as hostage at Rome. In Lycia the federal secretaryship was an important office, and men took pride in holding it. Another federal official of some importance was the treasurer, but we know less about him than about the secretary. In fact in many cases in which problems of finance are mentioned, the title of the official handling the money is not given. It seems safe to conclude, however, that treasurers, like other officials, normally were annual officials. Unlike the secretary, the treasurer does not seem to have been an eponymous official, but that need not mean that he was less important. The name of the secretary of the year must have been useful, for instance, for identifying records in the archives. All these officials must have had a certain number of assistants and some place to keep their records, which suggests that there was some sort of capital and government offices.

Further evidence for the need of some sort of federal capital is supplied by the virtual certainty that most federal states possessed a board or boards of officials charged with the drafting of laws and responsible for having them recorded correctly. It is even possible that such officials were charged with bringing to trial magistrates who violated or disregarded the laws, much as the Areopagus did at Athens before 462. A little is known about the *nomothetai* of Athens but very little about the *nomographoi* and *nomophylakes* mentioned for several Greek states.[1] Probably the one single best piece of evidence concerning them is a statement by Cicero in *De legibus* (iv. 46–47) in which he laments that in Rome there was no authority responsible for seeing that the texts of laws were preserved correctly. Instead the laws were whatever the attendants wished, thus implying that the clerks were careless or arbitrary in reporting the texts of laws. The Greeks did better. They had *nomophylakes* who not only kept watch on the text of the laws but also took action against individuals who disregarded the laws. This seems to imply that the *nomophylakes* exercised a certain guardianship of the laws. Cicero's proposal is that at Rome the task should be taken over by the censors, and that censors were to be in office continuously. He adds, however, that the Greek experience had shown that volunteer prosecutors were more effective than officials. This may mean that more irregularities had been checked by suits corresponding to the Athenian *graphe paranomon* than by the action of official guardians of the law. Yet, it is clear that in the Greece known to Cicero, such officials were common. It so happens that not *nomophylakes* but *nomographoi* and periodic revisions of the laws are known for the Achaean, Aetolian, and Acarnanian confederacies. This suggests that it was common in federal states to have such a board which functioned in connexion with the drawing up and revising of laws. The relatively great size of the Achaean board indicates that it was an important body. Nevertheless, as in other states, it was probably essentially a committee and the laws proposed by it probably were submitted to the federal council or assembly or both.[2] Alongside of the *nomographoi* there probably were also *nomophylakes* as there were at Cyrene. In any case the prevalence

---

[1] Not much has been added to the account of H. Francotte in the first chapter of his *Mélanges de droit public grec* (1910). The most important evidence that has come to light after its publication is probably *SEG* ix. 1, which shows that in the late fourth century Cyrene had nine *nomophylakes* and five or more—probably more—*nomographoi*.

[2] For comparison note that for the Athenian law against tyranny of 337–336 B.C. (*SEG* xii. 87; Pouilloux, *Choix*, no. 32; for further literature cf. *SEG* xv. 95; xvii. 26, xviii. 12) the *nomothetai*, as it were, drew up the *probouleuma* which afterwards was submitted to the people. Note also that in a letter of Antigonus Monophthalmus concerning a proposed synoecism of Teos and Lebedus, it is suggested that six *nomographoi* be selected to draw up laws which afterwards are to be submitted to the united *demos* of the synoecized community (*SIG*³ 344 (Welles, *Royal Correspondence*, no. 3), 44–50).

of *nomographoi* warns us to minimize neither federal laws and legislation nor federal administrative machinery.

Little is known about the staff of aides or subordinate clerks in the various branches of administration. This is not surprising when it is recalled how little is known about such functionaries in city-states. Almost all that it is possible to say is that they must have existed. In accordance with what seems to have been normal ancient practice, they probably were state slaves.[1] Thus there was enough administration to require a federal capital of sorts whether the federal council or assembly met there or not. In the Boeotian Confederacy the capital was Thebes; in the Arcadian, Megalopolis; in the Aetolian, Thermum; in the Achaean, Aegium; in the Lycian, Patara. As a matter of fact, the realization that there must be some way of communicating with the government, and some place where messages could be received, was older than Greek federalism. It is illustrated by the Athenian rule that one third of the *prytaneis* must be available at the *tholos* day and night.[2]

The two departments of the federal government about which we hear the most are the treasury—but not the treasurer—and the army. The commonest practice of the treasury department was to make collections depend on needs. This meant that assessments were normally heavy during wars but might be lightened if a great deal of booty were taken. The method followed was for the federal government to assess contributions upon the members in proportion to their representation in the federal council. The money was then collected by the local authorities and trasmitted by them to the federal treasury. This method of handling the finances is attested first for the Boeotian Confederacy of 447–386. At about the same time in certain other states there was a beginning of a system of direct taxes or income for the federal government. In the Chalcidic and Thessalian confederacies custom duties were collected for the federal government, but it was the Boeotian system which seems to have won general acceptance. It is attested clearly for Aetolia and Lycia and more indirectly for Achaea. For the latter state there is abundant proof that the cities collected and sent in their contributions. In 219 Dyme, Pharae, and Tritaea withheld their contributions and instead used the money for hiring mercenaries. Polybius (iv. 60) commends them for hiring mercenaries but condemns the withholding of contributions from the federal government. His statement implies that such extra expenses as those for the

---

[1] On state slaves see W. L. Westermann, *The Slave Systems of Greek and Roman Antiquity* (Philadelphia: The American Philosophical Society, 1955), 9 f. for Greece, 70 f. for Rome. The great development of the use of slaves and freedmen under the Empire (102 ff.) has less bearing on the problem.

[2] Arist. *Ath. pol.* 44. 1.

mercenaries could be recovered from the federal treasury. The next year Philip V of Macedonia came to the aid of the Achaeans. The latter voted him fifty talents to be paid at once as pay to his army for three months and seventeen talents for each additional month's campaigning in the Peloponnesus. Apparently, when they felt that they got their money's worth, the Achaeans were quite ready to pay. When the Macedonians returned home and the inefficient and unpopular Achaean general, Eperatus, was on his own, discipline broke down completely and the cities of the Confederacy were disinclined to send in their contributions. The demoralization continued till his successor, Aratus, took over in the summer of 217 and induced the Achaeans to engage a large force of mercenaries and to mobilize in addition a force of Achaeans. This must mean that, with confidence restored, the cities once more were ready to pay, but, as it happened, the season's campaigns brought in so much booty that they began to hope that not too much would have to be collected after all. It looks as if the money collected was mostly for military expenses and primarily for hiring mercenary soldiers. From the Achaean point of view the money paid the Macedonians was pretty much in the same category. If this is true, a federal state in which the citizens did most of their own fighting, such as the Aetolian Confederacy, need not collect any huge sums. All federal states, of course, had a certain amount of expenses even in time of peace and so something was collected every year.

Ancient states, as far as finances go, fell into two classes, those which accumulated reserves and those which did not. The first class drew on their reserves for unusual expenses; the second class, at least in theory, raised extra taxes or contributions to meet emergencies. There was no third way, since there was no opportunity to negotiate large loans or to finance wars by means of bonds.[1] Our federal states belonged to the class of states which did not accumulate reserves. This should not be held against them. So did the Roman Empire, which, no matter what it may have tried to do, never accumulated any reserve adequate for a major emergency. Moreover the failure of the Greek federal states to accomplish more than they did, does not seem to have been due to any great extent to their loose finances. They made mistakes enough, but their chief mistake was that they were so much smaller and weaker than the chief contemporary states. The practice of accumulating reserves by collecting normally more than was spent belonged essentially to monarchies, not only Persia but also other ancient monarchies including Macedonia. Thus it may be no accident that the federal states

---

[1] When Athens borrowed from Athene and other gods, these loans were loans only in name. Actually it was a case of the use of accumulated reserves.

which did have some direct federal collection of taxes, namely Thessaly and the Chalcidic Confederacy, were neighbours of monarchies.

The army was run on similar principles. It was composed of contingents from the various cities under the command of local officers with the central command in the hands of federal officials. At Delium in 424 the commander-in-chief of the Boeotians did not even decide how the troops of the various contingents were to be drawn up; the Thebans were drawn up twenty-five deep, the rest as they wished. The local authorities thus had a three-fold task, to provide contingents to the federal army, to maintain the permanent guard of the walls and gates of the city, and to defend the territory outside the walls against raids by robbers and pirates and sudden attacks by more official enemies. Thus about 200 B.C. Araxa in Lycia carried on regular wars against a robber baron and nearby cities, once even negotiating a peace or cessation of hostilities. In this case the federal government gave only diplomatic support and treated the fighting as border incidents. Achaean cities too at times acted on their own. Thus 204–201 there seem to have been border incidents between Megalopolis and Sparta arising out of the theft of a horse belonging to the Spartan tyrant Nabis. Two Boeotians—probably mercenary soldiers—and a groom had run off with his finest horse and fled to Megalopolis. When agents of Nabis followed in pursuit, the city allowed them to take back the horse and groom but not the Boeotians. Nabis retaliated by raiding and carrying off flocks. Then, when he in 201 attacked Messene, Philopoemen and the Megalopolitans came to the aid of the city. After that the Achaeans went to war with Nabis. That was the occasion of the secret mobilization of the entire Achaean army.

The quality of an army made up of contingents from various cities naturally would depend partly on the training and military system and partly on the morale and the confidence or lack of confidence of the local authorities in the federal commanders. The army of the Achaean Confederacy was often inefficient and lost many battles. Sometimes too it seems to have depended chiefly on mercenary troops rather than on citizen soldiers. At least in 219 B.C. some of the cities in disgust took matters into their own hands and engaged mercenaries themselves instead of depending on the federal authorities. And yet the citizens of the Confederacy were good military material. The Achaeans proper were efficient light armed troops, and particularly produced excellent slingers. They are said to have been better than the Balearic islanders. They could hit, so we are told, not only the head of an enemy but any part of the face they wished. Achaeans appear fairly often as mercenary soldiers serving abroad, but they lacked heavy armed troops suitable for pitched battles. Of the other citizens, it is unnecessary to say that both Dorians and Arcadians were excellent soldiers, but the Achaean system, if it can be called that, prevailed to the extent that the Confederacy was short of troops of the line. This was all changed with the military reforms of Philopoemen in 209 and 208 B.C. In 207 the Achaeans were able to defeat the Spartans in a pitched battle at Mantinea. The efficiency lasted for some time. In 201 Philopoemen was able to mobilize the entire army at Tegea without revealing the purpose of the mobilization and without allowing more time than just enough for all to reach their destination on the appointed day. At that time the Achaeans must have had an army ready for mobilization at a moment's notice. This must have consisted of all eligible men of a certain age group.[1] The men were to leave home with supplies and money for five days. In 197 the Macedonian commander at Corinth, who had 6,000 troops under his command, naturally was not afraid of the Achaean contingent of 2,000 infantry and 100 cavalry stationed at that time at Sicyon, but the Achaean general mobilized the contingents of the neighbouring cities, staged a surprise attack, and won a decisive victory.[2]

From the nature of the case in general and from what has been stated above, it is clear that in the division of labour between local and federal authorities, foreign affairs and diplomacy belonged primarily to the federal government. Local authorities could at times send embassies abroad after securing permission from the federal authorities, as when the Megalopolitans secured permission from the Achaeans to send an embassy to Antigonus Doson. The juridical situation is not altered by the fact that Aratus, who was the Achaean general at the time, was the instigator of the embassy. Otherwise, when cities seem to take independent action in foreign affairs, this action usually turns out to be connected with some such innocuous matter as the recognition of a religious festival or of the inviolability of a sanctuary. In these cases the federal government apparently often had acted in advance. The securing of further decrees from the cities was largely a matter of ostentation. Real, often treasonable, communications with foreign authorities are to be found in embassies sent from cities to Rome—but that is another matter.

---

[1] According to Pol. xvi. 36. 3 the men mobilized were τοὺς ἐν ταῖς ἡλικίαις ... πάντας. This has been translated 'all of military age', but the actual mobilization must have been much less inclusive. In all likelihood the men mobilized were those of the age group liable to service on short notice. According to a statement which Polybius reports that he himself made in 168 (xxix. 24. 8) the Achaeans could mobilize thirty or forty thousand, but he implies that this had never been done.

[2] Livy, xxxiii. 14–15.

PART I

FEDERALISM BEFORE THE
KING'S PEACE

CHAPTER I
THE RISE OF FEDERALISM[1]

THE normal Greek federal state was a sympolity or federation of city-states which had developed with little or no direct break from one of the tribal states set up by a group of Greek conquerors. The city-states had grown up within the tribal state, but the latter had never completely lost its unity and at some point had been given a closer organization based on a union of cities or other local units. The change may have come gradually—certainly the growth of cities was a natural and gradual process, not always proceeding at the same rate within the entire tribal area—but the change was so great that some conscious constitutional reform or reforms must be presupposed. There was a change from a state in which the government handled very little except foreign affairs to one in which local affairs were in the hands of city governments and the latter in turn had definite financial and military obligations to the central government. Certainly the fixing of the number of votes of the members in the federal assembly or council and the determining of the size of their military contingents and financial obligations did not come automatically.[2] To be sure, it

[1] The study of Greek federalism was greatly advanced by the work of Edward A. Freeman. His account was first published in 1863 as *History of Federal Government from the Foundation of the Achaian League to the Disruption of the United States*, vol. i: *General Introduction—History of the Greek Federations*. This was the only volume published. It is now most readily available as *History of Federal Government in Greece and Italy*, 2 ed. by J. B. Bury, 1893. In this edition there were added two chapters of hitherto unpublished material on Italy and Germany. So many advances have been made since Bury edited the volume that it makes little difference which edition is used by students of Greek history. Rather subjective, rhetorical, and diffuse but brilliant, the book has never been displaced as a general account of Greek federalism and still remains important for the study of federalism in general. Unexcelled for its time as guide to the study of federal institutions was Heinrich Swoboda, *Lehrbuch der griechischen Staatsalter-tümer*, 1913 (vol. i, Part 3 of K. F. Hermann's *Lehrbuch der griechischen Antiquitäten*, 6 ed.). Valuable for bringing the bibliography more up to date is the section on federalism in Georg Busolt, *Griechische Staatskunde*, vol. i, 1920; vol. ii (edited by Swoboda), 1926. Of the shorter accounts that of V. Ehrenberg is particularly valuable, not least for its bibliography; the most recent editions are *The Greek State* (1960) and *Der Staat der Griechen*[2] (1965). Useful for its bibliography and perspective is also Hermann Bengtson, *Griechische Geschichte von den Anfängen bis in die Römische Kaiserzeit*, 2 ed., 1960. A brief but inclusive 'Survey of Greek Federal Coinage' is given by Caspari (Cary), *JHS* xxxvii (1917), 168–83. On the assemblies see also J. A. O. Larsen, *Representative Government in Greek and Roman History* (1955).

[2] On tribal states and their relation to federal states see *Rep. Govt.*, ch. ii. Important articles not yet available when this was written are Marta Sordi, 'Le origini del koinon etolico', *Acme*, vi (1953), fasc. 3 and Fritz Gschnitzer, 'Stammes- und Ortsgemeinden im alten Griechenland', *Wiener Studien*, lxviii (1955), 120–44. The two articles will be cited by the

was possible for a tribal state to develop a strong government and still retain its tribal organization. In the cases of some states that eventually became sympolities, the development went far before the change took place or was completed. Aetolia certainly became a sympolity, but, when it first appeared as a strong state in the last part of the fifth century, it was still a tribal state. Likewise Thessaly, in the days of its strength and power appears to have been a tribal state rather than a sympolity, unless it should be called a territorial feudal monarchy. Such states as these which ultimately became sympolities will be called confederacies from the outset, even though the name may seem to belong more properly to the sympolities. With these included, it may seem that what is considered below is all Greek states other than city-states. As a matter of fact, the Greeks themselves grouped their states in two groups, city-states and ethnic (tribal) states and included the federal states in the second group.[1] Apparently the tribal state was more fundamental and had early established itself in the consciousness of the Greeks. Nevertheless, the true federal state is to be distinguished from it. The continued application of *ethnos*—in this connexion best translated 'nation'—to a federal state even after it had expanded far beyond its original tribal boundaries shows that it was felt that the people of such a state was being welded into a nation. The best example, with the most enduring results, is the transformation of Dorians and Arcadians into Achaeans perpetuated in the name of the Roman province of Achaea.

The fact that the tribal states seem to have been formed by invading tribes does not mean that the peoples of such states were groups with no infusion of foreign blood. Greece was inhabited before the Greeks came, and some of the pre-Greeks remained to be absorbed into the new people of the country. If then the first Greek invasion was followed by a second the population would be a mixture of pre-Greeks and two strata of Greeks. It is also likely that the invading tribes themselves were the product of earlier amalgamations. Specific evidence is the fact that one of the three Doric sub-tribes was named Pamphyloi, 'men of all tribes'. Then, after the arrival of new invaders, the process of mixing continued, and students of Greek dialects recognize particularly in communities with Doric dialects the survival of pre-Doric

names of the authors alone. Gschnitzer starts from the classification of states on the basis of names; Sordi argues that there is no break in the development from the Aetolian tribal state to the later federal state. Gschnitzer too places a healthy emphasis on continuity. Both tend to minimize the changes.

[1] On *ethnos* see *CP* xl (1945), 78 and n. 72; cf. Sordi, 13 f. A good example of Greek usage is found in the Epidaurus inscription connected with the renewal of the Hellenic League by Demetrius Poliocretes in 302. In this every member state is referred to as a *polis* or *ethnos* (*IG* iv². 1. 68).

elements.[1] Other indications of mixture will be noticed below in con-nexion with the accounts of individual federal states. The history of the Achaeans of the north shore of the Peloponnesus is particularly com-plicated. There seems to be no clearer example than Achaea of the name of a state or region derived from a tribal name. If we were to go exclusively by the name, the conclusion would be that there was at the outset an Achaean tribal state which later became transformed into a federal state. The difficulty is that Achaean has long been recognized as the name of a Greek people or group of tribes of the Mycenaean Age whose language was the ancestor of the Aeolic and Arcado-Cyprian dialects. The names of these dialects is enough to indicate a distribu-tion in northern Greece, on Aegean islands, on the coast of Asia Minor, in the Peloponnesus, and on the island of Cyprus. The recently deciphered Mycenaean language has been recognized as this Achaean or Old Achaean language. Before the coming of the Dorians this language was used on most of the Peloponnesus, and there certainly was a time when Old Achaean was the language of both Achaea and Arcadia. In the latter district it survived as Arcadian, the only dialect of this group to maintain itself in the Peloponnesus. The language of the district later known as Achaea became Doric or Northwest Greek. Thus, at the time of the Doric migration, there were enough invaders to impose their own language, while the old inhabitants retained enough influence so that the mixed population continued to call itself Achaean.[2] This little segment of the original Achaeans, swamped by the heavy infusion of men of another tribe and speaking their language, in the opinion of later Greeks constituted an *ethnos* (tribe or nation), but there seems to be no trace of sub-tribes. Instead, as far back as Homer, local place names within Achaea are known. When the Acha-ean Confederacy later began to absorb its Doric neighbours, it was natural for it to adopt the Doric *koine* or lingua franca of the Doric districts in Hellenistic times. Through this channel the Doric *koine* came to be widely used also by the Arcadians.[3] Thus the last victory of the Doric dialect in the Peloponnesus was due to the Achaeans.

What were the tribes and tribal states? The invading tribes may well have been groups which acquired their feeling of kinship from living together in some area before their invasion of Greece. Similarly within Greece old and new inhabitants of a district might become amalga-mated into what seemed a homogeneous people speaking a common

---

[1] For Sparta, Messene, Argos, and Crete respectively see A. Thumb, *Handbuch der griechischen Dialekte*, second ed. by E. Kieckers, vol. i (1932), secs. 91, 112, 120, and 140; on Sparta cf. also *RE* xix. 818.

[2] On Achaea at this time cf. *Rep. Govt.* 26 f. and nn. 8 and 9 on p. 201 f.

[3] C. D. Buck, *The Greek Dialects* (1955), 179.

language, though that language might well contain survivals from the languages of earlier submerged groups of inhabitants. Thus a tribe was pretty much an artificial creation of geography and politics. Nevertheless, it had a language of its own and its members felt akin to each other. A tribal state, when once formed, felt the same hesitancy as a city-state about admitting outsiders to its citizenship, or, if that term implies too highly developed a state, into its circle. Only the members of the three Aetolian tribes mentioned by Thucydides seem to have been members of the Aetolian tribal state.[1] Individuals, if they once were admitted into a community, were probably easily absorbed, but there is no reason to believe that early tribal states easily absorbed whole communities so that the tribal state was nothing but an artificial political creation.[2] The later ability of federal states to absorb alien communities is another matter.

The institutions of the various tribal states had much in common. In early times they all apparently were led—hardly governed—by kings, and possessed councils of elders or heads of leading families and assemblies of the men of arms of the community. The councils were the ancestors of the similar councils of the city-states and so indirectly of the later Greek *boule* and *gerousia*; the assembly, of the primary assembly of Greek cities and more directly of the primary assemblies of the Acarnanian, Aetolian, and other confederacies. With the king replaced by magistrates, the entire skeleton of later Greek government was there. The only difference was that in the tribal state this government was less developed and interfered little except in the conduct of foreign affairs. There was no written but only customary law, and protection against crime came from kinsmen and friends rather than from the government. The result was that men normally went armed even when they went to market. Thucydides remarks that in parts of Greece they were still doing so in his day and, in another connexion, states that the institutions of the Greeks in former times were similar to those of the barbarians of his own time.[3] The lack of organization went so far that private raids and piratical expeditions were the order of the day, something again which Thucydides recognized as surviving in parts of Greece in his own time. When the Illyrian queen Teuta in

---

[1] So Sordi, 24. Thucydides (iii. 94. 4–5) does not say this in so many words but implies it. Later, when he mentions two smaller groups (96. 3), they are subdivisions of one of these larger tribes. Sordi also refers to the evidence of Arrian, apparently *Anab*. i. 10. 2, but this is much less to the point. The fact that the Aetolian ambassadors sent to Alexander were chosen by tribes gives no information about the number and nature of the tribes.

[2] Cf. Gschnitzer, 132 f., who argues from the practice of the Aetolians and Achaeans in the fourth century and later.

[3] Thuc. i. 5. 3, 6. 6. Cf. the high praise bestowed on Thucydides for his statement of 'the principle of the comparative method in social anthropology' by George Thomson, *Studies in Ancient Greek Society*, i (1949), 142.

230 B.C. told the Roman ambassadors that she would try to see to it that the Romans suffered no wrong at the hands of the public authorities but that it was not lawful for the kings to prevent the Illyrians from profiting from private undertakings,[1] her answer represented a point of view once prevalent in Greece but at the time surviving only among the Illyrians and other more backward peoples. The government was there to lead co-operative undertakings and wars of the state, not to restrain and keep the subjects in order. Judging by the account of Polybius, this was understood neither by him nor by the Romans. Not that it would have made any difference to the policy of the Romans if they had understood it, but it might have been an aid to their ambassadors in handling the situation.

The lack of administration and government restraint in the tribal state left the field open to any agency which could fill the gap. In most cases this proved to be the city. There was a special reason for this. The people of the tribal state lived in unfortified villages. When a need for defence and closer association was felt, the villagers moved together and formed cities. This was not done equally early in all parts of Greece or even in all parts of the same tribal state. Thucydides, as already noted, remarked that the old mode of life prevailed in parts of Greece in his own time. It is hardly necessary to say that the lead in the cultural and economic life was taken by those parts of Greece in which cities had developed.

When the cities once were there, a number of courses of action were possible. If the cities made themselves completely independent and acquired control of the surrounding countryside, the old tribal state had been replaced by a group of city-states. If, on the other hand, the cities in a similar way acquired control of their various surrounding districts but did not allow the ties with the rest of the tribe to lapse, the result was a federal state. Obviously there would be disagreement at times as to which of the two alternatives was preferable. A good example is Boeotia, but there are other illustrations. Thus, in the Achaean Confederacy Pellene had a tendency to go its own way. A third possibility would be that one city should reduce the others to subjection and transform their inhabitants into perioeci. Unkind tongues might say that at times the real trouble in Boeotia was that Thebes was trying to reduce the people of the rest of Boeotia to this status.

With the development of the federal state something new and something different had been born. The Greeks finally indicated this by adopting a new name to describe the form of the federal state from one point of view. This word was *sympoliteia*, which can best be interpreted as a union of city-states or the common citizenship of citizens of

[1] Pol. ii. 8. 8.

several city-states. The word is so natural and simple and so closely related to common Greek words that it is hard to realize that there is no record of its use in literature in this sense before Polybius in the second century B.C. nor any example of its use in documents before the same century. The earliest example yet found is in a decree of the Lycian city of Araxa honouring a fellow citizen, which was first published in 1949.[1] The Greek historians and political scientists have told us so little about either the tribal or the federal state that it is from such incidental material as this that we must reconstruct the Greek views on federalism. The reason that a new word had to be created was that the older terms did not distinguish a federal from a tribal state.

It has already been mentioned that *ethnos* was used for tribal states and that it continued to be used also for federal states. This was a word which could be applied to a tribe or nation whether it constituted a state or not. Of course, when a document reports, for instance, action by the *ethnos* of the Lycians, it is clear that a tribal or federal state was in existence. *Koinon*, on the other hand, was frequently used for a federal state or a federal government, but this word, which could be used about almost any kind of corporation or association, certainly could be applied to a tribal state as well as to a city-state or a federal state. At any rate it is not a word that need mean a federal state and it is not safe to conclude, as often has been done, from the use of such an expression as the '*koinon* of the Aetolians' or the '*koinon* of the Macedonians' that an Aetolian or a Macedonian federal state was in existence at the time. Clearly it was because neither *ethnos* nor *koinon* meant a federal state distinct from any other form of state, that *sympoliteia* was adopted. The difference between it and *ethnos* can be seen in the expression 'the federal state (*sympoliteia*) of the nation (*ethnos*) of the Lycians' used in the Araxa inscription.

To understand the real significance of *sympoliteia* it is necessary to start with the Greek word for citizen, *polites*, which means a citizen of a *polis* or city-state. This derivation is in itself nothing unusual. Almost all Indo-European words for citizen are derived from words meaning city or fortified place,[2] but, though in English, for instance, this derivation is perfectly obvious, we usually are not conscious of it when we employ the word in speaking of a citizen of the United States or some other country. Nor do we intend to compare that country in any sense to a city. Similarly the Greeks may have applied *polites* also to a

[1] *SEG* xviii. 570. It is a slip when Sordi, n. 36 speaks of *sympoliteia* as used in *Hell. Ox.* 11. 3. The related verb is used here to indicate the union of other cities with Plataea, but it is not applied to the union of the cities in the Boeotian Confederacy.

[2] C. D. Buck, *A Dictionary of Selected Synonyms in the Principal Indo-European Languages* (1949), 19. 37.

citizen of a federal state, but *polis* remained definitely a city or city-state. There was an interlude during which it seems that *polis* was applied more widely to any kind of state including federal states. Some time before 389 B.C. the Achaean Confederacy had incorporated into the Confederacy the city of Calydon on the north shore of the Corinthian Gulf, a city which later became Aetolian. Xenophon, in reporting this, was able to say that the Achaeans had made the Caledonians their *politai*, thus applying the word to the citizens of a federal state. At about the same time federal states included in the Peloponnesian and Second Athenian leagues were classed as *poleis*. In an inscription at Athens, a list of the members of the Second Athenian League is given under the heading: 'the following *poleis* are allies of the Athenians', and among these the Acarnanians are listed.[1] Thus, *polis* was on its way to become the name for any Greek state, federal states included, and *polites* the name for a citizen of any kind of state. This tendency was soon checked, at least as far as the use of *polis* is concerned. It is likely that Aristotle himself called the Thessalian Confederacy a *polis*. If so, he was using the word in a sense that already had become or was becoming obsolete, and there is no reason to believe that the word is ever used in this sense in the *Politics*.[2] In 337 B.C. in an Athenian decree granting citizenship to a number of Acarnanians it was specified that also the names of their *poleis* be recorded.[3] By this time Acarnania, according to the usage of the time, was not a *polis* but contained several *poleis*. It has already been noted that in 302 B.C. all states belonging to the Hellenic League were classified as *ethne* and *poleis*, and in this classification the federal states were grouped with tribal states as *ethne*, while *polis* remained the name for a city-state. The federal state, which had been on its way to become classed as a *polis*, was, as it were, reclassified as an *ethnos*. It is likely, however, that the use of *polites* for a citizen of a federal state was retained. At least it was possible to say in a treaty that an Aetolian was to be a *polites* in Acarnania and an Acarnanian in Aetolia.[4]

The choice of *ethnos* was wise and natural. The Boeotians or Aetolians, for instance, constituted an *ethnos* before they were organized as a federal state, and there was no reason why they should not be considered an *ethnos* after the change. This made it possible to emphasize

---

[1] For the Achaeans and the Calydonians see Xen. *Hell.* iv. 6. 1; for the list of the allies of the Athenians, Tod, 123. The Acarnanians are not in the original list immediately under the heading but among the names later added in the margin. It is likely that in Tod, 144, a treaty of 362–361 B.C. between Athens and Peloponnesian states, the Arcadian and Achaean confederacies were spoken of as *poleis*. On the entire problem see *CP* lvii (1962), 250 f.

[2] See below under the Thessalian Confederacy, p. 16 f.

[3] Tod, 178. 34 f.   [4] *IG* ix². 1. 3. 12 f.

the continuity with the older and less developed tribal state. It also made it possible to use the word with a meaning much like 'nation', and with some of the same emotional overtones. All this could be done without interfering with local patriotism. There had been *poleis* within the tribal states for a long time. They could now continue as municipalities within the federal state, and it was to their cities that the citizens of federal states applied the term, *patris*, fatherland or, more strictly, paternal city.[1] What was lacking was some term to set off the federal state from the tribal state and to indicate that it was a union of city-states. This was found in *sympoliteia*, a word which clearly refers to a joint or federal citizenship, state, or constitution. Exactly when this term began to be used cannot be determined. All that can be said is that we have no example of its use before early in the second century B.C.[2]

The federal states which played the most important roles in Greek history were those which expanded farthest beyond the original tribal boundaries. A unitary state too could expand, as the city of Rome did, by adding new territory to her own and absorbing the citizens of such districts into her own citizen body. In the formative period tribal states must have expanded much in this way, but there came a time when it was felt that the tribal area extended so far and no farther, and that what lay beyond was foreign territory. Probably the extension of the frontier when possible at the expense of the neighbours remained the order of the day, but the absorption of large foreign elements became difficult or impossible. Federalization and urbanization made further expansion much more easy. Federalization meant that each city within the state had recognized duties and rights; urbanization, that the new communities to be absorbed already were cities which could be given rights and duties similar to those of the older members. For this too, however, it was necessary to overcome the old tribal particularism and admit cities belonging to other tribal groups. An early example of this was the absorption of Calydon and Naupactus by the Achaean Confederacy about 400 B.C. Thereafter this policy seems to have been accepted by the Achaeans without question and, when the Achaean Confederacy, after a short interruption, was revived in 280 B.C., it was scarcely a generation before the first non-Achaean city was admitted. In both periods the new citizens after their admission were called Achaeans. They became members of an expanding *ethnos* or nation. This seems to bring us back to the tribal state, but it was

---

[1] Cf. above, p. xxi, cf. xix, n. 1.

[2] Another word for federal citizenship is *koinopoliteia*, used in *SIG*³ 622 B, a letter from the Cretan city of Vaxos to the Aetolian Confederacy. This word, however, was used with a slightly different connotation.

federalism which had made the expansion possible by combining members of tribal groups once alien to each other.

By contrast it is well to remember the particularism of the city-state. There was no lack of lust for power in the larger cities, but this tended to express itself in the leadership of large alliances, such as the Peloponnesian League under the leadership of Sparta and the Delian and Second Athenian League under that of Athens. The citizens of the cities belonging to these leagues were not Spartans or Athenians and could not become so except under very unusual circumstances. Moreover, the leading city had a tendency to reduce its allies to the status of virtual subjects. Yet the treatment by Sparta and Athens of their immediate neighbours was even worse. Nothing need be said about the helots and perioeci of Sparta, but it is less well known that Athens had none too clean hands in such matters but had a string of subject communities along her borders—Oropus, Eleutherae, Salamis.[1] By contrast the policy of the Achaean Confederacy was liberal and enlightened. It is true that in its later days it forced the annexation of unwilling neighbours, but it at least tried to make the new citizens into Achaeans.

The statements about federal states so far have implied organization by cities, but cities are not essential to federalism. Organization by rural districts or tribes is also possible and actually was used. The Epirote Confederacy seems to have retained organization by tribes to the end. The Aetolians too, while still organized by tribes, seem to have developed a strong and efficient central government, as the Athenians learned to their sorrow in 426. Organization by cities was adopted later but the date cannot be fixed. Moreover, some of the units probably were not real cities. In spite of that, the Aetolians developed an unusually elastic and elaborate system for attaching and protecting friends, not by admission into the Confederacy as regular members, but by the grant of civil rights combined with potential citizenship through isopolity, and by the grant of immunity from attack at the hands of Aetolians and others residing in Aetolia. Most of this, of course, belongs to the later period of her history.

[1] U. Kahrstedt, *Staatsgebiet und Staatsangehörige in Athen* (1934), 346–62; Larsen, *RE* xix. 824 f., under 'Perioikoi'. Though treated under this heading, the communities are subject rather than perioecic communities. Gschnitzer, *Abhängige Orte*, 82–88 discusses Oropus and Eleutherae.

CHAPTER II
THE CHIEF CONFEDERACIES
OF THE PERIOD

THE accounts of the various confederacies in this chapter concern chiefly their form of government and their institutions and the evolution of these. Of historical events, those which have primarily local significance are included; those of wider significance are reserved for Chapter III. Sometimes it has been difficult to know where to draw the line. The result may at times involve a little duplication with certain events told more fully in this chapter and referred to more briefly in the next. The Chalcidic Confederacy may be a case in point. Its complicated history seemed to call for a longer treatment than was desirable in the general account of the period, and yet this history has a bearing on the broader questions of the time and on the relations of Sparta and Athens and their allies to each other. Also the order in which the various confederacies were to be taken up, involved difficulties. Thessaly seemed an obvious choice for the first place. Boeotia is taken next on account of its early development of a federal state with representative government. Yet it could also have been placed last, for nothing marked more clearly the end of a period in the evolution of federalism than the dissolution of the Boeotian Confederacy after the King's Peace.

I. THE THESSALIAN CONFEDERACY

The Thessalian Confederacy is taken first mostly on account of the importance of Thessaly in early Greek history. It was relatively late to develop a true federal state, and this development was preceded by a period of weakness and civil strife.[1] Before this there was first a strong feudal kingdom created by the conquering invaders who reduced the earlier inhabitants to serfdom. Later, we do not know just when, the Thessalians conquered their immediate neighbours, later known as the perioeci of Thessaly, and subjected so many other tribes that they at times exerted a controlling influence in the Amphictionic League, reduced Phocis, extended their influence through Boeotia to the

[1] Of the many works dealing with Thessaly some of the more important are: Eduard Meyer, *Theopomps Hellenika* (1909); the article 'Thessalia' ('Landeskunde' by Friedrich Stählin, 'Geschichte' by Hiller von Gaertringen) in *RE* vi A; A. Momigliano, 'Tagia e tetrarchia in Tessaglia', *Athenaeum*, x (1932), 47–53; F. Gschnitzer, 'Namen und Wesen der thessalischen Tetraden', *Hermes*, lxxxii (1954), 451–64; Marta Sordi, *La lega tessala fino ad Alessandro Magno* (1958); cf. also Larsen, *CP* lv (1960), 229–48.

Euripus and to Athens, and actually challenged Sparta's claim to supremacy in Greece. Later the central government was weakened while the cities grew in importance and Thessaly was transformed into a regular sympolity, though it retained one feature of the old monarchy —a chief magistrate elected for life. This, of course, was to prove an instrument for the restoration in the fourth century of the authority of the central government, which was accomplished without destroying the cities and the federal machinery. The result was a federal state which, at least in the federal exploitation of customs duties, was one of the most advanced of all Greek federal states, though it served as an instrument for the power of Macedonian kings.

The outline given above, involving as it does a strong Thessaly in the period before the Persian War, differs somewhat from the orthodox interpretation, which has taken the weakened Thessaly of the fifth and fourth centuries, so to speak, as the original Thessaly. That Thessaly was strong at an earlier date is shown by what it accomplished. Moreover, it may be well to recall that ancient Greece probably never again was so nearly united under Greek leadership as it was in the Mycenaean Age. Hence, it would not be unnatural for some of the succession states, whether organized by invaders or ruled by pre-Doric Greeks, to be relatively large and strong.

The greatness of Thessaly may in part have been due to its geography. Thessaly proper was a great plain, the valley of the Peneus river and its tributaries, divided into two by a chain of hills and boxed in on all four sides by mountains. The chief breaks were at the vale of Tempe in the north east, through which the Peneus reached the sea, and relatively easy access to the Gulf of Volo at ancient Pagasae, while also the pass to Lamia on the Malian Gulf was not too difficult. As Cary remarks; 'No other district of Greece was better fitted by nature to become the seat of a single territorial state'. He continues, however: 'Yet the Thessalians scarcely progressed beyond the cantonal stage of development until the fourth century'.[1] This is true in the sense that they hardly developed a sympolity before that date, but this did not prevent Thessaly from being a united and strong territorial state in the sixth century. In the mountains surrounding the plain lived tribes later reduced by the Thessalians and considered perioeci, that is, subjects or subject allies of the Thessalians.[2]

Apparently at the time of the Doric migration invaders coming from the west, from southern Epirus, entered this plain,[3] took it over as

[1] Cary, *Geographic Background*, 64.
[2] On the problem of the Thessalian perioeci see Larsen, *RE* xix 831. f.; Gschnitzer, *Abhängige Orte*, 1–6.
[3] On the early invasion of Thessaly cf. *CP* lv (1960), 229 f.

conquering landlords, and partly expelled and partly reduced to serf-dom the earlier inhabitants. Thus, Thessaly too, another of the strong states of early Greece, like Sparta was the result of the Doric invasion. In both cases the lowest stratum of the population was reduced to serfdom, namely the helots of Sparta and the *penestai* of Thessaly.[1] Yet there were marked differences. In the Lacedaemonian state, the entire population, the Spartiates, perioeci, and helots, all eventually spoke the Doric language of the conquerors; in Thessaly, the language was essentially Aeolic, the language of the earlier population. There were enough elements in common with West and Northwest Greek to indi-cate that there had been an invasion, but as a whole the language of the older inhabitants won.[2] The result of the conquest was the establish-ment of a feudal kingdom with estates so large that one nobleman, Meno of Pharsalus, in addition to a subsidy of twelve talents, was able to furnish two or three hundred horsemen from his own serfs for the campaign of 476–475 against Eïon in Thrace, at the time still held by the Persians.[3] This evidence is unique, but the many references to wealthy families and their flocks and followers[4] suggest that there were several families with similar large estates. These nobles apparently acquired their horses and horsemanship from the earlier inhabitants, whose descendants, judging from the example just mentioned, though subjected by the conquerors, continued to serve as horsemen. Thus the serfs (*penestai*) of the Thessalians probably were better off than most groups of this status. Yet, though horsemanship may have been acquired from the earlier inhabitants, it seems that the development of cavalry and cavalry tactics cannot be placed earlier than the seventh century and so belongs to the state established by the Thessalian conquerors.[5]

The head of the state was a king, who in Thessaly was designated by the local title of *tagos* (plu. *tagoi*).[6] There is evidence that from the middle of the fifth century the *tagos* was elected. In all likelihood the kingship was elective from the beginning, or at least from the last part

[1] Cf. *OCD* under 'Serfs' and 'Helots'.

[2] Buck, *Greek Dialects*, 149 classifies Thessalian as Aeolic but also lists West and North-west Greek charactersitics; cf. Bury-Meiggs, *History of Greece*[3], 60.

[3] Dem. xxiii. 199; ps.-Dem. xiii. 23. The first passage gives the number as 300; the second, as 200.

[4] E.g. Theocritus xvi. 34–39; cf. also Pindar, *Pythian* x and in general the evidence for families continuing powerful generation after generation.

[5] On the origin of the use of cavalry in Greece see ch. iii at pp. 106–8.

[6] In the earliest references to him in Greek literature he is called *basileus* (Pindar, *Pythian* x; Herod. v. 63. 3; Thuc. i. 111. 1), thus being designated by the commonest Greek term for 'king'. This evidence is authoritative for the contemporary Greek view on the nature of the office. Authoritative for the Thessalian usage is a fifth-century decree of a Thessalian city (*SIG*[3] 55; Buck, *Greek Dialects*, no. 35), which indicates that the Thessalian title was *tagos*. The title occurs several times also in Xenophon's *Hellenica*.

of the seventh century. This is indicated by the fact that various *tagoi* known to us came from different families and localities.[1] Beginning in the middle of the fifth century there occurred several lengthy periods in which the failure to elect a king produced a period of what the Thessalians called *atagia*, a term comparable to the Latin *interregnum*. This has led to the common belief that the *tagos* was merely an emergency commander elected for war, though it was evident that once elected he served for life. However, it should be clear that the existence of a name for a period without a chief executive need not mean that a long period of this kind was considered desirable. On the contrary, the accomplishments of the Thessalian Confederacy, particularly in the sixth century, show that the central government must have been considered a permanent organism. The Thessalian state at the time conquered extensive territories, collected tribute from the subjects, set up officials to supervise some of them, and had a conscious and fairly consistent foreign policy, so that it was possible to contract a treaty of alliance with the Thessalian state and rely on it to meet its obligations. Thus, when the Athenian tyrant Hippias called on the Thessalians for help against the Spartan intervention, he did so in virtue of a pre-existing treaty of alliance, almost certainly contracted with his father, Peisistratus, who went so far as to name a son, Thessalus.[2] The intervention of the Thessalians at the time amounted to a challenge to the claim of Sparta to supremacy in Greece. A state with such a policy cannot have intended to rely on a chief magistrate created only when an emergency arose or on a central government which from time to time was dormant. The office of *tagos* must have been considered permanent except for the lapse of a few days between the death of one *tagos* and the election of a successor. The long intervals observed later were due to weakness and civil strife.

In the first period after the conquest the organization must have been purely feudal with the king relying on the support of the various great nobles and their followers. But this sort of organization or lack of organization is none too reliable in the long run. The time was bound to come when the king could not always rely on his lords. Some of them may well have challenged his right to claim their allegiance. Out of this may have come the elective kingship, if it was not there from the outset. But even a system for selecting the king and settling disputed successions was not enough. The size of the contingents furnished

---

[1] See particularly Beloch, *GrG*[2] i. ii. 199–210; Sordi, *La lega tessala* disagrees with him on a number of points but is too inclined to attribute all Thessalian greatness to the Aleuadae of Larisa.

[2] The pre-existing alliance: Herod. v. 63. 3; Peisistratus' son, Thessalus: Thuc. i. 20. 2, vi. 55. 1, Arist. *Ath. pol.* 17. 3; cf. Sordi, 55.

might still depend on the whims of the nobles and their followers. An aggressive and conquering state needed a more stringent organization. This came in the form of the organization of Thessaly proper as four *tetrads*, Thessaliotis, Phthiotis, Pelasgiotis, and Hestiaeotis, each headed by a *tetrarch*. Like their successors, the polemarchs, the *tetrarchs* obviously were the commanders of the contingents of the four *tetrads*. Yet they were federal rather than local officials, and so were called '*tetrarchs* of the Thessalians'. Like the *tagos* they seem to have served for life or for an indefinite term. Some of the best information concerning the office comes from a set of inscriptions on statue bases at Delphi.[1] These give the genealogy of the male members of a prominent family of Pharsalus and the chief points in the careers of its members. The central figure was Daochus, who for twenty-seven years ruled all Thessaly, that is, was the *tagos* of the confederacy. He clearly belongs in the period of the Peloponnesian War. His grandfather, Acnonius, was a tetrarch and likewise his grandson, a second Daochus. The latter served after the office had been discontinued for a while and then revived by Philip II of Macedonia and need not concern us at the moment. Returning to Acnonius, it is noticeable that neither his father nor any of his sons served as tetrarch. In other words, the office was not hereditary but elective.[2] There were smaller units called *kleroi*, each of which were required to furnish forty cavalry men and eighty hoplites. The word *kleros* suggests some connexion with the allotments first assigned to the Thessalian nobles at the time of the conquest, but the uniform size of the contingents shows that some adjustment had been made. While smaller landholders might combine to make up the contingent of a single *kleros*, those who, like Meno of Pharsalus, could mobilize hundreds of horsemen must have controlled several.

It has already been implied that the four tetrads represent not preexisting smaller states that were united but subdivisions of a unitary state, and that the *kleroi* were further subdivisions of the tetrads. This conclusion, reached also on other grounds, is supported by a curious bit of evidence which usually has been misinterpreted or overlooked. Particularly important are two fragments of Aristotle, 497 and 498. In this connexion it is well to bear in mind that among the sketches of governments of various states prepared by Aristotle, there were a few dealing with federal states, one of these being Thessaly.[3] In frag. 498

---

[1] *SIG*³ 274.

[2] See the articles by Momigliano and Gschnitzer listed on p. 12, n. 1 above and cf. my own discussion in *CP* lv (1960), 237 f.

[3] Cf. *CP* xl (1945), 74 and n. 55, 78 and n. 72. The interpretation of *Pol.* 1261a28 given there in n. 72 is much like that given later by Barker in his translation.

Aristotle states that Aleuas, to whom the reorganization is attributed, when he subdivided the *polis*, ordained that each *kleros* was to supply forty horsemen and eighty hoplites. He may also have provided for contingents of peltasts, less heavily armed infantry, but that is uncertain.[1] In this connexion *polis* must refer to the Thessalian state, and thus we learn that the *kleroi* as well as the tetrads were regarded as subdivisions of it. This use of *polis* about a large territorial or federal state is so unusual that editors have sought to get rid of it by emendation but, in so doing, have only made matters worse. Better is the suggestion that the word refers to the territory of the state proper in opposition to perioecic territory.[2] But even this is unnecessary. To be sure, the area organized was that of Thessaly proper and did not include perioecic territory, but we do not know whether the perioeci had been reduced by that time or not. The explanation is simply that there was a tendency in the fourth century to adopt *polis* as a name for every kind of state, even a federal state. In our fragment Aristotle followed this usage, which was soon abandoned, and which otherwise does not seem to have affected his works.[3] The reorganization described above was attributed by Aristotle to a certain Aleuas the Red. Many have thought that this Aleuas was a purely legendary figure. It matters little. Here it is enough to note that Aristotle considered him a real personality whose career fell long before his own time.

Some information about the Thessalian military system can be deduced from a statement attributed to Jason of Pherae, who in the early fourth century sought to be elected *tagos* and so to revive the dormant Thessalian monarchy. He is reported to have said that when Thessaly had a *tagos* there would be available a cavalry force of about 6,000,[4] and the cavalry was always the most important element of the Thessalian army. At the rate of forty from each *kleros*, 150 *kleroi* were needed for a force of 6,000. If each *kleros* contained about ten square miles or twenty-five square kilometers, these 150 *kleroi* would require only about half the land of the four tetrads.[5] The 6,000 probably included all horsemen on the military lists, and it is likely that no

[1] Cf. *CP* lv (1960), 237 and n. 37.
[2] So Wade-Gery, *JHS* xliv (1924), 58, n. 16 followed by Sordi, 319, n. 4.
[3] Cf. *CP* lvii (1962), 250 f.
[4] Xen. *Hell.* vi. 1. 8. In the same passage the number of hoplites is given as over 10,000. Light armed troops were furnished by the perioeci. When Jason did become *tagos*, he is said to have had 8,000 cavalry and not less than 20,000 hoplites (ibid. 19), but these included allied troops. Thus 6,000 remains the largest number of cavalry given for Thessaly proper.
[5] Cary, *CAH* iii. 600 suggests that the 'individual allotments [*kleroi*] . . . cannot have fallen far short of five square miles'. This estimate seems low. Beloch, *GrG*² iii. i. 293 estimates the area of Thessaly as 15,000 square kilometres of which one-half belonged to the tetrads, thus giving them in all 7,500 square kilometres. Only 3,750 of these would be needed for 150 *kleroi* at 25 each.

2

more than half of this number could be mobilized at any one time. Even this may be too high. The Thessalian cavalry which crossed with Alexander to Asia is said to have numbered 1,800 and that which fought in the Lamian War and defeated the Macedonian cavalry, 2,000.[1] In both cases we must have near maximum numbers. Alexander, considering the importance of cavalry to his plans, must have taken along as large a force as he could, while in the Lamian War, when the Thessalian cavalry had deserted the Macedonians and was fighting against them on its own home territory, it must have called on all men available. It is possible that in the early days of enthusiastic expansion, somewhat larger forces were mobilized, but it is well to remember that when the Thessalians sent abroad a force of 1,000 cavalry, they sent one half or at least one third of the entire available cavalry. Thus, when they sent a force of this size to aid Hippias against Sparta, it was not a case of a casual dispatch of aid but a major operation which must have been due to a deliberate and conscious policy.

The reforms of Aleuas the Red were connected with the moulding of the military machine used to conquer territory and hold it in subjection. There is also a bit of information concerning the exploitation and control of the subjects. This involved the exaction of tribute and military service, and, at least in some cases, control through the taking of hostages and through supervision both by Thessalian officials and native agents. This information is gained from a few small but significant pieces of evidence. Connected with the fixing of the tribute of the perioeci—not necessarily with the first subjection of them, as it sometimes has been said—is a certain Scopas. We are told that Jason of Pherae ordered all perioeci to pay the tribute fixed by Scopas. Since Jason aimed at restoring the power of the *tagos* as it was before its collapse, and since this collapse came before the expedition of Xerxes in 480, this in itself points to the sixth century or the very beginning of the fifth. The Scopas to whom the reform is attributed is most likely the elder Scopas, the grandfather of the contemporary of Simonides. This places his work well back in the sixth century. The evidence for further control comes from a story of the revolt of Phocis. In a single day the Phocians murdered all Thessalian officials in their country and their 'tyrants'. These 'tyrants' apparently were native Phocian rulers serving under the protection of the Thessalians. The latter retaliated

[1] For the Thessalian cavalry with Alexander see Diod. xvii. 17. 4. At Gordium 200 additional Thessalian horsemen were brought up (Arrian, *Anab.* i. 29. 4), thus making a total of 2,000. For the 2,000 in the Lamian War, Diod. xviii. 15. 2. In a passage in which he wishes to represent the Thessalian forces as very great Isocrates speaks of over 3,000 (*On the Peace* 118).

by putting to death all the Phocian hostages they held.[1] The statements made by Xenophon about the military duties of the surrounding tribes and the tribute paid by them, all indicate that the services were performed and the tribute paid when there was a *tagos*.[2] This has been connected with the theory that the *tagos* was only an emergency commander chosen in time of war. Similarly the tribute has been interpreted as assessments collected in time of war. This is a system which would suit a peaceful state which went to war only when attacked. But all this is refuted not only by the long terms of service of some *tagoi*, but also by the story of the revolt of Phocis. There, in time of peace, the Phocians were under the thumbs of Thessalian officials and agents, and the war was begun by an attack on these officials.[3] No, Thessaly in the sixth century was an aggressive state which conquered and held others in subjection. The meaning of Xenophon's statement about Jason must be that if the old monarchy was restored and Thessaly reunited, it would be possible once more to subject and exploit the neighbours as in the 'good old days'. It is well known that Jason succeeded in doing this but that his power did not last long.

So far only the administrative and executive departments of the government have been considered, but there must also have been an assembly of some kind. Aside from the election of officials, there are indications that policies of state were sometimes decided by an assembly. In 424 B.C. the pro-Athenian group in Thessaly complained that Brasidas was crossing their country without securing the common consent of all. This must mean that there was an assembly to which the pro-Spartan oligarchic manipulators who co-operated with Brasidas failed to submit the question. Thus there was a body which claimed a right to determine questions of policy. This, or a forerunner, must have been the body which decided to send the king and a thousand horsemen to aid Hippias against the Spartans. This means that the assembly existed in the days of Thessalian greatness in the sixth century. Concerning its exact nature we have no information but it probably was in a sense a primary assembly but one attended or controlled exclusively by the nobles.[4] The aristocratic flavour of Thessalian society is seen also in the prominence of cavalry, though, as is implied in the story of

[1] For Scopas see Xen. *Hell.* vi. 1. 19 and cf. Sordi, 61; for the 'tyrants' in Phocis, Plut. *Mor.* 244B.

[2] Xen. *Hell.* vi. 1. 9, 12, 19.

[3] The story is told only by Plutarch, but he is writing about the affairs of his neighbours, a subject on which he was something of an expert. One of the commanders in the ensuing campaign was Daïphantes of Hyampolis, whose life Plutarch had written.

[4] For the assembly see Thuc. iv. 78. 3; Herod. v. 63. 3; cf. *Rep. Govt.* 41 and 206, n. 39; for a different view Sordi, 330 f. A representative assembly with cities represented in proportion to their size, such as she favours, was to come later.

Meno of Pharsalus, the lords may have used their *penestai* in the contingents they furnished. Since there was no cavalry in Homeric times, and since the earliest use of horseback riding by Greek soldiers was as a sort of mounted infantry using the horses to transport them to the scene of conflict, it is likely that the first use of real cavalry by the Greeks was its use by the Thessalians in the period of their expansion.

Such then was the early Thessalian state of the sixth and probably late seventh centuries B.C., a strong elective kingship with regional subdivisions, an assembly controlled by the nobles to elect the king and other high officials and to decide important questions of foreign policy, and an aristocratic army depending largely on cavalry consisting of the nobles and their dependents. This state should probably be called a unitary state rather than a federal state, though, on account of the subdivisions it possessed a certain federal flavour. The government was strong in a sense, but it handled very little except foreign policy and the control of subjects. One may conjecture that at first local administration was completely in the hands of the great nobles. Later the control shifted somewhat to the cities. When the minting of money began about 500 B.C., this was in the hands of the cities.[1] This naturally means that by this time cities had acquired some sort of self-government and corporate existence. Furthermore, a fifth century inscription suggests that foreign trade and customs duties were controlled by the cities. The small town of Thetonium, otherwise almost unknown, granted to a Corinthian, Sotaerus, his descendants and agents and property, immunity from seizure (*asylia*) and exemption from taxation (*ateleia*). *Asylia* meant that, at a time when it was common to seize the goods of foreigners as compensation for bad debts and other grievances, not necessarily against the person whose goods were seized but at times against a fellow countryman, the person granted *asylia* was promised that he and his property would not be molested. In the present case the guarantee was valid whether Sotaerus personally or an agent was in charge of the goods. The *ateleia* involved the right to import and export goods without paying duty. The inscription raises as many problems as it solves. Since Thetonium was well inland, it is difficult to see how a Corinthian merchant could trade there. Traders and travellers must have circulated freely in Thessaly at the time. The eponymous magistrate by whom the document is dated is a *hyloros*, a 'warden of the forests', a magistrate described by Aristotle as policing the countryside outside the city proper.[2] Thus it seems that whatever policing there was of the countryside, was in the hands of the

---

[1] Seltman, *Greek Coins*[2], 89, 160 ff.

[2] *SIG*[3] 55 (Buck, no. 35). On the *hylorus* cf. Arist. *Pol.* 1321b30. These two seem to be the only known references to the magistrate by this name.

cities. This may indicate some encroachment of the cities upon the former domain of the nobles, though it is natural to suppose that the nobles continued to control and discipline their own dependants.

The growth of cities did not necessarily mean loss of influence and power on the part of the nobles. It is clear that a considerable amount of strife and factionalism developed. This is seen most clearly in connexion with the crossing of Thessaly by Brasidas in 424, for which the description of Thucydides (iv. 78) clearly indicates leadership by a narrow clique of oligarchic, pro-Spartan manipulators, while there also existed a more popular and more numerous pro-Athenian opposition. It has been pointed out above that the *kleroi* required to fill the Thessalian army did not necessarily include all the land of the four tetrads. On the rest there was room for towns and probably also for small farms. The cities may, nevertheless, at the outset have been the creation of the noble families. The headquarters of one of the more influential families is likely to have been a village, and may well have attracted merchants and artisans. Since Thessaly produced and exported grain,[1] it is possible that aristocratic families even had a hand in foreign trade. Thus Larisa may well have grown up around the manor house or palace of the Aleuadae and Pharsalus around that of the family of the Meno who personally could contribute several hundred horsemen to a campaign. At any rate, it is clear that such families tried to, and largely did, control the government of the cities in which they lived or with which they were identified. The Aleuadae have the distinction of having been glorified by Pindar, Plato, and Theocritus,[2] and Pindar specifically praises the Aleuadae for preserving and strengthening the Thessalian way, that is, aristocratic government; 'in the hands of the good [the nobles] rests the inheritance of their fathers, excellent piloting of the cities'. Thus, according to

---

[1] The earliest specific statement concerning the export of grain from Thessaly seems to be Xen. *Hell.* vi. 1. 11, but of course trade in grain began much earlier than this, and in all likelihood Thessaly was involved in it. Evidence in literary sources for early trade naturally is scarce. When Hesiod counts among the blessings of those who give good judgements that they do not travel on ships because their land yields enough to make this unnecessary (*Works and Days*, 236 f.), this proves that by this time there were districts that imported grain. The same can be deduced from Solon's prohibition against exporting any agricultural products except oil (Plut. *Solon* 24). C. Roebuck, *Ionian Trade and Colonization* (1959), 128 lists from Herodotus evidence for movements of grain which indicate that the Pontic region and Sicily were looked upon as possible sources of supply. Otherwise the evidence for early trade is indirect and chiefly archaeological.

[2] Pindar, *Pythian* x; Plato, *Meno* 70; Theocritus xvi. 34. For the interpretation of Pindar's ode cf. the commentary of B. L. Gildersleeve and the translation of Richmond Lattimore (1947). The νόμος Θεσσαλῶν does not mean 'the law of the Thessalians' (so apparently Sordi, 313) but is correctly rendered by Lattimore 'the Thessalian way' ('they carry aloft the Thessalian way and increase it'). Furthermore, Gildersleeve certainly is right in that ἀγαθοῖσι is used in the political sense; Lattimore is not clear on this point.

Pindar, Larissa was guided by the nobles. Next to the Aleuadae, probably the most talked of Thessalian family was that of the Scopadae of Crannon. There were also the Menos of Pharsalus, probably all belonging to the same family.[1] First came the Meno who supported the campaign of Eïon of 476–475 and was granted citizenship at Athens. Next comes the Meno who was one of the commanders of the Thessalian cavalry sent to aid the Athenians in 431. He was probably a grandson of the first Meno.[2] Thucydides son of Meno of Pharsalus, an Athenian proxenus, who played a minor part in the events connected with the overthrow of the Four Hundred and the establishment of the Five Thousand in 411, was probably a son of the second Meno.[3] The name Thucydides suggests that there was more than patriotism connected with the intervention of the first Meno at Eïon and that the Pharsalian and the Athenian families may have had financial interests in common, not that Thucydides the son of Meno necessarily was named after the historian. Undoubtedly the Meno who gave his name to one of Plato's dialogues and appears in Xenophon's *Anabasis* belonged to the same family.[4] The case is strengthened by the fact that Plato represents him as present at Athens, which suggests membership in a non-Athenian family with close connexions at Athens. Last is the Meno who commanded the Thessalian cavalry in the Lamian War and was the maternal grandfather of King Pyrrhus of Epirus. He too, in all likelihood, belonged to the same family.[5] Powerful as this family was, no member, as far as we know, was ever *tagos*. Nor was this the only powerful family at Pharsalus. There was also the family of the Daochus who was *tagos* during the Peloponnesian War.

Though such families continued to be influential, and though Thessaly continued to be dominated by an aristocracy through Hellenistic and Roman times, there was enough social unrest to cause

[1] The Menos are taken up briefly by Sordi, 139, n. 3, except that she fails to include the one of the Lamian War.

[2] Thuc. ii. 22. 3. A. E. Raubitscheck, 'Menon, Son of Menekleides', *Hesperia*, xxiv (1955), 286–9 (summarized *Bull. ép.* 1958, no. 172) gives a very imaginative account of the Meno of the Eïon campaign, who, according to Dem. xxiii. 199, was granted Athenian citizenship. Raubitscheck identifies him with Menon son of Menekleides of the deme of Gargettos whose name appears on several *ostraka*, and thus deduces that he took up residence at Athens and was active in politics. From the *ostraka*, one of which refers to him as a traitor, and an obscure entry in Hesychius, R. deduces that he was ostracized and that the ostracism came in 457 after the Battle of Tanagra, in which the Thessalian cavalry went over to the enemy. This is plausible but by no means certain. R. (n. 14) further considers it possible that the commander of the Thessalian cavalry in 431 was identical with the Meno of the Eïon campaign about forty-five years earlier. This is extremely unlikely.

[3] Marcellinus, *Life of Thucydides* 28; Thuc. viii. 92. 8. Raubitscheck (n. 2 above) takes the Thucydides of Marcellinus to be an Athenian, but if he is identical with the one of Thuc. viii. 92. 8 he was a Pharsalian citizen and a proxenus of Athens.

[4] Diogenes Laertius ii. 6. 50 calls him a Pharsalian.

[5] See the sketch of his life by Kroll, *RE* xv. 926.

changes both in the city and federal governments. Thus we hear about the creation of new citizens at Larisa. Connected with this is the joke of the sophist Gorgias, who compared the makers of Larisaeans to craftsmen making mortars. This points to the fifth century as the most likely time for the reform and suggests a liberal or democratic movement which was a part of the same movement which produced radical democracy in Athens. Such movements tended to overstep boundaries and affect more than one state. The precise course it would take in any particular place, naturally would depend on local conditions. In the Thessalian cities, the creation of new citizens probably meant the extension of active citizenship to members of some of the lower classes in the cities; probably artisans and merchants. The emancipation of the *penestai*, the serfs of the large estates, did not come as early as this. The date is unknown but cannot be placed earlier than the very last years of the fifth century.[1] A further indication of civil strife is the report that in Thessaly there were cities with public squares (*agorai*) in which no buying and selling was permitted and to which no artisan or farmer was admitted unless summoned by the magistrates, in other words, except when called upon to stand trial before his betters.[2] The fact that this is reported by Aristotle indicates that this institution originated not later than the fourth century. It probably represents a counter move of the oligarchs against their more liberal opponents. Such an institution is less likely to have had its rules formulated when the nobles or oligarchs held undisputed sway than when their control had been challenged. Brief as the statement is, it indicates that the opposition to the oligarchy came both from the city and the country population, that is the *penestai*.

The first change in the federal government that can be dated approximately is the replacement by 457 B.C. of the four tetrarchs chosen for life by four polemarchs elected for a short term, most likely a year. The evidence consists of a Delphic inscription first published in 1958 which records a dedication dated by the name of the polemarchs.[3] This change must have meant a great increase in the power of the assembly in relation to the executive, and there is reason to believe that the assembly was no longer completely dominated by the great nobles.

[1] On Gorgias see Arist. *Pol.* 1275b26. Critias of Athens, who was an exile in Thessaly immediately before he became one of the Thirty Tyrants, took part in rousing the *penestai* against their masters (Xen. *Hell.* ii, 3. 36). Such an act would not be out of character for a man with the devious ways of Critias. Cf. Sordi, 141–6; this excellent discussion is marred only by the conviction that the *penestai* had been liberated in 457. On the latter point cf. *CP* lv (1960), 244.

[2] Arist. *Pol.* 1331a30.

[3] G. Daux, 'Dédicace thessalien d'un cheval à Delphes', *BCH* lxxxii (1958), 329–34; now *SEG* xvii. 243. The inscription is quoted and discussed by J. and L. Robert, *Bull. ép.* 1959, no. 189. Fuller discussion, with text reproduced, *CP* lv (1960), 241 f.

Likewise by 431 the organization of the army had been so changed that contingents were contributed by the various cities. In that year the force sent to Athens was made up of contingents from the cities under the command of local officers, such as the Meno of Pharsalus already mentioned. This probably meant a weakening of the power of the *tagos*. Not that the *tagos* need take part in such an expedition, but the impression is that the commanders were chosen by the cities which contributed the contingents. Later Jason of Pherae, when he became *tagos*, fixed the size of the contingents to be furnished by each city.[1] Thus the organization of the army by cities was retained but brought directly under the control of the *tagos*. Whatever happened in the intervening years, it is safe to conclude that Philip II and later Macedonian kings retained this control over the army. Another change was the substitution of *archon* for *tagos* as title for the head of the Confederacy. This is attested by a treaty with Athens of 361–360 B.C.[2] Since Jason of Pherae and his immediate successors claimed the title of *tagos*, the change must have been introduced after this time. The new title may have been intended to emphasize that the head of the Confederacy was a magistrate rather than a monarch. Otherwise, since the *archon* too appears to have been elected for life, the change was of little significance. The same document lists the *hippeis* or knights among those taking the oath ratifying the treaty on behalf of the Thessalians. One cannot well believe that all the thousands of Thessalians, required when called upon to serve in the cavalry, took the oath. Probably an upper class among them, determined by a property qualification, constituted an oligarchic council. More important are indications that the Confederacy was completely transformed into a sympolity, a true federal state made up of cities, though it may be well to recall that there is no evidence that the term *sympoliteia* was applied to a federal state as early as this. Two third century decrees passed by outside cities (Cos and Mytilene) refer to the cities of Thessaly in such a way as to indicate that the Confederacy was made up of cities,[3] but the change had certainly come earlier. In the fourth century customs duties and probably also market fees were collected for the federal government in the Thessalian communities. We learn this on account of the complaint that Philip II and Alexander the Great diverted this income to their own use.[4] This mode of collecting suggests both the existence of cities and the subjection of these to some extent under the central government. This implies as advanced a system of federal finances as any

[1] Xen. *Hell.* vi. 1. 19.
[2] *SIG*³ 184; Tod, 147; cf. *CP* lv (1960), 240 f. and 248, n. 48.
[3] Cited by Sordi, 331 and n. 1; discussed briefly also *CP* lv. 244 and n. 59.
[4] See especially Dem. i. 22.

known from ancient Greece—more advanced, in fact, than those of the Aetolian and Achaean confederacies. The change probably also affected the organization of the assembly, but just how we do not know. All that is known on the subject is that the Thessalian Confederacy organized in 194 B.C. had a representative *synedrion* and no primary assembly.

To summarize, it seems that there was in Thessaly, after the development of a strong elective, feudal monarchy, a double development. At first the central government was weakened by civil strife and disputed elections, while much of the local administration was taken over by the cities. Later there was the restoration of strong central government but on new lines, those of a true federal state, the strength of the central government being indicated by the collection of customs duties on its behalf throughout the ports of the Confederacy. The earliest stages of this development must remain conjectural, but what little is known suggests the creation of a strong monarchy by invaders coming to Thessaly from southern Epirus. At first the entire government must have been that of the king and the chief nobles, and the armed forces must have consisted of the immediate followers of the king and the contingents supplied by the nobles. The control of any foreign trade which may have existed must have been exercised by the various nobles for their estates, some as large as small principalities. In the days before coined money and regular tolls, foreign traders who came to barter undoubtedly sought to win the favour of the king or some influential noble by means of 'gifts'. Later came the reorganization of Thessaly proper into four tetrads, these, again, being subdivided into *kleroi*. The purpose obviously was the maintenance of the army, and the government remained interested chiefly in foreign affairs. The cities as such apparently were ignored. To use an illustration, if the men of Larisa served in the army, they served in the contingents of the *kleroi* controlled by the Aleuads and other nobles. This was the Thessaly of the great conquests, and this organization thus belongs to the sixth century and may extend into the seventh. By the beginning of the fifth century, cities, chiefly in the eastern parts of Thessaly, had acquired a corporate existence, and so, when money began to be minted in Thessaly, this was left to the cities. In the fifth century the cities likewise took over the control of foreign trade and the policing of their own territories. At that time, Thessaly was probably a conglomerate of cities and estates controlled by the nobles. Prominent noble families probably exercised leadership, and sometimes virtual control, within the cities in which they lived and at the same time ruled over their own estates like little principalities. The leading nobles may have held a position somewhat like that of the dynasts or 'tyrants' that later in parts of Asia Minor stood alongside of the cities and sometimes were associated with them.[1] In the fifth century there was a popular movement against the control of the nobles. This led to the substitution of polemarchs for tetrarchs and to the substitution of cities for *kleroi* in the organization of the army. By this time the estates of the nobles must, as it were, have been absorbed by the cities, though the nobles still struggled for leadership in the cities and even fought each other for control of the Thessalian state. The result was that the central government almost disappeared and that there were long intervals in which there was no *tagos*. Then came a period of reconstruction resulting in a strong federal state, which, since the head was elected for life, was pretty much a constitutional monarchy. Probably the clearest indication of the change is that, while in the fifth century the cities controlled and collected the customs duties, in the fourth century these, and probably also market fees in the cities, were collected for the federal government. The cities were there, and Thessaly can be classed as a sympolity, but the cities seem to have been markedly subordinated to the federal government. How far this development would have gone without Macedonian control, cannot be said. The rebuilding had begun before Philip II became head—whether he was called *archon* or *tagos*—of the Confederacy. He completed the process of establishing again the supremacy of the central government when he once more replaced polemarchs with tetrarchs and appointed them himself.[2]

2. THE BOEOTIAN CONFEDERACY

Boeotia was the home of the best known and most highly developed federal state of the second half of the fifth century before Christ. It is the one state of the period for which representative government is clearly attested. This is enough to rank it ahead of other contemporary federal states even though its financial system was less advanced than those of the Thessalian and Chalcidic confederacies. Our knowledge of its institutions is relatively new and is due to the fragments of a history of Greece, the *Hellenica Oxyrhynchia*, preserved on papyrus and first published in 1908. This contains a description of the constitution of the Boeotian Confederacy as it was in the period 447–386 B.C. It has added so much to our knowledge that any earlier account by a modern historian is practically useless.[3]

[1] See below under the Lycian Confederacy and cf. 'The Araxa Inscription and the Lycian Confederacy', *CP* li (1956), 151–69, especially 159–66.

[2] Theopompus, *FGrH* 115, frag. 208; Dem. ix. 26; cf. Sordi, 318.

[3] The account in Freeman, *Federal Government*, 120–32 is interesting chiefly as a demonstration of how little was known at the time he wrote. The account of the Boeotian constitution in the *Hellenica Oxyrhynchia* is found in what is chapter 11 of the Oxford text (1909) as edited

Boeotia had rather well-defined natural boundaries enclosing rich agricultural land, thus putting limits to its expansion and determining that it was to be primarily a land of farmers. This in turn was almost sure to make it a land of hoplites and of a moderately oligarchic government. It consisted essentially of the valley of a small river, the Asopus, and the lower valley of a somewhat larger river, the Cephissus, But for Lake Copaïs, this would have been one continuous plain broken only by slight elevations as it is today. As it was, the lake divided it into two districts, and Orchomenus, the chief city of the smaller district west of the lake, had a tendency to go its own way and to oppose Thebes, the chief city of eastern Boeotia. The Cephissus valley was the natural route for invaders coming from the northwest, though it narrowed in one place to less than a mile to form a sort of natural boundary between Phocis and Boeotia. These narrows and the plain between the lake and the mountains to the south were natural battle grounds, and here lay Chaeronea with its territory touching the frontier. Though this was the most vulnerable front, there seems to have been little fluctuation in the boundary between Boeotia and Phocis. Towards Attica the boundary seemed better marked by mountains, but, nevertheless, there was more fluctuation. Boeotia also had a coast line both on the Gulf of Corinth and on the sea between Euboea and the mainland, but these coasts were separated from the inland by mountains and contained no port of great importance. The one effort of Boeotia to build a navy, in the fourth century under the leadership of Epaminondas, was unnatural and had only shortlived success.[1]

Into this district the tribe of the Boeotians entered at about the time of the Doric migration, but they themselves were not Doric or Northwest Greek but an Aeolic speaking group dislodged from farther north by the Thessalians.[2] From Thessaly they brought with them the cult of

by B. P. Grenfell and A. S. Hunt. The discovery of an additional fragment has caused this to become ch. 16 in the Teubner edition of 1959 edited by V. Bartoletti. On the confederacy of this period cf. *Rep. Govt.* 31–40; 'The Boeotian Confederacy and Fifth Century Oligarchic Theory', *TAPA* lxxxvi (1956), 40–50; Luigi Moretti, *Ricerche sulle leghe greche* (1962), ch. ii. On questions of chronology the orthodox system as found, for instance, in Bengtson, *GrG²* is followed. For questions of political evolution it makes little difference whether a battle was fought a year earlier or later.

[1] See particularly Cary, *Geographic Background*, 69–73.

[2] Thucydides (1. 12. 3; cf. Gomme ad loc.) places this arrival sixty years after the fall of Troy. His remark that a group of Boeotians had arrived earlier is probably inserted to explain the presence of Boeotians in the *Iliad*, but such a supposition is unnecessary. Since the Boeotians spoke Aeolic, they must have been in Greece in Mycenaean times. Moreover, participation in the Trojan War, if historical, need not prove their presence in Boeotia. As Gschnitzer, 'Stammes- und Ortsgemeinden', *Wiener Studien*, lxviii (1955), 120–44 at 128 has argued, Boeotia is a place name derived from the tribal name, and thus the tribe bore this name before it entered the district. It is different with the entry in the Catalogue (*Iliad* ii. 494–510) in which they definitely are located in Boeotia. It is widely recognized that the

Athena Itonia, and to her a temple was built at Coronea in western Boeotia and there the national Boeotian festival, the Pamboiotia, was celebrated annually.[1] They undoubtedly came by way of Thermopylae, the pass of Hyampolis, and the narrows between Phocis and Boeotia. Thus the first place in Boeotia occupied by them was Chaeronea, as Plutarch (*Cimon* 1) says, that is, if it existed and had acquired the name by that time, but the people displaced were not, as he says, barbarians but Greeks who had arrived at an earlier date, probably Ionians like their neighbours in Attica.[2] The conquest apparently was slow, and that may be the reason the first Boeotian religious rallying point lay in western Boeotia. The districts bordering on Attica were not completely reconciled to being included in Boeotia even by the end of the sixth century. But this is not the whole story. It is known from archaeology and tradition that 'Minyan' Orchomenus, west of Lake Copaïs, was a strong centre in Mycenaean times. In the catalogue of ships in the *Iliad* (ii. 511–517) Orchomenus of the Minyans and Aspledon are listed separately and are not included among the holdings of the Boeotians. Apparently, when the catalogue was drawn up, Orchomenus had not yet been acquired by them. Since it was near the spot where they entered the country, it must have been strong enough to resist capture. At the time of the Peloponnesian War, the city was Boeotian, but it was remembered that it had not always been so.[3]

When the Boeotians entered Boeotia, they undoubtedly constituted a tribe headed by a king,[4] and this naturally led to the formation of a tribal state. Within this communities soon sprang up. The catalogue of ships in the *Iliad* lists twenty-nine, not including Aspledon and Orchomenus. This is so large a number that most of them must have been villages rather than towns or cities. By the fifth century many of them had been absorbed by larger towns so that the number of self-governing communities was much smaller. Many, however, retained their names, one of these being Chaeronea, which was under the control of Orcho-

distribution of the Greeks in the *Iliad* is pre-Doric and specifically that the Catalogue is on the whole Mycenaean. See M. P. Nilsson, *Homer and Mycenae* (1933), 90 f., 157; H. T. Wade-Gery, *The Poet of the Iliad* (1952), 53–57; D. L. Page, *History and the Homeric Iliad* (1959), 120–4; G. S. Kirk, *CAH* ii², ch. xxxix(b) (1964), 19 f. Nevertheless, it appears that Boeotia, Phocis, and Locris are given as they were after the Doric migration (Page, 152). For the language of Boeotia see Buck, *Greek Dialects*, 152–4.

[1] L. Ziehen, 'Pamboiotia', *RE* xviii. ii. 288 f.; for the Thessalian origin of the cult, see also M. P. Nilsson, *Geschichte der griechischen Religion*², i (1955), 434.

[2] Wade-Gery, *The Poet of the Iliad*, 5 considers it virtually certain that Poseidon Helikonios, worshipped at Mykale in connexion with the Panionia, derived his name from Mount Helikon in Boeotia, 'that is to say, that Boeotia had once been Ionian'. Cf. also C. Roebuck, *Ionian Trade and Colonization* (1959), 28, 31.

[3] Thuc, iv. 76. 3.

[4] A king is mentioned in Plut. *Cimon* 1 and Strabo ix. 393, not that this is too significant.

menus at least from the time of the Persian to the Peloponnesian War.[1]
Thus Orchomenus remained strong and at one point in the fifth century, when circumstances favoured her, was able to assume the leadership of Boeotia. Thebes, however, was the city which in the long run
became the more powerful. Progress in unifying Boeotia is indicated by
coins issued by various Boeotian cities in the sixth century. These show
on the obverse a Boeotian shield and usually on the reverse the first
letter of the name of the city. They are so much alike that they must
indicate a union of some kind. In fact, it has even been suggested that
all were turned out by a single mint, probably at Tanagra. But there
was one city that did not conform, namely, Orchomenus.[2] This must
mean that Orchomenus was not yet a member of the Confederacy.
Possibly the absence of archaic coins at Thespiae indicates that this
city too stood aloof.

Aside from the evidence of the coins, the first clear proof of the
existence of a political union in Boeotia is the attempt in 519 B.C. to
force Plataea to join the Confederacy.[3] The leaders of the Boeotians at
the time and the initiators of the aggression against Plataea were the
Thebans. According to the story told by Herodotus the Plataeans first
appealed to the Spartans under Cleomenes. The latter referred them
to the Athenians, who came to their aid. When the Thebans moved
against Plataea and the Athenians marched out to aid the city, some
Corinthians who happened to be present acted as arbitrators and ruled
that the Thebans should permit those of the Boeotians who so desired
to remain outside of the Confederacy. The Boeotians, nevertheless,
attacked the Athenians but suffered defeat. The Athenians then established the Asopus River as boundary between Thebes on the one hand
and Plataea and Hysiae—a town so far not mentioned in the story—on
the other.[4] Thus not only Plataea but also nearby Hysiae were lost to
the Boeotian Confederacy. This little town was apparently annexed by
Athens. The Asopus, however, was not made the boundary for its
entire length. Scolus, immediately east of Hysiae and south of the
Asopus, remained Theban or at least Boeotian, and so did undoubtedly
the district east of Scolus. There are difficulties connected with the story
of these events, but what matters is the outcome and the settlement,

[1] When the Persians crossed from Phocis to Boeotia, they certainly came first to Chaeronea, but Herod. viii. 34 states that they entered the land of the Orchomenians. According
to Thuc. iv. 76. 3 Chaeronea still belonged to Orchomenus in 424 B.C.

[2] Head, HN^2 343–55; Caspari, *JHS* xxxvii (1917), 172; Seltman, *Greek Coins*, 55. The
suggestion of a single mint is made by Seltman.

[3] For a sketch of the political history, primarily of Thebes, see Paul Cloché, *Thèbes de
Béotie des origines à la conquête romaine*, Paris, c. 1952. On the Plataea incident see also Moretti,
105–8.

[4] Herod. vi. 108. This version is followed in Thuc. iii. 55 in the speech of the Plataeans to
the Spartans at the time of their trial. The date is derived from Thuc. iii. 68. 5.

and these are confirmed by incidents and remarks connected with events of a later date.[1] Thus Thebes failed to secure the adhesion of Plataea, and the main obstacle had been Athens. No wonder that Athens for long remained the chief enemy of Boeotia. Probably also Orchomenus stood aloof. Thus the work of unification was not progressing quite as the Thebans would have liked. True, Herodotus (v. 79. 2) represents the Thebans as saying in 506 that the Tanagrans, Coroneans, and Thespians habitually co-operated with them, but of these the Thespians were not too reliable from the Theban point of view and went their own way in the Persian War, while Coronea was one of the smaller towns. This means that Tanagra was the only major Boeotian city on which the Thebans could rely. Events also show that Thebes and her associates were not a great power at the time. They were defeated by the Athenians both in 519 and in 506, when they joined the anti-Athenian coalition organized by Cleomenes of Sparta. On the latter occasion they attacked and captured the frontier posts of Hysiae and Oenoe while the Peloponnesians were invading Attica but reaped no lasting benefit from their initial success. When the Peloponnesians withdrew and the Athenians were free to deal with their other enemies, they defeated the Boeotians decisively and recovered the lost outposts.[2]

The relation of Boeotia to Thessaly in this period is a riddle that remains with us. The Thessalian cavalry must have passed through Boeotia on its way to aid Chalcis in the last campaign of the Lelantine War and again twice c. 510 B.C. on its way to Athens to aid Hippias against Sparta. It also appears that at one point the Thessalians had secured almost complete control of Boeotia before they suffered a decisive defeat at Ceressus in the territory of Thespiae. It is suggested below[3] that the Boeotians, that is, the Thebans and their associates, at the time were subordinate allies of the Thessalians and that they joined with them in an attack on the Thespians, which resulted in the defeat at Ceressus about 490 B.C. and the subsequent collapse of the power of Thessaly. The Athenians had been made the allies of the Thessalians or brought into their sphere of influence long before 519 by Peisistratus, who named one of his sons Thessalus.[4] Thus it was very likely fear of

[1] Hysiae is called a deme of Attica in Herod. v. 74. 2 in connexion with its recapture by the Boeotians in 506, but its exact status is difficult to determine. Incorporation with Plataea, as sometimes suggested, is excluded by Herod. ix. 15. 3 and 25. 3, which show that in 479 it was not a part of the territory of Plataea. In Herod. ix. 15. 2 Scolus is said to be on Theban territory. Whether this is to be taken literally, or simply means 'Boeotian', is not certain.

[2] Herod. v. 74–77. Herodotus says nothing about the recovery of Hysiae and Oenoe by the Athenians, but in 431 Oenoe was an Athenian frontier fort (Thuc. ii. 18. 1). Hysiae is not mentioned, but it is likely that it was recovered at the same time as Oenoe.

[3] In ch. iii; cf. CP lv (1960), 236 f.   [4] M. Sordi, La lega tessala, 55.

Thessaly which caused Cleomenes and the Spartans to refuse to protect Plataea. If this is correct, there is no mystery about the later passage of Thessalian forces through Boeotia on their way to aid Hippias.

The Persian War did nothing to improve and strengthen Boeotian unity. Among those who gave earth and water to the Persians were 'the Thebans and other Boeotians except the Thespians and the Plataeans'. This division was maintained and if anything rendered more acute by the war. Note that it seems that the tokens of submission were given by the cities and not by a central government of Boeotia. In Herodotus' account of the war, the Thebans and Thespians are frequently mentioned but Boeotians as such appear only in the Plataea campaign. In favour of the Thebans it can be argued that they did not actually go over to the Persians until after Thermopylae, but the fact remains that the Thespians are said to have sent 700 men to Thermopylae; the Thebans only 400, and there is some suspicion that the ruling pro-Persian oligarchs sent their opponents to meet their death.[1] At Plataea there were 1,800 Thespians in the Greek army while the 'Boeotians', that is, the Medizing Boeotians, fought on the side of the Persians and, says Herodotus, distinguished themselves, especially the members of the Medizing group at Thebes. As a result 300 of their 'best' men, members of the oligarchic clique, were slain. Even after the rest had given way, the Boeotian cavalry helped to protect those who fled.[2] This is the earliest evidence we have of the excellent military qualities which later characterized the Boeotians. Nevertheless, first prize among the Boeotians must be given to the Thespians, who had distinguished themselves at Thermopylae and after heavy losses there held out even after their city had been laid waste.[3]

Concerning the government of Boeotia at this time, very little information is available. What little there is suggests that there was a central government but one with very little authority. At one point Herodotus states that the Boeotarchs secured the services of some of those who lived near the Asopus river to serve as guides for the Persians.[4] Thus we learn that the magistrates known as 'Rulers of Boeotia' existed at the time, but we do not learn how many there were nor whether they were more than Theban officials whose title proclaimed the desire to rule all Boeotia. It has already been noted that the reply to the Persian demand for earth and water was given by the separate

[1] Herod. vii. 132. 1, 202. Diod. xi. 4. 7 reports that the party in control at Thebes sent out members of the opposition.

[2] Herod. ix. 30, 66–68. Of course all statistics in round numbers such as those given above are only approximate at best, but these seem acceptable and certainly give no evidence of the exaggeration which vitiates many of the statistics of Herodotus.

[3] Herod. viii. 50.   [4] Herod. ix. 15. 1.

cities and not by the central government. Moreover, the contingents of troops sent to Thermopylae were furnished by individual cities, but that was the mode of mobilization of the federal army even when the Confederacy was fully developed. Nevertheless, it appears that the activity of the central government consisted of little but the leadership in war exercised by the Thebans. Otherwise the chief evidence for the existence of a confederacy is the coinage already discussed. As to the form of government, Thucydides represents the Thebans later as excusing the Medism of their city on the grounds that at the time it was ruled by a *dynasteia* of a few, a narrow oligarchy but little removed from tyranny. This is confirmed by the manner in which the Greeks in 479 dropped their pressure on Thebes after the surrender of a group of pro-Persian leaders.[1] The governments of the other cities co-operating with Thebes must have been similar. Whatever unity existed before the war must have been lost. Certainly Thespiae and Plataea and the districts affiliated with them were definitely detached. Orchomenus is not heard of during the war, but there is no reason for believing that the city was any more friendly to Thebes than it had been. Thus the Boeotian Confederacy for practical purposes remained dissolved until two efforts to revive it were made in the middle of the fifth century. The first was an effort by Sparta to revive the Confederacy under Theban leadership as a counterweight against Athens. This led to defeat and the subjection of most of Boeotia by Athens. It now became necessary to wait for the initiative of Thebes' old enemy, Orchomenus, to liberate the country and give the Confederacy the constitution which, with minor changes, was to last from 447 to 386 and, paradoxically enough, was to serve as an instrument of Theban power.

In 457 the Spartans, who had been operating in central Greece, proceeded to strengthen Thebes and place her in control of Boeotia. The government set up by them certainly was oligarchic. Two months after the Spartans and their allies had defeated the Athenians at Tanagra and the Peloponnesian army had returned home, the Athenians in turn defeated the Boeotians at Oenophyta and as a result established control not only over Boeotia but also over Phocis and Eastern Locris. When the Peloponnesian army was in Boeotia, Athenian oligarchs had hoped to overthrow the democracy with its aid. Now the tables were turned, and the Athenians instead, with the aid of the local democratic or popular party, were able to set up democracies in the Boeotian cities.[2] At the time the leaders of the oligarchic party must have been driven into exile, but they apparently

---

[1] Thuc. iii. 62. 3; Herod. ix. 86–88.
[2] Thuc. i. 107 f.; Diod. xi. 81–83 (confused). Two references in speeches in Thucydides (iii. 62. 5, iv. 92. 6) indicate that the Athenians were aided by *stasis* in Boeotia.

managed to return almost immediately to Thebes, to secure the independence of the city from Athenian control, and to restore oligarchic government.[1] In the rest of Boeotia the democracies established by Athens lasted to 447. In that year exiles managed to make their way back and secured Orchomenus and the smaller town of Chaeronea located on the territory of Orchomenus. A relatively small force of Athenians led by Tolmides managed to regain Chaeronea but not the larger and more important Orchomenus. This, of course, meant that the expedition was a failure. Nevertheless, the Athenians left a garrison at Chaeronea and started homeward. At Coronea this force was attacked and defeated by exiles operating from Orchomenus aided by Locrians and Euboean exiles. After the defeat the Athenians made peace on the terms that their fellow citizens captured in the battle be released and they themselves withdraw completely from Boeotia. This was the first great victory of Boeotians over Athenians, and it was won under the leadership not of Thebes but of Orchomenus. No wonder that Orchomenus was able to take the initiative in organizing the Confederacy anew, and that she, undoubtedly in co-operation with other cities hostile to Thebes, arranged the apportionment of territory and representation in such a way that the resulting system was almost as anti-Theban as anti-Athenian.[2]

The government set up at the time is the best known federal government of early Greece. The Boeotia of the time is important as the one state which certainly possessed representative government. It is equally important as an example of moderate oligarchy. Active citizenship, the right to vote and hold office, depended on a property qualification. This was almost certainly the hoplite census, so that active citizenship was confined to those qualified to serve in the cavalry and the heavy infantry. The result was that over half of the adult male

[1] Thuc. i. 108. 3 implies Athenian control of all Boeotia; Diod. xi. 83. 1 states that Myronides secured control of all Boeotia except Thebes; Arist. *Pol.* 1302b29 reports that Thebes was governed democratically after Oenophyta and that the democracy was overthrown. For a fuller treatment see *CP* lv (1960), 9 and 17, n. 2.

[2] The chief source for the events of 447 is Thuc. i. 113. In Xen. *Mem.* iii. 5. 4 the younger Pericles couples the battle of Coronea—or Lebadea as he calls it—with Delium as the two battles which completely changed the attitude of the Boeotians to the Athenians. He might have added, had he seen the works of modern historians, that any reference to the great military reputation of the Boeotians at an earlier date is anachronistic. The constitution of 447 is the one described in *Hell Ox.* 16 (11) except that the latter gives the distribution of votes and duties not as they were in 447 but as they were after the representation of Thebes had been doubled by the acquisition of the representatives of Plataea and the other small towns grouped with it. For the events of 447 and the distribution of representatives at that time see 'Orchomenus and the Formation of the Boeotian Confederacy in 447 B.C.', *CP* lv (1960), 9–18. Otherwise for the constitution see *Rep. Govt.* 31–40; 'The Boeotian Confederacy and Fifth Century Oligarchic Theory', *TAPA* lxxxvi (1955), 40–50. On the role of Orchomenus cf. also Moretti, 130 f.; Ehrenberg, *Staat*, 151 (modifying somewhat *Gk. State*, 123).

3

citizens (the *politai*) were disfranchised.[1] Under this system the passive or disfranchised citizens differed from foreigners in that they possessed the civil rights of citizens, to hold property, to sue in the law courts as citizens, and to conclude legal marriages with citizens. For them to become active citizens, no enfranchisement was needed. All that was needed was the acquisition of sufficient property. Just how this was handled is not known, but it probably involved periodic assessments.[2] The authorities would take an active interest in the matter, since also the duty of military service was involved.

Within each city these active citizens were divided into four councils or *boulai*. Each of the four took its turn to serve as the council and prepare bills which were submitted to the other three. Apparently each of the four voted separately and unanimous agreement of the four was necessary for the adoption of any measure. Since the members of all four belonged to the same social class, this meant little and disagreement between them must have been very rare.

For the purposes of representation in the federal government Boeotia was divided into eleven units. In these units, in a number of cases, small towns had been grouped with or incorporated into larger cities. In this way, of the three larger cities Thebes ultimately controlled four units; Orchomenus, two; Thespiae, two, while Tanagra constituted one unit. The other two units were made up each of three small towns which took turns about supplying the Boeotarch of the unit. But this was not the distribution of units in 447. At that time Thebes controlled only two units, while two were assigned to Plataea, Scolus, Erythrae, and Scaphae, small towns near the frontier of Attica and south of the Asopus. Since this district extended from the territory of Thespiae to that of Tanagra, it cut Thebes completely off from contact with Attica. Orchomenus probably controlled three units at this time but lost one later when Chaeronea was detached. Yet, even if Orchomenus controlled only two units, the votes of the three cities opposed to Thebes were enough to give them a clear majority. Under the circumstances, it is likely that Plataea, in spite of her close association with Athens, considered herself a member and took active part in the affairs of the Confederacy.[3]

[1] That the disfranchised citizens outnumbered the active citizens can be deduced from the statistics of the troops at the battle of Delium (Thuc. iv. 93. 2) in which the light armed troops outnumbered the cavalry, hoplites, and peltasts combined.

[2] There is evidence for assessments of the kind at Cyrene in the last part of the fourth century B.C. (*SEG* ix. 1; cf. *TAPA* lxxxvi (1955), 42).

[3] Probably the most doubtful point in my article on Orchomenus in *CP* lv is the claim that Orchomenus at first had three Boeotarchs, something I characterized as 'highly probable' (p. 17). The judgement of others may be of interest. Moretti, 140 considers the three Boeotarchs possible ('è anche ammissibile l'ipotesi'); Ehrenberg, *Staat*, 151 accepts the eadership of Orchomenus in 447, states that Thebes at the time controlled only two electoral

Each of the eleven units supplied one Boeotarch, a member of the chief federal executive board, and sixty councillors and shared in the same proportion in all privileges and burdens of the federal government. Thus the chief organs of government were the federal board of eleven Boeotarchs and a federal *boule* or council of 660 members. Like the city councils, the federal council too was divided into four sections, which must have taken turns about conducting routine business and submitting its important findings to the other three. This federal council or councils had 'complete final authority', and there was no larger federal assembly. The council met in the Cadmea, the acropolis of Thebes, and Thebes undoubtedly was the administrative capital. The choice was apparently determined by geography. Thebes was much more centrally located than Orchomenus and Plataea and even than Thespiae. Each unit was expected further to supply 100 horsemen and 1,000 hoplites to the federal army. Though these numbers undoubtedly are only approximate,[1] it is clear that Boeotia at the time had a federal representative government with representation approximately in proportion to the size of the citizen body of the various communities. This constitution functioned pretty successfully for about two generations. In actual practice the council in most cases followed the lead of the Boeotarchs, and it was a great surprise to the latter when the council once refused to ratify their proposal. The quarter section of the council consisting of 165 members apparently was too large for efficient conduct of business and so largely left matters to the smaller body of Boeotarchs.

In turning to the functioning of the government, the army will be taken first. In theory each of the eleven units supplied equal contingents. Actually probably all active citizens of the proper age who were physically fit were liable to serve, so that the sizes of the contingents varied somewhat. Further information about the army is derived from the account by Thucydides of the Battle of Delium in 424 B.C. From it we learn that the army was under the command of the eleven Boeotarchs of whom one served as commander-in-chief. For how long he served or how he was chosen, we have not been told. Though the others served as a council of war, the word of the commander-in-chief apparently was decisive even when the others disagreed with him. At Delium, while the others were opposed to such action, he and only he was in favour of joining battle but he, nevertheless, persuaded the

units, but says nothing about the number controlled by Orchomenus; T. T. B. Ryder, *Koine Eirene* (1965), 14 f. mentions the temporary prominence of Orchomenus.

[1] Pierre Salmon's careful article, 'L'Armée fédérale des Béotiens', *L'Antiquité classique*, xxii (1953), 347–60 is marred somewhat by the fact that he takes these numbers as precise figures for the contingents required.

Boeotians to fight. In the line of battle the various contingents were assigned their places in the line, but the details of drawing up the troops were left to the local commanders. The Thebans were drawn up twenty-five deep; the others, as each contingent chanced. Thus the army suggests a rather loose federal organization.[1]

The same is true of the financial but not the judicial organization. The eleven units contributed equal portions to the federal treasury. As will be seen later, this system of payments to the federal treasury in proportion to representation became common and almost normal in Greek federal states. The expenses borne by the federal treasury were small except in time of war. The members of the federal council were given salaries or remuneration for expenses by their constituents.[2] The same must have been true also of the soldiers unless—and this is probably more likely—the men served at their own expense. The federal judicial system, on the other hand, suggests a fairly advanced state. The units again contributed equal numbers of judges or jurors. This is all the information we have, but it is enough to show that a federal judiciary system independent of the council existed. Finally, when judging the federal government, it is well to bear in mind that the great amount of administration left to the local authorities need not mean weakness. On the contrary, a federal state in which the local authorities are active under the direction of the central government can be very effective. In Boeotia, in spite of rivalries between cities and strife between oligarchs and democrats, the state seems normally to have followed the leadership of the Boeotarchs.

The Boeotian constitution of 447 was on the whole unusually successful. It lasted with little change for two generations—longer, for instance, than the period from the development of extreme democracy in Athens under Pericles to the oligarchic revolutions of 411 and 404. Yet it could not entirely do away with strife between oligarchs and democrats and rivalry between cities within the Confederacy. Most notably, Thebes could not be kept in a position of inferiority. Orchomenus was too remote from much of Boeotia to be able to perpetuate her leadership, and this city undoubtedly had too little in common with Thespiae and Plataea for the three to form an effective block. Thebes too had the advantage from the beginning of serving as the federal capital. The Thebans also seem to have developed their military system ahead of their neighbours and, furthermore, do not seem to have been afraid to act independently at times, though they undoubtedly preferred to give their actions a semblance of legality. In the attack on

[1] Thuc. iv. 91–93.
[2] This seems pretty clear, though other theories have been held; cf. *Rep. Govt.* 38 and 205, n. 33.

Plataea in 431 two Boeotarchs commanded the attacking force,[1] but the story of the surprise attack certainly gives the impression that the undertaking was a Theban rather than a Boeotian venture. Had mobilization orders gone out to various cities, the attack could not well have been secret. On the other hand, when the Thebans in 423 dismantled the walls of Thespiae on the charge of Atticism,[2] they undoubtedly had secured in advance a federal judgement against the city. In general, the great opportunity for the Thebans came with the Peloponnesian War, which enabled them to dispose of Plataea. When the inhabitants of the small towns east of Plataea, which had been grouped with her for purposes of representation, felt themselves too exposed, they sought refuge in Thebes, and their territory was annexed to that of Thebes. The process was completed with the destruction of Plataea, and thus Thebes secured control of two additional units of representation and thus doubled her representation on the board of Boeotarchs and in the federal council.[3] But the greatest day of all for Thebes must have been that of the Battle of Delium, the second great victory of Boeotians over Athenians, and a victory primarily due to the Thebans. The latter obviously made use of the prestige gained there to act against their opponents. Though the Thespians had distinguished themselves in the battle and had suffered heavy losses, their walls, as already mentioned, were dismantled next year on the charge of Atticism. This too was probably the time when Chaeronea was detached from Orchomenus and, in all likelihood, the representation of that city reduced.[4] It was probably at this time too that Thebes secured a practical monopoly in Boeotia of the minting of money, which is stamped as that of the city rather than that of the Boeotians.[5] Otherwise they acted perfectly legally, and the official acts regularly appear as acts of the Boeotians.

[1] Thuc. ii. 2. 1.

[2] Thuc. iv. 133. 1. The charge of Atticism had been levelled also against the Plataeans (iii. 62. 2).

[3] Hell. Ox. 17 (12). 3. In his account of the Battle of Delium Thucydides iv. 91 refers to eleven Boeotarchs but speaks of only two as Theban. This may be an anachronism, or, more likely, a distinction was made between the two who filled the two original Theban seats and the other two. This fits with the statement of Hell. Ox. 16 (11). 3 that Thebes furnished four Boeotarchs, 'two on behalf of the city and two on behalf of Plataea and Scolus, etc.'.

[4] Thuc. iv. 93, 96. The Thebans may have used as a pretext the fact that those Boeotians who plotted with the Athenians in 424 had planned to secure Siphae in the territory of Thespiae and Chaeronea in that of Orchomenus (Thuc. iv. 76), but these were merely convenient localities on the frontiers, and there is no proof that there were more democratic 'traitors' in these two cities than in the other Boeotian cities. The archplotter actually was a Theban.

[5] These coins are dated 426–395 by Cloché, Thèbes de Béotie, 80 citing Babelon. The issue is dated as beginning after 447 by Head, HN² 349 f.; Seltman, Greek Coins, 156. Such dates given by numismatists are only approximate and usually are based on their understanding of the political situation. In this case the later date (426 ff.) is by far the more likely.

This, of course, was the better part of wisdom and was not difficult. With the large block of votes they controlled directly, the Thebans must have found it easy to secure enough votes from the smaller communities to outvote the Orchomenians or Thespians if either city tried to obstruct their policies.

The influence of Thebes was now paramount in the Confederacy, and, as things developed, this was natural enough. With the great accession of territory, the Theban representation in the federal government was not out of proportion, and, judging by Delium, the military strength of Boeotia was largely due to the Theban troops. The leaders of the city paid their enemies at Orchomenus the compliment of retaining the constitution they had drawn up. Nevertheless, party strife and rifts between cities could not be avoided. Party strife is seen best in the history of Thespiae. There must have been advocates of democracy in most Boeotian cities as there always were advocates of oligarchy at Athens, but at Thespiae, situated relatively near both the sea and Attica, the danger of a democratic revolt was greater than in other Boeotian cities. When the Thebans demolished the walls of the city the year after Delium, this may have been due to more than mere vindictiveness. The Thespians had suffered heavy losses in the battle, probably losing as much as one-third of the hoplites they had sent on the campaign.[1] Since the troops that suffered these losses belonged to the active citizens, that is, the oligarchs who controlled the city, and since the disfranchised lower classes normally outnumbered the active citizens, these losses may have upset the balance so much that the danger of a democratic revolution was greatly increased. Nine years later, in 414, there actually was a democratic revolt at Thespiae. This was put down with the aid of Thebes, while those of the rebels that were not caught fled to Athens.[2] Since the democrats looked to Athens, there naturally is no democratic revolt reported for the rest of the Peloponnesian War after the Spartans had occupied Decelea.

The continued strife between cities is illustrated by the history of Orchomenus. There is no report of any special action on the part of the city during the Peloponnesian War, but in the Corinthian War beginning in 395, Orchomenus, in her efforts to cut loose from Boeotia, became a staunch ally of Sparta. In the campaign of 395, when Lysander, in command of Sparta's allies in central Greece, was to advance from Phocis and meet Pausanias, coming from the south, at Haliartus,

---

[1] *TAPA* lxxxvi (1955), 47. The estimate is based on the statistics of the Boeotian troops and casualties given by Thucydides iv. 93. 3, 101. 2, and the implication that most of the Boeotian casualties were Thespian.

[2] Thuc. vi. 95. 2.

the natural place for the Boeotians to try to intercept him was near Chaeronea, but the Orchomenians, obviously again in control of Chaeronea, joined forces with Lysander and took part in the battle of Haliartus.[1] It was probably at this time that a Spartan garrison was stationed in Orchomenus. The next year the Orchomenians joined the army of Agesilaus, and what he thought of them is indicated by his action in stationing them at the battle of Coronea on the left wing of his army opposite the Thebans.[2] On this occasion the Orchomenians suffered defeat at the hands of their old enemies, but they, nevertheless, persisted. In 391, as we learn from a speech by Andocides (iii. 13, 20), one of the Athenian negotiators, the Boeotians actually were ready to make peace on terms involving the freedom of Orchomenus, but the plan fell through, and the Orchomenians had to wait for their freedom to the time of the dissolution of the Boeotian Confederacy after the King's Peace. The examples of Thespiae and Orchomenus are enough to show that it is not correct to regard this dissolution as a purely arbitrary act imposed by Sparta on an unwilling Boeotia. Probably the majority was unwilling, but there were many Boeotians who welcomed the dissolution.

Thespiae and Orchomenus illustrate two disturbing factors always present in Greek states. Thespiae illustrates the tendency to place party in the broadest sense above loyalty to one's community so as to look to outsiders for help against fellow citizens of the opposite party. The democrats of this city looked to Athens, while the oligarchs accepted help from Thebes in putting down revolution among the lower classes in their own city. Of course, these oligarchs and democrats were more than mere political parties. They stood for completely opposite social ideals. The oligarchs, even in so moderate an oligarchy as Boeotia, believed in keeping the control of the state in the hands of safe and sound men of property and thus safeguarding their own interests. The democrats favoured giving political rights to all adult male citizens and tended to dream of improving the lot of the lower classes. Orchomenus illustrates the extremes to which Greek city-states would go in fighting for complete freedom, particularly when the fight was embittered by hatred. What makes the case all the more significant is that the city, at least when it rose and joined the Spartans in 395, could hope for no position of leadership. All that the Orchomenians could hope to accomplish was to get away from Thebes and the Boeotians, and to do this they were ready to subordinate themselves to the leadership of Sparta. Except for the brief period of their own leadership in the

---

[1] Xen. *Hell*. iii. 5. 6, 17; Plut, *Lys*. 28.
[2] Xen. *Hell*. iv. 3. 15–18; Plut. *Ages*. 18.

middle of the fifth century, it seems that the Orchomenians were never at heart Boeotians but remained 'Minyans'.[1]

3. THE PHOCIAN CONFEDERACY

The Phocian Confederacy, if there were more information available, probably would furnish a perfect illustration of the transformation of a tribal state into a federal state, the development apparently being stimulated rather than impeded by the conquest of Phocis by the Thessalians. The tribal state was the creation of a conquering tribe, and, when this once had been set up, its unity was never seriously threatened, except for the eternal problem of Delphi, until the Third Sacred War in the middle of the fourth century. Yet within this state cities developed early and, when Phocis was liberated from Thessalian domination about 490 B.C., the state that emerged was a federal state in which the federal government and the governments of the cities each had their allotted tasks. Any further information about Phocian institutions, unfortunately, is extremely slim.[2]

Phocis was relatively small and compact. It consisted of two sections, of which the larger included most of the upper part of the Cephissus valley. This river, emerging from Phocis through a relatively narrow gateway, continued its course through Boeotia. This pass was enough of a barrier so that the Phocian part of the valley constituted a natural unit by itself. Near the gateway to Boeotia a pass extended south to the later port of Anticyra on the Gulf of Corinth. The mountainous district along the coast to which this pass gave access constituted the second

---

[1] Studies published too late to be used in the above account indicate a considerable interest in the Boeotian Confederacy. Marta Sordi, 'Autonomia e egemonia nel koinon Beotico', *Atene e Roma*, 1965, 10–19 raises some interesting problems. One is the suggestion that the two representational districts connected with Plataea did not exist before the 'admission' of Plataea in 427, so that in this earlier period there were only nine districts. This is a plausible conjecture but not proved. Less is to be said for the argument that the system of four *boulai* originated after Delium. The claim that the timocratic pattern of the Boeotians was derived from the movement for a return to the *patrios politeia* seems almost absurd. Boeotia was not Athens, and there is no indication that the Boeotian oligarchy was preceded by democracy. Nor does it seem correct to conclude from the troublesome τὰ κοινὰ in *Hell. Ox.* 16 (11). 4 that there existed a federal primary assembly in addition to the *boule*. This point in n. 16 is derived from S. Dušanić in *Živa Antika*, xiii–xiv (1964), 119 ff. A glance at the English summary of that article indicates that the conclusion is based on the conviction that *koinon* frequently means a primary assembly. This is very unusual, and the examples cited are far from convincing. *Thespies et la confédération béotienne* (1965) by Paul Roesch has little of any value for this period in spite of its imaginative but unconvincing suggestion about the division of rights and duties in the case of cities controlling more than one representational unit, but the book contributes much to the understanding of Boeotia in the late third and the second centuries B.C.

[2] The modern literature is correspondingly slim. It includes Gawril Kazarow, *De foederis Phocensium institutis* (1899); F. Schober, 'Phokis', *RE* xx. i (1941), 474–96 and his dissertation, *Phokis*, (1924).

and smaller section of Phocis. At its western extremity were the Crisaean Plain and Delphi. In the angle between the route to Anticyra and
the main route up the Cephissus valley lay Mount Parnassus. When
Delphi belonged to Phocis, this was entirely Phocian, and the mountain
always remained a place of refuge to which the Phocians could withdraw when the country was overrun by foes. From the eastern extremity of Phocis, another pass, that of Hyampolis, led north to the
Locrian shore. On this coast the Phocians are said to have held the
port of Daphnus for some time.[1] The occupation of this port must have
been a part of an effort to strengthen the defences against invaders
coming from the north and to try to stop them before they reached
Phocis proper. In this connexion it is well to remember that the route
by the pass of Hyampolis was the only good route available for invaders coming by Thermopylae and was, in fact, the route used by the
Thessalians in their attacks on Phocis.[2]

Phocis seems to have been inhabited by Greeks before it was conquered by new invaders at the time of the Dorian migration. The result
was a mixed population upon which the conquerors imposed their
Northwest Greek language, though the dialect also revealed some survivals from the Aeolic language of its earlier inhabitants.[3] As a symbol
of their unity, the Phocians looked back to an eponymous hero, Pho-
kos.[4] Even without this legend, we should conclude that the conquerors
formed an ethnic unity which, aside from the mixture with the earlier
inhabitants, retained its unity throughout antiquity. Their exact relation to the Locrians, who also spoke a Northwest Greek dialect and
who must have come at about the same time as the Phocians, remains
uncertain. Probably the old theory that the Locrians came first and
that the Phocians came later and split them into two divisions is
essentially correct.[5] The Phocians obviously tried to hold in subjection
the Epicnemidian Locrians between Thermopylae and Hyampolis.
Evidence of this is the Phocian Wall, built, it was said, to hold back the
Thessalians,[6] and the Phocian tenure for some time of the port of

---

[1] Strabo ix. 416, 424 f., 426. Thus Strabo mentions the city three times in his description
of Phocis and Locris. Otherwise little is known of it; cf. Philippson, 'Daphnus' (4), *RE* iv,
2148 f.

[2] Evidence for the use of the route Thermopylae-pass of Hyampolis will keep turning up
down to the period of the Roman wars in Greece. For a discussion of its use chiefly by the
Thessalians, cf. *CP* lv (1960), 231–3.

[3] Buck, *Greek Dialects*, 156 f.

[4] Paus. x. 1. 10.

[5] Cary, *CAH* iii. 613; Glotz-Cohen, *Hist. grecque*, i. 101. The theory is based on the belief
that the invaders advanced down the Cephissus valley. It is much more likely that they
came by way of Thermopylae and the pass of Hyampolis. If so the Phocians may well have
subdued the Locrians who remained on the coast of the Malian Gulf and have driven the
others before them.

[6] Herod. vii. 176. 4.

Daphnus. This was the only notable attempt in our period to subdue land outside of Phocis proper.

It has already been noted that the unity of Phocis, after the tribal state had been established, was not seriously threatened in classical times. Two factors, however, prevented the unity from being quite complete and serene. One was the fact that a small portion of the upper Cephissus valley did not belong to Phocis but constituted Doris; the other, the anomalous position of Delphi and Crisa. As for Doris, it is true that the ancients placed the source of the Cephissus at Lilaea in Phocis,[1] but a glance at the map will reveal that Doris belonged fully as much to the valley of that river as did the region of Lilaea. An attempt to conquer Doris and thus extend Phocis on this side to its natural boundary was made in the middle of the fifth century but only led to Spartan intervention.[2] As for Delphi, the Homeric *Hymn to Pythian Apollo* implies that Delphi was under the control of Crisa.[3] In the Homeric catalogue, both Crisa and Delphi (Pytho) are classed as Phocian. Nevertheless, the First Sacred War seems to have been directed against Crisa rather than against the Phocians. This may mean that the rest of Phocis had already been conquered by the Thessalians and that only Crisa remained, or that the city had become independent for other reasons. Its profits on trade and on travellers bound for Delphi may have made the city strong enough to go its own way.[4] When Crisa was destroyed, Delphi, in so far as it was not under the control of the Amphictionic League, must have become an independent city. There is much to be said for the theory that, except for very early— almost mythical—times, Delphi was not subject to Phocis before 454 B.C.[5]

The earliest evidence for the unity of Phocis is the catalogue of ships in the *Iliad*, but this also attests the existence of numerous cities.[6] The

---

[1] *Iliad* ii. 523; *Hymn to Pythian Apollo* 240 f.; Strabo i. 16; ix. 407, 424; Paus. ix. 24. 1; x. 8. 10, 33. 5.

[2] Thuc. i. 107, 2; Diod. xi. 79. 4–6.

[3] Cf. Busolt, *GrG* i². 690 and n. 6; Pomtow, *RE* iv. 253; Beloch, *GrG²* ii. i. 178 and n. 1. Crisa and Pytho classed as Phocian: *Iliad* ii. 517–20.

[4] Aeschines iii. 107; Strabo ix. 418 f. We know nothing actually about the relative merits of the crusaders and the Crisaeans, for all our information concerning the war comes from those who destroyed Crisa.

[5] Beloch, loc. cit.

[6] *Iliad* ii. 517–23. The names are: Pytho (Delphi), Kyparissos, Krisa, Daulis, Panopeus, Anemoreia, Hyampolis, and Lilaia. Of these Kyparissos according to Paus. x. 36. 5 was the later Anticyra, and Anemoreia (or Anemoleia) according to Strabo ix. 423 was located under a spur of Parnassus at what became the boundary between Phocis and Delphi when Sparta detached Delphi from the Phocian federal state. Daulis and Panopeus were situated south of the Cephissus valley in the approaches to the pass leading to Kyparissos-Anticyra. Thus, except for Hyampolis and Lilaea, the places mentioned belong to southern Phocis near the Gulf of Corinth. Of the two Hyampolis is probably mentioned on account of its strategic location, and Lilaea because it marked the source of the Cephissus, while the rest

places mentioned are near the Gulf of Corinth and in the southern part of Phocis except for Hyampolis, at the pass leading north from eastern Phocis to the sea, and Lilaea at the source of the Cephissus. The reference to the others who dwelt along the Cephissus does not exclude —it rather suggests—the existence of other towns in the Cephissus valley. Thus we can conclude that there were numerous towns in Phocis as early as the eighth century.[1] The twenty odd cities that ultimately belonged to the Confederacy[2] were many for so small a district. None of them can have been very large, and no single city dominated the others. If Elatea later became the capital, it apparently was not because this city overawed the rest, but rather because the others chose her as conveniently located. The situation in some respects was ideal for the formation of a federal state—a compact territory with numerous towns that were more or less equal.

To the evidence of the *Iliad* for the early development of towns in Phocis there can be added the report that Crisa, even before the city had begun to exploit the pilgrims going to Delphi, had enriched itself through tolls on trade from Italy and Sicily. This means that Crisa was an important city exploiting foreign trade as early as the seventh century, that is, before the minting of money had begun in this part of Greece. Evidence for the greatness of Crisa is the fact that the Gulf of Corinth continued to be called the Crisaean Gulf even after the destruction of Crisa and was so called by Thucydides.[3] The example of this city indicates that in Phocis, as in Thessaly, when the imposition of regular customs duties began, these were imposed by the cities. In the case of Crisa, its relative isolation must have made the step easy. The development of the rest of Phocis, whether it was as advanced as Crisa or not, was checked by its conquest by the Thessalians in the sixth or seventh century. When the latter were expelled, Phocis resumed its development and thereafter apparently continued it without interruption to the end of the Third Sacred War in 346. At any rate, there is no evidence that the Phocian Confederacy was dissolved as a result of the King's Peace. This means that there is no reason for assuming any violent break in the evolution of its institutions in this period.

The existence of a Phocian tribal state of some kind before the Thessalian conquest is attested by the representation of the Phocians in the Amphictionic League. For the government of this state there is only the

of those dwelling along the Cephissus are lumped together. This should not be taken to mean that there were no other towns in the Cephissus valley.

[1] On the Catalogue see p. 27, n. 2 above under 'The Bocotian Confederacy'.

[2] Dem. xix. 123 gives their number as twenty-two; Paus. x. 3. 1–2 lists twenty as destroyed by Philip and one (Abae) as spared by him.

[3] Strabo ix. 418; Thuc. ii. 69. 1, 83. 1, etc.

evidence of the statement in the *Iliad* (ii. 517 f.) that the Phocians were under the command of a pair of brothers. Their father and grandfather are listed without any specific indication that they too were commanders or rulers of the Phocians, but, on account of the prominence of kingship in Homer, it is natural to see here the survival of a kingship going back to the time of the conquest. The two brothers mentioned may have been joint kings, or the older of the two may have been the king.[1] In either case, this is our only evidence for the survival of kingship in Phocis. Whether it survived to the Thessalian conquest is not known. The evidence of the *Iliad* and the example of Crisa indicates that the development of cities already was under way. This, if anything, was furthered by the Thessalian domination. In connexion with it we hear of Thessalian officials in Phocis and of tyrants. The latter must have been Phocians who were set up by the Thessalians as rulers in their home communities. The information comes to us from Plutarch, who was from nearby Chaeronea and secured from local sources information lost to the main currents of Greek historiography. Whether the communities over which the tyrants ruled were or were not cities, the Thessalian support of them must have tended to disrupt the unity of the country, while the hostages held by the Thessalians tended to intimidate the Phocians and prevent a rising. Nevertheless, opposition to the oppressors seems to have strengthened the sentiment for unity and co-operation. The revolt, probably of about 490 B.C., which led to the liberation of Phocis, began with a concerted action—the assassination of all tyrants and all Thessalian officials in Phocis on a single day—and was followed by the vigorous conduct of the war by the central government.[2]

The Phocian government of the period from the liberation to the dissolution of the Confederacy in the fourth century was characterized by a strong executive in the shape of a general or a group of generals, with one in times of emergency being given dictatorial powers as *strategos autokrator*, general with full powers. Yet this executive was subject to the control of the Phocian assembly on major issues and was even liable to be deposed by the assembly. In the revolt against the Thessalians, Daïphantus of Hyampolis, who was general at the time and next to the women the hero of the occasion, proposed the plan, in case of defeat to put to death all women and children, but it was a vote of the assembly,

---

[1] The king may have been Schedius, one of the two who in *Iliad* xvii. 306–8 is described as living at Panopeus and ruling over many men.

[2] This revolt will be considered in ch. iii; cf. *CP* lv (1960), 231–6. The chief source accounts are Plut. *Mor.* 244 and Paus. x. 1. 3–10. On the chronology, though not on all details of interpretation, I have followed Sordi, *La lega tessala*, 88 f.; Kazarow, 8 places the revolt shortly before 480.

undoubtedly the men in arms, which adopted the plan.[1] This story may have been embroidered somewhat, but the general picture corresponds to later usage. For an illustration it is necessary to jump to 356 B.C., when Philomelus induced the Phocians to claim the control of Delphi and elect himself *strategos autokrator*. Philomelus did not go into detail about how he would use his authority, but both his election and the decision to go ahead were due to the assembly. On this occasion it seems that Philomelus did not wait for a regular meeting at a fixed time but rather that the consultation took place and the decision was made when the situation demanded it. When Philomelus was killed, Onomarchus, who had been his colleague, carried on. Later, after the war had been allowed to lapse for a short time, Onomarchus persuaded the Phocians to resume the war and was himself elected *strategos autokrator*. This meant another major decision by the assembly. Then, when Onomarchus was killed, he was succeeded by his brother, Phayllus. The latter, in turn, left the command to his nephew, Phalaecus, the son of Onomarchus, with an older man as his guardian and actual commander. It looks as if the family of Onomarchus was trying to establish a dynastic rule. This makes it all the more significant that Phalaecus was deposed and replaced by a group of three.[2] Thus, though during a war Phocis might seem practically a monarchy, the assembly was able to depose the dictator and, when public opinion demanded it, actually did so. There is absolutely no information about the composition of the assembly. In all likelihood, it was a primary assembly consisting of the men who bore arms or had done so. In all likelihood it was more nearly democratic than that of early Thessaly. At least, we do not hear of serfs in Phocis. Whether, in addition to the assembly, there was a smaller council, a *boule* or *synedrion*, in the absence of evidence, is any man's guess and there would be no profit in recording the guesses made by various scholars. As for the assembly, the country was so small that a primary assembly could work perfectly as well, or rather better than, in Attica.

For the chief executive or executives of the Confederacy, the title commonly used was *strategos* or general, a title which it is hardly necessary to remind the reader was commonly used in Greek federal states for the official we should tend to call president. This, in turn, should serve as a reminder that the federal government was concerned chiefly with foreign affairs. For Phocis we know the title but have trouble with

---

[1] Plut. *Mor.* 244 C-D. M. P. Nilsson, *A History of Greek Religion*, 63 (Norton ed., 1964) considers the story of the proposal to kill the women and children in case of defeat an aetiological tale. This may well be the case, but it seems nevertheless that the sequence of battles as reconstructed is as nearly correct as such things can be.

[2] For these events see Diod. xvi. 23.4-24.1, 31.5-32.4, 36.1, 38.6, 56.3.

the question of the normal number of generals and the length of their term of office. During the wars in the middle of the fourth century there was normally a general with dictatorial powers in charge, and he seems to have had these powers delegated to him for an indefinite period. The story of the wars implies that all except Phalaecus, who was deposed and later recovered his authority, remained in office till their death. Thus the election may have been for life or for the duration of the emergency. The delegation of such powers, clearly was an emergency measure. In normal times there seems to have been a board of two or three generals. The evidence is as follows. In their accounts of an attack by the Thessalians after the revolt of the Phocians about 490 B.C., Plutarch speaks of Daïphantus of Hyampolis as one of three officials; Pausanias speaks of him as general of the cavalry and Rhoeus of Ambrossus as general of the infantry, thus, in the opinion of most interpreters, implying the existence of two generals.[1] Of the two, the one who speaks with the greater authority concerning anything connected with Daïphantus is Plutarch. Therefore, it is likely that he is right when he suggests three generals. Since three appear again when Phalaecus was deposed in 347, it is likely that three was the normal number except when a general with dictatorial powers was elected, something which apparently was done as often as the assembly saw fit to do so. This may seem less startling if it is recalled that the Achaean Confederacy, as late as the last quarter of the third century, created Aratus a *strategos autokrator*. The four famous Phocian generals of the fourth century, Philomelus, Onomarchus, Phayllus, and Phalaecus, between them served about nine years, all except Phalaecus serving to the day of their death. There seems to be no information concerning the length of the term of office of the generals under more normal conditions.

An indication that the Phocian government did more than conduct wars is found in the coinage. This, it seems, began immediately after the revolt early in the fifth century and was definitely the coinage of the federal or central government. The earliest coins were uninscribed, but later coins bore the name of the Phocians in abbreviated form (*ΦΟ*, *ΦΟΚΙ*). The coins were struck on the Aeginetan standard, the largest

---

[1] Plut. *Mor.* 244 C; Paus. x. 1. 8. Kazarow, 8 f. argues that the seer, Tellias of Elis, mentioned by Pausanias as holding the chief position among the magistrates, was the third general. H. Swoboda, *Staatsaltertümer*, 318, n. 6 considers it impossible that an Elean should be a general of the Phocians, thus adopting the rather questionable procedure of judging one part of Greece by standards known from other parts and times. Busolt, *Staatskunde*, 1451 is non-committal. It is also possible that Plutarch and Pausanias are not speaking about the same thing. Plutarch calls Daïphantus an *archon*, and *archon* may or may not refer to the same official as *strategos*, while Pausanias speaks of *strategoi*. Is it possible that there was a board of three chief magistrates (*archontes*) and that for an actual campaign one was selected to serve as general (*strategos*) of the cavalry and one of the infantry? But this is highly speculative, and the point is not important.

being three obol pieces and the smallest being half obols.[1] In addition one Phocian city, Neon, also struck small silver on the same standard but with ΦO on the obverse and NE on the reverse, while another city, probably Lilaea, even omitted the Phocian name. These coins apparently were issued according to the federal pattern and not in opposition to or rivalry with the federal issues. Delphi too minted on the same standard and in this period issued only coins from one quarter obol to one and a half obol except for a few larger coins possibly of about 480 B.C.[2] If Delphi was politically independent at the time, it at least belonged economically to the Phocian sphere. The minting of money, in turn, suggests the existence of some federal administrative machinery other than merely the generals. This would include control of finances, a treasury department of sorts. The earliest reference to a treasurer seems to be in connexion with a payment of indemnities to Delphi in 336 B.C.[3]

To conclude, the Phocian Confederacy was a genuine federal state from the time of the expulsion of the Thessalians or very soon thereafter. This emerges clearly from its history in spite of the almost complete lack of information about the government machinery. The conclusion is based on the facts that there were at the same time a vigorous federal government and cities with their own local administration. For the latter point the minting of money by one or two cities is useful evidence. The Confederacy is designated a federal state by a literary source for the first time in connexion with events of the middle of the fifth century.[4] This is found in an account of events not much more than a generation after the liberation. This rings true, though our source is relatively late. Then there is the report of the campaign immediately after the revolt for which two generals, Rhoeus of Ambrossus and Daïphantus of Hyampolis, are named. This too points to a federal state in which the officials were listed as citizens of their respective

[1] Head, HN² 338 places the beginning of the issue not much later than the middle of the sixth century. Similar views are expressed by Schober, RE xx. i. 480 and Seltman, Greek Coins, 159. Thus this has become the orthodox view. Against this, for a date in the fifth century, see Percy Gardner, A History of Ancient Greek Coinage 700–300 B.C. (1918), 361; Caspari (Cary), JHS xxxvii (1917), 176–7. Note, however, that those who favour a date in the sixth century also tend to believe that the Phocian rising against the Thessalians came at this time. M. Sordi, Riv. fil., n.s. xxxi (1953), 255, n. 1, on the other hand, places the first coins before the Thessalian conquest. Since other evidence had led to the conclusion that the revolt did not come till after 491 (CP lv. 236 f.), it seemed that also the Phocian minting of money must be placed after this date, as has been done by Gardner and Cary.

[2] Head, HN² 340–3, Caspari, loc. cit.; Gardner, 361, 363 f.

[3] SIG³ 233. This is an entry in a record inscribed at the temple of Athena Cranaea near Elatea. Thus it is a part of the records published by the Phocians themselves, but it belongs to a period beyond the one now under consideration.

[4] Strabo ix. 423 f. speaks of the time when Sparta detached Delphi from the Phocian federal state (ἀπὸ τοῦ κοινοῦ συστήματος τῶν Φωκέων).

cities. Pressure from Thessaly clearly served as a challenge to stimu-
late the development of the federal state, and it is likely that the cities
near the line of advance of the Thessalians were the first to band together. Of the two generals mentioned, one came from Hyampolis,
directly in the line of advance through the pass, while also the home
city of the other, Ambrossus, lay in eastern Phocis. Probably also the
troops who took part in the campaign were local troops. With this
line of development, the theory that the money was minted at Daulis[1]
fits well, for Daulis lay between Hyampolis and Ambrossus. Of course,
it is possible that troops from more distant parts turned up for the
campaign. It is also possible that some cities in the upper Cephissus
valley were responsible for the defence on that side. There may be
some significance in the fact that Lilaea appears to have minted
money at this time. Was it minted for use in paying expenses in connexion with the defence? Though Neon lay at the foot of the north
slope of Mount Parnassus, it is almost too fanciful to suggest that the
money minted there belongs to a time when much of the country had
been overrun by enemies and the Phocians had sought refuge on
Parnassus. Whether the development of cities affected the organization of and method of taking votes in the assembly is not known. My
own guess is the same as for the Aetolian Confederacy, that it did not
but that votes were counted by heads. Distances were not so great that
the interests of any city had to be safeguarded by having the votes
taken by cities.

4. THE LOCRIAN CONFEDERACIES

The Locrians were a small tribe even for Greece, and were divided
into two geographically separated groups, the East Locrians east of
Thermopylae along the coast of the Malean and Euboeic gulfs, and
the West Locrians along the north shore of the Gulf of Corinth from the
neighbourhood of Delphi to the narrows at Naupactus. The West
Locrians were given the reputation by Thucydides (i. 5. 3) of being
backward, neither group developed a strong federal state, and neither
played any great role in the events of the times. Yet the Locrians have
considerable interest for us. The East Locrians in the first half of the
fifth century had a federal organization decidedly advanced for that
time, while the West Locrians, with a looser organization, illustrate
that state of fluidity in which there existed in a tribal state a central
government with some authority while there also were cities claiming
authority and the lines of demarcation between the two sets of power
were none too clear.[2] Yet the West Locrians too were rather advanced

---

[1] Seltman, *Greek Coins*, 159.
[2] Cf. F. Gschnitzer, *Abhängige Orte*, 143 f.

in some respects. Our knowledge is derived from three well known and much discussed but somewhat obscure inscriptions, which shed light not only on the development of federalism but also more generally on Greek social and political institutions of the fifth century B.C. The three inscriptions have been found in West Locris, two of them at Galaxidi, the site of ancient Chaleum.[1] One of the two contains regulations adopted by the East Locrians for a group of colonists sent by them to Naupactus. A note appended at the end indicates that the same rules applied to colonists sent there by Chaleum. Thus Chaleum has borrowed a law drawn up by the East Locrians, and to this we owe most of the information we possess about the early government of the latter.

How the division of the Locrians into two parts came about remains a matter of conjecture. Their dialect was Northwest Greek and they—or those among them who brought in the language—belong to the same group of invaders as the Phocians, but it is likely that the Locrians came first and that their division was due to the later invasion of the Phocians.[2] Though separated, the two groups appear to have retained a surprisingly strong feeling of kinship and to have retained contact with each other. Thus, when early in the fifth century Naupactus, near the western extremity of Western Locris, was in trouble, the Eastern Locrians sent a colony to strengthen the city. In so doing, they drew up regulations governing the relations of the colonists to their former home and also including stipulations concerning their rights at Naupactus, undoubtedly arrived at through an agreement with the older inhabitants of the city. As already mentioned, the document containing these regulations also refers to a group of colonists sent by the city of Chaleum.[3] The dispatch of these two groups to one city suggests a very serious situation. Further evidence for conditions in West Locris is supplied by the enactment of an unknown town envisaging the possibility that their community might be forced to call in as settlers 200 men at arms, who with their families would mean a considerable addition to the citizen body.[4] It has been

---

[1] The inscriptions will be cited as Buck, nos. 57, 58, and 59, since Buck's *Greek Dialects* seems to be the only handbook in which all three are available. Nos. 57 and 58 can be found in Tod as nos. 24 and 34, and 57 is available also as *SIG*³ 47. No. 59, first published in 1924, is included in neither of the other two collections. Nos. 57 and 58 were found at Galaxidi, the site of ancient Chaleum rather than Oeanthea; cf. Gomme, *Commentary* on Thuc. iii. 101. 2.

[2] On the coming of the Locrians and Phocians, see above under 'The Phocian Confederacy' at p. 41 and n. 5; on the language, Buck, *Greek Dialects*, 157–9, who rejects the theory that the dialects of the two groups differed considerably in early times. Oldfather, in his article on 'Lokris' in *RE* xiii at 1186, holds that the division goes back to the time of the coming of the Locrians; at Mt. Oeta one group turned east, while another went south and followed the river Daphnus to the Gulf of Corinth.

[3] Buck, no. 57.

[4] Buck, no. 59. Buck is in doubt about the relative age of this document and his no. 57. Both are archaic. No. 57 has a record number of koppas; no. 59 does not use this letter but

4

suggested plausibly that the difficulties of the Locrians were due to an attack by the Aetolians.[1]

In the document containing the regulations for the colonists sent to Naupactus, there are three parties involved, the Eastern Locrians, the colonists, and the city of Naupactus, with which an agreement must have been reached in advance. The Eastern Locrians retain a certain vestige of control over the colonists. They specify that the colonists are to pay no taxes at Naupactus except those paid by Western Locrians, that is, they are not to be treated as metics and charged a special tax for permission to reside at Naupactus. They specify further that if a colonist does not have an heir on hand, his property can be inherited by a kinsman in Eastern Locris, who is given three months to go to Naupactus and claim the property. Only if he fails to do so are the laws of Naupactus to apply. Finally, the colonists are required to take an oath of loyalty to the Eastern Locrians. The document is in form a statute passed by the Eastern Locrians, but once the colonists have settled at Naupactus it almost becomes a treaty between the colonists and the Eastern Locrians and can be emended by an agreement between these two parties. Thus Naupactus became almost a double or split community, though it is specified at the outset that the colonist is to become a Naupactian, so that he will be treated as a foreigner if he visits his old home. If the colonists from Chaleum formed a similar distinct group, the situation must have been very complicated. Probably the conquest of Naupactus by the Athenians and the occupation of the city by the Messenians came so early that the new system was not given a fair trial.

The existence of a federal or central government for Eastern Locris is amply attested by the document just cited, but the evidence is complicated somewhat by the fact that the Eastern Locrians are sometimes called Hypocnemidian Locrians, that is, Locrians living under Mount Cnemis, and sometimes Opuntians. The latter name may seem to refer to the citizens of the city of Opus, the capital or chief city of the district, but it is used in such a way that it must be a synonym for the Eastern or Hypocnemidian Locrians.[2] Some of the rules laid down for all Eastern Locrians are the following (references by lines): A Hypocnemidian Locrian, when he becomes a Naupactian by going to that city as a colonist, has the right, if he visits his former home, to

is engraved boustrophedon, which no. 57 is not. The latter is dated in the first half of the fifth century on the ground that it must antedate the Athenian control of Naupactus and the settling of Messenians there. No. 59 fits into the picture so well that it is clear that it must belong to the same general period.

[1] Oldfather, *RE* xiii. 1195.

[2] This is in agreement with the normal use of ancient writers; see Oldfather, *RE* xiii. 1159 f.

take part in the religious rites of the community as a foreigner; he and
his descendants can exercise this right for all time (1–4). The colonists
are to pay no taxes among the Hypocnemidian Locrians unless they
return and resume citizenship among the Hypocnemidians (4–6). If a
colonist wishes to return to his community, he can do so without paying
a fee for admission to citizenship provided he leaves an adult son or a
brother to carry on among the colonists. Also, if the Hypocnemidian
Locrians are forcibly expelled from Naupactus, they may return without paying any fee to the particular communities from which they
came (6–10). The rule about the place of origin, specifically enun-
ciated here, no doubt applied to all cases of return including the participation in religious rites by colonists home on a visit. Whenever a
Hypocnemidian Locrian returns from Naupactus, this is to be announced in the assembly of Naupactus and again in the assembly
(*agora*) of the city (*polis*) from which he came and to which he now
returns (19–22).[1] Clearly, we have here a federal government legislating for a group of member communities. But these communities also
have laws of their own. In the case of certain specific groups of colonists
who retain property in their old homes, it is specified that the property
at Naupactus is to be administered according to the laws or usage of
Naupactus; that among the Hypocnemidians, according to Hypocnemidian laws or usage as administered in each case by the particular
city. If any of them return, they are to be subject to the laws of their
city (22–28). If any colonist does not pay his taxes at Naupactus, he is
to be excluded from among the Locrians until he has paid the Naupactians what is due to them. (14–16).

With all these indications that the colonists have their roots in a
number of different East Locrian cities, it is startling to note that they
swear loyalty to the 'Opuntians', and that, when there is a question of
a possible renewal of the oaths, the two parties in question are the
Opuntians and the Naupactians, that is, the colonists settled at Naupactus (11–14). It is out of the question that all these colonists from
various cities should take an oath of loyalty to the city of Opus. Hence
the 'Opuntians' here and in the statement that the terms of the document can be modified by an agreement between the colonists and 'the
majority of the one thousand of the Opuntians' (38–40) must mean the
same as the Hypocnemidian Locrians of other passages. The term may
indicate the prominence of Opus as the capital or chief city of the
Confederacy, but that is all. Likewise, when there is a question of

---

[1] Here *agora* must mean assembly rather than 'market-place' (Tod, Buck) or 'Marktplatz'
(Gschnitzer, *Abhängige Orte*, 57). This meaning fits the passage better, and nearby Delphi
was one of the places where *agora* continued to be used as the name for the assembly; for
illustrations see Busolt, *Staatskunde*, 442, n. 4 (on 443); *SIG*[3], Index.

privileges of the colonists in lawsuits 'in Opus' (32–33), the reference must be to courts in the cities throughout Eastern Locris, for the suits in question are civil suits of a kind which naturally would fall under the jurisdiction of the local courts in the various communities. On the other hand, the *archos*, who is charged with conducting the trial in the case of an illegal attempt to modify arrangements for the colony (41 f.), must be a federal official. The federal state implied in these regulations embraced only East Locris. The one reference to the exclusion by all Locrians of a colonist delinquent in his taxes at Naupactus, may indicate a dream of a united Locris. A state embracing both Eastern and Western Locris could hardly have functioned at this time. As will be seen below, the Western Locrians had some sort of union of their own, but a very loose one.

The existence of cities within Eastern Locris, as the reader may have noticed, is clearly indicated in the inscription just used as evidence for the federal government. When colonists that had gone to Naupactus returned, they went to their old communities and their return was announced by a herald in the assembly of their *polis*. References to laws concerning property imply that there were East Locrian laws or usages but with local variations. Yet, on account of the nature of the document, no East Locrian city is mentioned by name except Opus, and then it is not absolutely certain that the reference is to the city itself as such. For Western Locris, on the other hand, there is evidence for a number of cities. Besides Naupactus, Chaleum has already been noted. In addition we have on a bronze tablet a treaty between Chaleum and Oeanthea and an enactment of one these cities concerning the rights of foreigners in the city and the legal procedure for law suits involving foreigners.[1] Then from an unnamed city we have an enactment about the division of land and pasture rights and changes that might be made if a group of additional settlers were invited and admitted to citizenship.[2] These documents, on the face of it, record enactments of completely independent cities, but this in itself does not exclude the possibility of the existence of a loose central government. These documents make it possible to draw a somewhat clearer picture of urban than of federal institutions. Let us, nevertheless, turn first to the federal institutions.

Most of what can be known concerning the federal government of Eastern Locris is deduced from the decree concerning the colonists sent to Naupactus. From it we learn that the magistrates were annual officials, that the highest federal official was named *archos*, and that there was a federal assembly known as the Thousand. For a district as small as Eastern Locris, this implies a body of voters determined by a

[1] Buck, no. 58.　　　　　　[2] Buck, no. 59.

property qualification which was not excessively high.[1] It is interesting to note that the state is not referred to as a *koinon* (commonwealth) or *ethnos* (nation) but simply as the Hypocnemidian Locrians and occasionally as the Opuntians. Moreover, when the federal assembly is mentioned, it is called the Thousand of the Opuntians. This has commonly caused scholars to conclude that it was the assembly of the city of Opus and that this city had established its supremacy over the others.[2] However, since the assembly of a city in this document is called *agora*, the 'Thousand of the Opuntians' must be something else and can hardly be anything but the assembly of all Opuntian, that is, Eastern Locris. Moreover, since it is likely that the government was oligarchic, an assembly with a thousand members would be too large for even the largest city in such a small agricultural state as East Locris. On the other hand, it would fit well for the Eastern Locrians as a whole if active citizenship and membership in the assembly depended upon service as hoplites.[3] The Opuntian Locrians are said to have turned up in full force at Thermopylae and their contingent is said to have numbered 1,000.[4] This need not mean that the actual number of the members of the assembly was exactly 1,000. The name, of course, is an example of a usage common among the Greeks of employing a number as the name of an assembly or body of active citizens, such as the Five Thousand at Athens and the assembly of the Ten Thousand of the Arcadian Confederacy. In addition to the annual *archos* and the assembly, there is also evidence for the existence of a federal court. Charges of the violation of federal ordinances were brought by private individuals before the *archos*. The judges or jurors who passed on the case—it is not indicated whether it was a standing court or one appointed for the occasion—gave their verdict under oath and voted by secret ballot or, rather, voting tokens.[5] Thus we have here an early federal state in which the highest federal official known has a civil rather than a military title, in which there is evidence for annual magistrates, and in which there existed a special federal court or legal

---

[1] There is a general reference to annual magistrates in Buck, no. 57. 35. Here it is not clear whether the reference is to federal or city magistrates, but in lines 42–43 there is a statement concerning the duties that devolve on the *archos*—certainly a federal official—if as much as thirty days remain of his term of office. Thus he too can safely be put down as an official with a short term of office, most likely annual.

[2] Cary, *CAH* iii. 614; Busolt, *Staatskunde*, 1456 f.; Oldfather, *RE* xiii. 1240 mentions the predominance of Opus, but later refers to the Thousand as drawn from all East Locris but meeting at Opus (1244).

[3] Also Ehrenberg, *Gk. State*, 49; *Staat*, 59 believes that Opuntian Locris was a hoplite state.

[4] Herod. vii. 203. 1 states that they turned out in full force; Diod. (Ephorus) xi. 4. 7 that they numbered 1,000. The statement of Paus. x. 20. 2 that they cannot have numbered over 6,000 is a worthless guess based on the number of Athenians at Marathon.

[5] Buck, no. 57. 38–46.

machinery. It was also a federal state with a capital. The way in which
'Opuntian' is used, makes it clear that the assembly met at Opus and
that Opus was the capital of the Confederacy. How much of a permanent administrative machinery existed, is not known. The *archos*,
obviously could be approached any time during the year and, in the
case of certain lawsuits, was required, on penalty of the loss of citizenship and property, to secure their settlement within thirty days.

Also the government of the cities was highly developed. The evidence on the subject comes mostly from Western Locris. An early decree
from an unidentified city reveals an almost embarrassing wealth of
organs of government. It appears that decrees of the city had to be
passed by the assembly (*polis*) and two councils, the *preiga* and the
apoklesia.[1] Of the two councils, the *preiga* must be the older and more
aristocratic body; the *apoklesia*, a unique term as used here, must be the
more popular council. A reference to a decision by the 'One Hundred
and One' suggests that the latter council, the *apoklesia*, numbered 101
members. The existence of two councils is known for a number of
cities, notably Athens, sixth century Chios, and Cyrene in the late
fourth century,[2] but it is something new to find action by both councils
specifically required on bills passed by the assembly. It is equally startling at this early date to find the popular council containing an odd
number of members, apparently in order to reduce the chances of a tie
vote. After this it is scarcely necessary to stop to point out that the cities
had magistrates and law courts or, at least, a regular administration of
justice. For one city, as it will appear, there is even evidence for a
special court or justices to deal with cases involving non-citizens.

The individual cities seem to have enjoyed a remarkable freedom of
action. This is implied in the East Locrian decree concerning the
colonists sent to Naupactus which has been mentioned so often. Even
more remarkable is a document which is practically a treaty between
the two West Locrian cities of Chaleum and Oeanthea concerning the
right of seizure of foreign goods. Though it provides that, if a citizen of

---

[1] Buck, no. 59; cf. p. 49, n. 4 above. *Polis* probably strictly speaking does not mean
'assembly', but indicates the vote of the city or community, being used much as *demos* was in
Athens and other cities. In Buck, no. 57 *agora* is used for the assembly and *polis* for
the community. Of the two councils, the *preiga* clearly is a body of elders and is the old aristocratic council or its successor, corresponding to the *gerousia* at Sparta or the Areopagus at
Athens; the *apoklesia* (not in the index of Busolt, *Staatskunde*; rendered 'committee' in the
LSJ *Lexicon* Supplement) must be the more popular council, which was, as it were, a
committee of the assembly.

[2] On the problem of the two councils cf. Ehrenberg, *Gk. State*, 61 f.; *Staat*, 75. He adduces
another example, that of the 'eighty' of Argos alongside of the *boule* (Thuc. v. 47. 9). On the
Areopagus and Chios, cf. *Rep. Govt.* 18 f.; for the *boule* and *gerousia* of Cyrene see *SEG* ix. 1
and the literature listed there. The body of 101 members cannot be the assembly but is more
likely to be one of the two councils, which one is not entirely clear. Another, but less likely,
possibility is that it was an *ad hoc* commission.

one of the two cities remains over a month in the other, he is to use the local courts in any suit in which he is involved, yet it also refers to *xenodikai*, thus showing the existence of a special court or courts for handling law suits involving non-citizens.[1] What has been cited is already enough to indicate that the two cities laid down laws or rules to apply in the future.

In this connexion it is well to remember that the Locrians distinguished clearly between the existing body of laws and usages (*nomia*), probably mostly customary law, and new statute law, a statute being called *thethmios* or *tethmos*, the same word in two different forms. A bill adopted is also indicated in typically Greek form as that which has pleased, that is, been voted by, the voters in question. These statutes are enactments of the assembly, but their contents are such that they must be considered laws rather than mere executive decrees. How far legislation had gone in cities is shown by the reference in one statute to the existing statute on homicide, and this in an inscription which in other respects gives the impression of being archaic.[2] Apparently the Locrians had started legislating early and had progressed far. If the tradition is correct that one of the earliest Greek lawgivers was from Locri in Italy,[3] this may well have been due to a tradition brought along from Greece.

Is it possible to determine the relations to each other of the central and local governments in the two parts of Locris? The regulations laid down by the Eastern Locrians in connexion with the colonists sent to Naupactus indicate a federal government which could impose regulations on the communities within the Confederacy. The negotiations between Chaleum and Oeanthea suggest complete independence for the cities of West Locris. Then there is the case of the West Locrian city which contemplated inviting a group of settlers to join the community.[4] It is unlikely that cities in Eastern Locris would have acted equally independently. If a city there had needed to have its population reenforced, it is likely that the federal government would have taken a hand in it. At Naupactus too it seems that East Locris negotiated directly with the city without the intervention of any West Locrian federal government. The conclusion must be that the cities of West Locris possessed greater independence than those of East Locris. If there was any central organization there, it must have been very loose. Yet some sort of organization capable of acting on questions of war and

[1] Buck, no. 58.
[2] *Nomia*: Buck, no. 57. 19, 25 ff.; *thethmios, tethmos*: no. 57. 46; no. 59. 1, 14; references to voting: no. 57. 38; no. 59. 10; homicide statute; no. 59. 13.
[3] Arist. *Pol.* 1274a22; Diod. xii. 19–20; cf. R. J. Bonner and G. Smith, *Administration of Justice*, i (1930), 69 f.
[4] Buck, no. 59.

alliance there was, for in 426 the Athenians had been promised the aid of the entire military strength of the Western Locrians for their invasion of Aetolia. It must have been to this same organization that Eurylochus, the Spartan commander of the force that was to march from Delphi through their country to attack Naupactus, sent a herald in an attempt to detach the Western Locrians from their alliance with Athens. However, it was the individual communities which, beginning with Amphissa, came to terms with the Spartans and pledged help or neutrality.[1] Thus, even an organization as loose as that of Western Locris, had some sort of central authority with which outsiders could communicate.

Thus we have two organizations of which at least the one of East Locris can be considered a federal state of the kind later classed as a sympoliteia. The regulations allowing colonists under certain circumstances to return from Naupactus to their former communities and resume citizenship without paying an admission fee (*eneteria*), indicates both that there was a clean-cut idea of local citizenship, and that there were regulations for the admission of new citizens, in connexion with which an admission fee normally was charged.[2] The reference to individuals owning property in more than one community and having relatives in other communities than the one in which they resided, make it likely that the citizens of one community had the right to own property in any community within the Confederacy and to contract legal marriages with their citizens. Whether these rights had yet been defined as *enktesis* and *epigamia* or not, they were there in practice. On the question of taxation, our information is sadly inadequate. The East Locrian decree concerning the despatch of colonists to Naupactus refers to the taxes of both the Western and Eastern Locrians and regulates the payment of taxes to some extent. This may seem to imply that taxes were collected directly by the federal governments. That, however, is unlikely. The taxes must rather have been collected by the cities, but to some extent subject to regulation by the federal government at least in East Locris. The extent to which relations with outsiders were in the hands of the city governments certainly suggests that the latter also collected the customs duties, whatever they were.

There is evidence for extensive contacts on the part of the various Locrian cities not only with each other but also with outsiders. East Locris was so small, a narrow strip scarcely fifty miles long, that only

---

[1] Thuc. iii. 95. 3, 101. Eurylochus did not start on his march before hostages were deposited at Cytinium in Doris. Apparently he trusted the West Locrians less than Brasidas two years later did the Thessalians.

[2] Buck, no. 57. 7–10.

the most stubborn isolationists could have avoided contact at least with neighbours from other East Locrian communities. But there was also contact with the West Locrians. The very fact that colonists were sent from East Locris to Naupactus is proof enough. Moreover, the East Locrians expected to keep up contacts with these former citizens of theirs, allowed them to participate in religious rites, and offered them special facilities at the local courts. The proviso that the authorities were to assign a colonist as an aid to any East Locrian involved in a law suit with a colonist, means that it was not anticipated that there would be any difficulty in finding a visiting colonist.[1] This contact between East and West Locrians must have been by land. Apparently there was considerable freedom of movement for individual travellers through the intervening state or states, probably chiefly Phocis. For contacts of various West Locrian cities with each other, the case of Chaleum and Oeanthea has already been noticed. The same document furnishes evidence also for contacts with the outside world. Both cities were sea ports, both were visited by trading vessels, and both offered strangers certain facilities and protection. They promised each other by treaty not to carry off foreigners or their goods from each other's territory or harbour. To understand this stipulation, it is necessary to remember that the right of self-help in order to retrieve alleged wrongs long outlived the related practice of blood vengeance. Even where outright piracy had disappeared, the practice of private seizure of the property and even the person of foreigners was widely practiced, and the victim was not necessarily the wrong-doer but might be someone else from the same community.[2] States often guaranteed rights and regular legal procedure to certain other states, but this merely reduced somewhat the danger of the merchants, for they might be attacked on the way by men from a third state. If Chalcum and Oeanthea were the two chief ports of Western Locris, as they seem to have been, their agreement greatly reduced the danger but left foreigners open to seizure on the sea outside the two harbours. This, however, did not mean sanctioning outright piracy. There was a fine for unjust seizure, and if the property seized unjustly was retained more than ten days, the offender had to restore not only it but in addition half as much again. For these offences each city undoubtedly exercised jurisdiction over its own citizens. The wronged alien could bring his case before the special magistrates trying cases involving foreigners (the *xenodikai*). If the latter disagreed, the foreigner who was the plaintiff, selected an additional nine jurors for minor cases and fifteen when values of a mina or more were involved.

[1] Buck, no. 57, especially lines 33–35.
[2] Buck, no. 58; cf. the articles 'Syle' and 'Asylia' in *OCD* and 'Sylan' in *RE*.

In addition the city had an official *proxenos*, whose duty it was to see that the foreigners were given fair treatment. In case of fraud he was liable to a fine of double the sum involved.

To take stock again of what has been found, it appears that East Locris in the first half of the fifth century was organized as a federal state of a type quite far advanced for the time. West Locris may have had a looser organization but shows advanced legislation and ideas about legislation, as well as relatively humane and enlightened rules for the treatment of foreigners. It looks as if Thucydides (i. 5–6) was so enamoured of the city-state that he maligned those who, like the Ozolian (Western) Locrians, Aetolians, and Acarnanians, did not conform to the pattern, and modern scholarship has paid more attention to an *obiter dictum* of Thucydides than to the evidence of documents. Since this development of Locris came before the Athenian seizure of Naupactus, it also antedated considerably the organization of Boeotia in 447. It may be well to recall also that Locrians had joined the Orchomenians in the liberation of Boeotia at that time. It may even be possible that the authors of the Boeotian constitution had acquired some of their knowledge of federalism by observing their neighbours in Eastern Locris. And is it too fanciful to conclude that the high development in West Locrian cities of laws concerning foreigners and foreign trade, when coupled with the memory of the high development of Crisa, indicates that the ports along the Gulf of Corinth had retained contact with the colonies in the west and thus at an early date had advanced far in foreign trade?

5. THE CHALCIDIC CONFEDERACY

The Chalcidic Confederacy is important for having united Greek cities on the border of Macedonia into a strong federal state. Little is known about the machinery of its government, but it is clear that it went far in developing uniformity of law in the cities within its boundaries, in extending civil rights to citizens within all cities of the Confederacy, and in developing federal finances to the point of federal control over the customs duties and foreign trade. In addition it is clear that it was one of the earliest federal states to admit cities which did not belong to the same ethnic group as the original founders. Thus, on the face of it, the Confederacy seems to have possessed an organization capable of expanding indefinitely, and it is tempting to believe that but for Spartan interference it might have grown strong enough to hold its own against Macedonia. Yet this is hardly the case. At least in the early part of the Peloponnesian War, it was only the smaller towns that banded together while the larger cities stood aloof. Even its famous capital, Olynthus, was relatively small before the synoecism of 432 and, if it then became a great city, it was as the creation of a group of other small cities which united and made it their capital and chief fortified centre. This enlarged city has been excavated in recent times and thus has added much to our knowledge of Greek classical cities and architecture. Unfortunately few inscriptions were found, but one of these few helps to make clear that the state of the 'Chalcidians' was a genuine federal state and that the name was not merely a sort of pretentious misnomer for the citizens of the expanded but unified city-state of Olynthus.[1]

The Chalcidic peninsula on which this state developed was not a part of Greece proper but an area of colonization. The peninsula at its broadest was scarcely sixty miles wide. From its southern side three narrow peninsulas, each some thirty miles long, extended southeast into the Aegean. The most easterly of these was Acte, called Athos by Herodotus; the central one was Sithonia; the westernmost one, Pallene. The favourite sites for colonies on all three was the coast facing southwest, and here were located the larger cities, Mende and Scione on Pallene, Torone on Sithonia, and Dium and Thyssus on Acte. The colonists came largely from Chalcis on Euboea, but some also from Eretria and some from Andros, the island immediately south of Euboea. The conjecture of the late Jean Bérard that the colonies of Chalcis and Eretria were founded before the Lelantine War while the two cities still were on friendly terms, is probably correct. Though the Eretrians and Andrians were not strictly Chalcidians, they were Ionians and sufficiently closely related to the Chalcidians to coalesce fairly easily with them. Somewhat of an exception both on the score of location and on that of the founders was Potidaea, founded by Corinth on the isthmus connecting Pallene with the main peninsula. The claim

[1] The debate about Olynthus and the Chalcidians is an old one. Grote, *Hist.* x. 67–74 praises the liberal spirit of the 'Olynthian' confederacy early in the fourth century; Freeman, *Fed. Govt.* 150–3 considers Grote's picture too favourable and argues that Olynthus wished 'to reduce the Chalkidian towns to the condition familiar . . . as the *Civitas sine Suffragio*', that is, allow them private rights of citizens but no voice in the government; Emil Kuhn, *Ueber die Entstehung der Staedte der Alten* (1878), 283–300 argues at length that there had been no real synoecism and that the cities which joined Olynthus continued to exist; A. B. West's detailed *History of the Chalcidic League* (1919) is useful but marks little advance in the interpretation of institutions. Of the accounts in handbooks that in Swoboda, *Staatsaltertümer*, 212–18, classifying the Confederacy as one of the very earliest *sympolities*, is important; that in Busolt, *Staatskunde*, 1501–7 is sound and covers most essential points. Glotz, *La Cité grecque*, 424 f. calls the organization a *sympolity*. The theory of a unitary state rather than a confederacy was revived by F. Hampl, 'Olynth und der Chalkidische Staat', *Hermes*, lxx (1935), 177–96, but his arguments, which were not convincing, were still more weakened by the publication about the same time of an inscription which refers to the federal magistrates (Tod, no. 158). On this point cf. *Rep. Govt.* 42 f., 206, n. 44. Also Ehrenberg, *Staat*, 324 finds the thesis of Hampl unconvincing.

that Scione, aside from Potidaea the largest city on Pallene, was founded by Achaeans from Pellene is apparently based on nothing but the similarity of the two names, but it is impossible to say who the actual founders were.[1] The nearness to the sea of Olynthus, which remained Bottiaean to 479, and Spartolus, which remained Bottiaean even longer, shows that the Greek colonists did not penetrate inland to any extent.

Most Greek federal states developed from earlier tribes or tribal states. In the case of the Chalcidians it is possible to see a group of cities coalescing into a sort of tribal state and then developing further into a sympolitical federal state. These 'Chalcidians of Thrace' had no city named Chalcis but, nevertheless, must have adopted the name because so many of their cities were colonies of Chalcis on Euboea. References implying a tribal unity, however, caused one scholar to propound the theory that the name was derived from a Greek tribe which settled on the peninsula and not from colonists coming from Euboea. Ehrenberg, on the other hand, noting the different origins of the settlers of various cities within the Confederacy, maintains that the organization was not derived from a tribal community.[2] This, strictly speaking, is true, but, before the formation of the highly organized confederacy, the Chalcidians functioned much like a tribal state. There is no reason to doubt the account of the ancients to the effect that the coast of the Chalcidic peninsula, except for Potidaea, founded by Corinth, was colonized from Chalcis, Eretria, and Andros, all Ionic communities, and that the colonists from Chalcis formed the nucleus of the 'Chalcidians'. Since the ethnic name of the Chalcidians of Euboea and those of Thrace is the same, it sometimes is difficult to know which group is meant. The name, *Chalkideis, -es*, is clearly derived from the name of the city, *Chalkis*, and was carried to the coast of Thrace by the colonists. *Chalkidike*, the name applied to their land, in turn, is clearly derived from *Chalkideis*. At the time of the Persian War the Chalcidians are spoken of by Herodotus as though they constituted a tribe or tribal state. He reports that the Chalcidian *genos* furnished troops to the Persians, and later that Artabazus captured Olynthus, then held by the Bottieaans, put the Bottiaeans in the city to death, and turned it over to the Chalcidian *genos*, placing in charge of it a man

---

[1] On the geography see Cary, *Geographic Background*, 299; on the colonization, Beloch, *GrG* i. i. 253 f.; D. W. Bradeen, 'The Chalcidians in Thrace', *AJP* lxxiii (1952), 356–80; J. Bérard, *L'Expansion et la colonisation grecques* (1960), 66 ff., 94. An excellent map is map no. 5 in *CAH* v. Thuc. iv. 120. 1 states that the people of Scione themselves put forth the claim to Achaean origin, which apparently was a matter of pride.

[2] E. Harrison, 'Chalkidike', *Class. Quart.* vi (1912), 93 ff.; V. Ehrenberg, *Staat*, 151 f.; cf. also F. Gschnitzer in his important article, 'Stammes- und Ortsgemeinden im alten Griechenland', *Wiener Studien*, lxviii (1955), at p. 142, n. 37.

from Torone, the largest Chalcidian city on Sithonia.[1] In these passages the group is called a *genos* instead of *ethnos*, but *genos* suggests kinship equally clearly. Thus here there appears to be an example of how at least some Greek 'tribes' were formed. People living close together, speaking the same language, and having in common such interests as defence against neighbours, began to feel akin and to coalesce into a 'tribe'. The remarkable feature in the present case is that it happened to a group which already possessed cities. At the time of the Persian War the Chalcidians acted as a state in furnishing troops to the Persians and were treated as a state by them. The existence of a political entity known as the Chalcidians is attested also by a coin type of the fifth century.[2] This must have been a very small organization, probably confined to the peninsula of Sithonia. Olynthus, which remained Bottiaean until it was given to the Chalcidians in 479 was only a few miles inland near the isthmus connecting the more westerly peninsula of Pallene with the mainland. Also Potidaea, located on this isthmus, was outside the Chalcidian *genos*, for it revolted from the Persians after Salamis, withstood a siege successfully, is reported to have had troops at Plataea, and is listed on the serpent column among the Greek victors.[3] The other cities on Pallene supported Potidaea, and so they too must have remained outside the Chalcidic organization.

The case for the interpretation given above, that the Chalcidians of Thrace largely were colonists from Chalcis on Euboea who coalesced into something in the nature of a tribal state, is greatly strengthened by indirect evidence concerning the lawgiver, Androdamas of Rhegium, who drew up laws for the Chalcidians of Thrace. The adoption of the alphabet and the development of Greek states combined to produce a spate of recorders and makers of laws.[4] Their activity among the Locrians has been noted above. Best known, of course, are Draco and Solon of Athens. Otherwise the names of early lawmakers are largely connected with the Greeks of Sicily and Italy. Among them Aristotle mentions Charondas of Catane, who made laws also for other Chalcidic cities of Italy and Sicily, among them, undoubtedly, Rhegium. In another passage he reports that Androdamas of Rhegium served as lawgiver to the Chalcidians of Thrace. This suggests a remarkable solidarity on the part of the Chalcidian colonists from Sicily to Thrace, who probably all derived their impulse towards legislation from the mother city. To be sure, the rules or laws reported as connected with

[1] Herod. vii. 185. 2, viii. 127.
[2] West, *Chalcidic League*, 8 and n. 14.
[3] Revolt and siege of Potidaea: Herod. viii. 126–9; Potidaeans at Plataea: Herod. ix. 28. 3, 31. 3; serpent column: Tod, 19.
[4] On the lawgivers cf. R. J. Bonner and Gertrude Smith, *The Administration of Justice from Homer to Aristotle*, i (1930), ch. iii.

Chalcis tend rather to concern interstate than local law, but Chalcis was in any case one of the more advanced cities of archaic Greece.[1] The development of the colonies in the west, not unnaturally gave the leadership in lawmaking to the specialists in the new cities. Consequently, when the Chalcidians of Thrace had need of a lawmaker, he was found in Italy. Apparently as late as the time of Aristotle he was considered the author of laws that had been given to the Chalcidians of Thrace and that still were valid.

Olynthus, at the time of the Persian War was a small or moderately large city, much smaller than Potidaea, Mende, Scione, and Torone, and it remained so down to 432. This is shown clearly by the tribute paid by these cities in the Delian League and later in the Athenian Empire.[2] While Scione and Torone each paid six talents a year and Mende eight, Olynthus paid only two. This tribute was paid by the individual cities, and the Chalcidic state is never mentioned in the tribute lists. In other words, it is treated as non-existent, which proves at least that the Athenians did not wish it to exist. Whether it actually was completely dissolved or whether it continued to function to some extent, cannot be said for certain. In any case, it resumed functioning again in 432, but at that time was a petty organization made up of small towns.

In that year, when the Potidaeans decided to break away from Athens, the Chalcidians joined the movement and, on the advice of Perdiccas of Macedonia, demolished and abandoned their cities located on the coast and moved inland to Olynthus and made it their one great fortified centre. For the duration of the war, the king offered them land to till near Lake Bolbe in his own territory.[3] The decision to move to Olynthus was made and carried out by the state of the Chal-

---

[1] Arist. *Pol.* 1274a23, b23.

[2] This is pointed out by West, *Chalcidic League*, 15 ff. Some of his statistics need to be modified in the light of more recent studies by himself and others; see particularly B. D. Meritt, H. T. Wade-Gery, and M. F. McGregor, *The Athenian Tribute Lists* (1939–53), cited hereafter as *ATL*. The information about the tribute is summarized in the 'Register' in vol. i, where the communities are listed in alphabetical order and the records of payments, in so far as they are preserved, are given year by year, the sum listed being the first fruit given to Athene, that is, one-sixtieth of the tribute. Thus, when 200 drachmas are listed, the tribute was 12,000 drachmas or two talents. Statements about amounts of tribute will be based on the 'Register' and page references will not be given. For other material in *ATL* references will be given by volume and page. In the present case, two figures given by West are misleading. Scione probably never paid fifteen talents; it has been conjectured that this sum belongs to Potidaea, the payments of the two cities having been interchanged (*ATL* iii. 64 f.); in any case, the more normal payment of the city was six talents, which was raised somewhat after the revolt of Potidaea but not to fifteen talents. The fifteen talents of Potidaea belong to the period immediately before the revolt, the more normal tribute again being six talents. Thus Mende, paying eight talents, was probably the largest city on Pallene.

[3] Thuc. i. 58. 2.

cidians, and this state naturally continued to bear this name even after Olynthus became a great city. In his account of this incident it seems that Thucydides uses *polis* with a meaning related to the old one according to which the word meant the acropolis or citadel of a community, so that he does not mean that the Chalcidians transformed their incipient federal state into a unitary state, the city-state of Olynthus. Undoubtedly the inhabitants of several towns left their former homes, as is shown by a clause in the Peace of Nicias ordering the inhabitants of three of them to reoccupy their own cities. These three were Mecyberna, the seaport nearest to Olynthus, located a short distance east of that city, Singus on the northeast coast of Sithonia, and, most likely, Gale on the opposite coast of the same peninsula.[1] The three were all small. Singus had paid two talents tribute, the same as Olynthus; the others, less. The location of these cities help to determine the area involved in the revolt. It extended along the south coast of the main peninsula and included a large part of Sithonia, but it did not extend to Acte, while the fact that Torone continued to pay tribute and later resisted Brasidas shows that not all of Sithonia was involved. Also the two large cities on Pallene, Mende and Scione, remained loyal to Athens. The same is true even of a city of some size situated in a district that would seem to be in the very centre of the movement, namely, Sermylia, located a couple of miles inland between Mecyberna and Singus. True, this city paid no tribute in 432–431 but, apparently, on second thought decided not to join the revolt. Consequently it was attacked by Aristeus, the Corinthian who had been in command at Potidaea, and the Chalcidians. At the time of the Peace of Nicias it was under the control of the Athenians, who some time in the intervening period had placed a garrison there.[2] Sermylia had been paying a tribute of five talents and probably was the largest city in the neighbourhood, over twice as large as Olynthus before the expansion of that city beginning in 432. The larger cities obviously took no part in the merger. It is easy enough to understand that they would not wish to have their citizens transplanted, but apparently something was mismanaged in such a way that they were unwilling to join the Confederacy at all. Most striking is the case of Torone, which seems to have

---

[1] Thuc. v. 18. 6 as emended by West in *AJP* lviii (1937), 171–3 and accepted *ATL* ii. 118, T. 134. The manuscript text gives Sane, a town at the head of Acte which continued to pay tribute, and which resisted Brasidas in 424 (Thuc. iv. 109. 5) and thus clearly had not joined in the revolt. Gale, on the other hand, failed to pay tribute and is located in an area which shared in the revolt. Gomme rejects the emendation.

[2] Thuc. i. 65. 2, v. 18. 8. If anyone doubts that the Athenian control was exercised through a garrison, let him consider that the other two cities included in the same clause in the treaty are Torone, in which a garrison had been placed recently (Thuc. v. 3. 6), and Scione, which actually was being besieged at the time but soon was captured (Thuc. v. 32. 1).

been the leading city of the Chalcidians in earlier times. Even so it is likely that certain cities joined at the outset without having their population transplanted so that the Confederacy already was a federal state. A probable example is Eïon, a colony of Mende, which was attacked by the Athenians the year before the arrival of Brasidas and was won back by the united efforts of the Chalcidians and Bottiaeans.[1] If the Confederacy at first came near to being a unitary state, this must have been due to the boycott of the movement by the larger cities of the region. Potidaea, of course, was in a special position. It seems to have been the intention from the outset that it was to remain an independent city-state outside the Confederacy but closely allied with it.

The Chalcidic Confederacy, when once formed, displayed a positive leadership and definite foreign policy. It was probably at the time of the revolt in 432 that it entered into an alliance with Corinth.[2] In 429 an Athenian force of 2,000 hoplites and 200 cavalry and a few peltasts from nearby towns advanced, doubtless from Potidaea, against the Chalcidians and Bottiaeans. When they approached Spartolus in the hope that the city would be betrayed to them, enough hoplites were sent as reinforcements from Olynthus so that the force in Spartolus went out and faced the Athenians in pitched battle. In this the Chalcidic hoplites were defeated and withdrew to Spartolus, while their light-armed troops and cavalry were victorious. After the first engagement, additional peltasts arrived from Olynthus. This encouraged the light-armed troops and cavalry already at Spartolus to join them in a renewed attack on the Athenians, which ended in the complete rout of the latter. The Chalcidian light-armed troops, which included archers, gave way when the Athenians counter-attacked and charged again when the Athenians tried to withdraw, while the Chalcidian cavalry charged at will.[3] It seems that the Chalcidian hoplites took no part in the second action, which thus was a victory of light-armed troops and cavalry over hoplites. This defeat seems to have discouraged the Athenians sufficiently so that they remained relatively inactive in this theatre until Brasidas irritated them into action. An exception was the ineffective attack on Eïon, already mentioned, but, though the Athenians had garrisons in the region, they did not have enough ships

[1] Thuc. iv. 7. The location is not known, but it clearly was not like that of the mother city on Pallene, for the Chalcidians and Bottiaeans must have approached the city by land, and at this time Potidaea, in the hands of the Athenians, blocked the approach to Pallene by the land route.

[2] An alliance is indicated by Thuc. v. 30. 2. It must have been in compliance with this treaty that Aristeus later operated with the Chalcidians against Sermylia (Thuc. i. 65. 2).

[3] Thuc. ii. 79; cf. Gomme's excellent comments.

at Potidaea to stop Brasidas when he brought aid by sea to revolting Scione.

The positive character of the foreign policy of the Chalcidians is seen particularly in connexion with the intervention of Brasidas in the Chalcidic region in 424. His primary purpose, aside from any possible megalomania and desire to play an important role personally, was to strengthen Sparta's interests by weakening those of Athens. For aid he had to rely both on Perdiccas of Macedonia and on the Chalcidians. His actual operations began in western Macedonia, then, as it were, circled the Chalcidic Confederacy extending its influence or territory to the east and the south and then once more took him back to Macedonia. The aid given Perdiccas seems intended primarily to keep him in line. Otherwise the Spartans can have had no particular interest in strengthening the Macedonian kingdom. Their interests coincided more with those of the Chalcidians, since both were anxious to detach cities from their allegiance to Athens. The operations of Brasidas were bound to lead to an expansion of the Chalcidic Confederacy, and there may well have been an understanding on the subject at the outset. The Chalcidians had had a share in the advance negotiations urging that an expedition be sent and did their bit also in helping Brasidas get through Thessaly. The group of prominent men from Pharsalus who met him and helped manipulate things in his favour included a proxenus of the Chalcidians. When Brasidas had reached Macedonia and had marched with Perdiccas against Arrhabaeus of Lyncestis but wished to settle with him instead of fighting, Chalcidian ambassadors present agreed with this policy. They urged Brasidas not to do away with the difficulties that faced Perdiccas, hoping thus to keep him more active in the support of his allies. The result was that Brasidas withdrew without fighting and without any real settlement. This left him free to devote himself to winning over Greek cities adjacent to the Chalcidic Confederacy.[1]

When Brasidas next is heard of, he was approaching Acanthus, an Andrian colony on the very opposite side of the Chalcidic peninsula, just north of Acte. Possibly he had passed through the Confederacy without finding any city that needed his attention, but it is natural to suspect that his course of action was due to a special interest in the mouth of the Strymon and Amphipolis. He certainly must have by-passed Sermylia, which, located as it was near the centre of the Confederacy, must have been a thorn in the flesh as long as the city remained in Athenian hands. Be that as it may, the Chalcidians had been made to acquiesce and co-operate, for, when he approached Acanthus,

---

[1] Thuc. iv. 78–79, 83.

5

where the citizens were divided between a pro-Chalcidic oligarchic and a pro-Athenian democratic faction, the army of Brasidas contained Chalcidic troops in addition to his original force.[1] After Acanthus and Stagirus, another Andrian colony located somewhat farther north, had come over without fighting,[2] Brasidas, instead of turning to the peninsula of Acte, pressed on towards Amphipolis, again with the aid of the allies from the Thracian region, that is, largely Chalcidians. Again, except for a skirmish with the guards at the bridge over the Strymon, it was a bloodless victory followed by further defection from the Athenians of cities beyond the Strymon. Thucydides places the action in the winter and attributes the success largely to surprise resulting from a forced march all day and all night from a Chalcidic city, Arnae, the exact location of which is not known.[3] It looks as if his opponents thought that he had gone into winter quarters and so were taken completely by surprise. That same winter, after Amphipolis had been secured, Brasidas and his allies moved on, first to Acte, and then against Torone, the chief city on Sithonia. On Acte, Thucydides reports, there was a small Chalcidic element and one Andrian colony, Sane, located by the canal of Xerxes. Otherwise the peninsula was inhabited by 'barbarians' who had reached that stage in their Hellenization at which they were bilingual, speaking both their native language and Greek. Most of the towns, which all were small, came over to Brasidas, but Sane and Dium resisted.[4] After staying for some time and laying waste their fields, Brasidas moved on against Torone. Apparently he and his allies did not consider the reduction of the smaller cities worth the effort.

From the point of view of the history of the Chalcidic Confederacy, the reduction of Torone is the most important and most interesting of the operations carried out by Brasidas. So far the Chalcidians had cooperated and certainly had an interest in the ousting of the Athenians from Amphipolis, but there is no indication that the liberated cities were incorporated into the Confederacy. In fact, in the campaign with Perdiccas in Lyncestis the following year, the troops of Acanthus, the first city liberated, were distinct from the Chalcidic troops.[5] Torone, on the other hand, was claimed as rightfully belonging to the Confederacy, though there is no indication that the majority of the citizens were motivated by any strong desire to be incorporated in it. The capture was due to a surprise attack by night and the aid of traitors within the walls. These traitors were few in number and clearly were members of the oligarchic party. There was more fighting and bloodshed

---

[1] Thuc. iv. 84.   [2] Thuc. iv. 88.
[3] Thuc. iv. 102–3; for the location of Arnae see Gomme's *Commentary* on iv. 103. 1.
[4] Thuc. iv. 109.   [5] Thuc. iv. 124. 1.

than in the previous operations, but that was due mostly to the presence of an Athenian garrison which held a special fort, Lecythus, on a promontory connected with the mainland by an isthmus. It is the demand for the surrender of this fort which indicates that Torone was claimed as a *de jure* member of the Chalcidic Confederacy. The Athenians were told to give it up on the ground that it belonged to the Chalcidians.[1] The Athenians were, so to speak, trespassing on land belonging to the Chalcidians. It will be remembered that Artabazus in 479 had placed a Toronian in charge of Olynthus. At that time Torone must have been the leading city of the Chalcidic state. This may have been the basis for the later claim to the city, but it is also possible that the Chalcidians laid claim to all cities that ethnically were Chalcidic. Equally interesting is the fact that the traitors were few, and that there was a pro-Athenian party in Torone, some members of which were sufficiently committed to join the Athenian garrison when it withdrew to Lecythus.[2] This seems remarkable when it is observed that Torone, which for some time had paid a tribute of six talents, had had its tribute doubled to twelve talents and by the assessment of 425–424 raised further to fifteen talents or more. Under the circumstances the loyalty to Athens may have been due to the presence of a garrison and to fear inspired by the example of Potidaea. Yet, even so, it may be well to reckon with the tendency of the democratic lower classes to be pro-Athenian.

After the capture of Torone, Brasidas not only stayed there the rest of the winter but used the city for some time as his headquarters. He now had gone as far as he could with land forces alone. Most of Acte had been won over, and the reduction of Torone undoubtedly completed that of Sithonia. There remained the cities on Pallene, but now that the Athenians held Potidaea, this peninsula was inaccessible by the land route and had to be approached as though it were an island. Of course, Sermylia too remained, but that city had been bypassed before. In any case, Brasidas was still at Torone, intriguing in the cities that had not rebelled, when news reached him that Scione had come over to him. He thereupon made his way to that city by night in a small boat escorted by a trireme which was to serve as protection or, in case of the approach of a hostile trireme, as decoy. When he once had established contact, he seems to have brought troops across without difficulty. Apparently there was no sizeable Athenian naval patrol in the neighbourhood. When the news of the armistice of 423 between the

---

[1] Thuc. iv. 110. 1, 113. 2–114. In the first of these passages Thucydides had described Torone as Chalcidic. This might mean Chalcidic only in the ethnic sense, but in the second, no doubt, ownership by or membership in the Confederacy is meant.

[2] Thuc. iv. 113. 3.

Spartans and Athenians arrived, the troops were withdrawn again to Torone, but no steps were taken to restore Scione to her allegiance to Athens, the Spartans maintaining that the revolt had come before the armistice, and the Athenians, of course, maintaining the opposite. From now on Scione is a perfect example of how terribly a small state might suffer when involved in the rivalries of greater states, while the deliberate cold-blooded vengeance of the Athenians is fully as much a blot on their record as the better known Melian affair. The Athenians immediately, on the motion of Cleon, voted to destroy the city and put to death its citizens,[1] a decree carried out two years later. The situation was soon complicated by the revolt of Mende under the leadership of a small group of oligarchs. This Brasidas accepted, claiming that the Athenians already had violated the truce. He realized fully that this action would arouse the Athenians and consequently removed the women and children of both Scione and Mende to Olynthus, left 500 Peloponnesian hoplites and 300 Chalcidian peltasts to aid the two cities, and then hied himself off to western Macedonia with Perdiccas, taking along both Chalcidian and Acanthian troops.[2] Up to this point there has been no indication that Scione and Mende intended to join the Confederacy. It is always their relation to Brasidas which is stressed. However, with their women and children taking refuge in a Chalcidic city, if the two had been successfully defended with the aid of Chalcidic troops, it would seem inevitable that they should join.

Any such plans were completely spoiled by the Macedonian adventure of Brasidas, who accomplished nothing except to get into a difficult position because he was deserted by his Macedonian allies, to extricate his troops successfully, and to alienate Perdiccas so that he once more shifted to the side of the Athenians. When Brasidas returned to Torone, an Athenian expedition had arrived and had already recovered Mende. This was largely due to the members of the popular party who fell upon the Peloponnesian troops and their own pro-Spartan fellow citizens.[3] In fact, the pro-Athenian group seems to have been decidedly in the majority. Meanwhile Scione held out and became the last centre of opposition to Athens on Pallene. The arrival of the Athenian expedition had upset the balance so much that it was a serious matter that the Thessalians, in part influenced by Perdiccas, refused to let reinforcements for Brasidas pass through their state. Nevertheless, three commissioners arrived, bringing along Spartans of military age whom they were to appoint as officials in the cities. This Thucydides indicates, alas much too briefly, was

---

[1] Thuc. iv. 120–2.   [2] Thuc. iv. 123–4.   [3] Thuc. iv. 129–30.

an innovation.[1] It looks as if the home authorities were dissatisfied with the generous treatment of liberated cities by Brasidas and were intending to establish direct control by means of officials similar to the later harmosts leaving to Brasidas little but the command of the field army. Those reported appointed were Pasitelidas at Torone and Clearidas at Amphipolis. Of these at least Clearidas seems to have worked later more in the spirit of Brasidas than in that of the home authorities.

The next summer (422) was that of the Thracian expedition of Cleon and of the battle of Amphipolis with the death of both Brasidas and Cleon. The siege of Scione clearly was uppermost in men's minds at the time. Aristophanes in the *Wasps*, put on early that year, could jest that Bdelycleon, the young man who hated Cleon and strove to keep his Cleon-loving father from attending the law-courts, found it harder to keep watch on his father than to guard Scione (lines 209 f.). Nevertheless, Cleon, mover of the decree against Scione, was content to leave the city blockaded and to move against Torone. This move, apparently took the enemy by surprise. Brasidas was not there—we do not know where his headquarters were at the time[2]—the troops on hand were insufficient, and the city was captured without much difficulty. The women and children were sold into slavery while the men were carried off to Athens. Of these, the Peloponnesians were released after the Peace of Nicias and the Chalcidians exchanged for Athenian prisoners.[3] There clearly was not the same hatred against Torone as against Scione.

So far the Athenian campaigns of 423 and 422, though Scione remained uncaptured, had been successful. Not so the campaign against Amphipolis. Brasidas seems again to have been in full charge of the anti-Athenian forces and to have had the co-operation of Clearidas, the commander of the garrison at Amphipolis. For this campaign he had got together a force in which light armed troops outnumbered the hoplites.[4] The little detachment he picked for his surprise attack on the

[1] Thuc. iv. 132; cf. Gomme's *Commentary* and see particularly Grote, *Hist.* vi. 614 f.; Busolt, *GrG* iii. 1170 f. The adverb used is παρανόμως, which Jowett renders 'contrary to law'. This cannot be correct. Crawley's 'in violation of all precedent'' is better. If men of military age could not leave Sparta without authorization, there can have been nothing to prevent the government from sending them abroad on a mission. The innovation must have been in the form of control established.

[2] Gomme on Thuc. v. 2. 3 remarks that Brasidas was absent from Torone, 'though it apparently was his headquarters'. So it was the preceding year, but he apparently had moved his headquarters when Pasitelidas was put in command at Torone. The attempt to surprise Potidaea during the winter (Thuc. iv. 135) rather suggests headquarters in or near Olynthus.

[3] Thuc. v. 2–3.

[4] Thuc. v. 6. 4–5. The 1,500 Thracian mercenaries certainly were light armed troops. In addition there were 1,000 Chalcidian and Myrcinian peltasts. His hoplite force numbered

Athenian line consisted of hoplites,[1] but it was the Myrcinian and Chalcidic cavalry and light-armed troops which finally routed the right wing of the Athenian line after it had resisted the attack of Clearidas with the hoplites.[2] In the last important action before the Peace of Nicias the Chalcidians had acquitted themselves well, something of which no cognizance was taken at the peace negotiations.

The Chalcidic problem was treated at these negotiations pretty much as though only the interests of Athens and Sparta were involved. This is seen in the general rule that the two should restore to each other what they held before the war. Sparta was expected to restore not only Amphipolis but Chalcidic cities which at the time were without Spartan garrisons. In the negotiations the Chalcidians were treated with less consideration than Sparta's other allies, in fact, they were not treated as allies at all. Before the treaty was ratified there was a meeting at Sparta of the assembly of the Peloponnesian League. Of the allies who were not members of the League, at least the Boeotians had ambassadors at hand. Afterwards the representatives of the various states remained at Sparta, were present when disputes arose about the enforcement of the treaty, and left only after the adoption of a treaty of alliance between Sparta and Athens. In connexion with the original negotiating of the treaty of peace, there is no reference to the Chalcidians. They clearly had no representatives present and had no opportunity to register a negative vote. Only after the surrender of Amphipolis had been ordered and Clearidas, the Spartan commander there had stated that he was unable to do so against the will of the Chalcidians, did the latter send ambassadors to support Clearidas and to try to have the treaty modified. Needless to say, they met with no success.[3]

A large part of the treaty concerns the Chalcidic Confederacy, though this organization is never mentioned but ignored as nonexistent. Instead all stipulations apply to individual cities. First and foremost, it is stipulated that Amphipolis is to be restored to the Athenians. Then follows the proviso that in the cities surrendered by the Spartans to the Athenians the citizens are to be free to leave and take along their property, that is, the safety of the partisans of Sparta

2,000 'at most'. There seems to be some confusion in the passage, but the large number of light armed troops is clear.

[1] Thuc. v. 8. 4.

[2] Thucydides (v. 10. 9) does not explicitly state that the troops of Clearidas were hoplites, but this is implied in the statement that the Athenians did not give way before the cavalry and peltasts went into action. Once more, as at Spartolus in 429, hoplites were routed by peltasts and cavalry.

[3] Thuc. v. 17. 2: meeting and vote on treaty with negative votes of Boeotians, Eleans, and Megarians recorded but no mention of Chalcidians; 22. 1; later presence of allied representatives at Sparta; 27. 1: their departure; 21: Clearidas and the Chalcidian envoys.

was guaranteed, provided they could find a place to go. The cities are to be autonomous on the payment of the tribute assessed by Aristeides. In other words, they are to be tribute-paying subjects of Athens, but the tribute is not to be arbitrarily raised. The Athenians and their allies are not to be allowed to attack them after the treaty goes into effect. So far all the clauses seem to apply to all cities surrendered, but then comes a list of six cities including Olynthus, the Chalcidic capital, and Spartolus, the Bottiaean capital, followed by the statement that they are to be allies neither of the Lacedaemonians nor the Athenians, though if the Athenians persuade them, they may enrol the cities in question as allies. Thus the Spartans can under no circumstances demand military support from the cities, and the Athenians, only if it is furnished willingly. Apparently this clause guaranteeing the right of neutrality applied only to the six cities listed; the proviso that they were to be 'autonomous' but pay tribute, applied to all; the proviso that citizens of surrendered cities could leave their city, applied in theory to all. Actually it was limited in some cases. A special clause provided that the men of Mecyberna, Gale, and Singus were to dwell in their own cities. This obviously meant that residents of cities evacuated in 432 were to return to them. Thus the treaty tried to restore conditions as they were before the revolt of Potidaea but with some changes in detail. These included a guarantee against the arbitrary increase of tribute and a guarantee of the right of neutrality for six cities—a guarantee which probably would have meant very little if Athens had ever regained her power in this region. Finally, the Athenians were permitted to do what they wished with the cities which they had garrisoned and held. Those specifically mentioned included Torone, recently reduced, and Scione, still being besieged. In the case of the latter city, this meant that, when the Athenians captured it, they were free to do their worst.[1]

After such a treaty, it is no wonder that a state of war between Athens and the Chalcidic Confederacy continued. The Chalcidians, as already referred to, had induced Clearidas, the Spartan commander at Amphipolis, to report that he was unable to hand over the city against their will. They themselves also sent ambassadors to Sparta to support him and to try to get the terms of the treaty modified. Clearidas, however, was told to return to Amphipolis and surrender the city, or, if unable to do so, to withdraw the Peloponnesian troops. He set out immediately and the same summer brought back those that

---

[1] The interpretation of the details of the treaty in Thuc. v. 18 is extremely difficult. The one given above is based on repeated readings aided considerably by the comments of Gomme. However, on the point of changing Sane to Gale, I follow the emendation by West discussed above on p. 63, n. 1.

were left of the troops that had set out with Brasidas. Soon after this the authorities at Sparta insisted that they were not in control of Amphipolis and so were unable to turn the city over to the Athenians.[1] And quite right they were, for by withdrawing their troops they had given up their last hold on the city and thus rendered themselves completely unable to fulfil their promise.

A number of incidents in the summer of 421 indicate that the Chalcidians did not consider themselves bound by the Peace of Nicias, and that a state of war continued. During the period of diplomatic confusion of that year the Corinthians used as an excuse for refusing to accept the peace the oaths which they had exchanged with the Chalcidians at the time when the latter supported the revolt of Potidaea, and which they had renewed later.[2] This means that neither Corinth nor the Chalcidians were at peace with Athens. Soon after this the Chalcidians contracted an alliance with Argos. In this step it appears that they followed the lead of Corinth. There were also actual hostilities, though not on a large scale except for the Athenian capture of Scione. Some time during the summer the city of Dium on Acte absorbed its neighbour, Thyssus. This was probably a gain for Athens, for, when Brasidas in 424 approached Acte, he had been opposed by Dium while Thyssus was among the places that came over to him.[3] Another gain for Athens, but a short-lived one, was the temporary occupation of Mecyberna. This city was not Athenian at the time of the Peace of Nicias but must have been occupied by the Athenians before the time in the winter of 421–420 when the Olynthians captured the city and expelled their garrison.[4] This is the one gain for the Chalcidians reported for that year. Their hostility to Athens, however, continued. In the brief period in 418 when Argos and Sparta were allied, the alliance with Argos was renewed and Sparta too included. Also Perdiccas of Macedonia entered into an agreement with them, but did not immediately break with Athens. In the spring of the following year, the Chalcidians scored a major success. Dium revolted from Athens and joined the Confederacy. This was important, for Dium, after its absorption of Thyssus, was the largest city on Acte,[5] and

[1] Thuc. v. 21, 34. 1, 35. 5.

[2] Those with whom the oaths had been exchanged were οἱ ἐπὶ Θρᾴκης, who revolted with the Potidaeans (Thuc. v. 30. 2). This may have included the Bottiaeans as well as the Chalcidians.

[3] Chalcidians and Argos: Thuc. v. 31. 6; capture of Scione: 32. 1; Brasidas on Acte: iv. 109; 'capture' of Thyssus by Dium: v. 35. 1, an aggravatingly brief statement which involves difficulties. It describes Thyssus as an ally of Athens. If this is correct, we have the absorption of one Athenian ally by another, for Dium did not revolt until a few years later.

[4] Thuc. v. 39. 1.

[5] Thuc. v. 80. 2, 82. 1. There were no really large cities on Acte; Dium, Thyssus, and Sane had each paid a tribute of one talent a year.

control of it had formerly given Athens control of the better part of the peninsula.

It may, or it may not, have been the defection of Dium which caused the Athenians to increase their activities in 417. In that year they sent against the Chalcidians and Amphipolis an expedition under the command of Nicias, an undertaking which failed to accomplish anything, for the reason that Perdiccas, on whom the Athenians had counted, did not support them. Thereupon the Athenians arranged with the Chalcidians an armistice which could be cancelled by either party on ten days' notice. Next they turned upon Perdiccas and blockaded the coast of Macedonia. Later they established a garrison at Methone near the west coast of the Thermaic Gulf. When the Athenians in 415 sent a cavalry detachment to Methone, the Spartans, in turn, urged the Chalcidians to support Perdiccas, but they refused to break their truce with the Athenians.[1] The truce was broken late in the summer of 414—thus apparently having been in force a little less than three years—when the Athenians, in conjunction with Perdiccas and the Thracians, made an unsuccessful attack on Amphipolis. It may seem strange that the Athenians had energy for this attack while heavily involved in Sicily, but the Thraceward regions seem never to have been forgotten. Even in the *Birds*, produced in 414, Aristophanes could suggest that anyone desiring fighting could fly to Thrace.[2] Thereafter the Chalcidians more or less drop out of sight till the closing years of the Peloponnesian War. After Aegospotami Lysander sent an officer with a small squadron to Thrace and brought over the region. There is also a hint of returning former inhabitants to their old homes. The only city in the Chalcidic region mentioned by name in this connexion is Scione, but it is likely that the same measure was applied also to Potidaea and Torone, and that these three cities, and probably others too, were admitted into the Confederacy.[3]

The next great opportunity to expand came when Amyntas of Macedonia, the father of Philip II, was expelled from a large part of

---

[1] Thuc. v. 83. 4, vi. 7. 3–4. There is no report of the negotiations between the Athenians and Chalcidians—Thucydides simply reports the truce as in force in 415—but scholars generally agree that it must have been arranged before the Athenian blockade of Macedonia. The truce is described as δεχήμεροι σπονδαί, which may mean either a truce which had to be renewed every ten days or one which was 'terminable at ten days' notice' (West, *The Chalcidic League*, 90). The similar expression in Thuc. v. 26. 2 for a truce between Athens and Boeotia is usually taken to mean a truce which had to be renewed every ten days. In their case such a truce would be possible but hardly in the case of the Athenians and Chalcidians. The hostile armies were not so immediately face to face, and the distances involved were too great. West's interpretation must be correct.

[2] Thuc. vii. 9; Aristophanes, *Birds* 1368 ff. The Chalcidians are not mentioned by Thucydides, but they certainly must have regarded an attack on Amphipolis as a hostile act.

[3] Xen. *Hell.* ii. 2. 5: Plut. *Lysander* 14; cf. West, *Chalcidic League*, 94 f.

his kingdom by the Illyrians and turned much of it over to the Chalcidians, who later, when asked for it, refused to restore it. The district thus acquired by the Chalcidians included Pella, the later capital of Macedonia.[1] Amyntas turned to Sparta with his grievances. So did also the two cities of Acanthus and Apollonia, which were under pressure to join the Confederacy.[2] These appeals served as the occasion for the intervention of Sparta and the Peloponnesian League in 382, resulting in the temporary dissolution of the Confederacy. The resulting campaigns are well known and will not be traced here. It must suffice to note, as an index of the strength of the Confederacy, that the Peloponnesian League voted to send a force of 10,000, that this was augmented by troops furnished by the Thebans, by Amyntas, and by Derdas, a minor Macedonian prince, and that the combined force suffered a major defeat at the hands of the Chalcidians. It was only when still greater forces were sent so that the Chalcidians were completely outnumbered that they were forced to give in.[3]

The exact extent of the Chalcidic Confederacy at any given moment is difficult to determine. It has already been suggested that in 432 the Confederacy extended along the south coast of the main peninsula and included much of Sithonia but no part of Acte or Pallene. The reduction of Potidaea by Athens must have meant that for the next few years there was little chance for expansion, though the defeat of the Athenians at Spartolus in 429 also meant that the freedom of the Chalcidians and Bottiaeans was secure for the time being. The next opportunity for expansion came with the expedition of Brasidas in 424. The co-operation of the Chalcidians with him was such that it seems that they regarded the war as their own. Their interest in Amphipolis might even suggest that this important city was incorporated into the Confederacy. Thucydides, however, says nothing about this. On the

[1] Diod. xiv. 92. 3, xv. 19, 23; Xen. *Hell.* v. 2. 12–13. Xenophon does not give an account of these events but merely reports in the speech, said to have been delivered at Sparta by Cleigenes of Acanthus, that the 'Olynthians' have tried to liberate the cities in Macedonia and are in possession of Pella, while Amyntas has been expelled from almost the whole of Macedonia. There is no mention of the Illyrians, and everything is attributed to the Olynthians. However, that Amyntas and the Chalcidic Confederacy once were allies is proved by a treaty preserved, though imperfectly, on stone (Tod, 111). In Diod. xiv. 83. 2 the Chalcidians are listed among the members of the anti-Spartan coalition of 395, but there is no indication that they took any part in the war.

[2] Xen. *Hell.* v. 2. 11 reports the appeal from the two cities; Diod. xv. 19. 3, the appeal from Amyntas.

[3] Decision to send 10,000: Xen. *Hell.* v. 2 20; Eudamidas sent with 2,000: 2. 24; Peloponnesian troops brought up to 10,000 in all: 2. 37; Theban cavalry and hoplites added: ibid.; troops of Amyntas and Derdas: 2. 38–40. The cavalry of Derdas proved particularly important. It saved the situation on one occasion (v. 2. 41) and defeated the Olynthian cavalry on another (v. 3. 1–2). It is not mentioned in Xenophon's account of the defeat suffered under the command of the Spartan, Teleutas (v. 3. 3–6). Dispatch of additional troops and final campaign: v. 3. 8–9, 18–20, 26.

contrary, in his report of a campaign in 423 he lists the Acanthian troops apart from the Chalcidians in such a way as to imply that their city did not belong to the Confederacy. If Acanthus did not, Amphipolis certainly did not. Thus it seems that these cities never were incorporated into the Confederacy. On the other hand, at Torone, Brasidas acted as though the city belonged to the Confederacy, while the later transfer of women and children from Scione and Mende to Olynthus must have meant that these cities too were scheduled for membership. This is of little importance, for the three cities were soon recovered by Athens. The Chalcidians may also have annexed some smaller places not mentioned in our sources. Probably the part of Acte won over by Brasidas joined the Confederacy. To this Dium was added in 417. Otherwise there seems to have been little chance for further expansion before the collapse of the Athenian power at the end of the Peloponnesian War. When Amyntas later entrusted much of his kingdom to the Chalcidians, this meant expansion into western Macedonia. Thus, at the time of its greatest extent, the Confederacy extended from near Acanthus in the east to and including Pella in the west. Yet there were surprising gaps or enclaves of non-members. These included the large city of Mende on Pallene. The treaty of the Chalcidians with Amyntas, probably of about 393 B.C., shows that at the time neither Mende, nor the Bottiaeans, nor Amphipolis, nor Acanthus belonged to the Confederacy.[1] In this list, Mende is the only real surprise, but also the Bottiaeans call for attention. Their chief city, Spartolus, was less than ten miles west of Olynthus. Then, as soon as Spartan troops appeared on the scene in 382, Potidaea went over to them, and the Chalcidians thus had the headquarters of their enemy in a fortified city less than ten miles in another direction from their capital.

When we turn to the form of government of the Confederacy, we find no direct information concerning the machinery of government but evidence for two important features of their institutions, namely, that the customs duties were collected for the federal government, and that the citizens of the Confederacy possessed the civil rights of *enktesis* and *epigamia* in all cities of the Confederacy. These features are attested in a speech said by Xenophon to have been delivered by Cleigenes of Acanthus when he was appealing to the Spartans to intervene.[2] He argued that if the cities once had become accustomed to these advantages, the Confederacy would be difficult to dissolve. This point, and the reference to *enktesis* and *epigamia* as something which had been voted, may imply that these rights were recent innovations. These

---

[1] Tod, 111.   [2] Xen. *Hell.* v. 2. 12-19.

measures obviously tended to make the Confederacy an economic unit and to break down the particularism of the city-state. Yet, at the same time, their very existence, proves that the Chalcidic Confederacy was a federal state with cities as units of local government and not a unitary state such as Athens, where all Attica was the territory of the one city. Moreover, the existence both of the Chalcidic federal state and the city of Olynthus is proved by documents preserved in inscriptions.[1]

Another point which is clear is that the Chalcidic Confederacy was oligarchic. There are not only the general considerations that a state developed at the time of the Peloponnesian War in opposition to Athens and with the support of Sparta and Corinth is likely to have been an oligarchy, and that the prominence of the Chalcidic cavalry suggests an oligarchic or aristocratic society. There are also several incidents connected with the expedition of Brasidas which definitely show that the Chalcidians were oligarchic and that the democrats favoured Athens. When Brasidas approached Acanthus, there was strife within the city between those who wished to co-operate with the Chalcidians and the *demos*, which clearly was hostile. Likewise at Torone, those betraying the city to Brasidas seem to have formed a small group of oligarchs, while also at Mende the *demos* was pro-Athenian. Such incidental bits of information make it practically certain that the government of the Chalcidians must have been oligarchic. This, in turn, suggests that they followed the model of the best known oligarchic state of the time, namely, Boeotia, and that, like the Boeotians, they had a government which included a representative federal boule. This is made almost a certainty when the Bottiaean Confederacy, a small federal state known only from a few references, is considered.

The Bottiaeans possessed one city, Spartolus, which overshadowed the rest. Yet it was the Bottiaeans and not the men of Spartolus as such who shared with the Chalcidians and Potidaeans in the revolt of 432. For years they seem to have co-operated with the Chalcidians. It was against the two confederacies that the Athenians directed an expedition in 429, and it was near Spartolus in the territory of the Bottiaeans that they suffered a disastrous defeat. A few years later, when an

---

[1] In Tod, 111, the treaty with Amyntas, it is clear that the *koinon* referred to is a federal state and not the city-state of Olynthus. In Tod, 158, a treaty with Philip II, there is a reference to federal officials and ambassadors. The latter document belongs to the period after the Confederacy had been temporarily dissolved by the Spartans and revived again. This does not make it less effective as evidence for Chalcidian institutions. It should also be clear that the state of the Chalcidians referred to in these documents is not the same as the *polis* of Olynthus mentioned in another inscription, dated by the editor in the first half of the fourth century (*TAPA* lxix (1938), 52–55, no. 6; another treaty of the 'Chalcidians', ibid. 44 f. no. 2).

Athenian general gathered a force and seized Eïon, a colony of Mende, the Bottiaeans and Chalcidians expelled him. Some time after this—the date is disputed—the Bottiaeans entered into an alliance with Athens.[1] In this document there is a reference to the magistrates of the cities and several cities are listed by name, thus indicating the federal character of the organization. That it continued to be a confederacy is shown by the later treaty of the Chalcidians and Amyntas of Macedonia,[2] which names four states with which neither of the two parties are to enter into friendship without the other. The names are all those of cities except for the Bottiaeans. In such company it must be significant that they and not Spartolus is listed. On the other hand, the fact that the Peace of Nicias, as in the case of Olynthus and the Chalcidians, lists Spartolus and not the Bottiaeans, does not prove that the Confederacy did not exist but merely that the two contracting parties preferred to overlook its existence and deal with the cities. For information about the form of government, there is only the statement in connexion with the treaty with Athens that the oath ratifying the treaty is to be taken by the '*boule* of the Bottiaeans' and by magistrates in the cities. The inscription has been mutilated and heavily restored, but it is reasonably clear that the *boule* mentioned is the federal *boule*. Thus it is extremely likely that one of the chief organs of federal government, both for the Chalcidians and for the Bottiaeans, as for the Boeotians, was a federal *boule* or representative council. At least in the case of the Chalcidians this was a part of the government in a closely knit federal state.

The close organization is seen in the exchange of civil rights already mentioned. This gave the citizens the right to own real estate and to contract legal marriages within any city of the Confederacy. There is also a hint of the broader sharing of laws and of uniformity of laws in the implication in the speech of Cleigenes that the Acanthians, if they were forced into the Confederacy, would have to give up their ancestral law and adopt Chalcidian law. It is natural to believe that the Chalcidic law of the fifth and even the early fourth centuries was built in part on the legislation of Androdamas of Rhegium, who, as noted above, is reported by Aristotle to have legislated for the Chalcidians of Thrace concerning homicide and inheritance. As in Eastern Locris, there may have been some local differences in the administration of this law. On the other hand, the report that *enktesis* and *epigamia* had been adopted by vote indicates that there was some federal organ of government which was qualified to legislate. In all likelihood this was the *boule*. In one other respect the Chalcidic Confederacy was

[1] Tod, 68; for additional fragments and later literature see *SEG* x. 89.
[2] Tod, 111; cf. also Tod, 158, the treaty with Philip II.

decidedly advanced, even more so than the Boeotian Confederacy. The customs duties collected in the ports of entry by land and sea went to the federal government. This is reported in the speech of Cleigenes and is further attested by the treaty with Amyntas, which shows that the federal government controlled customs duties and trade and imposed charges on exports and goods in transit as well as on imports.

The control of the customs naturally made for the strength of the federal government, inasmuch as it supplied a regular income and did not leave it dependent on lump sums contributed by the cities. In this respect the Chalcidians, together with their neighbours, the Thessalians, were in the forefront among federal states. In both states the actual collection was probably in the hands of publicans. Otherwise little is known about the functioning of the government. The excavations at Olynthus have brought to light disappointingly few documents bearing on the city and federal governments, though there is enough to prove both the existence of a city of Olynthus and of the Confederacy. However, if there were any public archives or many important documents published by being inscribed in some public place, these have not been found. Finally, the Chalcidic Confederacy was one of the earliest to go beyond the original ethnic unit in admitting new members. It began as a sort of Chalcidic ethnic state but obviously at the outset was willing to accept Eretrian and Andrian colonies. Since these were Ionian, this did little violence to the ethnic unity, but when Potidaea and Pella, and doubtless other Macedonian cities, were annexed, the Chalcidians overstepped old ethnic lines as clearly as the Achaeans did when they admitted Calydon and later Sicyon. They may not have been as successful as the Achaeans in absorbing alien material. At any rate, in 382 Potidaea broke away as soon as a small Spartan force appeared in the neighbourhood.

6. THE AETOLIAN CONFEDERACY

Aetolia of the fifth century B.C. is the best example known of a Greek tribal state. Later it developed into a very efficient federal state on sympolitical lines, though, even then, it retained its primary assembly. The transformation cannot be traced in detail, but it is clear that, though the tribal organization was retained at the time, the Aetolians had developed an efficient control of foreign policy and of the army already by the time of the Peloponnesian War. Soon afterwards, again it is impossible to date the change precisely, Aetolia was reorganized on sympolitical lines with the local government in the hands of cities. The development was largely determined by geography. There was some fertile land in the country, but much of it was mountainous and pretty well cut off from the outside world. Most of the passes communicating with the outside world were difficult. There was a coastline on the Gulf of Corinth, but again conditions were not such that any great commercial port developed on Aetolian territory. Eastern Aetolia was separated from the coast by mountains, south of which lay Western Locris. Here there were several ports, among them, Naupactus, which later was to become one of the chief cities of the Aetolian Confederacy. Farther west the harbours tended to be obstructed by silting, and even here the most important port, Oeniadae, was considered Acarnanian. Into this country invaders brought a Northwest Greek dialect at the time of the Doric migration. No wonder that cities were slow to develop and that the organization remained tribal probably as late as the early fourth century.[1]

The development of Aetolia before the King's Peace can be treated very briefly. In connexion with the Athenian expedition into Aetolia in 426, Thucydides gives a description of the Aetolians which shows them to have constituted a typical tribal state. He mentions three main tribes, the Apodoti, Ophiones, and Eurytanes, and refers to subtribes. They lived scattered in unfortified villages. Yet the account of the campaign shows that their opponents were surprised by the efficiency of the conduct of the war by the Aetolians. Both this and the subsequent management of their foreign policy show that there existed an efficient central government of some sort for the conduct of war and foreign relations, though the organization on tribal lines still was retained.[2] Otherwise Thucydides tells nothing about their government, nothing about their chief magistrates or assemblies. The leaders who conducted the successful campaign against the Athenians remain nameless. The only Aetolians mentioned by name are the three ambassadors, one from each of the three tribes, sent to Corinth and Sparta later in the year.[3] Thus it is not known whether, as later, a single general was at the head of the central government, or what other officials there were. The assembly, if one existed, was pretty certainly a primary assembly. Even in Hellenistic times the Aetolian Confederacy had a primary assembly in which all adult male citizens appear to have had a right to vote, and in which it seems that the votes, as in the *ekklesia* of Athens, were counted by heads and not by voting units.

[1] For the geography see particularly W. J. Woodhouse, *Aetolia* (1897); Cary, *Geographic Background*, 60 f. On the institutions, Marta Sordi, 'Le origini del Koinon Etolico', *Acme*, vi (1953), fasc. 3, an excellent study, which, however, underestimates the changes from a tribal to a true federal state; cf. also E. Kirsten, 'Aitolien und Akarnanien in der älteren griechischen Geschichte', *Neue Jahrbücher für Antike*, iii (1940), 298–316.

[2] Thuc. iii. 94–98; cf. *Rep. Govt.* 69 f.

[3] Thuc. iii. 100. 1. It appears that the information of Thucydides came from observers who, as it were, looked on from outside and did not have any inside information. On the other hand, when three ambassadors went abroad, they came into touch with other Greeks and their names became known.

This assembly had two regular meetings a year, in the spring before the campaigning season began and in the autumn after it was over.[1] The members of the assembly and the men under arms seem to have been approximately identical. This, of course, hardly means that the older men who no longer went campaigning were deprived of their vote. Since the Aetolians of our period fought as light-armed troops,[2] the assembly would be rather democratic, much more so than that of the Boeotians, who confined the vote to the cavalry and hoplites and excluded the lower classes. This Aetolian assembly must go back to early times and must have assumed prominence as soon as the Aetolians began to be involved in wars with their neighbours.

It is not clear whether they at this time possessed a federal *boule* or council, or whether the conduct of joint business, except for the meetings of the assembly, was left to a few magistrates or a smaller committee. In all likelihood a *boule* did exist. The discovery a few years ago of an inscription mentioning the federal *boule* of the early Achaean Confederacy[3] supplies one more piece of evidence indicating that federal states at an early date, like city-states, commonly possessed a *boule*. To this can be added the example of the Bottiaeans, noted above in connexion with the Chalcidic Confederacy. However, the organization with cities represented in proportion to their population, which existed in Hellenistic times, cannot antedate the reorganization of the Confederacy on the basis of cities, but a *boule* with a somewhat different organization may well have existed. The adoption by the Confederacy of an organization by cities seems to have come early in the fourth century. It was completed by 367 B.C. and probably had been adopted somewhat earlier in connexion with the struggles centring around Acarnania and the development of other confederacies at the time.[4] Some of the 'cities' may have been 'country districts grouped round some village or hill fort'.[5] The earliest proof for the existence of an Aetolian *boule* is a reference in an Athenian inscription of 333–332 B.C. or thereabouts to an Aetolian *boularch*, a presiding officer of the *boule*.[6]

7. THE ACHAEAN CONFEDERACY

The Achaean Confederacy in its early stages is important primarily as an example of a confederacy which, at least as early as the beginning of the fourth century, overstepped the ethnic boundary and admitted non-Achaeans to citizenship. Thus it anticipated or initiated the policy

[1] These points will be discussed below in the section on the Aetolians in Part II, chapter i.
[2] Thuc. iii. 94. 4, 97. 3.
[3] *SEG* xiv. 375. This probably dates from the fourth century.
[4] *Rep. Govt.* 70 f.; cf. *Studies Presented to D. M. Robinson*, ii (1953), 814 f.
[5] Tarn-Griffith, *Hellenistic Civilization*[3], 71.
[6] *IG*, ii[2]. 358; cf. *Rep. Govt.* 212, n. 8.

which was to make possible the great expansion in Hellenistic times. It is likely that this development was prepared by the early mixture of different Greek groups already before and at the time of the Doric migration.[1] According to legend, Achaea, the long narrow strip extending along the south shore of the Gulf of Corinth from near Sicyon to some thirty miles beyond the narrows forming the entrance to the Gulf proper, had once been occupied by Ionians, who, in turn, were displaced by Achaeans. Archaeological evidence shows the penetration of western Achaea by Mycenaean civilization, apparently in the thirteenth century. This may well be connected with the displacement of Ionians by Achaeans. To this period, in all likelihood, belongs the Achaean colonization of Zacynthus and Cephallenia.[2] Since the Ionians certainly were not the earliest inhabitants of Achaea, the population must have become mixed already from the time of their arrival on the scene. The later arrival of the Achaeans must have continued the process. Apparently the Achaeans were numerous enough to preserve their name proudly even into classical times and beyond. Later there was enough penetration by Doric elements to give the local dialect a Doric flavour. Nevertheless, in spite of the blend of various elements, the later population might well have become narrowly exclusive. That it did not do so may well have been due to the memory of the process by which it had been formed. The very fact that the Achaean name was retained, argues in favour of this.[3] The earliest later admission of foreign elements may be connected with the destruction of Mycenae by Argos in the fifth century. At that time refugees from Mycenae were settled at Cerynea.[4] This is surprising, for Cerynea was located near the middle of the Confederacy not far from Aegium. Does this mean that a federal government was functioning at the time

---

[1] On the early Achaean Confederacy see Larsen, 'The Early Achaean League', *Studies Presented to David Moore Robinson*, ii (1953), 797–815; *Rep. Govt.* 26 f.; J. K. Anderson, 'A Topographical and Historical Study of Achaea', *BSA* xlix (1954), 72–92; Emily Townsend Vermeule, 'The Mycenaeans in Achaea', *AJA* lxiv (1960), 1–21. The reconstruction of the movements of the Ionians and Achaeans given above owes much to M. P. Nilsson, *The Prehistoric Migrations of the Greeks* ('Acta Instituti Atheniensis Regni Sueciae, series in quarto', ii, 1953, 1–8). Cf. also J. Bérard, *La Colonisation grecque de l'Italie méridionale et de la Sicile dans l'antiquité* (2 ed., 1957), 140 f., who suggests the expulsion of Pelasgians by Ionians and of Ionians by Achaeans. These reconstructions may be correct even if the Ionians now are regarded only as a branch or offshoot of the Achaeans.

[2] Thuc. ii. 66 refers to Zacynthus as an Achaean colony. This 'colonization' is usually placed in Mycenaean times. Vermeule (20) is inclined to think that Cephallenia was occupied at the same time; on Zacynthus cf. also Anderson, 77 f.

[3] Little is known about the dialect of Achaea in classical times, and little new on the subject has been added by the Achaean inscriptions published by J. Bingen in *BCH* lxxviii (1954), 74–88 and 395–409. However, the later Achaean documents employed the Doric *koine* (Buck, *Greek Dialects*, 179), and it is unlikely that they would have done so unless the Achaean dialect already was Doric.

[4] Paus. vii. 25. 6; cf. Anderson, 81.

and prepared the way for the refugees? Otherwise they would have to pass through a string of city-states to get to Cerynea.

As far as the form of government is concerned, the Achaeans, according to our ancient sources, passed directly from a united kingdom to a republican federal state.[1] These sources, though ancient, are centuries removed from these events, but they include Polybius, himself a former Achaean statesman, who undoubtedly knew Achaean history and institutions better than any other of our informants. His reputation as a historian is as a whole excellent, but he was a patriot, and his views may also have been coloured by the official Achaean interpretation of the history of the Confederacy. Nevertheless, the claim that there was once a united kingdom which was transformed into a federal republic may well be correct. If so, the transformation probably came gradually. Polybius, to be sure, states that the Achaeans went directly from monarchy to democracy. However, considering the way in which the latter term was used in Hellenistic times, this need not mean that they adopted immediately a form of government which would have been regarded as democratic in Athens in the time of Pericles. In fact, a period of aristocratic or oligarchic government is not excluded. On the contrary, such a period can almost be taken for granted. At the time Polybius wrote, any state with republican self-government, no matter how oligarchic, was called a democracy.[2] The adoption of a federal government at an early date need not mean that every unit was a fully developed city. Herodotus (i. 145) speaks not of twelve cities but of twelve parts or, we might say, districts. Thus, some of the units may have been districts without real urban centres. Nor does the existence of a federal government necessarily mean that every city was completely loyal. Some of them may well have gone their own way at times, as Pellene was to do from time to time at a later date.

It may be well not to speculate too much and not to try to determine exactly when the kingdom was organized and when it was transformed into a federal republic. Examples from other parts of Greece, notably Thessaly, suggest that a rather extensive kingdom would not be unnatural in the late Mycenaean Age and the period following immediately on the Doric migration.[3] In the Greek colonization in the

---

[1] Pol. ii. 41. 4–6; Strabo viii. 384.

[2] 'Representation and Democracy in Hellenistic Federalism', *CP* xl (1945), 65–97, especially 88–91; A. Aymard, 'L'Organisation de la Macédoine en 167 et le régime représentatif dans le monde grec', *CP* xlv (1950) at 102 and n. 33.

[3] On the common assumption that the Catalogue of Ships represents Mycenaean Greece (cf. above under 'The Boeotian Confederacy', p. 27, n. 2) it is tempting to believe that the part of Achaea up to Aegium which appears in *Iliad* ii. 574–5 as belonging to the domain of Agamemnon represents the original Mycenaean holdings in Achaea, and that the extension of Mycenaean influence into western Achaea as traced by Vermeule (who holds that the penetration came from the Argolid rather than Pylos) represents the extension of this

west, the Achaeans are credited with the foundation of several important cities including Sybaris and Croton. In these cases no metropolis, that is, mother or founding city, is recorded, but the colony in question is said to be a foundation of the Achaeans. To be sure, the name and city of the *oikistes*, the man in charge of the founding, may be recorded, but this does not mean that his city was the mother city. This is merely the normal way of indicating the home city of a citizen of a federal state, and so the *oikistes* of Sybaris is said to have been Is of Helice. Skeptics may question this and say that the accounts merely prove that the colonists were Achaeans, but the natural interpretation is that Achaea at the time was a united state either under a king or as a federal republic.[1] Their participation in the colonization movement must also mean that the Achaeans suffered from the same ills and restlessness as did other parts of Greece. Colonists, however, tended to keep in touch with the founding state, and so the Achaeans must have been drawn into the trade with the west, even though there is little archaeological evidence to substantiate it. The Achaeans may well have been one of the groups that took part in the carrying trade without themselves producing many of the goods carried. An example of this type of trade is the trade of Phocaea with Spain, and were not the Aeginetans carriers rather than producers? There undoubtedly were others too. In any case, it would be most surprising if the Achaeans did not have a share in the trade and contacts which caused the early development of Crisa and West Locris.[2] This interest in the western trade, the Achaeans still retained in the fifth century. In the rivalry for control of the Gulf of Corinth in that and the following centuries, the Achaean Confederacy cannot be considered a rival of the great powers in Greece, but it was more than a pawn in their hands. This point will be considered more fully below in connexion with the discussion of the participation of the federal states in the inter-state rivalries of the time.

The form of government of the Confederacy remains to be discussed, but first it is necessary to try to determine whether the Achaean

control over all Achaea. Such a course of expansion would go far to explain the existence of a state with the strange shape of Achaea. The result was a united Achaea either under the control of Mycenae or as an independent kingdom. If this was taken over later by a Doric ruler, he and his successors obviously continued to call their subjects Achaeans.

[1] For the opposite point of view cf. Anderson, 78. His statement, 'Sybaris ... was founded by Is of Helike', is strictly true, but there is nothing in the source (Strabo vi. 263) which implies that the city was not a colony of the Achaean Confederacy. According to Arist. *Pol.* 1303a29 Troezen shared in the foundation, but again the reference is to the Achaeans, except for the colonists from Troezen, who were later expelled.

[2] T. J. Dunbabin, *The Western Greeks* (1948), 250 mentions only Sicyon as a city which may have challenged Corinth for a short time, though its trade cannot be traced by surviving material. He notes, however, that in the eighth and seventh centuries many small places on both sides of the Gulf of Corinth had an interest in the west. On the Phocaean trade with Spain see C. Roebuck, *Ionian Trade and Colonization* (1959), 94–101.

Confederacy refounded in 280 was regarded as new or as a revival
and continuation of the earlier organization. If the latter was the case,
as it seems to have been, there must have been a continuity of institutions, though, of course, not every detail attested for the one period can
be transferred to the other. In favour of continuity is one point in the
account of Polybius of the renewal of the Confederacy. He states that
the first cities to unite were Dyme, Patrae, Tritaea, and Pharae. For
this reason, says he, there is extant no *stele* recording the union of these
cities. This statement at first seems meaningless, but this is due to un-
due compression on the part of Polybius and the omission of something
obvious to him but not to us. When it is remembered that the sanctuary
in which the official records of the Confederacy were posted was in the
territory of Aegium, and that Aegium did not join before five years
later, it becomes clear that the reason the four cities set up no record of
their union was that they did not have access to the federal sanctuary.[1]
This, of course, proves that the revived confederacy was regarded as a
continuation of the old. More than that, it proves also that the idea of a
federal capital had been so far developed that the sanctuary connected with it was considered the only proper place for the publication
of important federal records.

Nor was this conception of a federal capital new at the time that the
Achaean Confederacy was broken up early in the third century. It can
be traced back into the fifth century, when the Italiote Confederacy
was founded and modelled on the Achaean in other respects and in the
designation of a temple and precinct of Zeus Homarios as the federal
sanctuary at which meetings were to be held and deliberations take
place.[2] Thus it is clear that the meetings of the assembly and council of
the Achaean Confederacy were held at the Homarion at least as early
as the middle of the fifth century, and that the Confederacy had a
capital by this time, but how the capital developed or was chosen is not
equally clear.[3] The importance of the sanctuary has suggested that the
Confederacy may at the outset have been a religious amphictiony.

---

[1] Pol. ii. 41. 12–13, where Polybius does not mention that Aegium in a sense was the
capital but takes this knowledge for granted.

[2] Pol. ii. 39. 1–7; cf. the account of the Italiote Confederacy below.

[3] See particularly A. Aymard, 'Le Zeus fédéral achaien Hamarios-Homarios', *Mélanges
Navarre* (1935), 453–70; 'Le Rôle politique du sanctuaire fédéral achaien', *Mélanges Franz
Cumont* (1936), 1–26. Aymard points out that, while Polybius uses the form 'Homarios',
later inscriptions favoured 'Hamarios', but that the form 'Amarios' which is frequently used
is incorrect. This is found both in Tarn-Griffith, *Hellenistic Civilization*[3], 73 and Bengtson,
GrG[2] 442. While Tarn writes about 'the temple of Zeus Amarios at the capital Aigion'
already in the first edition of *Hell. Civ.* 66 (cf. *CAH* vii. 736), Bengtson states that 'weder die
Ätoler noch die Achäer besassen als Koinon einen Vorort'. On the point of the capital Tarn
is to be followed, though in the early days it was probably the sacred precinct rather than the
city which was the capital. The taking over of this institution by the Italiotes shows that the
capital was a part of the federal state in contemporary thought.

However, as stated above, there is reason to believe that the political unity of Achaea is old and it would hardly be out of character to have established a federal cult and sanctuary and to have given the god chosen as protector an epithet to suggest that he was the god who held together and put in order the federal state. Certainly the reorganization of the citizen body of Athens by Cleisthenes involved innovations fully as great as this. The emphasis on the sanctuary, naturally, was greater in the early days than later. It has been demonstrated that the revived Achaean Confederacy functioned for twenty years beginning in 276–275 under the leadership of one secretary and two generals with the assembly meeting in the sanctuary.[1] Not only the practice of holding meetings in the sanctuary but also the system of two generals and a secretary were apparently carried over from the earlier organization. Is it too much to suggest that the secretary probably maintained an office in the sanctuary or the nearby city and that there thus was the beginning of a federal administration at the capital?

That the idea of a federal citizenship was fully developed early in the fourth century, should come as no surprise. Some time before 389 the Achaeans had acquired Calydon, a few miles northwest of the narrow strait giving access to the Gulf of Corinth proper, and had made the Calydonians Achaean citizens.[2] This was the year in which the Achaeans appealed to Sparta for aid in the defence of Calydon against an attack of the Acarnanians. Indirect evidence in connexion with the operations which followed, makes it practically certain that the Achaeans also held Naupactus and the shore between the two cities, and had incorporated the citizens of this city too into the Achaean citizen body.[3] In his report concerning the incorporation of Calydon into the Confederacy, Xenophon speaks of the Achaean citizens as politai, a word which normally means the citizens of a city-state.[4] Thus we may have here the earliest application of a term originally meaning the residents or citizens of a city to the citizens of a federal or territorial state. After the Achaeans or some other Greeks had started the practice, many were to follow their example, witness citizen, citoyen, Bürger, etc. The most notable exception was Rome. The cives Romani, no matter how numerous or how much of the earth they inherited, were always citizens of the city of Rome.

[1] Aymard, Mélanges Cumont, 18–21 on the basis of Pol. ii. 43. 1–2 and Strabo viii. 385.
[2] Xen. Hell. iv. 6. 1. This account implies that the Achaeans had held the city for some time and in this particular year were forced to place a garrison in the city and to prepare to defend it against the Acarnanians.
[3] Studies Presented to Robinson, ii. 807.
[4] Ibid. 809; cf. above, p. 8f. In Hell. Ox. 16 (11). 2 the word is used about the citizens in the cities of the Boeotian Confederacy.

Concerning the form of government of the early Confederacy very little was known until the publication a few years ago of a fragmentary inscription found at Aegium, dating from the fourth or possibly the very beginnings of the third century.[1] At any rate it seems to antedate the revival of the Confederacy in 280 and also the dissolution of the older organization. The document is very fragmentary but apparently contains a treaty, the nature of which cannot be determined, with a city Coronea, which cannot be identified for certain,[2] but it does contain a clear reference to the *boule* of the Achaeans, that is, the federal council, and to their *damiorgoi*. Thus we have evidence for the existence of the federal *boule* and the board of *damiorgoi* for the early Confederacy. It is not certain that the *damiorgoi* numbered ten as they did later.[3] It can also be taken for granted that the two generals and the secretary whom the Confederacy possessed in the period 280 to 255 B.C. were parts of the machinery of the earlier period taken over at the time of the revival of the Confederacy. The same can be said with fair certainty of the federal primary assembly, though the evidence for that is later. Thus, though further details cannot be determined, the federal government already was highly developed.

To return to the events of 389, these display a positive policy as indicated not only by the absorption of non-Achaean cities across the Gulf but also by the demand for aid from Sparta backed up by the threat of secession from the Peloponnesian League in case aid was not forthcoming. This demand and threat on the part of the Achaeans were precipitated by an attack of the Acarnanian Confederacy on Calydon, doubtless with the intention of conquering and annexing the city.[4] For the conduct of affairs under these conditions it is likely that there already existed some authority functioning between the meetings of the council and assembly, some authority which could be approached at any time, which could make decisions on minor questions and could call special meetings of the federal council and assembly when needed. This can hardly have been anyone but the magistrates and *damiorgoi*. For the conduct of business of this kind, it would be advantageous to

---

[1] *SEG* xiv. 375; earlier editions, J. Bingen, *BCH* lxxviii (1954), 402, no. 18; P. Åström, in the *Opuscula Atheniensia* of the Swedish Institute at Athens, ii (1955), 4–9.

[2] The editors rightly consider neither Coronea in Boeotia, nor Coronea in Phthiotic Achaea, nor Corone in Messenia as a very plausible candidate. There remains a Coronea near Corinth and Sicyon listed by Stephanus of Byzantium but otherwise unknown.

[3] The list of names in the inscription, with the names in the nominative and with the ethnics of the cities given, cannot be a list of the *damiorgoi*. These should be given in line 4 in the genitive, but here there is no room for a list of any length. Possibly merely the name of the chairman was given in some such formula as 'those with—'. In addition, the plural form of the ethnics suggests more than one delegate per city and thus indicates that the list was too long to be a list of the *damiorgoi*.

[4] Xen. *Hell*. iv. 6. 1–2.

have a permanent capital, and this, we have already seen, the Achaeans seem to have had, though in 389 the city connected with the Homarion probably was not Aegium but Helice. Only when the latter city was destroyed by an earthquake a few years later, did Aegium become the capital.[1]

It is impossible to trace in greater detail the evolution of particular political institutions in the early Achaean Confederacy, but it is possible to follow to some extent the fluctuations between aristocracy or oligarchy and democracy. It has already been suggested that the transition from kingship to the republican government must have been marked by a period of aristocratic or oligarchic government. This can be deduced by analogy from the normal course of development of Greek states. Moreover, unless we place the overthrow of monarchy extremely late, or think that the Achaeans were centuries in advance of the Athenians, it follows also from the fact that real democracy of the Greek type did not develop before in the fifth century. From the time of Pericles on, Greeks commonly referred to Cleisthenes as the founder of Athenian democracy, but actually the state was not fully democratic in his days and *demokratia* had not yet been adopted as the name for popular government.[2] On the other hand, by 417, Achaea had become so democratic that the Spartans found it necessary to set things right.[3] This must mean that the Achaeans had adopted democracy in the fifth century, that is, approximately at the time when extreme democracy was developing at Athens, and they may well have done so at the time when they were allied with the Athenians. The report that things were set right in 417 indicates further that the Spartans at that time introduced oligarchic government. This oligarchy, when once established apparently lasted undisturbed to 367. In that year the Achaeans were brought over by Epaminondas without a change in government, but the home authorities at Thebes decided to send harmosts and establish 'democracies'. Here the use of the plural by Xenophon suggests that he was thinking of the government of the cities within the Confederacy. The result of this action was that oligarchs exiled at the time fought their way

---

[1] Paus. vii. 7. 2 speaks as if, at the time of the revival of the Achaean Confederacy, it was decided to hold the meetings at Aegium only because Helice no longer existed.

[2] On the use of the term *demokratia* see Larsen, 'Cleisthenes and the Development of the Theory of Democracy at Athens', in *Essays in Political Theory Presented to George H. Sabine* (1948), 1–16, and cf. 'The Judgment of Antiquity on Democracy', *CP* xlix (1954), 1–14 at 1 f. For Cleisthenes as the founder of Athenian democracy see Ehrenberg, 'Origins of Democracy', *Historia*, i (1950), 515–48 at 534, an article now available in the author's *Polis und Imperium* (1965). For the argument that for a few years after the reforms of Cleisthenes the *boule* remained so powerful that Athens practically had representative government, see *Rep. Govt.* 14–18.

[3] Thuc. v. 82. 1.

back, re-established oligarchies, and once more co-operated with the Spartans.[1]

What do these changes in the form of government involve? Unfortunately there is practically no evidence. For democracy the prominence of the primary assembly in democratic states in this period and the emphasis on the collective judgement of the masses in popular democratic theory, make it reasonably certain that the decisions on all major issues were reserved for the primary assembly, the *ekklesia*. Likewise we can be pretty certain that there was no property qualification for voting and holding office. Whether the Achaeans went as far as the Athenians in choosing magistrates in the cities by lot, or whether the cities had anything corresponding to the popular Athenian law courts with their hundreds of citizen judges, is not known. The federal officials, and the representatives of the cities in the federal council, on the other hand, certainly were chosen by vote and not by lot. At least, there appears to be no evidence for the practice of selecting federal officials by lot in any Greek confederacy. Thus it would seem that the one organ of the federal government for which the adoption of democracy mattered most was the *ekklesia*. Yet here it may have mattered little except in theory. On account of the distances involved, it is likely that only men of property with sufficient leisure normally attended the meetings of the federal assembly. The real influence of the lower classes may have been exercised more effectively in the election of representatives to the federal council. Thus it is likely that, even under the democracy, the federal government normally was directed by the moneyed upper classes.

The nature of the oligarchic revolution of 417 is equally difficult to define. It can be considered certain that it involved some limitation of the rights to vote and hold office, probably similar to that of contemporary Boeotia. Did the Achaeans follow the example of the Boeotians also in doing away with the federal *ekklesia* and relying exclusively on the *boule*? Since the *ekklesia* existed in the Hellenistic confederacy, this is unlikely. But there is another feature of the later constitution which may well go back to the oligarchic revolution, namely, the age qualification of thirty years for voting. This, at least judging by earlier Greek standards, is a very high age qualification for a state that claimed to be democratic. It seems natural to believe that it was adopted in 417 and never abolished. This raises another question. If a property qualification for active citizenship was adopted at the time, when was it abolished? Or was this too retained? The fact that Polybius considered the Achaean Confederacy democratic and that the

---

[1] Xen. *Hell.* vii. 1. 41–43.

Confederacy itself boasted of its democracy, does not prove that it was democratic by the standards of fifth century Greece. Thus it is possible that not only a high age qualification for voting but also a property qualification for active citizenship were introduced in 417 and retained by the Confederacy not only to its temporary dissolution but also throughout Hellenistic and Roman times.

8. THE ACARNANIAN CONFEDERACY

Before the King's Peace, Acarnania, later important in the contests for the control of northern Greece, is important chiefly in connexion with the westward expansion of the Greeks and the rivalry between Athens and Corinth for leadership in northwest Greece and beyond. This rivalry became acute in the middle of the fifth century and remained so through the Peloponnesian War. Hence it is no accident that the greatest land battle in the war before the battle of Delium seems to have been the battle of Olpae fought late in 426 just north of Acarnania proper. Nevertheless, Acarnania itself, before these events, was more or less an inland power facing Aetolia.[1]

Acarnania must be the land of the conquering tribe of Acarnanians. Their land consisted essentially of the mountainous district west of the Achelous river and of a part of the valley of that river. Here was the best agricultural land, and here was the capital or chief city, Stratus. The Acarnanians may well have looked upon their land as extending west to the sea, but the coast had been occupied by a string of Corinthian colonies, Sollium, Leucas, and Anactorium, and a little farther north the important Ambracia. Between Ambracia and Acarnania the territory of the partly Hellenized Amphilochians extended down to the Gulf of Ambracia. Farther south, Oeniadae, near the mouth of the Achelous, appears to have been regarded as Acarnanian but was subject to intrigues from the outside and stood aloof from the Acarnanian Confederacy, while Astacus, a little farther north, was under the control of a tyrant. During the Archidamian War the local objectives of the Corinthians and Ambraciotes were to extend their power and, if possible, gain control of all Acarnania; of the Athenians, to oust the Corinthians and to strengthen the Acarnanian Confederacy as a

---

[1] Acarnania is a somewhat neglected field. E. Oberhummer, *Akarnanien, Ambrakia, Amphilochien, Leukas im Altertum* (1887) remains fundamental. The recent publication of *IG* ix². 1, fasc. 2 (1957) by G. Klaffenbach is of great importance. It includes not only the inscriptions from Acarnania but also Acarnanian documents found in other places. The review by K. Latte in *Gnomon*, xxxi (1959), 30–36 discusses *inter alia* the language and nomenclature. N. G. L. Hammond, *A History of Greece* (1959) gives a relatively full account of Acarnania, but it is embedded in the general account of the period. For an excellent continuous account see E. Kirsten, 'Aitolien und Akarnanien in der älteren griechischen Geschichte', *Neue Jahrbücher für Antike*, iii (1940), 298–316.

counterbalance against them; of the Acarnanians to strengthen their Confederacy and to secure and incorporate the Acarnanian cities still remaining outside, including the Corinthian colonies. In this they were successful except for Leucas.

Acarnania, like other states of the kind, was the result of conquest by an invading host. The conquest might well have resulted in a mixed population in which any non-Greek elements would be likely to be Illyrian. Actually there are a number of Illyrian place names in Acarnania, but they are relatively few. The dialect was north-west Greek, not distinguishable from Aetolian.[1] How much cohesion there remained in the period between the conquest and the Persian War is not clear, but Acarnania was known as a cultural or ethnic unity at least as early as the last part of the sixth century. Peisistratus, when he fought his way back to Athens after his second expulsion, if we can believe the account of Herodotus, was inspired by an Acarnanian soothsayer to make a night attack on his opponents at Pallene. Even more interesting, another Acarnanian soothsayer, Megistias, a personal friend of Simonides, was with Leonidas at Thermopylae, refused to leave, and was afterwards honoured by an epigram by Simonides.[2] Acarnania, however, at this time seems to have stood aloof from Greek politics, while the Corinthian colonies, Ambracia and Leucas, are said to have contributed respectively seven and three ships to the fleet at Salamis, and these two and Anactorium between them, 1,300 men to the Plataea campaign.[3] This was probably due to the leadership of Corinth rather than to their own initiative. Some twenty-five years later, when Athens began to challenge the leadership of Corinth in the west and to try to extend her own influence all the way to Sicily, Acarnania was drawn into general Greek politics and became as a result one of the chief theatres of warfare during the first years of the Peloponnesian War. This is recognized by Thucydides, and as a consequence, he gives a fairly full account of the events involved.

Concerning the government and organization of the Confederacy at the time, little is known and Thucydides tells nothing directly. He does indicate, however, as in the case of Aetolia, that there was a central authority which could initiate policies and negotiate treaties. Furthermore, his statement that Stratus was the largest city of Acarnania,

[1] On Illyrian names, see Latte, *Gnomon*, xxxi. 32; on the dialect ibid. 31, Kirsten, 302. Note also that Buck, *Greek Dialects*, no. 67 gives the third-century Aetolian-Acarnanian treaty (*IG* ix². 1. 3) under the Northwest Greek *koine*.

[2] Herod. i. 62 f.; vii 219. 1, 221, 228. 3–4. It may be interesting to note that Sir Maurice Bowra, in the article on Simonides in *OCD*, lists this touchingly simple epigram as one of those most likely to be genuine.

[3] Herod. viii. 45; ix. 28. 5; their names on the victory monuments: Tod, 19; Paus. v. 23. 2 (Leucas not included).

combined with its importance in the campaigns, suggests that the city already was the capital of Acarnania. This is even clearer in the report that Agesilaus in 389 sent a communication to Stratus to the *koinon* of the Acarnanians.[1] Here *koinon* must mean the federal government, and it thus becomes clear that Stratus was the place to which communications intended for that government normally were sent. Olpae on Amphilochian territory was used as a common place of judgement.[2] The language suggests that this was the seat of a federal court—and it would be perfectly possible to have different seats for the federal executive and the federal judiciary—but it has also sometimes been taken to mean a place for the settlement of disputes between the Acarnanians and the Amphilochians.

Since so little is known about the Acarnanian government, it is a common view that the Acarnanians of the time constituted a loose tribal state.[3] Yet, there are signs that the development of cities had gone far. The statement of Thucydides about Stratus, which already has been cited, implies that there were other cities. Thucydides also states that after the battle of Olpae the booty was divided by cities, while for 389 Xenophon reports that Agesilaus attacked several cities but failed to capture them.[4] The Acarnanians contended with Ambracia for the control of Amphilochian Argos; in the period 431–424 they acquired the Corinthian colonies, Sollium and Anactorium, also Astacus, which possibly was Corinthian, and finally Oeniadae, an Acarnanian city which had stood aloof from the Confederacy. Of these cities, the one for which there is evidence of a functioning city government is Stratus, from which we have a proxenic decree of the late fifth century.[5] This document suggests a normal city government with an assembly, a council, and annual magistrates. The one magistrate listed, the chairman of the council (*boularchos*) was from Phoctiac, later a separate city. If this place, some ten miles west of Stratus, was a part of its territory, it was relatively large, and it would seem that Stratus was on its way to become a predominant city. The wars, however, do not seem to indicate any particular hostility between it and the other cities. The evidence has led at least one scholar to class Acarnania at this time as a sympoly or true federal state.[6] Be that as it may, what counts is that, while a number of cities had developed, the feeling for

---

[1] Thuc. ii. 80. 8, iii. 106; Xen. *Hell.* iv. 6. 4.
[2] Thuc. iii. 105. 1.
[3] So Busolt, *Staatskunde*, 1463; Bengtson, *GrG*² 82; Hammond, *History of Greece*, 500; Ehrenberg, *Staat*, 28.
[4] Thuc. iii. 114. 1; Xen. *Hell.* iv. 6. 12. On account of his many inaccuracies the statement of Diod. xi. 85. 2 that Pericles won over all cities of Acarnania except Oeniadae carries less weight.
[5] *IG* ix². 1. 390 = *SIG*³. 121.   [6] 'Bundesstaat' (Kirsten, 312).

Acarnanian unity had not been lost. The development of cities was likely to be accompanied by a certain slackening of the bonds uniting the original nation as the cities emphasized 'state rights' over against the central government. Yet there is nothing unique in the fact that in a line of battle the contingents from the various localities retained their unity and were drawn up in the battle order as each contingent or its commander chose. This was the practice of the Boeotians as late as the battle of Delium[1] and probably later. What is important is the extent to which the federal government could act for the Confederacy. This includes the negotiation of a treaty for a defensive alliance with Ambracia for a hundred years, and these negotiations seem to have been conducted by the Acarnanians themselves without Athenian guidance. True, the treaty provided that the Ambraciotes need not support the Acarnanians against the Peloponnesians nor the Acarnanians (including the Amphilochians)[2] the Ambraciotes against the Athenians. Thus the two parties to the treaty retained their affiliation with their old allies. For the Ambraciotes the 'Peloponnesians' meant primarily the Corinthians, who actually did send a garrison of 300 hoplites to the city. This looks ominous, but whatever Corinth wished, the local authorities apparently wanted this settlement to remain permanent. A special clause in the treaty provided that the Ambraciotes were not to help Anactorium. This must mean that the Acarnanians gave notice that they intended to reduce this Corinthian colony and that the Ambraciotes acquiesced in this plan. Though a conclusion from silence is dangerous, it is likely that the Acarnanians, in turn, were pledged to stay away from Leucas. Anactorium actually was reduced the next year by the Acarnanians with the aid of the 'Athenians from Naupactus', the inhabitants expelled, and the city colonized by Acarnanians. This obviously did not involve any major Athenian expedition. The Athenians had even less to do with the reduction of Oeniadae the following year (424). The Athenian general, Demosthenes, appeared in Acarnania before his projected raid on Siphae in Boeotia but found Oeniadae already brought over by the Acarnanians themselves. Apparently the local war was finished. There were Acarnanian troops with Demosthenes when he approached Siphae, and a few Acarnanians later served with the Athenians in Sicily.[3] while the Leucadians

---

[1] Thuc. iii. 107. 4, iv. 93. 4.

[2] The statement of Thuc. iii. 114. 3 that the Acarnanians and the Amphilochians made a treaty with the Ambraciotes *can* be taken to mean that these were two separate states, but in the summary of the treaty itself the Amphilochians are not mentioned except in a special clause providing for the restoration of Amphilochian posts and hostages held by the Ambraciotes. Otherwise it is simply a question of the Acarnanians, who thus include the Amphilochians, at this time obviously members of the Confederacy.

[3] Thuc. iv. 49, 77, 89. 1; vii. 57. 10, 60. 4, 67. 2.

and Ambraciotes gave some support to the other side,[1] but the war in and around Acarnania and Amphilochian Argos does not seem to have been resumed.

The alliance or entente with Athens remained essentially unbroken down to 388. With this affiliation, it was natural enough for the Acarnanians to join the anti-Spartan coalition in the Corinthian War. They even contributed light-armed troops to the allied campaign in the Peloponnesus.[2] Their attack on Calydon later in the war may have been part of an attempt on the part of the allies to break the hold of the Achaeans, the allies of the Spartans, on the entrance to the Gulf of Corinth. From the narrower Acarnanian point of view, it undoubtedly was an effort to expand the Confederacy and annex also the coast east of Oeniadae. After the expedition of Agesilaus of 389, the Acarnanians decided early in 388, before their country could be invaded a second time, to make peace with the Achaeans and to enter into an alliance with the Spartans. The account of Xenophon[3] indicates that the initiative came from the Acarnanians, whose ambassador arrived at Sparta when plans for a new campaign were under way. Their action at this time is comparable to their decision in 426 to withdraw from the general Greek war. The alliance with Sparta probably meant that the Acarnanians were pledged to follow the leadership of the Spartans, but they were so far removed from the normal area of Spartan campaigns that this was not likely to cause them serious inconvenience. As it turned out, it was probably this alliance which made it possible to survive the epidemic of dissolution of federal states which followed the King's Peace. Thus the Acarnanian Confederacy was able a few years later to join the Second Athenian League as a unit. To be sure, from the Spartan point of view, Acarnania lay so far afield that this might have been enough to keep the Spartans from taking action. In any case, the Acarnanian leaders of the late fifth and early fourth century seem to have exhibited no mean statesmanship.

Through what government machinery did these statesmen exercise their leadership? This is a question on which very little information is available, or rather what information there is dates from the late fourth and the third centuries. Yet this, in spite of some break in continuity, makes it possible to draw some conclusions also about the institutions of the earlier period. A treaty of the middle of the third century indicates that at that time there was a college of seven generals at the head of the Confederacy.[4] Since there was a tendency in Greek federal

---

[1] Thuc. vii. 2. 1, 7. 1, 58. 3.
[2] Xen. *Hell.* iv. 2. 17. [3] Xen. *Hell.* iv. 7. 1.
[4] *IG* ix². 1. 3 A (*SIG*³ 421). This will be discussed in the account of the Acarnanian Confederacy after the King's Peace.

states to replace such a body with a single head of state, it is almost certain that the board of generals represents a revival or survival from earlier institutions. Of the seven listed in the treaty no two are from the same city. In the absence of further evidence, it is impossible to say for certain whether there simply was a rule against having two generals from the same city, or whether the seven represent seven electoral districts. Probably the latter is more likely, though, in that case, there must have been more than one city in several districts.[1] The other officials listed, the hipparch, the secretary, and the treasurer, came from the same cities as some of the generals. The same document refers also to a federal *synedrion* or council. It is likely that this too goes back to the fifth century. The number of generals may not have been exactly the same at the time, and there may have been other changes in detail. In addition, it would be natural to have also a federal primary assembly, and for this there may actually be evidence. Cassander when he in 314 proposed to strengthen the frontier of Acarnania against Aetolia, is said to have laid his proposals before the federal *ekklesia*, and this appears to be a previously existing organization and not a new creation.[2] In favour of regarding this as a primary assembly is not only the name but also the late survival of the primary assembly in neighbouring Aetolia. In addition there is the consideration that, when the Acarnanian Confederacy comes into view in the fifth century before it had absorbed Oeniadae and the Corinthian colonies along the coast, it was a comparatively compact state so that a primary assembly could function effectively. In a treaty with Pyrrhus, a document which unfortunately never was published in full and now has been lost, this assembly is referred to as the *chilioi* or 'One Thousand'.[3] This may seem a small number for a primary assembly of a state of any size, but it is well to remember that such numbers as thousand, five thousand, and ten thousand, when used as names for assemblies and citizen bodies are round numbers and do not give the actual number, which may have been considerably larger. Moreover, the name may have been adopted at a time when the Confederacy was so small that

[1] Seven is a relatively large number in comparison, for instance, with the two generals of the early Achaean Confederacy or the three of the Phocians. Apart from the Acarnanian board, the one larger board known for this period is that of Boeotia, and there the eleven Boeotarchs represented eleven districts, of which some contained more than one city. The seven cities represented in our list include Oeniadae in the extreme south, Anactorium in the extreme north, Leucas on the west coast, Stratus on the Achelous river, and Phoetiae and Thyrrheum in the interior. The seventh general came from the Deries, who according to Diod. xix. 67. 4 in 314 were moved into Agrinium. Thus he seems to represent the district of Agraea east of the Achelous.

[2] Diod. xix. 67. 3–4.

[3] *IG* ix². 1. 207. The term appears again in *IG* ix². 1. 582 (*Inschriften von Magnesia*, 31) of the late third century.

the next number used in this way—apparently Five Thousand—seemed much too pretentious. It is also possible that there was a property qualification for active citizenship even if hoplite census might be a misnomer for a state which made extensive use of light-armed troops.[1]

To conclude, it is likely that the Acarnanians had the normal Greek government with magistrates, including a board of generals, a council, and a primary assembly, and that the essentials of this form of government endured from the fifth to the late third century. To this may be added a feature which is seldom attested for Greek federal states. There existed a federal court, which, in the period when the Amphilochians belonged to the Confederacy, was located at Olpae. The *koinon dikasterion* with seat at Olpae has long puzzled scholars, who have hesitated to accept the natural meaning that it was a federal court, and that, since its seat was at Olpae, the Amphilochians at the time were regular members of the Confederacy.[2] This interpretation gets some indirect support from the publication a few years ago of an inscription of the late third century including, alongside of much other valuable information, a reference to an Acarnanian federal court. This inscription will be discussed below in connexion with the Acarnanian Confederacy of that period. Here it must suffice to note that the existence of a federal court at a later date should make us less hesitant to accept its existence also for the earlier period. To be sure, this implies an advanced and developed federal state, but this is not the only evidence which shows that the Acarnanians were not as backward as scholars at times have thought.

9. THE ITALIOTE CONFEDERACY[3]

This union of Greek cities of southern Italy appears definitely to have been formed for mutual defence against the native tribes and specifically the Lucanians, as is shown by the report that they were all bound by treaty or agreement to come to the aid of any city whose land was raided by the Lucanians, and that the responsible officials of any city which failed to do so, were to be put to death.[4] This may suggest

---

[1] Busolt, *Staatskunde*, 1466, n. 1, though recognizing that the Acarnanians largely used light-armed troops, suggests a connexion between hoplite service and full citizenship. Another suggestion is that of Swoboda, *Staatsaltertümer*, 304, n. 11 that the number represents the quorum required for the transaction of business.

[2] Thuc. iii. 105. 1. It has been argued above on p. 92, n. 2 that also the treaty with Ambracia of 426 implies that the Amphilochians were members of the Confederacy.

[3] This organization is not included in the handbooks of Swoboda and Busolt but is frequently mentioned in histories, e.g., E. Meyer, *Geschichte des Altertums*, v (1902), 127 ff.; Beloch, *GrG²* iii. i. 113 f. A recent article with references to the literature on the subject is F. Ghinati, 'Ricerche sulla Lega Italiota', *Memorie della Accademia Patavina*, lxxiv (1961–2), 3–19.

[4] Diod. xiv. 101. 1. The rules mentioned were established by *synthekai* (treaties), and the troops involved are called *symmachoi*. However, the latter term seems applicable to any

that the organization was a symmachy or alliance rather than a federal state. On the other hand, such rules might well be adopted by a federal state in order to secure quick action in case of an emergency. Moreover, if it is correct that the Confederacy originated in the fifth century and copied the institutions of the Achaean Confederacy to the extent of taking over laws from it and following its example in creating a federal sanctuary and capital, then the original organization must be considered a federal state, and its establishment an important event in the history of federalism.

The report that the union was due to the initiative of the Crotonians, the Sybarites, and the Caulonians, and that the Achaean institutions were copied, is due to Polybius. Concerning the approximate date he indicates that the Confederacy was organized some time after the dissolution of the Pythagorean clubs in various cities, and further that it was broken up by Dionysius of Syracuse and the surrounding barbarians. The mention of Dionysius indicates that the organization did not last long into the fourth century and that the later co-operation of Italoite cities with each other was due to later arrangements. Furthermore, the imitation of Achaean institutions must be placed before 417, the year in which Sparta introduced oligarchy into Achaea. Thus the Italiote Confederacy in all likelihood belongs to the last quarter of the fifth century and the first decade or so of the fourth.[1]

To be told by Polybius little more than that the new organization copied that of the Achaeans is aggravating, since so little is known about the latter. There may also arise the suspicion that Polybius is distorting things a bit for the greater glory of the Achaeans, since the only purpose in reporting the incident is to prove the high regard in which the Achaeans were held. Yet there is one detail which is almost a guarantee of authenticity. This is the statement that the Crotonians and their associates designated a temple and precinct of Zeus Homarios as the federal sanctuary at which meetings were to be held and deliberations take place.[2] Since the federal sanctuary of the Achaeans was the pre-

troops aiding those of another city, and so cannot be used to prove that the cities in question were allied cities rather than members of a federal state. Similarly, *synthekai* could as well be applied to the agreements by which cities joined a federal state as to treaties between completely independent cities.

[1] Pol. ii. 39. 1–7; cf. Walbank, *Commentary*. Both Walbank (on ii. 39. 4) and Ghinati (p. 11 and n. 33) favour placing the formation before 417. Apparently only Walbank notes that ii. 39. 7 implies that the victory of Dionysius at Elleporus (389) ended 'the alliance on the Achaean model'. The Sybaris involved probably was neither the great Sybaris nor Thurii but Sybaris on the Traeis, as Walbank suggests.

[2] Ghinati, p. 10 takes the reference to be to the temple in the Peloponnesus which served as the federal sanctuary of the Achaean Confederacy. This is an impossible interpretation. If this were the meaning one would expect some indication—at least the definite article—to indicate that *the* temple of Zeus Homarios was meant. Ghinati, of course, does not believe that the Italiotes sailed to Greece to hold their meetings there, but the supposition that the

cinct of Zeus Homarios near Aegium, this suggests genuine borrowing. Yet, when we are told further that Achaean customs and laws were borrowed, this may not mean too much. Nevertheless it must mean that both confederacies were fully developed federal states, but it would be foolish to think the institutions identical in all respects. To give one illustration, Polybius states that for the first twenty-five years after the revival of the Achaean Confederacy in 280 its chief magistrates were two generals and a secretary.[1] The use of two generals was very likely carried over from the old Confederacy. But, if this was the usage of the fifth-century Achaeans, it may not have suited the Italiote organization and may not have been taken over by it. However, it is useless to speculate about the details of the Italiote institutions.

Thus, very little is known about the Italiote Confederacy, but what little is known is of great importance. To repeat, it illustrates the tendency, too often underestimated, of Greek cities to get together in the face of danger. In the second place, it shows that already in the fifth century it was considered normal for a Greek federal state to have something in the nature of a capital. The Greeks may not have had a name for it, but they did have the institution. There is nothing surprising in finding that a federal state had a federal sanctuary, but this was more than a mere sanctuary. It was also the place where political deliberations were held and, undoubtedly in addition, the place where federal enactments were recorded. Moreover, since the Italiote capital was modelled on the Achaean, the information from Italy has a bearing also on the institutions of the homeland.

10. THE EUBOEAN CONFEDERACY

Euboea, though extremely important in Greek interstate rivalries and wars, has little to teach concerning Greek federal institutions, but that little is of considerable importance. It concerns chiefly the problem of federal and local coins.[2] The lesson seems to be that one cannot judge the intensity of federal bonds by the amount of ostensibly federal currency in circulation.

The wonder is that a Euboean Confederacy ever should be organized, and, in spite of the coins, it is not certain that such an organization did exist in the late fifth and early fourth centuries. The long and narrow island lacked any satisfactory overland communications between the centre of the island and the northern and southern

---

meetings were not held in the sanctuary requires taking more liberties with the text. Polybius definitely indicates that the sanctuary was the place where the meetings were held.

[1] Pol. ii. 43. 1.

[2] W. P. Wallace, *The Euboean League and its Coinage* ('Numismatic Notes and Monographs', no. 134) (1956). On the geography and history of the island, see now also E. Meyer in *Der Kleine Pauly*, ii. 397–9.

7

extremities.[1] It must have been this configuration which caused it to be practically divided between four large city-states which lorded it over the smaller communities, namely, Chalcis and Eretria in the centre of the island, Carystus at the southern extremity, and Histiaea-Oreus at the northern. At any rate, when the Confederacy existed at its greatest extent, it seems to have been made up of these four cities.[2] Moreover, at times it seems that Histiaea and Carystus stood outside of the confederacy or alliance so that it was made up exclusively of Chalcis and Eretria. Thus it is tempting to consider the organization a revival or continuation of the early co-operation of Chalcis and Eretria. After the Lelantine War, the co-operation was followed by the domination or supremacy of one or the other. From the Lelantine War to their defeat by the Athenians in 506, the Chalcidians were supreme; after that, the Eretrians, their supremacy apparently lasting only to the capture of the city by the Persians in 490. These relative positions of the two cities seem reflected in their coinage. At first it was Chalcis that produced the more important issue; afterwards, Eretria, which on the obverse of tetradrachms and smaller coins placed a cow, apparently celebrating Euboea, the land of fine cattle, and thus, as it were, claiming to coin for all Euboea.[3] This need not mean that there existed any real federal state or that Eretria had subdued the entire island but merely that the city claimed primacy on this island 'rich in cattle'. This may actually be the meaning of the name, which seems to be an out-and-out place name and not a name derived from an ethnic group. In favour of this interpretation rather than against it, is the fact that at the same time Carystus was issuing coins with a cow and a calf on the obverse. On the reverse, each city had its own symbol, Eretria a cuttlefish, Carystus a cock.[4] The tendency to close contacts between Boeotia and Euboea

[1] Wallace, p. 6.

[2] *IG* xii. 9. 207, a document of the early third century. This, of course, is not fully conclusive for the earlier period, but an indication that conditions were much the same is the consistency with which any important political development is connected with one or more of the four cities.

[3] Seltman, *Greek Coins*, 54, 83 f. and Pls. iv, 16 and 17, xi, 1 and 2. Seltman maintains that the real activity of the Eretrian mint began only after Chalcis ceased issuing her 'eagles'. On the play of words involved, cf. also Wallace, 3, n. 6, who speaks of the federal coins of 411 and after as adopting 'Eretria's heifer', but if the cow or heifer involved a play on words in 411, why not earlier?

[4] Seltman, 84 and Pl. xi, 4. He suggests that the cock too may be a 'canting type', the cock representing the *Keryx*, 'the herald of day'. He considers the Carystian design copied from the Eretrian. It may be noticed that the issues of the two cities could be reconciled with a federation, the cities showing the design of the federal state on one side of a coin and that of the city on the other. If Histiaea stood aloof and Chalcis was in eclipse, there would only be two cities in the organization. Or is Dicaea (Seltman, Pl. xi, 3) to be considered a full-fledged member? On the name of Euboea, see Hesiod, *Aegimius*, frag. 4 and cf. Meyer, 398. That the name is old is shown by its occurrence in the *Iliad*, *Odyssey*, *Works and Days*, and the *Hymn to Pythian Apollo*.

noticeable in later history is seen early both in the literary tradition[1] and the coins, a Chalcidic issue showing the Boeotian shield and a Boeotian issue, the Chalcidic wheel.[2] In fact, at the time of the triple attack on Attica by Sparta, Boeotia, and Chalcis in 506, Boeotia and Chalcis may well have been formally allied.

The further history of the island in the fifth century down to the revolt of Euboea in 411 will not be discussed here except to note that under the Athenian Empire there always were Euboeans hoping to regain their freedom and sometimes plotting to do so, and that, as was to be expected after the planting of Athenian clerouchs not only at Chalcis but also at Histiaea, the lead in this movement was taken by Eretrians. When the Spartans had occupied Decelea, the very first to appeal to Agis for aid in a revolt were Euboeans, and Agis is reported actually to have summoned a small contingent of troops from Sparta for the invasion of the island. However, when an appeal came from Lesbos, the Euboean venture was given up. This did not put a stop to the intrigues of the Euboeans. Early in 411 Eretrians aided the Boeotians in the capture of Oropus. Immediately after that they appealed to the commanders of the Peloponnesian fleet off Rhodes, but again were disappointed when the fleet chose to proceed to Chios.[3] They probably also went to Sparta, for the fleet that ultimately did intervene is said to have acted on the invitation of the Euboeans. When the Peloponnesian fleet arrived off Euboea and established headquarters at Oropus, the Eretrians were busy again and, in spite of the presence of an Athenian garrison on their land, managed to signal to the attackers. Athenians fleeing to the city of Eretria were put to death, and only those who made their way to the Athenian held fort or to Chalcis were saved. Later these places too were liberated and only Histiaea, or Oreos, as Thucydides now calls the city, was retained by the Athenians. Thereupon at least Chalcis and Eretria proceeded to co-operate. Apparently one of their first acts was to join with the Boeotians in narrowing the Euripus so that only a single ship could pass through at a time, and to bridge the narrows. An Athenian expedition under the command of Theramenes sent to interfere failed to accomplish anything.[4] The organization of a confederacy is not reported in

[1] Hesiod's visit to Euboea: *Works and Days* 650 ff. If the author of the *Hymn to Pythian Apollo* was Boeotian, it is particularly significant that the god on his progress from Mt. Olympus to Crisa (216–86) visited the Lelantine Plain, for this certainly was not on the direct route from Olympus to Delphi.

[2] Seltman, 57 and Pl. v. 8 and 9, Seltman believes that there was a 'definite alliance'.

[3] Thuc. viii. 5. 1–2, 60. 1–2. The earlier appeal is characterized as an appeal by Euboeans, but the Eretrians were clearly the prime actors in 411.

[4] Thuc. viii. 91. 2, 95; Diod. xiii. 47. 3–6. Only Diodorus mentions the expedition of Theramenes, but this may have come so late that the failure of Thucydides to mention it is of

the literary sources, unless it be implied in the statement of Thucydides that the Spartans set everything in order. Its formation has been deduced from indirect evidence, particularly that of the coins. This, in turn, makes it impossible to date the formation exactly. There is extant a decree of the city of Eretria granting citizenship and special privileges to a Tarentine, undoubtedly the commander of the Tarentine ships in the fleet that liberated Eretria.[1] This is easily taken to be a decree passed before the Confederacy was formed, but this is by no means certain. The Euboean cities seem always to have retained considerable freedom of action even if they were united in some way, and Eretria was near the site of the decisive battle, its citizens had actually taken part in the action connected with it, and the city became something like the capital where the federal coins apparently were minted.[2]

The term confederacy has been applied to the Euboean organization, and there is evidence for the existence of a federal state, but this evidence dates from Hellenistic times. The inscription of the early third century cited above as evidence that the organization consisted of four large city-states, also indicates that there was a federal assembly of sorts and federal legislation,[3] but this is from the period when Euboea was under the control of Demetrius Poliorcetes so that the Confederacy was scarcely independent. Practically nothing further is known about the government machinery except that the head of the Confederacy was entitled *hegemon* and that there also was a federal treasurer and a secretary.[4] Even such evidence as this is lacking for the period before the King's Peace.

Turning to the evidence for the existence of a federal state after 411, the evidence is of the most tenuous kind. There were masses of coins issued, apparently at Eretria, with the legend EYB and with the cow or heifer known from earlier times. Obviously these coins claim to be the

no significance. Its historicity seems confirmed by the return to Piraeus of a squadron under the command of Theramenes reported by Xen. *Hell.* i. 1. 12; so E. Meyer, *GdA* iv. 608.

[1] Tod, 82. The presence not only of Tarentine but also of other Italiote and Sicilian ships in the fleet indicates that Sparta's role as champion of Greek freedom against Athens was taken seriously.

[2] The monuments at Olympia to the commanders of contingents in the fleet at Aegospotami commemorated two Euboeans, one from Carystus and one from Eretria (Paus. x. 9. 10). Part of the inscription on the pedestal of the Eretrain has been preserved (Tod, 94 g). Wallace (p. 6) is inclined to think that Carystus stood aloof from the Confederacy and that the Eretrian commanded the federal forces. It is also possible that the two were joint commanders of a federal force.

[3] *IG* xii. 9. 207; cf. Wallace, 27 f. A vote by a federal assembly is implied also in *IG* xii. 9. 898 recording a grant of federal proxeny.

[4] On p. 211 in the index of *IG* xii. 9 there are listed a number of 'Chalcidensium vel foederis ἡγεμόνες'. These clearly are eponymous magistrates. Except for 898 and possibly one other document, the decrees are those of the city of Chalcis, but the city may well have dated documents by the head of the Confederacy.

currency of Euboea, but similar coins were continued so long, even when other cities were issuing their own silver, that it looks as if the coins at times were issued as the currency of Eretria and as if at the time the existence of a confederacy was pure fiction. However, there were two important issues towards the end of the fifth century, both on the Aeginetan standard. When this is coupled with the statement of Thucydides already noted about the Spartans setting everything in order, it suggests the establishment of a union of some sort which even in its currency was anti-Athenian. Sparta, with two confederacies as allies, the Boeotian and the Achaean, would not be averse to a third. Also the action in narrowing the Euripus in conjunction with the Boeotians, looks like the action of a united Euboea, or at least of co-operation between Eretria and Chalcis and possibly Carystus. Histiaea was still in Athenian hands. Certainly the operations along the Euripus presupposes that Chalcis was a party to the deal. Nothing more can be said about the form of government, but a state or states allied with the Boeotians and Spartans is likely to have been oligarchic.[1]

In the evidence cited above there is really nothing which proves the existence of a federal government for Euboea in the fifth century. The fact that a city issued coins and stamped them as Euboean does not prove that they were the coins of a Euboean federal state. There would seem to be proof enough of this in the fact that in the fourth century a groups of cities including Rhodes, Byzantium, Samos, Ephesus, and others, issued coins with like obverses stamped ΣYN thereby indicating the existence of a symmachy not known from the literary sources. This usually is thought to have been formed immediately after Conon's victory over the Spartans at Cnidos in 394.[2] If, as some have argued, the coins merely indicate the existence of a commercial alliance,[3] the proof that an organization other than a federal state can issue what looks like federal coins, is equally clear. In the case of the cities referred to, their coins could serve as models for federal issues with the federal design on the obverse and that of a city on the reverse. As for the operations on the Euripus, all that they would require would be an alliance between Eretria and Chalcis and the Boeotians.

The new Euboean organization, whatever its form, at first was an ally of Sparta and Boeotia, whether or not formal treaties had been

---

[1] On the history and coinage of this period see Wallace, 1–7, 68 ff.; for Euboean coins issued even when no 'league' existed, p. 4. Tod in his commentary on his no. 82 considers the fact that the decree is a decree of the *boule* an indication that Eretria at the time was under an oligarchy.

[2] For the coins see Seltman, *Greek Coins*, Pl. xxxii, 4–12; *CAH*, Plates ii, 4 k–p; cf. Beloch, *GrG*² iii. i. 95 and n. 3; Cary, *CAH* vi. 49 f.; for references to further literature, Bengtson, *GrG*² 259, n. 1.

[3] S. Accame, *Il dominio romano in Grecia* (1946), 119.

negotiated. In the Corinthian War the Euboeans followed their Boeotian allies into the anti-Spartan camp. In connexion with this the Confederacy, if not formally dissolved, ceased to function, and the cities went their own way in interstate politics and negotiated their own treaties. Already in 394–393 Eretria contracted a treaty of alliance with Athens. To this period may belong also the mysterious treaty between Eretria and Histiaea.[1] When the Second Athenian League was formed, the Chalcidians, Eretrians, and Carystians joined the League very soon after its formation, each city by means of its own individual treaty of alliance. Eretria too, in spite of the earlier treaty, must have followed the same procedure, for, in the case of cities already allied with Athens, new treaties were negotiated making them allies also of the allies of Athens, that is, admitting them to membership in the League. The treaty admitting Chalcis into the League, has been preserved.[2] The admission of Chalcis, Eretria, and Carystus at about the same time—the admission of Histiaea came later—does suggest concerted action. Were the three cities joined in a loose alliance, or did they merely co-operate when occasion demanded it? The EYB coins might as well refer to a Euboean alliance as to a federal state. On the other hand, the simultaneous action may have been due to invitations and pressure from Athens. It was also the individual cities rather than a federal state which co-operated with Thebes after Leuctra and contributed troops to the army of Epaminondas on his first Peloponnesian campaign and again for the Mantinea campaign.[3] When the Euboean cities were brought back into the Second Athenian League in 357 or thereabout, it was again four cities which were admitted.[4] Thus, if any Euboean federal state was organized in 411 or soon thereafter, it was dissolved a few years later when the cities individually joined the Second Athenian League and thereafter continued to operate as

---

[1] Athens and Eretria: *IG* ii². 16 (Tod, 103); Eretria and Histiaea: *IG* xii. 9. 188 (Schwyzer, 805). Wallace, 6, n. 15 thinks that the alliance may have been contracted while the Confederacy was in existence. This is very unlikely. The expression ἡ Εὔβοια ἅπασα (Diod. xiv. 82. 3; cf. Xen. *Hell.* iv. 2. 17), used in connexion with the military operations, is not too clear but implies participation by all states of Euboea rather than by a single federal state.

[2] For the membership of these cities see lines 80, 81, and 83 of the Aristoteles decree (Tod, 123; references to later literature and emendations, not, however, affecting the present problems, *SEG* xvi. 44). Treaty with Chalcis; Tod, 124. On the membership of these cities cf. S. Accame, *La lega ateniese* (1941), 70–74. The position of Histiaea in the list of allies (line 114) shows that this city joined at a later date. The treaty with Methymna (Tod, 122) is the one extant example of a treaty by which an old ally joined the League. Also the later treaty of 357 with Carystus (Tod, 153), which mentions the *synedros* of Carystus and refers to embassies sent to Eretria, Chalcis, and Histiaea, indicates that the cities individually were members of the League.

[3] For the first campaign Εὐβοεῖς ἀπὸ πασῶν τῶν πόλεων (Xen. *Hell.* vi. 5. 23) is perfectly clear; for 362 *Hell.* vii. 5. 4 is less clear but certainly contains nothing which indicates a federal state.

[4] Tod, 153; cf. n. 2 above.

separate units. The federal state of which a brief sketch was given above, originated later, at the earliest, it seems, about 341.[1]

The sketches of federal states given in this chapter do not claim to be exhaustive, but it is to be hoped that no state which would throw further light on federal institutions has been omitted. On some of those included, the information is very scanty, but they have been included for special reasons. Thus the Italiote Confederacy was included in part because its very existence indicates how extensive the federal movement was. Euboea was included chiefly on account of the coins. This is a subject on which future studies by specialists may have much to contribute. Nevertheless, it seems that evidence from other sources is sufficient to prove definitely that coins alone are not enough to establish the existence of a federal state. Of other confederacies, the Bottiaean is of some importance for demonstrating the intensity of the federal movement in the Thraceward regions, but what little can be said about it has been included in the account of the Chalcidic Confederacy.

---

[1] To the period after this must belong *IG* ii². 149 recording a treaty of alliance between Athens and the Euboeans.

CHAPTER III

FEDERAL STATES AND INTERSTATE RIVALRIES

I. TO THE EXPULSION OF THE PERSIANS FROM GREECE

WHAT follows is not an inclusive narrative of the events of the period but merely an effort to bring out aspects and points commonly overlooked in histories of Greece. Federal and tribal states in general receive little attention, the chief exceptions being the Boeotian and Chalcidic confederacies, but even these two states do not receive the attention they deserve. The Boeotians contributed more to the development of Greek political institutions and to the defeat of Athens in the Peloponnesian War than most accounts indicate. Even more flagrant is the failure to indicate adequately the disgraceful way in which the Chalcidic Confederacy was treated, especially by Athens. For the earlier period, now to be considered, the state to suffer most from inadequate treatment is probably the Thessalian Confederacy. In passing it may be well to notice that no normal city-state ever exercised real leadership in Greece or the Aegean. Probably the city which came nearest to do doing so was Rhodes in the Hellenistic Age. That Athens and Sparta were not normal city-states —if there ever was such a thing as a normal city-state—does not need to be demonstrated. Moreover, they exerted their leadership by means of alliances with or domination over others.

The federal or tribal state which played the most important role in northern and central Greece was the Thessalian Confederacy, which, at least at one point challenged Sparta and probably was as strong a power as Sparta herself. To those who look upon early Thessaly as backward, this claim may seem absurd. But was Thessaly so backward? Certainly no history of Thessalian literature or art can be written, but it is well to remember that contributions to the Greek renaissance came from many parts of the Greek world from Asia Minor to Sicily, and, even after much of the Greek intellectual activity became concentrated at Athens, it is a mistake to think that in other places all activities of the kind suddenly ceased. As for Thessaly, it is well known that it took an active part in the development of the Amphictionic League and in the movements connected with it. To go back farther and touch on a problem frequently discussed, do not the prominence of Achilles in the *Iliad* and the Aeolic stratum in its language suggest that Thessaly had a prominent share in the development of the epic tradition?[1] And does not this get additional support from the horses and chariots which suggest the background of a land of horses? Moreover, the fact that the home of the gods was placed on Mount Olympus suggests more than an influence on the epic tradition. It shows that Thessaly had an important share in the shaping of Greek mythology and religion.[2] Near Olympus was also the old home of the muses, whose worship, at least according to one version, was brought from there to Boeotia. To turn to later times, Simonides had ties with Thessaly, and among the earliest patrons of Pindar were the Aleuadae of Thessaly, who are glorified in the Tenth Pythian ode. Then, to turn to the early sphere of Thessalian political influence, it embraced Locris, Phocis, and Boeotia, and so included not only Delphi but also the home of Hesiod, the earliest known Greek teacher of social justice.[3] Likewise, 'primitive' Locris is seen to have had advanced institutions and ideas of law in the fifth century.

The early prominence and peculiar history of Thessaly were due to special factors. A strong united state was developed at an early date. Possibly even more important, Thessaly seems to have developed genuine cavalry tactics earlier than any other Greek state, while on the economic side it had the advantage of being one of the few sections of Greece to produce enough grain for its own use and even for export. This undoubtedly helps explain the failure of Thessaly to take part in that movement of colonization which began in the eighth century.

As for the strong state, it has been argued above in the account of the Thessalian Confederacy that the invading Thessalians had created a large state headed by a king locally called *tagos*, that this state probably had started to weaken by the time it was given new life when the armed forces were reorganized on the basis of the four tetrads and the subdivisions known as *kleroi*. Thus Thessaly had been and remained an aristocratic state with a feudal nobility. The stronger families controlled large estates and great numbers of *penestai*, who usually are equated with the Spartan helots. However, in opposition to the helots, these *penestai* were the dependants of specific masters and were not the

---

[1] Cf. Denys L. Page, *History and the Homeric Iliad* (1959), 254.

[2] M. P. Nilsson, *Geschichte der griechischen Religion*, i. 330 (cf. *Homer and Mycenae*, 266–8) states that 'Olympos' apparently is a pre-Greek word for a mountain which later became a proper noun. Zeus was a mountain god, and the particular mountain would vary from place to place. The name was retained for Mt. Olympus in Thessaly for the reason that it was the highest in Greece. So it was, but in a country with so many fine mountains, does not the prominence of Olympus suggest a strong Thessalian influence?

[3] Ascra at the foot of Mt. Helicon, the home of Hesiod, must have lain within what later became the territory of Thespiae. The quadrennial festival of the muses and the contests in music celebrated at Thespiae and known from Hellenistic times may not be primitive but may be due to a combination of love of festivals and antiquarianism. See especially M. Feyel, *Polybe et Béotie*, 256–61.

property of the state. Moreover, according to what little information we have, they actually were used in the famous Thessalian cavalry, some nobles, like the Menon of Pharsalus, who sent help to the Athenians for the Eïon campaign, being able to muster regular little private armies.

The importance of the development of cavalry in northern Greece and especially in Thessaly has been obscured to some extent by the presence in other states of *hippeis* or horsemen, frequently translated 'knights'. It is generally recognized that these states went through a period of aristocratic rule, and that some of the members of the class in control were known as *hippeis* and continued, for instance at Athens, as a class with a property qualification higher than that of those who served as hoplites. From this it is easy to get the impression that all the young men of this class served their city as cavalry men and that where there were *hippeis* there was cavalry. Yet this was not always the case. The 300 elite troops of Sparta known as *hippeis* did not serve on horseback.[1]

To go back as far as possible, the *hippeis* of the *Iliad* were men that rode in or drove chariots, and, as every reader of the epic knows, the great champions rode to battle in chariots but usually descended from them and fought on foot. It has recently been argued that chariots continued to be used in this manner at the time when the epic was composed.[2] This theory gains support from the continuity of the development of institutions. The time was soon to come when chariots were used in most Greek communities only in ceremonies and chariot races. The charioteers, however, had been an aristocratic group, and an aristocratic group their successors remained and, even after they had given up their chariots, they continued to be called *hippeis*. After giving up their chariots they took to horseback but at first not as real cavalry men but rather as mounted hoplites who used their horses as means of transportation to the field of action. In other words, they formed a mounted infantry.[3] Undoubtedly the fighting was still at first

---

[1] Busolt, *Staatskunde*, 704 and 706; H. Michell, *Sparta* (1952), 249. It is true that Dion Hal. *Ant. rom.* ii. 13. 4 speaks of them as serving both on horseback and on foot, but this is only an incidental remark in a comparison with Roman institutions. All other evidence points the other way. To mention only some, Strabo x. 482 states definitely that they did not have horses. Probably indirect evidence is more valuable. The 'so-called' *hippeis* grouped around the king at the battle of Mantinea in 418 (Thuc. v. 72. 4) certainly were not mounted. It was an innovation when the Spartans in 424 equipped 400 horsemen (Thuc. iv. 55. 2). Before this there had been *hippeis* but no cavalry. Though the noun used is the same, it is clear that the new cavalry was distinct from the old *élite* corps which still served on foot at Mantinea.

[2] On the entire question see the concise and illuminating article by J. K. Anderson, 'Homeric, British and Cyrenaic Chariots', *AJA* lxix (1965), 349–52.

[3] E. Meyer, *Kleine Schriften*, ii (1924), 274 ff.; Busolt, *Staatskunde*, 344, 371 and literature cited there.

conducted as in Homeric battles as a series of contests between champions. Later, when heavy armour became more common, the *hippeis* either gave up their horses or were transformed into genuine cavalry. The Spartan *hippeis* mentioned above are an example of the former process. Still stranger, as far as the terminology goes, are the three hundred select hoplites called 'charioteers and companions', to use Grote's translation, who fought in the front ranks of the Boeotian line of battle.[1] Here the preservation of the names almost makes it possible to sketch the process of development. First the two actually served in a chariot, next they became champion and groom or companion, and finally both became hoplites but remained associated.

How early did Greek states develop cavalry? The example of the Spartan *hippeis* is enough to show that not all aristocratic *hippeis* served as cavalry. Even for Boeotia, where cavalry was adopted relatively early, the curious names applied to the select hoplites indicates that there was a period after chariots had been given up during which there was no cavalry. Thus the Solonian *hippeis* were not cavalry men. Mounted infantry they may have been or had been earlier, but not cavalry. When the Peisistratids used cavalry they relied on their Thessalian allies, and other evidence suggests that the Athenians did not have cavalry of their own before the fifth century. At the time of the expedition of Xerxes, aside from the Thessalians, the only Greeks to possess cavalry seem to have been the Boeotians.[2] At the beginning of the Peloponnesian War Thucydides lists the Boeotians, Phocians, and Locrians as those allies of Sparta that supplied cavalry.[3] Thus at the outbreak of the Peloponnesian War, there was no cavalry south of the Isthmus. From these bits of evidence, it is possible to reconstruct the approximate order of the adoption of cavalry by Greek states. First came the Thessalians, and next those with close contacts with the Thessalians. Of these the Boeotians developed cavalry before 480; the Locrians, Phocians,[4] and Athenians, before the Peloponnesian War, the Spartans during the war.

[1] Diod. xii. 70. 1 (line of battle at Delium 424 B.C.); Grote, *History*, vi (1849), 527. Since the Sacred Band too numbered 300 and was made up of pairs who, before Pelopidas took it in hand, were distributed throughout the front ranks of the entire phalanx (Plut. *Pel.* 18–19; Athenaeus xiii. 561 F; Polyaen, ii. 5. 1), it is likely that it was a revival or transformation of the older institution. Grote takes the 300 select hoplites to be the Sacred Band; Meyer, *GdA* v. 389 implies a connexion.

[2] Herod. ix. 68–69.

[3] Thuc. ii. 9. 3 and iv. 44. 1, where he indicates that the Corinthians had no cavalry in 425. On Sparta, cf. p. 106, n. 1 above.

[4] Possibly also the Locrians and Phocians had begun to use cavalry before the Persian War. The absence of evidence may be due to the fact that this cavalry played no important part in the campaigns of 480 and 479.

The exact time of the origin of the Thessalian cavalry naturally is not known. Systematically organized and drilled cavalry can hardly have gone farther back than to the seventh century and is probably to be connected with the reforms of Aleuas the Red discussed above in the sketch of the Thessalian Confederacy. The conquerors who entered Thessaly from southern Epirus about the time of the Doric migration cannot have been mounted warriors; the horses and horsemanship were acquired from the earlier inhabitants. The new lords of the land may soon have learned to use horses, but like others probably at first used them only for transportation. Later they probably began to lead bands of their own followers in raids on horseback, and there may have been mounted men in the feudal armies of earlier rulers, but the first systematic organization of cavalry for the entire state is likely to have been the one associated with Aleuas. The fact that hoplites were included in his system is not against this conjecture. What made the mounted infantry out of date was the increase in the number of heavy armed infantrymen and the development of the close formation of hoplites. When this change came, Sparta and Thessaly developed in opposite directions. Sparta perfected the hoplite technique and completely neglected cavalry; the Thessalians, though they retained hoplites, emphasized and developed cavalry. It is noticeable that the system of Aleuas the Red provided for only twice as many hoplites as cavalry men and that throughout our period the Thessalians always emphasized their cavalry. As a result, Sparta became the great power of southern Greece; Thessaly, of northern Greece. Had the two stood together in 480, the Greeks would have been in a much better position to meet the Persians on land. As it was, they had to fight on land in 479 with the much needed cavalry of Thessaly and Boeotia actually aligned with the invaders.

Neither the conquest by Thessalians of territory outside Thessaly nor the collapse of this empire can be traced satisfactorily. All that it is safe to say about the conquest is that by early in the sixth century Thessaly had acquired considerable influence in the Amphictionic League and at Delphi, had subjected Eastern Locris and Phocis, and had further extended her influence through Boeotia in such a way as to enable her cavalry to proceed unimpeded through Boeotia to the Euripus, when it crossed into Euboea and supported Chalcis in her final victory in the Lelantine War.[1] The only date fixed fairly securely

---

[1] The subjection of Eastern Locris is to be deduced from the facts that Phocis was completely subdued and that the line of advance from Thessaly to Phocis passed through almost the entire length of Eastern Locris from Thermopylae to the pass of Hyampolis; cf. p. 110, n. 1 below. Our only authority for the statement that Thessalian cavalry under Cleomachus of Pharsalus contributed to the victory of Chalcis is Plut. *Mor.* 760 E–761 A, but the account is plausible and is generally accepted. Plutarch states that the tomb of Cleomachus was still

is the end of the First Sacred War about 590. If the date of the end of the Lelantine War was known, it would be possible to reconstruct at least the order of the chief steps in the extension of the power of Thessaly, but unfortunately this date is a matter of dispute, the proposed dates varying considerably.[1] If we were sure that the Sacred War marked the first step in the advance of the Thessalians beyond Thermopylae—or rather the valley of the Spercheus—we should have to place the conquest of Phocis and the end of the Lelantine War farther down in the sixth century.[2] To anyone believing that the first advance was towards Delphi, this conclusion is inevitable. Though Greeks allowed the passage of troops of other states through their territory more freely than modern states would, one cannot believe that Thessalian cavalry could roam that far at a time when the influence of their state did not extend beyond Thermopylae. However, there is reason to believe that the order of events may have been the reverse, and that the advance on Phocis came before the First Sacred War.

The belief that the participation of the Thessalians in the First Sacred War came before their conquest of Phocis, apparently was based on the feeling that the natural line of advance for an army when it came from the north to the head of the Malian Gulf was south towards Doris, Amphissa, and Delphi instead of east through the difficult pass of Thermopylae. Hence the Thessalians must have established themselves in central Greece before they advanced down the Cephissus valley into Phocis. This seems logical enough if one only looks superficially at the map. Moreover, we have been misled by Herodotus who lets us believe that the Persians fought for days to clear Thermopylae and then turned back and took the other route. Even Beloch, who takes for granted that the advance of the Thessalian cavalry to aid Chalcis must have come after the First Sacred War, seems to have fallen into this error. A check of the evidence, on the other hand, shows that the reports of clashes between the Thessalians and

to be seen in his time in the agora of Chalcis. He states further that Aristotle had criticized a detail, thus indicating that the story was known to Aristotle.

[1] For some recent discussions see D. W. Bradeen, 'The Lelantine War and Pheidon of Argos', *TAPA* lxxviii (1947), 223–41; E. Will, *Korinthiaka* (1955), 391–404; W. G. Forrest, 'Colonisation and the Rise of Delphi', *Historia*, vi (1957), 160–75 at 161 ff. Bradeen places the Lelantine War *c.* 675–670; Forrest in the eighth century; Will, the end of the war in the sixth century. The argumentation of the three seem to agree only in placing emphasis on a particular one of several obscure and conflicting pieces of evidence. It will be suggested below that the Thessalian conquest of Phocis probably preceded the First Sacred War. This does little to fix the date of the Lelantine War, since the Thessalian expedition to Chalcis may have come soon, or not so soon, after the Thessalians had conquered Phocis and extended their influence into Boeotia.

[2] Beloch, *GrG*². i. i. 338 f. suggests about 570; Will (cf. n. 1) arrives at about the same date by a different line of reasoning.

the Phocians indicate that the Thessalians in their attacks on Phocis did not advance down the Cephisuss valley but came through the pass of Hyampolis. This means that they had advanced through Thermopylae and almost the entire length of Eastern Locris before entering Phocis by what may be called, somewhat crudely, the north-eastern corner of Phocis. Information about later movements of troops shows that as late as the Roman conquest of Greece this route was regarded as the only one feasible for the advance of an army from northern to central Greece.[1] Thus it would be natural for the Thessalians, when they advanced into central Greece, to take the normal route through Eastern Locris toward Phocis and Boeotia. Except for the relatively small tribe of Eastern Locrians, the first enemy they would encounter would be the Phocians. It would be natural for the latter to try to stop the invaders at Thermopylae. As evidence that this is what they did, there is the Phocian Wall.[2] When this had been turned, the next place to stop the invader was the pass of Hyampolis, the normal route from Eastern Locris to Phocis. That this was what the Phocians actually did is shown by the reports of three victories over the Thessalians. Of these, two were won in the pass, and the third too is also connected with the pass by one of the sources, obviously because the invaders came by this route and the opposing armies first faced each other there. Of the three battles, two are connected with a revolt of the Phocians against the Thessalians and the futile efforts of the latter to reconquer the district, thus apparently with the Phocian war of independence and the final expulsion of the Thessalians from Phocis. The third seems to be connected with the early advance of the Thessalians into Phocis.[3]

With the ground thus laid, it is possible to reconstruct very tentatively the story of the expansion of the Thessalians beyond Thermopylae. In the seventh century, or possibly even in the late eighth century, they began their attack. Apparently they met with sufficient difficulties so that the Phocians were able to build a defensive wall at Thermopylae. Herodotus relates further that they diverted the waters from the springs in such a manner as to cut up the terrain with gullies—

[1] For a discussion of the evidence, see 'A New Interpretation of the Thessalian Confederacy', *CP* lv (1960), 229–48 at 231 ff. To the evidence cited there add Pol. xxvii. 16. 6, where it is told that the Roman commander Aulus Hostilius, on his way to Thessaly in 170, landed at Anticyra. He too was going to take the route used by Flamininus in 198 in his advance to the Gulf of Corinth, but was to take it in reverse.

[2] Herod. vii. 176. 4 connects the wall with the first advance of the Thessalians into Thessaly. It is more likely that it is to be connected with the later advance against Phocis. The remains of the wall now standing suggest a defence against an advance from the opposite direction, but probably an original Phocian wall had been remade later. See W. K. Pritchett, *AJA* lxii (1958), 211–13.

[3] The evidence for the three battles and the battle of Ceressus is discussed *CP* lv. 231 f. and 235–7.

obviously an effective defence against cavalry. The works must have proved sufficient for some time, for it is reported by another source that Phocis for a time had a seaport in this neighbourhood, namely, Daphnus.[1] Nevertheless, the position was ultimately turned, according to Herodotus, by means of the very same path later used by the Persians.[2] This, of course, was not the work of men on horseback, but probably of light-armed troops furnished by the perioeci of the Thessalians, but it opened the way for the cavalry, which proceeded to advance through the pass of Hyampolis. Here, according to stories later told, they suffered a famous reverse when the Phocians prepared the ground by burying empty amphoras and thus broke or injured the legs of the horses. This can at most have meant a temporary setback, for the Thessalians were able to reduce Phocis so completely that they controlled the country through Thessalian officials and 'tyrants' and the taking of hostages.[3] The tyrants, in all likelihood, were Phocians who served as agents for the Thessalians. The one Phocian city to remain independent at first was Crisa with Delphi. Crisa, it is well to remember, was isolated and difficult to approach, particularly for an enemy relying largely on cavalry. It was captured and destroyed in the First Sacred War and Delphi placed under the protection of the Amphictionic League. This, needless to say, was largely controlled by Thessaly.

Thessaly was now the greatest power in northern Greece and probably in all Greece. This tends to be overlooked, probably in part because Thessaly was so different from other Greek states. To begin with, it was larger,[4] and instead of importing grain it actually produced more than was needed at home and early began exporting it. Thus the foreign trade was different from that of other Greek states. Moreover, the Thessalians did not send out colonists but instead reduced their neighbours. To some extent Sparta did the same, but at least at first the Thessalian system was more complicated than that of Sparta. Beyond Laconia and Messenia, Sparta had only allies and ultimately the Peloponnesian League, while Thessaly, beyond the perioecic territory had both subjects and allies. The exact status, for instance, of the Malians is not known, but Phocis was subjected. Beyond Phocis Chalcis and Athens under the Peisistratids were allies. The status of Boeotia remains uncertain, but Boeotia, in any case, did not really play

---

[1] Herod. vii. 176. 4. On Daphnus cf. above, p. 41; Strabo ix. 416, 424 f., 426 mentions the port in three passages.

[2] Herod. vii. 176. 4, 215.

[3] Herod. viii. 28; Paus. x. 1. 3; Polyaen. vi. 18. 2; Plut. *Mor.* 244 B.

[4] Beloch, *GrG*[2] iii. i. 285 and 293 estimates the area of Laconia at 5,820 square kilometres; that of Messenia, 2,600; that of Thessaly, 15,000, of which about half was included in the four tetrads, the rest being perioecic territory.

a major part in the interstate politics of this period before her revolt against Athenian control in 447. It is possible that most of Boeotia was reduced to subjection—the defeat at Ceressus suggests that the subjection was not completed—but the activities of the period rather suggest friendship or alliance of a sort. At the latest early in the sixth century the Thessalian cavalry crossed Boeotia on its way to aid the Chalcidians in the Lelantine War and again, late in the century, to go to the aid of Hippias against the Spartans. Since in ancient Greece troops crossed neutral territory rather freely, this may mean mere acquiescence, or friendship, or alliance. Since there were allies beyond Boeotia, some sort of understanding or alliance is likely. The alliance with Athens apparently goes back to the days of Peisistratus himself, since he named one of his sons Thessalus.[1] If so, the alliance or entente goes back quite a number of years before the attempt of Thebes in 519 to force Plataea into the Boeotian Confederacy, the attempt which led to the alliance of Plataea with Athens. It has been suggested that it was fear of Thessaly which kept Cleomenes and Sparta from assuming the protection of Plataea.[2] Athens, on the other hand, may have been able to do so precisely on account of her alliance with Thessaly. The strengthening of Athens meant the strengthening of the southermost ally of Thessaly. Thus, if Thebes too was an ally, she was not favoured to the same extent as Athens. The events of 519 had shown that under Hippias Athens was a power to be reckoned with.

All this was changed in a few years, and Thessaly became the only real strong power north of the Isthmus. After the murder of Hipparchus, it seems that Hippias lost his nerve. He became so suspicious of the people of Athens that he disarmed them and thereafter relied only on his mercenaries and the cavalry of his Thessalian allies.[3] Hence the seizure of Leipsydrium by the Alcmaeonidae[4] may not have seemed as desperate at the time as it has been judged in later accounts. The Alcmaeonidae may well have thought that they would be able to handle the mercenaries and to settle the entire affair before the Thessalians could arrive on the scene. As it turned out, it seems that the mercenaries sufficed to thwart them. Not so in 510, when the Spartans intervened. The first expedition was routed by a force of 1,000 cavalry

---

[1] Thuc. vi. 55. 1; Sordi, *La lega tessala*, 55.

[2] Cf. p. 29 f. above.

[3] Thuc. vi. 58 places the disarming of the Athenians on the very day of the assassination of Hipparchus. Arist. *Ath. pol.* 15. 3–4 attributes it to Peisistratus and places it soon after his victory at Pallene. Furthermore, in 18.4, though not mentioning his name, Aristotle is obviously criticizing the account of Thucydides. Nevertheless, the latter is certainly right in attributing the disarming to Hippias. The effectiveness of the Athenians against the Boeotians in 519 is enough to show that they had not yet been disarmed. Moreover, it is clear that the rule of Peisistratus was not a reign of terror over a disarmed citizen body.

[4] Herod. v. 62. 2; Arist. *Ath. pol.* 19.

sent by the Thessalians; the second, under Cleomenes, succeeded in defeating the Thessalian cavalry with the result that Hippias had to stand siege and ultimately withdraw.[1] This is the first dateable setback for the power of the Thessalians after it had been extended beyond Phocis. Athens did not become a Spartan vassal, as Cleomenes no doubt had planned, but it was lost also to Thessaly and began its development as a great republican and ultimately democratic state. Athens had been a power of some importance and with a positive foreign policy under Peisistratus, and it is impossible to say whether the original rapprochement was due to him or to Thessalian leaders, but during the last years under Hippias, Athens can have been little better than a vassal of Thessaly. With the expulsion of Hippias and the rearmament of her citizens, the city became once more a live and energetic power.

For Thessaly the setback at Athens was a serious check, but it was not calamitous. Thessaly remained a considerable power for another twenty years and about 490 was still strong enough to give asylum to her former enemy, Cleomenes of Sparta.[2] The collapse seems to have come soon after this. In the meantime, with the foothold at Athens gone, it is likely that the Thessalian government cultivated closer relations with Boeotia and especially Thebes as the most advanced post of Thessalian influence. Co-operation between the two aggressive and selfish powers would be natural enough. So it seems that the Thessalians joined the Thebans in an attack on Thespiae, a city that commonly tended to oppose Thebes. The Thespians took refuge at the stronghold of Ceressus on their own territory. Somehow the outcome was a disastrous defeat for the Thessalians. This touched off the great revolt in Phocis. The Phocians succeeded in putting to death on a single day all Thessalian officials in their country and all 'tyrants', apparently Phocians who were supported by the Thessalians. Thus Phocis was cleared of all officials and agents of the Thessalians, and the latter had to give up the country or reconquer it. They are reported to have begun by massacring the hostages they held and resolving to put to death all Phocian men and to enslave the women and children. As at the time of the earlier conquest, they advanced through the pass of Hyampolis, where they succeeded in destroying an advance guard of some 300 Phocians. In the battle that followed, the Phocians won a complete victory, but it was not decisive enough to drive the Thessalians out for good. They soon returned and this time were able to force the pass and overrun most of Phocis, while the Phocians took refuge on Mount Parnassus. The turning point came when the Phocians had a group of

---

[1] Herod. v. 63–65; Arist. *Ath. pol.* 19. 5–6.   [2] Herod. vi. 74. 1.

8

men estimated at 600 or 500 whiten their bodies and armour and attack by moonlight. In the confusion that followed the Thessalians were defeated with a loss, it is said, of 4,000 dead.[1]

This, as has been said, is a reconstruction involving a series of events for which exact dates have not been given in our sources. The accounts, furthermore, clearly contain anecdotal material but should not be completely rejected for that reason. Much comes from Plutarch, who lived in nearby Chaeronea and seems to have had access to local sources. It is impossible to go into the details of the reconstruction in the present account. It may be noted that dating Ceressus as late as is done here is unusual, but the battle is said to have resulted in the freedom of the Greeks. Thus it is natural to believe that it came just before the revolt of Phocis, and there are many reasons for dating the revolt of Phocis rather late. Of course, much remains doubtful. A loss of 4,000 Thessalians in the final victory of the Phocians seems excessive, but fighting with heavy losses shortly before the expedition of Xerxes would go far to explain the violent mutual hatred at that time of the Thessalians and the Phocians. Possibly the suggestion that Thebes joined the Thessalians in the attack on Thespiae before the battle of Ceressus will be considered the wildest guess in the entire reconstruction, but that too seems natural in virtue of the normal antagonism of these two cities. At any rate, before the attack. Thebes must have been subject to or allied with the Thessalians.

Turning now to the situation in 480, it may be well to recall that Thessaly had been one of the strongest powers in Greece a century before the Persian Wars and had still been strong in 510, when the Thessalian cavalry supported Hippias against the Spartans. By 480 the holdings beyond Thermopylae had been lost, but Thessaly was nevertheless by no means a negligible power. The Thessalian cavalry was still the strongest in Greece, in fact, except for the lesser body of Boeotian cavalry, the only Greek cavalry worth consideration. Thus, when the Persians approached, there were not only two but three kinds of armed forces to be taken into consideration by the Greeks in planning their strategy: hoplites, in which Sparta excelled; the fleet, to which Athens furnished the largest contingents; and the cavalry, in which the Thessalians excelled. The plan first adopted clearly was to meet the Persian army in Thessaly and thus have the advantage of the aid of the Thessalian cavalry and of campaigning in a region where it was relatively easy to provision an army. This plan was later abandoned in favour of one which aimed at winning the decisive victory at sea. Since this plan, in spite of the glorious victory at Salamis, failed to accomp-

[1] Herod. viii. 27; Paus. x. 1. 11.

lish its purpose of forcing the withdrawal of the Persians from Greece, the decisive battle after all had to be fought on land. The result was that the Greeks not only had to fight the Plateaean campaign without the aid of the Thessalian and Boeotian cavalry but even had to face this cavalry when it was ranged on the side of the enemy. At least the Boeotian cavalry was very active at Plataea.

Since all accounts in our sources are written from the point of view of Athens and Sparta, the Thessalian proposals for the conduct of the war have not been given adequate attention. Moreover, it is easy to conclude that the Thessalians never meant to oppose the Persians. This, apparently the almost unanimous verdict of modern scholars, is based on the fact that the *tagos* and the Aleuad family to which he belonged Medized in advance, and that the entire state did so after it had been abandoned by the other Greeks. As for the first of these two points, this was not the only time that there was disagreement within Thessaly. Herodotus indicates that the Aleuadae had communicated with Xerxes before he entered Greece and that Xerxes made the mistake of thinking that they spoke for all Thessaly.[1] Naturally, Herodotus cannot have known how much information reached Xerxes, nor what were his thoughts on the subject. What emerges from his statement is that the pro-Persian attitude of the Aleuadae was not shared by all Thessalians. Certainly, in a time of political ferment it would be natural enough for the king to look to the great king of Persia for support, and for his opponents to turn for aid to the free states of Greece.

It is difficult to reconstruct just what happened, but it looks as if the anti-Aleuad and anti-Persian majority in Thessaly thought that the Persians could be defeated by a combination of infantry from the rest of Greece and cavalry and other troops from Thessaly. Their presentation of the case must have made a strong impression on the congress of the Greeks assembled at the Isthmus, and this seems the most plausible explanation of the mysterious Thessalian expedition of 480. If a force of 10,000 hoplites was sent by sea and was to be joined by other infantry coming from nearby states and by the Thessalian cavalry 2,000 strong or better, this was no petty or hurried undertaking.[2] At any rate it was not a scouting expedition but probably a force fully as well or even

---

[1] Herod. vii. 6. 2, 130. 3.

[2] Our two source accounts, Herod. vii. 172–4 and Diod. xi. 2. 5–6, leave much to be desired. Only Diodorus tells that other troops besides those that came by sea were to be summoned, but it stands to reason that this should have been done. We are not told where the troops embarked, but they sailed through the Euripus. This means that they came from Attica or beyond. Troops from Boeotia, Phocis, and Locris, in addition to those of Thessaly, must have come by land. In spite of uncertainty whenever statistics are involved, and particularly such round numbers as 10,000, the impression remains that the force sent was large for Greece. This tends to be obscured by the impossibly high numbers attributed to the Persians.

better equipped to face the Persians than the army that defeated them the following year at Plataea. It may not have been quite as large, but it had the cavalry which the later army lacked, and this cavalry may well have been fully a match for that of the Persians. The army which actually entered Greece can hardly have numbered more than 50,000 including not over 2,000 cavalry.[1]

Even so, the invading army was undoubtedly the largest Greece had ever seen. Nevertheless, Greece was large enough so that with proper co-operation and organization it would be able to face any army that the Persians or anyone else could bring into the country. They could not overwhelm it with numbers but had to depend on quality and leadership. Nor was the Persian invasion a sudden and unexpected raid. The elaborate preparations of Xerxes gave also the Greeks time to plan and prepare. So why should they fear to face the Persians in Thessaly? And would it not be a great advantage to stop them before they penetrated farther? After all, the Athenians had defeated the Persians at Marathon without the aid of cavalry, while in Thessaly the Greeks would not lack cavalry.

The considerations presented suggest that the allied army did not withdraw from Thessaly because the Persians might arrive by some other route than that of the pass of Tempe, or because it was hopeless to

---

[1] Concerning the Persian military forces the most plausible reconstruction remains the one which finds in Herodotus indications that the Persians had mobilization plans for six armies, each containing 60,000 men—50,000 infantry and 10,000 cavalry—paper strength, and that three of these were mobilized by Xerxes. For a brief statement see J. A. Munro, *CAH* iv. 271–3. By means of a study of the water supply and conditions along the route taken by the Persians for the first seven days after crossing the Hellespont, F. Maurice, 'The Size of the Army of Xerxes', *JHS* l (1930), 210–33 has shown that the army cannot have been larger than the estimate of Munro, but he has given no positive reconstruction for determining its actual size. Munro's thesis that only three armies were mobilized is based in part on the fact that the later narrative of Herodotus mentions as present in Greece only three commanders of sufficient prominence to have been commanders of armies, namely, Mardonius, Artabazus, and Tigranes, but of these only Mardonius can be shown to have been active in Greece. Artabazus escorted Xerxes to the Hellespont and did *not* fight at Plataea, though Herodotus writes as though he were present in Greece (viii. 126; ix. 66, 70. 5); Tigranes commanded and fell at Mycale (ix. 96. 2, 102. 4). Surely it looks as if, of the three armies mobilized, that of Tigranes remained in Asia Minor, that of Artabazus occupied Thrace and Macedonia, and only that of Mardonius entered Greece. In size, all three probably were well below their theoretical numbers, particularly for the cavalry. For that of Mardonius, there seems to be some positive information. This comes from the story of the selection by Mardonius of the troops to remain with him in Greece. The story, of course, is pure fiction. The fact that Xerxes had to be escorted to the Hellespont is proof enough that he did not withdraw troops from Greece. Note, nevertheless, that Herod. viii. 113. 2 states that he included τὴν ἵππον τὴν χιλίην . . . καὶ τὴν [ἄλλην] ἵππον. Whether the bracketed word is read or not, it is clear that two divisions of cavalry are mentioned. Of these one, apparently the one which ranked highest, numbered 1,000. It is likely that these are the two divisions of 1,000 each mentioned in vii. 40–41. With the 10,000 horsemen of vii. 41.2, we are back in the never-never land of impossibly large armies. How many of the 2,000 cavalrymen dropped out before they reached Greece, it is impossible to say.

try to fight in Thessaly. It was rather because those who favoured placing reliance on the fleet, by hook or by crook, carried the day over those who wished to rely on the Greek hoplites and the Thessalian cavalry. The determining factor was probably that the commanders sent to Thessaly were out of sympathy with the undertaking and so failed to carry out the will of the assembly which had dispatched them. They were an otherwise unknown Spartan, Euaenetus, who probably shared the common Spartan aversion to distant expeditions, and Themistocles, the Athenian, who, above all others, was determined to challenge the Persians on sea rather than on land.[1] Thus the strategy of Themistocles was substituted for the original plan of the council of allies. The new plan, which now in turn must have been adopted by the assembly of the allies, it need hardly be said, called for an effort to win the decisive victory at sea and for a holding battle at Thermopylae to check the advance of the Persian army until the naval victory could be won. It was a highly imaginative plan, and few decisions in history are more impressive than that of the Athenians to abandon their city and to put all their available manpower aboard their ships.[2]

The withdrawal to Thermopylae meant the abandonment of a plan of defence under which the Thessalian, Phocian, and Bocotian confederacies, and especially the Thessalian and Bocotian cavalry, might have played an important part. At any rate, when the decision had been made, there was nothing for the Thessalians to do except to Medize, with what enthusiasm or lack of enthusiasm it is impossible to say. The greatest contribution of Thessaly to the cause of the Persians was that it served as their winter quarters. Not much is heard about the Thessalians in connexion with the actual campaigning. It undoubtedly is true that Thessalians served as guides for the Persians in Phocis, and they may well have induced the Persians to do as much damage there as possible. The Thessalians are also listed as present at Plataea, and that is about all. If the Thessalians in 479 urged Mardonius to invade Greece, as Herodotus states, this means little.[3] Their purpose may have been to get the Persians out of Thessaly or to bring about the decision in Greece as soon as possible. The later unsuccessful punitive expedition led by the Spartan king Leotychidas may not so

---

[1] In the brief reference to the expedition in Plut. *Them.* 7, Themistocles is represented as favouring a naval policy from the outset. The expedition was the result of opposition to his policy. When the army returned without accomplishing anything, the Athenians were more willing to listen to his advice. It looks as if Plutarch has preserved a correct tradition to the effect that Themistocles was opposed to the Thessalian venture from the outset. This is not disproved by the fact that he was chosen one of the commanders; cf. Nicias and the Sicilian expedition.

[2] At present its significance seems in danger of being buried by the controversy over the Themistocles decree—a subject not to be discussed here.

[3] Herod. viii. 32. 2; ix. 1, 31.5.

much be proof of guilt as of the hostility of the Spartans.[1] For the
Locrians, Phocians, and Boeotians, on the other hand, there was no
need to Medize as long as Thermopylae was held. Actually the Eastern
Locrians are reported by Herodotus to have been asked to come to
Thermopylae in full force and still to have sent seven penteconters to
Artemisium.[2] For so small a state this represented a considerable effort.
After Thermopylae they too obviously had no choice and are said to
have joined the Persians and to have taken part in the battle of Plataea.[3] The Phocians, though they have been blamed for failing to stop
the Persian division which turned the position of the Greeks at Thermopylae, did not have too bad a record. According to Herodotus, their
failure to stop the turning force of the Persians was due not to cowardice
but to an honest mistake. They thought the attack was directed against
them and prepared to take a strong position and sell their lives dearly
but, by so doing, gave the Persians a chance to bypass them.[4] Evidently it was a mistake to entrust the defence of this position to men
who were likely to consider it enough if they prevented a raid on their
own state by the back door, as it were, and who were used to fighting
their defensive battles in the pass of Hyampolis. After Thermopylae
the Phocians did not Medize at once but instead sought refuge on
Mount Parnassus and in Western Locris. In 479 they seem to have
avoided taking part in Mardonius' invasion of Attica but later sent
1,000 men, who were present at Plataea. Yet, even after their state had
gone over to the Persians, some of the Phocians held out on Parnassus
and continued to raid the Persians and the Greeks with them.[5] Moreover, the Thessalians, Locrians, and Phocians apparently all were
among the Greeks who were present at Plataea but avoided fighting
against their fellow-Greeks.[6] Of all the Greeks, only the Boeotians, that
is, primarily the Thebans, seem to have fought effectively on the side
of the Persians.

The record of the Boeotians up to Thermopylae is difficult to follow.
Herodotus states that, except for the Thespians and Plataeans, they
rendered allegiance to the Persians before the latter entered Greece,
that at Thermopylae the Thebans stayed behind for the final stand

---

[1] The date of this expedition has been debated extensively Recently Sordi, *La lega tessala*,
101 ff. and article cited there has argued for 469, but a date nearer 479 may be more likely;
cf. *CP* lv (1960), 248, n. 53.

[2] Herod. vii. 203; viii. 1. 2.

[3] Here Herod. viii. 66. 2 and ix. 31. 5 speaks of Locrians in general, but it is likely that
those who served with the Persians were chiefly or exclusively Eastern Locrians.

[4] Herod. vii. 203. 1, 217–18.

[5] Herod. viii. 32; ix. 17, 31. 5.

[6] The verb Herod. ix. 67 applies to them is ἐθελοκακεῖν, which literally should mean 'to
play the coward intentionally'. It probably means that they gave way without fighting;
cf. Herod. i. 271.

only under compulsion, and that as many as were able to do so surrendered. However, some doubt is thrown on this story by the fact that
the Persians branded them after their capture.[1] On the other hand,
after Thermopylae the Thebans and those Boeotians, if any, who
followed their leadership did all they could to help the Persians and
apparently also to use their Persian allies to do all the harm possible
to their own enemies. By contrast the Thespians and Plataeans held
out against the Persians to the end. The Thespians, according to
Herodotus, sent a larger contingent to Thermopylae than the Thebans—700 as compared to 400—voluntarily stayed behind with
Leonidas, and by implication were all killed. Nevertheless, their
fellow-citizens continued to hold out and turned up for the Plataea
campaign to the number of 1,800 light-armed troops, doubtless all the
surviving men fit for military service. The Plataeans in 480 were not
represented at Thermopylae but served in Athenian ships at
Artemisium. The next year they furnished 600 hoplites for the
Plataea campaign. On the monument erected at Delphi both the
Thespians and Plataeans were listed among the victorious Greek
states.[2]

The Thebans and their followers among the Boeotians began to co-
operate with the Persians immediately after Thermopylae. In fact, the
co-operation was so prompt that there may be reason to accept the
report that the Boeotians had given earth and water to the Persians in
advance and that consequently the Thebans had not given whole-
hearted support to the stand at Thermopylae.[3] When the Persians
entered Boeotia the cities there were saved from being ravaged by the
presence of Macedonian garrisons or officers, who had been sent in
advance and indicated to the approaching Persian troops that the
cities were friendly.[4] This arrangement must have taken time and
must have involved an understanding between the Boeotian authorities, the Persian officers, and the Macedonian king. Of course, when
the invading army approached Thespiae and Plataea, the fact that
these cities had been abandoned by their inhabitants and had not been
occupied by Macedonian troops would be enough to show that the two

[1] Herod. vii. 132, 222, 233. It is well to remember that when Herodotus hereafter speaks
of actions by the Boeotians by no means all Boeotians were involved.

[2] Herod. vii. 202, 222; viii. 1, 44; ix. 28. 6, 30; Tod, 19.

[3] This proves nothing concerning the attitude of the members of the contingent sent. They
may have been patriots who volunteered, or opponents of the government sent to be got rid
of. But there is no need to try here to solve this riddle.

[4] This seems to be the meaning of a passage (Herod. viii. 34) which has bothered translators and commentators and so commonly has been ignored by historians, including even
Grote. An exception is Thirlwall, who remarks that 'the cities, except Thespiae and Plataea,
had testified their submissive spirit, by receiving Macedonian garrisons' (Hist. of Greece,
ii. 296).

cities were not friendly and so could be sacked and burned. The report that the Thebans had lodged specific information against them may well be true.[1] The Thebans also joined the Persians in the invasion of Attica in 480 and played an important part in the campaign of the following year. The report that, when Mardonius came south from his winter quarters in Thessaly, the Thebans urged him to make their city his headquarters, may or may not be significant. They undoubtedly took part also in his invasion of Attica and, when he withdrew by a different route, the Boeotarchs secured natives of the district to serve as guides. By the way, the army of Mardonius cannot have been excessively large if it spent a night at Tanagra and then next day proceeded to Scolus. During the later operations a Theban is given credit for advising Mardonius to block the Cithaeron passes by which supplies were being brought to the Greek army, and it is likely that the Boeotian cavalry joined in harrying the Greek infantry. In the final battle the Boeotians fought well and suffered heavy losses, and, when others retreated, the cavalry continued to aid in protecting the retreating troops. The Theban cavalry in particular inflicted heavy losses on the Megarians and Phliasians.[2] It is not surprising that after the battle the allies marched on Thebes and demanded the surrender of the Medizing leaders. When these were given up, Pausanias had them executed without trial but withdrew the army. By this action the allies seem to have accepted, as it were, the claim later attributed by Thucydides to the Thebans, namely, that the guilt was not that of the people but of the narrow oligarchic clique which ruled at the time.[3]

To summarize, the only federal state to give more than the most necessary aid to the Persians was the part of Boeotia which was dominated by Thebes. The abandonment of the plan to meet the Persians in Thessaly meant the abandonment of a strategy which would have assigned an important role to the Thessalians. This, in turn, made it necessary for the latter to Medize. The control of Thessaly, which was used as winter quarters for their army, proved extremely valuable to the Persians, but this was hardly the fault of the Thessalians. In the operations which followed, Thessalians served as guides in Phocis and may have used the Persians to inflict as much damage as possible on their old enemies. Otherwise there is no indication that they were more

---

[1] Herod. viii. 50. 2. Cloché, *Thèbes de Béotie*, 41 and Moretti, *Ricerche*, 124 are disinclined to accept this report, but it would be in character for Thebes to use any means possible to break her Boeotian opponents. If the interpretation of the battle of Ceressus given above is correct, the Thebans had recently tried to use the Thessalians against Thespiae, but had suffered a set-back. Why not now use the Persians?

[2] Herod. viii. 66. 2; ix. 2, 15, 38, 67–69.

[3] Herod. ix. 86–88; Thuc. iii. 62. 3.

active in the campaign than necessary. For the other states discussed, there was no need to Medize before the Persians had been victorious at Thermopylae. The only ones suspected of having Medized earlier are the Boeotians. The Phocians, in spite of their fatal error at Thermopylae, from the point of view of Hellenic patriotism, had a fairly good record. They held out for some time after Thermopylae and, even after the state officially had gone over to the Persians, some of them refused to yield and took to the mountains, while the division of troops sent to join the Persians avoided taking part in the invasion of Attica and, like many others, seem to have fallen back at Plataea without fighting. Even a better record was that of the Plataeans and Thespians, who remained loyal to the Greek cause through thick and thin and took part on the Greek side in the battle of Plataea. By contrast, the Boeotians dominated by Thebes seem to have been glad to see the greatest possible damage inflicted on their Greek enemies and themselves were active at Plataea and in the campaign preceding the battle.

2. FROM THE PERSIAN WAR TO THE PEACE OF NICIAS

This unorthodox organization of the subject matter may surprise the reader. The justification is that, not least for the federal states of the time, the events of the period beginning about 460 prepare the way for developments and events of the first part of the Peloponnesian War. On the other hand, especially for the Chalcidic Confederacy, the Peace of Nicias marks the end of an epoch. The account given below is not intended to be an interpretation of Athenian and Spartan policies. Yet, since the various federal states were entangled in them, they cannot be entirely neglected. Special emphasis will have to be placed on the commercial and imperial rivalry of Corinth and Athens extending from the Isthmus to Italy, Sicily, and probably even Carthage. Involved in this, directly or indirectly, were the Phocian, Aetolian, Achaean, and Acarnanian confederacies. Also the Boeotian Confederacy might be included, since its territory touched the Gulf of Corinth, and since the triple attack on Boeotia in 424 included an attack from this side. Boeotia, however, seems to have been more interested in local issues, probably including Euboea. The Chalcidic Confederacy, on the other hand, probably would never have become particularly involved in the Peloponnesian War if it had not been for the Athenian provocation of Potidaea. It is difficult not to see in this a grave error which greatly complicated the war and diverted much energy from its chief issue. Finally, the Thessalian Confederacy, aside from now and then supporting Athens with her cavalry, would have counted for relatively little in this conflict it if had not been for the crossing of its territory by Brasidas. This too, of course, was an indirect result of the Potidaean affair.

When the break between Athens and Sparta began to develop in 462, Athens immediately entered into alliances with Argos and Thessaly.[1] These were the first steps taken by Athens in her effort to build up her power also on the mainland near home in spite of continued hostilities against Persia. Yet it was soon to be seen that the Athenian aggression was directed much more against Corinth than against Sparta and aimed at securing control over the Corinthian Gulf and the western trade. Directly involved in the resulting struggle were the Achaean and Acarnanian confederacies. A byproduct was the Athenian invasion of Aetolia. An early indication of this special interest was the Athenian alliance with Megara. According to Thucydides, a boundary dispute with Corinth caused this city to break away from the Peloponnesian League and approach the Athenians. The resulting alliance gave the Athenians access to the Megarian ports of Pegae on the Corinthian and Nisaea on the Saronic Gulf. The latter was now connected with the city of Megara by means of long walls.[2] The first open conflicts concerned Athenian and Corinthian rivalries in the Saronic Gulf. The Athenians were defeated by the Corinthians and Epidaurians when they raided Halieis at the southern extremity of the peninsula of Acte, but won two victories at sea which enabled them to besiege Aegina. This was followed by the unsuccessful attempt of the Corinthians to divert the Athenians by means of raids into the Megarid.[3] Yet, though the first clashes revolved around the Saronic Gulf, the centre of conflict was soon transferred to the Corinthian Gulf, and now the federal states bordering on it became involved. The course of events was soon to cause also Sparta to become involved, but, when the period from 462 to 432 is viewed as a whole, Corinth rather than Sparta was the prime actor among the states opposing Athens. Sparta, moreover, seems to have been more interested in communications over land north toward Thessaly than in the western interests of Corinth. Thus, there was some division of interests, but the activities of Sparta appear to have been more sporadic than those of Corinth.

The Spartans became involved when they intervened against the aggression of the Phocians in Doris. This was followed by an effort to organize Boeotia as a counterweight to Athens. In fact, the force sent was so large that it seems that the intervention was directed from the

[1] Thuc. i. 102. 4. For the events of the period no effort will be made to cite all the sources even when for convenience references to the pertinent passages in Thucydides are given.

[2] Thuc. i. 103. 4. This places the building of the long walls in the Megarid earlier than those in Attica. The building of the latter is reported in i. 107, 1; cf. Gomme on the two passages.

[3] Thuc. i. 105.

outset more against Athens than against Phocis. At the time the
Phocians were trying to conquer Doris and had captured one of the
little towns of that petty district, when the Spartans intervened with
1,500 hoplites of their own and 10,000 of their allies.[1] This certainly
was a force larger than was needed to deal with the Phocians. Nor does
the Phocian attempt to annex Doris appear in itself to have been too
heinous an offence by Greek standards. It might even be argued that
the Phocians were merely trying to extend their state to its natural
boundaries by gaining control of the upper end of the Cephissus valley.
True, the ancients placed the source of the Cephissus near Lilaea in
Phocis, but anyone glancing at a map of the region is likely to feel that
the tributary coming down from Doris has a better claim to be considered the headwaters of the river. Moreover, since the dialect of
Phocis was Northwest Greek, it cannot have differed too much from
that of Doris, and the Dorians under Phocis would hardly be any more,
if as much, under foreign control as the Orchomenians in a Boeotian
Confederacy dominated by Thebes. The Spartans may have had a
sentimental attachment to Doris as the Metropolis of the Lacedaemonians. There was also the additional consideration that only in connexion with the Metropolis was Sparta represented in the Amphictionic League. At first the Spartans had had no representation but
later, at least at times, were allowed to fill the position once reserved
exclusively for the Metropolis.[2] Nevertheless, the interest of Sparta in
Doris was probably more geographic than sentimental. The usual
route from central to nothern Greece went by the passes of Hyampolis
and Thermopylae, a route which could be approached through the
Phocian port of Anticyra. If this route was in hostile hands, the route
from Delphi and Amphissa to the head of the Malian Gulf would be a
possible but difficult alternate route. To have both routes controlled by
Phocis would have been a prospect unwelcome to the Spartans, even if
they were slow to intervene outside the Peloponnesus. If, as is likely, the
Athenians had already settled the Messenian refugees at Naupactus,[3]
the Spartans and their allies would have an additional reason to act.
The army sent was such that it is clear that the campaign must have
been preceded by a meeting of the assembly of the Peloponnesian

[1] Thuc. i. 107. 2; Diod. xi. 79. 4–6. The statistics are given by both authors.

[2] See G. Daux, 'Remarques sur la composition du conseil amphictionique', *BCH* lxxxi
(1957), 95–120 at 104–17, where references to earlier literature can be found.

[3] See Gomme, *Commentary*, i. 401–11; *ATL* iii. 165 f. An important consideration is the
fact that the narrative of Thuc. i. 103–7 implies that the settlement came before not only the
Tanagra campaign but also the alliance of Athens with Megara. In *ATL* there is added
the additional consideration that it is unlikely that the Athenians could have prevented
the return of the Peloponnesian army by the sea route across the Gulf of Corinth if they
had held no port on the Gulf except Pegae.

League, at which intervention was voted. Corinth too certainly must have been in favour of the intervention.

After the Phocians had captured one of the little towns of Doris, the Spartans intervened in 457 or thereabouts.[1] Considering the size of the intervening army, it is not surprising that the Phocians came to terms without fighting, thus enabling the Peloponnesian army to continue down the Cephissus valley into Boeotia, where its chief purpose was to reconstruct the defunct Boeotian Confederacy under Theban leadership. Even for this task, so large a force was scarcely needed. After the Persian War Plataea and Thespiae certainly and Orchomenus most likely stood aloof from the group of cities, if any, loyal to Thebes. Thus there was no danger of having to face a united Boeotia, and a smaller force would have sufficed for supporting Thebes against its Boeotian opponents. It must have been the danger of opposition from Athens which dictated the size of the army, and the Athenians did intervene, supported by 1,000 Argive soldiers and a detachment of Thessalian cavalry. In the battle the latter went over to the enemy, and, whether or not this was the cause, the Athenians were defeated. The Spartans, however, after the battle, merely withdrew from Boeotia by the land route through the Megarid, and the Boeotians were left to stand on their own feet. This they were unable to do. In a couple of months the Athenians invaded Boeotia, defeated the Boeotians at Oenophyta, and as a result secured virtual control of Boeotia (except Thebes), Phocis, and Eastern Locris.[2] Though this is not specifically stated, it is likely that they secured control also of Western Locris, located as it was, between Delphi and Naupactus. Thus Sparta had won the battle of Tanagra but lost the campaign. In the long run, however, these events may have had far-reaching influence on the future course of events, in that they united Boeotia in opposition to Athens, and, though the union was quickly shattered, the reduction by the Athenians caused the Boeotians to remain hostile to Athens and so prepared the way for a new union with the same orientation.

The reactions to these events by the several federal states involved varied. The Phocian Confederacy seems to have come over to the side of Athens without any opposition, to have been treated as a friendly power, and to have been allowed to assume the control of Delphi. On

---

[1] In *ATL* iii. 171 ff. the authors have argued that the battles of Tanagra and Oenophyta belong in 458, but their elaborate arguments have merely convinced me that absolute certainty is impossible. Under the circumstances it seems better to retain the conventional date. The chronology of the years after 458–457 offered by A. E. Raubitschek in 'The Peace Policy of Pericles', *AJA* lxx (1966), 37–41 is not convincing.

[2] Thuc. i. 107–8; Diod. xi. 79–84.

the other hand, whether there was any fighting in Eastern Locris or not, the Athenians did not similarly trust the Locrians and so took hostages from them.[1] The alliance of Athens with the Thessalian Confederacy apparently was not broken off as a result of the desertion of the cavalry at Tanagra. Dissension was not rare in Thessaly in this period, and the action of the cavalry was probably due to aristocratic officers hostile to Athens who disobeyed the orders given them by the home government. Not to mention the incidents connected with the crossing of Thessaly by Brasidas, similar dissension was seen a few years after Tanagra when the Athenians tried to restore Orestes, the son of Echecratides, the 'king of the Thessalians', that is, the *tagos*, but were prevented from doing so by the Thessalian cavalry.[2] Apparently Echecratides, who probably was the *tagos* with whom the Athenians had negotiated their alliance a few years earlier, was dead or in exile, and the Athenians were trying to restore his son. Again the cavalry was hostile to the Athenians while the family of the *tagos* was on their side. The alliance seems to have survived even this incident. There seems to have been no break, at any rate, after Tanagra. It is even likely that the Thessalians supported the Athenians at Oenophyta, took part in the subsequent dismantling of Tanagra, and dedicated a tithe at Delphi from the spoils taken there.[3] The events just mentioned show that Thessaly was not too reliable an ally, but this seems to have been due to the deterioration of the situation at home.

The Athenians, when riding high, naturally did all in their power to strengthen their position and to gain prestige. One step was to secure a strange treaty of alliance between themselves and the Amphictionic League or its members. The treaty, or rather an Athenian decree concerning the treaty, is contained in a badly mutilated inscription which used to be taken to refer to a treaty between the Athenians and the Phocians, though the name of the Phocians does not occur on the stone while there are several references to things Amphictionic. The reason undoubtedly was that a treaty of alliance with the Amphictionic

[1] Diod. xi. 83. 2–3 speaks of reduction and hostages also for Phocis, but Thuc. i. 108. 3 speaks of hostages only for the Opuntian Locrians. This in itself is not conclusive in an account so brief. More important is the fact that a few years later Delphi was under the control of Phocis (Thuc. i. 112. 5).

[2] Thuc. i. 111. 1; cf. CP lv (1960), 243 and n. 54 (where the date should be corrected to 457–456). It is best to follow Thucydides, who implies that the campaign came a few years later, rather than Diod. xi. 83. 2–4, who makes it a sequel to the Oenophyta campaign.

[3] SEG xvii. 243; J. and L. Robert, Bull. ép. 1959, no. 189. In addition to the literature cited there cf. CP lv (1960), 241–3. The suggestions about the nature of the monument and the participation of the Thessalians in the battle of Oenophyta are from the original publication of the monument by Daux, BCH lxxxii (1958), 329–34. A different interpretation is given by Miss Sordi, La lega tessala, 344–7. The bearing of the inscription on the constitutional development of Thessaly has been discussed above, p. 23.

League seemed unthinkable. A few years ago, however, two of our leading epigraphers, the late Adolf Wilhelm and B. D. Meritt, published independent restorations making it clear that the Amphictionic League actually was one of the parties to the treaty.[1] There can no longer be any doubt about the general contents, though many details remain uncertain. Most likely the Athenians, soon after their victory at Oenophyta, secured the adoption by the Amphictions of a proposal for a treaty between the League members and Athens. This undoubtedly was due to the manipulations of the Athenians, whose allies must have had a clear majority in the council of the League. The purpose must have been to give Athens whatever benefit it could receive from the Panhellenic prestige of the League. As a political document it cannot have affected directly any states except those with votes in the assembly, and, from that point of view, the Amphictionic League was a local rather than a Panhellenic organization,[2] but, even so, it must have enjoyed a considerable Panhellenic prestige as a result of its connexion with the oracle of Delphi. Thus the Athenian democrats, who had broken with the Panhellenic policy of Cimon, were now trying to acquire as much Panhellenic prestige as possible for their city and empire.[3]

The Athenians also had the more material aid of the Achaean Confederacy. This state was not represented on the council of the Amphictionic League and otherwise too for some time had stood aside from the main currents of Greek politics. It apparently had not even taken part in the Persian War. The Achaeans, nevertheless, seem not to have forgotten their old ties with the West and to have been interested in curbing the Corinthian control of the Gulf of Corinth and of the trade with Italy and Sicily. The Confederacy, at any rate, became the ally of the Athenians and thus helped to give them control of both sides of the entrance to the Gulf. The exact date of the alliance is not known, but it seems already to have been in existence by the time of the expedition of Pericles in the Gulf, the time he started from Pegae in the Megarid, debarked near Sicyon and defeated the Sicyonians, then took

---

[1] Meritt's first version appeared in *AJP* lxix (1948), 312–14; that of Wilhelm in *Mnemosyne*, 4 ser., ii (1959), 286–93. Wilhelm had seen Meritt's text in *SEG* x. 18 before his own was published and was able to add some comments on points on which the two differed. Later Meritt returned to the inscription in *AJP* lxxv (1954), 369–74 in a very judicious article in which he accepted some of Wilhelm's suggestions. In this article also both Meritt's own earlier version and that of Wilhelm are reprinted. The three versions are also found respectively in *SEG* x. 18; xii. 7; xiii. 3; cf. also *Bull. ép.* 1949, no. 40; 1951, no. 67; 1956, no. 79. A photograph is given *AJA* lv (1951), Plate 37.

[2] Cf. the article by Daux cited on p. 123, n. 2.

[3] For a completely different reconstruction of the course of events, see M. Sordi, 'La posizione di Delfi e dell' Anfizionia nel decennio tra Tanagra e Coronea', *Riv. fil.* (1958), 48–65.

Achaeans on board and sailed out the narrows to besiege Oeniadae unsuccessfully.[1] Thus the Achaeans were active and not merely passive agents in the efforts to bottle up Corinth. While the Messenians at Naupactus and forts held by the Athenians controlled the north shore of the narrows, the Achaeans held the south shore. They were to continue in a similar role as the allies of Sparta in the Corinthian War early in the fourth century, except that then the Achaeans for some time controlled both sides of the narrows.

To approximately the same time as the alliance with the Achaeans, belongs a group of Athenian treaties of alliance with Rhegium in Italy and with several cities on Sicily.[2] It is possible that the dreams of the extension of power in the west even included some thought of exerting control over Etruria and Carthage. The earliest evidence for plans on Carthage is found in the *Knights* of Aristophanes performed in 424 B.C. There the Sausage-Seller, who is to replace the Paphlagonian (Cleon) as the favourite of Demos, is told by Demosthenes that the area under his control will include Carthage, and later in the play the democratic leader Hyperbolus is said to be planning an expedition against Carthage. This has been taken to mean that such an expedition was being seriously discussed at the time.[3] This was not a new issue at the time, if we can believe the report of Plutarch that Pericles was opposed to dreams of aggression against Carthage and Etruria.[4] If Pericles actually was involved in such a controversy, this is likely to have been during the early part of his career as a leader of the state. Certainly such plans are more likely to have been advocated in the period of aggressive democratic imperialism beginning about 460 than in the more discreet last years of the career of Pericles. Whether or not responsible Athenian leaders ever went as far as this in their plans, the Athenian intervention in the west was directed largely against the interests of Corinth. Of the allies of the Athenians, those with the greatest stake in the issues would seem to have been the Achaeans. Later also other opponents of Corinth, particularly, Acarnania and Corcyra became involved.

It was not many years before the ambitious plans of the Athenians

[1] On these operations see 'The Early Achaean League', *Studies Presented to D. M. Robinson*, ii (1953), 797–815, especially 798–802.

[2] For Egesta see Tod, 31; for Leontini and Rhegium, 57 and 58 of 433–432 B.C. For these two cities there is evidence that the treaties were renewals of older treaties, probably of about 448; see particularly B. D. Meritt, 'The Athenian Alliances with Rhegion and Leontinoi', *Class. Quart.* xl (1946), 85–91, an article which also contains important emendations of the texts; *ATL* iii. 276 f., 304 f. For the date of the treaty with Egesta see A. E. Raubitschek, *TAPA* lxxv (1944), 10–14; cf. *Bull. ép.* 1946–7, no. 74. There probably were treaties which have not been preserved with other cities.

[3] *Knights* 174, 1303 ff. Cf. E. Meyer, *GdA* iv. 82; Swoboda, *RE* ix. 255; Glotz-Cohen, *Hist. grecque*, ii. 648.   [4] Plut. *Pericles* 20.

suffered setbacks and had to be abandoned or modified. The events connected with this do not concern the present study except in so far as they affected the various federal states. Thus, concerning the failure of the intervention in Egypt, all that need be said is that the losses were not so great as to slacken noticeably the energy of the Athenians. The Five Years' Truce of 451 seems to have been due not to exhaustion but rather to a return to the policy of Cimon involving friendship with Sparta and all out war against the Persians. The great break came in 447 with the rising of Boeotia, when Boeotian exiles seized Orchomenus and Chaeronea in northwestern Boeotia, Chaeronea being at that time a part of the territory of Orchomenus.[1] The Athenian general, Tolmides, intervened with a thousand Athenian and some allied troops and succeeded in occupying little Chaeronea, enslaving the population, and leaving a garrison there, but he did not succeed in reducing Orchomenus, which, of course, meant that the expedition was a failure at the outset. When Tolmides started the return march towards Athens, the Boeotian exiles using Orchomenus as head-quarters and receiving some aid from Locrians and Euboeans, attacked the Athenians at Coronea and captured those who did not fall in battle. After this the Athenians made peace on the terms that they secure the release of the prisoners in return for their own complete withdrawal from Boeotia. It is hardly necessary to say that this meant the collapse of most of the Athenian empire or protectorate on the mainland of Greece. The revolt of Boeotia was followed by that of Euboea, but, while Euboea was later reduced, the holdings on the mainland were for the most part lost. Thessaly seems to have remained an ally, but, as to the rest, even the Phocians were considered allies of the Spartans at the beginning of the Peloponnesian War. Naupactus, of course, remained and the events of 427 were to show that the Athenians retained also Chalcis and apparently a couple of other small forts on the north side of the entrance to the Gulf of Corinth.[2] Thus they did not completely renounce their interest in the Gulf of Corinth even though they gave up their alliance with the Achaean Confederacy at the time of the Thirty Years Peace. Thucydides writes as if they turned over Achaea to the Spartans, but that is misleading. The Achaean Confederacy was not a subject state to be handed over from one power to the other. Actually, at the beginning of the Peloponnesian War, only the easternmost Achaean city, Pellene, which often went its own way, was a firm ally of Sparta.[3]

---

[1] See above p. 33 and cf. 'Orchomenus and the Formation of the Boeotian Confederacy in 447 B.C.', *CP* lv (1960), 9–18.

[2] On this point cf. *Studies Presented to D. M. Robinson*, ii. 799 and 802.

[3] Thuc. i. 115. 1; ii. 9. 2.

Also events in another theatre of operations show clearly that Athens by no means abandoned her interest in the west at the time of the Thirty Years Peace. In fact, it was not many years before Athens intervened in Acarnania, a district of which the coast was studded with Corinthian colonies. Of these Ambracia was particularly aggressive. It was probably soon after 440 that the Ambraciotes, who had been given some sort of share in Amphilochian Argos, expelled the Argives proper—obviously Amphilochians—and themselves took over the city. Thereupon the Amphilochians attached themselves to the Acarnanians as allies or members of the Confederacy, and the latter, in turn, appealed to the Athenians. They thereupon sent an expedition under the command of the Phormio who was to become famous for his exploits in 429. With the aid of the Athenians the Acarnanians captured Argos, sold the prisoners into slavery, and resettled the city with Amphilochians and Acarnanians. This was followed by the first treaty of alliance between the Athenians and the Acarnanians.[1] This undoubtedly means that a formal treaty was negotiated as in the case of the alliances with the Sicilian cities mentioned above.

Thus Athens, when her land empire collapsed, by no means gave up her plans of a western extension of her power. This is indicated not only by the intervention in Acarnania and the later acceptance of the alliance with Corcyra. There is also the evidence of the renewal of the treaties with Rhegium and Leontini precisely in 433–432.[2] All of this makes it look almost as if the later Athenian ultimatum to the Potidaeans was a deliberate provocation of Corinth. If so it was a costly mistake which greatly complicated the rivalry of the two cities. At any rate, it was largely the clash of their western interests which brought on the Peloponnesian War, and the first part of that war, to a great extent took the form of a struggle for the control of northwest Greece. In the first year of the war, the most tangible successes gained by the squadron of a hundred ships sent out by the Athenians were in this area. Two cities on the coast of Acarnania, Sollium, a Corinthian colony, and Astacus were captured. The first of these, Sollium, was turned over to the Acarnanians of Palaerus. This apparently means that it was incorporated into a pre-existing Acarnanian city. This arrangement seems to have proved lasting. From Astacus, at the time under a tyrant, it appears that the tyrant was expelled only to be restored by the Corinthians and then expelled once more by the

---

[1] These events are reported in Thuc. ii. 68. 6–8 in connexion with the account of the campaign of 430. The chief reason for placing them after 440 is that, if Corinthian and Athenian interests had clashed recently, it is unlikely that the Corinthians would have opposed intervention against Athens at the time of the revolt of Samos (Thuc. i. 41. 2).

[2] Cf. p. 127, n. 2 above.

9

Acarnanians. At least a force of Athenians and Messenians coming from Naupactus in 429 could use the city as a port of debarkation.[1]

The following year saw only the prelude to more important operations in the Acarnanian theatre. The Ambraciotes, aided by the Chaonians, an Epirote tribe, and others of the nearby 'barbarians', made an attack on Amphilochian Argos but were repulsed. Later in the autumn or early winter the Athenian admiral, Phormio, came out to Naupactus with a squadron of twenty ships to guard the entrance to the Gulf of Corinth.[2] The coming season he was destined not only to win two famous naval battles but also to intervene in Acarnania. The naval battles do not concern us; the operations in Acarnania do. Yet, before turning to them, it may be well to recall that the year 429 also witnessed an important Athenian setback at the hands of another federal state. About May of that year 2,000 Athenian hoplites, 200 horse, and a few local peltasts under the command of three Athenian generals advanced against Spartolus, the Bottiaean capital. In the engagements which followed, the Athenian hoplites were disastrously defeated by the local light-armed troops and cavalry, including troops from Olynthus. This is apparently the first battle known in which hoplites fighting on relatively level ground were defeated by a combination of cavalry and light-armed troops.[3] Thus the efficacy of other troops than hoplites was being demonstrated also by the Chalcidians and Bottiaeans in the very same year that it was being demonstrated by the Acarnanians.

Phormio's squadron, to judge by the course of events, had been sent out to blockade the entrance to the Gulf of Corinth. It was scarcely large enough to perform this task and at the same time to prevent the crossing of troops farther west from the Peloponnesus to the Corinthian colonies on the coast of Acarnania. The Spartan Cnemus apparently accomplished his crossing before his opponents became aware that such a move would be tried. The Spartans had been induced to intervene by the Ambraciotes and Chaonians, who hoped to detach all Acarnania from the alliance with Athens and close the nearby waters to the Athenians. In response to this, Cnemus, the Spartan nauarch, was sent hurriedly with a few ships and a thousand hoplites. He must have proceeded directly to Leucas, where the ships of that city as well as of Ambracia and Anactorium already were gathered. Thither too a Peloponnesian fleet, which was being organized at Corinth and Sicyon, was ordered to proceed. This fleet, when it set out, numbered forty-seven ships, carrying troops to be used in landings on the coast of Acarnania. It was thus the plan to attack simultaneously from land

[1] Thuc. ii. 30, 33. 1–2, 102. 1.
[2] Thuc. ii. 68. 1 and 9, 69.1.   [3] Thuc. ii. 79, cf. above, p. 64.

and from sea, both attacks starting from the Corinthian colonies on the northern part of the coast of Acarnania. Phormio's contribution was that he intercepted the fleet and thus prevented the attack from the sea from materializing. Cnemus himself must have started from Ambracia with his thousand Peloponnesian hoplites, the men of the Corinthian colonies, Leucas, Anactorium, and Ambracia itself, and an imposing array of Epirote tribesmen. With this force he by-passed Amphilochian Argos and made for Stratus on the Achelous, the capital and largest city of Acarnania. To meet this attack, the men of Stratus were left to their own resources, the other Acarnanians remaining at home to defend their country against the anticipated attack from the sea. Under the circumstances the men of Stratus did remarkably well. They must have had scouts watching and reporting the advance of the enemy, so that they knew that the Chaonians were pressing forward impetuously ahead of the others. This gave them time to prepare an ambush so that, when the Chaonians approached the city, they were met by a double attack, by troops issuing from the city and others rising from the ambush. The result was that the Chaonians were defeated with such losses that all Cnemus could do was to safeguard the rest of his forces. The men of Stratus, on the other hand, were not strong enough to attack the hoplites, but they did make life miserable for them by peppering them with bullets or stones from their slings. After recovering his dead under truce, Cnemus retreated to Oeniadae, and the invading force broke up.[1] For the time being Acarnania was saved. Phormio's first naval victory, won at about the same time as the battle of Stratus, saved the coasts of Acarnania from an attack by the Peloponnesian fleet. His second victory, later in the season, saved them from attack by a larger fleet than the first.[2] In the following autumn or early winter Phormio proceeded from Naupactus to Acarnania and landed 400 Athenian and 400 Messenian hoplites at Astacus. The objective was the reduction of Oeniadae, the only Acarnanian city hostile to Athens. However, since the waters of the Achelous river made an attack in winter impossible, this had to be given up.[3]

This was not a very brilliant final action for a year which had been remarkably successful in this theatre both for the Athenians and for the Acarnanians. The latter must have realized that Phormio, though unable to intervene directly in Acarnania until after his two naval victories, had, by these victories, contributed largely to their salvation. Only this can account for his tremendous popularity, which can

---

[1] Thuc. ii. 80–82; the size of the Peloponnesian fleet; 83. 2.   [2] Thuc. ii. 85–92.
[3] Thuc. ii. 102. 1–2. That an attack on Oeniadae was the main objective is deduced from the statement that such an attack had to be given up.

hardly have been due exclusively to the aid given years earlier when he was instrumental in bringing about the first alliance of Athens and Acarnania. Next year, when Phormio was not available, the Acarnanians asked for a son or kinsman, and the Athenians sent his son Asopius. This time the Athenians and Acarnanians took the offensive. A joint attack on Oeniadae failed. Thereupon Asopius made a raid on the territory of Leucas but was defeated and killed.[1] The failure may have been due in part to the smallness of the Athenian fleet—only twelve ships—and in part to the difficulty of capturing fortified cities. Even so, the situation was completely different from that of the preceding year. This time there was no fear of the intervention of a large Peloponnesian expedition. Instead the initiative was on the other side.

In this manner the rivalry of Athens with Sparta and, above all, with Corinth, in northwest Greece and beyond, beginning at least as early as the middle of the fifth century, was continued during the early period of the Peloponnesian War and affected that war and incidentally also strengthened the Acarnanian Confederacy. The next year in which that confederacy was involved in important operations was 426, and at that time these operations were entangled with other operations and particularly with the Athenian invasion of Aetolia. Before taking up the events of that year, it is necessary to glance at the manner in which the events of the period affected the Boeotian Confederacy.

As already noted, the liberation of Boeotia in 447 had been followed by the organization of the most advanced and best known oligarchic federal state in early Greek history. At the time all Boeotia was more or less forced into the anti-Athenian and pro-Spartan camp. After the Persian War not only Plataea but also Thespiae stood aloof from Thebes, while Orchomenus was normally hostile. It would seem that it might have been possible for a discreet statesman to detach these permanently from the side of Thebes and secure them as allies of Athens. Later events were to show that there were strong democratic elements at least at Thespiae ready to co-operate with democratic Athens. As it was, however, the union manipulated by Sparta in 457 followed by the defeat at the hands of the Athenians at Oenophyta and the reduction to what must have been a status as subject allies, alligned the Boeotians in general against Athens. It will be remembered that the first act of war in 431 was an attack by Thebans on Plataea, the one city in Boeotia which continued to be an ally of Athens. In the organization and plan of representation of the Boeotian Confederacy drawn up in 447 it looks as if a place was made for the Plataeans. Was Plataea

[1] Thuc. iii. 7.

in the period from 447 to 431 a member of the Boeotian Confederacy and an ally of Athens at the same time? No one can say, but so many things that seem strange to us were done by the Greeks that it is not entirely impossible.[1] Aside from the Plataeans, the Boeotians were allies of the Spartans throughout the Peloponnesian War. Members of the Peloponnesian League they were not. They have often, but incorrectly, been so considered.[2] The trouble is that *symmachoi* is used with such a variety of meanings extending all the way from people who casually happen to fight on the same side to groups with formal treaties of alliance and even to fellow members of a league. Thus '*symmachoi* of the Lacedaemonians' does not always have the same meaning. In Thucydides ii. 9. 2 the Boeotians are listed as *symmachoi* and rightly so, for they supported the Spartans in war, but this need not mean that they were members of the League. After enumerating all those who supported Sparta, Thucydides concludes, 'This was the *symmachia* of the Lacedaemonians' (ii. 9. 3), but in this group of allies there certainly are included several who were not members of the Peloponnesian League. To complicate matters, he also reports consultations which seem to indicate that the Boeotians took part in meetings of the assembly of the League, and most certainly they did do so. On questions on which Sparta had to consult the members of the League, she might also wish to consult her most powerful single ally outside the League. When the Peace of Nicias was negotiated in 431, he states that the Boeotians, Corinthians, Eleans, and Megarians voted against it (v. 17. 3). If this passage were the only evidence, all would conclude that the Boeotians, like the other three states mentioned, were normal members of the Peloponnesian League, but what happened afterwards shows that they were not. The Boeotians did not consider themselves bound by the treaty and negotiated a separate truce. When the Corinthians later induced the Boeotians to intercede for them and secure a similar truce, the Athenians refused on the grounds that they were at peace with the Corinthians, since the latter were *symmachoi* of the Lacedaemonians, that is, as the word is used here, members of the Peloponnesian League.[3] Thus the Athenians considered the Corinthians, but not the Boeotians, to be members of the League and bound by the Peace of Nicias.[4]

[1] The point is discussed, inconclusively of course, *CP* lv. (1960), 12. More recently M. Sordi, *Atene e Roma*, 1965, 14 f. is positive that Plataea was not a member between 447 and 427, and that at the time the Confederacy contained only nine instead of eleven units.

[2] The Boeotians were considered members of the Peloponnesian League by Busolt *Staatskunde*, 1323; Gomme, *Commentary*, iii. 665 on Thuc. v. 17. 2. For a more correct view see U. Kahrstedt, *Griechisches Staatsrecht*, i (1922), 30 and n. 1.

[3] Thuc. v. 26. 2, 32. 6. On the nature of the truce see p. 148, n. 3 below.

[4] Even clearer is the evidence of the one year's truce negotiated in 423. The first clause guaranteed free access to the oracle at Delphi. Concerning this clause the Spartans promised

During the Archidamian War the Boeotian contributions to the conduct of the war were extremely important. The raids of the Peloponnesian army into Attica were made possible largely, probably even exclusively, by the support of the Boeotian cavalry. At this time the Athenians had cavalry of their own and, in addition, at least at the outset, the aid of Thessalian cavalry. The Lacedaemonians and their Peloponnesian allies for several years had none. Thus, if it had not been for the Boeotian cavalry, the Athenian and Thessalian cavalry could have made it impossible for the invading troops to raid and devastate the countryside. The statement attributed to the Athenian general, Hippocrates, before the battle of Delium, that without the Boeotian cavalry the Peloponnesians would not invade Attica, is not an exaggeration. The Thebans themselves, in their speech after the surrender of Plataea, are represented as referrring to the importance of their cavalry, stronger than that of any other state taking part in the war on their side. This undoubtedly is correct, since apparently the only other cavalry on the Spartan side in the first years of the war, was that of the Phocians and Locrians.[1] Yet the contributions of the cavalry was not such as to be mentioned frequently in the accounts of the events of this period. For 431 a skirmish between Boeotian cavalry on one side and Athenian and Thessalian on the other side is reported. In this the Athenians and Thessalians had the better of it until hoplites intervened in support of the Boeotians.[2] In this connexion it is impossible not to wonder why the Boeotians allowed the Thessalian cavalry to reach Attica apparently without trying to stop them on their way. For a number of years after this no action of the Boeotian cavalry is reported, but, even when it is not mentioned, it must have co-operated regularly with the invading Peloponnesian troops.

The great year for federal states was 426, the year in which the Athenians under Demosthenes suffered a disastrous defeat at the hands of the Aetolians, while they and their allies, the Acarnanians, under the command of the same Demosthenes, at Olpae in the territory of Amphilochian Argos, won a decisive victory over the Ambraciotes and their Peloponnesian allies in what was undoubtedly the greatest battle on land in the war before Delium. The events were closely interrelated: Demosthenes operated in Acarnania before he invaded Aetolia; after his defeat, Naupactus was saved by the Acarnanians; and, after that again, came the campaign culminating in Olpae. Yet an analysis of the events of the year will suggest that, had

that they would send ambassadors to the Boeotians and Phocians and do their best to induce them to accept it (Thuc. iv. 118. 2). Thus neither of the two confederacies had taken part in the negotiation or was bound by a treaty ratified by the Peloponnesian League.

[1] Thuc. iv. 95. 2; iii. 62. 5; ii. 9. 3.   [2] Thuc. ii. 12. 5, 22. 2.

the Athenians and Acarnanians seen eye to eye, the successes might have been greater. The Acarnanians might have secured Leucas, and the Athenians Ambracia. Thucydides does not indicate the plan of campaign, but the events recorded make it clear that the original objective was the reduction of Leucas, the largest and most powerful Corinthian colony on the coast of Acarnania.

The force that came out from Athens was not large. In fact, it was the smaller of two fleets sent out that summer, consisting of thirty ships under the command of Demosthenes and Procles. These two were expected also to assume leadership of allied troops and ships. The first major operation was an attack on Leucas with the support of the Zacynthians, Cephallenians, fifteen ships from Corcyra, and the total mobilization of the troops of the Acarnanian Confederacy.[1] Such an attack can hardly have been undertaken on the spur of the moment but must have been planned in advance. Obviously the plan was that the Acarnanians were to attack on land and the ships of the Athenians and the Corcyraeans were to cut off communications by sea. It seems that all was going well and that the Acarnanians favoured completing the blockade of the city, when Demosthenes was induced to raise the siege and proceed to invade Aetolia. From Leucas he sailed to nearby Sollium, where he had some kind of conference with the Acarnanians, whether it was with the board of generals or a larger body, it is impossible to say. Though the Acarnanians disapproved, and the Corcyraeans, too, withdrew, Demosthenes went on from there with his other forces to invade Aetolia. With the blockade by the fleet abandoned, there naturally was nothing for the Acarnanians to do except to give up the siege. It was probably this experience which caused the Acarnanians, who had no navy, at the end of the year's campaigns, to make peace with their neighbours on terms which involved renouncing for the time being any hope of reducing Leucas.[2]

The Athenian expedition into Aetolia is too well known to require any detailed account. Undoubtedly the common view that Aetolia was more backward than Acarnania is correct. Yet it may be well to recall that the Aetolians were able to plan a campaign, to fall back before the invader, and ultimately to fight a battle in a place of their own choosing. Moreover, they obviously observed the same usages in interstate relations as other Greeks, so that the Athenians were able to arrange a truce to recover their dead. Later in the year they sent ambassadors to Sparta to induce the Spartans to attack Naupactus and took part in the campaign which followed. Obviously the Aetolians

[1] Thuc. iii. 91. 1, 94. 1–2, who states that all Acarnanians, except for Oeniadae, took part, but Oeniadae was not a member of the Confederacy at the time.
[2] Thuc. iii. 94–95.

already had developed an efficient central government. Probably it was new, for the efficiency of the Aetolians came as a surprise even to the Messenians of Naupactus, who prophesied an easy victory for Demosthenes and the Athenians.[1] However, the organization at the time appears still to have been on tribal lines. The sympolitical organization by cities or communities treated as cities came somewhat later.

For the expedition against Naupactus organized in response to the appeal from Aetolia, the Spartans sent a force of 3,000 allied hoplites under the command of Eurylochus. Of the entire force only he and two other officers were Spartiates. When to this force there were added Locrians and Aetolians, it must have seemed formidable and a real threat to Naupactus. To meet it Demosthenes, with some difficulty, induced the Acarnanians, who still resented his withdrawal from Leucas, to send a thousand hoplites. This force, added to the local Messenians, was enough to deter Eurylochus from attacking the city. He now withdrew, but not back in the direction of Amphissa and Delphi. Instead he proceeded to Proschium, a town a few miles from the mouth of the Achelous. The reason was that he had been induced by the Ambraciotes to support them in an attack directed against Amphilochian Argos and Acarnania in general. Therefore he dismissed the Aetolians and awaited the signal to act.[2] In order to understand what followed, it will be well to remember that Ambracia was north of Acarnania, that also Amphilochian Argos was north of Acarnania proper, while Proschium was near its southern extremity.

The campaign that followed belongs in the winter or late autumn. It began with an invasion of the territory of Amphilochian Argos by three thousand Ambraciote hoplites who captured Olpae, a fortified town located on the coast. The Acarnanians thereupon mobilized and occupied two positions, one at Argos and one a little farther south, in the hope of intercepting the Peloponnesian troops of Eurylochus as they approached. Meanwhile they sent to Demosthenes at Naupactus and to a squadron of twenty Athenian ships cruising off the Peloponnesus to come to their aid. Eurylochus and his Peloponnesians arrived first, marching north through Acarnania, which, except for forts that were garrisoned, was now denuded of troops, and managed to effect a junction with the Ambraciotes without being intercepted. Soon both the Athenian ships and Demosthenes put in their appearance, Demosthenes too obviously coming by sea to the Gulf of Ambracia. He

---

[1] Thuc. iii. 94. 3, 96–102.

[2] Thuc. iii. 100–2. Later in 109. 2 Thucydides refers to mercenary soldiers in such a way as to suggest that Peloponnesian troops were largely mercenaries rather than contingents supplied by the various cities.

brought only two hundred Messenian hoplites and sixty Athenian archers. He does not seem to have suffered much in his personal reputation on account of his defeat in Aetolia and was elected to command the allied forces in conjunction with the Acarnanian commanders.[1]

There are difficulties, particularly topographical ones, connected with the campaign which followed, but the main course of events seems fairly clear.[2] Eurylochus, after he had combined his troops with the Ambraciote forces, took up a position outside but near Olpae. Demosthenes, in turn, brought up his troops and took up a position near but with a ravine separating the two armies. Before the arrival of Eurylochus, the Ambraciotes had sent word to the home government to come to their aid with the entire forces of the state. When Eurylochus had arrived, the combined forces outnumbered the enemy and did not fear to accept battle without waiting for the additional troops. The battle seems to have been largely an old-fashioned hoplite battle except that Demosthenes had planted four hundred hoplites and light-armed troops in an ambush.[3] This proved the decisive factor, and the Acarnanians and their allies won a conclusive victory. The losses of the Ambraciotes and Peloponnesians were heavy, Eurylochus and one of the other two Spartiates present being among those fallen.

The next day Menedaïus, the only survivor of the three Spartiates, was induced to enter into a secret agreement with Demosthenes and the Acarnanian generals by which the Mantinean contingent and the more prominent of the other Peloponnesians were to be allowed to get away and leave the Ambraciotes in the lurch. When it came to carrying out the agreement, there was some confusion, for the departing Peloponnesians did not succeed in getting away entirely unobserved. In the confusion which resulted when the Ambraciotes tried to follow, some Peloponnesians as well as Ambraciotes were killed. The rest of the Ambraciotes made their way into the hilly country to the east. This proved an advantage to the Acarnanians, for it meant that they were farther removed from the scene of action when the Acarnanians and Amphilochians had to deal with the rest of the Ambraciote levy, which

---

[1] Thuc. iii. 105–7. The number of invading hoplites from Ambracia is given in Diod. xii. 60. 4 as 1,000, and some historians have thought this number more nearly correct than the 3,000 of Thucydides, but cf. Gomme on Thuc. iii. 105. 4. Since the combined Peloponnesian and Ambracian army outnumbered the Acarnanians, the larger number is the more likely.

[2] The only source account of any value is that of Thuc. iii. 107–13. For discussions of the topography see particularly Kirsten, *RE* xvii, s.v. 'Olpai'; N. G. L. Hammond, 'The Campaigns in Amphilochia during the Archidamian War', *BSA* xxxvii (1936–7), 128–40; Gomme, *Commentary*, ii. 426–8. Hammond has an excellent description of the terrain but makes the unlikely claim that the Olpe of Thucydides is distinct from Olpai.

[3] On the prominence of hoplites in the battle and the use of hoplites by the Acarnanians, cf. Gomme on iii. 107. 4. They, however, also used light-armed troops, as they did the preceding year (Thuc. ii. 81. 8).

was now approaching Olpae. The very day the Peloponnesians were allowed to escape, Demosthenes sent forward troops to prepare ambushes. Next morning, while it still was dark, he staged a surprise attack on the Ambraciotes, who were quickly put to flight and, when they fled, found the paths by which they tried to escape blocked by ambushes of Amphilochian light-armed troops. The result was a massacre from which few escaped. The casualties were probably even greater than they had been in the main battle two days earlier. Thucydides makes a statement strange for him, that he has not given the total because it was so unbelievably great in proportion to the size of the city.[1]

The results of this campaign were great gains for the Acarnanians rather than for the Athenians. It also marked the end of the efforts of Corinth and her colonies to secure control of Acarnania. After Demosthenes and the Athenians had failed the Acarnanians at Leucas, the latter apparently had kept their own councils even more than before. When Naupactus was in danger, they had saved the situation in response to the appeal of Demosthenes, though they probably acted chiefly on account of the realization that it would be dangerous for themselves to have Naupactus fall into the hands of the Peloponnesians. When the army under Eurylochus approached, they were glad to have the aid of the Athenian fleet and to have Demosthenes as commander, but that apparently was about all. When the victory had been won, they took matters into their own hands. Demosthenes wished to capture Ambracia, and Thucydides undoubtedly is right when he states that this would have been an easy task. At Ambracia, aside from women and children and men beyond the military age, there can have been only a small group of survivors from the final action. The survivors from the first battle had made their way to Oeniadae, where they were separated from their home by the entire length of Acarnania. Nevertheless, the Acarnanians and Amphilochians refused to attack the city because they realized that it would then be taken over by the Athenians and feared that they would be worse neighbours than the Ambraciotes. At the time both Acarnanians and Ambraciotes seem to have been ready to make peace and to withdraw as much as possible from the war.

After Demosthenes and the Athenians had left, the Acarnanians and Amphilochians first allowed the Ambraciotes to return home under an armistice and then negotiated a defensive alliance for a hundred years, however with the special stipulation that the Ambraciotes would not be required to fight against the Peloponnesians nor the Acarnanians against the Athenians. In addition, the Ambraciotes

---

[1] This last statement is found in iii. 113. 6. It is probably best to leave it at this.

promised not to help Anactorium. This clearly meant that the Acarnanians were resolved to reduce this city.[1] The following year it was
captured by the 'Athenians at Naupactus' and the Acarnanians, the
Corinthian colonists expelled, and the city occupied by Acarnanian
colonists. A year later, when Demosthenes appeared off Oeniadae, he
found that the city already had been won over by the Acarnanians.[2]
In reporting this, Thucydides places the emphasis on the resulting
alliance with Athens, but it undoubtedly was as a member of the
Acarnanian Confederacy that Oeniadae now became an ally of
Athens. Too much emphasis on Athens at times warped the vision
even of Thucydides. As for Acarnania, the Confederacy now apparently had gained all its immediate objectives except Leucas, and,
something very rare in ancient Greece, had learned to be satisfied
with what was attainable and to withdraw as much as possible from
unprofitable rivalries.

To return to the Boeotians, in addition to the contribution of their
cavalry to the Spartan war effort, they inflicted upon the Athenians
the most serious defeat on land during the Archidamian War, namely
that of the battle of Delium in 424. This was considerably more serious
than the defeats suffered in the Thraceward region, at Spartolus in 429
and at Amphipolis in 422. Earlier in the summer, when Brasidas came
to the relief of Megara with troops furnished by nearby allies, the
Boeotians furnished 600 cavalry and 2,200 of the total of 6,000 hoplites.
This detachment of cavalry surprised the light-armed Athenian troops
who were raiding the countryside and afterwards fought a drawn battle
with their cavalry. According to Thucydides the Boeotians had planned to intervene even before Brasidas requested their aid. In fact, they
had mobilized their entire army at Plataea but sent home again those
not needed for the expedition.[3] Thus the Boeotians at the time had an
independent foreign policy and did not need to get directions from
Sparta before they acted. On this occasion they undoubtedly contributed not a little, but their great victory came when the Athenians
invaded their country.

The Athenians, when they entered Boeotia, were not planning to
fight a major battle. Instead they planned, with the aid of the democratic and anti-Theban groups in Orchomenus and Thespiae, to
establish themselves in three different places on the border of Boeotia
and from there gradually subvert the oligarchy in all Boeotia. Siphae,
the port of Thespiae on the Gulf of Corinth, was to be betrayed to the
Athenians; Chaeronea, on the boundary towards Phocis, was to be
surrendered by the Orchomenians; while the Athenians were to

---

[1] Thuc. iii. 114.   [2] Thuc. iv. 49, 77.   [3] Thuc. iv. 72.

march out and fortify Delium near the south-east corner of Boeotia. This was all to be done on the same day to prevent the Boeotians from concentrating all their forces in one place. According to Thucydides, the Boeotian leader in the plot was a Theban exile,[1] and so he may well have been, but the majority of the plotters were Orchomenians and Thespians. Thucydides notes particularly the activity of exiles from Orchomenus, with whom also some Phocians were co-operating. Thus leadership belonged again to a large extent to the same city as in 447. The chief trouble with the plot was that it could not possibly be kept secret. A force for seizing Chaeronea could hardly be organized without some information leaking out, particularly not if it is true that some of the eventual participants were actually being brought from the Peloponnesus, nor could the Athenians mobilize their manpower without some information crossing the border into Boeotia.[2] Possibly the operation that on the face of it offered the best chance of success was the plan to surrender Siphae to a group of triremes which was suddenly to approach the city, but this plot was foiled. A Phocian from Phanoteus —less than five miles from Chaeronea as the crow flies—revealed the plot so that the Boeotians were able to make preparations both at Siphae and Chaeronea. Moreover, since the Athenian generals failed to co-ordinate their actions properly, Demosthenes with the Athenian triremes arrived off Siphae ahead of the proposed time so that the Boeotians were able to foil the plot against Siphae before they had to deal with the Athenian army at Delium.[3]

The battle of Delium had a peculiar effect on Boeotian affairs. The Boeotian losses fell largely on the Thespians, and, since the fallen were hoplites, this meant the weakening of the oligarchic element in the city and the corresponding growth in the influence of the lower classes favouring democracy. This, in turn, provided the Thebans with an excuse for taking action against Thespiae and thus strengthening her own position within the Boeotian Confederacy.[4] The very next year the Thebans dismantled the walls of Thespiae on the charge of Atticism.[5] This is one of those stray bits of information which Thucydides from time to time gives us concerning the secondary actors in the

---

[1] Thuc. iv. 76. 2. Gomme notes that two manuscripts have an alternative reading in the margin making the leading plotter a Thespian. This in itself is possible, but there was practically no Greek community without an opposition, and so there may well have been democratic plotters also at Thebes.

[2] For comparison it may be noted that during World War I the movements of German troops were sometimes deduced from information concerning the movement of trains that reached Denmark.

[3] Thuc. iv. 89–90. 1.

[4] These events are discussed at greater length in 'The Boeotian Confederacy and Fifth-Century Oligarchic Theory', *TAPA* lxxxvi (1955), 40–50 at 47–50.

[5] Thuc. iv. 133. 1. For another example of Atticism, cf. *Hell. Ox.* 17 (12). 1.

war. They are bricks without straw or mortar, but such material must be utilized if the version of Greek history resulting from excessive concentration on Athens and Sparta is to be corrected. In the present case the reference to the charge of Atticism, combined with what is known of Boeotian institutions, makes it safe to conclude that the Thebans secured some sort of federal condemnation of Thespiae before they took action. Thereafter, Thespiae lay defenceless at the mercy of her enemies. Apparently the only hope for some of the despairing Thespians seemed to lie in adopting democracy and turning to Athens for help—a plan that must have been at best the last desperate hope of men who cannot have been unacquainted with the fate of Plataea. In 414 there was a democratic revolt in the city which was put down with aid from Thebes. Of the rebels, some were seized and some fled to Athens.[1] Thus the battle of Delium was a double victory for the Thebans. They inflicted on the Athenians a defeat in which they lost 1,000 men, not including light-armed troops and baggage carriers, while the Athenians, on the wing on which they were at first victorious, obligingly inflicted such heavy losses on the Thespians that they made it relatively easy for the Thebans to deal with these rivals.

The same year the actions of two other federal states affected the course of the war considerably, the Chalcidic Confederacy, which with the aid of troops sent by Sparta under the leadership of Brasidas proceeded to detach numerous cities from the Athenian Empire, and the Thessalian Confederacy, which contributed equally decisively to the outcome by permitting Brasidas to pass through its territory on his way to Thrace. Since the Thessalians were allies of Athens, this is so surprising that their action calls for a little special consideration. The decision to let him pass was due largely to the high-handed manipulation of the pro-Spartan faction which allowed him to pass in spite of the opposition of the more numerous pro-Athenian faction, but also certain peculiarities of Greek international law entered into the decision. Greek defensive alliances originally did not oblige a party to a treaty to do more than to defend an ally against invasion and direct attack. The distinction between an offensive and a defensive alliance is to be seen in the report of Thucydides on the treaty of 433 between Athens and Corcyra. The Athenians refused to negotiate an offensive alliance pledging them to have the same friends and enemies for fear that the Corcyraeans should involve them in war with Corinth and thus cause them to violate their treaty with the Peloponnesians (the Thirty Years Peace). Instead they entered into a defensive alliance (*epimachia*) by which the two parties promised to aid each other in case

[1] Thuc. vi. 95. 2.

of an attack either on the Corcyraeans or on the Athenians and their allies.[1] A defensive alliance did not at first involve even the duty of stopping a hostile force from crossing the territory of a state on the way to attack its ally, though, as the Brasidas incident shows, the exact rights and duties of belligerents and allies had by this time begun to be a matter of dispute.

Even before the expedition of Brasidas, it seems that some antagonism had been aroused in Thessaly by the Spartan occupation of Heraclea in Trachis. According to Thucydides the impetus for the colonization of Heraclea was an appeal from the Trachinians, who were looking for protection against the Oetaeans of the mountains overhanging their land. This may be true, though the Spartans clearly realized the value of the location. So did the Athenians, who feared that it might be used as a base for an attack on Euboea. However, in the long run, Heraclea was rendered relatively harmless by the repeated attacks of the Thessalians on the new settlers. This, of course, means that the Thessalian state of the time controlled the country practically up to Thermopylae. Thus its territory was still extensive, though there were signs of dissension and consequent weakness. Thucydides reports that one of the considerations that induced the Spartans to establish the colony was its strategic position on the route to Thrace. It would be interesting to know whether this is true or whether even in Thucydides this is merely a consideration suggested by later events. In any case, Heraclea was used by Brasidas as a base for his march across Thessaly to Macedonia and the Chalcidic region. It was from Heraclea that Brasidas sent a messenger not to the government of the Thessalian Confederacy but to pro-Spartan friends in the city of Pharsalus requesting them to escort him and his troops across Thessaly.[2] Their success in doing so made possible the later success of Brasidas in Chalcidice. It was a strange situation. The Thessalian Confederacy was allied to Athens, the hostility of the Thessalians had been aroused by the founding of Heraclea, and the majority of the Thessalians were friendly to the Athenians. Nevertheless the pro-Spartan plotters were successful, simply because they belonged to the oligarchic gang which more or less ran Thessaly at the time. They were aided by the fact that it had been customary for the Greeks to allow armed forces to cross neutral territory so that to refuse passage might seem a hostile act. This was the old usage. In the days of petty raids, armed forces must have crossed the territory of third states without much ceremony. Nor is it likely that smaller neighbours would interfere with the passage of

---

[1] Thuc. i. 44. 1; on this passage cf. *CP* xliv (1949), 260 in a review of Gomme's *Commentary*, i.

[2] Thuc. iii. 92–93; iv. 78.

Spartan hoplites or Thessalian cavalry. It was when both parties were relatively strong that protests began to be heard to the effect that armed forces should not cross the territory of a neutral state without securing permission in advance.

The crossing of Thessaly had been carefully planned by Brasidas and his local friends, and with good reason. As Thucydides remarks, it was not easy for an armed force to cross Thessaly without an escort, and there had been developing among the Greeks a feeling against crossing a neighbour's land without securing permission.[1] From Heraclea Brasidas had sent a messenger to the pro-Spartan leaders at Pharsalus. A number of them met him at Melitaea in Phthiotic Achaea, apparently a day's march from Heraclea. These led him on another day's forced march from there to Pharsalus. On the way they were met at the river Enipeus by a group of opponents, who objected that it was wrong to proceed without the assent of the federal assembly. To this the Thessalian escorts of Brasidas replied that they would not conduct him through the country against the will of the people. As guest friends (*proxenoi*) they were merely escorting Brasidas, who had turned up unexpectedly. Brasidas, for his part, stated that he came to the land of the Thessalians as a friend, that he was bearing arms not against them but against the Athenians, and that he knew of no hostility between the Thessalians and the Lacedaemonians to prevent them from crossing—literally, using—each other's land. Notice that this presupposes that neither the alliance of the Thessalians with Athens nor the actual help given the Athenians by Thessalian cavalry had resulted in a state of war between the Spartans and Thessalians. Brasidas assured the latter that he neither would nor could proceed contrary to their will, but that he did not consider it proper for them to refuse passage. After these exchanges the objectors withdrew, and Brasidas, on the advice of his friends, hurried on and passed through Thessalian territory with forced marches before the opponents could mobilize to oppose him.

It may be well to notice briefly the future of the question of the right of passage through Thessaly. The next year, Perdiccas of Macedon stirred up so much opposition in Thessaly that the Spartans abandoned the plan of sending re-enforcements through Thessaly. Behind this apparently was also Athenian diplomacy.[2] A year later (422) a force

---

[1] The account of the crossing is given in Thuc. iv. 78–79. On the crucial passage (78. 2) concerning the growing sentiment against crossing neutral territory without permission, see *CP* liii (1958), 124 f. The interpretation given there may not be acceptable to all. Even so it is perfectly clear that the claim was put forth on one side that an army which wished to cross had a right to do so and that any interference would be a hostile act.

[2] Thuc. iv. 132 mentions only the activity of Perdiccas except for the statement that Nicias, the Athenian general, had urged him to do something to show his friendship. In Aristophanes, *Wasps* 1265–74 there is a none too helpful reference to an Athenian going to Pharsalus as ambassador.

of 700 hoplites was sent to reinforce Brasidas, but the commander wasted time setting affairs at Heraclea in order. They did not advance into Thessaly before the beginning of the winter, and then turned back partly on account of the opposition of the Thessalians and partly because the news of the death of Brasidas at Amphipolis had reached them.[1] Such incidents could not settle the question of the right of passage through neutral territory. That may well be why it became customary to include in treaties of alliance a clause by which the contracting parties bound themselves to prevent armed forces from crossing the territory of one in order to attack that of the other. It may not be pure chance that such a clause was inserted in the treaty of 420 between Athens, Argos, Mantinea, and Elis.[2] Their experience with the Thessalians may well have made the Athenians aware that some such clause was desirable.

To return to the events of 424, the expedition of Brasidas was a typical Spartan expedition for distant operations, the force consisting of one Spartiate, Brasidas himself, 700 helots, and 1,000 mercenary troops, all hoplites. The mercenary troops undoubtedly were engaged in the Peloponnesus and probably consisted largely of Arcadians and Achaeans. These apparently were already beginning to be known as a source for the supply of mercenary soldiers.[3] Already in 432 the Corinthians had been able to engage mercenary soldiers in the Peloponnesus to be sent to Potidaea, and now the Spartans drew upon the same or similar supply. Apparently the troops sent were all hoplites, though they were sent to operate in a region strong in light-armed troops and cavalry. An account of the campaigns of Brasidas has already been given above in the sketch of the Chalcidic Confederacy and will not be repeated here. It will have to suffice to mention that the accounts preserved do not always give very satisfactory information about the troops engaged. However, for the battle of Amphipolis in 422, the battle in which both Brasidas and Cleon fell, Thucydides makes it clear that the final rout of the Athenians was due to the cavalry and peltasts of the Chalcidians and their neighbours, the Myrcinians.[4]

---

[1] Thuc. v. 12–13. The Spartans advanced as far as Pierium, an otherwise unknown place. We can do no better than follow Gomme in conjecturing that it was located in southern Thessaly or probably rather south of Thessaly proper.

[2] Thuc. v. 47. 5 (Tod, 72). For the right of passage δίοδος seems to have become a technical term; cf. Aristophanes, Birds 189; Thuc. v. 47. 5; Pol. iv. 5.7, 7. 4; OG 437. 67, 71 (with no comment on the word!). Corresponding to the noun was διιέναι 'to let pass', used in a number of treaties as in Thuc. v. 47. 5; Pol. xxi. 32. 3, 43. 2, which Livy xxxviii. 11. 2, 38. 2 translates transire sinito; cf. also IGR iv. 1028.

[3] Thuc. iv. 78. 1, 80. 5; in vii. 57. 9 it is implied that at the time of the Sicilian expedition it already was common for Arcadians to serve as mercenaries. Xen. Anab. vi. 2. 10 indicates that over half of the 'Ten Thousand' were Arcadians and Achaeans.

[4] Thuc. v. 10. 9–10.

In connexion with the Chalcidic operations neither Athens nor Sparta had done much to win the affection or confidence of the Chalcidians. It is hardly an exaggeration to say that the Athenians had goaded the Potidaeans into revolt, and that they, when later rebellions occurred in the region, were interested in little except suppressing and punishing the offenders. This is seen at its worst in the case of the massacre of all the adult males at Scione and the selling of the women and children into slavery.[1] The Spartans, on their side, seem to have been interested first and foremost in causing the Athenians as much trouble as possible with the least effort on their own part. Except for the aid given by Brasidas and his detachment, the Chalcidians and their neighbours did most of their own fighting. After the arrival of Brasidas, no Spartan reinforcements, except a few officers, came through Thessaly. Thus, why should the Chalcidians feel bound to comply with terms agreed upon by the Athenians and Spartans? Nevertheless, this is precisely what they seem to have done at first in connexion with the armistice of 423. The only dispute was that concerning the date of the revolt of the city of Scione on the peninsula of Pallene. In negotiating the treaty, both the Athenians and the Spartans must have had the Chalcidian question in mind, and yet the Chalcidians were not represented in the negotiations and were not mentioned in the treaty. The one clause that could be applied to them was the general proviso that the parties to the treaty should remain in possession of what they held when the treaty went into effect.[2] The Chalcidians could have argued that, though they in a sense were allies of the Spartans, they were not members of the Peloponnesian League and thus not bound by the treaty. The Athenians and the Spartans, on the other hand, assumed that the treaty was binding on all belligerents, and two commissioners, one from each of the two states, were sent to the Chalcidic peninsula to supervise the application of its terms. Their point of view was accepted by the Chalcidians, undoubtedly because it would leave them in possession for the time being of the cities that had come over to them the preceding year. In the case of Scione, it seemed to be enough to insist that it had rebelled before the armistice began. This was denied by the Athenians, who were also particularly aroused by the fact that a city practically situated on an island should revolt. This dispute led to the resumption of warfare. The Athenians prepared to send an expedition immediately and on the motion of Cleon voted to reduce Scione and put its inhabitants to death. On the disputed point, Thucydides remarks that the truth was on the side of the Athenians, for the revolt took place two days after the beginning of the armistice.

[1] Thuc. v. 32. 1. [2] Thuc. iv. 118. 4.

10

On such a point, Thucydides can be trusted, but, even if the Athenians were in the right on this particular point, this does not excuse their inhuman decree about Scione, and still less the cold-blooded way in which it was carried out a few years later.[1]

It appears to have been largely on account of their trust in Brasidas that the Scionians held out and that Mende soon after revolted, and Brasidas fully understood the seriousness of the situation. He had the women and children of the two cities removed to Olynthus and garrisoned them with 700 Peloponnesian and 300 Chalcidic troops. Thereupon he hied himself off with Perdiccas to western Macedonia, where he accomplished nothing except to extricate his troops from a difficult position and lose once more the friendship of Perdiccas. When he returned he found Mende captured and Scione besieged, decided that he was unable to help, and withdrew to Torone on the peninsula of Sithonia. These events cannot have enhanced the reputation either of Brasidas personally or of the Spartans in general, and it cannot have helped the situation any that the next spring they failed to prevent the recapture of Torone by the Athenians. True, the Chalcidians continued to co-operate with Brasidas at Amphipolis, but that must have been due largely to their common hatred of the Athenians. The battle of Amphipolis was, in fact, largely a Chalcidic victory, something completely disregarded in the peace negotiations and the treaty itself.

In the Peace of Nicias the Spartans and the Athenians disposed blithely of holdings both of the Chalcidic and Boeotian confederacies. The Boeotians at least were represented at the conference and were able to register a negative vote. The Chalcidians did not even have that dubious satisfaction. Instead, in their absence, the contracting parties disposed freely of Amphipolis and Chalcidic cities. Though this subject must not be taken up again here, one point may be mentioned. In a list of cities held by the Athenians which they were free to treat as they wished, Scione was included.[2] Yet, at the time, the city was not held by the Athenians but was being besieged by them. The clause, of course, meant that when the city was captured the Athenians were free to wreak their vengeance as cruelly as they wished. The fact that the Athenians insisted on the insertion of this clause in a peace treaty and that the Spartans acquiesced, shows the complete callousness of Greek states when the lives of citizens of other states were at stake. This is set off in even more lurid light by the fact that another clause provided that the Peloponnesian soldiers and others brought to Scione by Brasidas should be released. Scione actually was captured later in the

[1] Thuc. iv. 122; v. 32. 1.   [2] Thuc. v. 18. 8.

summer and the adult males executed while the women and children were sold into slavery—a blot on the record of Brasidas, Cleon, and all those who had negotiated the Peace of Nicias.[1] Hence it is no wonder that the Chalcidians considered themselves at war with Athens until at some time, probably in 417, a truce was arranged which could be cancelled by either party on ten days' notice. This truce was called off or broken in 414 when the Athenians and Perdiccas staged an unsuccessful attack on Amphipolis.[2]

The Peace of Nicias and the complicated plots that followed indicate the breakdown of the dualism which long had been the dominating concept in the foreign policy of Athens and Sparta, and which had found official expression in the Thirty Years Peace. The two states, of course, were aware of the existence of Argos, but Argos, most of the time as it were, sat on the sidelines and watched the contest between the other two. They were aware also that there were other states that did not belong to either of the two great symmachies, but none of these seemed a challenge to the leadership of Sparta and Athens and, if any of them became involved in difficulties or adopted an ambitious foreign policy, it sought to establish some sort of ties with one of the great powers, as Corcyra did with Athens and Boeotia with Sparta. But such states were not going to remain subservient for ever. The Boeotian Confederacy, as already noted, had shown signs of independence in its foreign policy. The same is true also of the Chalcidic Confederacy, while the tendency of Corinth, though a member of the Peloponnesian League, to go its own way and to attempt to lead others, was potentially fully as dangerous. In spite of all of this, Athens and Sparta tried to maintain the old dualism and acted on the supposition that all were bound by treaties negotiated by themselves. Since the Boeotian and Chalcidic confederacies had fought against Athens, the result was that Sparta made promises to Athens on their behalf. By any standard of international law except the self-centred outlook of Athens and Sparta, the two confederacies were completely justified in refusing to honour these commitments.

A detailed analysis of the Peace of Nicias does not belong here. It may be enough to note that the clauses causing most offence were the ones ordaining that 'the Lacedaemonians and their allies' were to surrender Panactum to the Athenians and again that they were to surrender Amphipolis. The former clause meant that Sparta and Athens were regulating the boundary between Attica and Boeotia without the consent of the Boeotians, who held Panactum at the time.

---

[1] Thuc. v. 32. 1.
[2] The evidence for this period is scant and some points, particularly that of the nature of the truce, are debated; cf. above, p. 73 and n. 1.

The latter clause, coupled with the detailed arrangements for the Thraceward regions, meant that all gains from the operations of Brasidas were to be surrendered. In fact, the references in the treaty to separate cities imply that the contracting parties did not even recognize the existence of the Chalcidic Confederacy. Except for the brutal treatment of Scione and the recognition of some sort of right of neutrality on the part of six cities, the treaty tried to restore conditions approximately as they were before the revolt of Potidaea. If the terms of the treaty had been enforced, it would have meant a decided victory for Athens, but they could not be enforced short of a united military action on the part of Sparta and Athens, and that was out of the question. Yet that was the general line which the statesmanship of the two great powers took, but they did not go farther than to try joint persuasion, not joint military intervention.

The first clear demonstration that the treaty was unworkable came from Amphipolis. Clearidas, the Spartan commander of the Peloponnesian—not Spartan—garrison of this city returned home stating that he was unable to use force against the Chalcidians, and this would be necessary if he were to surrender the city to the Athenians.[1] Thucydides, to be sure, implies that he assumed this attitude in order to please the Chalcidians. At Sparta he was told to return and either surrender the city or else withdraw the Peloponnesian garrison, and, naturally, the course he later adopted was to withdraw the garrison.[2]

As a consequence of these developments the Chalcidians continued to be in a state of war with Athens. Meanwhile the Boeotians and Athenians got along with a truce subject to cancellation by either party at any time on a ten days' notice,[3] and Corinth had suspended hostilities but had no treaty or agreement with Athens of any kind.[4] Thus, though members of the Peloponnesian League, the Corinthians refused to be bound by a treaty negotiated by that organization.

3. FROM THE PEACE OF NICIAS TO THE KING'S PEACE

The period of unstable peace beginning in 421 is so full of diplomatic intrigues that it is difficult not to lose sight of the main issues involved. Nevertheless it appears that the old struggle for supremacy in

---

[1] Thuc. v. 21. 2. The phrase βίᾳ ἐκείνων must mean that the Chalcidians would have resisted any attempt to surrender the city and that he was unable to use compulsion.

[2] Thuc. v. 34. 1.

[3] ἐκεχειρία δεχήμερος (Thuc. v. 26. 2) is usually taken to mean a truce renewed every ten days. However, a similar term is applied to the later truce between the Athenians and the Chalcidians, and in that case, as already noted (p. 73 and n. 1), a truce requiring renewal every ten days would be impossible. The phrase must mean the same in both cases, namely a truce subject to suspension on ten days' notice.

[4] Thuc. v. 32. 7, where the state of affairs is designated as an armistice without a treaty.

the west continues. This is seen in the grievances of the Corinthians against the Peace of Nicias. Those of the Boeotians and Chalcidians have already been discussed. They consisted largely in objections to clauses by which the Spartans promised to surrender to the Athenians places which were held or claimed by each of the two confederacies. In opposition to this, the grievance of the Corinthians was that the Athenians had not been made to restore to them Sollium and Anactorium, two of their old colonies on the coast of Acarnania.[1] Hence the western question remains prominent. From that point of view, the chief issue decided within the next few years was that of the status of Achaea. An effort was made to bring the Achaean Confederacy into the coalition opposing Sparta. This failed, and their victory at Mantinea enabled the Spartans to establish their control over the Achaeans.

The wording of the grievances of the Corinthians as given by Thucydides indicates that they were based on the acceptance of the old dualism in Greek interstate politics, but with this went also the demand that the leaders of the two groups champion the interests of their allies. The Corinthians objected to the treaty on the ground that the Athenians—not the Acarnanians—were not made to surrender the cities in question. Undoubtedly the Acarnanians, like the Chalcidians, had been without representation at the peace conference, but in their case no stipulations unfavourable to them had been included in the treaty. This was precisely the grievance of the Corinthians which caused them to take the lead in the formation of a coalition against Sparta. Their task seemed facilitated by the fact that the thirty years peace between Argos and Sparta had expired so that the Argives were free to act as the banner-bearers in the new organization. Feelings were further embittered by the action of the Spartans, who countered opposition to the treaty by contracting a defensive alliance with the Athenians.[2] Apparently the two old hostile powers preferred to co-operate with each other rather than to run the risk of having the leadership usurped by some upstart third state.

Circumstances offered Corinthian representatives an opportunity to act. It seems that the Peace of Nicias had been negotiated at Sparta, and that delegates from various states had remained there until the treaty of alliance with the Athenians had been negotiated. Thus, the delegates from Corinth on their way home were able to stop at Argos and urge the Argives to invite other states to join them in a defensive

[1] Thuc. v. 30. 2. There can be little doubt that this was their real grievance, though Thucydides indicates that it was not mentioned in their negotiations with the Spartans.

[2] Expiration of thirty years' peace: Thuc. v. 14. 4; alliance of Sparta and Athens: v. 22–24. Sparta seems to have taken the initiative in the negotiations in order to prevent a coalition of the Argives and the Athenians.

alliance. The Argives accepted the proposal and created a commission of twelve authorized to validate such treaties with any state except Athens and Sparta. A treaty with one of these two states would have to be submitted to the popular assembly. This sounds ideal—a purely defensive alliance consisting chiefly of Peloponnesian states. However, as it turned out, every state which joined had some special interest to protect, and this at times meant perpetuating abuses. The first city to join, Mantinea, was anxious to assure her own recent conquests. Elis was anxious to recover Lepreum, which the Spartans had declared free and had garrisoned. Other allies were the Corinthians and the Chalcidians, both of whom had grievances enough of their own. Meanwhile the Megarians and the Boeotians stood aloof.[1] Thus, instead of being merely an alliance for the mutual guarantee of peace and neutrality, it proved to be a combination of states with special interests seeking to maintain their advantages, while Athens, when it later joined through the influence of Alcibiades, was interested primarily in furthering her own power. None of these states could be trusted to support its allies unless it suited its own interests to do so. Nevertheless, the summer of 421 was devoted chiefly to diplomatic activities, including an effort by the Argives and Corinthians to bring over Tegea. When this effort failed, the Corinthians in turn lost their interest. Thus, in the Peloponnesus, Argos retained as allies only Elis and Mantinea. Meanwhile the Spartans invaded Parrhasia, the district recently subjected by the Mantineans, and laid it waste. The Mantinaeans entrusted the defence of their own city to their allies, the Argives, and themselves planned to defend Parrhasia but on second thought withdrew without fighting. Thereupon the Spartans declared the Parrhasians free, thus liberating the people whose land they had just been devastating. In this manner the Mantineans had already lost the conquests which they had been so anxious to protect, though it was only after the battle of Mantinea in 418 that they officially renounced their claim.[2]

The most important development of the year 420 was the negotiation of the treaty of alliance between Athens, Argos, Elis, and Mantinea which produced the coalition which was to oppose Sparta two years later at Mantinea. Strange to say, the complicated chain of negotiations which was to result in the alliance was set in motion by a pair of Spartan statesmen, namely, Cleobulus and Xenares, who were opposed to the Spartan treaty of alliance with the Athenians. They were members of a new group of ephors elected to office in the autumn of 421. The two are said to have approached ambassadors of the Corinthians and Boeotians who were then at Sparta with an elaborate scheme intended to bring about an understanding between Sparta and

[1] Thuc. v. 27–31.   [2] Thuc. v. 32–33, 81. 1.

Argos. Of these the Corinthians were chosen because they already were allies of Argos; the Boeotians, obviously because they were at odds with the Athenians and might be counted upon to join a large coalition opposed to Athens. On their way home, the Boeotians were approached, very opportunely from their point of view, by two Argive representatives, who urged the Boeotians to become the allies of Argos. When the ambassadors came home and reported to the Boeotarchs, the latter were pleased with the proposal. To be adopted, however, a treaty had to be approved also by the federal *boule*. This was where complications arose. The Boeotarchs, apparently were so used to having their proposals accepted by the *boule* that it never occurred to them that the latter body might reject a measure if the policy behind it was not explained. The Boeotarchs did not immediately suggest a treaty with Argos, but instead proposed alliances with the Corinthians, Megarians, and Chalcidians. The treaty with Argos was to follow. It was never even submitted to the council. When the other treaties were submitted, the members were so appalled at the idea of contracting an alliance with the Corinthians, who had broken with the Spartans, that they voted them down. After this rebuff the Boeotarchs dropped their entire plan.[1]

The intrigues of the year 420 cannot be followed in detail. When the Spartans asked the Boeotians to give up Panactum, the latter demanded in return a special treaty of alliance with the Spartans such as the one they had negotiated with the Athenians. When this was granted, the Boeotians demolished the fortifications at Panactum, with the result that all the Spartans could turn over to the Athenians was the empty site. Even though they did secure the release of Athenian prisoners still held by the Boeotians, this made for bad feeling and prepared the way for the alignment of Athens with the enemies of Sparta. Before this was arranged, the Argives, the original leaders of the anti-Spartan coalition, had themselves sought an alliance with the Spartans. From this they were diverted by the diplomacy of Athens under the leadership of Alcibiades. The result was the treaty of alliance of the Athenians with the Argives, Mantineans, and Eleans. In spite of this alliance with the enemies of the Spartans, the Athenians did not renounce their own alliance with Sparta.[2] The resulting situation was not as impossible as it tends to seem to modern observers. Since the two treaties of alliance were essentially defensive, it was possible to be pledged to defend both the Spartans and their opponents against aggression. The new feature of the treaty between Athens and the

[1] Thuc. v. 36–38. The bearing of this incident on the Boeotian constitution has been touched on above, p. 35, and discussed more fully *Rep. Govt.* 35 ff.

[2] Thuc. v. 39–48; Tod, 72.

Peloponnesian states was the clause pledging the parties to the treaty not to allow the passage of hostile forces by land or sea unless the right of passage had been voted by all four powers. When later the Spartans managed to send 300 soldiers by sea to Epidaurus, the Argives complained to the Athenians that they had failed to do their duty as stipulated in this clause.[1] Their allies clearly expected the Athenians to stop any hostile movements by sea. The alignment of Athens and Argos with Elis and Mantinea, two states breaking away from the Peloponnesian League, must have seemed an aggressive alliance to the Spartans, no matter how much the treaties took the form of defensive alliances.[2] Moreover, if, as Thucydides indicates, the Eleans, Argives, and Mantineans had transformed their triple alliance into an offensive alliance, pledging the three parties to have the same friends and enemies, and if this had been done before the treaty with Athens was negotiated,[3] Alcibiades obviously must not be given all the blame or credit for the hostilities that followed.

Of the few incidents reported by Thucydides for 419, the two to which he devotes least space are the most important for the history of federal states and probably also for that of Greece in general. These are the intervention of the Boeotians in Heraclea in Trachis and of the Athenians and their allies in Achaea. The action at Heraclea shows the Boeotians trying to take over from the Spartans the control of that strategic post. The Spartan commander at Heraclea, Xenares, who had been a leader of the party anxious to break with Athens, was killed in the winter 420–419 in hostilities against neighbouring tribes. The following spring the Boeotians ousted his successor on the grounds of incompetence and took charge themselves. They are said to have done so lest the Athenians should make use of the opportunity offered by the confused situation in the Peloponnesus to occupy the city,[4] but it seems safe to conclude that the Boeotians were acting in their own interest and were anything but disinterested supporters of the Spartans. It is hardly necessary for Thucydides to tell us that the Spartans were displeased with their action.

Probably even more important was the attempt of the Athenians

---

[1] Thuc. v. 56. 1–2. This is the earliest known use of such a clause in a treaty.

[2] On this point cf. the sane remarks of Glotz-Cohen, *Hist. grecque*, ii. 666.

[3] Thuc. v. 48. 2, where the treaty merely is referred to as already in existence. It is noted by Busolt. *GrG* iii. 1225. This passage must have been overlooked by Meyer, *GdA* iv. 478 when he wrote about the peaceful attitude of the two groups of powers, each united by purely defensive alliances.

[4] Thuc. v. 51–52. On the earlier activities of Xenares cf. v. 36–38, 46. 4. As ephor he had helped to hatch the plot to secure a treaty with Argos through the aid of the Boeotians, and in the negotiations of 420 had insisted that Sparta make no concessions to Athens. He must have gone to Heraclea when his term as ephor expired. His presence there testifies to the interest of the more aggressive Spartans in the city.

and their allies under the leadership of Alcibiades to secure the active co-operation of the Achaean Confederacy and with its aid establish control of both sides of the entrance to the Gulf of Corinth.[1] This is another incident of which Thucydides gives an aggravatingly brief report. It may be remembered that the Achaeans had been allies of the Athenians in the middle of the fifth century, and that this alliance had been terminated by the Thirty Years Peace, but this did not make the Achaeans members of the Peloponnesian League. In 419 Alcibiades brought a small force of Athenian hoplites and archers to the Peloponnesus, secured aid from the Argives and other allies, marched across the peninsula, and induced Patrae to extend its walls to the sea, while he himself prepared to build a fort at Rhium, on the Achaean side of the entrance to the Gulf of Corinth, a fort undoubtedly to be garrisoned by Athenian or other non-Achaean troops. The plans for Patrae, on the other hand, show that the project had Achaean support. From the Athenian point of view, it was a return to the policy of the fifties of hemming in Corinth and securing complete control of the entrance to the Gulf. Had this venture been successful, it would have gone far to break the power both of Sparta and of Corinth. As it turned out, it aroused immediate opposition. The Corinthians, Sicyonians and others who would have been adversely affected by the fortification of Rhium, intervened and prevented the completion of the fort. The intervening force probably accomplished its purpose without actual fighting. Nevertheless, the setback suffered by the allies was probably fully as important as the more spectacular setback in the battle of Mantinea the following summer. The Spartans clearly indicated their realization of the importance of the control of Achaea by their intervention in 417.

In the year of Mantinea, the best picture of the alignment of powers is not furnished by the operations immediately preceding the battle but by the earlier invasion of the Argolid which ended with negotiations and the withdrawal of the invaders. Here only the parts played by the Boeotians and Achaeans will be noted. Of the Achaeans, only the Pellenians are mentioned. Apparently the other Achaeans did not take part. This means that the Confederacy as a whole stood aloof and was not a member of the Peloponnesian League or a close ally of Sparta. The Boeotians, on the other hand, are said to have sent 5,000 hoplites, 5,000 light-armed troops, 500 horsemen, and 500 troops trained to work with the cavalry.[2] This contingent certainly did not include every Boeotian of military age but, for a force sent abroad, must have been near the maximum and so is something of a measure of the Boeotian

---

[1] Thuc. v. 52. 2. On Achaea at this time see 'The Early Achaean League', in *Studies Presented to Robinson*, ii (1953), 797–815.

[2] Pellenians; Thuc. v. 58. 4, 59. 3, 60. 3; numbers of Boeotian contingents: v. 57. 2.

interest in the campaign. That they cannot have been motivated chiefly by loyalty to Sparta, is shown by the intervention at Heraclea the preceding year. They must rather have been influenced by opposition to Athens, with which was now coupled opposition to Argos, the ally of Athens. This attitude seemed justified by what followed. The Argives had been granted a four months truce for negotiating. Instead, the allies of the Argives caused the hostilities to be renewed, and the responsibility for this seems to have rested chiefly with the Athenians and largely with Alcibiades personally. The allies now took the offensive and moved first against the Arcadian Orchomenus and, after its surrender, against Tegea.[1] Here the story will not be retold, of how Sparta came to the aid of Tegea, or how the allied effort was largely frustrated by dissension within their ranks, the Eleans withdrawing before the offensive against Tegea and the Athenians sending forces inadequate for so important an action. It is enough to recall that the battle was a complete victory for Sparta and restored its supremacy in the Peloponnesus, and that, though Athenians fought against Spartans and suffered casualties that were heavy for their small contingent, this did not lead to renewal of the war between Athens and Sparta.[2] The reason is probably simply that neither power desired to undertake major operations against the other. If this action, or lack of action, was rationalized, it may have been explained by the old practice of allowing a state to send troops to aid in defence of another state without thereby becoming involved in war with the aggressor. Since the battle was fought on Mantinean territory, it might be argued that the Athenians were trying to help defend Mantinea against the invading Spartans.

Actually the allies were aggressors, and, in spite of the failure at Mantinea, had posed quite a threat to Spartan supremacy in the Peloponnesus. Nor was the Spartan victory as decisive as it sometimes has been regarded. Argos had not been eliminated or brought over to the side of Sparta, and the alliance between the two old enemies negotiated soon after the battle proved shortlived. Probably even more important, the capture of Orchomenus posed a double threat to Spartan interests. The release of Arcadian hostages deposited there loosened the hold of Sparta on its Arcadian allies, while the Orchomenians in turn had to furnish hostages to their new allies, the Mantineans. The supremacy of Mantinea over Orchomenus, of course, came to an end when Mantinea soon after the battle was compelled to

---

[1] Thuc. v. 60–61.

[2] Thuc. v. 61. 1 reports the arrival of 1,000 Athenian hoplites and 300 horse under two generals; Thuc. v. 74.3 gives the losses of the Athenians together with the Aeginetans (apparently a part of the Athenian contingent) as 200 including both generals.

renounce its supremacy over other Arcadian communities.[1] From these few facts there emerges a lurid picture of conditions in the great eastern valley or plain of Arcadia before the defeat of Mantinea. In the centre Mantinea was trying to build a miniature empire of her own in opposition to Tegea on the south and Orchomenus, closely tied to Sparta, on the north—conditions that do not seem very propitious for the future formation of an Arcadian federal state. To return to the events of 418, from the Spartan point of view, the threat to the communications north to the Gulf of Corinth involved in the loss of Orchomenus was probably even more serious than the release of the Arcadian hostages.[2] If Sparta was to be more than a minor south Peloponnesian power, it was necessary to keep this line of communications open. That this was the sentiment of the Spartans themselves is shown by the actions which followed.

Already in the winter of 418–417, during the short period when Sparta and Argos were allies, the two states intervened at Sicyon and set up a government more narrowly oligarchic than the preceding government, and one very closely tied to Sparta. This is reported by Thucydides in one short sentence. In an even briefer statement he reports under the summer of 417 that the Lacedaemonians set right the affairs of Achaea.[3] This must mean the establishment of an oligarchic government friendly to Sparta and the inclusion of the Achaean Confederacy in the Peloponnesian League. This condition was to last to 367. Thus, with Mantinea humiliated, Orchomenus recovered, and close control established over Sicyon and Achaea, the Spartans had for the time being secured their northern communications including the control of the south side of the entrance to the Gulf of Corinth. On the opposite shore, Naupactus was still under Athenian control.[4] Since it is known from later events that the Achaean Confederacy was pledged to unquestioning obedience to Sparta in foreign affairs, it seems that the defenders of Greek freedom against the Athenians already in 417 began to transform their own allies into subject allies. Probably the Arcadian hostages should be considered evidence for an even earlier step in that direction. The best known single step was the treaty of 404 with the Athenians by which the latter were pledged to have the same friends and enemies as the Spartans and to follow their leadership on land and sea.[5]

---

[1] Arcadian hostages: Thuc. v. 61. 4–5. Orchomenus is not specifically mentioned in the report about the Mantinean renunciations in 81. 1.

[2] Thucydides has nothing on the subject except the statement in v. 63. 1 that the loss of [3]chomenus intensified greatly the anger of the Spartans against Agis.

[4] Thuc. v. 81. 2, 82. 1.

[5] Thuc. vii. 17. 4, 19. 5, 31. 4–5, 34. 1 refers to Athenian ships stationed at Naupactus. Or Xen. Hell. ii. 2. 20.

The developments just discussed prepared the way for the alignment of powers in the Corinthian War. The close ties established between Sparta and Achaea, may have contributed to the later antagonism of Corinth and Sparta. By the defeat of Athens in the closing years of the war, Sparta carried her supremacy across the Isthmus and Gulf of Corinth into central Greece. In the years that followed, it was to try to extend its control even farther. In these efforts Sparta made use of two federal states, the Achaean and Phocian confederacies, and apparently helped to strengthen the first of the two. In 389 the Achaean Confederacy was in control of Calydon and, apparently, Naupactus north of the Gulf of Corinth and appears to have exercised this control for some time.[1] At the same time, the Spartans were also endeavouring to extend their influence north beyond Thermopylae. The Boeotians had made use of the confusion of 419 to seize Heraclea and had thereby antagonized the Spartans.[2] The latter naturally made use of their first opportunity to re-establish their control of Heraclea and even to extend their influence farther. In the autumn of 413, Agis led an expedition from Decelea to the Malian Gulf. In addition to planting a garrison at Heraclea, he established control over Echinus in Malis to the north of the gulf and exacted hostages and money contributions from the Malians and Phthiotic Achaeans. This was done against the protests of the Thessalians, who considered these tribes their subjects.[3] In this way the Spartans for the time being extended their control up to the border of the Thessalian Confederacy. Thus did the more aggressive Spartan leaders give an indication of the extent of their designs. In this case their control did not long go unchallenged. A few years later the Oetaeans rose against the Heracleotes and, when also the Phthiotic Achaeans joined the movement, defeated them with a loss of 700 including the Spartan harmost.[4] For the time being the Spartan control was ended but it was soon restored. In 399, on the occasion of a stasis, the Spartans sent a certain Herippidas to set things right. It was probably at this time that a Spartan garrison was planted also at

[1] The exact time of the acquisition of these cities cannot be determined. If it is correct that the Spartans, when they expelled the Messenians from Naupactus at the end of the Peloponnesian War, turned the city over to the Locrians (Diod. xiv. 34. 2), then the acquisition must have come some time later, probably during the Corinthian War.

[2] Thuc. v. 52. 1; cf. p. 152 above.

[3] Thuc. viii. 3. 1, in his brief report, mentions neither Heraclea nor Echinus by name, but the regarrisoning of Heraclea can almost be taken for granted and is confirmed by later events. Spartan control of Echinus and Malis as a whole is implied in Aristophanes, *Lysistrata* 1168–70, performed early in 411. This expedition, so important as an indication of the Spartan policy, seems to be overlooked in most histories but is noted briefly in Busolt, *GrG* iii. 1415 and Meyer, *GdA* iv. 551.

[4] Xen. *Hell.* i. 2. 18 speaks of the Achaeans as betraying the Heracleotes in such a way as to suggest that they changed sides on the field of battle.

Pharsalus in Thessaly. At any rate, this was done before 395.[1] The primacy of Sparta in this part of Greece was inevitably challenged by the Boeotians. In the contest which followed the Spartans were greatly aided by the Phocian Confederacy and by dissension within the Boeotian Confederacy. They were aided also by Lycophron of Pherae, who apparently had tried to become *tagos* of Thessaly but had not succeeded in winning general acceptance. In 404 he had inflicted a bloody defeat on the Larisaeans, but in 395, when the Corinthian War began, Larisa under a certain Medius was at war with the tyrant of Pherae.[2]

In the face of Spartan policies, some such war as the Corinthian War was bound to come. At the time it certainly was not desired by the Spartans, who just then were involved in war against Persia. It is probably correct that Persian gold exerted some influence in bringing on the war at the precise moment by strengthening the hands of the various anti-Spartan leaders.[3] Yet, even without this stimulant, the war would have come sooner or later. Previous events had made it clear that the Boeotians would seize any good opportunity to challenge the Spartan supremacy, and almost equally clear that the Corinthians, Argives, and Athenians would support the effort. The Corinthians were antagonized by the Spartan efforts to control the Gulf of Corinth, the Argives were always ready to better themselves, and the Athenians would seize any opportunity to regain a little of their former power. Thus would old enemies be united in common opposition to Sparta. So, to recall some well known incidents, it is not surprising that the Boeotians and Corinthians who in 404 had desired the destruction of Athens in 403 refused to follow Pausanias into Attica. Earlier Thebes had given refuge to the Athenian democratic exiles under the Thirty, not because they were pro-Athenian but for other reasons, that is, on account of their opposition to the Spartan supported Thirty Tyrants, the author of the *Hellenica Oxyrhynchia* informs us.[4] A few years later the Corinthians and Boeotians failed to support Agis of Sparta in an expedition against Elis in which other allies of Sparta, including even the Athenians, took part. Finally, there was the insult to Agesilaus in 396, when the Boeotarchs sent a detachment of cavalry and prevented

[1] The intervention of Herippidas: Diod. xiv. 38. 4–5; Spartan garrison at Pharsalus in 395: Diod. xiv. 82. 6; cf. Sordi, *La lega tessala*, 150 f.; Herippidas is mentioned several times in the *Hellenica* in connexion with the operations of Agesilaus.

[2] Xen. *Hell.* ii. 3. 4; Diod. xiv. 82. 5.

[3] Xen. *Hell.* iii. 5. 1; Paus. iii. 9. 8; briefer references in some of Plutarch's lives; cf. Beloch, *GrG*² iii. i. 67, n. 1. While other sources tend to emphasize the Persian gold, *Hell. Ox.* 7 (2) minimizes its influence in comparison with pre-existing rifts but in 18 (13) states that the anti-Spartan leaders in Boeotia were confident that the King would supply money.

[4] Xen. *Hell.* ii. 2. 19, 4. 30. *Hell. Ox.* 17 (12). 1 states that the leaders of the anti-Spartan faction were accused of Atticism on account of the hospitality extended to these exiles but that they were not really pro-Athenian. The further explanation of their action is lost in a lacuna.

him from completing the sacrifice which, in imitation of Agamemnon, he was performing at Aulis before sailing for Asia.[1] When to this is added the fact that Sparta, in spite of such signs of discontent, and in spite of being involved in war in Asia Minor, was nevertheless attempting as late as 395 to act as arbiter between all her allies, outside as well as inside the Peloponnesian League, it is easy to accept the report of contemporary ancient sources that the anti-Spartan leaders at Thebes purposely brought on the war. On other details they disagree, but the main line of events can be reconstructed with fair certainty.

The war grew out of disputes about pasture lands. Both the Phocians and West Locrians had been pasturing flocks on Parnassus, where there apparently was a sort of no man's land or common pasture between the two states. It seems that they not infrequently had carried off each other's flocks but had normally reached a peaceful settlement. This time, when the Phocians raided the Locrians, the latter counter-raided, whereupon the Phocians invaded Locris. Apparently the earlier actions had been confined to carrying off flocks from the disputed pasturage. Now, with their country invaded, the Locrians appealed to the Boeotians, and the Boeotians promptly decided to help.[2] Thereupon the Phocians sent ambassadors to the Spartans to request them to forbid the Boeotians to attack Phocis. The Spartans responded by sending ambassadors to the Boeotians to instruct them not to make war upon the Phocians, but if they had any grievance, to seek justice in some sort of meeting of the allies.[3] Though the report thus implies that also Sparta's allies were to have a hand in the settlement, it, nevertheless, seems that this was the kind of arbitration or trial in which a stronger power wished to supervise its dependents. As it turned out, the Boeotians disregarded the Spartan request and invaded Phocis, plundered the land of the cities near the border as far as

---

[1] Xen. *Hell.* iii. 2. 25, 4. 3–4.

[2] The two chief accounts of these events are *Hell. Ox.* 18 (13) and Xen. *Hell.* iii. 5. 3–5; cf. also Paus. iii. 9. 9–10. The account given above relies chiefly on *Hell. Ox.*, which clearly gives the best account. Xenophon was in Asia at the time of these events (Plut. *Ages.* 18) and may not have had the most accurate sources of information. Xenophon gives the Locrians involved as the Opuntian or eastern Locrians, but the entire history of the region makes a quarrel with the western Locrians more likely, and the reference to the pastures on Parnassus practically settles the question. Also Pausanias, who mentions Amphissa, points to the western Locrians. Both our chief sources place the responsibility for the outbreak of the general war on the anti-Spartan leaders at Thebes. *Hell. Ox.* 18 (13). 2 states that they induced some of the Phocians to invade Locris; Xenophon, that they stirred up the Locrians. It is doubtful whether these two peoples needed the suggested stimulus, but there can be no doubt about the readiness of the Boeotians to go to war.

[3] This attempt of the Spartans to settle the affair without fighting is reported only in *Hell. Ox.* 18(13). 4, while Xen. *Hell.* iii. 5.5 represents the Spartans as glad for an excuse to march against the Thebans. On this point he was probably led astray by the later hostility between the two cities. As indicated above, the situation was such that it is unlikely that Sparta desired a war in Greece, and the version of *Hell. Ox.* should unhesitatingly be accepted.

to Elatea, and made some attempts on the towns themselves. After that they withdrew. No major battle was fought, the Phocians obviously postponing such action until help should arrive. Meanwhile, in preparation for the war that they knew was coming, the Boeotians secured an alliance with Athens. When the Spartans marched and summoned their allies, the Corinthians refused to follow, and before the year was over also the Argives joined the coalition.[1] The preserved fragments of the alliance between the Boeotians and the Athenians show that it was a defensive alliance. Since the Spartans in 395 invaded Boeotia, this naturally obliged the Athenians to come to the aid of their allies. Treaties of this kind involved no legalistic decision about who was responsible for the outbreak of the war but simply stipulated, as in this case, that 'if anyone goes against the Boeotians in war, by land or by sea', the Athenians were obliged to answer their summons to aid, and *vice versa*.

When it was clear to the Spartans that war was inevitable unless they were to allow the Boeotians to bully the Phocians and thus allow their own control of central and northern Greece to collapse, they planned a bold and apparently devastating pincer movement against the Boeotians. Lysander was to advance into Boeotia from the west; King Pausanias, from the south. The former was to draw on Sparta's allies west and north of Phocis; the latter, on the Peloponnesian allies. Lysander obviously crossed to Phocis by sea and was able to assemble troops not only from Phocis but also from more northerly allies. His advance was facilitated by the fact that Orchomenus came over without resisting. Undoubtedly this city resented the manner in which Thebes had managed to readjust representation within the Boeotian Confederacy in its own favour and had assumed almost complete control of that organization, as witnessed by the treatment of Thespiae. The defection of Orchomenus meant that the northwest part of Boeotia lay open to the invader. It also meant that the Orchomenians joined Lysander in his further advance and thus were ready to fight against their former fellow-citizens of the Confederacy. It is no wonder that the little town of Lebadea, though it resisted, fell easily and was plundered. Nor does Coronea, which came next, appear to have caused any trouble. After that Lysander moved against Haliartus, but first he sent a letter to Pausanias, now at Plataea, to meet him at Haliartus. This letter was intercepted by Theban scouts. This enabled the Boeotians to rush troops to the city before the arrival of Lysander. The latter,

---

[1] Alliance between the Boeotians and Athenians: Xen. *Hell*. iii. 5. 7–16; failure of the Corinthians to follow the Spartans: ibid. 17; for Argos see the account of the year's campaign; a fragment of the treaty between the Boeotians and Athenians made 'for all time', Tod. 101.

arriving ahead of Pausanias, advanced carelessly, was caught between the soldiers within the city and those without, and so was defeated and killed. The casualties were heavy on both sides. The rest of the story need not detain us. It is well known that, when Pausanias did arrive, he was soon followed by the Athenians. Thereupon he negotiated a truce allowing him to remove the bodies of the fallen and withdrew. Thus the first round had gone to the opponents of Sparta. Nevertheless the Spartans did retain one of their gains. They retained a footing in Orchomenus, where they placed a division of Lacedaemonian troops —a clear proof that they were serious about retaining a foot-hold in this part of Greece. The troops had probably been stationed there by Lysander before his advance on Lebadea and Haliartus. There was hardly an opportunity to make such arrangements after the batttle, and the troops were in Orchomenus at the beginning of next season's campaigning.[1]

The three states already mentioned as opponents of Sparta, namely, Boeotia, Athens, and Corinth, were joined by Argos in organizing for the conduct of the war an alliance with a *synedrion* sitting at Corinth. Invitations were then sent to other states, and the organization was joined by the Acarnanian, Chalcidian, Euboean, and Locrian confederacies, and the cities of Leucas and Ambracia. Other states may have been added later. Apparently the league so formed was a temporary symmachy for the conduct of the war rather than a permanent organization. It appears that its assembly either was permanently gathered at Corinth or could be summoned on short notice. It seems to have directed the campaign of 394 and is last heard of in 393, when Pharnabazus and Conon appeared before it and delivered Persian subsidies to the allies.[2]

An appeal from Medius of Larisa in Thessaly for aid against

---

[1] The account of Xen. *Hell.* iii. 5. 6–7 and 17–25 needs to be supplemented by Plut. *Lys.* 28–29. Often on matters concerning Boeotia Plutarch seems to have had access to good material not used by others. Diod. xiv. 81 adds nothing of value. To take up some details, Xen. *Hell.* iii. 5. 6 states that the day for the rendezvous of the two forces at Haliartus had been fixed in advance. That is not likely and would be impossible unless the Spartans were assured of the defection of Orchomenus. It looks more as if it was the defection of Orchomenus which made it possible to fix on Haliartus and to arrange some sort of schedule. Plutarch specifically places the message of Lysander to Pausanias on the subject after the fall of Lebadea. Concerning the casualties, Xenophon mentions only those of the Thebans, which he gives as over 200; Plutarch gives 300 for the Thebans, 1,000 for their opponents. Xenophon also relates that Lysander tried to induce the Haliartians to secede from Boeotia and implies that they would have been willing to do so if it had not been for Thebans who were present and prevented it. If this is correct, dissatisfaction with the leadership of Thebes was not confined to Orchomenus and Thespiae.

[2] The only account of the formation of the symmachy is that of Diod. xiv. 82. 1–3. To the list of members given there, the Locrians, whose membership could almost be taken for granted, are added on the basis of the reference to their contingents in the campaign in the Peloponnesus in 394 (Xen. *Hell.* iv. 2. 17). The appearance of Pharnabazus and Conon before the synedrion is reported in Diod. xiv. 84. 5; Xen. *Hell.* iv. 8. 8 and cf. 10.

Lycophron of Pherae came to this assembly probably already in 395. In response a force of 2,000 was despatched. Judging by what followed, the force contained some Argives but otherwise consisted largely of Boeotians. Since both the Phocians and Orchomenians sided with Sparta, this expeditionary force most likely took the coast road from Boeotia through East Locris. Though not large, it was sufficient to enable Medius to capture Pharsalus. Thereupon the Boeotian and Argive troops captured Heraclea, which was turned over to the native Trachinians but garrisoned by the Argives. Meanwhile the Theban commander, Ismenias, proceeded to raise troops from tribes farther afield and to plan an invasion of Phocis. This must have involved an effort to enter Phocis by the pass of Hyampolis. The Phocians, however, met the attackers at Naryx on Locrian soil. The Boeotians are reported to have been victorious but withdrew and did not enter Phocis.[1]

To take stock of the first year's campaigning, it had been a failure for the Spartans but not disastrously so, though they had lost one of their greatest commanders and all control beyond Thermopylae. The losses included two cities which they had garrisoned, Heraclea and Pharsalus. This was counterbalanced by the defection of Orchomenus from Boeotia. For the Boeotians, on the other hand, the year at first glance seems highly successful. After gaining their first allies, their defeat of the Spartans had enabled them to gain more allies. These had established an organization for co-operation in the conduct of the war and had secured additional allies, largely federal states. The new organization had begun operations with a successful campaign, which had detached from the Spartan alliance all holdings north of Thermopylae. Against this must be placed the secession of Orchomenus and the failure of the attack on Phocis. As long as the Spartans could count on Orchomenus and Phocis, they had a strong foothold in central Greece enabling them to invade Boeotia from the west. Yet the allies had met with sufficient success to encourage them to aim a blow directly at Sparta. This occurred in the campaign which culminated in the battle variously known as the battle of Corinth or the battle of Nemea, but, probably better, of the Nemean river.

The remarkable feature of the league of the Corinthian War is that it at first worked well and was able to get the co-operation of even

---

[1] The only account of these events is Diod. xiv. 82. 5–10. Since neither Lysander nor Agesilaus was directly involved, it is not surprising that Xenophon passes them over completely, and even less so that they are not mentioned in Plutarch's lives of these two leaders. Naryx, the site of the battle, is placed by Oldfather (*RE* xvi. 1774) in the Boagrios valley, that is, on the short cut from Thronium to Elatea. This must be wrong. The account in Diod. xvi. 38. 2–3 of fighting around Naryx in 352 shows that it was near Abae, which means that it was near Hyampolis. The chronology in Diodorus is confused, but these events seem to belong late in 395 rather than early in 394.

rather distant states in the bold plan of marching against the Spartans and catching them isolated near their home before they were able to march out and add their allies to their army. Twenty-four years earlier an attempt had been made to break Sparta's power through revolts in the Peloponnesus, and twenty-four years later Epaminondas was to invade Laconia, but on those occasions, much of the peninsula was already in revolt. Now an attack was planned at a time when Sparta had brought the entire Peloponnesus, except Corinth and Argos, under control. For this purpose there was mobilized an army which probably was the largest Greek army to march against a Greek state up to this time. There were hoplites from Athens, Argos, Boeotia, Corinth, and Euboea and light-armed troops from as far away as Acarnania. The allied army probably numbered well over 20,000, and the Spartans apparently managed to mobilize an army of about the same size. Though the armies may have been about equal in the number of hoplites, the Boeotians and their allies were superior in light-armed troops and cavalry but these do not seem to have been effectively used in the battle, which is described as essentially a hoplite battle. Probably the allies lacked a strong central command to co-ordinate properly the efforts of the various contingents. The most serious failure of the allies, however, was the failure to move fast enough to catch the Spartans before they had gathered their allies. This failure was probably inevitable, for the elaborate plans of the allies could hardly have been kept secret. In any case, the Corinthians and their allies had got no farther than Nemea, approximately half way between Corinth and Argos, when the Spartans and their allies appeared at Sicyon. This made it necessary for their opponents to descend the valley of the Nemean river. The Spartan army, when on rough ground, suffered some losses at the hands of the light-armed troops of its enemies, but, when both armies descended into the plain, no more is heard of the light-armed troops. In the battle that ensued, the right wing of both armies bore to the right and outflanked the left wings of their opponents. In this way the Spartans on their own right defeated the Athenians, while on the other wing the allies of the Spartans were defeated by the Boeotians and their allies. The losses on the Spartan side are said to have been about 1,100; those of their opponents, about 2,800. The result of the battle was that the members of the coalition made no further attempt to march on Sparta. On the other hand, they were not defeated so decisively that they gave up the struggle.[1]

---

[1] The fullest account of the campaign is that of Xen. *Hell.* iv. 2. 9–23. The numbers of those fallen are from the shorter account of Diod. xiv. 83. 1–2. Xen. *Ages.* 7. 5 gives the Lacedaemonian losses as only eight (so also *Hell.* iv. 3. 1) and those of the enemy as almost 10,000. For monuments of Athenian cavalrymen fallen in the battle see Tod, 104 and 105.

Later in the summer came a battle equally important though not on as large a scale. King Agesilaus of Sparta, obedient to instructions from home, was returning from Asia approximately by the route once taken by Xerxes. His admirer, Xenophon, was with him and thus was an eye witness to the events. When Agesilaus entered Thessaly, he began to lay waste the land as hostile territory. Xenophon lists Larisa, Crannon, Scotussa, and Pharsalus as allies of the Boeotians. The Thessalians harried the forces of Agesilaus during the crossing of their country, but he seems to have got through without much difficulty. Then, after crossing the last mountain chain in Phthiotic Achaea, Agesilaus, according to Xenophon, proceeded through friendly territory to the frontier of Boeotia.[1] Here it might have been more correct to have said to the frontier between the territory of Orchomenus and the rest of Boeotia.

The unimpeded advance from the boundary of Phthiotic Achaea was, of course, due to the loyalty of Phocis and Orchomenus. The East Locrians may not have been friendly but were too weak to interfere. The loyalty of Orchomenus was in part inspired by the presence of a Spartan garrison, and also Phocis may have been supervised by Spartan officers. The support of Orchomenus most likely brought with it the support of the smaller towns in western Boeotia, notably Chaeronea, so that the most advanced community supporting Thebes was Coronea. Before the battle, Agesilaus was reinforced by the contingents of Phocis and Orchomenus, half of the Spartan division stationed at Orchomenus, and one division which was brought over 'from Corinth'. This, incidentally, suggests that the two hostile armies which had fought at the Nemean river, or parts of them, were still facing each other near Corinth. Though most of the states which had had contingents in the earlier battle, are said to have been represented also at Coronea, the sizes of the contingents are not known. In the course of the battle the right wing of the army of Agesilaus swept everything before it, while on his left wing the Orchomenians were defeated by the Thebans. Since the Thebans had advanced westward, while the rest of the army had retreated in the opposite direction to Mount Helicon, the Spartans now stood between the Thebans and their allies. Thereupon the Thebans proceeded to cut their way successfully through the opposing army. Xenophon, of course, emphasizes the losses of the Thebans, but does not conceal the fact that Agesilaus himself had been in great danger and was severely wounded. The Boeotian Plutarch, on the other hand, tells how proud the Thebans were of the fact that they

[1] The above account is based chiefly on Xen. *Hell.* iv. 3. 3–9. According to Plut. *Ages.* 16 Agesilaus reached some sort of agreement with the Larisaeans, and this agreement may explain their inactivity.

were undefeated. However, since the Thebans removed their dead under a truce, Agesilaus could claim a technical victory. A real victory it was not. The army of the coalition was not destroyed, and Agesilaus had not opened a way for himself through Boeotia. He himself went to Delphi to deliver a tithe of his booty from Asia, while his army withdrew into Phocis under the command of a Spartan officer, Gylis. The latter met his death raiding western Locris. Thereafter Agesilaus dismissed his troops and 'sailed home', that is, crossed the Gulf of Corinth.[1]

While the campaign on land thus was inconclusive, a decisive victory was won at sea in the battle of Cnidus, which definitely decided the war as far as Sparta and Persia were concerned. In its ultimate effects this may seem an Athenian victory, since Conon and Pharnabazus came to Greece the following year with Persian subsidies for the allies, and Conon was allowed to go to Athens and spend Persian money on the rebuilding of the long walls between Athens and Piraeus.[2] The answer to this is the King's Peace. This is enough to indicate that after Cnidus it was just a question of which Greek state should win the Persian ear, and, strange as it may seem, it was Sparta, the real loser in the war, that finally won the diplomatic war and appeared supreme in Greece. After Cnidus, however, the Spartan power in Asia collapsed completely, as Pharnabazus and Conon expelled Spartan harmosts from various cities and informed these cities that they were to be free from garrisons and autonomous. This liberation seems to have been greeted with enthusiasm, as is shown by monuments and honours bestowed on Conon—proof, if not of trust in Persia, at least of the depth of hatred of Sparta.[3]

The one sphere in which Sparta was successful in the Corinthian War was in maintaining control of the Gulf of Corinth and communications across it to her allies to the north, where she retained ties with Phocis and Orchomenus. The latter city remained garrisoned by the Spartans down to the King's Peace,[4] while Phocis apparently still was an ally at the time of the expedition of Cleombrotus in 371 which preceded the battle of Leuctra. When it is remembered that it was these

[1] Xen. *Hell.* iv. 3. 15–4. 1; Plut. *Ages.* 18 f.; Diod. xiv. 84. 1–2. Xenophon does not tell which Locrians were raided by Gylis, but the movements of the army after the battle make it clear that it must have been the western Locrians.

[2] The chief accounts of the battle, Xen. *Hell.* iv. 3. 11–12 and Diod. xiv. 83. 4–7, are far from satisfactory. For the other sources see Beloch, *GrG*² iii. i. 76, n. 1. The decisiveness of the battle is emphasized by Meyer, *GdA* v. 239. For Pharnabazus and Conon in Greece in 393 see Diod. xiv. 85. 2–3; Nepos, *Conon* 4. 5. Cf. also A. T. Olmstead, *History of the Persian Empire* (1948), 387 f.

[3] Xen. *Hell.* iv. 8. 1–3; Diod. xiv. 84. 3–4. Honours and monuments to Conon: Paus. vi. 3. 16; Tod, 106 (decree of Erythrae). On the unpopularity of the Spartans and the liberation of the Greeks in Asia, see Cary, *CAH* vi. 43 f.; Glotz-Cohen, *Hist. grecque*, iii. 86.

[4] Xen. *Hell.* v. 1. 29 gives as one reason for Sparta's desire for peace the burden of maintaining one *mora* in Orchomenus and one in Lechaeum.

ties which enabled Lysander in 395 to invade Boeotia from the west and Agesilaus in 394 to continue on to Sparta though he could not force his way through Boeotia, it is not surprising that the enemies of Sparta made a very special effort to break this control and that Sparta fought back with dogged determination. The operations were on a relatively small scale, and they are so briefly and unsatisfactorily reported by Xenophon that they have commonly been overlooked.[1] After Pharnabazus and Conon had brought Persian subsidies to the allies, the Corinthians made use of these to equip a fleet with which, operating out of Lechaeum, they established temporary control of the Gulf as far as to the Achaean port of Rhium, which they apparently occupied and used as a naval station. The Spartans in the long run successfully met the challenge but only after a good deal of fighting. The commander of the first Spartan fleet to intervene was killed in action and the officer next in command wounded. No further details are known except that the second Corinthian commander withdrew from Rhium, and that the Spartans then took over the port and in their turn used it as a naval station. Thus the Spartan-Achaean control of the entrance to the Gulf of Corinth was restored. Apparently the restoration of the Corinthian 'thalassocracy' in the Gulf belongs in 393 and the withdrawal of the Corinthians from Rhium in 392. From that time on it appears that the Spartans maintained a fleet of twelve ships in the Gulf.[2]

The outcome of the naval war for the control of the Gulf, in all likelihood, was decided on land. It is strange that Xenophon, who reports the death of a Spartan commander in the fighting over Rhium, reports the later withdrawal of the Corinthians from Rhium without mentioning any Spartan naval victory, and it is difficult to believe that he would have failed to report such a victory had it occurred, especially since the last Spartan commander he mentions is Teleutias, the brother of Agesilaus. Hence it is likely that the withdrawal from Rhium was caused by the capture of Lechaeum by the Spartans.[3] The loss of

---

[1] The report of the naval warfare in the Gulf of Corinth is given in Xen. *Hell.* iv. 8. 10–11. The events reported there apparently belong to the years 393 and 392. In iv. 7 Xenophon has carried the story of the campaigns on land down through 388, then in iv. 8. 1 he shifts to naval operations after the battle of Cnidos of 394. Needless to say, this procedure is confusing. There is an obvious connexion between the naval operations and the contests for the control of Lechaeum, the harbour town of Corinth on the Gulf, but, since the latter are land operations, they are described before the naval operations are mentioned. For discussions of the chronology see particularly Grote, *History*, ix (1852), 455, n. 2 on pp. 455–7 and J. Beloch, *Die attische Politik seit Perikles* (1884), 346–59.

[2] In 390, when the Spartan fleet in the Aegean was in difficulties, the admiral Teleutias was ordered to bring to its aid 'the twelve ships which he had in the gulf off Achaea and Lechaeum' (Xen. *Hell.* iv. 8. 23).

[3] That the withdrawal of the Corinthians from Rhium was due to the capture of Lechaeum has been suggested by Beloch, *GrG*² iii. ii. 220.

Lechaeum probably also explains the failure of the Corinthians and their allies to challenge the Spartan control of the Gulf during the rest of the war. Probably it would be more correct to say that the first step was to try to recover Lechaeum and that, when this attempt failed, any naval operations were out of the question. At any rate, a few years later, any challenge to Spartan communications across the Gulf came not from Corinth but from an Athenian squadron stationed at Oeniadae at the southern extremity of Acarnania.[1]

The opportunity to capture Lechaeum came to the Spartans as the result of an act which, depending on the point of view, was either treason or extreme party politics. After the war party had massacred or driven into exile many of those who favoured peace with Sparta, two of the remaining pro-Spartans communicated with the Spartan commander stationed at Sicyon and arranged to admit him and his troops in between the long walls connecting Corinth and Lechaeum. At this time Sicyon was the headquarters of the Spartan front; Corinth, Lechaeum, and the long walls, of the allies. Apparently it had been an inactive front for some time. There was one Spartan *mora*[2] stationed at Sicyon at this time, under the command of a Spartan polemarch, Praxitas. This *mora* was about to be withdrawn when its commander was approached by two Corinthian acquaintances who offered to admit him and his men into the corridor between the walls. When they had been admitted, they proceeded to fortify themselves, and were left unmolested for one day, while Argive troops were being brought to Corinth, for this happened at the time the two cities were merged. The next day, when they were attacked by the Corinthians, Argives and mercenary troops under the command of the Athenian Iphicrates, the Spartans and Corinthian exiles operating with them, carried the day, inflicted heavy losses on the enemy, and captured Lechaeum, which was being defended by a Boeotian garrison. Thereupon Praxitas demolished enough of the long walls to leave a clear passage for troops to pass, and then proceeded to the frontier towards Megara and captured two forts, Sidus and Cromyon located on the shore of the Saronic Gulf in Corinthian territory, and garrisoned them. After completing these operations he dismissed his troops and himself returned to Sparta.[3]

[1] After the expedition of Agesilaus to Acarnania in 389 this squadron kept him from crossing at Calydon.

[2] According to Xen. *Lac. pol.* 11. 4 there were six *morai* of hoplites and apparently the same number of units of cavalry. The *mora* defeated by Iphicrates is said to have contained about 600 hoplites; the number for the cavalry is not given (*Hell.* iv. 5. 12). It probably is safe to accept these statistics for this period, though the size and composition of the Spartan army at various times continues to be debated. For a convenient survey, see Busolt, *Staatskunde*, 704–12; cf. also H. Michell, *Sparta* (1952), 234–74.

[3] The account of these events depends almost entirely on Xen. *Hell.* iv. 4. 1–13. The capture of Lechaeum is reported also in the contemporary speech of Andocides, *On the Peace* 18.

Thus the year's campaigning ended with the Spartans in control of the Gulf of Corinth and forts on the frontier of Megarid. This situation called for vigorous counteraction by the enemy, and this came the following year.

The campaigning of the year began with raids by Iphicrates and his peltasts from Corinth against Phlius and into Arcadia, and counter raids all around Corinth by a Spartan *mora* stationed at Lechaeum and Corinthian exiles. A later development was that the Athenians came in full force, recaptured Lechaeum, and rebuilt the long walls. The recapture of Lechaeum, which involved the dislodging of a Spartan *mora*, must have been a victory of some importance, but it is not even mentioned by Xenophon but can be deduced from the facts that Lechaeum earlier in the year had been in Spartan hands and then again was recaptured by them later the same year. The Athenians and Corinthians may have begun to prepare also to regain naval supremacy in the Gulf, but did not retain Lechaeum long enough to accomplish anything. The very same year Agesilaus, after a raid on the Argolid, marched north, destroyed the sections of the walls rebuilt by the Athenians, and recaptured Lechaeum once more. In the latter operation he was aided by a Spartan flotilla of about twelve ships.[1] Thus the Spartans had successfully met the challenge to their control of the Gulf of Corinth. Nor was the general situation too much changed by the sensational defeat of a Spartan *mora* by Iphicrates in 390. Agesilaus took home the remnants of the defeated *mora* but left another one at Lechaeum. However, on account of the success of Iphicrates, communications between Lechaeum and Sicyon were now kept up by the sea route and not by land.[2]

In the following year the centre of interest shifts to the west, where the Achaean control of the entrance to the Gulf of Corinth—or the Spartan control exercised through the Achaeans—was being challenged by the Acarnanian Confederacy, possibly spurred on by the Athenians. By this time, though the date of acquisition or admission is not known, Calydon and Naupactus were members of the Achaean Confederacy. In 389 the Achaeans complained to the Spartans that, though they were being attacked by the Acarnanians and their allies, the Athenians and Boeotians, they were receiving no help. Unless help were forthcoming, they threatened to drop the alliance, that is, secede from the Peloponnesian League. This, clearly, was not the first year the Acarnanians had attacked with the objective of taking the two ports mentioned away from the Achaeans and thus beginning to open up the Gulf. Since only Calydon is mentioned at first in Xenophon's

---

[1] Xen. *Hell.* iv. 4. 14–19.
[2] Xen. *Hell.* iv. 5.

account, this city must have been the first objective. The Spartans yielded to the ultimatum of the Achaeans and sent out Agesilaus with two *morai*, approximately one third of the Spartan army, and some allied troops. The Achaeans themselves joined the expedition with all their available troops. When it is remembered that there was one *mora* at Lechaeum, one at Orchomenus, and lesser garrisons in other places, it is clear that not many Spartans of military age were inactive, and that the Acarnanian affair was taken seriously.[1]

The account of the campaign by Xenophon by no means belittles the achievements of Agesilaus but shows clearly that the Spartans suffered considerably at the hands of the Acarnanian peltasts, and that the Achaeans were dissatisfied because he failed to capture cities. He withdrew from Acarnania through Aetolia, after reaching an agreement with the Aetolians, and crossed to the Peloponnesus at Rhium. He took this route instead of sailing from Calydon for the reason that Athenian triremes were lurking at Oeniadae. The friendly attitude of the Aetolians is said to have been due to the hope—a hope that was to be disappointed—that Agesilaus would help them secure Naupactus. Before he left Acarnania, Xenophon reports, the Achaeans asked him to remain long enough into the autumn to prevent the fields from being seeded. To this he replied that the suggestion was mistaken. He intended to come back next year, and the bigger the crops the Acarnanians expected, the more anxious they would be for peace. If this prediction was actually made, it proved correct. When Agesilaus next spring prepared for another invasion, the Acarnanians sent ambassadors to Sparta and made peace with the Achaeans and an alliance with the Spartans. In other words, they deserted the anti-Spartan coalition and joined the Peloponnesian League. Thus, in spite of the losses suffered the preceding year, the Acarnanian venture was, from the Spartan point of view, one of the most successful of the entire war. Likewise, though the Achaeans had threatened secession, as the Corinthians had done in 432, the alliance with the Achaeans, or their membership in the League, was one of the most successful of all those manipulated by Sparta. The reason was simply that there was little conflict of interests between the greater and the lesser state.[2]

Thus the Spartans approached the end of the Corinthian War with their control over the Corinthian Gulf as firm as ever. Their control of Lechaeum excluded any naval ventures on the part of the Corinthians, while the Achaean absorption of Calydon and Naupactus gave them control of both sides of the entrance into the Gulf. Beyond the Gulf, the

---

[1] Xen. *Hell*. iv. 6. 1–3; cf. *Studies Presented to Robinson*, ii. 807 f.

[2] Xen. *Hell*. iv. 6.4–7.1. The request that Agesilaus prevent the Acarnanians from seeding their fields is, of course, based on the practice of seeding in the autumn.

alliance with the Phocians and Orchomenus gave them access to central Greece and lay Boeotia open to attacks from the west. These advantages had been gained largely through the co-operation of two federal states, the Phocian and Achaean confederacies, while a third, the Acarnanian Confederacy, was brought over in 388. The one federal state which suffered a setback during the war in spite of success on the field of battle was that of the Boeotians.

The Peace of Antalcidas or the King's Peace of 386 is one of the great turning points in Greek history, marking, as it does, the cessation of efforts to secure the freedom of the Greeks of Asia Minor and in-augurating, in theory, a period of efforts to secure a general peace and freedom for all Greek *poleis* except those subject to the Great King and a few others listed in the treaty. It was the result of the diplomacy of Sparta and specifically of Antalcidas, but it was imposed upon the Greeks by the proclamation of the king of Persia, though the king, of course, was merely a figure head during the negotiations. The general plan was first suggested by Antalcidas to the Persian satrap Tiribazus in 392 or possibly even 393. It was simply that the Spartans would lay no claims to the Greek cities in Asia but would be satisfied if the islands and the other Greek cities were free. This latter clause must have been erected into a sort of general principle or policy, for, though Tiri-bazus found the terms acceptable, they were rejected by the Athenian ambassadors for fear that they would have to give up Lemnos, Imbros, and Scyros; by the Thebans, for fear that they would have to set free the cities of Boeotia; and by the Argives, for fear that Corinth would once more be separated from their city.[1]

The Spartans apparently were emboldened by their success in capturing Lechaeum and breaking through the long walls to renew negotiations, this time making some concessions to their chief op-ponents, the Boeotians and the Athenians. In this connexion we hear for the first time of a common or general peace (*koine eirene*) and free-dom for all Greeks,[2] though the treaty proposed actually violated these principles. Not to mention the subjection of the Greeks in Asia to Persia, Athens was given control over Lemnos, Imbros, and Scyros, while the Boeotians were to retain their confederacy on condition that

---

[1] Xen. *Hell.* iv. 8. 12–15. Olmstead, *Persian Empire*, 388 speaks of Tiribazus at Sardis as announcing 'the peace which the king was willing to grant', but later events were to show that what was proposed was not yet the king's policy; it was rather the policy of Sparta and Tiribazus, and Xenophon seems to be right in indicating that the Spartans took the initiative in wooing the Persians.

[2] F. Hampl, *Die griechischen Staatsverträge des 4. Jahrhunderts v. Christi Geb.* (1938), 10 insists that the term *koine eirene* was not adopted as an official title before considerably later than the King's Peace. This may be true, but the term occurs in Andocides, *On the Peace* 17 and so was used in political propaganda as early as 391. See now T. T. B. Ryder, *Koine Eirene* (1965), 27 ff.

they renounce their claims to Orchomenus.[1] By these concessions the Spartans appear to have expected to win over the two states and thus make it impossible for Argos to continue the war. The Boeotians were willing, and the Athenian envoys favoured the treaty, but the Athenian assembly rejected it, and so the war went on. Instead of making peace, the Athenians set out to recapture Lechaeum and rebuild the long walls, but Agesilaus struck back the same year and all the advantages gained by the Athenian energy and initiative were lost again. From then on it was merely a question of keeping on till general exhaustion overtook all combatants. When Antalcidas and Tiribazus finally got the peace for which they had been working, the concessions to Athens but not to Boeotia were retained, but undoubtedly not only Boeotia but also Athens would have been better off if the treaty offered earlier had been accepted.[2]

The treaty, of course, did not accomplish its alleged purpose of bringing freedom to all Greek cities except those to remain subject to Persia and to Athens, at least not in so far as the existence of federal states was considered a violation of the treaty. Actually a number of federal states were allowed to continue to exist. Apparently the real test was largely whether Sparta did or did not object to the continued existence of a particular federal state. This statement does not refer to the Peloponnesian League. This organization was not a federal state but in theory an alliance of free cities and thus its continued existence could not be questioned. Similarly, the Second Athenian League could be organized a few years later without violating the King's Peace. Yet facts and theory were not the same. Sparta had become more and more domineering and was engaged in transforming her free allies into subject allies. Athens, too, trying to rebuild its empire, had been contracting alliances in which the partners were really subject allies and had even tried to restore tolls on ships passing through the Hellespont.[3] Such treaties now had to be cancelled, though the subjection was hardly more severe than that imposed by Sparta on some of her allies.

---

[1] Andoc. iii. 12–13, 20; the statement that the Boeotians were willing to make peace on these terms implies that an agreement had been reached with the Spartans.

[2] Xen. *Hell.* v. 1.31; shorter statement, Diod. xiv. 110.

[3] On the Athenian policy during the Corinthian War see particularly Beloch, *Attische Politik*, 344–6, where the evidence both from literary and epigraphical sources is marshalled. The inscriptions, of course, are cited from old editions. Among those indicating subjection is Tod, 114, an Athenian decree honouring the people of Clazomenae. Ambassadors had been sent from there to Athens to secure a ruling on some matter or other. The Clazomenians are told to pay the five per cent tax imposed by Thrasybulus—probably a tax on exports and imports to take the place of tribute—but are permitted to settle themselves their relations to their political exiles in a nearby town and to that town itself. The Athenian *demos* is to take a special vote to decide whether Clazomenae is to be garrisoned or not. A later vote decided against imposing a garrison. Further details can be deduced from the mutilated inscription. For the withdrawal of a garrison from Carpathus, see Tod, 110; for a ten per cent toll imposed on traffic from the Black Sea through the Bosporus: Xen. *Hell.* iv. 8. 27.

However, it was in deciding whether federal states were to be allowed
to continue as such or were forced to set their cities free that Sparta
proved particularly arbitrary.

The only major federal state dissolved at the time was the Boeotian
Confederacy. The Spartan intervention against the Chalcidic Confederacy was based on the principles of the King's Peace but came a
few years later. The Spartans certainly took pleasure in the dissolution
of the Boeotian Confederacy, but to condemn the act as an arbitrary
action of Spartan tyranny would be a mistake. On the contrary, it is
safe to say that many Boeotians favoured the dissolution. At the congress of ambassadors gathered for the ratification of the treaty, the
Thebans wished to take the oath on behalf of all the Boeotians. For
some time Thebes had been aggrandizing her power so that the Boeotian Confederacy had become pretty much a caricature of what it once
had been. To give in to the Thebans at this point, would, for instance,
have meant abandoning Orchomenus, which had been separated from
the Confederacy for nine years, to the mercy of the Thebans. When the
Boeotian ambassadors left for home with the question unsettled,
Agesilaus induced the Spartan ephors to order mobilization. He himself led the Spartiates to Tegea in Arcadia and summoned thither the
perioeci and contingents of the members of the Peloponnesian League.
Before he could start from Tegea, he received word from Thebes that
the Thebans would grant autonomy to the cities of Boeotia.[1] That was
the only sensible course for them to take. In case of hostilities, Agesilaus
could have counted on the help not only of the Spartan *mora* still at
Orchomenus but also of the Orchomenians themselves, and possibly
of the Thespians and other Boeotians who had suffered in the past at
the hands of the Thebans.

In addition to the dissolution of the Boeotian Confederacy, the
King's Peace was also followed by the detaching of Corinth from
Argos, but that can hardly be called the dissolution of a federal state.
More important was the dissolution of the Chalcidic Confederacy a
few years later. On the other hand, the Achaean and Phocian confederacies, which had proved so useful to Sparta, were allowed to
continue their existence uninterrupted. Also the Acarnanian, Aetolian,
and Thessalian confederacies were allowed to continue as they were
probably because they were so remote that they did not matter too
much from the Spartan point of view. Most important was Thessaly,
but Thessaly was not a menace at the time.[2]

When there actually was so little done at the time to dissolve federal

[1] Xen. *Hell.* v. 1. 32–33.

[2] On the Achaean, Acarnanian, and Aetolian confederacies, see *Studies Presented to
Robinson*, ii. 814 f.; *Rep. Govt.* 66 f. As indicated above, it appears that the Thessalian Confederacy too was allowed to continue. In its case the vigour of the central government or its
approximate dissolution depended primarily on local conditions.

states, it may seem strange to take the King's Peace as marking the end of one period in their development and the beginning of another. Yet, the fact that the Boeotian Confederacy was dissolved as a direct result of the peace and the Chalcidic Confederacy as a more remote result, is enough to warrant this division. The Boeotian Confederacy had, after all, been the most influential federal state in Greece in the fifth century, while the Chalcidic Confederacy was the one which, had it been left to itself, was the Greek state with the best chance to hold its own against Macedonia. Moreover, the dissolution of these two confederacies put an end to the early development of representative government in Greek federal states. The Boeotian Confederacy certainly and the Chalcidic most likely had adopted representative government for the federal government and in other respects possessed quite advanced institutions. The confederacies which survived were of the kind which relied on a primary assembly even for the management of federal affairs. Likewise, the federal states organized soon after the King's Peace, the new Boeotian Confederacy and the Arcadian Confederacy, adopted direct government with federal primary assemblies rather than representative government. This development was helped along by the general acceptance in theory of democracy. In this connexion it is well to remember that the one feature of the democratic theory which was long accepted even by those who otherwise tried to undermine democratic government was the belief that the collective judgement of the masses was better than that of the experts,[1] a belief which naturally led to the retention or adoption of primary assemblies. Hence, as far as representative government was concerned, the federal states had to make a new start, and it was not before late in the third century that representative government was adopted again and became normal in federal states.

[1] Cf. 'The Judgment of Antiquity on Democracy', *CP* xlix (1954), 1–14.

PART II
FEDERALISM AFTER THE KING'S PEACE

CHAPTER I

THE CHIEF CONFEDERACIES
OF THE PERIOD

I. THE BOEOTIAN CONFEDERACY

THE Boeotian Confederacy has a unique position among the
federal states of the period. As far as is known, it was the first confederacy organized or reorganized after the King's Peace. In
addition, it marks clearly the change that came with the theoretical
acceptance throughout Greece of democracy with its emphasis on
primary assemblies. The early development of federal states with
representative government had been stopped by the dissolution of the
Boeotian and Chalcidic confederacies, and this check came so early
that no theory of representative government had been developed.
Instead democracy won general acceptance at the time of the restoration of democracy in Athens after the rule of the Thirty Tyrants. This,
of course, was less of a victory than it seemed at first, for *demokratia*
tended to become a laudatory term for any form of republican government in contrast to monarchy, and soon many a so-called democratic
state actually was an oligarchy.[1] Meanwhile, the democratic form of
government, with power resting in the popular assembly, was found
to be an admirable instrument for the control of a federal state by a
large city. Thus, as long as the Boeotians used a primary assembly with
meetings in Thebes and counted the votes by heads, the Confederacy
was pretty completely controlled by Thebes. At the same time, the
retention of Boeotarchs as heads of the state gave the Thebans another
advantage. There now appears to have been seven Boeotarchs most
of the time, and of these at least three were elected by the Thebans.
This was the Confederacy as refounded in 378. When the system was
changed so that no more than one Boeotarch came from any single city
and the vote in the assembly was counted by cities, the predominance
of Thebes was greatly reduced. This development will have to be
sketched briefly.[2]

---

[1] On this development cf. 'The Judgment of Antiquity on Democracy', *CP* xlix (1954),
1–14.

[2] The study of both the history and institutions of Boeotia is complicated by information
gleaned from scattered references and from masses of inscriptions of which many have not
yet been included in any systematic collection. No effort will be made to refer to all even of
those with direct bearing on the subjects discussed. Boeotia still remains a fruitful but difficult
field for research. Of special studies M. Feyel, *Contribution à l'épigraphie béotienne* (1942)
and *Polybe et l'histoire de Béotie au IIIe siècle avant notre ère* (1942) offer very useful studies of

The revival of the Boeotian Confederacy was the result of the liberation of Thebes through the expulsion of the Spartans from the Cadmea late in 379. The Theban leaders began immediately to try to secure control of all Boeotia, but the nature of the state created has been disputed. Some have taken it to be merely an expanded Thebes or the incorporation of all Boeotia into the city-state of Thebes; others have taken it to be a federal state from the outset, but one in which the influence of the capital predominated.[1] The trouble apparently is that the attitude of Thebes was not too clear at the time. Thebes as a city joined the Second Athenian League in 378 and was still a member in 373–372.[2] Furthermore, the Thebans employed force against cities that were unwilling to join them. At the same time, no sooner had the Thebans liberated their city than they elected Boeotarchs, probably four in number.[3] Four was the number of Boeotarchs that Thebes had furnished to the Confederacy before the King's Peace, and so the election of Boeotarchs looks like an indication that the Thebans intended to revive the Confederacy,[4] but it could also mean that Thebes intended to control Boeotia. Possibly the leaders were not too clear themselves. Their purpose may well have been to make Thebes as powerful as possible either through direct control of Boeotia or by assuming leadership of a federal state. As already stated, a federal state with a primary assembly was to prove well adapted to leadership by the capital.

Whatever was the original plan of the Theban leaders, a federal state had been created by 365 if not before. For this period, the account by the contemporary Xenophon tends to speak of Thebans rather than Boeotians; Isocrates, another contemporary, accuses the Thebans of having subjected Boeotia; and even the incident of the famous peace conference at Sparta in 371, when the Thebans, after having taken the oath ratifying the treaty, asked to have their designation changed from Theban to Boeotian, can be interpreted to fit a unitary state or a synoecism of Boeotia under Thebes fully as well as a

detail rather than a broad interpretation. P. Cloché, *Thèbes de Béotie des origines à la conquête romaine* (c. 1951) covers so much ground that the institutions are treated rather superficially.

[1] For references to the different views see Busolt, *Staatskunde*, 1426, n. 2. Busolt himself came out in favour of a *Bundesstaat*.

[2] Thebes appears as one of the early members of the League in Tod, 123; for an inscription showing a Theban serving as chairman in a meeting of the assembly of the League in 373–372 see S. Accame, *La Lega Ateniese del sec. IV A.C.* (1941), 230; cf. *Rep. Govt.* 61 f.

[3] Plut. *Pel.* 13 lists Melon, Charon, and Pelopidas; in 14, Pelopidas and Gorgidas. Of these Pelopidas and Melon are mentioned also in Plut. *Ages.* 24. All four are prominent enough in the events connected with the liberation to have been elected.

[4] For this point see already Grote, *History*, x. (1852), 121.

federal state.[1] However, if we can rely on reports in late sources that there were seven Boeotarchs present at Leuctra, the Confederacy must have been organized by that time. The story is that Epaminondas and two others voted to join battle, while three Boeotarchs voted against doing so. The tie was broken when the seventh Boeotarch, who had been on detached service, turned up and cast his vote on the side of Epaminondas.[2] Further proof of the existence of a federal state is to be found in two proxenic decrees of the Confederacy of 364–363 or thereabout.[3] Both are decrees passed by the *damos*; one, and probably both, listed the *archon*, apparently the nominal head of the Confederacy, as eponymous magistrate; and both list seven Boeotarchs, of whom two are identical in the two lists showing that they belong to the same period. One of the two is the famous decree honouring Nobas of Carthage—a decree almost certainly connected in some way with the naval policy of Epaminondas. These decrees thus bear witness to the existence of a federal state with a primary assembly, an *archon* at its head, and a board of seven Boeotarchs. The story of Leuctra referred to above indicates that the real leadership lay with the Boeotarchs. The *archon* appears as eponymous also in a document listing contributions to the expenses of the Sacred War.[4] This is about the extent of the information available concerning the institutions of the Confederacy before Chaeronea and the destruction of Thebes by Alexander. This destruction and the subsequent restoration of Thebes, dated about 316 B.C.,[5] must have led to some changes, at least in the position of Thebes within the Confederacy. These changes were largely connected with the college of Boeotarchs. In addition, at least for the period between the destruction and the refounding of Thebes, it is clear

---

[1] Isoc. *Plat.* 9–11. Xenophon, for instance, states that in 371 the Thebans (not Boeotians) were induced to send an embassy to the congress (*Hell.* vi. 3. 2) and that after the exclusion of the Thebans from the settlement, Cleombrotus led the Spartan army into Boeotia against the Thebans (vi. 4. 3). Such and other similar entries may mean nothing more than the *de facto* predominance of Thebes. It may be more significant that at the congress the delegates at first could designate themselves as Thebans (vi. 3. 19–20). On the other hand, the fact that Diodorus, who in some passages refers to the subjection of Boeotia (xv. 38. 3–4, 50. 4), in at least one passage refers to a *symmachia* (xv. 57. 1) may be more significant. Diodorus actually has more information about fourth-century leagues and the like than Xenophon. Since a federal state was largely concerned with foreign affairs, and since the historian who served as source for Diodorus had not read nineteenth-century studies on Greek political institutions, he may well have applied *symmachia* to an organization which others would call a *sympoliteia*, while his statements implying subjection place the emphasis on actual conditions rather than constitutional theory.

[2] Paus. ix. 13. 6–7; Diod. xv. 52. 1, 53. 3.

[3] *IG* vii. 2407 and 2408 (Michel 217 and 218; the first also *SIG*³ 179). The mention of *ateleia* in these inscriptions gives little or no information concerning federal finances; cf. below p. 232, n. 5 under 'The Achaean Confederacy'.

[4] *SIG*³ 201 naming three *archons*, one for each of three years.

[5] Diod. xix. 54. 1; Paus. ix. 7. 1–2.

that the place of meeting of the assembly was changed. Otherwise there seems to have been no change in the position of the *archon* or in the functioning of the assembly. The *archon* is mentioned chiefly as an eponymous magistrate both before and after Chaeronea.[1]

The assembly is extremely important for showing the difference between the newer organization and the one dissolved at the time of the King's Peace. The earlier organization had no federal primary assembly, while the formulas used in the decrees of the later period, both before and after Chaeronea, show that the decrees were voted by the *damos*.[2] This must mean a primary assembly in which all active citizens had a right to vote. It seems, furthermore, that the votes were counted by heads, so that the city in which the meetings were held had a great advantage. Since before 338 the city was Thebes, this meant that the assembly at the time normally was controlled by Thebes. There unfortunately is no record of a vote giving direct evidence on this point. The conclusion is based on the general conditions of the times combined with the fact that all records of the taking of votes by cities in federal assemblies are relatively late. The direct evidence for Boeotia on this point dates from 197. The absence of a reference to a *boule* suggests that the old federal council simply had disappeared and had been replaced by the primary assembly.[3] Thus the direction of affairs fell to the assembly and the Boeotarchs, which obviously meant that, except when public opinion had been aroused, the Boeotarchs were nearly omnipotent. Probably, however, the assembly was summoned to meetings more frequently than in larger federal states. Here a word of warning may be added. The language of the decrees suggests a democratic government. Yet, the most that the references to the *damos* can prove is that all active citizens had a right to vote in the assembly. It does not prove that the old property qualification for active citizenship had been removed.

The one feature in which a change probably was introduced relatively early, was the composition of the college of Boeotarchs. The decrees of the middle of the fourth century show each a group of seven. The literary tradition likewise points to seven Boeotarchs at Leuctra. However, since the lists do not indicate the origin of the Boeotarchs, they give no further information about the composition of the board. On this point the only information is the report about the election of several Boeotarchs at Thebes at the time of the liberation of the city.

---

[1] Some illustrations in addition to those already cited: *SEG* i. 101, 102, 104, 108–10, 116; iii. 351–3 and apparently also 343, 345–9 (decrees of the city of Thisbe); xv. 282.

[2] Some examples: *IG* vii. 2407 and 2408 already discussed; *SEG* i. 101, 105–6, 109; xv. 282.

[3] Does not the fact that the motion of an individual sometimes is practically called a *probouleuma* (*SEG* i. 115 and 116) suggest that there was no probouleutic council?

This has led to the theory that there were seven Boeotarchs of whom four were Thebans.[1] Such a distribution might result from the modification of the old system of eleven by eliminating the representation of cities which had opposed Thebes. Some such distribution is very plausible and would help to explain the obvious predominance of Thebes. It is likely to have lasted until Chaeronea.

All evidence for the later period indicates a system under which there never was more than one Boeotarch from any single city. There actually is only one list of Boeotarchs for the period and this was first published in 1955.[2] This list contains eight Boeotarchs and a secretary, thus showing that the board had been increased by one, or if the secretary was counted as a member, by two additional members. This document helped confirm conclusions already drawn from lists of officials called *aphedriateuontes*, who had been taken to be the Boeotarchs under another name or a college paralleling that of the Boeotarchs. These lists show seven and sometimes eight members from so many cities. All lists include Thebes, Orchomenus, Tanagra, and Thespiae, which also occur in the list of Boeotarchs mentioned above.[3] Additional confirmation is derived from a list of Boeotian hostages honoured by the Achaeans probably about 225.[4] This list too shows eight men from eight different cities including the same four leading cities listed above. It is most unlikely that the Boeotarchs themselves went to Achaea as hostages, but it looks as if for any important task or mission a board paralleling that of the Boeotarchs was employed. Thus, to return to the Boeotarchs, it is clear that the number for a time was seven and that, at least for some time, it was raised to eight and possibly even nine. The manner in which distribution of seats over and above the four leading cities varied, suggests that the election was not by cities but that it took place in the federal assembly. It is possible that the representation of Thebes, Orchomenus, Tanagra, and Thespiae was prescribed by law and that these cities were permitted to select their representatives in advance.

Two later changes must be noted. At a date which cannot be fixed with certainty the colourless *archon* was replaced by a *strategos*, who was more like the generals at the head of the Achaean and Aetolian confederacies. There is certain proof of his existence in 177–176, and the

[1] Busolt, *Staatskunde*, 1429 has four Theban Boeotarchs; Cary, *CAH* vi. 70 has three.

[2] *SEG* xv. 282, first published in 1955 by Mitsos in *Arch. ephem.* for 1952; cf. *Bull. ép.* 1956, no. 121, inscription 13, where attention is called also to *SIG*³ 519 with a list of eight Boeotian hostages.

[3] The documents with lists of *aphedriateuontes* were gathered and discussed by M. Holleaux in *BCH* xiii (1889), 1–23 and 225–9. His interpretation has won general acceptance.

[4] *SIG*³ 519. For a discussion of the date with references to the earlier literature, see Feyel, *Polybe et Béotie*, 123 f.

office may go back as far as to the middle of the third century.[1] The second change was the introduction of the practice of taking the vote in the assembly by cities. The use of this procedure is reported for 197 for the meeting at which the Boeotians were induced to come over to the side of the Romans.[2] This has generally been taken to mean that the count was one vote per city, and the statement about the unanimity of the vote may seem to favour this interpretation. On the other hand, the development of federal institutions suggests a vote weighted in proportion to the strength or populations of cities. With this new method of taking the vote combined with the practice of having no city furnish more than one Boeotarch, there should no longer be any predominant city. Nevertheless, the intrigues during the Roman intervention in Greece seem to indicate that the political leadership and political intrigue still centred in Thebes.[3]

2. THE ARCADIAN CONFEDERACY

The Arcadian Confederacy was a product of the anti-Spartan revolt following the defeat of Sparta at Leuctra in 371. In form of government it was democratic with the ultimate power residing in a primary assembly. Just how democratic it was in practice, it is difficult to say, but it can definitely be claimed as democratic in opposition to the more oligarchic, pro-Spartan elements in the Peloponnesus. This is clearly seen from developments immediately preceding the formation of the Confederacy and the civil wars connected with its founding. In order to follow these events it is necessary to glance hurriedly at some features of the geography and earlier history of Arcadia.

The best land in this mountainous region is the plain of eastern Arcadia, which is relatively narrow from east to west but extends some forty miles north and south. Near the southern extremity lay the city of Tegea; farther north, beyond the narrowest portion of the plain, lay

---

[1] *SGDI* 1872, a manumission record published at Delphi, lists the Boeotian *strategos*, Eureas, as contemporary with the Delphic *archon* Melisson. The latter is dated 177–176 by Daux, *Delphes*, 191. If Pol. xx. 4. 2 is right in calling Abaeocritus, the commander defeated by the Aetolians in 245, *strategos*, and if he uses the word as a technical term, then the change had taken place by this time. Plut. *Arat.* 16. 1 calls him the Boeotarch. Gilbert, *Staatsalterthümer*, ii. 55, n. 3 follows Polybius and accepts the early date; Busolt, *Staatskunde*, 1436, n. 3 thinks the version of Plutarch more correct; so also Feyel, *Polybe et Béotie*, 198, n. 4. But note that also Plutarch refers to Abaeocritus, so to speak, as a monarchical commander, and that c. 250–245, shortly after the Achaean change from two generals to one, would not be too early for the reform.

[2] Livy xxxiii. 2. 6: 'rogatio ... omnium Boeotiae civitatum suffragiis accipitur iubeturque'.

[3] Unfortunately Paul Roesch, *Thespies et la confédération béotienne* (1965) became available only after the above account was written. The material presented there hardly necessitates changes in what was written but would have made it possible to elaborate the account both of the federal and of the local governments for the late third and the second centuries B.C. Of particular importance is the demonstration that a federal *synedrion* existed by about 220 B.C. The treatment of earlier periods is less convincing.

Mantinea. Through the territories of these two cities passed the normal route of communications from Sparta towards the Gulf and Isthmus of Corinth. Thus, it is easy to see that, if both were hostile to Sparta, they might cause considerable difficulty. It is also easy to see that, if one caused trouble, it was natural for Sparta to play the other off against it. North of the two lay Orchomenus. This city too was astride a route to the Gulf, but it had a less strategic position as there was an alternate route turning off east farther south.

The Arcadians appear early as an ethnic group. In the catalogue of ships in the *Iliad* their land seems to be approximately that which later was known as Arcadia. Probably the best evidence that the name is old is the fact that there were Arcadians and an Arcadia also in Crete.[1] This seems sufficient to show that the name existed before Crete was occupied by the Dorians. This use of the name also suggests a certain feeling of unity or kinship. More concrete proof is to be found in a series of coins with the legend ARKADIKON either in full or abbreviated. There is so little evidence for political unity in this period that it has commonly been suggested that the coins were issued by an Arcadian religious organization.[2] This is probably correct. Also the example of Euboea demonstrates that coins with legends of this kind cannot by themselves prove the existence of a federal state. It has been argued, however, that the coins rather suggest a political organization, and that the Spartan king, Cleomenes, then in exile, in 490 B.C. 'almost certainly organized an anti-Spartan Arkadian League'.[3] The king, who was active in Arcadia at the time, may well have organized the Arcadians as a support for himself against enemies at Sparta and possibly also as a step in a transformation of Sparta's organization of her allies. If so, the Arcadian organization must have collapsed with the overthrow of Cleomenes. Certainly no effective union existed during the campaigns of 480 and 479 when the contingents of the Arcadian cities operated independently of each other.

The history of the relations of Mantinea and Tegea to each other and to Sparta is curious and complicated, though few details are known.[4] It was the Tegeans who for long resisted the extension of

---

[1] *Iliad* ii. 603–14; R. F. Willetts, *Aristocratic Society in Ancient Crete* (1955), especially 147, n. 1.   [2] So Head, *HN*² 444; Seltman, *Greek Coins*, 97.

[3] W. P. Wallace, 'Kleomenes, Marathon, the Helots, and Arkadia', *JHS* lxxiv (1954), 32–35. In trying to accumulate evidence for joint action by the Arcadians, Wallace has strained the evidence and misinterpreted it in one case. As evidence for joint action he cites the presence at the Isthmus of Corinth in 480 of Ἀρκάδες πάντες (Herod. viii. 72). But surely it is evidence for just the opposite. The phrase rather means 'Arcadians of every division' (Macaulay's translation) or 'of every community'. With this correction made, any evidence for joint action in 480–479 disappears.

[4] See Gustave Fougères, *Mantinée et l'Arcadie orientale* (1898) for problems connected with the history of Mantinea.

Spartan power in the sixth century, but, after they had come to terms with Sparta, they appear to have been faithful allies and later, much of the time, the most trusted members of the Peloponnesian League. Nothing is known about the relations of the various cities to the plots of Cleomenes, but ten years later the Tegeans were prominent in the Persian War. They, as well as the Mantineans and Orchomenians, were represented initially at Thermopylae, and Tegeans and Orchomenians took part next year in the battle of Plataea and were registered among the victors on the serpent column at Delphi. The Mantineans, on the other hand, came too late for the battle and were not listed among the victors.[1] Yet a few years later, Tegea was the leader in an anti-Spartan movement and opposed Sparta in two battles; in the first as the ally of Argos; in the second, together with all the Arcadians except the Mantineans. The latter are also reported to have aided Sparta in supressing the revolt of the helots.[2]

In the next anti-Spartan movement, the one culminating in the battle of Mantinea of 418, the roles were reversed. For some time the Mantineans had been busy subjecting their neighbours. In the winter of 423–422 the Mantineans and Tegeans with their respective allies had even fought an inconclusive pitched battle with heavy losses on both sides. In the years that followed, the Mantineans were on the losing side and had to give up their conquests but, even so, the Spartans apparently were not able to break their power as fully as they would have liked. Instead they negotiated a thirty years treaty with them, probably the peace treaty after the battle.[3] This obviously precluded any further action against the Mantineans for the period involved and, it seems, filled the Spartans with pent up resentment making them ready for action when the treaty expired.

The treaty expired about the time of the King's Peace, whereupon the Spartans besieged Mantinea and compelled its citizens to break up their city into four villages. These were governed oligarchically, and it is easy to believe Xenophon that the rich landowners, when they had become used to the situation, were rather pleased with it, living nearer their estates, having the kind of government they wished, and being rid of the demagogues. Meanwhile the leaders of the popular party had been allowed to go into exile, and the situation thus was ripe

[1] Herod. vii. 202, ix. 77; Tod, 19; cf. Paus. v. 23 for the corresponding monument at Olympia.

[2] Herod. ix. 35. According to Xen. *Hell.* v. 2. 3, when the Spartans were preparing to break up Mantinea into villages, Agesilaus excused himself from the command of the necessary expedition on the grounds that the city had aided his father against Messene.

[3] Account of the battle: Thuc. iv. 134. The expiration of the thirty years' treaty is reported in Xen. *Hell.* v. 2. 2.

for intrigue,[1] with the oligarchs controlling the villages being pro-Spartan; the popular or democratic party, for the moment out of power and with its leaders in exile, being anti-Spartan and watching for an opportunity to act. Tegea meanwhile was governed by an oligarchy co-operating closely with Sparta, but here too there was a democratic element ready to join with democrats in other cities in their opposition to Sparta.

All details of the events which followed, and even the chronology, are not too well established.[2] The peace conference at Sparta and the battle of Leuctra took place early in the summer of 371. The Mantinean villagers at first remained loyal to Sparta, but it was probably already in the autumn of the same year that the Mantineans decided to rebuild their city. With this went the organization of the city as a democracy, though the details are not known. The Spartans protested, but, when their protest was ignored, did not intervene. Apparently it was the next year that the movement for further unity came to a head and for the time being progressed successfully, though it was marred by civil war, bloodshed, and coercion—the rather common accompaniments of Greek political strife. The lead was undoubtedly taken by Mantinea and, it appears, that Lycomedes of Mantinea was the leader from the outset, but the first details reported concern Tegea.[3] In this city two leaders, Callibius and Proxenus, proposed that all Arcadia should unite in a single state, or rather that Tegea should support the movement in this direction proposed by Mantinea. When their proposal was turned down by the board of magistrates called *thearoi*,[4] probably a small board consisting of five members, who were the highest officials

---

[1] Xen. *Hell.* v. 2. 1–7.

[2] Of the two chief ancient accounts, that of Xenophon in *Hell.* vi and vii suffers from partiality and omissions and lacks clear chronological organization. That of Diodorus xv. 50 ff., though it contains fewer details, places events under specific years but appears to contain mistakes even in chronology.

[3] Xenophon (*Hell.* vi. 5. 6) writes as though the proposal for a union of all Arcadia stemmed from Callibius and Proxenus of Tegea and does not mention Lycomedes until considerably later (vii. 1. 23). Diodorus (xv. 59. 1) relates under 370 that Lycomedes of Tegea induced the Arcadians to organize a federal state. Here Tegea undoubtedly is a slip for Mantinea, since under the next year he tells of the activities of Lycomedes of Mantinea (xv. 62. 2). The fact that the Tegean advocates of federalism had reached an agreement with the Mantineans before they acted at home (*Hell.* vi. 5. 8) shows that the latter already were known to be committed to the cause.

[4] *Thearoi* is a dialect form of the more common *theoroi*, usually a name for envoys to religious festivals, but in Arcadian cities used as a name for regular city officials. In the treaty of 420 between Athens, Argos, Mantinea, and Elis, the oath is to be administered at Mantinea to the *boule* and other magistrates by the *theoroi* and the polemarchs (Thuc. v. 47. 9); a document from Orchomenus is dated by the names of the five *thearoi* and the five *polemarchs*, and a third-century decree of the same city is dated by the chairman of the board (Schwyzer, 664 and 667). The pairing off of polemarchs and *thearoi* suggests that the latter, originally at least, were religious officials, but at Tegea they seem to have broadened their activities.

of the city, the advocates of federalism appealed to the people. This actually meant a call to arms and civil war. In the fighting that ensued the oligarchic government in power at first had the upper hand, and one of the democratic leaders, Proxenus, and a few of his followers were killed, while the others withdrew to the northern section of the city by the gate to the road leading to Mantinea. The fighting was renewed when aid to the popular party came from Mantinea, and now it was the turn of the oligarchs to flee, which they did through the gate to the road to Pallantium and Sparta. The bloodshed appears to have been considerable, and Xenophon, of course, lays the blame on the democratic-federal party. He gives 800 as the number of the opponents who fled to Sparta.[1] When it is remembered that the lukewarm and less openly committed stayed behind, this will give some idea of the strength of the oligarchic pro-Spartan group. Thus was Tegea brought into the new confederacy.

The Spartans now found it necessary to intervene 'on behalf of the dead and exiled Tegeans'. Their plan was to strike both from the north and from the south while the Confederacy as yet consisted only of Mantinea, Tegea, and a few minor cities. Polytropus, an officer otherwise unknown, was to organize at Corinth a force of mercenaries, which may have been joined also by Argive and Boeotian exiles, and with it go to the aid of Orchomenus, while Agesilaus was to invade Arcadia from the south. The Arcadians disposed their troops accordingly. The Mantineans under Lycomedes were to deal with Orchomenus and the troops of Polytropus, apparently considered the chief menace, while the rest of the troops of the Confederacy gathered at Asea, southwest of Tegea near the Spartan border. The troops of Heraea in western Arcadia and Lepreum near the west coast of the Peloponnesus co-operated with the Spartans. The army of the latter under Agesilaus entered Arcadia and occupied Eutaea, only a couple of miles from the border. This position he fortified, and there he settled down to wait for the troops of Polytropus. Meanwhile the Mantineans under Lycomedes attacked Orchomenus unsuccessfully but defeated the Orchomenians and the mercenaries when they pursued the Mantineans as they were withdrawing. The losses were considerable, Polytropus himself fell, and only the intervention of the cavalry of Phlius prevented an even greater slaughter. After this Agesilaus moved north and took up a position west of Mantinea, where he was joined by the troops of Orchomenus and the cavalry of Phlius, which had saved the day in the action not far from their city. He was also supported by two future members of the Arcadian Confederacy,

---

[1] Xen. *Hell.* vi. 5. 10.

Heraea and Lepreum. Thus the two armies seemed mobilized and ready for battle near Mantinea, but no battle followed. Agesilaus apparently did not feel strong enough to risk battle and withdrew without fighting, while the Arcadians decided to await the arrival of aid from Boeotia.[1]

The new Confederacy had weathered the first storm but obviously, aside from Tegea, had not yet induced other recalcitrant cities to join. After the Spartan army withdrew, the Arcadians attacked Heraea in western Arcadia but, though they burned houses and cut down trees,[2] they clearly failed to bring over the city. Orchomenus too, undoubtedly remained aloof, but this in turn brought in Cleitor, the old enemy of Orchomenus, with which it had been at war as late as 378.[3] Possibly also a smaller community or communities west of Orchomenus joined so that there was direct communication between this far northern city and the rest of the Confederacy. At this time too it appears that the Confederacy took the step of at least planning its new capital, Megalopolis. This step fits best a time when there were two and only two really important cities in the Confederacy and it was clear that to make one of these the capital would be certain to lead to trouble. Moreover, the Mantineans, by building a fort in Parrhasia during the Peloponnesian War,[4] had shown that they realized the importance of establishing a fort on this route from Sparta into Arcadia, and what better time than now when the Spartans had withdrawn from Arcadia without fighting? As a commission for founding the city, two men were chosen from Tegea, two from Mantinea, two from Maenalia, immediately west of Mantinaea, and two from Parrhasia, a region to be absorbed into the territory of the new capital. The territory of these four formed a compact block in southern Arcadia including the entire boundary between Arcadia and Laconia. In addition, there were two representatives from Cleitor in the far northern mountains of Arcadia, a city apparently ready to join with others in exerting pressure on its old enemy, Orchomenus. Thus the plans for founding Megalopolis must belong between

[1] Xen. *Hell.* vi. 5. 10–21; Diod. xv. 62. 1–2. Almost the only point of any importance from Diodorus is the statement that Lycomedes was in command of the forces attacking Orchomenus. For the troops of Polytropus Diodorus lists 1,000 'citizen soldiers' and 500 Argive and Boeotian exiles. It is Xenophon who states that they were mercenaries (vi. 5. 11), and it is likely that he would not have represented the Spartans as using mercenaries unless they actually had done so. Of course, it is possible that Boeotian and Argive exiles joined the force.

[2] Xen. *Hell.* vi. 5. 22. The season was obviously so far advanced that the grain already had been reaped.

[3] War between Cleitor and Orchomenus was called off when the troops were needed for a Peloponnesian expedition into Boeotia (Xen. *Hell.* v. 4. 36–37). The participation of Cleitor in the founding of Megalopolis (see n. 1 on p. 186) makes it almost certain that the city joined the Confederacy about this time and certainly before Orchomenus.

[4] Thuc. v. 33. 1.

the withdrawal of Agesilaus and the arrival of the Boeotians and their allies in the autumn of that year.[1] It is natural to see in this project the initiative of Lycomedes. Under his influence the Arcadians are said to have begun to boast that they were the only autochthonous inhabitants of the Peloponnesus, that they were the largest nation among the Hellenes, and the strongest and bravest in the lot, so that neither did the Spartans invade Attica without the aid of the Arcadians; nor the Thebans, Lacedaemon.[2]

The Confederacy was pressing boldly forward on its own initiative, but its expansion was undoubtedly greatly aided by the Peloponnesian expedition of the Boeotians and their allies under the command of Epaminondas. This expedition of the winter 370–369, given prominence in every history of Greece, need not be described here. Undoubtedly it helped to bring many new members into the Confederacy. Moreover, Epaminondas and the Thebans are to be credited with the refounding of Messene and the liberating of all Messenia from Sparta.[3] The Arcadians, in any case, were not strong enough to have put such a plan into execution. Moreover, they would be more likely to have concentrated on the expansion of their own state rather than on creating a formidable new state on their own border. Such an act, however, would suit Thebes, intent on breaking the power of Sparta.

The new Confederacy is one of the most interesting in Greek history, but there is a lack of precise information, for the reason that our chief informant, Xenophon, omits so much. The Confederacy, like the revived Boeotian Confederacy was founded in the period in which democracy, so to speak, was the rage and in which statesmen commonly acted on the theory that the collective judgement of the masses was superior to that of the experts. Therefore, the ultimate action on major issues was reserved for a primary assembly, the *Myrioi* or Ten Thousand, in which all active citizens of the Confederacy had a right to take part. Unfortunately it is not known how often this met. What little is known of the troubled history of the Confederacy during its few

---

[1] Paus. viii. 27. 2 actually gives four members on the commission from Tegea, but for two of these he has repeated the names of the two members from Mantinea. Thus it is clear that each of the five cities furnished two commissioners. The impetus is often thought to have come from Epaminondas. The evidence is the statement of Pausanias that Epaminondas 'might be called'—not that he was—the founder, and that he sent Pammenes with 1,000 picked soldiers to defend the Arcadians against the Spartans. The dispatch of Pammenes actually came some ten years after the battle of Mantinea (Diod. xv. 94. 1–3). Thus the connecting of Epaminondas with the founding of Megalopolis is just one more example of the tendency to credit great men with anything accomplished during their lifetime. There is also disagreement in the sources concerning the date of the founding; cf. Busolt, *Staastkunde*, 1401 f.

[2] Xen. *Hell.* vii. 1. 23.

[3] Diod. xv. 66. 1; Paus. ix. 14. 5. For other literature and discussion see Beloch, *GrG*² iii. i. 178, n. 3; C. Roebuck, *A History of Messenia from 369 to 146 B.C.* (1941), 31, n. 21.

years of existence suggests that, when an issue arose, the assembly could be called on short notice. This could be done rather easily when Megalopolis, Tegea, and Mantinea were the major cities of the Confederacy. Undoubtedly the meetings were regularly held in the huge congress hall, the Thersilion in the new capital, Megalopolis,[1] though it is likely that meetings at times were held in other cities. But, of course, there was also a federal council or *boule*, in which the cities were represented approximately in proportion to their population. The best source of information on the subject is a decree of 369–367 in which it is recorded in good democratic style that 'it was voted by the *boule* of the Arcadians and the Ten Thousand' to bestow certain honours upon an Athenian.[2] After the body of the decree follows a list of fifty *damiorgoi* listed by cities. Of these, the majority, seven in all, including Tegea, Mantinea, and Orchomenus, have five representatives each; one city has two and another three, while Megalopolis has ten. These fifty are best taken as a committee corresponding to the *prytaneis* or presiding committee of the council of a city-state.[3] Fifty is too small a number to include all the members of the council of a rather large federal state and too large to be that of a board of magistrates like the eleven Boeotarchs. They correspond better to the *apokletoi* of the Aetolians—also a sort of committee of the council. Like the latter also these *damiorgoi* may have had considerable power and may well have been the magistrates (*archontes*) who, according to Xenophon, played a leading part in directing the policies of the state.

The composition of the *boule* naturally raises the question whether also in the assembly of the Ten Thousand the vote was taken by cities as in some later confederacies, or whether it was taken by heads as, for instance, in the *ekklesia* of Athens. On this point there is no direct evidence, and there would be little object in citing the views of various scholars. It must suffice to say that the impression given by what little is known concerning proceedings in the assembly suggests that the votes were counted by heads. Moreover, to judge by the example of Athens, the democratic way at the time was to have proportionate representation in the council but to count the votes in the primary assembly by heads. This procedure, as far as the assembly is concerned, seems to have been adopted by the contemporary Boeotian

---

[1] Paus. viii. 32. 1; for a plan of Megalopolis see R. E. Wycherley, *How the Greeks Built Cities* (1949), fig. 24 on p. 85; Wycherley remarks (p. 34) that neither Megalopolis nor the rebuilt Mantinea was laid out on the Hippodamian plan.

[2] Tod, 132; for the date see Cary, *JHS* xlii (1922), 188–90; cf. *Rep. Govt.* 73.

[3] For references to various interpretations see Busolt, *Staatskunde*, 1408. Beloch, *GrG*² iii. i. 175 identifies the federal *damiorgoi* with the *boule*; Busolt sees some connexion between them and the *damiorgoi* of the cities; and it has even been suggested that they were at the same time city officials and representatives of their cities in the federal council.

Confederacy and to have been retained in Aetolia to a much later date.

The Arcadian Confederacy also had a strong executive department headed by a general (*strategos*), apparently elected for a one year term and eligible to re-election.[1] In addition there was a board of magistrates of some sort. These were powerful and could be approached at any time. They were not afraid of making important decisions on their own authority and arresting individuals who opposed them. Their decisions, however, could be overruled by the Ten Thousand, and they could be called to account and brought to trial after their term of office was over. The proof for these statements will be found below in the account of the events leading to the fragmentation of the Confederacy only a few years after its formation. The power of the federal authorities was strengthened by the fact that they had at their disposal a standing army, the *eparitoi*. This could be used not only against foreign enemies but also for police work within the Confederacy. Since this force is mentioned in the first year of the Confederacy, it must have been created when the Confederacy was formed.[2] The only statement concerning the number gives it as 5,000. This seems large for a standing army but it has commonly been accepted.[3] If, as is likely, the soldiers were former mercenaries or men ready to take service as mercenaries, they would render allegiance to their paymasters rather than to the state. Thus, with the aid of the *eparitoi*, the magistrates might even be able to defy the will of the majority of the assembly. The pay for the troops at first came from regular federal funds made up by contributions from the cities within the Confederacy. Later, at one point, officials appropriated money for the purpose from the treasures at Olympia. Objection against this was first raised by the Mantineans, who proceeded to send to the federal authorities their own share of the pay for the troops. This was soon followed by a vote in the assembly of the Ten Thousand against the use of the sacred money, and this again by the abolition of pay and the substitution of the volunteer system.[4]

---

[1] Lycomedes was general at the time of the attack on Orchomenus in 370 (Diod. xv. 62. 2). Thus he was certainly the first *strategos* of the Confederacy. He is again reported elected *strategos* after the first expedition of Epaminondas and the refounding of Messene (Diod. xv. 67. 2). This would fit immediate re-election to a second annual term. There was time for five generalships between the founding of the Confederacy and the death of Lycomedes in 366. One of these was held by Aeneas of Stymphalus (Xen. *Hell.* vii. 3. 1).

[2] These *eparitoi* are mentioned repeatedly by Xenophon. They are clearly the same as the *epilektoi* of Diod. xv. 62. 2, 67.2; cf. Busolt, *Staatskunde*, 582, n. 2.

[3] The number is given by Diodorus. It is accepted by Cary, *CAH* vi. 88; Glotz-Cohen, *Hist. grecque*, iii. 156; Bengtson, *GrG²* 273. The suggestion that they were 'soldiers of fortune' comes from Cary.

[4] Xen. *Hell.* vii. 4. 33–34. This incident will have to be treated more fully below.

This one incident is enough to show that there were no taxes collected directly by the federal authorities but that instead the cities were
expected to contribute to the federal treasury according to its needs.
Since there was representation according to population in the federal
council, it is pretty safe to conclude that the size of the contributions
was in proportion to the representation, a system definitely attested
for the Early Boeotian Confederacy and for the Aetolian Confederacy.
The alleviation following the appropriation of money from Olympia
shows further that there was no fixed payment which was the same in
all years but that the size of the contributions varied according to need.
This recalls the hopes of the Achaeans at a later date that booty would
make it possible to decrease the payments of the cities to the federal
treasury.[1] To be sure, there may have been a fixed regular contribution for current administration to be supplemented by additional
contributions when the need arose.

The Arcadian Confederacy was thus organized with a strong executive department with armed forces at its disposal but subject to the
decisions on major questions of the primary assembly of the Ten
Thousand. This organization might have proved successful but
for the old antagonism between Mantinea and Tegea which led to
a split in the Confederacy before the Mantinea campaign of 362. In
the events of the time it is difficult to assign blame and even to know
which of the two was the more oligarchic and which the more democratic. Two points that seem clear are that the federal administration
was dominated by Tegea while the party of Mantinea had a
majority in the federal assembly, and that the Thebans, when both
parties appealed to them, chose to support Tegea and the administration against Mantinea and the assembly. The situation was further
complicated by a conflict with Elis over the control of border territories.

Such a conflict was not particularly new. The communities involved may have found the claims of the Arcadians somewhat more
attractive than those of the rivals. The Arcadians offered membership
in the Confederacy, while Elis offered only subjection. Elis had long
claimed a considerable territory east and south of Elis proper. In 399
Sparta had forced it to renounce these claims. Under the circumstances, it was only natural that, after the defeat of Sparta at Leuctra,
Elis should try to recover what had been lost, but now the Arcadian
Confederacy stood in the way. It was probably at this time that the
myth arose—obviously manufactured out of whole cloth—that the
Triphylians on the coast south of Elis were descended from Triphylos

[1] Pol. v. 94. 9.

the son of Arkas.[1] When the Eleans attacked Lasion, a town formerly
subject to them but now a member of the Arcadian Confederacy, this
led to protracted hostilities that cannot be discussed here except to
note a couple of points. When the war was complicated also for the
Eleans by civil strife, it was the democratic party which plotted to
betray the city to the Arcadians, thus bearing witness that the Arcadian Confederacy was regarded as democratic.[2] When the Eleans
were hard pressed by the Arcadians, they appealed to their old enemies, the Spartans, who invaded Arcadia to create a diversion.[3] Thus
the two old enemies were brought together through common hostility
to the Arcadians and by a similar desire to subdue their former subjects; the Eleans, Triphylia, etc.; the Spartans, Messene. At the same
time Lycomedes succeeded in arranging an alliance for the Arcadians
with the Athenians. Lycomedes himself was murdered on the way
home, but the alliance he had negotiated was ratified.[4] Thus was prepared the new alignment of powers. The nationalistic policy of Lycomedes had led to a break with Thebes and an alliance with Athens.
This was the line that was later followed by the group of Arcadians
which followed the leadership of the Mantineans.

Serious developments followed when, some time after the Olympic
Games of 364, Arcadian federal officials began to draw upon the
treasures of Olympia to pay the *eparitoi*. This, of course, made the
officials who appropriated the money and the troops who received
the pay companions in crime and tended to make them rely on each
other. Thus any change in this system would be resented by the guilty
officials, both because it implied a criticism of their action and because
it would loosen their hold on the troops. Abolition of pay, when it
eventually came, completely changed the composition of the *eparitoi*.
The first step was taken by the Mantineans who voted to condemn the
action of the officials and themselves to send to the federal government
their city's share of the pay. This amounted to a suggestion that all
members of the Confederacy do likewise and that the troops should
once more be paid with Arcadian money. The officials hit back claiming that they were being maligned and ordering the leaders of the
Mantineans to appear and stand trial before the Ten Thousand. When
they did not appear, they were condemned *in absentia* and *eparitoi* were
sent to arrest them as convicted criminals, whereupon the Mantineans
closed their gates and refused to admit the troops. This condemnation

---

[1] For the perioeci of Elis see *RE* xix. 825–8; Gschnitzer, *Abhängige Orte*, 7–17; arrangements of 399, Xen. *Hell.* iii. 2. 30–31; Triphylos son of Arkas, Pol. iv. 77. 8; Arcadian claims
to Triphylia, etc., Xen. *Hell.* vii. 1. 26. The Triphylian city of Lepreum was soon to become
a member of the Confederacy and appears as such in Tod, 132.
[2] Xen. *Hell.* vii. 4. 12–15.   [3] *Hell.* vii. 4. 13 ff.   [4] *Hell.* vii. 4. 1–2.

theoretically must have been due to the Ten Thousand thus showing that the magistrates claimed for that body jurisdiction in cases of offences against the federal authorities, and that it could be summoned on short notice when needed.

So far the federal officials had managed to carry the assembly with them, and Mantinea was practically in revolt, but soon opinion shifted and others spoke up in the meetings of the Ten Thousand condemning the appropriation of money from the sacred treasures. Again this looks like an extraordinary or at least very opportune meeting of the assembly. Soon it was also voted to abolish pay for the *eparitoi*, whereupon those soldiers who could not afford to serve without pay dropped out, while members of more wealthy families joined up. Thereupon those federal officials who had laid hands on the money and probably had kept some for themselves, realizing that, if they were to try to pass their audit after laying down their offices, they stood a good chance of being condemned to death, sent word to the Thebans that, unless they intervened, there was danger that the Arcadians would again go over to Sparta. Their opponents succeeded in securing the sending of ambassadors officially representing the Arcadian Confederacy to notify the Thebans not to intervene in Arcadia unless requested to do so. This official action must have been due to the Ten Thousand, who thus for a second time overruled their magistrates. The Thebans obviously preferred the appeal from the magistrates and sent a Theban officer with three hundred Boeotian hoplites to Tegea. Thus we learn that the federal officials whom the Mantineans and the assembly were opposing were closely identified with Tegea.[1]

The final break was precipitated by a treaty of peace. Probably during the winter 363–362 or early in 362 a treaty was negotiated with Elis. No details of the negotiations have been preserved, but it is clear that the Arcadian leaders in the peace movement were the same as those who had secured the ruling against the use of the sacred treasures, namely, the Mantineans and their supporters, and that they had again carried the day in the federal assembly, while the same set of officials who had opposed the earlier measures also opposed the peace negotiations. The treaty was nevertheless duly accepted and ratified

---

[1] The account given above is based on Xen. *Hell*. vii. 4. 33–35. There is no report here of the sending of the Theban officer and his troops. They simply are found to be present a little later, and this is likely to be the time they were sent. They can hardly have been stationed in Arcadia at the time the Confederacy was under the influence of the local patriotism of Lycomedes. There is little to be learned from the other sources. Diod. xv. 82. 1 states that individual Mantineans enriched themselves at Olympia, but it would be rash to conclude on this basis that they embezzled more than others, such as the federal officials who had handled the money. The statement may well be derived from the propaganda of the time.

by oath by representatives of all the cities in the Confederacy including Tegea. Even the Theban commander of the Boeotian troops at Tegea took the oath. The final ceremony of ratification took place at Tegea. It is not clear whether representatives of all cities came to Tegea to take the oath on behalf of their communities, or whether it was only the Tegeans themselves who took the oath within their city.[1] If the latter was the case, the representatives of the other cities were present as witnesses. When the ceremony was over, there was general rejoicing and celebration until the Theban commander in collusion with those Arcadian federal officials who feared the audit of their accounts and some of the *eparitoi* proceeded to close the gates of the city and to seize the leading men of other cities who were present.[2] Soon the prisons and other accommodations available for prisoners became overcrowded. Yet the plot failed, for it was aimed chiefly against the Mantineans, and Mantinea was so near that most of its citizens had gone home and so escaped seizure. The Mantineans naturally sent a protest to Tegea and asked for the release of those of their fellow-citizens who were being held there. At the same time they protested that no Arcadian should be imprisoned or put to death without a trial. They also guaranteed to turn over to the federal authorities[3] those they might summon. There-upon the Theban officer released all those who had been seized. The local authorities let this pass at the time but sent ambassadors to Thebes to lodge capital charges against him. At Thebes, the reaction of Epaminondas is said to have been that the officer had done better when he seized the persons in question than when he released them. The Arcadians, in making a separate treaty with Elis had betrayed the Boeotians. This was followed by the announcement of his forthcoming expedition to Arcadia.[4] When this was reported to the Arcadian federal government and published throughout the cities, the Manti-neans and those who shared their views got together with the Eleans and Achaeans and negotiated alliances with the Athenians and the Spartans. Co-operating with the Boeotians in addition to Tegea were also Megalopolis, Asea, and Pallantium, and from outside Arcadia, Argos and Messene, two cities that could be trusted to remain firm in

---

[1] Xen. *Hell.* vii. 4. 35–36. The interpretations vary greatly. Thirlwall, *History of Greece*, v. 141 states that the ratification took place at Tegea; Grote, *History*, x. (1852), 445, that the oath had been taken in other cities before Tegea; Cary, *CAH* vi. 99 thinks that the 'Arcadian executive' had placed the ceremony at Tegea by collusion; E. Meyer, *GdA* v. 466 calls the gathering at Tegea a *Bundestag*; so also Busolt, *Staatskunde*, 1407 and n. 1. It is much more likely that the ceremony of ratification was distinct from a meeting of the Ten Thousand.

[2] Xen. *Hell.* vii. 4. 36.

[3] εἰς τὸ κοινὸν τῶν Ἀρκάδων (Xen. *Hell.* vii. 4. 38), literally, 'to the commonwealth of the Arcadians'.

[4] Xen. *Hell.* vii. 4. 35–40.

their hatred of Sparta.[1] Thus was the stage set for the Mantinea campaign. This will not be described here.

The Arcadian Confederacy was now divided into two parts, the one containing besides Tegea and the two little towns of Asea and Pallantium, the federal capital, Megalopolis; the other, the greater part of the old confederacy.[2] The first group had on its side the federal magistrates who, for some time, had been acting in opposition to the majority of the assembly. The second group controlled the majority in the assembly and thus, it seems, should be considered the legitimate Confederacy, while the group headed by Tegea, even though it did control the federal capital, should be considered the secessionists. In fact, the federal officials, when they appealed to Thebes, seem to have acted without proper authorization simply to save their own skins.

After the battle of Mantinea, each of the two parts apparently continued to claim to be the Arcadian Confederacy. It was undoubtedly the one headed by Mantinea which contracted a formal alliance with Athens, Achaea, Elis, and Phlius.[3] Concerning the other group we are told that towns which had been merged with Megalopolis began to break away and appeal to Mantinea for support, while Megalopolis appealed to Thebes. Thereupon the Thebans sent a force of 3,000 hoplites and 300 horse to check the secessionist movement. Otherwise little is known about the later history except that the two parts apparently remained apart.[4]

And now a few final observations about the Arcadian Confederacy. Its brief and troubled history can only be understood by taking for granted the existence of a strong federal executive which could be approached at any time, could manage the affairs of state between meetings of the assembly, and could call extraordinary meetings of that body. These officials, unfortunately nameless, unless their mainstay were the *damiorgoi*, the managing committee of the council of the Confederacy, were ever available like the Boeotarchs of Boeotia, to plan, to lead, and to intrigue. And there was a name for the federal government, namely, *koinon*, that word of many meanings, which in some cases clearly means the commonwealth or the federal government. The clearest case is the statement that the reaction of the Thebans was

[1] Xen. *Hell.* vii. 5. 1–5.

[2] This statement is based on the conclusion that Xenophon lists the members of the Tegean-Megalopolitan block because they were so few and gives no list of the cities on the side of Mantinea simply because they included the rest of the Confederacy.

[3] Tod, 144; cf. Tod's commentary for the debate whether the treaty is to be placed before or after the battle. The arguments for a date after the battle seem the stronger.

[4] Diod. xv. 94. 1–3. Beloch, *GrG*[2] iii. ii. 173–7 argued for a reunion of the two parts by Philip II of Macedon. The argument depends on dating the inscription already cited as Tod, 132 under Philip. However, if the inscription belongs in 369–367 as stated above on p. 187, there remains no evidence for the reunion.

13

reported 'to the *koinon* of the Arcadians and to the cities', where *koinon* certainly refers to the federal government. Similarly, when the Mantineans a little earlier offered to surrender individuals accused to the *koinon* of the Arcadians, this means to the federal authorities.[1] There even was built a new capital for the federal government. Yet this capital, though it was given a huge territory as territories of city-states went, does not seem to have become a domineering capital such as Thebes was in Boeotia. It is even possible that the federal magistrates, during the quarrels between Tegea and Mantinea, established their headquarters at Tegea and that communications to the federal government for the time being were sent there instead of to Megalopolis.

How democratic was the Arcadian Confederacy? It has been stated that it was built on the democratic pattern with a federal council and a federal primary assembly,[2] but magistrates, council and assembly were fully as much at home in a moderate oligarchy as in a democracy. Thus the answer to the question will depend on the composition of the Ten Thousand. Were all adult male citizens admitted to this body, or were there certain requirements excluding some of them? In their case it is impossible to know for certain whether *myrioi* means an indefinitely large number, a myriad, or whether it has the force of a numeral meaning a body of approximately 10,000. If so, there must have been some qualification for membership, most likely the hoplite census.[3] There is one passage in one of the sources in which the plans for the Confederacy seem to include an assembly 'consisting of ten thousand men,'[4] but this one brief statement by a late historian is not much to go by. More important is the fact that such numbers as five- and ten thousand, when mentioned in connexion with constitutions, are associated with moderate oligarchies. First there is the government of the Five Thousand established at Athens in 411 after the overthrow of the Four Hundred. Then half a century after the founding of our Confederacy, there were issued regulations at Cyrene substituting the 'Ten Thousand' for the 'Thousand'. In this case there was a change from an extreme to a moderate oligarchy. The 'Ten Thousand' were a special body of active citizens (*politeuma*) selected on the basis of a

---

[1] Xen. *Hell.* vii. 5. 1; vii. 4. 38 (cf. p. 192, n. 3). Less clear is the statement that the plan for the Confederacy included the proviso that what was decided in the *koinon* was to be binding for all the cities (*Hell.* vi. 5. 6). Here undoubtedly action in the assembly is meant; so also when it was voted in the *koinon* not to use the sacred funds and when leaders later persuaded the *koinon* to send ambassadors to Thebes (*Hell.* vii. 4. 34–35). Even so it is likely that the word rather means the state or commonwealth than specifically the assembly.

[2] So Busolt, *Staatskunde*, 1406.

[3] Busolt, *Staatskunde*, 1462, n. 3 estimates the hoplites of Arcadia at about 10,000–12,000 and cites Beloch. However, the account of the latter in *GrG*² iii. i. 279 f. implies a number somewhat larger.

[4] Diod. xv. 59. 1.

property qualification from a larger body of citizens.[1] Moreover, even if there were no property qualifications for active citizenship, in a state involved in almost constant warfare and waging its wars largely with hoplites, the control of the state must, for practical purposes, have been in the hands of the middle and upper classes. Yet, even so, the prominence of the assembly may well be due to the acceptance of the democratic doctrine that the collective judgement of the masses is superior to that of the experts. Finally, since this was a period in which *demokratia* had become a laudatory term, and in which some 'democracies' adopted conservative reforms, it is likely that the Arcadian Confederacy, no matter what the qualifications for active citizenship may have been, called itself a democracy. Unfortunately direct evidence is lacking.

3. THE AETOLIAN CONFEDERACY

The Aetolian Confederacy developed on lines almost the direct opposite of those of the Achaean Confederacy. If the Achaean Confederacy was one of the earliest, if not the earliest, to adopt representative government after its abolition, notably in Boeotia, after the King's Peace, the Aetolian Confederacy was the most important confederacy to retain a very active federal primary assembly to a late date. Yet along with this went a strong central government with considerable initiative and freedom of action. A special feature was its use of *isopoliteia* for binding to the Confederacy states that were not given complete membership. This institution will require special attention. Otherwise the institutions are relatively well known, while the Confederacy itself, from the time of the Lamian War to the establishment of Roman supremacy in Greece, is so closely tied up with the chief rivalries and conflicts that its history must be included as an important part of the general history of the period. Thus, apart from the constitution and institutions, only a few special aspects of its history will be considered in the present chapter.

The institutions of Aetolia as an ethnic state have been sketched above in the account of Aetolia before the King's Peace. The transformation into a sympo[l]ity in which the ultimate subdivisions were cities or rural communities treated as the equivalent of cities, can neither be dated nor sketched in any detail. It may no longer be fashionable to place as much emphasis on such transformations as once was common, and it is now realized that a state with tribal organization can develop a vigorous executive and an active central government at least for the conduct of foreign affairs; witness the Aetolian

[1] *SEG* ix. 1; cf. *CP* xxiv (1929), 351–68; *Rep. Govt.* 3.

Confederacy itself at the time of the Peloponnesian War and the Epirote Confederacy somewhat later. Yet a transformation did take place, and in this transformed state Aetolian officials were usually listed by the city from which they hailed as in other sympolities. This transformation is now known to have come somewhat earlier than used to be thought. Thus, not so long ago, it was argued that, because ambassadors sent by the Aetolians to Alexander early in his reign were chosen by tribes (*ethne*), the old ethnic organization was still unchanged. On the other hand, the reference to the *koinon* of the Aetolians in connexion with the events of 314 showed that the *sympoliteia* had been organized by this time.[1] This obviously leads to the conclusion that the transformation took place between *c.* 335 and 314 B.C., but there are two fallacies involved in this argument. Even after a confederacy had been organized on the basis of cities, it would be possible to have some regard for the old tribal subdivisions, for instance, in the choice of ambassadors. In the second place, *koinon* is a word which can be applied to almost any kind of corporation, association, or state. Thus its use does not prove that the Aetolian state was organized at the time as a sympolity rather than as an ethnic state. Proof of the relatively early organization by cities has been furnished, however, by an inscription containing an Athenian decree of 367 ordering the sending of ambassadors to the *koinon* of the Aetolians to protest the arrest of religious envoys from Athens by one of the cities of Aetolia.[2] Here the transformation is clearly attested, not because the organization is called a *koinon*, but because the transaction presupposes the existence of a central government able to make agreements on behalf of the entire state and able to intercede against violators of the agreements, and, not least, because the offender is one of the constituent cities of the Confederacy. It was soon noticed that the date of this inscription fell in the period when Thebes was at the height of its power, and so the inevitable suggestion was made that the development of the Aetolian government was due to the influence of Epaminondas, though there actually is very little evidence for any influence of Boeotia in Aetolia at the time.[3] It is more likely that the change came earlier and was connected with the movement that caused the development of the Acarnanian and Achaean confederacies. At the time of the expedition

---

[1] On the embassy to Alexander (Arrian, *Anab.* i. 10. 2) cf. Swoboda, *Staatsaltertümer*, 327, on the events of 314 (Diod. xix. 66. 2), 328; Busolt, *Staatskunde*, 1509 f.

[2] Tod, 137; cf. *Rep. Govt.* 69 ff.

[3] Cf. Tod's commentary on his 137 and Tarn-Griffith, 71. The only evidence for Boeotian influence in Aetolia is the statement of Diodorus (xv. 57. 1) that Epaminondas in 370 secured the friendship of the Phocians, Aetolians, and Locrians. Note, however, that in Xenophon's rather full list of allies who took part in the Peloponnesian expedition of that year the Phocians and Locrians are included but not the Aetolians (*Hell.* vi. 5. 23).

of Agesilaus against the Acarnanians in 389, the Aetolians possessed a government with which Agesilaus was able to negotiate and arrange for unmolested passage through Aetolian territories.[1]

Aetolia seems to have possessed a rather unique feature, a system of districts intervening between the federal government and the cities, based to some extent on the old ethnic subdivisions. The name for such a district was *telos*. Two such districts are known from inscriptions. For 234–233 or thereabouts there is a record for the *telos* of Stratus of a boundary dispute between two cities of the district, Oeniadae and Metropolis, being settled by judges from Thyrrheum.[2] This district is named after Stratus, the former capital of the Acarnanian Confederacy, and also the other three cities involved were originally Acarnanian. Thus the district must have consisted of that part of Acarnania which had been annexed by Aetolia and formed a long, narrow ribbon along the west bank of the Achelous. The other district of which a record is preserved is the Locrian *telos*, which consisted of West Locris. The record of a manumission at Delphi in 189–188 by an Amphissan is dated by the *boularch* of the Locrian *telos* and the archon of Delphi. Another manumission record of the same period is dated by the same two officials, though it is not indicated that the *boularch* is an official of the Locrian *telos*. From this evidence the conclusion has been drawn that all Aetolia was divided into districts and that every district had its own council headed by a *boularch*.[3] This is likely but not entirely certain, since the only two districts mentioned represent ethnic units annexed by the Aetolians. Yet, if the evidence for these two units is combined with the evidence for the continued use of the three old Aetolian tribal names and the tendency to speak of ethnic groups later annexed as Aetolian tribes, it appears that the three tribes mentioned by Thucydides remained as districts after the Confederacy had been organized and that the territories later annexed were organized in districts on ethnic lines.[4] It has already been noticed that in 314, after the Confederacy had been organized as a sympolity, it sent ambassadors chosen by tribes to Alexander. In this connexion the names of the tribes are not given, but the names given by Thucydides, Apodotoi, Ophiones, and Eurytanes, appear in the works of others, while also the Agraeans and the Amphilochians are spoken of as Aetolian tribes.[5]

[1] Xen. *Hell*. iv. 6. 14; cf. *Rep. Govt*. 69–71.
[2] *IG* ix² 1. 3 B.
[3] *SGDI* 2070 and 2139; the Delphic archon Xenon is dated 189–188 by Daux, *Delphes*, 189; Busolt, *Staatskunde*, 1513.
[4] On this point cf. M. Sordi, 'Le origini del Koinon Etolico', *Acme*, 1953, fasc. 3, 28 ff.
[5] In Pol. xviii. 5. 8 Philip V is represented as saying that the *ethnos* of the Agraeans, as well as that of the Apodotoi and that of the Amphilochians, was not really Greek. The Eurytanes, Agraeans, and Ophieis (Ophiones) are mentioned in Strabo x. 451, 465. Individual Ophieis

Thus ethnic units, when annexed by the Aetolians, appear to have been given a considerable amount of local autonomy and an opportunity to keep alive loyalty to the old unit. Larger and more distant states were connected with the Confederacy by the looser bonds of *isopoliteia*. This will be discussed below.

It was stated above that the Aetolian institutions are well known. On the whole, this is true, but the sources involve many difficulties of interpretation, which, in turn, have given rise to numerous disputes. The chief literary sources are Polybius and Livy, and, when it comes to Greek institutions, Livy's statements normally are rehashed Polybius. There are also rather many inscriptions, often clarifying matters, but at times causing trouble. Most notable is the fact that, while it is known that the Aetolians had a council (*boule, synedrion*) and a primary assembly, the two bodies are never mentioned together in the record of the passing of a decree. In other states it was common to use some such formula as 'it was voted by the council and the assembly'; in the Aetolian decrees the usual formula is 'it was voted by the Aetolians', without any mention of the council. Over against this can be placed a single decree of the *synedroi*. The existence of a council is also attested by the mention in documents of the secretary of the *synedroi* or of the *boule* and the instructions and authorizations directed to the *synedroi* in decrees. The prominence of the *synedrion* actually led one scholar to conclude that all decrees of the Aetolians were decrees of the *synedrion* and that the Aetolian Confederacy lacked a primary assembly. This theory, so attractive, particularly to one with a special interest in the development of representative government, unfortunately has to be rejected. A number of decrees contain instructions to the *synedrion* worded in such a way that it is clear that they must emanate from a larger body with higher authority delegating some of its authority to the smaller body. Moreover, the literary sources contain accounts of meetings that clearly are mass meetings of a primary assembly. An examination of the accounts of these meetings supplies an explanation of the failure to mention the council in the decrees of the assembly. The decrees passed were formulated at the meetings and were not drawn up in advance by the council.[1] Thus the council was not so much a committee of the assembly as a representative assembly supervising the government between meetings of the larger body and itself qualified to make the final decision on a great number of questions. The assembly

---

are listed in inscriptions, e.g. *SGDI* 1862 and 1978. The reason for listing Ophians in this manner—something apparently not done for the citizens of the other two chief tribes—is probably that their district was the least urbanized part of Aetolia.

[1] Of course someone must have prepared the business in advance. Probably the general and/or other officials presented definite proposals to the assembly.

had two regular meetings a year scheduled in such a way as to emphasize the martial character of the Confederacy. The spring meetings, the *Panaeitolika*, were held in different places from year to year and were at times so scheduled as to constitute both a meeting and the mobilization of the army for the coming campaign. In 197 the spring meeting was held at Heraclea on the route by which the Romans were marching north to Thessaly. The Aetolian army, which joined the Romans at Xyniae, two days after the assembly had made its decision, must have come directly from the meeting at Heraclea. In the autumn, after the year's campaigns were over, the assembly met regularly at Thermum, a place that was more a sanctuary than a city but yet, in a sense, the capital of the Confederacy. In addition to these two regular meetings, extraordinary meetings could be summoned when needed.[1]

In the council the constituent cities were represented in proportion to population. The evidence comes from an arbitration by federal judges between the city of Melitaea in Phthiotic Achaea and the nearby smaller town of Perea, at the time merged by special *sympoliteia* into one city. The boundary between the territories of the two was fixed, and the relations of the Pereans to the larger community and their rights while the union lasted were defined. But provision was made also for the possible future separation of the two communities. In that event, Perea, the smaller town, was to retain one *bouleutes* in the federal council and was to contribute a proportionate share to the Aetolian treasury. A similar proviso was made also for the assumption by the Pereans of their share of the indebtedness of the united community. From these provisos it can be seen that Melitaea-Perea, when united, sent several representatives to the federal council. If the two severed their connexions, the smaller town would send one representative, while the larger would retain the rest. From this it is further seen that the cities elected their representatives to the federal council and that they were represented in proportion to their population.[2] The inscription dates from the late third century, but the arrangements for representation must go back to the time when the Confederacy was first organized as a sympolity. Perea, be it noted, with only one representative, must have been very small, almost microscopic. The federal council was so large that in 167 two Aetolian leaders, with the aid of Roman soldiers, surrounded the 'senate', put to death 550

---

[1] For a fuller statement with citation of the evidence and references to the modern literature on the subject see 'The Assembly of the Aetolian League', *TAPA* lxxxiii (1952), 1–33.

[2] *IG* ix[2] 1. 188 (*SIG*[3] 546 B). The point concerning the Aetolian representation seems to have been accepted by most of those who have studied the problem. Some early statements are E. Kuhn, *Ueber die Entstehung der Staedte der Alten* (1878), 125; E. Szanto, *Griechische Bürgerrecht* (1892), 152; G. Gilbert, *Staatsalterthümer*, ii (1885), 29. A more recent statement, Busolt, *Staatskunde*, 1524 and n. 5.

members, and exiled others.[1] This presupposes a council with a thousand or more members.

Such a large council must have delegated much of the work that came its way to a smaller body. This smaller body is not mentioned in the documents preserved but is prominent in the accounts of events of this period in the literary sources. This smaller body consisted of the *apokletoi* (*apocleti* in Livy), men specially selected, as the name implies. We learn from Livy, who certainly depends on Polybius, that they constituted a smaller council in comparison with a larger council, that they were elected, and that their meetings were secret. From one incident in connexion with the campaign of Antiochus III in Greece in 192, it is seen that the *apokletoi* themselves were so numerous that they could detach thirty of their members for service at the headquarters of Antiochus.[2] The members of the federal council (*boule*, *synedrion*), like the officials of the Confederacy and the members of most Greek councils, were certainly elected to serve for a year, and the *apokletoi*, in turn, were elected from among the members of the council. They constituted the body that was the first to be consulted on questions which the general of the Confederacy and other officials could not decide on their own authority. Consequently the *apokletoi* are frequently mentioned in connexion with diplomatic negotiations. On the other hand, the decrees recorded in inscriptions required action by the assembly or, at least, the entire *synedrion*, and in these the *apokletoi* are not mentioned. Yet they probably did many times as much work as the rest of the council and made most of its decisions for it. Nevertheless it is impossible to determine just how far they could go on their own authority for the reason that many times, when our accounts mentioned only the *apokletoi*, they may have had their decisions confirmed by the council or even the assembly.

It is easier to distinguish the authority of the primary assembly from that of the council and *apokletoi*. It is clear that major decisions on war and peace were reserved for the primary assembly, but, once a decision had been made, the implementing of the policy might be left to the *apokletoi*. In 192, after it had been voted by the assembly to invite Antiochus to liberate Greece and to arbitrate between the Aetolians

---

[1] Livy xlv. 28. 7.

[2] The clearest indication that the *apokletoi* formed a smaller elected council is found in the following statement by Livy; 'ita vocant sanctius consilium; ex delectis constat viris' (xxxv. 34. 2). A little later he refers to the council as secret (35. 4) and again as elected (xxxvi. 28. 8). Probably many of his references to the leading men (*principes*) refer to the *apokletoi*. Thirty of them assigned to staff work with Antiochus: Pol. xx. 1; Livy xxxv. 45. 9. For further evidence see Busolt, *Staatskunde*, 1526 and nn. 3–8; for various older theories, Swoboda, *Staatsalter-tümer*, 361, n. 5. A more recent ingenious but not entirely successful interpretation is that of W. Schwahn, 'Die Apokleten der Ätoler und die Apoklesia der Lokrer', *Wiener Studien*, xlviii (1930), 141–9, but cf. *TAPA* lxxxiii. 3, n. 8.

and the Romans, it was left to the *apokletoi* to stir up trouble in Greece.[1] This involved plots to secure the cities of Demetrius and Chalcis as well as intrigues with Nabis of Sparta. These undertakings were belligerent enough, and yet, at the meeting which decided to invite Antiochus, a vote of war against Rome in so many words had been avoided. Hence, when Antiochus arrived in Greece, another meeting had to be held to take up this question. This was an extraordinary meeting called at Lamia some time after the regular autumn meeting. Antiochus was present and addressed the meeting. After his departure, there seems to have been a real debate, in which one party, led by the general, Phaeneas, advocated calling on Antiochus merely to arbitrate. Had this policy prevailed it would have meant a complete reversal of the policy adopted in the spring, As it was, the more belligerent policy prevailed, and Antiochus was elected commander-in-chief, probably with the title *strategos autokrator*. Since this was too late in the autumn for a major campaign, the meeting broke up and the voters went home, leaving further details to the *apokletoi*. The day after the meeting broke up, they had a conference with the king. It was at this conference that it was decided to bring over Chalcis, where Antiochus established headquarters later in the autumn. For future consultations with the king, the assembly had decided to attach thirty of the *apokletoi* to his staff.[2]

The division of labour between the various organs of government is illustrated further by the events of 191 and 190. In 191 the Aetolians had decided to throw themselves on the mercy of the Romans through unconditional surrender. When their general and ambassadors went to the headquarters of Glabrio, the Roman commander, to report the decision and the Aetolians objected to some of the Roman demands, Glabrio ordered chains and iron collars placed on Phaeneas and the ambassadors to illustrate what *deditio* meant. After this rather crude lesson in semantics, Phaeneas remarked that he and the *apokletoi* would do what they were told to do, but that the arrangements made, to be valid, had to have the approval of 'the many'. Obviously, the negotiations so far had been carried on by the general and the *apokletoi* and they felt personally bound by the terms they had arranged, but the final validation of a peace treaty required action by the assembly. In the present case, the anger over the treatment of their general and ambassadors, caused the Aetolians to reject the treaty. Finally, to show how far the authority of the *apokletoi* extended, it may be noted that the

[1] Livy xxxv. 33. 8, 34. 2.

[2] The account of Livy xxxv. 43. 7–46. 2 naturally does not contain the Greek term *strategos autokrator*, which is directly attested only by Appian, *Syr.* 12, but Livy's *imperator* is a natural translation of the term. For the *apokletoi* assigned to serve with Antiochus see n. 2 on p. 200.

six months armistice negotiated by the Scipios in 190 seems to have been contracted by the *apokletoi* without consulting the popular assembly. Thus they could even arrange a six months armistice on their own authority, but a decision to go to war or to make peace required action by the assembly.[1]

The Aetolian federal assembly seems to have functioned much like the *ekklesia* of a democratic city-state with votes counted by heads and not taken by cities or other voting units.[2] The close association of assembly and army suggests that the young men voted and that there was no thirty year age requirement as in the Achaean Confederacy. Nor is there anything to suggest that there was any property qualification for voting. Thus it seems that any adult male citizen who turned up at the meeting could vote. Though some of these voters came from communities that had not originally been Aetolian, the Confederacy and its assembly appears always to have remained Aetolian in spirit. Apparently the true Aetolians met up in such numbers, even when meetings were held outside of the original Aetolia, that they were not swamped by the new citizens. The Aetolians probably should also be given credit for absorbing and assimilating conquered and annexed groups successfully.

The Aetolians, however, did not annex all communities brought under their influence. Many were granted the status of *isopoliteia*. Communities with this status did not send representatives to the council of the Aetolians and their citizens could not vote in the assembly, but they enjoyed a privileged status in Aetolia, and individual citizens who transferred their residence could register as citizens in an Aetolian community and thus assume active Aetolian citizenship.[3] Yet there apparently were several grades of absorption and subjection.[4] What was the real status of a city which possessed Aetolian citizenship or potential citizenship, probably in the form of *isopoliteia*, but which was blessed with the presence of an Aetolian commander and so apparently a garrison of some sort? Were such cities not in reality subjects rather than allies or members of the Confederacy?

[1] Abortive peace negotiations of 191: Pol. xx. 9–10; Livy xxxvi. 27–29. Negotiation of armistice in 190; Pol. xxi. 4–5: Livy xxxvii. 6–7. For a further discussion of the roles of the *apokletoi* and the assembly see the article cited on p. 199, n. 1 at pp. 23–31.

[2] A similar conjecture is that of Dittenberger, *Hermes*, xxxii (1897), 171 f. Counting votes by heads is implied also in Bruno Keil's statement in Gercke-Norden, *Einleitung*, iii². 414 concerning the democratic character of the Confederacy with a 'Bundesbürgerversammlung mit primären Beteiligungsrecht des einzelnen Bundesbürgers'.

[3] Cf. 'Isopoliteia' in *OCD* and 'The Aetolians and the Cleomenic War', *Studies in Honor of Harry Caplan* (1966), 43–57. On the use of *isopoliteia* by the Aetolians, cf. Busolt, *Staatskunde*, 1510–13.

[4] Freeman, *Federal Government*, 267–71 is still worth reading, though he did not have all the evidence now available.

Difficulty in answering such questions is caused by the fact that Polybius at times uses expressions that imply *sympoliteia* or full membership in the Confederacy when the city in question was connected with it by some looser tie such as *isopoliteia*. It is easy to accuse him of inaccuracy, but this may not be entirely fair, for *sympoliteia* could well be applied to any kind of sharing of citizenship. As for *isopoliteia*, in the extant parts of his history, Polybius simply fails to apply the term to the Aetolian connexions, though it was known to him.[1] The word became a technical term for a mutual grant of potential citizenship to each other by two states, but the institution developed first and the name came afterwards. Early examples of reciprocal grants are two treaties of the early fourth century of Ceos with Eretria and with Histiaea.[2] In neither treaty does the term *isopoliteia* seem to have been used. The earliest known use of the word for a reciprocal exchange of privileges is found in a Messenian decree of about 240 B.C. concerning a treaty arranged between Phigalea and Messene on the advice of the Aetolians. In this case the two cities are near each other. Yet the treaty provides for *isopoliteia* and rights of intermarriage and specifies that another special treaty is to arrange for the trial of law suits between citizens of the two states. By the time this document was drawn up, the term apparently was so well known that it was unnecessary to go into details about the registration of anyone who transferred his citzenship from one city to the other. That these arrangements were due to Aetolian diplomacy is indicated by the clause that if the Phigaleans do not remain true to their friendship with the Messenians and the Aetolians, the entire agreement is to be invalid.[3] Of the cities, it was Phigalea which already was tied in with the Aetolians and Messene which was brought more loosely into the Aetolian sphere by means of the treaty.

This one example should be enough to make it clear that the Aetolians made use of *isopoliteia* and sometimes called it by that name. There seems to have been at least two ways in which it could be employed. If the grant was arranged between an outside state and an Aetolian city, the right to take up Aetolian citizenship was apparently limited to citizenship in that one city. If the grant was made by the federal government, the new citizen apparently could register in any community of the Confederacy.

The grant of citizenship by an Aetolian city is illustrated by the grant of Naupactus to Ceos. The decree of Naupactus has been lost, but it is known from the Cean decree that citizenship and the right to

---

[1] In xvi. 26. 9 Polybius reports the voting of *isopoliteia* by the Athenians to the Rhodians.
[2] *SEG* xiv. 530 and 531, the latter an emended form of Tod, 141; cf. *Bull. ép.* 1955, no. 180.
[3] *SIG³* 472.

acquire real property had been voted the Ceans by the Naupactians. In return the Ceans vote the Aetolians similar rights, thus indicating that they considered the grant of the Naupactians as giving them the status of Aetolians of a sort. This status is also recognized in the Aetolian decree granting the Ceans immunity against seizure by Aetolians and residents of Aetolia. Nevertheless, it seems that a city could not exclusively on its own authority bind the Confederacy by a grant of *isopoliteia* to an outside city. The decree of the Ceans shows that their ambassadors had been accredited to Naupactus and the council (*synedroi*) of the Aetolians. Obviously the approval of the federal government had been secured.[1]

The more common grants by the federal government are illustrated by an Aetolian decree in favour of the citizens of Heraclea—probably Heraclea by Latmus in southwestern Asia Minor—of some time in the middle of the third century. Though only the Aetolian decree has been preserved, action also by Heraclea and thus the existence of *isopoliteia* can be taken for granted. A reciprocal grant between the Aetolians and the city of Tricca in Thessaly is recorded in a somewhat later inscription.[2] Still later is an Aetolian decree in response to a letter from Vaxos in Crete. In this letter the Vaxians state that a citizen of theirs had served as a mercenary soldier on Cyprus and had married there and raised a family. After his death his son Epicles, and the latter's mother had been taken prisoners and sold into slavery at Amphissa. There Epicles had bought his freedom and was living with two sons and a daughter. Both he and the children are claimed as citizens of Vaxos and in virtue of this the Aetolians are asked to see that they suffer no wrong and that their federal citizenship (*koinopoliteia*) be recorded. In response, the Aetolians vote to set up copies of the Vaxian letter at Delphi and Thermum. It is the copy set up at Delphi which has been preserved, though, of course, mutilated. A reference to *isopoliteia* with Vaxos in another fragmentary inscription shows that Aetolian citizenship was claimed for Epicles in virtue of *isopoliteia* of long standing between Aetolia and Vaxos.[3] A very complicated problem has been raised by the fact that one document records an Aetolian *boularch* and another a general who have been taken to be citizens of the Cretan Vaxos. From this it was concluded that citizens of distant

---

[1] The decree of the Ceans is *SIG*[3] 522. iii; that of the Aetolians, 522. i. Formerly 522. ii was interpreted as the decree of Naupactus, but it has been shown to contain a second copy of the Aetolian decree. i and the last part of ii are now best consulted in *IG* ix[2]. 1. 169.

[2] Decree for Heraclea: *IG* ix[2]. 1. 173. Which Heraclea is concerned is none too clear, but the fact that the Aetolians promise to appeal on its behalf to Ptolemy fits Heraclea on Latmus; cf. Beloch, *GrG*[2] iv. ii. 609. Grant to Tricca: *IG* ix[2]. 1. 136.

[3] Aetolian decree and letter of Vaxians: *SIG*[3] 622; Aetolian decree also *IG* ix[2]. 1. 178; letter of Vaxians: *Ins. Cret.* ii, p. 65, no. 19; *isopoliteia*, ibid., p. 64, no. 18.

cities with *isopoliteia* could be elected to the highest offices in Aetolia. This is almost unthinkable. It is much more likely that the two officials came from a Locrian town with a similar name.[1] Hence there is no evidence supporting the theory that citizens from distant cities with *isopoliteia* could be elected to federal offices in the Aetolian Confederacy.

This, however, does not solve the riddle of the *koinopoliteia*. Why was so much fuss made about the registration of the *koinopoliteia* of Epicles, if it brought him no additional privileges? *Koinopoliteia* should mean federal citizenship, and it is possible that some who transferred their residence from communities with *isopoliteia* at first had their federal citizenship registered without registration as citizen of a particular community. This may have involved some rights otherwise not open to them. It is hardly worth while to speculate concerning the nature of such rights except to note one possibility. If, for instance, the city of Amphissa, where Epicles lived, had refused to accept as citizen a former slave coming from Cyprus, it might help to have the federal authorities publicly recognize him as a citizen, especially when this was published at Thermum and Delphi.

Next some steps in the extension of the Aetolian power will be considered briefly. The amount of territory annexed outright was considerable. Thus, of the cities mentioned above, neither Melitaea and Perea nor Naupactus nor Amphissa were originally Aetolian. The steps in the expansion have been traced through the study of the number of *hieromnemones*, representatives in the council of the Amphictionic League, that are listed as Aetolians. It is held that the Aetolians never acquired membership in their own name. The representatives listed as Aetolian are those of districts that have been absorbed into the Confederacy.[2] The policy probably fluctuated considerably. When they negotiated their treaty of alliance and *isopoliteia*—the latter term is not used in the document—with the Acarnanians shortly before the middle of the third century,[3] the Aetolians apparently chose to employ the looser ties even in relations with larger states among their immediate neighbours. Another large and somewhat stronger state which the Aetolians seem to have virtually controlled for some time without annexing it was Boeotia. It appears that the Achaeans and

---

[1] See particularly Daux, *Delphes*, 487, n. 1. For the two officials see *IG* ix². 1. 6 and 99. As Daux implies, it is still more unlikely that the vendor and two witnesses in a Delphic manumission record (*SGDI* 1951) who are 'Axians' are Cretans. M. Guarducci, *Ins. Cret.* ii, p. 46 considers all these individuals Cretans.

[2] See particularly Beloch, *GrG*² iv. ii, *passim*; R. Flacelière, *Les Aitoliens à Delphes* (1937) (cited hereafter by the name of the author alone); G. Daux, 'L'expansion étolienne vers le nord . . .', *Mélanges Salač* (Prague, 1955), 35–39, who points to the many pitfalls and uncertainties involved.

[3] *IG*. ix². 1. 3 A.

Boeotians for some time, just how long is not clear, had been allied against Aetolia. In 245 Aratus, during his first term as general of the Achaean Confederacy, had been conducting raids on the Locrian shores. When the Aetolians invaded Boeotia, Aratus mobilized the Achaean army, 10,000 strong, it is said, to go to the aid of the Boeotians, but the battle was fought at Chaeronea before the arrival of the Achaeans, and the Boeotians were defeated with heavy losses. After their defeat, the Boeotians gave up their alliance with the Achaeans and went over to the Aetolians but remained free.[1] Sometime in this period in which the Aetolians were practically masters of the Amphictionic League, the Phocians appear with three *hieromnemones*. This probably means that at the time they had annexed East Locris and had received an extra representative for this district.[2] This must mean further that at the time the Phocians were high in favour with the Aetolians but not full-fledged members of the Confederacy. The treaty between the Aetolians and Acarnanians suggests that these larger states, Acarnania, Phocis, and Boeotia, during their periods of close association with the Aetolians enjoyed the status of *isopoliteia*. Nor is it likely that this was all. Like the Acarnanians, the others too undoubtedly were also allies. Aside from these three states, it appears that states in central and northern Greece won over by the Confederacy were annexed. This was later the fate also of much of Acarnania.

The more distant connexions fall into groups, among them one group encircling the Aegean Sea and one consisting of states in the Peloponnesus. The latter, in turn, falls into two groups. South of Elis, for long closely associated with the Aetolians, the cities of Phigalea and Messene were connected with the effort of the Aetolians to extend their influence south along the west coast of the Peninsula. The contacts with them were of long standing when they in 220 entered prominently into the intrigues preceding the Social War. Connected with this southward movement was also the island of Cephallenia, which for years was represented on the council of the Amphictionic League, a sign of independence but also close relations with Aetolia, probably

[1] Pol. xx. 4–5; Plut. *Arat.* 16. 1, the latter giving the date, i.e., the first generalship of Aratus. Only Plutarch mentions the raids on the Locrian coast. These raids and the Achaean expedition to Boeotia must have been distinct operations. The Achaeans certainly did not have ships to transport an army across the Gulf even if, as Feyel (*Polybe et Béotie*, 80) remarks, the 10,000 must be an exaggeration. The freedom of the Boeotians is to be deduced from the fact that they continued to be represented in the Amphictionic council (Flacelière, 244 and App. i, nos. 24 ff.). Porter on *Arat.* 16. 1 holds that they 'entered into isopolity with them [the Aetolians]'. This probably is correct.

[2] Flacelière, App. i, nos. 14, 15, and 16 dated by him 266, 265, and 264 B.C. No. 17 for the autumn of 262 shows only the normal two for Phocis and an increase of one in the representation of the Aetolians. This has been taken to mean that East Locris had been transferred to Aetolia (Flacelière, 198; Beloch, *GrG*² iv. ii. 401).

isopoliteia and alliance.[1] The Arcadian sub-group, including at least Tegea, Mantinea, and Orchomenus, was affiliated with the Aetolians only a few years, and, though Polybius speaks of alliance and *sympoliteia*, it clearly was very loosely connected with Aetolia.[2]

In the Aegean group a new complication enters in, namely the grant of *asylia*, a guarantee against arbitrary seizure of persons and goods.[3] In the case of the *isopoliteia* with Ceos discussed above, though it is clear that there was a mutual grant of potential citizenship, the Aetolian decree is a decree of *asylia*;[4] the grant of citizenship was embodied in a decree of the city of Naupactus. A grant of *asylia* appears to have been made to Delos about 250,[5] but so little of the decree has been preserved that it is impossible to tell whether also *isopoliteia* was included. In the grant of *asylia* of about the same date to Chios, *isopoliteia* was included.[6] This grant is mentioned in a Chian decree of about 243 thanking the Aetolians for granting the city a seat in the Amphictionic council. In the introduction reference is made to the earlier Aetolian decree conferring citizenship upon the Chians and forbidding seizure of Chians and their goods. In return the Chians had voted citizenship and other privileges to the Aetolians. Some time later came the grant of an Amphictionic vote. In both cases the initiative came from the Aetolians, who, obviously, were seeking connexions with a port which could be used as a base for Aetolian ships in the Aegean. This must belong to the very beginning of the extension of Aetolian influence in these waters. The grants of privileges to Ceans and others who took the initiative and appealed to the Aetolians are likely to belong to a later period after the Aetolian ships had begun to make their influence felt in the Aegean. Though the two are often coupled, the grants of *asylia* did not always involve *isopoliteia*.[7]

---

[1] Flacelière, 284 and n. 3, 314; he notes that in his App. i, no. 42 a citizen of Pronni on Cephallenia is listed as an Aetolian representative. This should mean that the Pronnians in a sense were Aetolians.

[2] See especially Pol. ii. 46. 2 and cf. the treatment of *isopoliteia* above and in the article cited on p. 202, n. 3.

[3] On the decrees of *asylia* cf. the article cited on p. 199, n. 1 at pp. 14 f.

[4] *IG* ix². 1. 169.   [5] *IG* ix². 1. 185.

[6] The information is contained in a Chian decree known from the copy posted at Delphi. The version of *SIG*³ 443 has been greatly expanded by later finds and studies; cf. *SEG* ii. 258. The first twenty-one lines have been further improved by the find of a fragment containing the upper left-hand corner of the stone. This was published by Daux, *BCH* lxxxiii (1959), 475–7, no. 8, now *SEG* xviii (1962), 245; cf. also *Bull. ép.* 1961, no. 345. The new fragment helps to make clear that in the various negotiations involved the initiative came from the Aetolians (Daux, 477). The approximate date is determined by the fact that the first Chian *hieromnemon*, Gannon, whose name appears in line 48 of the decree, appears in a list dated 242 (Flacelière, App. i, 25).

[7] Cf. the grants to Mytilene and Teos in *IG* ix². 1. 189 and 192.

Three cities with a status all their own were Lysimachea on the Gallipoli peninsula, Chalcedon on the Bosporus, and Cius on the Propontis. The information concerning them comes from the report by Polybius of the taking over of the cities by Philip V of Macedon, and, for the moment, he is more intent on damning Philip than the Aetolians. To be sure, he does belabour the Cians and implies that they are to blame themselves for their calamities.[1] Then in the next two chapters he condemns Philip's treatment of them in the strongest language and bases his criticism mainly on the violation by Philip of the rights of the Aetolians. He had just made peace with them and had 'stretched out his hands to their nation'. Yet, though Lysimachea, Chalcedon, and Cius had recently become friends and allies of the Aetolians, he had first brought over Lysimachea and detached it from the alliance with the Aetolians, had next done the same with Chalcedon, and then had enslaved Cius, though there was an Aetolian *strategos* in the city in charge of affairs.[2] Thus Polybius speaks of alliance in connexion with the status of the cities, but it is likely that all three, like Cius, were actually subject allies under the control of an Aetolian commander and garrison. In fact, the presence of an Aetolian commander is attested also for Lysimachea.[3]

What so far has been told about the functioning of the Aetolian Confederacy is enough to show that its central government was busy but primarily with foreign affairs. One indication of the increase of business is that, while the Confederacy from its early days had one secretary, it was found necessary to add a second secretary who was specifically the secretary of the council. The earliest certain reference to two secretaries occurs in a decree of about 207.[4] It was apparently the original secretary who was the more important and sometimes was called the secretary of state.[5] Evidence of his importance is the fact that the treaty with Rome of 189 listed him with the general and hipparch as one of the three officials who could not be seized as hostages. Several phases of the activities of the federal government are reflected in the decree of 182 honouring Eumenes of Pergamum and his brothers and queen, accepting the festival of the Nicephoria, and declaring the sanctuary of Athena Nicephoros inviolable. It is ordered that Aetolians or residents of Aetolia violating the sanctuary are to be subject to the jurisdiction of the federal council (*synedroi*), and that a person wronged or someone acting in his interest, can bring suit

---

[1] Pol. xv. 21. 3–8.   [2] Pol. xv. 22–23, especially 23. 7–9.

[3] Pol. xviii. 3. 11 shows that Lysimachea was under an Aetolian commander.

[4] *SEG* xii. 217. 7–8, though fragmentary, has a clear reference to the two secretaries. Before this inscription was published, the earliest known clear reference to two secretaries dated from 194–193; cf. *TAPA* lxxxiii (1952), 12, n. 19.

[5] δημόσιος γραμματεύς (Pol. xxi. 32. 10); *scriba publicus* (Livy xxxviii. 11. 7).

according to a special procedure open to non-citizens. Included were
also provisions for the dispatch of Aetolian *theoroi* to the festival and
the entertainment of visiting *theoroi* announcing the festival. The general
and other officials were also instructed to see that these regulations
were incorporated in the laws. This must mean at the time of the next
revision of the laws, a procedure referred to in an earlier decree.
Copies of the decree were to be inscribed on stone pillars and set up at
Thermum and at Delphi. The money for the necessary expenses was
to be furnished by the federal treasurer.[1] Thus in this decree the
general is seen acting as the chief executive supervising even rather
routine business, the council is seen acting as a court for the trial of
citizens and foreign residents who have committed crimes in violation
of the immunity granted by the Confederacy, and a federal treasurer is
seen instructed to take care of expenses, but also local authorities are
seen assuming much of the expense of entertaining foreign religious
envoys. Of special interest is the clause seeking to secure permanency
for the enactment by having it incorporated in the law code of the
Confederacy. A somewhat earlier decree concerning the *asylia* of Teos
shows that there was a board of *nomographoi* in charge of the laws and
that there were periodic revisions of the laws. The *nomographoi*, in fact,
were instructed to incorporate certain measures at the time of the next
revision of the laws. This periodic revision of the laws must mean that
the official copy of the code of laws was no longer, as often in early
Greece, posted in an inscription or inscriptions. One can hardly
imagine the code reinscribed on stone after each revision nor amend-
ments added at the end of a long document on a stone added to the
old complex or reserved for the purpose. Moreover, the clause about
inserting something in the laws, implies insertion in the context in
which it belongs. A decree from an Aetolian city shows that also the
cities—or some of them—had similar revisions of laws.[2] This must
mean that what we may call the master copy of the laws of the state
was to be found in some government archives or record office. This in
turn means that there must have been a federal capital of a kind
somewhere or other.

Another activity of the federal government which seems to call for a
capital is the jurisdiction of the federal council as a law court. The
council, in fact, seems to be the only federal court mentioned anywhere

[1] *IG* ix². 1. 179, a corrected version of *SIG*³ 629. Particularly important is the correction of
line 25 due to L. Robert. This removes a mysterious reference to an official called a *proxenos*
and shows that the word is the name of the Aetolian general Proxenus, who was in office in
183–182 and is mentioned also in *SGDI* 2133.
[2] Decree concerning Teos with reference to *nomographoi*: *IG* ix². 1. 192; *nomographoi* of a
city: *IG* ix². 1. 186. On the problem in general cf. in Introduction p. xxiv f. with notes 1
and 2.

14

in our documents. Hence when three judges arbitrated between Melitaea and Perea or again between Melitaea and Xyniae, they must be taken as delegates chosen by the council. Moreover, it appears that the federal government did not normally have jurisdiction in such cases but acted upon the invitation of the parties involved.[1] The jurisdiction of the *synedroi* is mentioned normally in decrees granting *asylia*. Of the goods illegally appropriated, those which were readily available were subject to summary seizure by the general, while the rest was subject to the jurisdiction of the *synedroi*. In this connexion, the general must mean the general and his staff, that is, the federal executive. Clauses of the kind have been recognized in six decrees, three of these involving states which also were granted *isopoliteia*.[2] Thus, though citizens of states with *isopoliteia* to a certain extent were looked upon as Aetolians, when it came to protection against abuses perpetrated by Aetolians, they were subject to the same procedure as foreign states that had been granted *asylia*. In other words, they too were essentially foreign. This is further indicated by the fact that in proxenic decrees immunity was often included, and, when not specifically expressed, probably was implied.[3] Undoubtedly offences against such individuals, if committed abroad, came under the jurisdiction of the *synedroi*. This, in fact, seems to concern chiefly offences committed outside Aetolian territory. The jurisdiction in other matters, seems to have fallen to the courts of the cities. If, as has been stated above,[4] the citizens of federal states normally possessed civil rights, including the right to hold property and to sue in the courts, in all cities of his confederacy, civil suits between citizens of different cities need involve little difficulty.

There obviously is some connexion between the judicial activities of the council and the question of the 'piracy' of the Aetolians. Probably seizures ruled legitimate by the Aetolian authorities were considered rank acts of piracy by others. Yet the Aetolians too knew that there were times when it was advisable to maintain peace. It is clear that from the time Antigonus Doson had re-established the Hellenic League in 224 and thus brought peace to all Greece, the Aetolians had discontinued their raids. They were dissatisfied, it is alleged, with the peace which deprived them of a source of income. Concerning one of their leaders, Dorimachus, at the time stationed at Phigalea, Polybius reports that 'a crowd of pirates flocked to him at Phigalea; and being unable to get them any booty by fair means, because the peace between

---

[1] *IG* ix². 1. 177 and 188 (*SIG*³ 546).

[2] *IG* ix². 1. 4c and d (Magnesia, *isopoliteia*), 169 (Ceos, *isopoliteia*), 179 (sanctuary of Athena Nikephoros at Pergamum), 189 (Mytilene), 192 (Teos), 195 with corrections in *SEG* xviii. 245 (Chios, *isopoliteia*). All these have been discussed above.

[3] Some examples *IG* ix² .1, nos. 6, 12d and e, 16a, 19.

[4] See p. xviii.

all Greeks which Antigonus had concluded was still in force, he was finally reduced to allowing the pirates to drive off the cattle of the Messenians, though they were friends and allies of the Aetolians'.[1] Thus they had maintained peace for a number of years, but in the long run it was too much for many of them. The result was a string of outrages which ultimately led to the Social War of 220–217. Since this usually is thought of as a contest in which no holds were barred, it is interesting to observe how gentlemanly and well behaved both the Aetolians and Philip were when it came to negotiate peace, but that is a story which cannot be taken up here.

Thus the piracy was not outright piracy but seizure of goods as reprisal against alleged injustices and privateering, the difference between Aetolians and other Greeks being that the Aetolians, whether they themselves were belligerents or not, did privateering in any war against either belligerent and without any sort of letter of marque or other authorization. Here two types of raids conducted by private individuals can be distinguished. In the first place, it was not uncommon in times of peace to proclaim the right of reprisal against a state against which one had a real or fancied grievance. This might or might not lead to war. A good example is the action of the Cretan city of Eleutherna in 220. When it felt that it had a grievance against Rhodes, it first proclaimed the right of reprisal and afterwards went to war. In the second place, in time of war governments authorized privateering as the Achaeans did against the Aetolians the same year.[2] Other Greeks, at least when they were on their best behaviour, did not exercise the right of reprisal except when authorized to do so,[3] and did not go privateering except against those with whom they were at war. The Aetolians, on the contrary, whenever any state was at war, even when they themselves were not involved, felt free to go privateering against either belligerent and to do so without authorization from any government, their own or any other. If we can believe Philip V as quoted by Polybius, both he and 'other Greeks' had sent ambassadors to them urging them in vain to prohibit the practice of seeking plunder when other states had authorized privateering.[4] In such cases even their own friends and allies were victimized according to the accusations of their enemies. These practices apparently explain the many ties with cities in the Aegean. In the period of the growth of Roman

[1] Pol. iv. 3. 8–9, Shuckburgh's translation.
[2] Action of Eleutherna: Pol. iv. 53. 2, the phrase used is ῥύσια καταγγέλειν for ῥύσια, cf. also Pol. xxii. 4.13, xxxii. 7. 4. Action of the Achaeans: Pol. iv. 26. 7.
[3] For example, in connexion with action against the Boeotians in 187–186, the Achaean general, Philopoemen, is said to have issued authorizations to those who asked for them (Pol. xxii. 4. 13).
[4] This seems to be the meaning of ἄγειν λάφυρον ἀπὸ λαφύρου (Pol. xviii. 4. 8, cf. 5. 1–3).

power and the Punic Wars, there cannot have been too many opportunities for plunder in the waters west of Greece. In the Aegean, on the other hand, if all that was needed was a war, there was seldom a long period in which there was no opportunity to loot. Ships operating far away from their homeland, however, needed harbours which they could enter for repairs, supplies, etc., but cities could hardly be expected to welcome such ships unless they were sure that the visitors would not stage a surprise raid in their harbour or on their territory. Hence the many grants of privileges and assurances.

In addition to their indiscriminate privateering, it is likely that the Aetolians, when there was no war in progress, made more free use of self-help than most Greeks and did so not only if the government had proclaimed the right of reprisal against another state. Reprisals and self-help appear to have been used also by individuals who felt themselves wronged by a citizen of another state. In early Greece such retaliation against real or fancied wrongs must have been common. *Asylia* was essentially a promise not to employ such self-help but to substitute legal procedure. When granted to an individual, it meant that, though his fellow-citizens still might be fair game, he personally was exempt. Probably the more common substitute was the negotiation of *symbola*, treaties arranging for the settlement of disputes between citizens of different states or of one state and citizens of another. Yet whatever others did, the Aetolians did not normally negotiate such treaties. A fragmentary treaty with Athens mentions such an agreement,[1] but this is a treaty drawn up by the Athenians and accepted by the Aetolians. Otherwise, the latter seem to have relied upon grants of *asylia* and *isopoliteia*. As already noted, Aetolians and foreign residents who violated the grants of immunity were subject to the jursidiction of the *synedrion*. The handling of the correspondence connected with this and other business of the council must have made the office of the secretary of the *synedrion* a busy place.

Another activity which must have been centred in some way was that of the federal treasury. As far as collecting revenues was concerned, its task was to receive payments sent in by the cities of the Confederacy. The evidence on this point comes from the arbitration between Melitaea and Perea already mentioned several times.[2] In this it was provided that, if the two cities severed their connexions, Perea, the smaller of the two, was to retain one representative in the federal council and contribute to the federal government the amount of money which, as it were, went with one representative. This is enough

---

[1] *IG* ix². 1. 176, the term used being συμβολά (fem. sing., dialect form). The document, however, does imply the existence of at least one other such treaty.
[2] *IG* ix.² 188.

to show that in the Aetolian Confederacy the member states contributed to the federal treasury in proportion to their number of
representatives in the federal council. The size of the contributions
probably varied according to the need, but the treasury apparently
was expected normally to have on hand enough petty cash for minor
expenses. Thus the decree concerning the Nicephoria at Pergamum
included a clause instructing the treasurer to take care of the expense
of posting copies of the decree at Thermum and at Delphi.[1] This is the
one document preserved in which a single federal treasurer (*tamias*) is
mentioned in so many words. The one other reference to Aetolian
treasurers in an inscription occurs in the third century treaty with
Acarnania, which complicates matters by listing seven treasurers.[2] It
is impossible to be sure how the discrepancy is to be explained. Was
there once a board of seven later replaced by a single treasurer? Or
was there always a board of seven and does the single *tamias* of the one
document represent the chairman?

The treasury probably had some supervision also of the minting of
money. The Aetolian issues were on two standards. Tetradrachms
were issued on the Attic standard and gold staters on the closely related
Macedonian standard. The tetradrachms, it seems, were intended for
foreign trade and would go well with trade and other ventures in the
Aegean. For local use, silver was minted on a lighter standard in
general use in northwest Greece.[3] This suggests a more advanced
economic policy than normally is associated with the Aetolians. Yet
there is little evidence that Aetolian money travelled far.[4] On the
other hand, the fact that gold was minted suggests wealth. The same is
true of the relatively large booty brought to Rome in 187 by Fulvius
Nobilior after he had defeated the Aetolians and reduced Cephallenia.
According to the statistics of Livy the value was over 8,000,000 denarii
after probably another million had been used up in a distribution to
his soldiers. This was as large a sum as any brought home from
the Balkans before the booty of over 50,000,000 after the Third
Macedonian War.[5] The list includes 118,000 Attic tetradrachms. The

[1] *IG* ix². 1. 179.   [2] *IG* ix². 1. 3A.

[3] For brief statements and references to older literature see 'The Chief Types of Coins in
Circulation in the Last Two Centuries B.C.' in *Econ. Surv. Rome*, iv. 326–34 at 329; Seltman,
Greek Coins, 254 f.

[4] The finds indexed by S. P. Noe, *Greek Coin Hoards*² (1937) list only an occasional Aetolian
coin.

[5] Livy xxxix. 5. 14–17; cf. *Econ. Surv. Rome*, iv. 319 f.; booty from various wars tabulated,
p. 323. Both the late Tenney Frank and I, after the independent investigations, concluded
that these statistics concerning booty 'apparently derive from fairly accurate copies of
treasury accounts' (*Econ. Surv. Rome*, i. 127; iv. 325). On the role of the booty in the transfer
of the accumulated wealth of the Mediterranean world to Italy, see Aymard in A. Aymard
and J. Auboyer, *Rome et son empire* (1954), 147.

explanation is that in the lists of booty other issues of the same standard are listed as Attic, so that many or most of these 'Attic' tetradrachms actually may have been Aetolian.[1] Similarly the Philippei undoubtedly included gold coins of Aetolian as well as of Macedonian mintage.

To sum up, the Aetolian Confederacy was something of a paradox. There was extreme local independence involving not only a great deal of freedom for the cities but also some district organization on ethnic lines. When absorbed into the Confederacy not only West Locrians and Acarnanians but, apparently also Agraeans and Amphilochians, not only were allowed to retain their city governments but also were allowed some sort of ethnic organization. The federal government dealt with little but foreign affairs, and even its legal jurisdiction over its citizens seems to have been concerned mostly with offences committed against outsiders in violation of the privileges granted them by the Confederacy. Hence there seems to have been no federal lawcourt aside from the *synedrion*, the same body which had an important share in negotiating with other states and in directing the government in general. These activities were so numerous that it must have been possible at all times to communicate with some delegate or officer of the council. This could be arranged most conveniently if the secretary had a permanent office in some locality, and the most convenient locality would seem to be the city where the record office or archives were located. There are also other considerations which suggest that the Aetolians must have had something in the nature of a capital. The references to the laws suggest the existence of archives where the law code was kept, while the federal treasury department must have had both a treasury and a records office. To be sure, the headquarters of the various branches of the government need not have been in the same place.

If there was a capital, where was it? The favourite places for publishing documents through inscriptions were Delphi and Thermum. Of these Delphi was conveniently located for communication with the outside world, but it was scarcely Aetolian enough to serve as capital. Publication of documents there was somewhat like the publication of documents at Olympia in order to reach a Panhellenic audience. Thermum, on the other hand, as seat of an annual fair and festival, with which was combined the autumn meeting of the federal assembly

---

[1] *Econ. Surv. Rome*, iv. 331. Conclusive proof is derived from the statement that Manlius Vulso brought 127,000 'Attic' tetradrachms from Asia Minor (Livy xxxix. 7. 1), where Attic coins did not circulate. In the booty of Nobilior, Aetolian and other silver coins other than the tetradrachms on the Attic standard must be included in the 83,000 pounds of silver listed.

and the election of the general and other federal officials, seems a better candidate. Also the publication of so many documents there suggests that it was frequented by the citizens who could see the inscriptions. If it is true that Philip V found over 15,000 suits of armour or military outfits there,[1] the buildings must have housed some sort of arsenal. And yet the account of Philip's raid and other evidence suggest that between the autumn meetings the place was almost deserted.[2] Yet, as far as sentiment is concerned, Thermum came nearer to being capital than any other city of the Confederacy. Nevertheless such a place cannot have been the site of normal government administration. The archives may have been located there but hardly the various administrative offices. Where these were located it is impossible to say. Moreover for major negotiations with foreign governments and decisions about Aetolian policies, the capital of the Confederacy for practical purposes moved to the place where the general and the *apokletoi* chose to establish themselves. Thus, after the defeat of Antiochus at Thermopylae in 191, for the rest of that year and for 190 down to the armistice with the Romans, the capital practically was at Hypata in the Spercheus valley. There negotiations with the enemy were conducted, and thither the assembly of the Aetolians was summoned when a decision by that body became necessary.[3]

4. THE ACHAEAN CONFEDERACY

The Achaean Confederacy in many ways is the most important of all Greek federal states. Certainly it is the best known and the object of the largest literature,[4] but the Arcadian and Aetolian confederacies attained prominence somewhat earlier. The Achaean Confederacy was dissolved for practical purposes early in the third century and was

---

[1] Pol. v. 8. 9. Just exactly what these *hopla* were is none too clear. The translators take them to be suits of armour dedicated and hanging in the porticos, while the historians ignore them, except for Tarn, who states that '15,000 stands of arms [were] burnt' (*CAH* vii. 767). Whatever they were, they were too numerous to be spoils taken from enemies. Moreover, at least some seem to have been in better condition than the outfits of some of Philip's soldiers, who accordingly re-equipped themselves with what they found.

[2] Cf. Walbank on Pol. v. 7–8.

[3] On these events see *TAPA* lxxxiii (1952), 26–29.

[4] The chief literary sources are Polybius, Livy, and Plutarch's life of Aratus and, to a lesser extent, the lives of Agis and Cleomenes. Of modern works the most indispensable are André Aymard, *Les Assemblées de la confédération achaienne* (1938), cited as *ACA*, a model of conscientious scholarship with detailed references to earlier literature; F. W. Walbank, *A Historical Commentary on Polybius* (1957—); and E. A. Freeman, *History of Federal Government in Greece and Italy* (2 ed. by J. B. Bury, 1893), which, with all its faults, is almost unique in its effort to sketch the history of the period from the point of view of federal states. For the Achaean assemblies, see also my *Representative Government in Greek and Roman History* (1955). For more recent statements on the assemblies, see Walbank on Pol. ii. 37. 8, especially p. 219 f.; V. Ehrenberg, *The Greek State* (1960), 129 f.; *Der Staat der Griechen* (1965), 157 f.

revived again in 281–280 but did not attain prominence until some time later. It has been argued above that the revived or refounded Confederacy was regarded as a continuation of the earlier organization. The period of dissolution, or rather coma or trance, had not lasted long. The Achaean Confederacy was in existence in 302, when the Achaeans were listed among the members of the Hellenic League at the time of its revival by Demetrius Poliorcetes.[1] After this came a period in which some cities were garrisoned by Demetrius and some had tyrants imposed upon them by his son, Antigonus Gonatas. The beginning of this period can probably be connected with the change of policy by Demetrius indicated by his capture and garrisoning of Athens in 294. The planting of garrisons in Achaean cities must have come a little later. The account by Polybius of the revival of the Confederacy mentions tyrants in Cerynea and Bura and a garrison at Aegium, but it is unlikely that this is an exhaustive list of the cities over which the kings had established control by such means. There does not, however, appear to have been any formal dissolution of the Confederacy. What happened was merely that so many cities were controlled from the outside that the federal government ceased to function. Hence it could be made to function again without any elaborate constitution-making, though some sort of understanding must have been reached between the cities which, so to speak, wound up and started the clock again.

In 281–280 the initiative in the revival came from Dyme and Patrae, the two leading seaports of western Achaea outside the Gulf of Corinth. With them were joined the two inland cities of Tritaea and Pherae, which on account of their location quite naturally joined with the seaports. Five years later Aegium expelled its garrison and joined the Confederacy. The same year or soon after the Achaeans under the leadership of Margus of Cerynea, probably an exile from his home city at the time, intervened at Bura and put to death the tyrant, whereupon the city joined the Confederacy. This is the first recorded military action of the reconstituted federal government. The tyrant of Cerynea, when he observed what was going on at Aegium and Bura, arranged to lay down his office and have also his city join.[2] The first union of the four cities had brought together the western part of Achaea; the addition of Aegium, Bura, and Cerynea gave the Confederacy control of the central section; the eastern section must have been brought in before Aratus joined Sicyon to the Confederacy in 251–250.

---

[1] *IG* iv². 1. 68; cf. A. Aymard, 'Un ordre d'Alexandre', *REA* lix (1937), 5–28, who demonstrates that it was a mistake to interpret Hypereides, *Against Demosthenes* 18 to mean that Alexander ordered the dissolution of the Achaean Confederacy.

[2] Pol. ii. 41. 1 and 12–15.

The constitutional development of the period is sketched by Polybius in two short sentences. For the first twenty-five years (280–255) the cities elected a federal secretary and two generals on some system of rotation, apparently with the city whose turn it was to furnish an official electing him and having the choice confirmed by a federal assembly. The details of the system are not known. Probably the *damiorgoi*, attested by an inscription for the Confederacy before the dissolution, functioned again from the beginning of the revival. A statement by Strabo adds further that from the time Aegium rejoined the Confederacy the assemblies—and this probably means both the council and the primary assembly—met in the Hamarion near Aegium.[1] This undoubtedly was the meeting place of the Confederacy before the dissolution. What place was substituted the five years before Aegium joined is not known.

The passage of Polybius just discussed also reports an important change introduced in 255. It was decided to choose a single general and entrust the entire leadership to him, the first general so chosen being Margus of Cerynea. It is clearly implied that, as far as the general was concerned, the system of rotation was now abandoned and replaced by the free choice of the best man. A second change probably came at this time or soon after. The place of meeting was transferred from the sanctuary to the city of Aegium. The statement of Livy concerning the later challenge to this monopoly of Aegium, implies that the custom of meeting in the city was of long standing.[2] The transfer of the meetings to the city does not mean that Zeus Hamarios ceased to be the special patron deity of the Confederacy but merely that for convenience the political assemblies were transferred to the city.

A detailed account of the expansion of the Achaean Confederacy does not belong here. The expansion was complicated by entanglements with the great powers of the time, as is illustrated by the relations of Aratus not only with the Macedonian kings from Antigonus Gonatas to Philip V but also to Ptolemy Philadelphus. On much of this considerable information is available in Plutarch's lives of Aratus and of his Spartan opponents, Agis and Cleomenes. Polybius too has much to tell, but his narrative is coloured by his devotion not only to the

[1] Pol. ii. 43. 1–2; Strabo viii. 385. For the *damiorgoi* see *SEG* xiv. 375 and cf. above, p. 86. For election of officials by rotation, cf. Aymard, *ACA* 390, n. 3 and Walbank on Pol. ii. 43. 1. For a demonstration that the twenty years of Strabo is not a contradiction of the twenty-five of Polybius, since the latter's period begins in 280, while Strabo's covers only the period after Aegium joined, see Aymard, *ACA* 297 f. The term *koinoboulion* used by Strabo strictly speaking might cover only the federal council, but undoubtedly also the *ekklesia*, the primary assembly, met in the same place.

[2] On the place of meeting, cf. Aymard, *ACA* 294–300. When Livy xxxviii. 30. 2 speaks of Aegium as chosen for the meetings on account of the standing of the city or the convenience of its location, he is clearly speaking of the city rather than the sanctuary.

Achaeans collectively but to Aratus personally. Much of the information is ultimately derived from the memoirs of Aratus himself. Incidentally, the devotion of Polybius to the Achaean Confederacy colours his entire history. The emphasis on the greatness and importance of the Achaean achievement is such that he treats the rise of the Achaeans as second in importance only to the rise of Rome. This even affects his attitude to the question of causation and the role of *tyche* (fortune, luck, chance, etc.) in human affairs. In his first two books *tyche* looms large, but when he comes to the question of how the little Achaean nation succeeded in imposing its constitution and name upon the entire Peloponnesus, he remarks that it would not be proper to attribute it to *tyche*. To do so would be *phaulon*—a cowardly or stupid act. The cause is then found in the fine qualities of the Achaeans and their devotion to democracy. Thus the Achaean expansion ranks with the Roman as a major achievement calling for careful study of causation.[1] These statements obviously were written before the fall of Corinth and the dissolution of the Achaean Confederacy. Naturally a detailed study of events would reveal that *tyche* managed to influence events now and then. Thus, the Achaean general Philopoemen was inferior to no one in manly qualities but only in *tyche*, though *tyche* had favoured him most of his life.[2]

The first step in the expansion beyond Achaea proper came when Aratus in 251 freed the city of Sicyon from the rule of a tyrant and soon after brought it into the Confederacy.[3] From the story and related material much can be learned concerning conditions in Greece at the time. The cities in this part of Greece were largely ruled by tyrants, good, bad, and indifferent, who were agents of one of the kings and looked to him for support. From this time on the story of Achaean expansion and of Achaean vicissitudes is tied up closely with the chief trends in Greek interstate politics. Thus the liberation of Corinth by Aratus in 243 seemed definitely to affiliate the Achaeans with the anti-Macedonian forces. To this period belongs the liberation of other cities from tyrants and the voluntary relinquishing of their rule by other tyrants, whose cities thereupon joined the Achaean Confederacy. This movement culminated with the admission of Argos in 229. This marks

---

[1] Importance of Achaeans: Pol. ii. 37. 7–11, 40. 1; *tyche* and causation as applied to Achaeans: ii. 38 and cf. Walbank on 38. 5; rise of Rome not due to *tyche*: i. 63. 9. Walbank's most recent statement on *tyche* is found in *Latin Historians* (1966, ed. T. A. Dorey), 56 f.

[2] Pol. xxiii. 12. 3.

[3] For the date see Pol. ii. 43. 3; for the story, Plut. *Aratus* 4–9, undoubtedly derived from the memoirs of Aratus; Cic. *De officiis* ii. 81–82. For the career of Aratus see Walbank, *Aratos of Sicyon* (1933) and W. H. Porter, *Plutarch's Life of Aratus* (1937), an edition with a very full introduction and commentary.

the greatest advance of the Achaeans, as it were, under their own steam. Soon after this they found Sparta under Cleomenes too powerful for comfort and so turned to Macedonia. Thus the Confederacy became a leading member of the Hellenic League (*symmachy*) as organized or reorganized by Antigonus Doson in 224–223. It is probably not unfair to say that next the Achaeans, that is, Aratus, in an effort to use the League against the Aetolians, brought on the Social War of 220–217, thus doing no good either to themselves or to anyone else. When the Romans appeared in force in Greece, the Achaeans in 198 switched sides, and thereafter their history is closely interwoven with the story of the Roman intervention in Greece.

For the institutions of the Achaean Confederacy, no first class ancient description exists. Polybius himself probably took a knowledge of Achaean institutions for granted and so wrote no such description. At any rate, none has been preserved. Yet from odds and ends it is possible to acquire a more many-sided view of the Confederacy than of most ancient federal states, though the interpretation involves several debated problems. The most prominent of these problems is that of the nature and composition of the Achaean assemblies. Nevertheless, the most lasting contribution was probably the union of the Peloponnesus, and we may share some of the wonder of Polybius at the fact that Laconians, Arcadians, and others who had been incorporated into the state of the Achaeans and been included under their name were content with this arrangement. The various tribes of the Peloponnesus had, as it were, been merged into one nation.[1] This unity may seem artificial and unnatural, but it still remains true that Achaia became not only the name of the Peloponnesus but also of the chief Roman province in Greece, so that, for instance, it was possible to speak of Nicopolis as a city of Achaia.[2] Later the name was revived in the Middle Ages as the name of a Frankish principality. Polybius obviously wrote this laudation of the accomplishments of the Achaeans before the Achaean War and after the Third Macedonian War. A little later, he wrote of Aratus as the author of the plan, Philopoemen as the one who realized it, and Lycortas as the preserver of the unity.[3] If one who knew Rome as well as Polybius did, could regard the Achaean Confederacy as a going concern as late as this, the efforts of the Achaean leaders to have an independent policy may not have been as absurd as they often are considered.

In speaking of the unity of the Peloponnesus, Polybius mentions the use of the same laws, weights and measures and coins, and, in addition,

---

[1] Pol. ii. 37. 7–38. 4. The various ἔθνη of the Peloponnesus had been merged into one ἔθνος.

[2] Tac. *Ann.* ii. 53. 1. [3] Pol. ii. 40. 1–2.

the same magistrates, councillors (*bouleutai*), and dicasts.¹ In fact it differed from a city-state only in that it did not have a single central fortification for all its inhabitants.² Helpful as this statement is, it is hardly necessary to say that it is exaggerated. Undoubtedly there was a uniform system of weights and measures and coins, but this did not prevent cities from minting at times without any federal symbol. There were federal laws and magistrates, but there were also city magistrates and undoubtedly special local regulations in some cities. The mention of federal laws and dicasts indicates that the federal administration of justice was more highly developed than in some federal states. The mention of common *bouleutai* indicates the existence of a federal *boule* or council.

Now to turn to the institutions in more detail and to begin with the magistrates, after the shift in 245 from two generals to one, the head of the Confederacy was a general (*strategos*, translated *praetor* by Livy), elected annually. Down to the beginning of the Social War in 220, he was elected and assumed office some time in the spring but so late that, in case of war, hostilities might begin before the new general took office.³ Soon after this the election was shifted to the autumn. The change had been made by 208 and probably actually was introduced in the autumn of 217 at the end of the Social War. This would mean that Aratus, who was in office at the time, laid down his office and allowed Timoxenus, one of his lieutenants, to succeed him.⁴ Other federal officials are listed in a decree of about 234 concerning the admission of Orchomenus into the Confederacy. It is stipulated that the agreement is to be sworn to on behalf of the Achaeans by the general, *hipparch*, and *nauarch*. Of these, the *hipparch* was the second highest official of the Confederacy. Less is heard about the *nauarch* or admiral, but he seems to have been a regular member of the government. Before the three titles there is a lacuna in which some additional title must have been included. This was almost certainly that of the important board of *damiorgoi*,⁵ who will be mentioned frequently below. Another high military official, a *hypostrategos*, a commander of the troops of a

¹ Pol. ii. 37. 7–11; cf. Walbank on 8–11.

² On this point cf. *Robinson Studies*, ii. 810, n. 55.

³ In the spring of 220 Aratus for this reason assumed office five days ahead of time (Pol. iv. 7. 10).

⁴ The report in Pol. xi. 10. 9 that Philopoemen had almost eight months for training the citizens before mobilization in the spring shows that he had assumed office in the autumn. Pol. v. 106. 1 implies the election of Timoxenus in the autumn of 217; cf. *Rep. Govt.* 93. Walbank ad loc. considers it unlikely that the Achaeans should have introduced the reform at a time when it would have cut short the term of Aratus by half a year; cf. also Aymard, *ACA* 240–7.

⁵ *SIG*³ 490, where in the text οἱ σύνεδροι τῶν ᾿Αχαιῶν has been restored. This is certainly incorrect; cf. Swoboda, *Staatsaltertümer*, 388, n. 2; Busolt, *Staatskunde*, 1567, n. 3.

district (*synteleia*) is mentioned occasionally. The one such district known is that of Patrae, which included besides Patrae also Dyme, Pharae, and Tritaea. This is known from the Social War and played a part also in the campaign of 146.[1] Since this is the only *synteleia* adequately attested, it is possible that it was unique. The four cities mentioned were the ones which revived the Confederacy in 281–280, and it is possible that the *synteleia* is a survival from this original union. Nor would it be unnatural to have a separate military district comprising these cities on the border of Elis.

From the manner in which Polybius, in his brief statement about the government of the period 280–255, lists the secretary ahead of the two generals, it has been concluded that at the time the secretary was an official of great importance. From the absence of much information concerning him for the later period, it has been concluded that he lost much of his importance after 255. In this he differed from the chief Aetolian secretary, who retained his political importance much later.[2]

The Achaean organ of government which seems to have ranked next to the general in importance was the board of ten *damiorgoi*. This is mentioned in the fourth century fragment of a treaty, which also attests the existence of a federal *boule* at the time, but this document does not help to determine the number of members. Thus it is not certain that the number always was ten.[3] The evidence for the connexion of the *damiorgoi* with the conduct of foreign affairs is rather extensive. It has already been noted that they appear to have been listed ahead of the general among the officials who ratified by oath the agreement by which Orchomenus was admitted to the Confederacy. In 224 they joined with Aratus, the general of the time, in the oath ratifying the agreement with Antigonus Doson. In 183, Flamininus, when he

---

[1] Pol. iv. 59. 2, in connexion with the independent action of Dyme, Pharae, and Tritaea in 219, lists Mikkos of Dyme as *hypostrategos*. Two years later Lykos of Pharae was ὑποστράτηγος τῆς συντελείας τῆς Πατρικῆς (Pol. v. 94. 1). Here Hultsch, Büttner-Wobst, and Paton print the adjective without a capital, thus making Lykos *hypostrategos* of his ancestral or home *synteleia*, not the *synteleia* of Patrae. As Walbank ad loc. points out, the latter meaning is the more likely. In its favour is also the report of the Achaean mobilization in 146. The contingents of Elis and Messene were kept at home, while also the men of Patrae and the *synteleia* to which the city belonged failed to appear (Pol. xxxviii. 16. 3–4). This implies that the *synteleia* of Patrae bordered on Elis.

[2] See especially A. Aymard, 'Recherches sur les secrétaires des confédérations aitolienne et achaienne', *Mélanges Iorga* (1933), 71–108. Of the inscriptions listed p. 98, n. 2, two have since had their texts considerably improved; cf. *SEG* xiii. 273 and 327. Important as these emendations are for other purposes, they do not alter the evidence concerning the secretary.

[3] The evidence for ten members is relatively late (Livy xxxii. 22. 2 referring to 198). In *SEG* xiv. 375 the names of the *damiorgoi*, if preserved, should have been in the genetive. The names in the nominative must represent something else; cf. above, p. 86 and n. 3.

wished to secure the summoning of an extraordinary meeting of the Achaean *ekklesia*, wrote to the general and *damiorgoi*. Apparently they normally announced dates and places for meetings. On one occasion in 188 the *damiorgoi* scheduled the meeting for Aegium; the general, Philopoemen, for Argos.[1] Their role in the procedure at meetings will be taken up in connexion with the assemblies.

The incidents in connexion with which the *damiorgoi* are mentioned show them to have been so prominent that it is virtually certain that they were included in the body of officials called the *synarchiai* and sometimes referred to more loosely. This body, acting as a sort of cabinet, met in secret meetings and at times made decisions of great importance. In the autumn of 172 Roman envoys arranged with the general and the *synarchiai* to have the Achaeans send 1,000 troops to hold Chalcis.[2] Undoubtedly they were prominent in many decisions, but it is far from certain that the *synarchiai* always comprised the ten *damiorgoi* and the general, no more and no less. Probably both the *hipparch* and *naurach* took part. On the other hand, important decisions were made by smaller bodies or bodies of a different composition. When Psophis was captured in the winter of 219–218, the Achaean officials present with the army arranged to garrison both the citadel and the city. In 182, for the final negotiations with the Messenians, Lycortas, general at the time, called together his fellow officials or fellow officers, probably chiefly the latter. In 219 the three cities, Dyme, Pharae, and Tritaea, when they felt that they were not adequately defended, first sent messengers to the general and later sent ambassadors to the federal government to bring up the subject.[3] Sending ambassadors (*presbeutai*) 'to the Achaeans' was the regular method used by cities for laying matters before the federal government.[4] In the present case, the ambassadors of the three cities must have been sent to complain of the incompetence or neglect of the general, the younger Aratus. There must have been many communications both from members and from abroad. Entries such as the one just mentioned do not indicate to what officials they were addressed, but the example of the letters of Flamininus suggests that at least important communications largely concerned the *damiorgoi*. These appear to have been connected with the permanent administration in

---

[1] Exchange of oaths with Doson: Plut. *Arat.* 43. 1, 44. 1; Flamininus and Achaeans: Pol. xxiii. 5. 16–17; Philopoemen and the *damiorgoi*: Livy xxxviii. 30. 4.

[2] Secrecy of meetings of *synarchiai*: Pol. xxxviii. 13. 4–5; decision concerning Chalcis: Pol. xxvii. 2. 11; Livy xlii. 44. 7–8, which implies a *synkletos*, is misleading.

[3] Psophis: Pol. iv. 72. 9; Lycortas at Messene: xxiii. 16. 6; *presbeutai* of the three cities: iv. 60. 1.

[4] For the dispatch of ambassadors to the Achaeans by Megalopolis, Mantinea, and Stymphalus see Pol. ii. 48. 5–6, 58.1; *SEG* xi. 1107. A similar usage can be observed in the Lycian Confederacy.

Aegium rather than with the army in the field. Thus it may not be due entirely to chance that one of the two documents in which they are eponymous is a decree granting proxeny.[1] The other is the fourth century treaty mentioned above.

The most extensively debated problem of Achaean institutions has been the composition of the Achaean assemblies. The verdict on whether the ancients were or were not acquainted with representative government used to depend largely on the interpretation of the Achaean assemblies. Now that the representative character of the governments of the Lycian and Thessalian confederacies and the four Macedonian republics has been clearly established, the question of the Achaean assemblies is no longer equally vital but still continues to be important.[2] In connexion with the meetings, the term *synodos* occurs frequently; *synkletos*, seeming to mean a specially summoned or extra-ordinary meeting, once in Polybius and once in an inscription referring to events of about 155.[3] In both cases a *synodos* was followed by a *synkletos*, and in Polybius xxix. 24. 6 this is described as a meeting attended not only by the *boule* but by all citizens over thirty. This, sup-ported by certain other evidence, led to the theory that *synodoi* were regular meetings attended only by the federal *boule*, while *synkletoi* were extraordinary meetings of the primary assembly. This meant that most of the work of the government was performed by the representa-tive body. The use of *synkletoi* was much like submitting important questions to the voters by means of a referendum. This was a view widely held in the first part of the present century. Then in 1938 came the very learned and acute study of the late André Aymard, in which he argued that also the *synodos* was in theory a primary assembly. This, however, proved mistaken in large part. It has now been demonstrated that for the period down to 220 the Achaeans regularly relied on primary assemblies. Later, beginning at least as early as 200 and probably in 217, they began to rely chiefly on the representative *boule* and to summon the *ekklesia*, the primary assembly, only from time to time for extraordinary meetings. The change introduced at this time was so radical that it practically amounted to the adoption of represen-tative government. The key to the solutions was the realization that, when Polybius used the words *boule* and *ekklesia* in his statements con-cerning Achaean affairs, the words had their normal meaning, *boule* meaning a council and *ekklesia* a primary assembly in which all male citizens of the proper age were allowed to take part. *Synodos*, on the

---

[1] *SIG*[3] 519, an Achaean decree granting proxeny to Boeotian and Phocian hostages.
[2] For a fuller discussion than can be given here see *Rep. Govt.* 75–102 and 165–88 and for a very detailed treatment Aymard, *ACA*.
[3] Pol. xxix. 24. 6; *SIG*[3] 675.

other hand, meant a meeting—it is a widely used term for that—and could be a meeting of the *boule* or of the *ekklesia* or both, while *synkletos* meant a specially summoned or extraordinary meeting. For the year 220 it appears that there were four regular meetings or *synodoi* during the year, and, as far as we know, this was normal.[1] For the earlier period there is evidence that these meetings, at least often, were meetings including a primary assembly and that at them business of the kind later reserved for extraordinary meetings of the *ekklesia* was transacted. In other words, a primary assembly with several regular meetings during the year was competent to act on all questions that arose.

The change came when a law was passed to the effect that 'the many' were not to be summoned to a meeting of the *ekklesia* except to deal with a question of alliance or war. This, of course, also meant that decisions on these questions were reserved for the *ekklesia*. Later there was added the additional provision that the *ekklesia* could be summoned if a Roman representative with a written statement from the senate arrived. The information on this point is given most clearly in connexion with the visit of Caecilius Metellus in 185. He demanded that the officials summon 'the many' to an *ekklesia*. Thereupon the officials asked for the statement from the senate and, when he had none to present, refused to call the meeting since the laws forbade them to do so unless a written statement from the senate was presented. Subsequently, before the senate at Rome, Achaean ambassadors defended the action of their officials on the ground that the laws forbade them to summon such a meeting except for a question of alliance or war or if someone arrived with a written statement from the senate.[2] The proviso concerning written statements from the senate must have been contained in an amendment added to an older law. Descriptions of meetings, to be noted below, show that this law must have been passed before 200. The date may well be the same as for the transfer of elections from the spring to the autumn.

The difference in procedure before and after this change, can be seen in the descriptions of meetings. In 229, when Aratus and the other officials felt that Spartan aggression had gone too far, they convoked the Achaeans and in conjunction with the *boule* decided to go to war with the Lacedaemonians. This must have been an extraordinary meeting attended by both the *boule* and the *ekklesia* and one in which the *boule* acted as a probouleutic body.[3] The decision made at this meeting would later have been reserved for a *synkletos* of the *ekklesia*.

---

[1] For an analysis of the evidence see *Rep. Govt.* 79–81.

[2] Pol. xxii. 10. 10–12, 12. 5–7; Livy xxxix. 33. 5–7, obviously derived from Polybius.

[3] Pol. ii. 46. 6; fuller treatment, *Rep. Govt.* 78 f. and 165 f.

Also other *synodoi* of the period made decisions on questions of war and peace and alliances. It was at a *synodos* at Aegium that Antigonus Doson was recognized as *hegemon* of the allies, that is, as head of the revived Hellenic League. This is best explained as arranged at a constitutional convention of sorts held in conjunction with an Achaean *synodos*.[1] Also at least two of the *synodoi* of 220 made decisions of the kind later reserved for an extraordinary meeting of the *ekklesia*. At one, the Achaeans, gathered in their *ekklesia* at Aegium, voted to give aid to the Messenians. The general was to mobilize the Achaeans and any decision made by the men in arms was to be valid. Thus the decisions later made by the mobilized soldiers was to be valid by virtue of this previous authorization.[2] At the next *synodos*, the third of the year, the mass (*plethos*) voted to select 5,000 Achaean infantry and 500 cavalry.[3] This might possibly be considered an administrative measure. Not so, however, the ratification of the declaration of war by the Hellenic League against the Aetolians which was voted at the fourth and last *synodos* of the year. With this went the authorization of privateering against the Aetolians.[4] In all these decisions the primary assembly must have had a share. Yet the *boule* too seems to have been important. In connexion with the last *synodos* mentioned it is even reported that Philip V appeared before the *boule* and addressed it.

With the change eliminating the use of the primary assembly except for a few extraordinary meetings, the importance of the *boule* naturally increased. It seems even to have taken over the election of the magistrates. The elections had been transferred from a spring to the autumn *synodos*, and they continued to be held at that time though only the *boule* attended the meeting. It has often been maintained as a sort of self-evident law that the elections must have been conducted by a primary assembly. This attitude should be abandoned now when it is known that also the electoral assembly of the Lycian Confederacy was a representative assembly. Though there were several fixed meetings of the *boule*, it stands to reason that it could be summoned at times to extraordinary meetings. Apparently there is a record of one such meeting when it was summoned in 170 to meet with visiting Roman ambassadors.[5]

The Achaean *boule* was clearly a body of considerable size. This is

---

[1] Pol. ii. 54. 3–4.
[2] Pol. iv. 7. 1–6; on this much debated assembly cf. *Rep. Govt.* 79 f., 82 f.
[3] Pol. iv. 14–15; especially 14. 1 and 15. 3.　　　　　[4] Pol. iv. 26. 7–8.
[5] συναχθείσης αὐτοῖς τῆς βουλῆς εἰς Αἴγιον (Pol. xxviii. 3. 10) seems clear enough, but it must be admitted that the passage has been given several interpretations. Polybius had just stated that the ambassadors had planned to accuse certain Achaean leaders before the *ekklesia* but dropped the plan. It seems that the *ekklesia* was not summoned but only the *boule*. Cf. *Rep. Govt.* 88, 93 f. and nn. 18 and 19 on p. 216.

15

implied in the reports of meetings and is suggested also by the examples
of other federal councils. That of the Aetolians at the time of the Third
Macedonian War numbered well over 550; that of the Thessalians in
the reign of Tiberius, 334. These large councils were made up of delegations from cities varying in size according to the population of the
city. It is safe to conclude that also the Achaeans followed this rule of
representation in proportion to population. This system was widely
used in the councils of city-states and in the early Boeotian, the Aetolian, the Lycian, and Thessalian confederacies. However, the most
convincing argument for its use by the Achaeans is to be found in the
system of federal finances. It will be shown below that the Achaean
federal treasury depended on payments sent in by the cities. In the
cases in which direct evidence for the use of this system is available, the
size of the contributions of a city was in proportion to the number of its
representatives in the federal council. It was so in the early Boeotian,
the Aetolian, and the Lycian confederacies.

It is impossible to determine the size of the *boule* more precisely. In
185 Eumenes of Pergamum offered the Confederacy 120 talents to be
invested and the income used for paying the members of the *boule* at the
meetings. Efforts have been made to determine the size by figuring out
how many could be paid from the income thus derived, but this is a
hopeless task. No one knows either the number of days spent at the
meetings nor the suggested rate of pay. Moreover, the sums handed
out would probably have been more like favours distributed on special
occasions than like actual pay. The offer was made and rejected at a
synodos and the mob hysteria at the meeting suggests that the *boule* was
anything but small, but the 8,640 members suggested by one scholar is
fantastic and obviously much too large.[1] The members certainly had
been unpaid and so they remained. The history of the Confederacy
with its fear of social revolution is enough to show that it was dominated by men of means. What Eumenes proposed to do was not to
relieve the federal treasury of a burden but to introduce something
new.[2]

Boule also suggests *boularchs* or *proëdroi* presiding over the council, but
there seems to be no record of such officials. Instead the accounts of
meetings give the impression that the same federal officials who pre-

---

[1] The *synodos* at which the offer of Eumenes was made: Pol. xxii. 7–8. G. De Sanctis in his
article, 'Le assemblee federali degli Achei', *Riv. fil.* xxxvi (1908), 252–60 suggests that 120
talents at twelve per cent would yield 86,400 drachmas. If then the members received a
drachma a day and were in session ten days during the year, this would suffice for 8,640
members (p. 257, n. 1).

[2] On the basis of the offer of Eumenes, E. Szanto, *Das griechische Bürgerrecht*, 125 argued
that the members were paid. The theory has commonly been rejected; see particularly
Aymard, *ACA* 331 ff. Unfortunately it has been revived in Tarn-Griffith, 74 f.

sided over the *synkletoi* of the primary assembly also took charge of the meetings of the *boule*. This procedure may have been adopted early. Meetings are recognized as meetings of the *boule* by the procedure followed and the nature of the subjects considered. If several unrelated subjects are taken up, it is the *boule*; if the subject is not one of those reserved for the *ekklesia*, it is the *boule*; if the procedure of a *synkletos* of the *ekklesia* calling for a three-day consideration of a subject is not followed, it is the *boule*, that is, if the meeting belongs after the great reform. In 218 there was an extraordinary meeting at which the procedure employed after the reform was not followed. In fact, when things did not go too well, the meeting was transferred from one city to another. This was the year in which Macedonian influence had resulted in the election of Eperatus as general and the defeat of the candidate of Aratus. When Philip was in need of supplies, he secured the summoning of the Achaeans to a meeting at Aegium. When he could accomplish nothing here on account of the obstruction of Aratus and his supporters, Philip changed tactics, induced the officials to transfer the meeting to Sicyon, the home town of Aratus, staged a public reconciliation with Aratus and his like-named son, and thus got what he wanted.[1] Here there is a looseness of procedure that could not be found at a *synkletos* after the reform.

Probably the best example of a regular meeting of the *boule* after the reform, is the *synodos* at Megalopolis at which the offer of Eumenes was submitted and rejected. There were ambassadors present not only from Eumenes but also from the Ptolemaic and Seleucid courts, while also an Achaean embassy back from Rome presented its report. A question of some importance was the proposed renewal of a treaty of alliance with the Ptolemies, advocated both by a Ptolemaic ambassador and by an Achaean embassy headed by Lycortas, which was just back from Alexandria. Apparently the rule reserving questions of alliance for the *ekklesia*, did not apply to the renewal of existing treaties. In the present case the general, Aristaenus, prevented action on the grounds that there were many former treaties and no one could tell which particular treaty was being renewed.[2] This action was more significant for politics than for constitutional law. Lycortas belonged to the group that favoured as independent a foreign policy as possible; Aristaenus, to those who believed in subordinating the entire foreign policy to the Romans and avoiding ties with other powers.

[1] Pol. v. 1. 6–12; cf. *Rep. Govt.* 168 f. The reference to the calling of the meeting at Aegium according to the Achaean custom may give the impression that down to this time also all extraordinary meetings were held there. However, there is evidence for holding such meetings at other places, for instance, the meeting called at Argos to negotiate with Cleomenes.

[2] Pol. xxii. 7–9.

An almost equally complicated meeting is reported for 169. At this Archon, the general of the year, proposed the total mobilization of the Achaean military forces to be sent to Thessaly to co-operate with the Roman army there. When this had been voted, it was decided that Archon was to take charge of the mobilization, and that Polybius, the *hipparch* of the year, was to head an embassy to the Roman commander in Thessaly. The same meeting also dispatched ambassadors to Eumenes of Pergamum and to Egypt. The account of Polybius does not apply any name to the meeting, but the number and variety of the subjects handled shows that it was a *synodos*, a regular meeting of the *boule*. The question of the projected expedition to Thessaly may look important enough for a *synkletos*, but, since the Confederacy already was at war with Macedonia, the *synodos* undoubtedly was authorized to make plans in detail.[1]

The chief aid in differentiating between the two types of meetings in the second century is the account of a *synodos* at Corinth and a *synkletos* at Sicyon, both in 168. Ambassadors from the Ptolemies appeared before the *synodos* requesting that the Achaeans send them 1,000 infantry and 200 cavalry under the command of Lycortas and Polybius. This plan was opposed by Callicrates, who managed to hold up action on the ground that it was contrary to law to consider a question of military aid at the meeting. The result was the summoning to Sicyon of a *synkletos*, which was open not only to members of the *boule* but to all citizens over thirty. This is the only passage in the preserved parts of the history of Polybius in which he applies the term *synkletos* to an Achaean assembly or meeting.[2] It is from this passage that our information of the age limit for voting and on the composition of the primary assembly is derived. The report also helps confirm information from other sources about the procedure followed at meetings of the *ekklesia* when it states that on the second day anyone who wished could propose a decree. At this meeting there were two opposing motions submitted by Lycortas and Callicrates.

The best source of information concerning the procedure at the extraordinary meetings of the *ekklesia* is the account of the meeting at Sicyon in 198 at which the Achaeans decided to break with Macedonia and the Hellenic League and go over to Rome. This is supplemented somewhat by a shorter report of a meeting at Argos in 200. For both we have only the account of Livy, which, however, clearly is based on

---

[1] Pol. xxviii. 12. The Achaeans were to mobilize πανδημεί, but it is often difficult to know how complete such total mobilization really was.

[2] Pol. xxix. 23–25 with συγκλήτου occurring in 24. 6. The difficulties of interpretation are treated more fully in *Rep. Govt.* 87 f. Also in *SIG*³ 675, a decree of Oropus of about 154, there is a report of a *synodos* followed by a *synkletos*, but it adds no further information about the nature of the meetings.

Polybius. The subject to be taken up at such a meeting was announced in advance and no action could be taken on any subject except the one so announced. This is indicated by the accounts of both meetings.[1] The regular procedure at such a meeting consumed three days. The first was devoted to a statement or statements concerning the issue to be settled, the second was given over to the formulation of decrees, and on the third the vote was taken. Frequently foreign ambassadors were present and addressed the meeting on the first day of the session. At Sicyon in 198 there were present Roman, Pergamene, Rhodian, Macedonian, and Athenian ambassadors, and the entire day was devoted to their speeches.[2] At Sicyon in 168 only one set of foreign ambassadors was involved. Though the Ptolemaic ambassadors already had presented their case at the meeting of the *boule* at Corinth, and though their presence at Sicyon is not specifically mentioned, it can almost be taken for granted. Probably much of the first day was devoted to statements by Achaean dignitaries. On the second day of the meeting of 198 the call for those who wished to present their motion, according to the report of Livy, was issued by a herald (*praeco*), as was the custom of the Greeks.[3] Thus there was no formal *probouleuma*. The motion to be passed could be formulated at the meeting after the debate. At Sicyon in 168 there were two motions submitted, one by Lycortas to the effect that the aid requested by the Ptolemies be sent; one by Callicrates, that ambassadors be despatched to reconcile the Ptolemies with Antiochus. Probably neither of the two movers was the general of the year. Lycortas certainly was not,[4] and yet the majority of those present favoured the motion of Lycortas, and Callicrates carried the day only with the aid of a letter from the Roman proconsul in Macedonia. The absence of a formal *probouleuma* does not mean that everything was left to chance. Officials and prominent Achaeans knew in advance what measures they wished adopted. At the meeting just discussed, the motion of Lycortas apparently represented what might be called the government policy; that of Callicrates, the point of view of the opposition.

Decisions were normally greatly influenced by the advice of the general. In 181, when the Achaeans seemed to have settled the Messenian question and the Romans seemed to have given in to them, Achaean leaders tried to assume an independent policy also towards Sparta. At a *synodos* Spartan exiles had presented a letter from the

---

[1] Livy xxxi. 25. 9, xxxii. 20. 4.   [2] Livy xxxii. 19. 10–13.   [3] Livy xxxii. 20. 1.

[4] It is not known who was general in 169–168, but Lycortas certainly could not have thought of going to Egypt as commander of an Achaean detachment if he had been general. As for Callicrates, his opponents had been strong enough to elect Archon and Polybius as general and *hipparch* for 170–169, and it is hard to believe that they would have allowed Callicrates to be elected the following year.

Roman senate concerning their restoration. At the time the Achaeans put off action till their own ambassadors should return. When they did come, the Achaeans at a *synkletos* decided to make no changes, that is, to do nothing for the exiles. This happened when Lycortas was general and represented his policy. In the autumn of the year, the new general, Hyperbatus, called another *synkletos* hoping to have the policy changed, but in this case the prestige of office does not seem to have helped. Lycortas still prevailed, and it was decided to send an embassy to Rome to present his point of view. Yet, at this juncture, Hyperbatus won after all. Callicrates was one of the three ambassadors sent.[1] The most important decision ever made by a *synkletos*, that of 198 to go over to the side of the Romans, was made on the advice of the general, Aristaenus.

From this meeting comes also the best statement available concerning the taking of votes on the third day of the meeting. On the second day, Aristaenus had advocated becoming allies of the Romans. Already on that day, while five of the *damiorgoi* favoured putting the motion to vote, five indicated that they would not allow this to be done, since it was contrary to law for the magistrates to put to vote and for the assembly to decree anything conflicting with the alliance with Philip. This verdict must have been based on the pledges taken when the Achaeans joined the Hellenic League. The deadlock was broken when the father of one of those *damiorgoi* who opposed putting the motion threatened to lay violent hands on his son if he persisted. It then became clear that most of the cities—the vote was taken by cities— favoured the motion. Thereupon the men of Dyme and Megalopolis, and some of those of Argos withdrew before the voting took place. All those who remained favoured the motion. The result was alliances with Attalus and Rhodes and ultimately with Rome. The taking of votes by cities is reported also in connexion with a declaration of war on Sparta in 189. Though this is not stated in our sources, it is pretty certain that the votes of the cities normally were weighted in proportion to the numbers of their representatives in the *boule*.[2] Instead of mentioning this, the accounts of Livy (from Polybius) of the voting on the two occasions emphasizes the unanimity of the cities voting. Obviously this was regarded as highly desirable, and it may have been

---

[1] Pol. xxiv. 2. 1–5, 8. 1–8. On the meetings of 181 cf. *Rep. Govt.* 179–81.

[2] Livy xxxii. 22, xxxviii. 32. 1. Opinions of scholars have varied. See Busolt, *Staatskunde*, 1559, n. 1; Aymard, *ACA* 381, n. 4. Aymard has disproved the theory that *IG* iv². 1. 73 shows representation in proportion to population on the board of *nomographoi*. He is uncertain about the voting in the *synkletos*. On p. 382 and n. 3 he notes that the argument from analogy is inconclusive. For equality he lists the Peloponnesian and Athenian leagues; for proportion, the 'Macedonian symmachy' and the Lycian and Aetolian confederacies. But do not these very examples show the advance of the system of proportion?

in part for that reason that the men of Dyme and Megalopolis abstained from voting. One other detail emerges from the account of the meeting of 198. When points of order arose, they were decided by the *damiorgoi* alone. When it is reported that a general ruled that some measure could not be put to vote, it probably means that his ruling was not challenged or, if it had been challenged, was upheld by the *damiorgoi*. It need not mean that the general, who normally presided over the meetings, personally had the final decision.[1]

Two other councils, namely the *gerousia* and the *nomographoi* must be mentioned for the sake of completeness. The *gerousia* is mentioned only once. At Corinth in 146, after the general, Critolaus, already had opposed the other magistrates, he became so abusive to the Roman ambassadors that the members of the *gerousia* sought to lay hands on him and restrain him.[2] Though they failed, the story implies action by a body which felt that it had a right to control the behaviour of any speaker, even the general. This can hardly have been anyone but the *damiorgoi*. Hence, of the various theories concerning the *gerousia*, the most plausible is that the word designates the college of *damiorgoi*.[3]

The *nomographoi* are known largely from an inscription listing twenty-four members from seventeen cities and a secretary. Most of these cities had one representative each, two had three each, and three two each. Soon after the publication of this document, Heinrich Swoboda advanced the theory that the composition of the board was based on representation in proportion to population. This theory won wide acceptance. Since then, however, Aymard has demonstrated that it seems impossible to find a time when representation of cities according to population would produce such a distribution of seats as that shown in the inscription.[4] Another mention of the *nomographoi* is found in a decree of Megalopolis of the late third century preserved at Magnesia on the Maeander,[5] but this gives little or no help in determining the

[1] For rulings by the general, Aymard, *ACA* 358, n. 5 cites Livy xxxi. 25. 9 and Pol. xxii. 9. 12. In his opinion the *damiorgoi* and general constituted the presiding board (*bureau*). At the Sicyon meeting in 198 Aristaenus was excluded from taking part in the decision because he had participated in the debate (357–61). This is possible but unlikely. At any rate, active participation in the debate on the part of the general was not rare.

[2] Pol. xxxviii. 12. 7, 13. 1. This passage is difficult, but it does seem clear that Critolaus was defying other magistrates.

[3] Aymard, *ACA* 153 f. somewhat hesitatingly indicates this as the preferred interpretation.

[4] *IG* iv². 1. 73. See especially Swoboda, *Hermes*, lvii (1922), 519–22; Aymard, *ACA* 383–5; cf. also *Rep. Govt.* 217, n. 22.

[5] *SIG*³ 559. At the end is the statement that other Arcadians passed similar decrees. This is followed by a list of eighteen cities, not all Arcadian. The list undoubtedly is due to the Magnesians and has nothing to do either with a revival of the Arcadian Confederacy or with an Arcadian district within the Achaean Confederacy.

composition of the board. Its connexion with laws and law-making will be considered later.

The *boule* and *ekklesia* of the Achaeans suggest democracy. In addition there is the boast of the Achaean democracy on the part of Polybius.[1] But this does not mean that the Achaeans had a government as democratic as that of Athens in the fifth century. It should no longer be necessary to argue that the meaning of *demokratia* had changed, so that in Hellenistic times states which once would have been considered oligarchic could be called democratic. In the Achaean Confederacy the right to vote was limited to men over thirty.[2] This limitation combined with the absence of pay for magistrates and for attendance at meetings might be enough to place control of the state in the hands of the men of property. But this may not have been all. The total number of men at arms that the Confederacy could raise is once given as 30,000 or 40,000 at a time when it included practically the entire Peloponnesus, and this is given in such a way as to suggest a theoretical maximum, never actually mobilized. Since this is not a large number for the entire peninsula, it is possible that there was a property qualification for active citizenship.[3] Except when inspired by such a leader as Philopoemen, the Achaean men of means may not have been anxious for military service, but the ease with which mercenaries could be raised indicates that there was a mass of poorer men ready to serve if there was any money to be made.

The federal finances is a subject of special importance for the functioning of the government, but it is also an elusive and difficult problem. There was a federal treasurer, but he is seldom mentioned[4] and seems to have been relatively unimportant. There must normally have been a little money in the treasury to provide for minor current expenses—a sort of petty cash fund made up of sums sent to the treasury by the constituent cities. There is no proof that there existed any tax which was collected directly by the federal government.[5] At

[1] Especially Pol. ii. 38. 6; cf. Walbank ad loc.

[2] Pol. xxix. 24. 6.

[3] Pol. xxix. 24. 8. Beloch, *GrG*[2] iii. i. 285 estimates the population of the Peloponnesus as about 1,140,000 in 400 B.C.

[4] In inscriptions the *tamias* apparently is mentioned only in *Inschriften von Magnesia*, 39. 46.

[5] Busolt, *Staatskunde*, 1317, n. 6 (on p. 1318) mentions permanent direct taxes among the Achaeans but cites no evidence. Later (1549, n. 1) the closing lines of *SIG*[3] 531 are cited as proof of the obligation to support payments to the federal treasury. This may be correct, though much of the text has been restored, but this still does not prove the existence of a special federal tax. On p. 1554, n. 3 it is stated that the Confederacy imposed payments on the cities and not individuals, and that these communities collected the money and sent it to the federal government. This last statement is correct but is not given sufficient emphasis, while the earlier statements are misleading. The grant of *ateleia* in *SIG*[3] 519 tells little about federal finances. It is not even clear whether the taxes involved were collected by federal or local officials. The example of Acarnania should be a warning not to attribute rashly to a

most there were taxes or fees collected by the cities that were destined
for the federal treasury, but it is much more likely that the cities merely
sent sums of various sizes depending upon the circumstances. To judge
by the examples of the early Boeotian, the Aetolian, and Lycian confederacies, they simply paid a certain sum for each representative in
the federal *boule*. This sum could be increased when the demands were
heavy and lowered when the demands were few. In the case of a wind-
fall, payments might be completely eliminated. These payments were
called *eisphorai*, a term which tends to suggest extraordinary payments,
and which certainly indicates payments of lump sums by the cities. In
219, when the three cities of Dyme, Pharae, and Tritaea felt that they
were not adequately defended by the federal general, they decided
not to pay their *eisphorai* but to engage mercenaries themselves. Polybius praises them for this initiative but blames them for failing to keep
faith with the federal government, especially since their right of recovery of the outlay was undisputed.[1] This implies that if the members
undertook expenses which properly belonged to the federal government, they had the right to be reimbursed. Undoubtedly also the
federal government theoretically had a right to compel the cities to
send their contributions. This was under the generalship of the
younger Aratus.

Next year, under Eperatus, conditions were no better. Therefore the
refusal to pay *eisphorai* was more general. As a result, there was a shortage of money for the pay of soldiers so that the mercenary force of the
Achaeans was seriously demoralized. Such were still the conditions in
the spring of 217 when the elder Aratus once more took over as general.
What happened next shows that the condition was due to neglect and
disorganization. Aratus, at what must have been an extraordinary
meeting of the assembly, secured the adoption of a resolution to keep
mobilized a mercenary force of 8,000 infantry and 500 cavalry and a
detachment of Achaean citizen troops numbering 3,000 infantry and
300 cavalry. It was also arranged to put half a dozen ships into service
along the coast. This must mean that the cities were able and now,
when there was prospect of action, willing to pay *eisphorai* for the support of the armed forces. Later, when considerable booty had been
secured through the raids by the ships, the soldiers were cheered because they felt that their pay was assured; the cities, because they hoped
not to be burdened with *eisphorai*.[2] Clearly there were assessments
for special purposes when the need arose. During the generalship

---

federal government the direct collection of customs duties. Such a system for Achaea would
have involved an elaborate federal bureaucracy. The federal government may well have
had the right to grant exemption even if the duties were collected by local authorities.

[1] Pol. iv. 60. 4–10.   [2] Pol. v. 30. 5–8, 91. 4–8, 94. 6–9.

of Eperatus the cities refused specifically to contribute to pay for
the army. Yet the Achaeans voted to give the Macedonians fifty
talents as pay for three months for their army in the field, to supply
them with grain, and, if necessary, to pay seventeen talents a month
for any time they remained in the Peloponnesus beyond the three
months. Undoubtedly this required a special assessment.[1] This
manner of financing federal undertakings worked well enough when
the Confederacy had able leadership which enjoyed the confidence of
the citizens. Under incompetent leadership, the system collapsed.

The Achaean system of coinage went well with the system of taxation. Polybius has made famous the fact that members of the Confederacy used 'the same coins', that is, they had a uniform system of
coinage. Yet there was no federal mint, but the constituent cities
minted coins which bore on the reverse the Achaean monogram and
the monogram or symbol of the cities issuing them. The standard
silver coin was an Aeginetan triobol, which apparently was the chief
coin in use in the entire Peloponnesus. Many cities also issued autonomous triobols, that is, coins without any federal insignia. Some of
these may have been issued before the city joined the Confederacy,
but it is clear that several cities issued autonomous coins as well as
federal coins after they had joined. Such a demonstration of local pride
clearly was considered neither treasonable nor objectionable. Most remarkable was the case of Megalopolis, which, in addition to federal
and autonomous coins also minted coins marked as Arcadian. This
city, at the very time when its citizens played a prominent part in the
leadership of the Achaean Confederacy, liked to keep alive the impression that it was the chief city of Arcadia. Finally, it may be noted
that the use of the Aeginetan standard and the triobol as the chief
denomination minted made the Peloponnesus somewhat a land apart
within Greece.[2]

The systems of taxation and coinage indicate that most of the
details of administration were handled by local authorities. Hence it
need hardly be demonstrated that the cities had laws and law-making
machinery of their own. There were city as well as federal *nomographoi*.[3]
This must mean that there were differences in details between the laws
of the cities. Hence, when Polybius (ii. 37. 10) states that the Achaeans
used the same laws or had uniform laws, this, strictly speaking, is not
true about local laws but only about federal laws. The latter largely

---

[1] Pol. v. 1. 11.

[2] For brief statements on the Achaean coins with references to earlier literature see *Econ.
Surv. Rome*, iv. 328 f. and Walbank, *Commentary on Polybius*, i. 218. For autonomous coinage
and the Arcadian coinage of Megalopolis, Margaret Thompson, 'A Hoard of Greek
Federal Silver', *Hesperia*, viii (1939), 116–54, especially 142–4.

[3] Summary of evidence in Busolt, *Staatskunde*, 1572, n. 6.

concerned constitutional law, such as the law frequently mentioned which regulated the meetings of the *ekklesia*. The latter is an example of a piece of legislation altering the constitution of the Confederacy. This need not mean that constitutional law was clearly distinguished from other law, but law and decree were distinguished. Another constitutional change came in 188, when the old custom of holding the regular *synodoi* at Aegium was abandoned and a law passed to the effect that thereafter meetings were to rotate between cities.[1] The meeting, a *synodos* or regular meeting of the *boule*, undoubtedly adopted a decree which the *nomographoi* were instructed to register among the laws. Such details are not reported in our literary sources but can be deduced from the legislative practices of the times as well as the existence of *nomographoi* in the Confederacy. Another important, though less far-reaching law, was one forbidding the acceptance of gifts from a king on the part both of private citizens and officials. This is mentioned in connexion with the offer of 120 talents by Eumenes. It probably had not yet been adopted at the time when Aratus was receiving an annual subsidy of six talents from Ptolemy.[2] It can be inferred that there were laws regulating the *eisphorai* and the minting of money. The laws concerning military service went so far that the general could order complete mobilization without indicating the purpose or objective. An example is the time when Philopoemen ordered a mobilization in such a way that no one knew where he was going until the last day when all converged on Tegea.[3]

Concerning law-making, it may be noted that the Achaean Confederacy was one of the federal states for which there is evidence for a board of *nomographoi* which staged periodic revisions of the laws. Directions to the board to register a particular decree as law was common. There is evidence for this for the late third century both for the Confederacy and for cities belonging to it.[4] Thus the board may have been in existence when the time for the Achaean elections was changed, and when the new rules about summoning the *ekklesia* were adopted, and, without any doubt, existed in 188 when the law concerning the rotation of the place of meetings of the *boule* was adopted. It seems safe to

---

[1] Livy xxxviii. 30. 1–6. The law was passed at the meeting which the *damiorgoi* had called at Aegium and the general, Philopoemen, at Argos, where the meeting actually took place. Livy does not say in so many words that the law proposed by Philopoemen was passed, but this is implied by the manner in which all opposition broke down. On the meeting, cf. *Rep. Govt.* 174 f. Aymard, *ACA* 302–5, who was inclined to class the meeting as a *synkletos*, also began to see arguments for considering it a *synodos* (p. 323, n. 6).

[2] Law against gifts: Pol. xxii. 8. 3; subsidy of Aratus: Plut. *Arat.* 41. 5.

[3] Pol. xvi. 36. A law making it illegal to fail to answer the summons of the general is mentioned by Paus. vii. 12. 6.

[4] The Achaean Confederacy: *Inschriften von Magnesia*, 39. 43 f.; Megalopolis: ibid. 38 (*SIG*3 559). 47 f.; evidence for other cities, Busolt, *Staatskunde*, 1572, n. 6.

conclude that at least the latter reform was embodied in a decree which the *nomographoi* were instructed to include among the laws.[1]

The federal courts naturally had jurisdiction in cases of treason and the like. Sometimes also special regulations for single cities were imposed at the time of their admission into the Confederacy. An example is the agreement by which Orchomenus was admitted. This provided for the trial of certain cases before a federal court, which was competent not only to impose fines but also to inflict the death penalty.[2] The federal assembly or council sometimes took upon itself to condemn an individual, but jurisdiction was normally in the hands of special federal judges. How many they were and how they were chosen, is not known, though there is reason to believe that any individual court contained only a small number of judges. That the activities of the courts were extensive is suggested by the fact that the Achaeans at times employed foreign judges. This is known from an incident connected with a decree ordering the abolition of the excessive honours of Eumenes of Pergamum. The task of determining which honours were excessive was left to a court, in which the judges were Rhodians, who had their own grudge against Eumenes. The result was that all his honours were cancelled. Editors and translators have commonly refused to believe that the judges were Rhodians, but the story rings absolutely true. Foreign judges appear again in connexion with the Roman ruling in 183 that the Achaeans were to have jurisdiction over the Spartans except for capital charges, which were to be submitted to foreign judges.[3] That the use of foreign judges by the Achaeans was extensive is suggested by the fact that the Rhodian judges who handled the question of the honours of Eumenes were not summoned to deal with this particular problem but already were on hand when the question came up.[4] The case apparently was handled by a panel consisting of only the two judges named by Polybius. In fact, small panels were common when foreign judges were employed.[5] There is reason to believe that this tendency to use small panels of judges applied also to the native Achaean judges. Thus, when the general, Diaeus, during the death struggle of the Confederacy engineered the execution of the *hypostrategos* Sosicrates, he secured the organization of a panel of dicasts to render the verdict. This suggests

---

[1] Livy xxxviii. 30. 3 speaks of a *lex* and implies that it was passed.

[2] *SIG*³ 490.

[3] Honours of Eumenes: Pol. xxviii. 7. 8–9; settlement of 183: Paus. vii. 9. 5. For a fuller discussion see *CP* xliii (1948) 189 f. in a discussion of '"Foreign Judges" in Cicero *Ad Atticum* vi. 1. 15'. To the literature cited there in n. 6 add A. Heuss, *Stadt und Herscher des Hellenismus*, *Klio*, Beiheft xxxix (1937), 72, n. 1.

[4] ὑπάρχοντας κατ' ἐκεῖνον τὸν καιρόν (Pol. xxviii. 7. 9).

[5] For brief accounts of foreign judges cf. *CP* xxxviii (1943), 249–53; Tarn-Griffith, 88 f.

the existence of a group of federal judges from among whom the panels for particular cases could be made up.[1]

Such was the normal system of federal administration of justice. Yet much is heard of sentences imposed by an assembly. In this connexion the word 'assembly' will be used whether the body referred to is the old *boule-ekklesia* of the early Confederacy or the *boule* or *ekklesia* of the later period. In general, verdicts due to an assembly seem to have been incidental to politics. The assembly did not sit as a court but, when it saw fit, passed a decree imposing the death penalty or banishment upon some individual. Sometimes it is not easy to distinguish. However, when in 183 there were ambassadors at Rome representing Spartans condemned to death or exiled according to the decrees of the Achaeans, it is likely that the decrees laid down the general rules and that judges or other officials decided what particular individuals were affected by the ruling.[2] In such cases the assembly probably legislated rather than acted as a court. Also when the former general Cycliadcs was exiled on account of his pro-Macedonian leanings, it is safe to conclude that he was exiled by the assembly and that the action was primarily political.[3] On the other hand, when a certain Leonidas is referred to as *exul, damnatus frequenti concilio Achaeorum litteris ad Persea deprensis*, it looks more as if the assembly made some pretence of acting as a court and considering the evidence before giving its verdict, though it probably did little more than hear a report concerning the incriminating correspondence with Perseus.[4]

In the division of labour between the federal and local governments, the conduct of foreign affairs naturally fell to the federal government, though even here the prominence and influence of individual cities can be observed. Thus the hostility between Megalopolis and Sparta coloured Achaean politics for years. An obvious rule was that embassies of political importance must be sent by or at least have the approval of the federal government, though this approval might be given by federal officials. This rule probably did not apply to religious matters. Thus the recognition of the festival of Artemis Lycophryene at Magneisa on the Maeander and the inviolability of the sanctuary and the city was voted not only by the Achaean Confederacy but by many of the cities belonging to it.[5] In such matters the city controlling a sanctuary obviously took pride in securing as many decrees as

---

[1] Pol. xxxviii. 18. 3. Though Diaeus was responsible in this case, it need not mean that the general normally supervised the selection of dicasts.

[2] Pol. xxiii. 4. 5, 8, 14.

[3] Pol. xviii. 1. 2; Livy xxxii. 19. 1–2, cf. 32. 10.

[4] Livy xlii. 51. 8.

[5] *Inschriften von Magnesia*, 38 (Megalopolis), 39 (Achaean). At the end of 38 are listed eighteen 'Arcadian' cities said to have passed similar decrees.

possible, and there is no indication that any federal government objected to having such decrees passed by the cities. In the decree of the city of Aegira, included in the mass of decrees of 242 recognizing the inviolability of the sanctuary of Asclepius of Cos, it is indicated that the city's decree had been preceded by a federal decree.[1]

Embassies of political importance sent abroad by cities, as already indicated, required the approval of the federal authorities. To be sure, this rule was later frequently violated by cities sending embassies to Rome without the approval of the central government, but that meant that the city in question was in open revolt, or on the verge of revolt, or, and this was much the same, was appealing to Rome against the federal government. There are so many instances of this in the second century that it is not necessary to cite examples. A good example of the proper procedure is the embassy of Megalopolis to Antigonus Doson in 227. At the time Aratus, the general of the year, was beginning to feel that it might become necessary for the Achaeans to call in the Macedonians for help against Cleomenes of Sparta. Consequently he arranged with two Megalopolitan friends to have their city send ambassadors—*presbeutai*, the usual term for envoys from cities to the federal government—to the Achaeans to secure from them permission to proceed to Macedonia to ask for Macedonian intervention. The permission was promptly granted and the ambassadors continued on their way.[2] The speed with which the permission was secured, shows that it was given by federal officials and that it was not necessary to wait for a meeting of an assembly. From Doson the ambassadors obtained a promise of help in case also the Achaeans desired it. The Megalopolitans submitted this reply to an assembly of the Achaeans with the recommendation that they invite Antigonus. Aratus, however, secured a decision from the Achaeans to make no change for the time being but to try to carry on the war by themselves.[3]

An excellent illustration of the supervision by the federal government of the relations of an Achaean city with an outside city is to be seen in the affair of exiles from Elatea given refuge at Stymphalus in Arcadia. When the Elateans had been driven into exile, probably in 194, the Stymphalians took them in, supplied them with food, gave them land to cultivate, and allowed them to share in the religious life of the community. This is known from the copy posted at Stymphalus of a decree passed by the Elateans after their return home.[4] The begin-

---

[1] *SEG* xii. 371. 41–51.   [2] Pol. ii. 48. 5–8.
[3] The ambassadors before Antigonus: ii. 48. 8; his reply: 50. 1–2; the *synodos*: 50. 4–51. 1.
[4] *SEG* xi. 1107. The section telling of the exiling of the Elateans has been lost and so both the Romans and the Aetolians have been blamed by various scholars. The problem will come up in the narrative of the events of the period.

ning of the document is lost, but it is reasonably clear that permission to bring the Elateans into the territory of the Achaeans must have been secured from the federal government. Later, when the Romans had secured control of Phocis, the Stymphalians, according to the normal practice of cities, sent ambassadors to the Achaeans, who in turn sent ambassadors to the Roman commander in Greece concerning the return of the Elateans to their old home. When they were preparing to leave, another difficulty arose. On account of an embargo on grain, it was impossible for the Elateans to take along their own grain. Again this was taken care of by an embassy which arranged for a special permit. This undoubtedly was granted by a federal magistrate or board of officials. This incident indicates that cities retained their individuality, and that it was possible for a city, with the permission of the federal government, to have intimate relationships with a city outside of the Confederacy.

In the Achaean Confederacy, in spite of the marked individuality of some of the cities, the citizens possessed civil rights in all the cities of the Confederacy. There is evidence that Aratus of Sicyon owned property at Corinth and that a certain Hiero of Aegeira owned a house in Argos.[1] This, however, is not conclusive for the general grant of civil rights, for the individuals in question may have been granted the right to hold property as a special privilege. More conclusive is the casualty list for Epidaurus for the battle of the Isthmus in 146. The list contains 156 names of which fifty three are the names of Epidaurian citizens and 103 of Achaeans and other residents. The 'other residents' may include non-Achaean metics, but the 103 must have been made up largely of Achaeans from other cities. One can hardly imagine so many moving to Epidaurus and affiliating themselves closely enough with the community to serve in its contingent in the army, unless they possessed civil rights.[2]

There remains the question of the capital of the Confederacy. Bengtson denies that either the Achaeans or the Aetolians possessed a capital,[3] but he has in mind the lack of any hegemony within the Confederacy, that is, the absence of any city that dominated it as Thebes did the Boeotian Confederacy. That is not what is meant by a capital in the present discussion, and so our views are not too far apart. By capital rather is meant the administrative centre, above all the place where 'ambassadors' from Megalopolis, Stymphalus, and other places could communicate with the federal authorities. Most likely the archives and treasury were in the same city. That there must have been a place to which communications to the federal government

[1] Plut. *Arat.* 41. 4, 42. 3; *Cleom.* 19; *SIG*³ 675.
[2] *IG* iv². 1. 28. [3] Bengtson, *GrG*² 442.

could be sent at any time is obvious. In this connexion it may not be out of place to recall the Athenian rule that one third of the *prytaneis* must be available in the *tholos* at all times of day and night, and that in the Hellenic League of the late fourth century the *proëdroi* functioned as a committee between the meetings of the assembly.[1] A federal state probably did not have a perpetual watch like that of the Athenian *prytaneis*, but they must have had an official or board at least as accessible as the *proëdroi* of the Hellenic League. That the Achaean capital for such purposes was Aegium is shown by an anecdote concerning the negotiations between Aratus and Cleomenes. When the negotiations broke down, Cleomenes sent a herald declaring the resumption of hostilities not to Argos, where Aratus and the other officials were at the time, but to Aegium. This, as Aratus remarked in his memoirs, was clearly a trick to gain time,[2] but Cleomenes could argue that he had acted perfectly properly, for he had sent his message to the capital. Further proof is to be found in the law of 188 ordering that thereafter the regular *synodoi* should be held in various cities in rotation. So far all regular meetings had been held in Aegium. This change did not mean that the city ceased to be the capital. There still was need for a centre of administration.

5. THE LYCIAN CONFEDERACY

In this mountainous and, except for contacts by sea, rather isolated little country near the western end of the southern coast of Asia Minor, there had developed by 200 B.C. a federal state which by 100 B.C. at the latest, had done away with the federal primary assembly and thus had adopted representative government.[3] This was developed by a non-Greek people, which retained its native language to a late date[4] but

---

[1] The Athenian *prytaneis*: Arist. *Ath. pol.* 44. 1; the *proëdroi* of the Hellenic League are discussed *CP* xx (1925), 325–8 and, with some new evidence, *IXe congrès international des sciences historiques*, i (1950), 403 f.

[2] Plut. *Cleom.* 17. 2 quoting Aratus; cf. Walbank, *Aratos of Sicyon*, 94 f. For comparison note that the report of the battle of Lake Trasimene was brought to Philip at Argos by a letter from Macedonia (Pol. v. 101. 6). Clearly the Macedonian intelligence agents in Italy sent their reports to the home office and not directly to the king.

[3] O. Treuber, *Geschichte der Lykier* (1887) and G. Fougères, *De Lyciorum communi* (1898) have in part been rendered obsolete by later discoveries. For more recent introductions see A. H. M. Jones, *The Cities of the Eastern Roman Provinces* (1937), ch. iii; D. Magie, *Roman Rule in Asia Minor* (1950), ch. xxii; L. Moretti, *Ricerche sulle leghe greche* (1962), ch. iii, cf. review in *CP* lix (1964), 137–9. The works of Fougères, Jones, Magie, and Moretti will be cited in this section by the names of the authors alone. The inscriptions for parts of Lycia are now collected in *Tituli Asiae Minoris* (*TAM*). For others it is still necessary to go to *Inscriptiones graecae ad res romanas pertinentes* (*IGR*) and special collections.

[4] What the language was seems to remain a matter of dispute. For a statement citing earlier theories see Deeters, *RE* xiii. 2282–91. Some more recent opinions follow: belongs to a group of Anatolian languages, neither Indo-European nor Semitic (Beloch, *GrG*². i. i. 97); probably not Indo-European (Moretti, 173); descended from Luvian, an Indo-European

developed under Greek influence a culture with something of a flavour of its own known to all students of Greek art. Probably this non-Greek background is in part responsible for the fact that the Lycian Confederacy commonly has been passed over in handbooks on Greek political institutions.[1] Moreover, there were local developments in this part of Asia Minor which may suggest even to the careful student that the Lycian Confederacy was Anatolian rather than Greek, Nevertheless, it is clear that Lycia ultimately became thoroughly Hellenized and that the political institutions conformed closely to Greek institutions even if the impulse to federalism at the outset may not have been Greek. In short, the Lycian Confederacy belongs to Hellenistic federalism fully as much as the Achaean and Thessalian confederacies. To mention an example of a striking similarity in terminology, the noun *apoteleios*, used as the title of a commander of a local contingent in the Achaean federal army, is used with the same meaning in a decree of the Lycian city of Araxa of the early second century B.C.[2]

Two organizations which may have had some influence on the development of Lycian federalism are the Chrysaoric Confederacy in Caria to the northwest of Lycia and the Cibyrate Tetrapolis on its northern border.[3] The chief literary source for the two organizations as for the Lycian Confederacy itself is Strabo, who is known to have drawn on Artemidorus of Ephesus, who wrote about 100 B.C. or a little later. Thus Strabo's account largely describes conditions of the early first century B.C., though there are some references to later events. The Chrysaoric Confederacy is important as illustrating one manner in which representation in proportion to population might have developed. The history of federalism or approaches towards federalism in Caria is very complicated and cannot be taken up here in detail. It appears that an earlier Carian organization was made up of Greek or Hellenized cities, while the Chrysaoric *ethnos* originally was made up of native Carian villages. Another feature appearing in Caria and common in this part of Asia Minor is the juxtaposition of constitutional government of a kind and a powerful individual often later called a tyrant or a dynast. An early example is the Mausolus who was

language which came into Asia Minor about the same time as Hittite (L. R. Palmer, *Mycenaeans and Minoans* (1961), 229 f.); belongs to a group of Indo-European languages probably established in Asia Minor at the same time as Hittite and Luvian (O. R. Gurney, *The Hittites* (revised, 1961), 18, cf. 127).

[1] The Lycian Confederacy is omitted in Swoboda, *Staatsaltertümer* and Busolt, *Staatskunde*.

[2] First published by G. E. Bean, 'Notes and Inscriptions from Lycia', *JHS* lxviii (1948), 40–58 at 46–56. Later editions: L. Moretti, *Riv. fil.* lxxviii (1950), 326–50: J. Pouilloux, *Choix d'inscriptions grecques*, 4; *SEG* xviii. 570. Cf. the discussions of J. and L. Robert, *Bull. ép.* 1950, no. 183 and by myself, *CP* li (1956), 151–69.

[3] On these two organizations see 'Representation and Democracy in Hellenistic Federalism', *CP* xl (1945), 65–97 at 76–81; also Magie, *passim*.

'satrap' and is mentioned in a decree of the city of Mylasa.[1] In Caria, which was only partially urbanized, the cities probably early formed a sort of federal state. Somewhat later the Carian villages in the rural areas organized a confederacy of their own. Then, when the villages were absorbed into the territories of the cities, the two organizations more or less merged. According to Strabo the villagers held their meetings at the temple of Zeus Chrysaoreus in the territory—not inside the city—of Stratonicea. Apparently the villages each had one vote, for, says Strabo, the cities that controlled most villages carried most weight in the organization. Thus there developed a system of representation of cities in proportion to the number of Carian villages acquired. Stratonicea, a Macedonian colony, though its citizens were not Carians, held membership through the Carian villages it controlled.[2]

The Cibyrate Tetrapolis apparently went a little farther in the direction of representation in proportion to population. According to Strabo it consisted of four cities, Cibyra, Bubon, Balbura, and Oenoanda. Of these Cibyra had two votes (psephoi) and each of the others one. For the present purpose this general sketch will suffice. It is not necessary to go into the problem of other towns which seem once to have belonged and to have been absorbed by or merged with one of the others. It is more important to notice the strange combination of constitutionalism with tyranny attested by Strabo, who praises the excellence of the laws but states that the Tetrapolis was always under a tyrant, though the tyrant ruled with moderation, the last tyrant, Moagetes, being ousted by Murena, one of Sulla's lieutenants, in 84 B.C. At that time, while Cibyra itself was joined to the province of Asia, Balbura and Bubon and, undoubtedly, Oenoanda were given to the Lycians.[3] At the time of the expedition of Manlius Vulso in Asia in 189, another Moagetes ruled at Cibyra, and it is likely that he and his descendants ruled continually from that date to 84.[4] To this period belongs a treaty of alliance with Rome in which the two contracting parties are the people (demos) of Rome and the people of Cibyra. There is no mention of the dynast or tyrant.[5] Thus there appears again the combination of republican government with control by a dynast or tyrant. On the question of representation, the only safe conclusion to be drawn from the statement that Cibyra had two votes and each of the other three one vote, is that Cibyra had twice as great

---

[1] Tod, 138.

[2] Strabo xiv. 660. The *ethnos* is mentioned in *OG* 234, an Amphictionic decree of about 200 B.C.

[3] Strabo xiii. 631.   [4] Pol. xxi. 34; Livy xxxviii. 14.

[5] *OG* 762. The absence of any mention of the tyrant has led to the theory that tyranny was abolished earlier than the time given by Strabo, but see *CP* xl. 80, n. 80.

a share in the government of the Tetrapolis as any one of the other three. Strabo, as will be noted below, uses the same word in stating that the cities of Lycia each had three, two, or one *psephos* in the *synedrion* of the Confederacy. In Lycia, with twenty-three cities, it is possible to imagine a council in which each city had one, two, or three representatives, but one can hardly speak of a *synedrion* with five members. Hence it is clear that the statements indicate proportion rather than the exact number of representatives.

The origin and early development of the Lycian Confederacy cannot be traced, though there are indications that there was a movement towards union and concerted action already when Lycia was successively under the Ptolemies, Antiochus III, and Rhodes. The evidence was rather tenuous[1] until the publication in 1949 of a honorific decree from the city of Araxa in honour of one of its citizens, Orthagoras, who had been active in warfare against a local dynast about 200 B.C.[2] This document shows that the Lycians possessed an active federal government ready to intervene when desirable and necessary both with diplomatic and military support of members that were attacked, though much of the frontier defence was left to the cities along the border. Sometimes these operations were on such a scale that they actually amounted to little wars. This was largely on account of the presence of landowners or barons who controlled large estates and sometimes enrolled large bands of retainers. From time to time, one of these magnates would get control of a nearby city and thus become its real ruler, even if the city retained its magistrates and assemblies. Alternately he might become a robber baron and raid his neighbours. One of the most powerful of such rulers was, of course, the tyrant of the Cibyrate Tetrapolis. Also the Ptolemaeus, son of Lysimachus, who controlled Telmessus in Caria, apparently belongs pretty much in the same class. It may be noted in passing that the region remained one with many large estates right down into Roman[3] and, it is safe to add, Byzantine times.

Araxa lay in a strategic or exposed position near the northern end of the valley of the Xanthus river, just at the foot of a range of mountains running east and west. Across the range, just a few miles away, lay the towns that for some time were incorporated in the Cibyrate Tetrapolis. Of these, Bubon was only about a dozen miles away as the crow flies. About 200 B.C. this town was under the control of a certain Moagetes, in all likelihood the Moagetes who was soon to control the

---

[1] Cf. *CP* xl. 71–76 for an effort to trace this earlier development.
[2] For editions and literature see p. 241, n. 2 above. In what follows it will be taken for granted that the date of the document is about 180 B.C., which is now the generally accepted date.   [3] Cf. T. R. S. Broughton in *Econ. Surv. Rome*, iv. 663–76.

Cibyrate Tetrapolis. At the moment he obviously was tyrant of Bubon, though the city possessed enough self-government so that in their early undertakings the two appeared as partners. Together they had raided the territory of Araxa sufficiently to have the resulting operations referred to as a war. For this war Orthagoras was elected commander by his city. He was also sent as ambassador to Cibyra to complain of the conduct of Moagetes and the Bubonians, who, at the time, in some way must have been subject to Cibyra. At this point the war was called off, clearly through the influence of Cibyra, but hostilities were soon resumed.

When Moagetes renewed his raids, the city of Araxa sent Orthagoras as its ambassador (*presbeutes*) to the federal government. The result was that the federal government in turn sent him as its ambassador to lodge its complaint against Moagetes and to Moagetes himself to negotiate concerning the goods he had carried off and the crimes he had committed. The fact that an attempt was made to negotiate with Moagetes suggests that he may have claimed to have some grievance justifying his use of self-help to gain restitution. The fact that a complaint was lodged at Cibyra, shows that Moagetes was still regarded as a subject of that city. This time, however, the result of the appeal was that the Cibyrates joined Moagetes in the war. In the hostilities that followed and obviously lasted for some time, Orthagoras alternated between service in the cavalry and repeated embassies to the federal government in an effort to induce it to intervene with military aid, but these efforts were not successful. The federal government continued to regard the hostilities as frontier disorders to be handled by the local authorities. Ultimately some settlement must have been reached. At any rate, when war later broke out in another part of the Confederacy, Araxa was able to send its contingent to the federal army.

Two individuals, otherwise unknown, named Lysanias and Eudemus, seized the city of Xanthus, staged a massacre, and proceeded to set up tyranny there. This time the Confederacy as a whole intervened and Orthagoras served as commander of the contingent of Araxa. At first the federal troops do not seem to have met with much success. Instead the conspirators were able to secure also Tlos, situated farther up the Xanthus valley. This renewed success of the would-be tyrants stimulated the Lycians to continue the war until the tyranny was overthrown. If while a dynast controlled Telmessus and a tyrant was securing control of Cibyra, other tyrants had secured two of the leading cities in the centre of Lycia, it would have been a sorry day for the Confederacy and Lycian freedom. Later a war of the Confederacy against Termessus, probably Termessus Major in Pisidia, is mentioned.[1] For this war neither any great success nor any great setback is reported. Yet, as a whole, after the expulsion of the tyrants from Xanthus and Tlos, better days seem to have arrived. At any rate, less warlike measures are reported. After his service in the war against Termessus, Orthagoras is next reported to have played a prominent part in securing from the federal government—apparently a federal court—a settlement favourable to Araxa of a dispute with another member of the Confederacy over a bit of land, and again in securing the admission of the nearby town of Orloanda into the Confederacy. Since the latter action involved the liberation of Orloanda, it is possible that the expulsion of a tyrant or some other drastic action was involved, but there is no indication of any serious hostilities.

A serious situation arose a few years later as the result of the defeat of Antiochus III by the Romans. After the Seleucid king had extended his control over southern Asia Minor, he planted a garrison at least in the Lycian port of Patara, where royal troops (regii milites) are reported to have been present in 190. In that year it was attacked by a mixed Roman and Rhodian squadron. A second larger attack is said to have been planned but abandoned. The following winter, Polyxenidas, the commander of the fleet of Antiochus, when he heard of the defeat at Magnesia, sailed to Patara, abandoned his ships there and made his way to Syria overland. The ships left behind to the number of fifty decked ships were destroyed by the Romans in 188.[2]

When the decision once was made, the Lycians clearly were anxious to gain the favour of Rome as soon and as thoroughly as possible. Undoubtedly they were among the many states that appealed to Rome through embassies, but their involvement in the war, willing or unwilling, made it desirable to think of some special way of currying favour. This special way was found in the deification of Roma. This mode of appeal apparently was used first by Smyrna, where a temple of Roma is reported to have been erected in 195 B.C.,[3] five years before Roman troops entered Asia. After Smyrna had shown the way, a number of other states followed the example. The cult established by the Lycians was one of Roma Goddess Manifest (Rhome Thea Epiphanes),[4] in whose honour pentaëteric festivals were organized.

---

[1] In CP li (1956), 162 I was inclined to believe that the city was Termessus Minor located near Bubon and Cibyra. Later I heard from Professor Bean that he had visited the site of Termessus Minor and considered it very unlikely that there could have been a city there large enough to have maintained a war against the Lycian Confederacy. Also the Roberts in Bull. ép. 1950, no. 183 are inclined to believe that Termessus Major is meant.

[2] Livy xxxvii. 15–16. 45, 2; later destruction of ships: Pol. xxi. 44. 3; Livy xxxviii. 39. 2–3.

[3] Tac. Ann. iv. 56. 1.

[4] Line 71 of the Araxa inscription cited on p. 241, n. 2. On this and other cults of the period see 'Some Early Anatolian Cults of Roma', Mélanges A. Piganiol (1966), 1635–43.

Orthagoras of Araxa served as envoy to the two first such festivals. The epithet *Epiphanes* must refer to Rome's intervention in Asia and so indicates that the cult must have been established after the battle of Magnesia. Moreover, it cannot have been organized while Lycia was still under the control of Antiochus. On the other hand, it is almost certain to belong to the period before Lycia was assigned to Rhodes. This makes the date of origin almost certainly 189 and the years of the two festivals attended by Orthagoras 189 and 185.[1]

If deification and the establishment of cults were ever used for political purposes, this cult belongs in that class. In the Hellenistic monarchies, cities could rather easily indicate the shift of allegiance from one king to another through their cults. In the case of Rome, since there was no Roman king, another way had to be found, namely, the creation of a goddess Roma. This accorded well with the practice of using a cult as an expression of gratitude for past favours or a request for future favours. States acquainted with the Roman use of *deditio* often sought the aid of Rome by an offer to surrender coupled with an appeal to the *fides*, the better nature, of the Romans. In Asia Minor, it seems, that the establishment of a cult of Roma was used as an alternate mode of requesting help or favours from Rome. From the point of view of the states establishing the cults, this may have seemed to have had the advantage of not involving as abject surrender as *deditio*.

As an instrument for securing the favour of Rome, the cult did not prove very effective. In the settlement of Asian affairs in 188, the criterion on which the decisions of the Roman commissioners were based, was whether a city had come over to Rome before the battle of Magnesia or not.[2] Thus Smyrna, which not only had established her cult in 195 but even earlier had communicated and intrigued with Roman authorities and had openly opposed Antiochus, was not only declared free but given favoured treatment. Lycia, on the other hand, was turned over to Rhodes. After the troubles and diplomatic negotiations which followed, the status was somewhat modified in 177, when the senate declared that the records of the ten commissioners showed that Lycia had been given to the Rhodians not so much as a

---

[1] Another argument for the early date of the Araxa inscription is the reference to two Roman *legati* by their *praenomina* alone. The two names, Appius and Publius, fit members of the group of ten commissioners who co-operated with Manlius Vulso in the settlement of Asian affairs. In *CP* li (1956), 154 examples of similar uses of *praenomina* are cited, including what was then an unpublished inscription. This is now *SEG* xvi. 255. It contains a decree of Argos honouring Gnaeus Octavius, who together with Gaius [Popilius Laenas] had been sent by Aulus [Hostilius Mancinus] as an ambassador in the autumn of 170. Note that the *praenomen* and *nomen* of the man honoured are given, while for the other Romans mentioned only the *praenomina* are given. This seems to correspond to the normal usage of the time.

[2] E. Bikerman, 'Le statut des villes d'Asie après la paix d'Apamée', *REG* l (1937), especially p. 227.

possession but rather as friends and allies.[1] This was probably not so much a definition of what had been done in 188 as an adoption of a new policy, but, since Rome tended to retain a ruling once made, the new policy was worded as a mere definition of the old. It undoubtedly was fully as much aimed at curbing Rhodes as at favouring Lycia. It was followed in 167, a year in which states were declared free right and left, by complete liberation.[2] This freedom was retained to A.D. 43, when Lycia was joined with Pamphylia to form a province.[3] If freedom was recovered after that, it was ephemeral and was soon lost. Yet the Confederacy continued as an instrument of local government and its chief offices continued to be objects of ambition and competition.

The Araxa inscription contains considerable information concerning the nature of the Confederacy about 200 B.C. At first glance it seems disappointingly lacking in information about federal institutions and organs of government. No federal assemblies or federal officials are mentioned by name or title. Nevertheless, the document gives a vivid impression of a live and active federal government. The many communications between the city of Araxa and the federal government, commonly referred to as the koinon, shows that there was a federal administration to which communications could be sent at almost any time and which, apparently, could settle minor questions— and some not so minor—by executive decree without waiting for a meeting of an assembly. A local representative sent to lay matters before these authorities was called an ambassador (presbeutes), as was the usage also in the Achaean Confederacy. It is seen further that the federal government had pretty definite ideas about what should be handled by itself and what should be left to the cities. Araxa was given diplomatic support against Moagetes but otherwise, even after Cibyra became involved in the hostilities, was left to its own resources to handle the affair as a bit of local frontier defence. On the other hand, when an attempt was made to set up tyranny in the very centre of Lycia, this was treated as a matter concerning the entire Confederacy. Araxa, be it noted, does not seem to have resented the lack of further support against Moagetes and contributed its share to the later wars of

[1] Pol. xxv. 4. 5.

[2] Pol. xxx. 5. 12; Livy xlv. 25. 6. On these events and the status of Lycia at the time, cf. CP xl (1945), 71 ff. Little need be added except that the Araxa inscription confirms the conclusion that an active Lycian Confederacy existed in the period of ties with Rhodes and even earlier.

[3] Suet. Claud. 25. 3; Dio Cassius lx. 17. 3. On the basis of a statement in Suet. Vesp. 8. 4, repeated by later historians, in which Lycia is included among states deprived of their freedom by Vespasian, it has frequently been held that Lycia had been proclaimed free again by Nero or Galba. Magie, 530 and 1387, n. 50 considers the evidence inadequate.

the Confederacy. Probably the most startling evidence of the strength of the federal government is the fact that when Araxa was involved in a dispute over the possession of some land, this was settled by a law suit before or arbitration by federal authorities. The Araxans commemorated the services of Orthagoras in bringing the affair to a successful conclusion but had the tact not to record the name of the unsuccessful rivals.[1] It may be of interest to note also that the Araxa inscription, in connexion with the admission of Orloanda into the Confederacy, contains the earliest known example of the use of *sympoliteia* as a technical term for a federal state or federal citizenship.[2]

Of the institutions, the federal assemblies remain the most interesting and important. For Roman times there is ample evidence for the existence of a federal *boule* and a federal electoral assembly, the *archairesiake ekklesia*, which in spite of its name, was a representative assembly in which the votes were cast by electors (*archostatai*) representing the various cities in the Confederacy. Strabo, on the other hand, who wrote under Augustus but apparently essentially sketched conditions as they were early in the first century B.C., mentions only one *synedrion* in which each of twenty-three cities had one, two, or three votes (*psephoi*), thus giving us only one instead of two representative assemblies.[3] This raises the question whether there had been a change in institutions or whether there was continuity but that Strabo for some reason or other failed to mention both bodies. Unfortunately the records of the period of independence tell very little about the assembly or assemblies. One inscription of the period honours a man who, among other services, included service as 'Lyciarch of the nation at the three meetings of the federal assembly',[4] thus indicating that a federal assembly of some sort met three times during the year, but it is not even clear whether this means meetings held at three different times of the year or three sessions in close succession. Another honorific decree would be more useful if we could be absolutely sure that it belongs to the period of independence. Since it contains a reference to *archostatai*, the electors known chiefly from inscriptions of the second century after Christ, it would be certain that the *archairesiake ekklesia* was a representative assembly already in the period of independence.[5] However

---

[1] Cf. Bean's comment on line 50 of the inscription and *Bull. ép.* 1950, no. 183, inscription 11, comment on section 11.

[2] *Rep. Govt.* 24 and 201, n. 4.   [3] Strabo xiv. 664.

[4] *TAM* ii. 583. Here as commonly *ethnos* refers to the nation or people and *koinon* to the federal government or state.

[5] *TAM* ii. 508. The difficulty is that the inscription contains the title *semnotatos dikaiodotes*, which many think must belong under the empire. However, those who emphasize this usually fail to mention that the document also contains a reference to a Lycian *hipparch* on active service, a phenomenon which definitely suggests the period of independence. For dis-

desirable as it would be to have such direct and positive proof, it is hardly needed. In the period in question the government of a federal state would tend to become less rather than more complicated. In the period of independence, the Lycian Confederacy, according to Strabo, had a single *synedrion* made up of representatives of the cities. Now if the Lycians had one and only one such assembly in the first century B.C., it is almost unthinkable that they later should have added another. If there were two such bodies later, they must have existed also at the earlier date, though, for some reason or other, Strabo mentions only one. Since he emphasizes the election of officials by this body, this must be the *archairesiake ekklesia* rather than the *boule*.

The name *archairesiake ekklesia* itself makes it possible to reconstruct some of the history of its development. *Ekklesia* indicates that the assembly had once been a primary assembly, which later was changed into a representative body. The change had taken place by the beginning of the first century B.C., as is implied by the Strabo-Artemidorus account, which speaks of the *synedrion* of the time as normal and not as a recent innovation. Now it is possible to add that important business was handled by a federal representative assembly a century earlier, when, in connexion with the admission of Orloanda into the Confederacy, Orthagoras was sent by Araxa as an 'ambassador' to the cities in Lycia and to the federal authorities. Obviously he first argued the case in the cities to induce them to send representatives favourable to the proposal and afterwards presented it before the federal assembly. Of course, the body before which he appeared may have been the federal *boule*. As for the term *archairesiake ekklesia*, it seems at first to have been fully as much an indication of the date of the meeting as the name of an assembly. It was common to use the term *kyria ekklesia* as a name for important sessions of an assembly.[1] Even more important was the *archairesiake ekklesia*, the meeting at which magistrates were elected. There probably was only one such session a year. In view of the weakness of ancient dignitaries for high sounding honours, it is obvious that they would take special pleasure in honours voted at the most solemn session of the year. As it happens, the few decrees of the Lycian *archairesiake ekklesia* that have been preserved,[2] are all honorific decrees. The practice of passing such decrees at this session may go back to the days when the meeting was a mass meeting of all Lycian citizens who could turn up and was retained when it was transformed into a

---

cussions see *CP* xxxviii (1943), 177–90 and 246–55 (edition and discussion); xl (1945), 93–97 (further discussion of date); *Bull. ép.* 1944, no. 171; 1946–7, no. 188; Moretti, 211.

[1] According to Arist. *Ath. pol.* 43. 4 there was at Athens one such session each prytany.

[2] *IGR* iii. 474; *TAM* ii. 905, documents 12, 15, 17, 20, 21, 22, 23, 30, and 32; of these 21, 22, 23, and 32 are joint decrees with the *boule*.

meeting of representatives. If this is correct, the *archairesiake ekklesia* should meet only once a year.

There is some indirect evidence that this was the case. This is found in the records of endowments established with the purpose of using the interest for a distribution of largesse to those attending the meetings,[1] the implication being that this distribution took place once a year. Then there are the dates of the decrees of the *archairesiake ekklesia*. The year is normally indicated by the name of the high priest of the year. In some cases also the month and day of the month are indicated.[2] In the few cases in which the date has been preserved, it falls in the month of Loos (October) though not on the same day of the month, except for one decree dated in Panemos (September, the day of the month not given).[3] This would fit well with a system of holding elections soon after the autumn equinox but not on exactly the same day every year. If, for instance, the phases of the moon were taken into consideration, this would necessitate the shifting of the date.

One of the statements concerning the distribution of largesse at the time of elections contains the statement that the distribution was to take place in the *koinoboulion*.[4] This can hardly mean anything but the federal boule or its quarters, thus suggesting that the meeting of the electoral assembly was regarded as an expansion of or an appendix to a meeting of the *boule*. If the members of the *boule* voted at the elections, the electoral assembly was an expansion of that body; if they did not, it was an extra event closely associated with the *boule*. That the *bouleutai* were on hand at the time of the elections is shown by the relatively many joint decrees of the *boule* and the *ekklesia*, and by the fact that they shared in the largesse distributed. The size of the *boule* cannot be determined with certainty. It is not impossible that the cities had one, two, or three representatives each—the *psephoi* of Strabo—though it is also

---

[1] The records of these gifts are discussed *CP* xl (1945), 91–93. (On p. 92 under '21' near the end read 'second entry' for 'second century'.) Of the documents cited, *IGR* iii. 739 is now available as *TAM* ii. 905. Document 18 is now dated 131 by the editor, and this would then be the year of the much publicized gift by Opramoas to the Confederacy.

[2] The Macedonian names of the months were used, but the calendar was readjusted so as to correspond to the Julian calendar, the month Dios corresponding to January. That the high priest entered into office in January is indicated by a list of honours for the year of Veranius Priscus, the earliest being Dios 20 and the last Hyperberetaios (December) 18 (*IGR* iii. 704. i. 14–18). For the years of the high priests (Lyciarchs) the table in *TAM* ii, pp. 349 f. will be followed.

[3] This was noted already by Fougères, 58. In *TAM* ii. 905 at least the months of the following decrees are fairly certain: no. 15, month Loos, but day of month and year uncertain; no. 21, joint decree with *boule*, year of Licinnius Longus (133), Loos, day of month not preserved; no. 22, joint decree, year of Demetrios son of Embromos (134), Loos 12; no. 23, joint decree, year of Killortas (135), Loos 23; no. 30, year not indicated, month Panemos.

[4] *TAM* ii. 905. vi. 61 in no. 21. The word occurs again in no. 66 (xx. 10), where the reference may be to a meeting of the *boule* alone, and again in *TAM* ii. 572, a short statement honouring a consul of A.D. 244.

possible that their delegations were multiples of these numbers. In any case the *boule* was supplemented for elections by an additional group of representatives. Certainly the *archairesiake ekklesia* was the larger of the two bodies.

In his statement concerning the work of the *synedrion*, as he calls it, Strabo mentions first and foremost the election of a Lyciarch and other officials, and records of individual dignitaries confirm that there was quite a staff of federal officials. These were particularly active in the period of independence. Among them were commanders of the armed forces, who either disappeared or changed their titles after the loss of independence. Strabo calls the head of the Confederacy Lyciarch. Earlier he was called general (*strategos*), as were the heads of several Greek federal states; or else the two titles may have designated the same official, one emphasizing the civil, the other the military side of the office. In any case, except for a strange revival in the second century after Christ, the title of *strategos* disappeared except in so far as later dignitaries liked to boast that they numbered *strategoi* among their ancestors.[1] While *strategos* disappeared, another title began to rival that of Lyciarch. It will be remembered that a cult of Roma had been established in or about 189 B.C. Later, at an unknown date, a cult of the Sebastoi (Augusti) was established. Not unnaturally the head of the state, the Lyciarch, took charge of this cult as high priest. For dating documents he was also the eponymous official, and as such was normally called high priest,[2] though he could also be called Lyciarch. However, if high priest was the title most frequently used while a man held the office, the title of Lyciarch was retained for life. Since former high priests remained prominent in the affairs of the state and its *boule* and continued to bear the title of Lyciarch, there are a number of documents dated by the name of the year's high priest in which another Lyciarch figures.[3] This caused scholars at first to consider the high priesthood and Lyciarchate as distinct offices, and that would be the conclusion reached by almost any student taking up the study of

[1] The one record of a man who had served as general is from the period of independence (*TAM* ii. 261). In most cases in which the title is used, it is applied to ancestors. Commonly the lists of distinguished ancestors contain Lyciarchs or generals, but in one document (*TAM* ii. 905, no. 17) both are included. This, however, is so unusual that it seems likely that the two titles refer to the same office and that the use of both words is pleonastic. Most striking are two dedications by Opramoas to his parents (*TAM* ii. 915 and 916). In the one his father is called father of Lyciarchs; in the other, his mother, mother of *strategoi*, obviously with reference to the same office. The use of *strategoi* here suggests that the title had not been abolished but had merely fallen into disuse.

[2] Note as an exception that in *TAM* ii. 497, a relatively late document, the eponymous official is called Lyciarch.

[3] Examples are documents 18 and 19 of *TAM* ii. 905, each a letter addressed by the governor to a Lyciarch who was not the high priest of the year.

the question without any previous knowledge or briefing. Later two scholars, Theodor Mommsen and Gustave Fougères, who already in published works had favoured this point of view, detected evidence indicating that the two titles were variant titles for the same official, and that the title of Lyciarch was the one retained for life. This is not the place to go into the arguments in detail except to note the statement of the jurist Modestinus, quoted in the *Digest*, defining such offices as Asiarch, Cappadociarch, and Bithyniarch as priesthoods of a nation bestowing certain privileges upon the holder *as long as he is in office*, thus implying both that the title is that of a priest and that it is retained by him after he has given up the office. Though the Lyciarchate is not specifically mentioned, this statement added to the other evidence is conclusive.[1]

Among the ancestors of later Lycians there are mentioned alongside of *strategoi* also *hipparchs* and *nauarchs*. These seem to have been active commanders who disappeared after the loss of independence. On the analogy of other federal states, it is natural to think of the *hipparch* as the virtual vice president of the Confederacy, but there is no evidence that this was the case. On the other hand, the existence of a subordinate cavalry commander, attested by an example from the last part of the period of independence,[2] rather suggests that the emphasis was on the actual command of the cavalry. Undoubtedly the *strategos-Lyciarch* served as the commander-in-chief of the armed forces of the Confederacy. Under him, as far as we can judge from the example of Orthagoras of Araxa, the contingent of each city was commanded by an *apoteleios*. Corresponding to the *hipparch*, there was a *nauarch* in command of the fleet of the Confederacy. The title occurs not only in the lists of ancestors of later dignitaries. There are monuments commemorating the services of a certain Aichmon of Xanthus, who as *nauarch* had won a double victory by land and sea at the Chelidonian Islands off the southwest corner of Lycia.[3] The location suggests action against the Cilician pirates. It is anybody's guess whether these victories belong to one of Rome's wars against the pirates or to a separate war carried on by the Lycians.

Numerous other federal offices are mentioned in inscriptions. The office of secretary (*grammateus*) was closely associated with that of high priest or Lyciarch. In fact, the two offices were commonly held con-

[1] *Dig.* xxvii. 1. 6. 14. For fuller statements see *CP* xl (1945), 85, n. 103; *Rep. Govt.* 118–20.

[2] *TAM* ii. 420, a honorific decree of Patara for one of its citizens who had served as a *hypohipparch* of the Confederacy.

[3] *TAM* ii. 264, 265, and 319, all from Xanthus. The title appears in 265 and 319, the latter being a sepulchral dedication by those who had served under Aichmon when he was *naurach*.

currently, though they clearly remained distinct.[1] The explanation probably is that the high priest, when he also served as secretary, chiefly looked after the correspondence with the Roman governor and, on occasion, the emperor, while the more routine business was taken over by subordinates. One such subordinate, a *hypogrammateus*, is mentioned a few times, and one, at least, was highly honoured.[2] The clerks in the offices and archives undoubtedly were state slaves.

Information concerning the federal treasury is very scarce. There are a few, but very few, records of men who had served as treasurers of the Confederacy.[3] Either the members of prominent families seldom held the office or, if they did hold it, did not care to commemorate it. Nor, apparently did anyone ever boast that federal treasurers were numbered among his ancestors. One explanation probably is that the duties of the treasurer were not too extensive. There were no taxes collected directly by the federal government. Instead the cities contributed to the federal treasury, the contributions probably varying according to needs—a certain amount regularly for petty cash to take care of current expenses and larger sums when needed. The only direct evidence on this point is Strabo's statement that the cities contributed payments and shared in the liturgies in proportion to their representation in the federal assembly,[4] but when this is considered in connexion with the evidence from other federal states, such as the Boeotian and Aetolian confederacies, it is sufficient. Direct collection of taxes by a federal government was the exception and not the rule. To the treasury department fell also undoubtedly the administration of government property. Thus there were several foundations the capital of which had to be invested and the interest used for specific purposes. Two such, founded to supply money for the distribution of largesse at the time of the federal elections, were the result of gifts by Opramoas of 55,000 denarii and by Licinnius Longus of 110,000, both in the early second century after Christ.[5] The deeds of the gifts have not been preserved, but from what is known from other donations,[6] it

---

[1] The two offices seem to have been held simultaneously by Opramoas (*TAM* ii. 905, *passim*). On the other hand, C. Licinnius Fronto, who served as federal secretary early in the second century (*IGR* iii. 493), never became high priest; cf. *Journal of Near Eastern Studies*, v (1946), 59.

[2] *TAM* ii. 660.

[3] At Tlos there is the record from the period of independence of a Lyciarch who had also served as treasurer (*TAM* ii. 583). The treasurer mentioned in *TAM* ii. 496 apparently was the treasurer of a city.

[4] Strabo xiv. 665. Here τὰς εἰσφορὰς εἰσφέρουσι clearly points to sums contributed by cities and not to taxes collected directly by the federal government.

[5] The gift of Opramoas is mentioned in several of the documents of *TAM* ii. 905; that of Licinnius Longus, in *IGR* iii. 492.

[6] *Econ. Surv. Rome*, iv. 361–8 under 'Roman Greece'.

is pretty certain that the money had to be let out on good security at the rate of interest specified in the deed. The income thus secured was to be used for the distribution of largesse. Thus the money from these foundations could not be used for the ordinary expenses of the government. For that purpose, a little money derived from other sources must have been kept on hand. Sometimes it seems that even a little surplus accumulated. At one time Vespasian ordered the money thus accumulated to be spent on the baths at Patara.[1] According to the inscription recording the transaction, Vespasian built the baths through the agency of the governor, but the money came from the federal and city treasuries. The fact that federal money was spent for the baths of a city, suggests a special interest in the city, in fact, that Patara was the federal capital, but more of that later. Another activity which must have concerned the treasury department, directly or indirectly, was the minting of money. There was silver money stamped as Lycian and, particularly in the third century after Christ, bronze money with the initials of the names of cities and with or without the name of the Lycians. To go into details and try to determine exactly what cities minted would require a specialized study which would not add correspondingly to our knowledge of Lycian federal institutions.[2]

Officials with the titles of *archiphylax*, *hypophylax*, and *paraphylax* are mentioned in a number of documents. The titles suggest police officials. Most likely the *archiphylax* was at the head of the federal police system and a *hypophylax* was one of his subordinates, while the *paraphylakes*, though city officials, co-operated with them.[3] The federal courts in Lycia appear to have been more active than those of most federal states, and so it would not be surprising if Lycia also had a more highly developed police system. These offices carried enough prestige so that the holders at times were honoured by their home communities. Sometimes service as *archiphylax* was mentioned also in federal honorific decrees even after the dignitary honoured had served as Lyciarch.[4]

In the administration of justice, the federal courts appear to have been active, to have had a considerable jurisdiction, and to have intervened in disputes between cities as a matter of course and not only by

---

[1] *TAM* ii. 396.

[2] Head, *HN*[2] 693–8. Discussions of cities issuing coins: Jones, 102–4; L. Robert, *Hellenica*, x (1955), 188–222; Moretti, 203 f.

[3] *CP* xxxviii (1943), 247–9. Magie (p. 531) renders the two first titles 'Chief-guardian' and 'Under-guardian'.

[4] *IGR* iii. 463 and 489 are decrees of cities, each honouring a citizen who has served as *hypophylax* and *archiphylax*. In *TAM* ii. 905, in documents 30 and 59, federal decrees honouring Opramoas after he had served as Lyciarch, there are references to his service as *archiphylax*.

invitation. In his brief account of Lycian institutions, Strabo mentions among the tasks of the *synedrion* the organization of federal courts. If the plural *dikasteria* is to be taken seriously and considered accurate, there was more than one court.[1] The earliest evidence for their activity comes from near 200 B.C., when Orthagoras of Araxa successfully pleaded the cause of his city before a federal court in a dispute with another city over the possession of some land. This is all the information available. Not even the name of the rival city is given. Undoubtedly disputes of this kind might easily arise at a time when there were many large estates which might seem as closely connected with one city as with another. In the document from which the story of Orthagoras is deduced, the villain of the piece is Moagetes, who appears closely associated with Bubon but also in some way subject to Cibyra. If his estate was to be attached to a city, it is easy to imagine a dispute between the two. Otherwise the information about Lycian federal courts comes largely from notices concerning the use of foreign judges. This Hellenistic practice of making use of impartial legal experts brought in from abroad was apparently extensively used by the Lycians. These visiting judges were aided by a Lycian official or commissioner called an *epistates*, who undoubtedly introduced the cases to be submitted to the judges and otherwise acted as a liaison officer between them and the local authorities. Usually information about foreign judges is derived from decrees honouring the judges and the cities that sent them, but for Lycia there are no such records. Instead there are records of the honours bestowed upon the Lycian *epistates*. There are three such records preserved. Of these two are from the period of independence and one is from the beginning of the second century after Christ, the *epistates* in the latter case being Apollonius, the father of Opramoas.[2] Foreign judges apparently were invited frequently and possibly even regularly in sufficient numbers to constitute more than one panel. This is implied in the statement that the *epistates* presided over the summoned courts (plural). One document, unfortunately difficult to interpret, seems to show four panels. Such activity implies that not only disputes between cities but many cases involving individuals came under the jurisdiction of the federal courts and the foreign judges. One document shows the man honoured —not the *epistates*—bestowing largesse upon the foreign judges, going bail, apparently for fellow citizens about to be tried before these

[1] Strabo xiv. 665.
[2] These entries are discussed and a brief statement concerning foreign judges given *CP* xxxviii (1943), 247–55. For *TAM* ii. 508 see the text given ibid. 181; for *IGR* iii. 736 there is now an improved text in *TAM* ii. 915. The commonest Lycian name for these courts seems to be *metapempta dikasteria*, 'summoned courts'. The plural suggests that the judges were numerous enough to be organized in several panels.

judges, and afterwards acting as their advocate. The use of foreign judges certainly originated in the period of independence. That it was continued under the Empire is shown by the record of the father of Opramoas, while the report that Opramoas as *archyphylax* decided certain cases himself, shows the continued activity also of the Lycian officials themselves.

All the activities noted must have centred somewhere. Where did Orthagoras go on his many missions from Araxa to the federal government? In other words, where was the central office of the executive administration? Where was the list of pending law suits kept? Where were the national archives? Where was the federal treasury? In short, what city was the federal capital? What little information is available points to Patara, which Livy calls the *caput gentis*, the capital of the nation.[1] To the evidence adduced earlier, there is only one item to be added, namely, the fact noted above that Vespasian directed the expenditure of federal funds on the baths of Patara, an act which certainly suggests a special interest in the city on the part also of the federal authorities. Finally, surveying the activities of the federal government has heightened the impression that there must have been a federal administrative centre of some kind.

The most important question connected with the federal citizenship is that of the extent of rights possessed by citizens in other cities than their home community. For Lycia, the evidence, indirect of course, is fuller than for most federal states, but the situation is rendered a bit piquant by the use in many honorific inscriptions of a phrase which seems to imply citizenship in all the cities of Lycia. However, that this is not the meaning, is shown by the fact that honorary citizenship in a Lycian city could be granted over and above the status described in this phrase, which probably can best be rendered 'having performed public services in all the cities of Lycia'. Naturally this can hardly be taken in every case as literally true.[2] For determining further what rights Lycians actually had in the various cities of the Confederacy there are available numerous records concerning the activities and property of individual Lycians, material much too extensive to be surveyed here. What is clear is that Lycians possessed civil rights, the right to own real estate (*enktesis*) and conduct business and the right of intermarriage (*epigamia*) in all cities of the Confederacy. Records of men who owned property in the territories of more than one city are not rare,[3] and there is even a record of property in the territory of one

---

[1] Livy xxxvii. 15. 6.

[2] See especially 'Lycia and Greek Federal Citizenship', *Symbolae Osloenses*, xxxiii (1957), 5–26; cf. Moretti, 195–8.

[3] *Enktesis* in all the cities of Lycia was noted already by L. Robert, *Études anatoliennes* (1937), 382.

city being willed to another city as income bearing property. As for intermarriage, there are numerous records of marriages between citizens of different cities. However, when it came to active citizenship, the right to vote and hold office, this right was exercised only in one city, normally the city of a man's father. This was the *patris* of a man, his fatherland, while the Lycian Confederacy was his nation, *ethnos*, or commonwealth, *koinon*. There may have been a sort of secondary interest in the city of one's mother, once at least, actually called the *patris* on the mother's side, but that did not mean active citizenship. Opramoas went as far as to serve as gymnasiarch in Corydalla, the city of his mother, but no farther. In other cities which granted him honorary citizenship he did not even serve as gymnasiarch. Gifts and benefactions were another matter but had no connexion with citizenship.

An interesting feature of Lycian society is the prominence in our records of women, suggesting that, at least, the control of property by women was not uncommon. To give some examples, a carefully constructed tomb is that of the estate manager of Claudia Platonis. On another tomb, prepared by a man of some prominence for himself, he mentions as an honour that he is the guardian of this lady. Clearly Claudia Platonis was a lady of some importance. Another such lady was the Lyciarchissa, Marcia Aurelia Chrysion or Nemeso, who apparently was from Patara, was married to a man from Sidyma, and after the death of him and their son controlled property at Sidyma. Certainly, in spite of the one reference to a *kyrios*, the impression remains that such women handled their properties themselves.[1] The same is true of women, who, though married, seem to have performed acts of liberality and services in their own name. This was probably in virtue of property inherited from their parents. Similarly, when Opramoas of Rhodiapolis owned land in Corydalla, the city of his mother, he must have inherited it from her.[2] Lately information about another woman of prominence was discovered. This lady, Iunia Theodora, was a Roman citizen living at Corinth during the last years of Lycian independence, who entertained Lycians coming to Corinth, both private citizens and ambassadors and exiles, and bestowed some sort of benefaction upon the Confederacy in her will.[3] This woman, if

---

[1] Claudia Platonis: *TAM* ii. 518 and 522; Marcia Aurelia Chrysion: *TAM* ii. 188, 189, and 190.

[2] Artemios of Bubon had served as priestess (municipal) of the Sebastoi when her husband was priest, but is honoured as a benefactress in her own name (*IGR* iii. 464); similarly at Arneae, Lalla appears to have served as gymnasiarch in her own name (*TAM* ii. 766).Opramoas actually gave title to land at Corydalla to the city of Tlos (*TAM* ii. 578 and 579).

[3] *SEG* xviii. 143.

17

not a Lycian citizen, was exceedingly prominent in the affairs of the Confederacy.

Marcia Aurelia Nemeso has, so to speak, mothered a strange theory. Not only is she called Lyciarchissa, but her less exalted husband is described as the husband of the Lyciarchissa. Inevitably this produced the theory that she had served as Lyciarch in her own name and so also that women were eligible for office.[1] Surely the explanation of her title is that she had been married twice and that her first husband had served as Lyciarch. The fact that the family of her second husband was less distinguished undoubtedly caused the lady's title to be emphasized.

In the functioning of the Confederacy there was an obvious difference between its problems and activities in the period of independence and under the Roman Empire. In the days of the contests between the Seleucids and Ptolemies for the control of this part of Asia Minor, politics must have been complicated and did not become less so when Rome intervened. Concurrently there was also the problem of local dynasts or tyrants. In those days the federal government was very active and had to cope with questions of war and military undertakings. The ill-defined relations with Rhodes did not make matters any easier. When these bonds were severed, there came, if anything, a more difficult period, that of wars against the Cilician pirates. The Lycians must have been affected by these almost continuously. Reference has already been made to the *nauarch*, Aichmon, who undoubtedly took part in these wars. The few known details tell very little about what the Lycians must have done and suffered. The Romans, not too efficient in the conduct of these wars, early began to draw on the Hellenistic east for their sailors and naval supplies. In fact, not only the wars against the pirates but also the other naval wars of the period were largely fought with men, ships, and money raised in the Aegean and adjoining areas.[2] The plan to make the suppression of pirates and policing of the seas a task of subject, allied, and friendly states in the east is clearly revealed in the Roman law of 100 B.C. concerning piracy, and the mention of Lycia in the document is enough to show that the Lycians were expected to contribute their bit.[3] Some insight into what actually went on is furnished by a monument in Piraeus recording honours bestowed on an Athenian of the prominent family of the Kerykides. His record included service as *nauarch*, and for

---

[1] Ruge, *RE* xiii. 2279; Kalinka, commentary on *TAM* ii. 188.

[2] See Broughton, *Econ. Surv. Rome*, iv. 519–25 on 'Cilicia and the Pirates'; on Roman use of eastern naval resources, C. J. Starr, *The Roman Imperial Navy 31 B.C.–A.D. 324* (1941), 1 ff.

[3] *SEG* iii. 378. It is pretty clear that Lycia was mentioned in frag. A.

this he was honoured not only by the Athenian sailors who had served under him but also by the *koinon* of the Lycians and by several Lycian cities including Phaselis and Myra.[1] Clearly an Athenian contingent had taken part in one of the campaigns against the pirates in the first century B.C. and on that occasion had served together with the Lycians or had rendered some special service to the Lycians, such as helping to defend the coast against pirate raids. It is impossible to be more specific.

More precise information is available for the period of the Roman civil wars. The course of these wars cannot be traced here more than to note that when the pirate wars were replaced by the civil wars conditions grew worse rather than better. The Lycians had the courage or stupidity to resist the demands of Brutus at the time of the exactions of Brutus and Cassius in Asia Minor. The result was that their country was invaded by Brutus, who had no difficulty in defeating the federal army, which met him in the field near the frontier, but met with desperate resistance at Xanthus, which seems to have functioned as the centre of national resistance. Though the defenders made sorties, burned siege engines, and caused the besiegers considerable trouble, the city was finally taken by storm with such bitter fighting that the city was destroyed by fire and that there were few survivors. As the story is told, the climax took the form of self-immolation by the inhabitants, men, women, and children.[2] After this Patara and Myra came over without resistance, and the federal government came to terms. Further money contributions were imposed, and the fleet of the Confederacy was ordered to sail to Abydus and there join the fleet of Brutus and Cassius. After Philippi, Antony proclaimed the Lycians immune from tribute and urged them to rebuild Xanthus.[3] When and how this was done is not known, but the city was once more of some importance under the Empire.

The loss of freedom of Lycia is dated A.D. 43, but it is clear that freedom had been circumscribed long before this. Ever since the defeat of Antiochus III at Magnesia, the extent of freedom enjoyed by Lycia, as well as by many other states, depended on the whim of the Romans, who in many ways employed freedom as a weapon. Thus, when after assigning Lycia to Rhodes, the Romans in 167 declared the Lycians free, this probably was done not so much in order to free the Lycians as in order to deprive the Rhodians of all control over them and all profit

[1] *IG* ii[2]. 3218. The man honoured had also gone on an embassy to L. Furius Crassipes, but this does not help fix the date. In *MRR* ii. 464 Furius is listed as praetor or promagistrate at an uncertain date.

[2] Appian, *BC* iv. 76–82; Plut. *Brutus* 30–32; Dio Cassius xlvii. 34. On the exactions of Brutus and Cassius see Broughton, *Econ. Surv. Rome*, iv. 582–5; Charlesworth, *CAH* x. 23, who characterizes them as 'the last expiring act of old Republican brutality'.

[3] Appian, *BC* v. 7.

derived from such control. In this period the Lycians were much in the same position as the Achaeans were after they had gone over to the side of the Romans in 198. They were free to govern themselves as long as they did nothing to offend Rome. Since they were farther away than the Achaeans, they probably were left more to themselves. On account of the proximity of the pirates, the task of the government must often have been difficult. From time to time they were called upon for contributions and suffered exactions, but to try to trace these developments would be too intricate.

It seems surprising at first to be told that Claudius deprived the Lycians of their freedom on account of their bitter internal strife.[1] The explanation is probably to be found in the concentration of land in large estates. Some of the landowners, it will be remembered, were so powerful that they set themselves up as dynasts or tyrants. Probably much, or most, of the land of many cities was controlled by less powerful estate owners who constituted the local aristocracy and ran their communities. As long as this element remained supreme and controlled the state, the Roman authorities considered it well governed and were glad to allow it to govern itself as far as all routine matters were concerned. But the time came when the lower classes began to rebel. The tendency to social revolution, always present in the Hellenistic world, made itself felt also in Lycia. When that happened, the Roman authorities stepped in and deprived the Confederacy of its freedom. That this was the case is indicated by information concerning Lycian exiles who were given aid at Corinth by a certain Iunia Theodora, a woman rich enough and influential enough to entertain ambassadors of the Confederacy and of the cities, as well as other Lycians, and to influence Roman authorities in the interest of Lycia.[2] The lady herself is something of a mystery. She is described as a Roman citizen residing at Corinth,[3] but she possessed interests in Lycia and bestowed some sort of benefit upon the Confederacy in her will, just how it is impossible to say.[4] Exiles received by such a lady cannot have been

---

[1] Suet. *Claud.* 25. 3; cf. Moretti, 192 ff.

[2] *SEG* xviii. 143; cf. the commentary of L. Robert, *REA* lxii (1960), 324–42. The document seems to refer to the disorders that preceded the loss of freedom, but, since it shows the Lycian government passing decrees and dispatching ambassadors without consulting Roman authorities, it must be dated before the loss of freedom. Apparently a social revolution, resulting in the exile of rich and influential Lycians, caused the latter to appeal for aid to the Romans, who intervened and once more restored a conservative government controlled by the wealthy. Afterwards the Confederacy was deprived of its freedom and placed under close control to prevent the recurrence of such a revolution. See J. Deininger, *Die Provinziallandtage der römischen Kaiserzeit* (1965), 71 ff.

[3] In the letter of the city of Myra to Corinth, she is called a citizen of Corinth. The editors undoubtedly are right in considering this an error on the part of the people of Myra.

[4] Robert (p. 330) believes she owned estates in Lycia and willed some of them to the Confederacy. This is plausible and may well be correct.

members of the proletariate but must have been members of the upper classes driven into exile by a revolt of the lower classes. Such exiles would naturally appeal to the Roman authorities to intervene, and Iunia Theodora may well have helped them to win the favour of Roman officials—not that it was difficult to induce the Romans to intervene against a rising of the lower classes. Since she is thanked for the favours bestowed upon the exiles, it is clear that they had been restored or, at least, the party to which they belonged brought back into power, before the decrees in question were passed. All this seems to have happened while the Lycians still were nominally free, for the documents give the impression that the Lycians passed decrees and dispatched ambassadors without any supervision by Roman officials. Then, later, to prevent a recurrence of the revolution, the Lycians were deprived of their freedom and their government placed under close supervision.

Though this reconstruction is based on rather scanty evidence, it seems reasonably secure. Such a fear of revolution as it implies goes far to explain the very detailed supervision imposed on the Lycian government as revealed in documents of the second century after Christ. The first impression received from the enactments of the period is that the Lycians had little to do except to elect each other to office and to vote each other honours. However, even the honours proposed in the federal assembly had to be submitted to the governor of the province for approval. Naturally, references to such approvals have not been preserved in all records of honours, but there are enough, particularly in the full record of the honours of Opramoas, to imply that such permission was regularly sought and commonly obtained, but that at times the governor vetoed honours as excessive. In such cases the Confederacy could appeal to Rome and, in at least two cases, the emperor overrode the governor's veto and approved of the honours.[1] The mass of evidence concerning honours may be deceptive. The recording was often due to the vanity of the person honoured. Probably more important acts, also subject to the approval of the governor, have been lost for the lack of anyone interested in giving them publicity. Nevertheless, a couple of examples can be cited. Thus, when Opramoas gave 55,000 denarii to endow largesse to be distributed at the time of the federal elections, the governor in a letter authorized the acceptance, the fund to be permanently administered according to the terms specified by the donor.[2] Also the cities of the Confederacy needed the approval of the governor for important acts. Thus, when Sidyma late in the second century after Christ organized a

---

[1] See particularly Magie, 533 f. and 1391, n. 61.
[2] *TAM* ii. 905, no. 18.

gerousia, a body which was probably a club of mature and respected citizens rather than an organ of government, the approval of the governor was sought and gained.[1] The first group of members consisted of about equal numbers of commoners and members of the city council (*bouleutai*), who at this time served for life. Also the commoners (*demotai*) undoubtedly did not come from the lower classes. Thus it was an association of the members of the upper classes of the community—the kind of organization that Roman officials were glad to give their approval.

In line with this was a transformation of the government largely under the Roman influence. There can be little doubt but that in the original Lycian Confederacy the members of the *boule* served for a short term, most likely a year, just as they did in normal Greek city-states. Under the Roman Empire it is clear that in most cities the membership was transformed into life membership. In Lycia it is reasonably certain that the same change was introduced in the federal government. This is attested by the lists of those who were to receive largesse at the time of the elections. For the second century after Christ these lists never specify former magistrates, though these remained exceedingly prominent in federal affairs. This must mean that they were included under some other designation, and this must have been as members of the *boule*.[2] Whether also the *archostatai* served year after year or actually were elected annually, it is impossible to say. At any rate, the officials they elected seem to have come regularly from old, wealthy families. Probably the election of a *novus homo* to high office was as rare in Lycia at this time as it had been in the Rome of the late Republic.

Yet with all this men sought office, and there are indications that not all succeeded in attaining to the office they sought. Holding office clearly was a financial burden. On this point it may be enough to recall that fathers sometimes were honoured for performing offices on behalf of their sons—an act which clearly means assuming the financial burdens connected with the office. Naturally the way to seek office was by a show of liberality. There are records of prominent Lycians who had shown liberality πρὸ τῆς Λυκιαρχίας, which clearly means before holding the office of Lyciarch and with the purpose of being elected to that office, but the service was performed several years before the election. The service of Opramoas so designated was the gift of 55,000 denarii to the Confederacy in or about A.D. 131, while his service as Lyciarch came in 136. Similarly Licinnius Longus presented animal

---

[1] *TAM* ii. 175 and 176; cf. J. H. Oliver, *The Sacred Gerusia* (1941), 36; Magie, 563 and passim.

[2] Cf. *CP* xl (1945), 84 f., 91–93; *Rep. Govt.* 154 f.; A. H. M. Jones, *The Greek City from Alexander to Justinian* (1940), 171.

hunts and gladiatorial combats in 116 and served as Lyciarch in 133.[1] His younger brother, Licinnius Fronto, served at his own expense as an ambassador to Trajan. Undoubtedly this was part of his campaign for office, but, though he served as *archiphylax*, priest of the cult of the Augusti, and secretary of the Confederacy, he never was elected Lyciarch.[2] Thus he can be considered a defeated candidate. That was undoubtedly the situation also in other cases when men were honoured for lesser dignities. Since they did not succeed in becoming Lyciarchs, they made the best of what they had. In fact, the manner in which service even in the lesser federal offices was paraded, is the best proof that federal offices continued to be sought.

The rivalry for office in Lycia is probably to be explained by the survival of a good deal of national pride. As Hellenized as the Lycians were, it looks as if they still were conscious of being Lycians so that it meant something to be the head of the Lycian nation. In addition, in spite of the close supervision by Roman authorities, the administrative work of the government cannot have been totally negligible, and this administration was in the hands of a wealthy aristocracy apparently not averse to the Roman supervision and support. At the same time the members of this aristocracy—or, at least, many of them—were ambitious to become Roman citizens, but in this many must have been disappointed, for the roster of Lyciarchs contains several names of men who were not Roman citizens. Many documents connected with Opramoas show that an effort was being made to call him to the attention of the Roman officials, obviously in the hope of securing citizenship for him, but this failed, and Opramoas remained non-Roman to the end. Those who did obtain Roman citizenship, and even those who held high office in the service of Rome, did not thereby lose interest in Lycian affairs, and did not scorn to return to Lycia and serve as Lyciarchs. Marcius Titianus, the father-in-law of the Lyciarch Licinnius Longus mentioned above, after serving as *primipilarius* in a Roman legion; Gaius Iulius Demosthenes, after a rather impressive equestrian career; and even Tiberius Claudius Agrippinus, after a senatorial career, all served as Lyciarchs.[3] Thus did the Lycians take an interest in the affairs of their nation to the end.

---

[1] For the evidence see *CP* xl (1945), 86, n. 105. The dates are taken from the table of high priests in *TAM* ii. pp. 349 f.

[2] *IGR* iii. 493 and 500. The failure to mention the Lyciarchate in 500 is proof enough that Fronto never held the office. This is a genealogical inscription in which the dignities of the members of the family are paraded.

[3] For Marcius Titianus see *IGR* iii. 500. iii. 28–32; for C. Iulius Demosthenes, *IGR* iii. 487; 500. ii. 53–60; for Tiberius Claudius Agrippinus, *TAM* ii. 422–5, 495; cf. *PIR*², C, 776. For the first two *IGR* iii. 500 shows clearly that the career in the Roman service preceded the Lyciarchate.

6. THE ACARNANIAN CONFEDERACY

The information from this Confederacy concerning federal institutions, particularly the courts and the collection of customs duties normally by cities rather than by federal authorities, is important and comes somewhat as a surprise. The first impression from the history of the period is that the Acarnanians were so buffeted about by the Aetolians, Epirotes, and Macedonians that they had little chance for peaceful development. This exposure to attacks culminated in the division of Acarnania between the Aetolians and Alexander of Epirus about 250 B.C., and consequently also in the dissolution of the Confederacy. It was refounded again about 230. Yet, to the earlier period of conflicts belongs the remarkable effort to reach a permanent understanding with the Aetolians on the basis of alliance and *isopoliteia*, which already has been mentioned above in the section on the Aetolian Confederacy. To the later period belongs some interesting information concerning federal institutions largely derived from an inscription first published in 1957. This period was not much more peaceful than the earlier one. In political institutions, as in other phases of their cultural developments, the Greeks had to learn to live dangerously and continue their activities between and during wars.

The Acarnanian Confederacy was one of the federal states not dissolved at the time of the King's Peace, apparently because at the time it was an ally of Sparta. In 375, as the result of the operations of Timotheus in northwest Greece, it was induced to join the Second Athenian League.[1] The Confederacy joined as a unit, but this time there does not seem to have been complete unanimity. Three years later the Athenians under Iphicrates intervened and supported cities friendly to themselves against Thyrrheum. Since the Acarnanians joined the Second Athenian League at a time when also Thebes was an ally of Athens, it is not surprising that they are found to have contributed a contingent to the army of Epaminondas at the time of his first Peloponnesian expedition.[2]

With the intervention of Philip II in Greece[3] a new period with a new orientation began for the Acarnanians. So far they had largely been affected by the contest between Athens and Corinth. Hereafter they were to be affected by the policies of the Aetolians, Macedonia, and Epirus. When Philip had acquired direct control of Thessaly by

[1] Xen. *Hell.* v. 4. 65–66; Diod. xv. 36. 5. The Athenian decree concerning the admission of the Acarnanians and others into the League (Tod, 126) was voted in the second prytany of the archonship of Hippodamas, that is, about August 375 B.C.

[2] Iphicrates in Acarnania: Xen. *Hell.* vi. 2 37; Acarnanians with Epaminondas: vi. 5. 23.

[3] See particularly C. Roebuck, 'The Settlement of Philip II with the Greek States', *CP* xliii (1948), 73–92, where references to earlier literature can be found.

becoming head of the Thessalian Confederacy and had established his brother-in-law, Alexander the Molossian, as king of Epirus, he continued to extend his influence southward along the entire front. In central Greece he was satisfied to turn Naupactus over to his ally, Aetolia, but farther west he aimed at more direct control. In 341 Demosthenes was able to state in his *Third Philippic* that Philip had moved against Leucas and Ambracia and had promised Naupactus to the Aetolians.[1] Under the circumstances it is no wonder that the Acarnanians joined the anti-Macedonian coalition and sent troops to take part in the Chaeronea campaign.[2] The arrangements following Philip's victory included the planting of a garrison in Ambracia and the transfer of the control of Acarnania to a pro-Macedonian faction and the exiling of the anti-Macedonian leaders.[3] This was the beginning of a period of strong Macedonian influence. When Philip's death caused Greeks to hope for release from the Macedonian control, the Aetolians sought to undo his work in Acarnania and restore the leaders exiled by him. Later they also attacked and captured Oeniadae the most southerly port in Acarnania.[4] This, in turn, was the beginning of Aetolian aggression in Acarnania and hostility against Macedonia. Their intervention in Acarnania after Philip's death must have been checked or counteracted when Alexander secured recognition in Greece, and the attack on Oeniadae must have come after he had crossed to Asia. The result was that Acarnania came to look upon Macedonia as a protector against the Aetolians.

During the time that Acarnania was under the protection of Macedonia, Cassander in 314 induced the Acarnanians to abandon a number of smaller settlements and to concentrate the population in a few cities. Actually the change at the time seems to have been confined to eastern Acarnania, the cities involved being Stratus, Oeniadae, and Agrinium, and the purpose obviously to strengthen the defences against Aetolia. At the same time Leucas was brought over but was not incorporated in Acarnania. Instead, Cassander placed a garrison of his

---

[1] Dem. ix. 34.

[2] The Acarnanians are not mentioned in Demosthenes' own list in xviii. 237, followed by Plut. *Dem.* 17, but they are found in Aeschines iii. 97–98, where they are said to have sent 2,000 hoplites. Their presence in the campaign is attested by an Athenian decree (Tod, 178).

[3] This is deduced from the report in Diod. xvii. 3. 3 of the expulsion after Philip's death of his garrisons from Ambracia and the resolution of the Aetolians to restore those exiled by Philip, and further from the Athenian decree (Tod, 178) in favour of Acarnanians who had sought refuge in Athens; cf. Roebuck, 76.

[4] Besides the report of the action of the Aetolians in Diod. xvii. 3. 3, their restlessness at the time of the revolt of Thebes is mentioned by Arrian, *Anab.* i. 7. 4. The date of the capture of Oeniadae is not known. Diod. xviii. 8. 6 indicates that it preceded the decree of Alexander ordering the return of the exiles; Plut. *Alex.* 49, that it preceded the execution of Philotas and Parmenio.

own in the city.[1] No sooner had Cassander returned to Macedonia than the Aetolians attacked Agrinium, the one Acarnanian city east of the Achelous. At this point the Aetolians are seen advancing from the fertile regions around Lake Trichonis. The city attacked surrendered on condition that the inhabitants be permitted to withdraw, but the Aetolians, it is said, violated their pledge and fell upon and massacred the unsuspecting Agrinians.[2] After such an act it is surprising to find the Acarnanians and Aetolians half a century later united by a treaty not only of alliance but of *isopoliteia*, the mutual exchange of rights to citizenship.

The events leading to this surprising development began with the reign of Pyrrhus in Epirus and the transfer of Acarnania from the sphere of influence of Macedonia to that of Epirus.[3] It looked as if the status of the Confederacy was to be changed from alliance with Macedonia to subjection under Epirus. The subjection, however, did not last even the entire reign of Pyrrhus. Acarnania was set free again, probably in 283 when Pyrrhus was defeated by Lysimachus. In all likelihood this was followed soon by a treaty of alliance between Pyrrhus and the Acarnanians. Hence, Pyrrhus was able to raise mercenaries in Acarnania for his expedition to Italy, and, since the treaty remained valid after his death, his son, Alexander II, when expelled from Epirus, could take refuge in Acarnania. Since Pyrrhus had been on good terms also with the Aetolians, it is likely that the allies who helped restore Alexander to his kingdom included both the confederacies.

To this period belongs the treaty of alliance etc. between the Acarnanians and the Aetolians. With the two confederacies pledged to maintain friendship for all time and to defend each other against attack, a peaceful future seemed secure as far as these two powers were concerned, particularly since Acarnania, except for Aetolia, had reached its natural boundaries and by this time had secured Leucas, the one

[1] Diod. xix. 67. 4–5. This account tells nothing about placing a garrison in Leucas, but its presence there can be deduced from the report of its expulsion two years later (Diod. xix. 89. 3).

[2] Diod. xix. 68. 1.

[3] The grant of Acarnania to Pyrrhus by Alexander, son of Cassander, is reported by Plut. *Pyrrhus* 6. For the later developments down to the treaty between the Aetolians and Acarnanians see especially G. Klaffenbach, 'Die Zeit des ätolisch-akarnanischen Bündnisvertrages', *Historia*, iv (1955), 46–51 and P. Lévêque, *Pyrrhos* (1957), 165–71 and 189–95. Earlier reconstructions failed to take into consideration the evidence for a treaty between Pyrrhus and the Acarnanians which long remained unpublished (*IG* ix². 1. 207). Some other crucial elements in the reconstruction are: evidence for the defeat of Pyrrhus by Lysimachus (Paus. i. 9. 7); the fact that Dion. Hal. *Ant. Rom.* xx. 1. 2–3 in his account of the troops of Pyrrhus calls the Acarnanians mercenaries; the statement of Justin xxvi. 3. 1 that Alexander, the son of Pyrrhus, when exiled from Epirus, fled to Acarnania and was restored with the aid of his allies.

Corinthian colony on its coast which long had remained independent. There is no information about the time and circumstances under which Leucas was acquired, but it may well have been during the period of the alliance with Pyrrhus. By making the Achelous river the boundary between the two confederacies, the treaty guaranteed the Aetolians the continued possession of the land they had conquered in 314. The Acarnanians, the weaker partner, may have been willing to renounce their claims in return for peace. After all, if friendship was maintained and the citizens of the two confederacies possessed full civil rights in the other and even had the right to transfer their citizenship from one to the other, boundaries did not matter too much.[1] Unfortunately this sensible arrangement did not last long.

Instead the king whom the Acarnanians had received when he was in exile and whom they had helped restore to his kingdom, and the Confederacy with which they had been allied, about 250 B.C. divided Acarnania between them.[2] A little later, about 239, the Aetolians attacked the part of Acarnania held by the Epirotes and at the time apparently conquered Thyrrheum.[3] This division of the Confederacy must have meant its dissolution. A federal state might retain its government relatively intact while subject to a stronger state, as several confederacies did under the dominion of Rome, but it could hardly survive fragmentation and subjection combined. Later, when on the collapse of the monarchy in Epirus the section of Acarnania which had been subject to that kingdom regained its independence in 231, the Confederacy had to be organized anew, and this is the time at which there are signs of some break in the development of institutions, though there also are signs of some survivals. Meanwhile the Aetolians, except for the loss of Thyrrheum at some unknown date, apparently not only retained the part of Acarnania they had annexed earlier but also tried to reduce the rest. Consequently the famous siege of Medeon in 231 when the city was saved by the intervention of Agron of Illyria.[4] In connexion with this incident, it is a question of help to the city, not to the Acarnanians in general. The Confederacy, apparently, had not yet been reorganized. Though defeated before Medeon with great losses, the Aetolians did not give up. When Antigonus Doson died in 221, the Aetolians, obviously hoping that the power both of Macedonia and of

---

[1] *IG* ix². 1. 3 A.

[2] The division is attested by Pol. ii. 45. 1; ix. 34. 7, while Justin xxviii. 1. 1 implies that Alexander retained his part to his death.

[3] Justin xxviii. 1. 1 mentions the attack but reports no conquest. The conquest of Thyrrheum is deduced from the fact that a few years later the city is seen from an arbitration record to have been a member of the district of Stratus within the Aetolian Confederacy (*IG* ix². 1. 3 B). Cf. Klaffenbach in *IG* ix². 1, fasc. 2, p. xx.

[4] Pol. ii. 2–3.

the Hellenic League would collapse, struck on various fronts. Included was an attack on Thyrrheum, apparently a failure.[1]

Thus the revived Acarnanian Confederacy was much reduced, was continuously faced with the threat of attack from Aetolia, and naturally itself was anxious to regain the lost territory. Much, including the central city of Phoetiae and the port of Oeniadae, was recovered in 219 with the aid of Philip V of Macedonia.[2] There must also have been some later fluctuations. Thyrrheum was still Acarnanian in 216 but must have been Aetolian at the time when a copy of the treaty of alliance between Rome and Aetolia was published there in 211 at the earliest. However, by the time the Aetolians again made peace with Philip in 206, the city was once more Acarnanian. The recovery undoubtedly belonged to the last period of the war, when the Romans withheld their aid and Philip and his allies had the better of the Aetolians.[3] On the other hand, Stratus, the old capital of Acarnania, when once taken over by the Aetolians, remained permanently under their control and was still Aetolian when the city was the objective of an important raid by Perseus during the Third Macedonian War.

The institutions of the Confederacy before its dissolution have largely been described above on the theory that the assembly, the council, and the system of seven generals already existed in the fifth century. To this a few points can be added. In the treaty with Aetolia, in addition to the generals and the *hipparch*, also a secretary and a treasurer are mentioned. This indicates some development of government machinery but not as elaborate as that of the later period. The same treaty indicates also that, when help had to be sent to the Aetolians, this could be done by the generals and the council without consulting the primary assembly. Thus, though the primary assembly was retained, considerable authority was vested in the generals and the council. The fact that the secretary and treasurer are included among the eponymous magistrates in this treaty, indicates their relative importance. There seems to be no further information for this period concerning federal finances, but in the light of later Acarnanian institutions and the normal practice of Greek federal states, it is certain that there were no direct federal taxes but that the federal treasury was supported by contributions levied on and paid by the cities of the Confederacy.

---

[1] Pol. iv. 6. 2.   [2] Pol. iv. 63–65.

[3] Thyrrheum appears as an Acarnanian city in the decree of 216 or thereabouts concerning the sanctuary at Actium (*IG* ix². 1. 583 and cf. p. 269, n. 3 below). On the posting of the Roman-Aetolian treaty at Thyrrheum, see G. Klaffenbach at pp. 21–26 in the *editio princeps* of that treaty in *Berlin Sitzungsberichte*, 1954, no. 1. In a list of cities appended to an Acarnanian decree of 207 (*IG* ix². 1. 582) Thyrrheum is again Acarnanian.

For the period before the dissolution there exists evidence for the grant of citizenship both by cities and by the federal government. There have been preserved three proxenic decrees of cities, one of Thyrrheum and two from Stratus. In addition there is also a federal decree published at Stratus. The privileges granted in the two decrees of Stratus and in the federal decree include citizenship, in the federal decree in such a form that the man honoured could choose to become a citizen of whatever Acarnanian city he wished.[1] In addition the treaty with Aetolia included the mutual exchange of the rights of citizenship between the two confederacies. The federal decree bestowing citizenship within any city that the new citizen desired, is unusual and probably unique. Undoubtedly most grants of citizenship remained purely honorary and potential.

The government of the reduced Acarnanian Confederacy after 230 showed several changes. Since the old capital, Stratus, had been lost, a new capital had to be found. This seems to have been Leucas down to the loss of that city in 167 in the settlement following the Third Macedonian War; after that, Thyrrheum.[2] In this period the Confederacy acquired also, as it were, a religious capital. Formerly the sanctuary of Apollo at Actium had been under the control of the city of Anactorium. During the Social War the city found itself unable to finance the festivals. Hence, when peace was restored, and so most likely in 216, the Confederacy arranged to take over the temple as a federal temple and to keep up the festival. This was arranged after negotiations between the Confederacy and the city and the drawing up of an agreement, almost a treaty, between the two. This and the federal decree embodying and ratifying the agreement are contained in an inscription found at Olympia and published only a few years ago.[3] In accordance with the common Greek practice of publishing important documents also at Panhellenic sanctuaries, the decree had provided for publication on *stelai* at Olympia and Actium. It was undoubtedly after the Confederacy had taken over the sanctuary that the Acarnanians began at times in dating documents to place the *hierapolos*, the high priest of the temple at Actium, at the head of the list of magistrates instead of the general of the Confederacy. To judge by the few

---

[1] *IG* ix². 1. 243 (Thyrrheum), 391 and 392 (Stratus), 393 (federal).

[2] Leucas is attested as capital in 191 by Livy xxxvi. 11. 9; detached in 167; Livy xlv. 31. 12. Concerning Thyrrheum Head, *HN*² 332 states that after 167 'it became the chief place for mintage of Silver in Acarnania'. The legends mark the coins as those of the city, but the types seem to be those of the earlier federal issues.

[3] Published by C. Habicht, *Hermes*, lxxxv (1957), 86–122 and almost simultaneously by Klaffenbach as *IG* ix². 1. 583 and later by J. Pouilloux, *Choix d'inscriptions grecques* (1960), no. 29. Cf. also *Bull. ép.* 1958, no. 270 and for more recent literature *SEG* xviii. 261. For the date see Habicht, 92–98.

documents preserved, the two were never listed together, and there was no fixed rule to determine which official was to be listed.[1]

The most important change in the reorganized Confederacy was in the executive department, which was now headed by a single general (*strategos*) instead of the former board of seven. This, in turn, makes it virtually certain that the *hipparchos*, listed with but after the general, was the vice president. A *promnamon* is also regularly listed and with him sometimes three *sympromnamones*. These apparently were annual officials presiding over the federal council.[2] The secretary of the council, mentioned in the same inscriptions, undoubtedly kept the records of that body.[3] Another secretary, called either the secretary of the general or of the magistrates,[4] indicates that the federal executive department had enough business to transact to need a special secretary. The presence of a *nauarch* in the decree concerning the sanctuary at Actium probably means that, when Philip V was trying to develop a navy, his Greek allies were asked to join in the effort.

In addition to the council mentioned above, there was also a federal primary assembly in which the vote was taken by cities.[5] It may seem strange that a federal state reorganized as late as 230 B.C. should employ a primary assembly. The reorganization, however, came several years before the great change in the Achaean Confederacy and so at a time when primary assemblies still were normal in federal states. It is not known how many regular meetings there were during the year, but it is clear that, in addition to these, also extraordinary meetings could be called.[6] The federal finances also provide almost certain information concerning the composition of the council and the method of

[1] In *IG* ix². 1. 583 the first eponymous official is the *strategos*, and the *hierapolos* is not listed, though he is mentioned in the body of the document. In 208, 209, 588, and 582 the usage varies from document to document.

[2] In all inscriptions listed in n. 1 a *promnamon* is listed; in some, also *sympromnamones*. This must mean that sometimes the entire board, sometimes only the chairman, is listed.

[3] In *IG* ix². 1. 582 he is called the secretary of the *synedrion* but more commonly of the *boule*.

[4] In *IG* ix.² 1. 582 this secretary is called the secretary of the *strategos*. The secretary of the *archontes* in 583 must be the same official.

[5] This is implied in two passages in Livy in which he uses *populi* to indicate the peoples of the various communities in the Confederacy. In his statement about Leucas as capital (xxxiii. 17. 1) he tells that *omnes populi* used to convene there; in his account of the meeting at Leucas in 197 debating the question of going over to the Romans, he states that all *populi* did not meet up and those that were present did not all agree and so the decree passed was unofficial, a *privatum decretum* (xxxiii. 16. 3). This implies that for important decrees a unanimous vote of the cities was required. The listing of Acarnanian cities at the end of a federal decree concerning the festival of Artemis at Magnesia on the Maeander (*IG* ix². 1. 582) may not be as convincing as it once was regarded, e.g. in *Rep. Govt.* 217, n. 27. It may not be a list of votes cast in the federal assembly but a list of cities which had passed their own decrees after that of the federal government. Cf. p. 231, n. 5 under the Achaean Confederacy.

[6] The meeting at Leucas in 197 mentioned in the preceding note was an extraordinary meeting, so also a meeting at Thyrrheum in 170 (Pol. xxviii. 5).

counting votes in the assembly. The federal treasury, as will be demonstrated below, was normally supported by contributions or assessments sent in by the cities. In those cases for which there is direct evidence of the use of this system, namely, the early Boeotian, the Aetolian, and the Lycian confederacies, the size of the contributions was in proportion to the representation in the federal council. Hence, where this system of finances was in vogue, it is virtually certain that representation in the federal council was approximately in proportion to the population or, probably rather, the number of citizens, and so also in Acarnania. It would be natural to apply the same principle to the counting of votes in the assembly. However, there are indications that on vital issues, such as the question of breaking with Macedonia and going over to the side of the Romans, a unanimous vote of the cities was sought.

Before the publication of the decree concerning the sanctuary of Apollo at Actium, the information from inscriptions concerning federal finances involved such routine matters as supplying money for a sacrifice or for paying the expense of having the document published.[1] This decree too contains some material of this kind. More important are the special regulations concerning customs duties and other fees collected during the Actian Games. The regulations in question show clearly that the federal government normally did not collect either of these taxes. When the federal government became responsible for the upkeep of the temple and for the annual games, it thereby assumed expenses that formerly had been borne by the city of Anactorium. Hence it was only proper that some of the income that formerly had gone to the city should be diverted to it. Therefore, it was arranged that half of the *pentekoste*—the two per cent duty on imports and exports—and of all other tolls collected during the festival should go to the federal government and the other half to the city of Anactorium. Obviously the *panegyris* was not merely a religious festival but included also an active market. Apparently a special income to be divided in the same way, came from the manumission fees of slaves manumitted during the festival.[2] The market was to be run as a sort of joint venture of the Confederacy and the city, each partner supplying four collectors and four secretaries to collect and keep record of the taxes and fees collected, while one market supervisor (*agoranomos*) from each sufficed for the general management and direction. But notice that this is a

---

[1] *IG* ix². 1. 582 and 583.

[2] Taking τῶν ἄλλων τῶμ πιπτόντων ἐκ τᾶς τῶν σωμάτων πωλήσιος (l. 32 f.) to refer to manumission fees; Habicht, 106 f. takes it to refer to the sale of slaves, but the phrase indicates a special source of income and is added almost as an afterthought. Manumission in the form of a sale at a sanctuary of Apollo, of course, is well known from Delphi.

special arrangement exclusively for the festival and market connected with it. A special clause provides that otherwise the Anactorians are to have complete control of their harbours and all tolls.[1] This should be enough to demonstrate that the Acarnanian federal government normally collected no taxes within the territory of any city of the Confederacy. There may have been fees in connexion with the administration, and there may possibly have been some income from property owned by the commonwealth, but otherwise the income of the federal treasury must have been derived from contributions from the cities or other constituent states, if any. With this state of federal finances, it is not surprising that also the minting of money was largely left to the cities. The beginning of federal coinage is dated about 400 B.C., but the cities too continued to mint. After 167 B.C. the minting by the federal government seems to have been discontinued. In its place came coins with federal types minted by Thyrrheum and stamped as issues of the city.[2]

The adoption of regulations concerning the temple and festival amounted to an act of legislation establishing rules binding on all Acarnanians. They were not to be invalidated either by law or decree proposed by either a city or an individual. Such prohibitions against future action may not have proved very effective, but it does show that some enactments were considered permanently binding laws. After all of this, it is surprising to learn from the very last lines of the document that sacred laws, that is laws concerning cults and sanctuaries, can be emended whenever a *nomothesia*,[3] or systematic revision of laws, comes around, provided nothing is enacted contrary to the present document. Thus one brief sentence provides evidence for a periodic checking and revision of laws.

If there were federal laws, there must have been a federal court or courts for their enforcement, and again the same document supplies evidence. A city violating the decree was to be fined 500 minas—a truly large sum for a small town—while an offending individual was to be put to death after condemnation by the *dikasterion* or law court, and, in this connexion, this can only mean a federal court.[4] Strictly construed the reference to the law court applies only to trials of individuals, but this court must have had jurisdiction also over the cities, unless that was assumed by some other authority such as the federal officials and council. A chance reference in Thucydides[5] shows that a federal court

---

[1] There are lacunae in the statement in lines 43–45, but the general meaning is clear; cf. the translations of Habicht and Pouilloux.

[2] On Acarnanian local and federal currency see Head, *HN*[2] 328–34.

[3] The LSJ *Lexicon* gives 'legislation' as the primary meaning, but the examples show that this is legislation in the sense of enacting laws.

[4] Lines 72–74; cf. Habicht, 115.   [5] Thuc. iii. 105. 1.

existed as early as 426. Thus it seems safe to conclude that the Acarnanian Confederacy during its period of existence from the late fifth century to the end possessed a federal court. For the periodic revision of laws, there seems at present no evidence to show that it can be carried farther back than to the re-establishment of the Confederacy about 230.

7. THE EPIROTE CONFEDERACY

This curious state, which combined monarchy, federalism, and tribal organization, deserves some consideration in any general account of Greek Federalism. It does not matter much whether the Epirotes were Greeks or closely related tribes which later became Hellenized.[1] The records that have been preserved are in a Greek dialect, and the political institutions seem to be normal Greek, but like those of the Macedonians and the Thessalians, to have preserved much of the older tribal monarchy. The history of Epirus, associated intimately with the history of both Macedonia and Rome, bristles with difficulties. Most of those connected with the narrative history need not concern us. Those connected with the political institutions are troublesome enough. The sources consist of a few references in ancient literature, chiefly the historians, and a surprisingly large number of inscriptions. These are usually short and compact and, in some cases at least, do not reproduce the entire text of the document in question but merely report the action taken. This may in part explain the great variety of the modes of expression. The most convenient and indispensable single collection remains that in Volume II (1899) of the *Sammlung der griechischen-Dialekt-Inschriften.*[2] These are largely from Dodona. Later discoveries there and other places have been published in works not readily accessible. Some of these are extremely important. So far there seems to be a lack of an adequate general account taking all this new material into consideration.[3] The sketch given below will have to be brief and tentative.

Epirus developed into what might be called an ethnic or tribal sympoly under a constitutional monarchy. The relation of the

---

[1] Beloch, *GrG*[2] i. ii. 33–44 argues that the Epirotes, like other tribes whose Hellenism has been challenged, were Greeks, but also on p. 37 he refers to several scholars who have held the opposite point of view.

[2] This collection will be referred to as *SGDI*, but at times the inscriptions will be cited by numbers alone.

[3] Of the older works particularly M. P. Nilsson, *Studien zur Geschichte des alten Epeiros* in 'Lunds Universitets Årsskrift' for 1909 and C. Klotzsch, *Epirotische Geschichte bis zum Jahre 280 v. Chr.* (1911) are important. Some newer works are G. N. Cross, *Epirus: A Study in Greek Constitutional Development* (1932); P. R. Franke, *Alt-Epirus und das Königtum der Molosser* (1955); P. Lévêque, *Pyrrhos* (1957). These books will be cited by the name of the author alone. For a discussion of recent literature see Lévêque, *REG* lxx (1957), 488–99.

18

central government to the members was much as in a normal federal state, but most of the constituent states were tribes rather than *poleis* in the usual sense of the word. It has been noted long ago that the very fact that Aemilius Paulus is said to have destroyed seventy *poleis* in Epirus, most of these Molossian, is proof that these numerous *poleis* cannot have been real cities.[1] The Epirote state consisted essentially of the three tribes, Molossians, Chaonians, and Thesprotians, the subdivisions of which, in turn, were smaller tribes and villages rather than cities. The scarcity of cities was largely due to the nature of the country with a harbourless coast and most of the inhabited districts consisting of mountain valleys. Of these the most fertile, with rich fields and excellent pastures, lay in the territory of the Molossians. This, in addition, had easy communication along the valley of the river Arachthus with the Gulf of Ambracia.[2] These advantages may to some extent explain the prominence of the Molossians.

The earliest description of Epirote institutions is given by Thucydides in connexion with his account of the attack of Ambracia, the Chaonians, and others on Acarnania in 429, a description which not only gives information about Epirus but also in doing so suggests a typical devolution from monarchy to republic. The Chaonians at the time were without kings and were led by two *prostatai*, elected for a term of one year from a single family; also the Thesprotians were without a king, while the Molossians were commanded by the guardian of their king, Tharyps, who was a minor.[3] A *prostatas* is specifically mentioned only for the Chaonians, but one can be taken for granted for the kingless Thesprotians. For the Molossians there is a great deal of later evidence that they had a *prostatas* who stood alongside of the king. It does not matter whether the Molossians had a *prostatas* in 429 or not—they probably did. In any case it seems that in Epirus the process of devolution began with the placing of one or more elected *prostatai* alongside of the king. It was completed when the kingship was abolished and elected officials became the heads of the state. By 429 this process had been completed among the Chaonians and Thesprotians. It was not to be completed among the Molossians before almost two centuries later. Meanwhile the Molossian kings were to extend their power until they became kings of all Epirus. With this went also the development of the Epirote Confederacy.

The development of a federal state covering Epirus was due to the extension of the power of the Molossians. The resulting federal state was at first known as the Molossian Confederacy and later became

---

[1] Emil Kuhn, *Ueber die Entstehung der Staedte der Alten* (1878), 150 f.; Nilsson, 66.
[2] Cary, *Geographic Background*, 57 f.; Hammond, *History of Greece*, 10.
[3] Thuc. ii. 80. 5–6.

known as the Epirote Confederacy. This statement simplifies considerably a very complicated history. One of the most difficult problems is that of the expanded Molossian Confederacy which resulted from the admission of non-Molossians without changing the name of the state. The existence of such an organization has been proved from the fact that the *prostatas* of the Molossians was not always a Molossian. In all likelihood the expanded Molossian Confederacy for a time included the Thesprotians but not the Chaonians, who were added later, probably at the time of the change of name of the larger organization. This all depends on the identification of the affiliation of the *prostatas* and other officials. The difficulty is that the ethnic added to the names of most officials is not that of one of the major tribes but of a subdivision,[1] and it is not always easy to know to which of the major tribes a community belongs. A particularly important ethnic is that of the Omphales. According to the *Geography* of Ptolemy, Omphalion was a town of inner Chaonia, and so scholars have commonly classed the Omphales as Chaonians. In so doing they have overlooked the evidence of an inscription in which the Omphales are clearly classed as Molossians.[2] On such a point the contemporary evidence of a document should count much more than the statement of a geographer writing centuries later, and, with the Omphales transferred to the Molossians, the evidence for Chaonian magistrates in the Molossian Confederacy seems to evaporate. The most important evidence comes from documents in which the *prostatas* of the Molossians is listed alongside of the king as an eponymous magistrate. From the reign of Alexander, apparently Alexander I (342–330 B.C.), there are four such documents. Two have the same *prostatas* and secretary, both Omphales, one has a Thesprotian *prostatas*, and in one the ethnic is lost.[3] Thus there is evidence that a Thesprotian could hold this office, but there is no such evidence for the Chaonians. The results gained from the examination of a list of ten *damiorgoi* from about 370 B.C. to be discussed below are the same: evidence for at least one Thesprotian but no evidence for a Chaonian. Here too, it must be admitted, the conclusion depends on the classification of the Omphales.

Turning to the federal institutions, recent finds indicate a high development rather early. Tharyps, the Molossian king who in 429 was a minor, was sent to Athens to be educated and on his return was said to be the first to formulate laws for the Epirotes, to establish a

[1] To avoid circumlocutions, 'ethnic' will be used throughout this section to designate a word indicating the tribe or city to which a person belongs.

[2] Ptol. *Geog.* iii. 14. 17; *SGDI* 1347.

[3] In 1334 and 1335 the *prostatas* is an Omphalian, i.e. a Molossian; in 1346 he is an Opernian, and 1351 shows that the Opernians were Thesprotian; in 1337 the ethnic has been lost.

'senate' and annual magistrates, and, in general, to organize the state.[1] It is known further from an Athenian inscription that Tharyps was granted Athenian citizenship, that his son and successor, Alcetas, inherited the citizenship, and that, when Arybbas, the grandfather of Pyrrhus, was driven from his kingdom by Philip II of Macedon, this citizenship was recognized as valid for him and his descendants by a special decree, which even imposed upon the Athenian generals the impossible task of restoring him and his sons to their ancestral domain.[2] Alcetas, the father of Arybbas, is said to have been brought over to the side of Athens in 375, and he and his son, Neoptolemus, the older brother of Arybbas, were registered as members of the Second Athenian League.[3]

Lest developments in Epirus seem too strange, it may be well to recall that the last part of the fifth century and the first part of the fourth were a period of political experimentation and innovations. At Athens there were the oligarchic revolutions and the restoration of democracy. Outside of Athens, it was the period of the highest development of the Chalcidic Confederacy as well as of important but less publicized advances in the Aetolian, Achaean, and Acarnanian confederacies. After the temporary check of the restored power of Athens and the dissolution of *some* (not all) federal states as the result of the King's Peace, came the forming of the Second Athenian League as well as many internal reforms at Athens. A better atmosphere for the modernization of Epirote institutions could hardly be imagined. It may even be true that the Athenian educated Tharyps systematically reorganized the government. At any rate, two documents, which date from about 370, from the period when Neoptolemus, the older brother of Arybbas, was sole king, reveal the existence of highly developed institutions.

The two documents are contained in an inscription published a few years ago.[4] Both follow what was to become the common practice of dating by the names of the king and the *prostatas* of the Molossians, the *prostatas* being identical in the two and the king being Neoptolemus the son of Alcetas. Thus both belong to the same year of this king's reign. One of the two bestows citizenship upon a woman from an unknown

---

[1] Justin xvii. 3. 11–12; Plut. *Pyrrhus* 1.

[2] Tod, 173.

[3] Diod. xv. 36. 5; Nepos, *Timoth.* 2. 1; Tod, 123. 109 f. In *Hell.* v. 4. 64–66 Xenophon reports the expedition of Timotheus without mentioning Epirus or Alcetas but later shows that Alcetas was an ally of Athens (vi. 2. 10–11).

[4] Published and discussed by D. E. Evangelidis, *Arch. ephem.* 1956, 1–13, now *SEG* xv. 384; see also G. Daux, *BCH* lxxx (1956), 433–5, text with brief but important discussion; Lévèque *REG* lxx (1957), 495–9. I follow Daux in holding that the last name in the first decree is not that of a *damiorgos* but rather that of a month. Thus the total number of *damiorgoi* is ten and not eleven.

place named Arronos, who is married to a man who already possesses citizenship. The second document on the same stone may contain a similar grant, but the case it not equally clear.[1] This matters little. One example is enough to show that the Molossians at this time could grant citizenship to a woman, apparently to insure the legitimacy of her children. The name of the organization granting the citizenship is not given, but it is clear that it must be the Molossian Confederacy, but a Molossian Confederacy which already had admitted non-Molossians. This is deduced from the list of officials, the *prostatas* of the Molossians, the secretary, and the ten *damiorgoi*,[2] thus twelve officials in all. A majority were Molossians, but there was also at least one Thesprotian but apparently no Chaonians.[3] Thus the Molossian Confederacy had expanded to include Thesprotians already early in the fourth century.

The change from the Molossian Confederacy to the Epirote Confederacy came about 300 B.C. The new name is seen first in a grant of *ateleia*, exemption from paying taxes, from the reign of Neoptolemus II, who for some time was joint king with Pyrrhus but later was put out of the way by him. In this document the new organization is referred to as a *symmachia*.[4] This has caused scholars to fall into the trap and to consider it a looser organization than the earlier Molossian Confederacy, though an examination of this very document, short as it is, reveals the opposite. In this the Epirotes grant *ateleia* in Epirus to an Atintanian, a member of a nearby tribe. Since this was granted to an outsider, the taxes from which he was granted exemption must have been primarily duties on imports and exports. The control over such duties by a federal government was so rare that it can hardly have existed except in a state with a rather strong and centralized government. Thus it can be said that, from the point of view of ordinary Greek usage, *symmachia* is a misnomer. The Confederacy was rather a

[1] To interpret the second document as a grant to a woman it is necessary to take γενεᾶι in line 22 to mean 'wife'. Unusual as this is, the close parallelism of the documents convinced me that this was the meaning and, further, that there were other Epirote documents in which the word meant wife or woman. For a fuller statement see *CP* lix (1964), 106–7 and lxii (1967), 255, but cf. the criticism of G. Daux, *BCH* lxxxviii (1964), 677 f.; and J. and L. Robert, *Bull. ép.*, 1965, no. 228.

[2] All ten *damiorgoi* are listed only in the first document; in the second only six are given.

[3] For discussions of the affiliations of the officials, see Evangelidis and Lévêque. Of special interest are the Arktanes, who furnished the *prostatas*, the secretary, and one *damiorgos*. Evangelidis thinks that they were Molossians; Lévêque, that they may have been Thesprotians. A certain example of a Thesprotian is an Opernian, since the Opernians are known from *SGDI* 1351 to have been Thesprotians. On the other hand, if the Omphales are classed as Molossians, there appears to be no example of a Chaonian.

[4] *SGDI* 1336. The grant was made by οἱ σύμμαχοι τῶν Ἀπειρωτᾶν, which, of course, means 'the allied Epirotes' and not 'the allies of the Epirotes'.

sympoliteia.[1] It should also be noticed that the fact that the grant was made for Epirus shows that 'Epirus' had been adopted as the name for the new state. The change of name was all the more meaningful if the guess is correct that the change in name was connected with the affiliation of the Chaonians with the federal state. The federal state so constituted continued to have a king at its head to about 235 B.C., when a pure republican government was set up.[2]

Turning to the government machinery, it may be well to recall that the two grants of citizenship of about 370 reveal a highly developed government in the early days of the expanded Molossian Confederacy. Most surprising of all is the grant of citizenship to women, which suggests that the Molossians had even copied the law of citizenship of Pericles requiring that for citizenship within the state both parents must be citizens. There is not much object in speculating about the activities of the officials mentioned in the documents. The *prostatas*, mentioned in several later documents, obviously was the highest official next to the king. Concerning the *damiorgoi*, it is hardly possible to say more than that their existence heightens the impression of a rather advanced and complicated government. The fact that they do not appear in later documents, may be due to the brevity of these and need not mean that the board had been discontinued. The character of the government as a limited monarchy was symbolized by an annual exchange of oaths between the king and the people at Passaron in Molossis, the king swearing to observe the laws; the people, to maintain the kingship. This did not prevent a king with a strong personality, such as Pyrrhus, from making all or most decisions personally and practically ruling as an absolute monarch.[3]

The very idea of a limited monarchy calls for some form of a council or assembly to elect officials and to make decisions on behalf of the state. That there existed a primary assembly of sorts is attested by two documents from the reign of Alexander I and so from the third quarter of the fourth century, both recording grants of citizenship. Though the formulas differ considerably, the identity of the *prostatas* shows that they belong to the same year.[4] The name *ekklesia* applied to the assem-

---

[1] Cf. *Rep. Govt.* 207, n. 50; also Lévêque, 221 speaks of the Epirote tribes as strongly united with 'une cohésion vraie, qui fît de leur symmachie un État au sens plein du terme'.

[2] In connexion with the events of 230 Polybius (ii. 7. 11) refers to the democracy of the Epirotes, which, as he uses the term, simply means republican government.

[3] Plut. *Pyrrhus* 5, referring to Pyrrhus but implying that the usage was old. On the power of Pyrrhus, cf. Nilsson, 67 f.; Cross, 58; Lévêque, 224.

[4] *SGDI* 1334 records the action as that of the *koinon* of the Molossians; 1335, as printed, has ἔ]δοξε τ[α]ῖ ἐκλησίαι τῶν ['Απειρωτᾶν]. This restoration is clearly wrong, since 1334 shows that the organization of the time was known as the *koinon* of the Molossians. Consequently, its assembly must have been called the *ekklesia* of the Molossians rather than that of the Epirotes. So already E. Szanto, *Das griechische Bürgerrecht* (1892), 145; Nilsson, 60, n. 3.

bly indicates a primary assembly, but it is impossible to tell how extensive participation actually was. Probably only the wealthier and more
influential members of the tribes actually met up. It is also impossible
to say how many regular meetings there were during the year. The
annual exchange of oaths at Passaron indicates at least one such
meeting. It is also clear that extraordinary meetings could be called.
When Aeacides, the father of Pyrrhus, during his absence on a campaign, was banished by a decree of the assembly,[1] this must have been
done at an extraordinary meeting called for the purpose. The calling
of the meeting may have been an act of revolt and so does not prove that
any of the elected officials had the right to call a meeting without the
consent of the king. The material to be presented to the assembly must
have been prepared in advance. In the period of the kings, it is not
certain whether this was done by a federal council or by a group of
magistrates, probably the latter.[2]

With the change to the republican form of government, the king
was replaced by an annually elected general (*stratagos*), or probably
rather a board of three of whom one was the chairman or commander-
in-chief. His name was used as that of an eponymous magistrate alone
or together with that of the *prostatas*.[3] In one case the *prostatas* was
called the *prostatas* of the Molossians. It is impossible to determine the
significance of this. Was he the *prostatas* of the entire Confederacy or
only of the *ethnos* of the Molossians? In general there is a minimum of
information available about the magistrates of the republican period.
The secretary of the *synedrion* is mentioned in a couple of documents,[4]
but that is about all. Yet the business transacted testifies that there
must have been officials to take care of it. Thus the secretary or a
secretary or some board of officials could receive written statements
concerning matters to be brought before the assembly of the Epirotes.
In one case it is specifically indicated that the appeal was brought
before the *ekklesia*, thus indicating that the primary assembly continued to function.[5] Similarly the existence of a *synedrion* in the

[1] Diod. xix. 36. 4.

[2] Justin xvii. 3. 12 credits Tharyps with the organization of a senate, and it is not entirely
impossible that he did organize a council, but there seems to be no epigraphical evidence for
the existence of such a body before the republican period. Formerly 1337 was cited as
evidence for a *synedrion* under Alexander I, but this was due to a very doubtful emendation;
cf. the later emendation of Nilsson, 59, n. 2.

[3] 1349 (alone), 1338 (?), 1339 (general and *prostatas*), 1350 (general and *prostatas* of the
Molossians). The most direct evidence for three generals is Livy xxix. 12. 11, where three
praetores are listed by name. This is undoubtedly from Polybius, *praetor* being Livy's normal
translation of *strategos*. Some confirmation is to be found in the reference to the *strategos* and
his *synarchontes* in *Inschriften von Magneisa*, 32.

[4] He is one of three eponymous magistrates in 1339 and is mentioned in *Inschriften von
Magnesia*, 32. In 1367 a secretary is mentioned, but nothing further can be determined
concerning his position.   [5] *SGDI* 1338 and 1339.

republican period is attested by the documents already mentioned as referring to the secretary of the *synedrion*.

Evidence for the subdivisions of the citizen body is extensive. Much of it comes from the period of the kingship, but it seems clear that in this respect conditions remained the same under the republic. To begin with, there were the three large tribes, the Molossians, Thesprotians, and Chaonians. At the battle of Asculum, the Epirotes were marshalled in tribal contingents,[1] recalling, for instance, the way the Boeotians were drawn up in city contingents at the Battle of Delium. One rather striking bit of evidence for two of these tribes is a document in which the witnesses to a manumission are divided into two groups, one Molossian and one Thesprotian.[2] In addition to the military organization, there are other indications that the three large tribes had their own federal organization on a smaller scale.[3] In various documents the ethnics following the names of individuals suggest that the three tribes were divided into smaller sub-tribes. New finds have a tendency to turn up new names. Thus one inscription contains a decree of the Aterargoi, a tribe or community unknown until the discovery of this document. In it friendship and community proxeny with the Pergamioi is renewed. It is dated by the *prostatas* of the Molossians and that of the Aterargoi themselves and, in addition, mentions also the *prostatas* of the Pergamioi.[4] Thus this title is used for magistrates of political organizations of all sizes. The document itself shows that the Aterargoi were Molossians, while the Pergamioi seem to have been located near Buthrotum and so to have belonged to Chaonia or possibly Thesprotia. Thus, whatever the exchange of proxeny between entire communities meant, it is seen that it was possible for a community within one of the three tribes to be on terms of special friendship and intimacy with one belonging to one of the other two tribes. To complicate matters, two different ethnics are applied to the ambassadors of the Pergamioi, thus implying that the latter themselves contained two or more smaller groups united by a sort of sym-

---

[1] Dion Hal. *Ant. Rom.* xx. 1. 2 and 5, 2. 4.

[2] *SGDI* 1351.

[3] Thus in 1590 a *koinon* consults the oracle at Dodona concerning *sympoliteia* with the Molossians, obviously the tribal organization. This apparently belongs to the republican period. An inscription, probably of the fourth century, published by Evangelidis in *Arch. ephem.* 1953–4, 99–103, quoted in full in *Bull. ép.* 1958, no. 286, records the consultation of the oracle by the *polis* of the Chaonians. Evangelidis takes this to be Phoenice. It is more likely that it means the state of the Chaonians and is another example of the short-lived tendency of this period to apply *polis* to any state, even a federal state; cf. above, pp. 9 ff.

[4] See L. Robert, 'Pergame d'Épire'. *Hellenica*, i (1940), 95 ff., where the inscription is quoted as first published and is followed by important corrections and interpretations; cf. *Bull. ép.* 1956, no. 114 for further discussion of some debated points.

polity. Evidence such as this suggests that the government of the smaller groups possessed considerable vitality of their own, and, be it noted, the evidence cited is far from exhausting the material available.[1]

For the government machinery of the tribes and smaller sub-divisions, little evidence is available. Apparently the title *prostatas* could be used for a magistrate in any organization large or small. In the smaller units, he was probably the head of the government. In the expanded Molossian Confederacy and the later Epirote Confederacy, he was outranked by the king and later by the general. Concerning other officials, it is impossible to say much more than that they existed. And yet their tasks must have been considerable. The grant of citizenship to a woman about 370 B.C. suggests a law of citizenship requiring both parents to be citizens. If that rule was maintained and applied in all Epirus, it must have involved carefully kept lists of citizens, probably kept locally in the subdivisions of the tribes, but this is decidedly uncertain. The evidence for the collection of customs duties by the federal government seems more conclusive. It consists of grants of *ateleia*, exemption from the payment of taxes, by the federal government.[2] The fact that such grants can be dated all the way from the fourth century down into the republican period, suggests that the kings collected such duties at least for their Molossian kingdom probably even before the formation of a confederacy. When the Molossian Confederacy expanded and finally became the Epirote Confederacy, the collection of these duties must have required a staff of some size. At any rate, it seems safe to conclude that the Epirote Confederacy is to be coupled with the Chalcidic and early Thessalian confederacies as examples of federal states in which the customs duties were collected for and by the federal government.

8. THE THESSALIAN CONFEDERACY

Thessaly from the Second Macedonian War at least down through the first two centuries after Christ was somewhat of a land apart. The Confederacy had retained its old organization with a monarchic head through the period of Macedonian domination. After the Second

---

[1] One group of inscriptions containing new geographic names was found near Buthrotum and published by L. M. Ugolini in *Albania antica*. See the full notice in *Bull. ép.* 1948, no. 98 and the review of J. H. Oliver, *AJA* li (1947), 101–5.

[2] The earliest example is a grant of proxeny, *ateleia*, and other privileges by the Molossians to a citizen of Pherae in Thessaly, dated by the original publisher, Evangelidis, in the fourth century; cf. *Bull. ép.* 1939, no. 153; Franke, 40; Lévèque, 210. *SGDI* 1336, a grant for Epirus from the reign of Neoptolemus II, belongs to the Epirote Confederacy while still under a king. 1339, a grant of proxeny to a citizen of Brundisium, and *Inschriften von Magnesia*, 32, are republican. In the latter the ambassadors of Magnesia are rewarded with proxeny and other privileges including *ateleia* and citizenship.

Macedonian War, it was set free, and in 194 was given a new organization and government by Flamininus.[1] This organization, though it owed its origin to a Roman statesman, was completely Greek. Territorially this Thessaly was not quite the same as that of the earlier period. It had lost some of its northern 'perioecic' subject territory but had gained territory to the south. The proclamation of freedom issued by Flamininus at the Isthnian Games in 196 listed among those who were to be free, the 'Phthiotic Achaeans, Magnesians, Thessalians, and Perrhaebians'. It would seem that these were all to be treated alike. However, in the settlement of Greek affairs which followed, the others were left free as independent states, but most of Phthiotic Achaea was added to Thessaly.[2] Later the territory of the Confederacy was extended to Thermopylae and Mount Oeta. This expansion can be traced to some extent, mostly by deductions from documents dated by the names of the generals of the Thessalian Confederacy. From such inscriptions it can be seen, for instance, that Lamia was Thessalian as early as 186 B.C. Before this extension, the Thessalians had suffered setbacks. Much of the territory Philip V was permitted to conquer as a reward for his aid to the Romans against Antiochus III was taken from them. It may have been as a sort of compensation that the Thessalians were given Lamia and probably other territory which had been under Aetolian control.[3] Aetolia, however retained the Aenians, the East and West Locrians, and the Dorians of central Greece, as is shown by the fact that the representatives of these tribes in the Amphictionic council in 178 B.C. were Aetolians.[4] At an unknown date, the Aenians gained their independence and formed a state of their own, which is usually considered a confederacy but which was completely dominated by Hypata. A vote of honours by the *koinon* of the Aenians to Lucullus when he served as quaestor in Greece shows that it was in existence about 85 B.C. An interesting feature of the government is that its chief magistrates were a board of five Aeniarchs.[5] Later the Aenians were

[1] Livy xxxiv. 51. 4–6; cf. *Econ. Surv. Rome*, iv. 278 f. for the activities of Flamininus at the time. The list of Thessalian generals given by Eusebius begins in 196, but Livy's account implies at least a major reorganization in 194. For a reference in a *senatus consultum* of *c*. 140 B.C. to the laws of the Thessalians given by Titus Quinctius, see *IG* ix. 2. 89 discussed below on p. 288, n. 2.

[2] Proclamation of freedom: Pol. xviii. 46. 5; Livy xxxiii. 32. 5. Disposition of Phthiotic Achaeans: Pol. xviii. 47. 7; Livy xxxiii. 34. 7.

[3] The treaty of peace with the Aetolians specified that they were not to take back any districts or cities which had been taken from them and had gone over to the Romans in 192 or later (Pol. xxi. 32. 13; Livy xxxviii. 11. 9). Lamia, captured in 190 (Livy xxxvii. 4. 8–5. 3), is seen from inscriptions dated by Thessalian generals to have been Thessalian as early as 186 (*IG* ix. 2. 64–7).

[4] *SIG*[3] 636; cf. Daux, *Delphes*, 307 f.

[5] Honours to Lucullus, *SIG*[3] 743; other important inscriptions: *IG* ix. 2. 4–8; cf. especially Swoboda, *Staatsaltertümer*, 437 ff.

absorbed into the Thessalian Confederacy, and one of the leading families of Hypata is known to have furnished several generals to the Confederacy.

The Third Macedonian War restored to the Thessalian Confederacy those cities which had been taken away from it by Philip V during the war of the Romans against Antiochus III and the Aetolians, but it must have been a period of real hardship for the young state. As in the Second Macedonian War, Thessaly again became the chief theatre of operations from 171 to the time in 169 when the Romans finally made their way into Macedonia. The Thessalians, moreover, took an active part in the operations. The only contingent mentioned as serving with the Roman army was a cavalry contingent numbering three of four hundred, which, according to Livy, in co-operation with Pergamene troops who served as a reserve, saved the day in the battle of Callicinus in 171 and kept the Roman defeat from being worse than it was.[1] Since Livy can be trusted not to exaggerate the contributions of allies, their service must have been important, even though he suggests that their contingent was smaller than it should have been. Yet, for a small state which had a hostile army within its territory and had to stand guard over its own cities, this was not an inconsiderable number. The end of the war brought peace for a few years, but this was broken again in connexion with the revolt of Andriscus in 150. Later, with the Mithridatic wars and the Roman civil wars, military operations became almost endemic until peace returned with the reign of Augustus. In this period the Thessalians, from the point of view of the ultimate victor, were not always on the right side, but they weathered it all, their freedom was recognized by Augustus, and the Confederacy continued long after that as an important instrument for local government and apparently with the constitution given it in 194. In fact, the policy of freedom seems to have worked better in Thessaly than in most Greek states. Unlike the Aetolians, the Epirotes, and the Achaeans, the Thessalians alone among the more favoured Greek states do not seem ever to have brought the wrath of Rome down upon themselves. In 173 a Roman representative had come out to quell incipient social revolution, which was affecting Thessaly, as most parts of contemporary Greece. This time, though a Roman arbitrator can hardly have been excessively leftist or even democratic, it seems that a sensible compromise was arranged. The moneylenders cancelled claims to excessive interest, and arrangements were made to have the rest of the debts paid in ten annual instalments.[2]

[1] Livy in xlii. 55. 10 gives the number as not over 300; in the account of the line of battle, as 400 (xlii. 58. 14); their share in the battle is given in 59. 4-5.
[2] Livy xlii. 5. 8-9.

The constitution of the Thessalian Confederacy, though drawn up under Roman patronage, was, as already noted, thoroughly Greek. It was not, however, a direct copy of any single existing federal state but had some features of its own, notably a greater independence of the cities over against each other. This was probably due to the blending of old Thessalian institutions with features borrowed from other Greek federal states, probably largely from the Achaean Confederacy. The most striking feature of the new Thessalian constitution was the adoption, apparently from the outset, of representative government with a *synedrion* of a moderate size and no federal primary assembly. Now the Achaean law practically transforming the government of that confederacy into a representative government had been passed a few years before 200, and the negotiations with the Achaeans must have made Flamininus personally well acquainted with their institutions, though his brother, Lucius, had had more direct contact with the Achaeans than the consul. He, like a modern statemsan, probably had an assistant or expert to tend to the details of the constitution. It would be interesting to know whether this expert was a Greek or a Roman. He may well have been a Roman. If the Sicilian Commonality (*Commune Siciliae*) was organized as early as 212 B.C.[1] there is reason to believe that Roman statesmen of the time were well acquainted with Greek political institutions. Moreover, the constitution given to the Magnesian Confederacy at about the same time shows that they did not have a single cut and dried pattern which they applied to any state. Naturally, there was a great deal of difference between this tiny state and the Thessalian Confederacy.

For the study of the Thessalian government there are available relatively many inscriptions and not infrequent references in the literary sources. This material does not answer all questions, but it is still so extensive that no effort will be made to cite all of it.[2] One point is clear. The Thessalian Confederacy was an oligarchic or aristocratic state. Livy reports that, when Flamininus went into Thessaly in 194, he not only was faced with setting free the cities but also with bringing some order into a confused situation. His settlement involved selecting senates and judges or officials in the cities on the basis of a property qualification and, in general, strengthening the position of the propertied classes, in whose interest it was to maintain peace and order. Since this statement specifically mentions property qualifications for office, and since records from the various cities refer to the *demos*, it has

---

[1] *Rep. Govt.* 128.
[2] The inscriptions known at the time were collected in *IG* ix. 2 published in 1908, but many have been found since and have been published, largely in *Arch. ephem.*

been held that there was no property qualification for voting.[1] This hardly follows. The references to the *demos* and its resolutions merely shows that there was a primary assembly open to all active citizens. It tells nothing about the qualifications for active citizenship. At any rate, the supremacy of the propertied classes is clear both from the passage in Livy under discussion and from the one report, already mentioned, of the active intervention of the Romans in 173 in the internal affairs of Thessaly, when they had to cope with troubles growing out of indebtedness and excessive interest rates. Since the citizen body of the Confederacy was made up of the citizens of the various constituent states, what has been said of the citizenship of the cities applies also to the federal citizenship.

One interesting feature of the government of the cities is the use of the title of *tagos*, once the proud title of the king of the Thessalians, for members of a board which clearly contained the highest municipal magistrates. The number of *tagoi* varied but was commonly five. All that can be said about the date of the adoption of this title is that it was in use before the Roman intervention. When Philip V wrote to the city of Larisa in 220 and again in 215 urging the expansion of the citizen body by the admission to citizenship of Thessalians and other Greeks residing in the city, there were five *tagoi* at Larisa; they are listed, not in the king's letters, but in the local decrees passed as a result of the letters.[2] The fact that the citizens obviously were reluctant to comply shows the exclusiveness of the local citizen body, while the fact that three of the *tagoi* of 220 were serving also in 215 suggests that within this body actual control was vested in a small group of leaders or politicians. Likewise, when Flamininus wrote to Cyretiae, also probably before the Roman reorganization, he addressed the letter to the *tagoi* (number not given) and the *polis*.[3] Numerous inscriptions testify to the presence of *tagoi* in various cities. This, then, was a feature of local government that the Romans did not change. In fact, they probably did not change the governments of the cities at all but merely gave their support to the upper classes and favoured such exclusiveness as that displayed at Larisa. Otherwise there is little to be said

---

[1] Livy xxxiv. 51. 4–6; comments, *Rep. Govt.* 218, n. 30. For the suggestion that there was no property qualification for active citizenship see Swoboda, *Staatsaltertümer*, 241, n. 10. The confusion in Thessaly before the arrival of Flamininus seems to have involved questions concerning titles to land. An example of the handling of this situation is afforded by the letter of Flamininus to the city of Cyretiae (*SIG*³ 593). The crucial section is quoted and discussed in *Econ. Surv. Rome*, iv. 311.

[2] *SIG*³ 543; for the dates see Walbank, *Philip V*, 297 f. For what seems to be a slightly earlier example of a list of *tagoi* see the decree of Crannon published by E. Mastrokostas, *REA* lxxxvi (1964), 312–15. Cf. *Bull. ép.* 1965, no. 216.

[3] *SIG*³ 593.

about the government of the cities except that it is clear that they possessed primary assemblies, though the assemblies were not open to all members of the lower classes. For city councils there is little evidence except the report that the arrangements of Flamininus provided that a high census qualification was needed for membership in the 'senate' of a city.[1] References in documents to the *boule* of a city are very rare.

A striking feature of the new federal government is that the head of the Confederacy is now an annually elected general (*strategos*), a title which in Latin is rendered *praetor*. That the term of office was a year is shown by the fact that the general was the eponymous magistrate of the Confederacy. Since a goodly number of records of transactions, particularly the manumission of slaves, have been preserved, the names of many are known, and not a few can be dated with more or less accuracy.[2] Unfortunately, the city from which the general hailed is not always indicated, but this is done often enough to show that most generals came from the cities of old Thessaly proper and not from the districts annexed later. An exception is a family from the Aenian city of Hypata, which furnished several generals, the earliest probably serving in 28–27 B.C. At least one branch of the family, which remained prominent into the third century after Christ, later received Roman citizenship.[3] There is no evidence for a primary assembly, the only deliberative body attested being the *synedrion*. Thus it appears that the Confederacy possessed representative government from the time it was organized in 194.[4] From a settlement of a dispute between the cities of Cierium and Metropolis from the reign of Tiberius it is known that the *synedrion* at the time numbered at least 334 members.[5] By this time the Confederacy had completed its expansion and the *synedrion* too presumably its growth. Though the exact number of cities in the Confederacy is not known, it certainly was considerably less than the number of representatives. This can only mean representation in proportion to population. On this point it is hardly necessary to recall

---

[1] Livy xxxiv. 51. 6. A decree from Halos in Phthiotic Achaea, *IG* ix. 2. 107, contains a reference to the *boule*.

[2] See the list of generals in *IG* ix. 2, which, however, should be supplemented by that given by Arbanitopullos in *Arch. ephem.* 1917, 146–50.

[3] 'A Thessalian Family under the Principate', *CP* xlviii (1953), 86–95. The names of the generals of this family are Eubiotus and Cyllus. Of these names Cyllus is very rare, but Eubiotus is not. Hence, since the origin of the Eubiotus who served in 28–27 is not given, it cannot be absolutely certain that he belonged to the family of Hypata, but the chances are very good that he did.

[4] This has been recognized by the majority of the scholars who have dealt with the subject but has been questioned by A. Aymard, 'L'organization de la Macédoine en 167 et le régime représentatif dans le monde grec', *CP* xlv (1950), 96–107 at 105; but cf. *Rep. Govt.* 218, n. 30.

[5] *IG* ix. 2. 261. There were 298 votes for Cierium, 31 for Metropolis, and 5 invalid.

the examples of the early Boeotian, the Aetolian, and Lycian confederacies, the Hellenic League of the time of Philip II and his successors, and the Roman efforts to adjust the representation in the Amphictionic League.[1]

The report of the action of the *synedrion* on the dispute between Cierium and Metropolis supplies what little information is available about the procedure in the *synedrion*. The case had been referred to the council by the Roman governor, and both the general of the Confederacy and the secretary of the *synedrion* wrote separate letters to the governor reporting the action taken. Both letters report that the meeting was held in the month of Thyios in such a way as to imply monthly meetings. The report on the voting shows further that, at least on important questions, the vote was taken under oath by secret ballot or probably rather voting tokens.

This machinery indicates that the federal government was equipped for handling a considerable business, and this, in turn, suggests a strong central government. On the other hand, the Thessalian cities seem to have had greater independence over against each other and the federal government than was the case in most federal states. Contrary to the normal usage, the citizens of one city did not normally possess the right to hold real property (*enktesis*) in the other cities of the Confederacy. This is shown by the fact that when cities voted honours to citizens of other communities of the Confederacy, they at times included this privilege. Thus Larisa granted *enktesis* to a citizen of nearby Scotussa and even sent ambassadors to that city to report the action.[2] Since there seems to be some direct continuity in local institutions between late Macedonian and early Roman times, the letters of Philip V to Larisa of 220 and 215 B.C. can be used for information about conditions in the capital city. At the time there were numerous metics, both Thessalians and other Greeks, resident at Larisa. In his first letter Philip advised enrolling them as citizens; in the second, he almost threatened compulsion. As a result, they were enrolled. Whether they retained their citizenship when Philip's power in Thessaly collapsed is another question. The list of new citizens has been preserved only in part, but the part preserved contains the names of numerous former citizens of the Thessalian cities of Crannon and

---

[1] On the adjustments in the Amphictionic League by Augustus and Hadrian see 'Cyrene and the Panhellenion', *CP* xlvii (1952), 7–16 at 13 ff.

[2] *IG* ix. 2. 519. iii. Other examples are given by W. Kolbe, 'Das griechische Bundesbürgerrecht der hellenistischen Zeit', *Zeitschrift der Savigny-Stiftung*, xlix (1929), 129–54 at 150 f. Kolbe attributes this restriction to the Romans, but he has failed to consider the bearing on this question of the many metics residing at Larisa at the time of the letters of Philip V to that city (*IG* ix. 2. 517).

Gortyn, as well as one man from Samothrace. The lost part undoubtedly contained transfers from a number of other cities. Larisa as
capital may have had a special attraction, and other cities may have
had fewer metics, but it seems clear that citizenship in one city did not
bring with it civil rights in the other cities of the Confederacy. Thus,
when the Confederacy granted foreign judges from Miletus and their
secretary citizenship, *enktesis*, and other privileges in all the cities of the
Confederacy, this can mean only potential citizenship in all cities so
that if they chose to register as citizens in some city, that city could not
refuse to accept them.[1] Certainly they could exercise the rights of
citizenship in no city without advance registration.

Another feature which seems to indicate greater freedom for the
cities over against the central government is the practice of a number
of them of having border disputes arbitrated by an outside power and
even sending their own ambassadors abroad to plead their cause. In all
cases, however, Rome or Romans were indirectly or directly involved,
so that the resulting story, so far as it can be traced, throws as much
light on the 'freedom' of the Greeks under Roman protection as on
Thessalian institutions. Most important and most difficult is a case
involving two cities in two of the small ethnic units south of Thessaly
proper, Melitaea in Phthiotic Achaea and Narthacium in Malis. The
two were separated by mountains, and the land in dispute was a part
of the mountain wilderness. The dispute was settled in 140 B.C. or
thereabouts by a decree of the Roman senate in accordance with the
laws of the Thessalians given them by Titus Quinctius, that is,
Flamininus. The *senatus consultum* was recorded at Narthacium, the
city in whose favour the decision was rendered. The inscription is
badly mutilated, but the chief steps in the litigation can be traced.[2] The
dispute, like so many others settled by arbitration, had already been up
before various arbitrators several times in the past. The references to
these earlier settlements made by the Melitaeans in their statement to
the senate, and the emphasis on the fact that the later settlements in
favour of Narthacium were based on laws given the Thessalians by
Flamininus, suggest that the earlier settlements had favoured Melitaea
and that some ruling by Flamininus was responsible for the reversal
of the earlier decisions. Thus already the settlement of Flamininus
interfered in what should have been the domestic affairs of the
Confederacy. A settlement by the senate of a case of a different nature

---

[1] *IG* ix. 2. 508. Kolbe takes it to mean full citizenship in all cities so that they could go from
one to another and exercise the rights of citizenship at will without ceremony.

[2] *IG* ix. 2. 89 (*SIG*³ 674); cf. A. Raeder, *L'Arbitrage international chez les hellenes* (1912), no.
xix; M. N. Tod, *International Arbitration amongst the Greeks* (1913), no. xxiv; for the date,
MRR ii. 643, addendum to i. 480.

concerns Pteleum in Phthiotic Achaea. Its citizens had been bothered by accusations brought against them by the nearby city of Larisa in Phthiotis, and, when these accusations were carried to Rome, the Pteleans were aided by a citizen of the more famous Larisa in northern Thessaly, who volunteered to go to Rome as an ambassador.[1] A different procedure resulted from the border dispute between Cierium and Metropolis in the reign of Tiberius. The case was referred to the *synedrion* for settlement by the governor. Apparently, under the Principate the Roman government at first did more to encourage the successful functioning of local governments than it had done under the Republic. A different spirit inspired the settlement between Lamia and Hypata carried out in the reign of Hadrian by the governor on instructions from the emperor.[2] This illustrates the fact that, alongside the emperor's encouragement of Hellenism, the reign of Hadrian marks the encroachment of bureaucracy.

Since the Roman government had a hand in the settlement of these disputes, there is nothing in them to disprove the existence of a strong and active central government. One stray bit of evidence suggests a continuity between the earlier administrative system and that of the Confederacy in Roman times. It has been argued above that the system of *tetrades* was imposed on early Thessaly as an administrative measure in connexion with army reforms so that the *tetrarchs* were federal officials and not officials locally elected. There may not be any evidence for *tetrarchs* for the Roman period, but an anecdote indicates that the *tetrades* continued as administrative units. In his *Precepts of Statescraft* Plutarch tells that a certain Hermon refused to be elected to office—apparently the generalship—on account of poverty, whereupon the Thessalians voted that each *tetras* was to supply him with a *lagynos* (a measure of unknown quantity) of wine and a *medimnos* of meal each month.[3] Thus the old administrative units continued to exist, though they are seldom mentioned in documents. There are, however, a number of cases in which men were identified as from 'Larisa of Pelasgis', probably to distinguish between this city and the Larisa of Phthiotic Achaea.[4] Normally the affiliation of a citizen is indicated merely by the ethnic of his community.

---

[1] *IG* ix. 2. 520 is a decree of Pteleum in his honour.

[2] Dessau, 5947a. Q. Gellius Sentinus Augurinus in the commentary is called proconsul of Macedonia but probably rather was proconsul of Achaia (*PIR²*, G 135). For the transfer of Thessaly from Achaia to Macedonia see *Econ. Surv. Rome*, iv. 439.

[3] Plut. *Moral.* 822E, a passage which seems to have been misunderstood by editors and overlooked by historians; cf. *CP* lviii (1963), 240. The most plausible guess concerning the *tetrades* of the time is probably that they still were the old divisions of Thessaly proper and did not include the southern districts acquired later.

[4] *IG* ix. 2. 528, 530, and 534.

19

A large part of the activities of the *synedrion* seems to have been judicial. The Greek federal states fell into two groups, those with a separate federal court or courts, and those in which the council was the sole federal court. Thessaly seems to have belonged to the second group. It was the *synedrion* which passed on the dispute between Cierium and Metropolis, and it seems to have been this body too which acted as a court in the dispute between Narthacium and Melitaea when it was brought up the first time after these cities became members of the Thessalian Confederacy. Further judicial activity is indicated by two decrees honouring foreign judges, one group from Mylasa in Caria and one from Miletus. Of these, the first has been tentatively dated about A.D. 130.[1] In both groups the number of judges was small, in the case of those from Miletus, two judges and a secretary. In the decree for the judges from Mylasa there is a clause praising them for having reconciled most of the litigants without formal trials—a feat which seems always to have been highly regarded. The cases handled by these judges probably normally would have come under the jurisdiction of the local courts in the various cities, but it was the federal government which invited the judges and later honoured them. Another bit of evidence for judicial activities is an imperial rescript of the second century addressed to the *koinon* of the Thessalians and ruling that, when there is a question of force and one of control of property, the question of the use of force is to be decided first.[2] This seems to suggest that the Thessalian authorities were permitted to handle cases which in other provinces might have been brought before the governor. In any case it seems strange to find in the *Digest* a rescript translated from Greek to Latin cited for a ruling on legal procedure. Finally, it may be said that, since no doubt the mass of ordinary law suits were settled in the local courts, the *synedrion* with its monthly meetings may well have been able to take care of all legal business that came before the federal authorities.

The city in which the business of the government was transacted normally, and where the *synedrion* met, in short, the capital, was clearly Larisa in Pelasgiotis. This is where the few Thessalian decrees which have been preserved were published. Even more significant is that meetings held here are reported in such a way as to imply that Larisa was the normal place for the meetings. In 191 Antiochus III sent ambassadors to Larisa to appear before a meeting of the Thessalians. Again, in 172, the Roman ambassadors sent to Greece and Macedonia to make ready for the Third Macedonian War, appeared before

---

[1] *IG* ix. 2. 507 and 508.
[2] It is given in *Dig.* v. 1. 37 as a rescript of Hadrian; in xlviii. 6. 5. 1 as one of Antoninus Pius. In both places it is said to have been written in Greek.

a session at Larisa.[1] The city was also the place of meeting when the case of Cierium and Metropolis was brought up. Equally important is the impression received from following the history of Thessaly that, except for such interludes as that of Jason of Pherae, Larisa was the focal point for almost all activities.

For the financial administration and the economic life, the coins of Thessaly are of considerable interest.[2] The Confederacy minted silver on two standards, the Attic and one according to which the drachma weighed about three fourths of an Attic drachma so that a tetra-drachm was worth only three Attic drachmas or three Roman denarii. Apparently the silver on the Attic standard was minted to serve foreign trade while the lighter standard was used locally and, as records show, was counted by staters (didrachms) and obols. Numismatists used to say that these issues ceased in 146 B.C. This conclusion was based on the unwarranted supposition that all freedom and privileges were cut short at that date. In any case, the old silver continued to circulate and the fees for manumitting slaves continued to be given in staters. Thus, most likely, the minting of silver was not discontinued abruptly. Under the Principate Thessaly, like so many units in the eastern provinces, continued to mint bronze. In fact, probably most of the small change came from local mints.[3] Sometimes, when payments later were made with denarii, the fractional currency used was the local bronze. In that case a denarius naturally was considered the equivalent of eight obols and a half denarius of four obols. Since bronze coins were token coins rated well above their metallic value, there was profit in minting bronze, and in Thessaly the profit seems to have accrued to the federal government.

Manumissions of slaves took place throughout the cities according to a Thessalian law, often referred to in the documents, which fixed a manumission fee of fifteen staters, which was paid to the city in which the manumission took place. About new year 27 B.C. an amendment or adjustment was introduced by which twenty-two and a half denarii were to count as fifteen staters.[4] A reference to staters as late as A.D.

[1] Livy xxxvi. 8. 2; xlii. 38. 6.

[2] For slightly fuller statements and bibliography see *Econ. Surv. Rome*, iv. 329 f., 448; 'The Policy of Augustus in Greece', *Acta Classica, Proceedings Class. Ass. of South Africa*, i (1958), 123–30 at 127 f.

[3] H. Mattingly, *Roman Coins*[2] (1960), 190 ff.; A. R. Bellinger, 'Greek Mints under the Roman Empire', *Essays . . . Presented to Harold Mattingly* (1956), 137–48 especially 143–8.

[4] *IG* ix. 2. 415 from Pherae lists manumissions under several generals. After having listed manumissions for the first half-year of Eubiotus, 28–27 B.C., the predecessor of Augustus, there is a statement concerning the *diorthoma* making twenty-two and a half denarii the equivalent of fifteen staters. After that comes the record of one manumission in the month of Hermaios (December–January). Apparently the new ruling took effect at the beginning of the second half of the year of Eubiotus.

131–2 indicates that the fee probably officially remained fifteen staters.[1] Thus the Roman denarii were treated as foreign currency which the Thessalian authorities graciously allowed to serve as a legal tender. Another detail of interest is that sometimes the fee paid is listed as twenty-two staters and four obols,[2] thus supplying evidence that the petty change tended to be local bronze.

Thus, as far as currency and manumission procedure are concerned, Thessaly continued to go its own way. The fact that under Hadrian it was included with free cities in a group of states to which the emperor sent a special envoy of the kind usually called a *corrector*, shows that Thessaly still was regarded as free, that is, as free as any state could be when it once had come under Roman influence.[3] This makes it likely that the Confederacy was a free state also in having its own system of custom duties. It will be remembered that the earlier Thessalian Confederacy had developed a system by which these duties were collected by the federal government, and that one of the charges against Philip II of Macedon was that he diverted them to his own use, but he doubtless did so as head of the Confederacy. When Thessaly was severed from Macedonia, it would be natural to continue the system but to place it under the control of the elected republican officials of the Confederacy. Nor is there any reason to believe that the Romans, with their ostentatious emphasis on the freedom of Thessaly, ever discontinued the system and substituted their own *portoria*. To be sure, on this point there is no direct evidence but only silence in the sense that there is no record of any Roman official authorized to collect *portoria* in Thessaly.[4] On the other hand, Greece had been proclaimed free so early and was so much in a class by itself that it would not be surprising if several Greek states were allowed to retain control of their custom duties.

In conclusion, the Thessalian Confederacy, organized under Roman patronage in 194 B.C. continued as something of a land apart down into the third century of the Christian era. Its constitution and administration preserved much that was old Thessalian or, at least, features developed before the Roman intervention, such as city governments with a council and a primary assembly and a board of *tagoi* at the head of the administration. It even seems to have preserved the four old

[1] *IG* ix. 2. 546. On the manumissions see also *Econ. Surv. Rome*, iv. 456, n. 21; *Acta Classica*, i. 127.

[2] Some examples: *IG* ix. 2. 1295 and 1296 (several payments); however, 3 obols in 1042. 74.

[3] Dessau, 1067.

[4] S. J. De Laet, *Portorium: Étude sur l'organisation douanière chez les Romains* (1949), 295, in the extremely brief statement—brief on account of absence of information—concerning the *portorium* of Achaia under the Empire has nothing concerning Thessaly, and likewise nothing concerning Macedonia and Greece under the Republic (70 f.).

Thessalian subdivisions known as *tetrades* as administrative subdivisions. The cities retained a good deal of local patriotism and did not readily admit other Thessalians to local citizenship or even grant them the right to own real property within their territories. The federal government, at the same time, was strong and laid down rules applying to all the cities of the Confederacy, such as those applying to the manumission of slaves. In general the federal government followed the pattern of the most advanced federal states, with the sovereignty within the state exercised by a representative *synedrion*, and the head of the state being a general (*strategos*). Nor was this entirely an empty title.

The Confederacy was hardly founded when it was attacked by Philip V in connexion with his support of Rome against Antiochus III. It was active again in the Third Macedonian War. To pass over other actions, Thessaly became particularly important in the Roman civil wars. In the campaign between Caesar and Pompey, though the Thessalians were divided, the majority probably supported Pompey, and the Thessalian general of the time was able to marshal sufficient troops to try to hold Caesar at Gomphi until Pompey should arrive.[1] In the war of Octavian and Antony against Brutus and Cassius, the Thessalians, by choice or compulsion, largely supported Brutus and Cassius. In fact, in addition to infantry, 2,000 Thessalian cavalrymen are reported to have served with them[2]—a larger number than that of the famous division of Thessalian cavalry which accompanied Alexander the Great to Asia. These, however, were probably pressed into service by Roman recruiting officers rather than mobilized by Thessalian magistrates.

Yet Thessaly was not penalized for this support of the losing side. After Pharsalus, Caesar, before he went in pursuit of Pompey, proclaimed Thessaly free,[3] which undoubtedly meant that the government was allowed to continue or resume functioning. Augustus later made a more formal settlement with the Confederacy when he allowed himself to be listed as its general precisely for the year 27–26 B.C.[4] It was not too unusual for an emperor or a member of his household to allow himself to be listed as a local office holder, but, coming at this particular time, the generalship must have served as a part of the general settlement of 27 B.C. It must have symbolized his recognition of the Thessalian Confederacy and his peace with it after its rather dubious record in the civil wars. And Augustus did even

---

[1] Caesar, *BC* iii. 34–35, 80–81. On these events and the treatment of Thessaly by Augustus, see *Acta Classica*, i. 125–30.
[2] Appian, *BC* iv. 88. [3] Plut. *Caesar* 48. 1; Appian, *BC* ii. 88.
[4] For the date see A. S. Arbanitopullos, *Arch. ephem.* 1917, 146–50.

more. Thessaly, with Nicopolis and Macedonia, was one of the three units allowed six votes each in the Amphictionic League.[1] Actually this may have reduced the representation of the tribes belonging to the Thessalian Confederacy,[2] but it must have been an advantage to have all seats consolidated and classed as Thessalian.

Thus Augustus not only allowed the Thessalian Confederacy to continue as a Greek organization but even gave it a privileged position in that special Greece in which he himself was under the protection of Apollo, the Apollo of Actium and Delphi. But the Hellenism of Thessaly was shown also in other ways. There were Thessalians who acquired Roman citizenship, and there were Roman citizens among the generals of the Confederacy, but the majority of the generals of the first and second centuries after Christ of whom the names have been preserved, were not Roman citizens. The records imply further that the office was sought after and prized. Furthermore, when Thessalians rose higher, it was commonly as Greeks holding office in the Amphictionic League and, after Hadrian, in the Panhellenion. Participation in Amphictionic affairs was an old habit of Thessalians, and this might also quite naturally incline them towards the Panhellenion. A family from Hypata, whose history can be tentatively reconstructed from inscriptions, supplied several generals to the Thessalian Confederacy, more than one *epimeletes* to the Amphictionic League, and an *archon* of the Panhellenion. A lady in the family, which by her time had acquired Roman citizenship, married a man— probably of Thessalian origin—prominent at Athens. Their son became eponymous archon of Athens and later acquired consular rank some time in the third century, but it is interesting to note that the route from Thessaly to the consulship went via Athens. Otherwise services in the Amphictionic League and the Panhellenion seem more natural for Thessalians, but it was also natural to be attracted by the Panhellenic aristocracy of Athens.[3]

---

[1] On the reorganization of the Amphictionic League by Augustus, see also *CP* xlvii (1952), 16, n. 42.

[2] There is no information available for the composition of the council just before Augustus. For the second century B.C. cf. *SIG*[3] 692, 704E, 826B; Daux, *Delphes*, 344–8. The representatives from the area of the Confederacy shown in 692 and 826B are: Thessalians 2, Phthiotic Achaeans 2, Aenians 2, Malians 1, Perrhaebians 1. There is some difficulty involved in 704E.

[3] See the article cited on p. 286, n. 3. The family studied in it was from the Aenian city of Hypata, a city which seems to have had close ties with Delphi and the Amphictions. Families from the older parts of Thessaly, or old Thessaly proper, seem to have held Amphictionic offices less frequently. A. B. West, *CP* xxiii (1928), 267 lists five *epimeletai* from Hypata for the first two centuries after Christ and none from any other Thessalian city. Actually he lists three from Hypata and two 'Thessalians', but these two are Cyllus and Eubiotus, whom we now know to have been from Hypata.

9. THE MAGNESIAN CONFEDERACY

The Magnesians in question are those of the Magnesian peninsula off Thessaly and along the coast north of the peninsula. Their confederacy will have to be treated very briefly in spite of the preservation of a rather large number of documents emanating from it and its chief city, Demetrias. These documents are interesting in themselves but add little of importance for the study of federalism. The two most obvious features are that it was a federal state with one predominant city, and that it had a federal primary assembly even though it was founded at a time when other federal states had begun to do away with such assemblies. The Confederacy was founded first at the end of the Second Macedonian War, but Demetrias was soon captured first by the Aetolians and then in 191 by Philip V of Macedon. After the Third Macedonian War the Confederacy was revived or refounded. It remained sufficiently favoured for Claudius, and possibly some other emperor, to allow himself to be listed as the general or head of the Confederacy. The last record of it is a decree of A.D. 283 honouring the emperor Carinus.[1]

The government of the Confederacy included a general, a *synedrion*, and an *ekklesia*.[2] In the short period in which the Confederacy was in existence in the nineties of the second century, the head was entitled Magnetarches.[3] From the statement of Livy, who, of course, took his information from Polybius, it is clear that this was the title of a single magistrate and not a member of a board or committee. The *ekklesia*, obviously a primary assembly, is mentioned regularly in the federal decrees, but in such a way as to suggest that most of the work was actually done by the *synedrion*. It seems that only this body is mentioned in the transitional clause marking the beginning of the decree proper,[4] while at the end of the document the vote of the *synedrion* is recorded first and this is followed by the record of the vote of the *ekklesia* almost as an afterthought.[5]

10. THE FOUR MACEDONIAN REPUBLICS

The formation of the four Macedonian republics in 167 B.C. as a part of the settlement after the Third Macedonian War is normally reported in histories of Rome. Such accounts naturally tend to

---

[1] Claudius as *strategos*: *IG* ix. 2. 1115, cf. 1117 and 1120 where the name of the emperor has been lost. Decree honouring Carinus: *SIG*[3] 896.

[2] Fuller treatment and documentation can be found in Swoboda, *Staatsaltertümer*, 429–37; Busolt, *Staatskunde*, 1492, f.

[3] 'Magnetarchen summum magistratum vocant' (Livy xxxv. 31. 11; cf. 43. 5).

[4] See especially *IG* v. 2. 367 and cf. also ix. 2. 1102 and 1103.

[5] *IG* ix. 2. 1101, 1103, and 1106.

view the incident from the point of view of Roman foreign policy and sometimes note that it meant 'for the first time the dissociation of *libertas* and *immunitas*',[1] for Rome declared these states free but still demanded the payment of taxes. These accounts, however, usually say little or nothing about the form of government imposed.[2] On the other hand, the authors of manuals and studies of Greek political institutions normally omit them entirely. An exception is the recent account of the Greek state by Ehrenberg, who lists the four republics as examples of 'representative government in the form of a federal state'.[3] This neglect of the Macedonian republics is unfortunate. They were as Greek or Hellenistic as most federal states of the time, and, when taken together with the contemporary institutions of the Achaean, Thessalian, and Lycian confederacies, they help to demonstrate the tendency of the time to do away with primary assemblies and instead establish representative government. They are important also for illustrating the elasticity of Roman policy, the settlement imposed differing from those of the Thessalian and Magnesian confederacies. The chief new element, illustrated by taxes and restrictions, was the harsher and more arbitrary attitude which dominated Roman policy after Pydna.

Our information concerning the formation and the institutions of the four republics is derived from the account of Livy, which, in turn, is derived from Polybius. Since the latter in 167 was a mature man, active in the affairs of the Achaean Confederacy, and later at Rome was a member of the Scipionic circle, his account was that of a contemporary who was close to some of the living actors. The extent to which Livy supplemented the account of Polybius with material taken from the Roman archives, remains an open question. According to Livy, the senate ordered that the Macedonians were to be free but that, in order to avoid the danger that would be connected with a large state, Macedonia was to be divided into four parts, each with its own assembly. The word used for assembly in the only manuscript of this part of Livy extant is *consilium*. If *consilium* and not *concilium* was the word used in the *senatus consultum*, and if it was used with the meaning it is usually thought to have when applied to Greek institutions, then the decree of the senate itself ordered that each of the four states was to have a representative assembly as its chief organ of govern-

---

[1] This is the expression of E. Badian, *Foreign Clientelae* (1958), 97.

[2] Exceptions are F. F. Abbott, *Roman Politics* (1923), 84 and H. H. Scullard, *The History of the Roman World from 753 to 146 B.C.* (1935), 296 f., both drawing on T. Frank, *Roman Imperialism* (1914), 208 f. and *CP* ix (1914), 49 ff.

[3] V. Ehrenberg, *Gk. State*, 131; the same statement also in *Staat*, 159.

ment.[1] That this was the form of government adopted is shown by the later ruling that senators, 'whom they call *synedroi*' were to be elected and the state administered according to their decisions.[2] This rule obviously was to apply to each of the four republics. This combined with the patronizing remark by Polybius concerning the Macedonians as unaccustomed to 'democratical and representative government',[3] makes it clear that the four republics had representative government. Note, however, that the words of Polybius do not mean that they were democratic as democracy was understood in the fifth century, but merely that these states were republican and were not under a king.

The four republics had no names of their own but were merely known as parts of Macedonia. The division was approximately as follows:[4] The First Meris contained the land between the rivers Nestus and Strymon with a small amount of land east of the Nestus and a very little west of the lower Strymon. Apparently this entire 'part' consisted of land acquired by Philip II and included Philippi and the adjoining mines. The capital was Amphipolis. The Second Meris included the land between the Strymon and the Axius except for the district mentioned as belonging to the First Meris. The capital was Thessalonica. The Third Meris extended from the Axius to the Peneus, which means that it included the rest of the coast of Macedonia from the mouth of the Axius a few miles west of Thessalonica to the vale of Tempe. Its capital was Pella. The Fourth Meris was inland, north of the Third; its capital is given as Pelagonia. In spite of the presence of cities there is reason to believe that some of the subdivisions of the states were tribal districts rather than cities. This was particularly true of the Fourth Meris, known under the Empire as Free Macedonia.[5]

In order to understand the problems of these states it is necessary to bear in mind their relation to Rome and to each other. Though declared free, they were obliged to pay to Rome one half of the tribute they had formerly paid to the king. This was laid down in the decree

---

[1] The *senatus consultum* is given in Livy xlv. 18, the crucial clauses being in 18. 6–7. This and the other chief passages in Livy's account of the settlement are quoted, translated, and discussed in *Econ. Surv. Rome*, iv. 294–9. Later literature on the subject: M. Feyel, 'Paul-Émile et le synedrion macédonien', *BCH* lxx (1946), 187–98; Larsen, 'Consilium in Livy xlv. 18. 6–7 and the Macedonian *synedria*', *CP* xliv (1949), 73–90, summarized and discussed in *Bull. ép.* 1950, no. 131; A. Aymard, 'L'organisation de la Macédoine en 167 et le régime représentatif dans le monde grec', *CP* xlv (1950), 96–107.

[2] Livy xlv. 32. 2.

[3] Pol. xxxi. 2. 12. The translation, quoted also *Rep. Govt.* 104, is that of Thirlwall.

[4] The division is described in Livy xlv. 29. 5–9 (further information, xlv. 30); Diod. xxxi. 8. 8–9. The word used for 'part' is μερίς, which is found on a coin discussed by C. Edson, *CP* xli (1946), 107, in an inscription from the Flavian period (*SEG* xvi. 391), and the *Acts of the Apostles*, xvi. 12; cf. *Rep. Govt.* 109.

[5] *Econ. Surv. Rome*, 443.

of the senate concerning the settlement to be made and was later proclaimed by Aemilius Paulus at Amphipolis.[1] This, of course, meant that the Macedonians not only were to pay tribute but that they were expected to be ready to listen to directives coming from Rome, and that any hostile action would be looked upon as rebellion. Nor is it likely that the reduction of the tribute brought any relief. It apparently meant that half of the taxes formerly used locally now went to Rome and that only one half remained for local needs, including the defence of the country against their rather bellicose neighbours. This task was not made easier by the fact that the Romans destroyed or carried off the military stores of the king. However, the states which bordered on barbarians were permitted to have armed guards on the frontier. This applied to all except Macedonia III. Lest there should be any temptation to build ships of the line or pirate crafts, the cutting of timber for ships was forbidden. Other economic and social restrictions did nothing to ease the situation. Though the mining of iron and copper was permitted, the gold and silver mines were closed and remained closed to 158 B.C.[2] No one was permitted to own property in more than one of the four states, and intermarriage between citizens of the various states was forbidden. On the other hand, trade between them was not cut off except for salt, and even for it there were special provisions for having salt brought into Macedonia IV.[3] Nevertheless it is clear that the four states were expected pretty much to go their own separate ways.

Little is known about the machinery of government except for the representative assemblies already discussed. At the head of each of the four states was a single supreme magistrate corresponding to the general, who was the head of so many federal states.[4] The statements that money was to be gathered or tribute brought in to the four capitals[5] make it clear that the cities or other subdivisions of the states collected the taxes locally and sent the required sums to the capitals. This is rendered practically certain by some of the details of the organization imposed upon Illyria at about the same time. The Illyrians too were declared free but had imposed upon them a tribute half as large as that formerly paid to their king. Illyria furthermore, like Macedonia, was divided into parts—three in its case—and within these parts some units were declared immune as well as free, while the

---

[1] Livy xlv. 18. 7 and 29. 4.   [2] *Econ. Surv. Rome*, iv. 302.

[3] In Livy xlv. 29. 10 *commercium agrorum aedificiorumque* refers only to ownership of land and buildings. Furthermore, the special restrictions on the trade in salt (29. 11–13) show that not all trade across the boundaries was forbidden.

[4] The only evidence is Diod. xxxi. 8. 9, where four ἀρχηγοί are mentioned and connected with the capitals in such a way as to make clear that they were the heads of the four states.

[5] Livy xlv. 29. 9; Diod. xxxi. 8. 9.

rest had tribute imposed upon them.[1] So undoubtedly also in Macedonia each city or other unit within the Merides had tribute imposed upon it and was required to bring it to the capital. The difference was that in Macedonia there apparently were no immune communities. The general features of the system were undoubtedly derived from that of the kings. The most important change must have been that the communities sent their payments not to a central treasury of all Macedonia but to the capital of their particular Meris. There is no information concerning how and by whom the tribute was transferred to Rome.[2]

The information about the tribute tells nothing about the finances of the federal governments except that, as in other federal states, they depended upon collections made by local authorities and sent by them to the federal treasury. It is possible that the communities continued to send the same sums as they had sent to the king, and that of these half went to Rome while the other half was retained by the governments of the Merides. The money and treasures found on hand and carried off by the Romans shows that the kings had collected what the traffic would bear and had deposited the surplus in the royal treasuries. Since the new governments started out with empty treasuries, they cannot have found it easy to finance their administration with half of the direct taxes formerly collected for the benefit of the king. Also the other income of the state was greatly reduced. The mines and royal estates were confiscated and became the property of the Roman state. The senate at first decreed that no contracts were to be let for the exploitation either of the mines or of the estates. Later, however, when it came to the detailed settlement, the ban on the mining of gold and silver was maintained but the mining of iron and copper permitted. Again it is stated that the operators were to pay a *vectigal* of half of what they had paid to the king. This can hardly be correct. The right to exploit mines and estates would normally be leased out on contracts, and there must thus have been variations in the payments from time to time. Hence the most plausible guess seems to be that of the sums paid by the lessees one half went to Rome and one half to the government of the state in which the mines or estates were located. If, when the gold and silver mines were reopened in 158, the same system was used, especially Macedonia I had its income greatly increased, and

[1] Livy xlv. 26. 11–15; Diod. xxxi. 8. 2–5. The immune communities are mentioned only by Livy.

[2] In 167 the booty was transported from Macedonia to Italy by the fleet (Livy xlv. 33. 7). It is unlikely that the tribute was sent by the same route. The Macedonian republics certainly cannot have maintained a fleet to transport and guard it. Possibly the four Macedonian and three Illyrian states sent their tribute overland to a port on the Adriatic where the Romans picked it up, but this is pure conjecture.

this explains the copious minting of silver by this state.[1] This must have gone far to bring back prosperity both to the governments and individuals. It is also likely that trade with the tribes north of Macedonia was resumed, and this too would mean additional income.

This is not the place to review the disorders which plagued the new states in their first period or to follow the hostilities resulting from the revolt of Andriscus or Pseudo-Philip. As a result of these events, Macedonia was organized as a Roman province. In the list of governors drawn up by scholars, Q. Caecilius Metellus, who reconquered Macedonia in 148 is counted the first governor.[2] The creation of a province did not, however, mean the end of the four republics, which continued as units of local government at least down to the time of the Flavian emperors. At some time there was superimposed on them a Macedonian League. This was in existence as early as the reign of Claudius and possibly that of Augustus.[3] It may go back even farther, but the events connected with the revolt of Andriscus suggest that no such organization existed at the time.

11. THE PHOCIAN CONFEDERACY

For the Phocians the great crisis came with the Third Sacred War and the settlement of the affairs of Phocis by the Amphictionic League in 346 after the Peace of Philocrates. The terms were, of course, actually dictated by Philip II. They included a prohibition against maintaining either cavalry or hoplites and the breaking up of all cities except Abae near Hyampolis, and this weakened organization was to pay sixty talents a year as indemnity to Apollo at Delphi.[4] Three years later the Phocians actually began to pay, and it is these payments made by them as a unit which show that even under these conditions they were allowed to retain some sort of organization. Soon conditions were improved to the extent that in 338 the annual indemnity was reduced from sixty to ten talents, that cities were consolidated again, and that the Phocians were listed as a unit with three representatives in the *synedrion* of the Hellenic League organized by Philip.[5]

---

[1] The confiscation of estates and mines is implied in Livy xlv. 18. 3. The permission to mine iron and copper is reported in Livy xlv. 29. 11; the opening of the mines in 158, in Cassiodorus, *Chron. minora*, ed. Mommsen, ii. 130; cf. *Econ. Surv. Rome*, iv. 312 f.; on the coins, ibid. 328; Edson, *CP* xli (1946), 107.

[2] List given by Geyer, *RE* xiv. 764–5; somewhat emended for 148–27 by W. F. Jashemski, *The Origin and History of the Proconsular and the Propraetorian Imperium to 27 B.C.* (1950), 129–31.

[3] *Rep. Govt.* 109, 113–15.   [4] Diod. xvi. 60. 1–3; Paus. x. 3. 1–3.

[5] Accounts of payments to Delphi: *SIG*³ 230–5 (later edition of 230, Tod, 172); Phocians in the Hellenic League: Tod, 177. 32.

An effort to study the institutions of the Confederacy at this time is not very rewarding, but there are a few points to be noted.[1] The heads of the government are mentioned off and on, but their number and title varied, and there is little information about their specific duties and functions. In the records of their payments posted by the Phocians at Elatea, one entry is dated by a single *archon*, another by four *archons*.[2] Probably this means a group of four of whom only the chairman was listed in the one document. In each case the home city of the officials is indicated. The single *archon* listed in one document was from Medeon; of the four in the other, two were from Elatea. Later three Phocarchs appear.[3] What little is known about these officials suggests annual elections by a primary assembly. There is no information about a smaller federal council and probably none existed. Phocis continued to be small enough for a primary assembly to function fairly effectively. There is, however, evidence that the Phocians had a board of *nomographoi*, and that the assembly could direct them to register an act among the laws.[4] This suggests periodic revisions of the federal laws and an active federal government.

This was the government of Phocis from the restoration of the Confederacy about 338 to the absorption of Phocis by Aetolia after the Second Macedonian War. The subjection to Aetolia lasted to the defeat of Antiochus and the Aetolians in 191. Evidence of the Aetolian supremacy is found in manumission records at Delphi in which manumissions by Phocians are dated by the Aetolian generals.[5] The Confederacy as reorganized seems to have followed the prevailing style of the times in having at its head a *strategos*. This official is known from numerous entries in the Delphic manumission records, several later than 146 B.C.[6] This suggests that, at least as far as the head of the Confederacy was concerned, the system of the period down to 146 was retained after that date. This raises the question whether this is true also for other organs of government, and specifically whether the *synedrion* directly attested only under the Empire goes back to this

---

[1] Besides the normal handbooks see G. Kazarow, *De foederis Phocensium institutis* (1899).

[2] *SIG*[3] 231 (Tod, 172B), 232. Kazarow, 16 takes the single *archon* of the one document to be the head of a college of four.

[3] *IG* ix. 1. 99. To the early third century belongs an elegy inscribed at Delphi (*SIG*[3] 361) in which a certain Xanthippus is said to have been elected *tagos* by the Phocians ten times. Is this title more than a poetic expression for an influential leader whose official title may have been *archon* or Phocarch? The reference to being elected ten times by the Phocians indicates that the office, whatever the official title, was a short-term office, most likely annual, and that the incumbent owed his position to election by what most likely was a primary assembly.

[4] *Inschriften von Magnesia*, 34.

[5] See the list given by Kazarow, 23 f. The latest datable entry is for the second generalship of Phaneas (192–191).

[6] See the list given by Daux, *Delphes*, 640–3. The latest entry is for 49–48.

earlier period.[1] Possibly as good a guess as any is that it was introduced at the time of the reorganization about 190. Undoubtedly too at some time, just when it is impossible to say, the old primary assembly ceased to function.

For the second century independent activity on the part of the cities within the Confederacy is indicated by the record of the union by sympolity of the two cities of Stiris and Medeon. The agreement, binding for all time, stipulates the merging of the *ekklesias* of the two cities, their joint election of magistrates, and goes into some detail about the local government but gives little information about the federal government. Nevertheless, the membership of the two cities in the Confederacy is proved by the dating of the document by the *strategos* of the Phocians. The agreement does not seem to have been supervised by the federal authorities but was witnessed by two citizens of Lilaea and one of Tithorea. In addition a sealed copy of the document was deposited with one of the witnesses from Lilaea.[2] The cities involved were not the nearest neighbours. Medeon was on the coast near Anticyra and Stiris a few miles inland from it, Lilaea and Tithorea in the Cepissus valley. Clearly our two cities were on good terms with the rest of the Confederacy, though they negotiated with each other almost as with a foreign state and only called in some of their fellow Phocians as witnesses.

----

[1] Paus. x. 4. 1 and 33. 1 refers to membership of two towns, in one case specifically mentioning the sending of *synedroi* to the meetings. In x. 5. 1 the hall in which the meetings were held is mentioned.

[2] *SIG*³ 647.

CHAPTER II

MACEDONIAN, AETOLIAN, AND
ACHAEAN RIVALRIES TO 217 B.C.

T HE period from the King's Peace to the Roman conquest naturally
falls into two periods, the one before and the one after the beginning
of the Roman intervention in the Balkans. In spite of the First
Illyrian War the Greek states and Macedonia continued their rivalries
on traditional lines, apparently with no thought of danger from the
western powers, to the end of the Social War in 217, when there came a
sudden and complete change. In this rivalry, the powers that counted
most were the three mentioned in the title of this chapter. Sparta's
bid for leadership ended with the defeat of Cleomenes, and this state
remained chiefly an instrument for intrigue and trouble, particularly
for the Achaeans. Another Peloponnesian state which once had been
important, Elis, seems to have been reduced to being a subject and
agent of Aetolia. Apparently it was not annexed outright, but it seems
to have been deprived of any freedom of decision of its own on major
questions of foreign policy. Its troops were often under the command of
Aetolian officers, who at times did not seem to mind too much the loss
of Elean troops provided they could save their own skin.

1. TO THE FORMATION OF ANTIGONUS DOSON'S
HELLENIC LEAGUE

The King's Peace, as already noted, did not lead to the dissolution
of all Greek federal states. Yet, on account of the dissolution of the
Boeotian Confederacy and the subsequent dissolution of the Chalcidic
Confederacy, it marks the greatest break in the history of Greek
federalism, much more so than the establishment of Macedonian
supremacy in Greece. During the forty years between the liberation of
Thebes and the battle of Chaeronea, federalism was on the rise again,
and Philip II, with his creation of the Hellenic League, did nothing to
discourage it. Nor did any of the Hellenistic monarchies become so
domineering that federalism disappeared, but it was a different
federalism. The two great federal states that had been dissolved were
the most advanced of that time. Moreover, the prevalence of the
democratic theory with its emphasis on primary assemblies tended to
check the development of representative government. Thus the two

most important new federal states of the fourth century, the Boeotian and Arcadian confederacies, both relied on primary assemblies. In the case of Boeotia this was probably in part because the use of a primary assembly meeting at Thebes was an easy way of placing control of the Confederacy in the hands of the Thebans, at least as long as votes were counted by heads, as they appear to have been in the fourth century.

The two confederacies mentioned were the most important creations of the period. The history of the supremacy of Boeotia is too well known to need to be retold here. On account of the brilliance of Epaminondas and the excellence of the Boeotian military machine, the Boeotian Confederacy had an unnatural prominence for a short time. The most important result was the breakup of the Peloponnesian League. Otherwise, as has been shown in connexion with Aetolia and Arcadia, Epaminondas and the Boeotians had less influence on the development of federalism than it used to be thought. The influence in the Peloponnesus was considerable, but even there the formation of the Arcadian Confederacy does not seem to have been due primarily to the Boeotian intervention—a point discussed above in the account of that Confederacy.

In the early third century Epirus and Acarnania were deeply involved in the rivalries between various princes for the control of Macedonia and adjoining parts of Greece. With the expansion of the Achaean Confederacy in the middle of the century and the development of it and the Aetolian Confederacy into two of the most powerful states in Greece, the history of federalism acquires a broader interest. It almost becomes the history of Greece. The interest is deepened also by the presence of strong and colourful personalities such as Aratus of Sicyon, Agis and Cleomenes of Sparta, and some of the Antigonid kings, not least Antigonus Gonatas and Antigonus Doson. There is also the advantage that for this period we have the account of Polybius, even if some of it belongs to the more compact, introductory part of his history. In using it, however, it is necessary to remember that he tends to be pro-Achaean and anti-Aetolian.

The Aetolians in Hellenistic times became prominent before the Achaeans. It is only necessary to recall their share in the Lamian War and later in repelling the Gallic invaders of Greece. They were involved in two of the most promising developments in the history of federal states, two combinations of states which looked like an advance in peaceful co-operation within Greece and which, if kept functioning, might have led to better times. The first was when the Aetolians about 262, instead of attempting to conquer Acarnania, entered into an alliance with the Acarnanian Confederacy even involving *isopoliteia*, the exchange of potential citizenship between the two confederacies.[1] In this case the failure seems to have been due to the aggressiveness of the Aetolians, the stronger of the two states. The other and even more promising development was the alliance between the Achaeans and Aetolians, which was sufficiently cordial for the Aetolians to serve with the Achaeans on Achaean ships against the Illyrians. The alliance began with the co-operation of the two confederacies against Demetrius II of Macedonia (239–229) and lasted, in spite of some antagonism, to the outbreak of the Social War in 220. It was all the more remarkable for the reason that the two confederacies had clashed a few years earlier, and that the new alliance had been preceded by a period in which the Aetolians had been allied with the Macedonians against the Achaeans.

At the time of the liberation of Sicyon by Aratus in 251, the cities in this part of Greece were largely ruled by tyrants who more or less were agents of one of the great kings and looked to him for support. Nearby Corinth was the centre in the peninsula of the power of Antigonus Gonatas, and undoubtedly the tyrant ousted from Sicyon by Aratus, and the predecessors of that tyrant were vassals of Antigonus. A little port nearby, Arsinoe-Methana on the Methana peninsula north of Troezen, was occupied by a Ptolemaic garrison and continued to be so to the middle of the second century.[2] This must have been a centre for intrigue and for recruiting mercenaries for the Ptolemaic army. Probably it was with the aid of the garrison stationed there that Aratus as a teenager was able to curry favour with Ptolemy II by sending him objects of art.[3] Thus the country teemed with Antigonid, Ptolemaic, and other intrigues. In fact, there was so much restlessness and so many irregularities that Aratus could make preparations at Argos for his coup at Sicyon and even have scaling ladders built without arousing any particular suspicion. There even were professional robber chiefs through whom men could be engaged to take part in the raid. As bait they were given to believe that a royal stud was to be raided. Under such circumstances it is no surprise to learn further that the gates of Sicyon were closed at night and that the walls were guarded by sentinels and a watch making the rounds. Apparently at this time cities of any importance maintained watch regularly even in time of peace.

The story of the rise of Aratus also tells something about the type of men who assumed leadership at the time. When living in exile at Argos, the young Aratus, not yet twenty, was able to send paintings as gifts to Ptolemy Philadelphus and, when he prepared his coup, to

---

[1] The treaty, *IG* ix². 1. 3A, is treated more fully in the accounts of the two confederacies.
[2] E. Meyer, *RE* xv. 1375–9 for Methana; 1382–4 under 'Methone (4)' for Mothone in Messenia and 'Methone (5)' for this name as a varient of Methana. [3] Plut. *Arat.* 12. 6.

20

supply thirty men from his own household while other exiles supplied ten each. Such men were hardly poor. Aratus himself obviously belonged to the class from which tyrants had sprung. His own father and uncle, who had ruled Sicyon for years, are not called tyrants, but that may be because the source of information about them ultimately is Aratus himself. They may have been benevolent despots, but, as far as their constitutional position is concerned, they probably were as much tyrants as any of the rest. Now, as always, it was possible to be a good 'tyrant', a term probably never used by these rulers themselves or their supporters but affixed to them by their enemies. A further indication of the wealth of Aratus is the story that, when he needed to raise sixty talents in connexion with his plans for the seizure of Acrocorinthus, he was able to do so on the security of his household plate and his wife's jewellery.[1] The story seems to be derived from the memoirs of Aratus. If so, it is equally significant whether he is telling the truth or is stretching it a bit in order to magnify his own achievements.

By bringing Sicyon into the Achaean Confederacy, Aratus gave a new direction to Achaean politics. The admission of a non-Achaean city was not anything new in itself for the Confederacy which once had incorporated Calydon, but it started expansion in another direction. With Corinth added later, the Confederacy was embarked on a policy which ultimately led to an effort to control the Peloponnesus instead of centring its efforts exclusively around the Gulf of Corinth. Before this, however, the first clash reported did involve the Gulf. In his first generalship of the Confederacy in 245, Aratus is said to have been responsible for raids on the coast of Western Locris and Calydonia and later to have led the entire Achaean army to Boeotia to support their allies against the Aetolians, but the Achaeans did not arrive in time for the battle, and the Boeotians were badly defeated at Chaeronea.[2] The next important step in the expansion of the Confederacy came as the result of the seizure of Acrocorinthus and the liberation of Corinth by Aratus in 243 during his second generalship.[3] This was accomplished by a surprise night attack in time of peace. He had been able to gather at Sicyon a force so large that he could select from its members 400 picked men for his night attack. With these he was able to secure both Acrocorinthus and the city. At dawn the rest of the force arrived from Sicyon, and Aratus was able to appear before the Corinthians in the theatre, of course with Achaean troops stationed in key positions to guard against any possible outbreak or attack. He thereupon persuaded the Corinthians 'to become Achaeans' and turned

[1] Plut. *Arat.* 19. 2.
[2] Pol. xx. 4; Plut. *Arat.* 16. 1. Only Plutarch mentions the raids on the coast.
[3] Pol. ii. 43. 4; Plut. *Arat.* 18–24.

over to them the keys of the gates of the city, the first time since the days of Philip II that these keys had been in the hands of local officials. Thus the adhesion of Corinth to the Achaean Confederacy, at least in appearance and probably in reality, was voluntary, even if Acrocorinthus was garrisoned by 400 Achaean hoplites and fifty watch dogs and their keepers. Also the harbour town of Lechaeum was seized but probably turned over to the Corinthians for their control. The latter may not have liked the fact that their citadel was held by a federal garrison, but they had more local freedom than they had had for years, since now only the citadel was garrisoned while the rest of the city was subject to the local authorities. As a sort of by-product of the success at Corinth, Megara, Troezen, and Epidaurus were brought into the Confederacy. Thus it now had a common boundary with Attica, and Aratus was able to begin to try to detach Athens from Macedonian control. His first raid on Attica belongs to the same generalship, probably to the spring of 242.[1]

The seizure of Corinth naturally resulted in a state of war between the Achaeans and Macedonia. The one action on the part of Antigonus Gonatas reported is an alliance with the Aetolians directed against the Achaeans.[2] To counterbalance this, the Achaeans received aid from the Spartans led by the reforming King Agis. It appears that shortly before this the Aetolians, who apparently already had established something like permanent control over Elis, had made a raid on Laconia in which they advanced all the way to Cape Taenarum and, though they failed to capture Sparta, according to one account, carried off 50,000 prisoners.[3] At about the same time the Aetolians also arranged an *isopoliteia* treaty between Phigalea and Messene, thus extending their influence in this area on a more permanent basis.[4] Hence it was natural for the aggressive Aetolians to join with Antigonus and derive any possible advantage they could from this alliance, though in their invasion of the Peloponnesus they seem to have acted by themselves. It was equally natural for the Spartans to ally themselves with the Achaeans to try to stop an Aetolian attack from a new direction, namely, southward across the Isthmus.

[1] For the chronological problems connected with the career of Aratus, see Walbank, *Aratos*, 167–211.

[2] Reported briefly in Pol. ii. 45. 1 and referred to in ix. 34. 6 and 38. 9.

[3] Pol. iv. 34. 9; ix. 34. 9; Plut. *Cleom.* 18. The latter account by contrasting conditions of the time with later conditions indicates that the raid occurred before the rise of Cleomenes. Walbank, *Commentary* on iv. 34. 9 places the raid after the death of Agis and gives the date as 'probably 240'. The earlier date is suggested in 'The Aetolians and the Cleomenic War', *Studies in Honor of Harry Caplan* (1966), 43–57 at 48 f., actually written a couple of years ago. It still seems to me the more plausible date, but complete certainty is impossible.

[4] *SIG*³ 472. The approximate date is deduced from the fact that the Aetolian commission included Timaeus, who was one of the commanders of the force invading Laconia.

At the same time it was natural for the states allied against Macedonia to seek the support of Ptolemy Euergetes, and it must have been at this time that he was given the title of *hegemon* of the Achaeans by land and sea.[1] How much aid, if any, was derived from Ptolemy is not known.

Their alliance resulted in one effort at co-operation between the Spartans led by Agis and the Achaeans led by Aratus. It must have fallen in the next generalship of Aratus after the liberation of Corinth, namely in 241. On the part of Aratus, it was a typical performance resulting in the defeat of an enemy that already seemed victorious. An added feature was the failure to co-operate cordially with Agis. This was probably due to the prejudice of a rich conservative against a king tainted with ideas of social reform. The Achaeans were expected to hold the frontier of the Megarid against the Aetolians, and Agis, eager for battle, brought the Spartans to their support, but Aratus refused to give battle and allowed the Aetolian army to pass into the Peloponnesus, where it captured and sacked Pellene, the easternmost of the towns of Achaea proper. Thereupon Aratus and the Achaeans fell upon them while they were disorganized and defeated them with heavy losses—700 dead according to Plutarch.[2] These losses seem to have been enough to discourage the enemy, and peace was soon negotiated. Thus, the campaign of Aratus, though the citizens of Pellene cannot have liked his methods, and though he practically sent Agis home to defeat and death, was in a sense highly successful. The peace apparently included Macedonia. In addition, a treaty of alliance between the two confederacies was arranged by Aratus and the Aetolian leader, Pantaleon. This alliance probably was not negotiated until after the death of Gonatas and is to be connected with the beginning of the co-operation of the two confederacies in the war against Demetrius II of Macedonia, which lasted the greater part of his reign (239–229).[3]

Very little is known about the course of the war of the two confederacies against Demetrius but considerably more concerning contemporary efforts to get rid of tyrants in the Peloponnesus and to incorporate their cities into the Achaean Confederacy. At this time monarchical heads of states, called tyrants by their enemies, were common in the Peloponnesus. These rulers normally were agents of the Macedonian king or at least friendly to him. They may even have been so closely tied to him that they automatically were considered at war with any state with which the Macedonian king was at war. The

[1] Plut. *Arat*. 24. 4.

[2] Plut. *Arat*. 31–32, *Agis* 13–15. In Paus. ii. 8. 5 and vii. 7. 3 the roles are confused and the Spartans made the enemies of the Achaeans and captors of Pellene.

[3] Plut. *Arat*. 33. 1–2; Pol. ii. 44. 1.

attack on Argos by Aratus in time of peace for which the Achaeans were condemned to pay a fine, occurred in that short period towards the end of the reign of Antigonus Gonatas during which the Confederacy was at peace with the king. There is no indication that the other attacks and intrigues of Aratus against tyrants were condemned in the same way. The two most important cities involved were Megalopolis and Argos.

Megalopolis had been ruled by Aristodemus 'the Good' about 260–250 B.C. He had to his credit a victory over a Spartan army in which their king Acrotatus, the son of Areus, was defeated and killed.[1] There seem to be no tales of cruelty connected with him, but he was undoubtedly an agent or ally of Antigonus Gonatas and he was a 'tyrant'. Consequently the philosophical tyrannicides, Ecdelus and Demophanes, who aided Aratus in the liberation of Sicyon and who greatly influenced Philopoemen, suborned assassins against him.[2] Obviously at this time not a few who considered themselves intellectuals with high principles thought that anything was fair provided the victim was a tyrant, but take the same man and make him a general of the Achaean Confederacy and he became a statesman no longer a legitimate object of such plots. This was the point of view of Aratus, as is seen most clearly in his relations with the tyrants of Argos. It was later the point of view also of Polybius, who states that right minded people consider the murder of a tyrant even in time of peace as praiseworthy, and here he obviously is speaking not primarily of attacks from within the community but of attacks engineered by outsiders.[3] From this point of view, if a man was dubbed a tyrant, anything was permitted. But, to return to Megalopolis, Aristodemus was soon succeeded by an even more famous tyrant, Lydiades, who later served three years as general of the Achaean Confederacy. In 251, in the interval between the two reigns, a Spartan army was defeated at Mantinea by the combined efforts of Arcadians, Achaeans, and the Sicyonians under Aratus. In this battle Lydiades appeared as one of the two commanders of the contingent from Megalopolis.[4] A few years later

[1] Plut. *Agis* 3; Paus. viii. 27. 11. When Pausanias calls Acrotatus the son of Cleomenes, he undoubtedly, as Niese, *Geschichte*, ii. 241, n. 4 remarks, is confusing him with a namesake.

[2] Pol. x. 22. 2–3; Plut. *Philop.* 1. 3, *Arat.* 5 and 7 (only Ecdelus); Paus. viii. 49. 2. The names of the two vary in the sources.

[3] Pol. ii. 60. 2. in the discussion of the guilt of the younger Aristomachus of Argos (ii. 59–60).

[4] Paus. viii. 10. 5–10, 27. 13–14 (a siege of Megalopolis, apparently a part of the same campaign). The historicity of this battle has been doubted, but it should be noted that Pausanias reports seeing the trophy commemorating the battle. See especially Beloch, *GrG*[2] iv. ii. 523–7, who, however, dates the battle *c.* 249. It remained for Walbank, *Aratos*, 36, 176 f., to note that Pausanias presupposes that Sicyon was free but not yet a member of the Achaean Confederacy. Hence the battle must have fallen between the liberation of Sicyon and its admission into the Confederacy.

he was tyrant. He seems to have ruled quite a number of years before he in 235 forestalled intervention from Aratus by giving up the tyranny and bringing Megalopolis into the Confederacy. He was immediately elected general and served three terms, he and Aratus serving in alternate years.[1] Soon after Megalopolis, also Orchomenus joined. Apparently a tyrant named Nearchus gave up the tyranny but continued to live in the city. Other Arcadian cities too may have come over at the time, among them Mantinea.[2]

The relations of Aratus and the Achaeans with the tyrants of Argos were considerably more complicated and irregular. This city at the time was headed by a regular dynasty of which three members, probably a father and two sons, Aristomachus, Aristipus, and the younger Aristomachus, were involved in the career of Aratus. In addition, it is pretty clear that the Aristippus who was head of the pro-Macedonian party at the time of the intervention of Pyrrhus in 272[3] was the father of the elder Aristomachus and that he was tyrant at the time. When the latter succeeded his father is not known, but it is known that Aratus began plotting against him about 240. Plutarch reports—and his most likely source is Aratus himself—that he tried to smuggle daggers into Argos from Corinth for use by assassins. The would-be assassins quarrelled and one informed on the others, most of whom, however, escaped to Corinth. A short time later the tyrant was murdered by his own slaves. Aratus thereupon hurried to Argos with all the troops he could raise at a moment's notice, expecting the Argives to open the gates to him. Instead he found Aristippus, most likely the son of Aristomachus, established as tyrant. Consequently Aristippus was able to accuse the Achaeans of making war in time of peace, the case was submitted to arbitration before representatives of the city of Mantinea, and the Achaeans were condemned to pay a fine of thirty minas. The assassination of Aristomachus and the raid of Aratus most likely occurred in the spring of 240. After this it is not surprising that Aristippus is said to have tried to secure the assassination of Aratus, and further that Antigonus is said to have approved. The accusation against Antigonus may be based on nothing but the suspicion of Aratus, but it would be surprising if Aristippus did not repay Aratus in kind and plot against him.[4] Concerning the fine

---

[1] Pol. ii. 44. 5; Plut. *Arat.* 30.

[2] The Achaean decree concerning the membership of Orchomenus (*SIG*³ 490) implies that Megalopolis already is a member. It has been plausibly conjectured that the Nearchus mentioned in the document was a tyrant who had abdicated.

[3] Plut. *Pyrrhus* 30.

[4] Plut. *Arat.* 25. The reference to Antigonus shows that the incident occurred while he was still alive. The fact that the charge was brought against the Achaean state shows that Aratus was general at the time. This must have been his third generalship, that of 241–240. Historians commonly say that it was Aratus personally who was fined for breach of peace,

imposed on the Achaeans, it has commonly been held that, because a tyrant was involved, the judges, hostile to tyrants, imposed merely a nominal fine.[1] If so, it means that the violation of international law was so flagrant that even friendly judges could not avoid condemning it.

The efforts to get rid of the tyrant of Argos continued. On one occasion Aratus with a few followers scaled the wall with the aid of ladders and killed the guards that tried to dislodge them. Though himself wounded, he maintained the position throughout the following day but withdrew the following night. Next he tried a pitched battle advancing to the neighbourhood of Argos with what must have been a considerable force. In the battle, it is said, that the Achaeans had the better of it along most of the line, but that Aratus retreated none the less. His dissatisfied troops shamed him into preparing for battle the next day, but, when the time came, he found that the enemy had received re-enforcements and so retreated once more and arranged a truce to remove the fallen Achaeans, thus admitting defeat. On the way home, Aratus again staged a coup. He secured Cleonae, whereupon the Achaeans conducted the Nemean Games there. Later the Argives in turn celebrated the games. In this connexion the Achaeans violated the right of inviolability of participants in Panhellenic games. Participants in the games conducted by Argos who crossed Achaean territory were seized and sold into slavery. A little later, clearly the same year, Aratus received information that Aristippus was intent on recovering Cleonae but was afraid to act while Aratus was at Corinth. Consequently the latter laid a trap for Aristippus. He mobilized a force and took it to Cenchreae, where supplies for several days as if for an expedition had been accumulated. Then, during the night, he secretly brought his troops to Cleonae and thus next morning was able to face Aristippus with a force in battle array. The result was that the Argives were defeated with heavy losses—over 1,500 dead including Aristippus himself, as compared with no Achaean losses according to the obviously exaggerated report of Plutarch, undoubtedly derived from the account of Aratus himself. Yet this time too Aratus failed to liberate Argos, where the younger Aristomachus, most likely a brother of Aristippus, set himself up as ruler and probably began his reign with the execution of eighty Argives suspected of complicity with the Achaeans.[2]

but the charge was brought against the Achaeans, and it must have been the Achaean Confederacy which was condemned to pay; cf. Porter on Plut. *Aratus* 25. 5.

[1] Freeman, *Fed. Govt.* 302; Raeder, *L'Arbitrage international*, 79 f., no. xl; Walbank, *Aratos*, 56; Tarn, *CAH* vii. 735.

[2] Plut. *Arat.* 27–30. These events, with the possible exception of the night attack with scaling ladders, belong to one year, and this must be a year in which the Nemean Games,

Thus the defeat and death of Aristippus did not bring Argos into the Confederacy, but it seems that it was these attacks on Argos which convinced Lydiades of Megalopolis that it was wisest to give up the tyranny and join the Achaeans. At least according to Polybius, while other tyrants waited till the death of Demetrius II before they gave up, Lydiades, analyzing the situation correctly, acted earlier. Then in 229 an agreement was reached with Aristomachus. It seems that Aratus, had begun the negotiations, and that Lydiades, who was general 230–229 for the third and last time, took over, maligned Aratus to Aristomachus as a hater of tyrants, and tried himself to get credit for the settlement. This so angered Aratus that he induced the Achaean assembly to reject the proposal. Later, no doubt, when he himself was general, he reversed his position and supported the proposal, and the Argives were admitted without further trouble. Plutarch (Aratus?) may be right in saying that Aristomachus was motivated by the feeling that it would be better to be general of the Achaean Confederacy than the hated tyrant of a single city. As a matter of fact, he was elected general for 228–227, a year in which Aratus was unqualified to serve. The wave which swept away the tyranny at Argos swept away also those of Hermione and Phlius.[1]

Along with the plots against the tyrants, Aratus kept up almost constantly his efforts to liberate Athens from Macedonian control. His first raid came soon after the liberation of Corinth. The peace negotiated with Antigonus Gonatas did not cause him to cease, and it is said that the Achaeans themselves blamed him for attempting to seize Piraeus in time of peace. Repeated raids, continuing after the war against Demetrius got under way, but about which nothing further is known, followed. Apparently these attacks and those on the tyrants in the Peloponnesus caused a Macedonian army to be sent to the Peloponnesus, probably in 233. Probably operating out of Argos it inflicted on the Achaeans at a place named Phylacia a defeat sufficiently spectacular for the rumour to circulate that Aratus was dead or captured. But even this defeat cannot have been too disastrous, for Aratus was able immediately afterwards to raid Attica and advance as far as to the Academy in the suburbs of Athens. Later, after the death of Demetrius, the Athenians called in Aratus to help negotiate for the withdrawal of the Macedonian garrisons in Attica. Aratus is even said

---

celebrated in odd years, were held. Since Aratus, after the death of Aristippus, began plotting against Lydiades (*Arat.* 30), and since the latter joined the Confederacy early enough to be elected general in the spring of 234, the latest possible date for the Cleonae incidents is 235. Pol. ii. 59. 8–9 connects the execution of the 80 by Aristomachus with an attack in which Aratus had entered Argos but had had to withdraw. The only such attack reported came under Aristippus. Conjectures about just what actually happened vary.

[1] Pol. ii. 44. 2–6, 60. 4; Plut. *Arat.* 35. 1–5.

to have contributed personally twenty talents to the sum needed to pay the mercenary soldiers that were discharged. Nevertheless, Athens did not join the Confederacy but chose to remain neutral. Aegina, however, joined.[1]

In this way the Achaean Confederacy had reached the height of its power and its greatest extent before the Roman intervention in Greece, but there were already signs of dangers ahead. This very year was the one in which the first great Roman armament intervened in Illyria, some time after the defeat of a joint fleet of the Achaeans and Aetolians by the Illyrians, a defeat in which Margos of Cerynea, the elder statesman of the Achaeans, fell.[2] Thus ended the most hopeful period in Achaean and Aetolian history, a period in which the two confederacies co-operated and were called upon for help by other Greek states when in need. Formally the alliance lasted to the outbreak of the Social War in 220, but the period of real co-operation seems to have come to an end in 229. Polybius has not done justice to the movement. Was it because it was the policy of Margos rather than of Aratus and that it died with Margos? Or was it that the coming of the Romans obscured everything else?

The year 229 saw also the beginning of the Cleomenic War, during which there may have been a decline in cordial relations between the Achaeans and Aetolians. During the war against Demetrius it seems that the co-operation was so close that when the defences of eastern Arcadia seemed endangered after the battle of Phylacia, the Achaeans permitted the transfer of Tegea, Mantinea, Orchomenus, and apparently Caphyae to the protection of the Aetolians.[3] Thus, at this time when Argos was still under the control of a tyrant supported by Macedonia, the Achaeans arranged to have along this frontier a series of buffer states allied with Aetolia. When Argos was brought into the Confederacy, this must have caused trouble, since these cities formed a line almost cutting the Confederacy in two. As long as the other state was a faithful ally, this did not matter too much, and the cordial relations seem to have continued down to the co-operation against the Illyrians in 229.

[1] Plut. Arat. 33–34; Paus. ii. 8. 6. The battle of Phylacia has been variously dated, Ferguson, Hellenistic Athens, 201 tentatively placing it in 235; Beloch, GrG² iv. i. 633 and Walbank, Aratos, 64 in 233; Feyel, Polybe et Béotie, 99 f. in 237. The reason for placing it in 233 is that it seems that there must have been some connexion between this defeat and the transfer of the eastern Arcadian cities to the Aetolians.

[2] Pol. ii. 9–10.

[3] For the transfer of the three cities from the Aetolians to Cleomenes, see Pol. ii. 46. 2; for the 'voluntary' or peaceful transfer of Mantinea from the Achaeans to the Aetolians, Pol. ii. 57. 1. The other cities undoubtedly were transferred at the same time. The capture of Caphyae by Aratus (Plut. Cleom. 4) shows that this city too was among those taken over by Cleomenes.

Thus at the outbreak of the Cleomenic War the situation was as follows. The Achaeans and Aetolians were still allies and, as can be seen in the complicated negotiations of 220, they were still formally allies down to the outbreak of the Social War. This, however, did not cause the Aetolians to give up their ambition to control at least the west coast of the Peloponnesus. Thus they can hardly have viewed with favour the growth of Spartan power under Cleomenes. At the same time, the Aetolians were heavily involved in hostilities against Macedonia. Their expansion in Thessaly, best known from their later claims, seems to have belonged to the last part of the reign of Demetrius II. Next, early in his reign, probably in 228, Antigonus Doson inflicted a severe defeat on the Aetolians and drove them out of Thessaly.[1] Just when peace was negotiated is not known, but it certainly was before 224 when Doson asked permission to take his army south by Thermopylae, but at the time of the outbreak of the Cleomenic War, the Aetolians and Macedonians were still at war. Hence it would seem that nothing could be more impossible at the time than a joint plot of the Aetolians, Doson, and Cleomenes directed against the Achaeans. Yet this is precisely what Polybius charges.

The seizure by Cleomenes through surprise or treason of the Arcadian cities affiliated with the Aetolians, and the failure of the Aetolians to resist the seizure, gave some plausibility to the charge of Polybius, undoubtedly derived from Aratus.[2] But what could the Aetolians have done? These cities, entirely surrounded by foreign territory and not regular members of the Confederacy, cannot have been worth much to them, certainly not the effort of a war of reconquest. Striking at Sparta by advancing through Elis and Messenia would not have been a very effective mode of intervention in the interest of cities located in eastern Arcadia. More practical would have been intervention from the north, but that would have involved crossing Achaean territory and could hardly have been undertaken except in co-operation with the Achaeans. If such a plan was ever proposed, it was rejected by Aratus and the leaders of the Achaeans without being brought before the assembly.[3]

---

[1] Justin xxviii. 3. 11–16; Frontinus, *Strategemata* ii. 6. 5; cf. S. Dow and C. F. Edson, *Harv. Stud. Class. Phil.* xlviii (1937), 165–8; Feyel, *Polybe et Béotie*, 115.

[2] In ii. 45. 2 Polybius specifically charges an understanding of the Aetolians with Doson and Cleomenes, though his account in ii. 46. 2 indicates that Cleomenes secured the cities through surprise or trickery. For the relation of these cities to Aetolia see pp. 202 ff. under 'The Aetolian Confederacy'; on the relation of the Aetolians to the Cleomenic War, see the article cited on p. 307, n. 3.

[3] According to Pol. ii. 46. 4 Aratus and the other leaders decided not to begin war against anyone but to resist Spartan attacks. This can only mean that they would not declare war on account of the seizure of these cities, which after all were not Achaean. If Achaean territory was attacked, they would act. They, of course, could make such negative decisions at any time without submitting them to the assembly.

The decision of these leaders was not to go to war on account of the Arcadian cities seized by Cleomenes. Only when Cleomenes a short time afterwards seized and fortified the Athenaeum claimed by Megalopolis, was an extraordinary meeting of the Achaean assembly called. At this it was voted to take up the war openly. In other words, war was declared late in 229 or early in 228, though the language of Polybius implies that hostilities had begun before the declaration.[1] The seizure and fortification of the Athenaeum by Cleomenes had been followed by night attacks by Aratus on Tegea and Orchomenus. Possibly also the capture of Caphyae preceded the declaration.[2] Be this as it may, it seems clear that the initiative in the aggression came from Sparta. There is extant a version which places the blame on Aratus and the Achaeans, but this too states that Cleomenes desired the war and began it but had an excuse in the plots of the Achaeans.[3]

Only some of the more pertinent points connected with the Cleomenic War can be considered. It was a war which almost brought the dissolution of the Achaean Confederacy and, though it survived and later expanded considerably, actually greatly reduced its real power and importance. Hereafter the Confederacy became a sort of vassal first of Macedonia and later of Rome. In the first part of the war down to 227 the Achaeans held their own fairly well. Reverses are reported, but defeats were closely followed by some success. If the defeats had been too devastating, the speedy recovery would have been impossible. According to the information available, the worst Achaean mistake was the failure to fight when conditions were favourable. In 228, when Aristomachus, the former tyrant of Argos, was general, an Achaean force said to have numbered 20,000 infantry and 1,000 cavalry was prevented by Aratus from joining battle with a force of less than 5,000 under Cleomene. Some have blamed Aratus for interfering with the conduct of the campaign by the responsible commander; others, Aristomachus for his weakness in yielding. Considering the hold of Aratus on Achaean public opinion, it is likely that Aristomachus found it impossible to act against his advice. Later, Lydiades brought charges against Aratus and ran against him at the elections in the spring of 227. Nevertheless, Aratus won and was elected general for 227–226.[4]

[1] Pol. ii. 46. 6; cf. Walbank's *Commentary* and *Rep. Govt.* 78 f., 165 f. The seizure of Tegea etc. by Cleomenes, the fortification of the Athenaeum, and the Achaean declaration of war, all belong in a single generalship of Aratus and this must be that of 229–228.

[2] Plut. *Cleom.* 4, undoubtedly from Phylarchus. The account of the attacks on Tegea and Orchomenus and of the insulting letters exchanged by Cleomenes and Aratus implies underhand actions in peace-time by both leaders. [3] Plut. *Cleom.* 3.

[4] The statistics found in Plut. *Cleom.* 4 are undoubtedly derived from Phylarchus, who may have exaggerated the difference in the sizes of the forces in order to belittle the Achaeans and Aratus. The charges of Lydiades and the contested election are reported in Plut. *Arat.* 35. 7.

It seems, however, that not a follower of Aratus but Lydiades was elected to serve as *hipparch*, that is, commander of the cavalry and virtual vice-president of the Confederacy.[1] Aratus began the year's campaigning with an expedition against Elis. On the way back he was met near Mount Lycaeum, west of Megalopolis, by Cleomenes and the Spartans and defeated, it is said, with heavy losses. Yet, immediately afterwards he surprised and captured Mantinea, where now 300 Achaean settlers were introduced and the Achaean hold on the city was further strengthened by a garrison of 200 mercenary soldiers.[2] In spite of the defeat in battle, this important acquisition meant that so far the Achaeans had the better of it. Later in the year the picture was somewhat changed. Cleomenes marched against Megalopolis, where he was met by the Achaeans under Aratus, the Achaean light armed troops in a sortie met with some success, but Aratus checked the pursuit and refused to join a general battle. At this, Lydiades in disgust charged with the cavalry and at first met with success but was drawn onto difficult terrain and defeated and killed, the defeat ultimately involving the entire Achaean force. Again the loss in this battle, usually called the battle of Laodicea, as far as casualties are concerned, may not have been too devastating. Yet the death of Lydiades caused a great stir. In a meeting of the assembly at Aegium it was voted not to furnish supplies to Aratus and not to maintain mercenaries. How much this was allowed to interfere with the conduct of the war is not known. Aratus retained his office and later—probably early in 226—was able to meet Megistonous, the stepfather of Cleomenes, at Orchomenus and defeat and capture him.[3] This looks like an expedition starting from old Achaea and striking south at the northern end of the Spartan corridor. Since the Achaeans already had recovered Caphyae and Mantinea, Orchomenus and Tegea must have been about all that the Spartans retained.

It was probably in 227 that Aratus made the first overtures to Antigonus Doson. It took the form of suggesting to two personal friends at Megalopolis, Nicophanes and the Cynic philosopher and poet, Cercidas, that Megalopolis appeal to Antigonus for help. Such an appeal from a city to a foreign power required the permission of the federal government. Thus the embassy involved three steps, the decision of the Megalopolitans to act, the despatch of Nicophanes and Cercidas as ambassadors (*presbeutai*) to the federal government to

[1] This has been deduced from the fact that Lydiades commanded the cavalry in the battle in which he was killed. Cf. Beloch, *GrG²* iv. i. 699 and n. 1.

[2] Plut. *Cleom.* 5, *Arat.* 36. 1–2; Pol. ii. 51. 3, 58. 1–3. The Achaeans of 58. 2 were settlers rather than a garrison proper; cf. Walbank on Pol. ii. 58. 4.

[3] Plut. *Arat.* 36–38, *Cleom.* 6; Pol. ii. 51. 3. The only report of the victory at Orchomenus seems to be that of Plut. *Arat.* 38. 1.

secure its authorization, and the further despatch of the two as ambassadors of Megalopolis to Antigonus Doson. Polybius gives at length the reasoning which prompted Aratus to act and the arguments which were presented to Doson. All of this consists of variations on his leitmotif of hatred and suspicion of the Aetolians. Involved is material of a kind concerning which it is impossible for an outsider to have accurate knowledge. Concerning Aratus, it might have been more truthful to say that it is impossible to know his reasons, 'but this is what he himself wrote'. The result of the embassy was that Doson promised to help if invited by the Achaeans, that is, by the federal authorities. Thereupon the Megalopolitans appeared at a regular meeting of the Achaean assembly and urged that such an invitation be sent. Aratus, however, induced the Achaeans to postpone action and for the time being to carry on the war by themselves. This decision would fit best after the success at Orchomenus and before the news arrived that Ptolemy had dropped the Achaeans and had transferred his subsidy to Cleomenes.[1] The chief advantage to Aratus resulting from the embassy was the knowledge that the seizure of Acrocorinthus had not made a future understanding with the Macedonian king impossible, though he was to learn that such an understanding would involve the return of Corinth and thus the repudiation of the policy which had inspired the seizure.

The Achaean general elected in the spring of 226 was Hyperbatas. During his term of office, Cleomenes first recovered Mantinea and then invaded the western extremity of Achaea proper, advancing through Arcadia south of the range of mountains separating it from Achaea. At Hecatombaeum near Dyme he met and inflicted a crushing defeat on the total levy of the Achaeans. In such cases it is impossible to tell how 'total' the mobilization actually was, but in this case it is clear that the defeat was serious. It was after it that Aratus sent his son, the younger Aratus, to negotiate with Antigonus Doson, and it was at this time that Doson stipulated the surrender of Acrocorinthus as pay for his intervention—a demand which caused the Achaeans to delay, for the Corinthians did not fancy being subject to Macedonia once again.[2]

---

[1] The chief source is Pol. ii. 47–51; briefer, Plut. *Arat.* 38. 11–12. The date of the appeal of Megalopolis is now commonly given as 227; cf. Walbank on Pol. ii. 47. 6 and the literature cited there. It is clear that it belongs to a year when Aratus was general, and 229–228 is too early and 224–223 too late. Moreover, early in 226 before the disasters that came later that year seems to be the latest date at which the Achaeans can have voted to carry on the war by themselves.

[2] Plut. *Arat.* 39. 1 barely mentions Mantinea and Hecatombaeum; *Cleom.* 14 is fuller. Pol. ii. 51. 3–6 so definitely connects the sending of the younger Aratus with Hecatombaeum that this mission must be accepted and kept distinct from the inclusion of the younger Aratus among the hostages later sent to Doson. Cf. Walbank on Pol. ii. 51. 5.

At the time of this crisis Aratus refused to be elected general for 225–224 in his normal turn, every second year. He has sometimes been accused of shirking responsibility, but it is doubtful whether this is justified. The general of the year, Timoxenus, was one of his followers, and Aratus kept in close touch with the conduct of affairs. At one time, when it became known that many at Sicyon and Corinth favoured Cleomenes, he was sent to the two cities with extraordinary judicial authority. At Sicyon he simply had those guilty put to death— startling evidence of the length to which the federal government would go at least in the case of war. When he tried a similar procedure at Corinth, though an Achaean garrison held Acrocorinthus, he was lucky to escape with his life.[1] This came after the failure of the first peace negotiations between Cleomenes and the Achaeans. These negotiations seem to have been opened soon after the battle of Hecatombaeum. A preliminary peace, or at least an armistice was arranged, and the Achaeans seemed quite ready to accept the terms offered by Cleomenes even when he demanded the *hegemonia*. There is no further explanation of what this meant, but, if it is interpreted as similar to the *hegemonia* of the kings in the Hellenic League, it meant some sort of permanent supremacy over the Confederacy. An extraordinary meeting of the Achaean assembly had been called to make the final arrangements, when a sudden illness prevented Cleomenes from attending. A second meeting was called at Argos, but this time Aratus imposed such terms concerning the armed escort of Cleomenes or the hostages to be furnished that Cleomenes stayed away and sent a declaration of war, not to Argos where the Achaean magnates were at the time, but to Aegium, the capital of the Confederacy.[2] It looks as if Aratus deliberately provoked Cleomenes in order to block the agreement. By this time he must have decided that he preferred dependence on the more distant Macedonia to vassalage under Sparta. Probably he also thought that he could influence, not to say manipulate, Doson more effectively than Cleomenes. Doson showed, however, by his demand for the return of Acrocorinthus and his first campaign in the Peloponnesus that his purpose was to re-establish Macedonian supremacy in Greece. The liberal terms of the Hellenic League as re-established by him were dictated not by pure idealism but by policy. After all, though the allies were permitted to remain neutral in case of a League war, it was, nevertheless, forbidden to do anything in opposition to the alliance with the king.[3]

---

[1] Plut. *Arat.* 40. 1–6.

[2] Plut. *Cleom.* 15–17, *Arat.* 39. 1–4. The two accounts differ about the exact nature of the quarrel between Aratus and Cleomenes.

[3] Pol. iv. 16. 5; Livy xxxii. 22. 3.

When the war was reopened, events moved rapidly. Cleomenes began by capturing Pellene and a couple of posts on the way to this city. By so doing he extended the corridor controlled by the Spartans to the Gulf of Corinth and cut the Achaean Confederacy in two. Soon he also secured control of Argos without too much difficulty.[1] It is no wonder that the pro-Spartan elements in Sicyon and Corinth began to show signs of restlessness. It was in this connexion that Aratus was sent to the two cities with extraordinary judicial authority. His expulsion from Corinth was followed by an invitation from the Corinthians to Cleomenes to take over their city.[2] The Corinthians by their invitation, and Cleomenes by accepting it, actually played into the hands of Antigonus, for this gave the Achaeans an excuse to surrender Acrocorinthus to him. Meanwhile Cleomenes, after Corinth and other cities had come over to him, laid siege to Sicyon, where the elder and the younger Aratus were at the time. This was most likely in the spring of 224. While the siege was in progress, the Achaeans called an extraordinary meeting of their assembly at Aegium and summoned Aratus to appear. He, together with his son, managed to make his way there by sea. At the meeting it was voted to invite Antigonus Doson, to surrender Acrocorinthus to him, and to send hostages. Among those sent was the younger Aratus.[3] Doson was completely prepared and went into action immediately.

Cleomenes did not succeed in reducing Sicyon or Acrocorinthus but had such control of the rest of the eastern part of the Peloponnesus that he could prepare to face the Macedonian army at the Isthmus and practically ignore the remnants of the Achaean Confederacy. When he heard that the Achaeans had reached an agreement with Doson, he discontinued the siege of Sicyon and began to prepare the defences of the Isthmus. This included digging trenches and erecting ramparts.[4] These defences held up the advance of Doson for some time but ultimately failed because Argos once more changed sides.

The Macedonian army which Doson brought south is said to have numbered 20,000 infantry and 1,300 cavalry.[5] Many of these troops undoubtedly were mercenary soldiers or other auxiliaries. The army came south by the route which crossed northern Euboea and then passed through Eastern Locris. Phocis, and Boeotia. It would seem that the natural route to take was the one by Thermopylae, but the use of this route was denied Doson by the Aetolians, who threatened to use force if necessary. For this reason it became necessary to take the

---

[1] Plut. *Cleom.* 17. [2] Plut. *Arat.* 40. 6; *Cleom.* 19; Pol. ii. 52. 3.
[3] Plut. *Arat.* 42, *Cleom.* 19; on the meeting at Aegium cf. *Rep. Govt.* 166 f.
[4] Pol. ii. 52. 5; Plut. *Cleom.* 20.
[5] Plut. *Arat.* 43. 1; cf. Pol. ii. 65. 1–5 for the troops in the Sellasia campaign.

army across to northern Euboea, and, since there are no roads suitable for an army to march from northern Euboea to the Euripus, it was necessary to cross again to the mainland. Like Philip V in 219, Doson probably landed at Cynus in Opuntian Locris and then proceeded through the pass of Hyampolis into Phocis and continued down the Cephissus valley.[1] The denial of passage on the part of the Aetolians was hardly a friendly act but does not warrant all the accusations lodged against them by Polybius. Yet it may have been enough to have prevented a complete understanding between them and Doson and thus to have kept them out of the Hellenic League when it was founded.

When the efforts to break through the defences of Cleomenes at the Isthmus failed, Antigonus undertook the slow and laborious task of collecting enough ships to ferry his large army across the Gulf. For this purpose he used as his headquarters Pagae, the port of Megara on the Gulf. Thither Aratus and the *damiorgoi* of the Achaeans made their way in boats with some difficulty, and there Antigonus and the Achaean leaders exchanged oaths. So far this was the only direct contact between the Achaean and Macedonian governments. The deadlock at the Isthmus might have continued for a considerable time but for the revolt of Argos. The pending revolt was reported to Aratus, who thereupon was sent by Antigonus with 1,500 men—undoubtedly a contingent of the Macedonian army—by sea to Epidaurus to proceed from there to Argos. This force came too late to take part in the fighting that ensued and did not end until Antigonus was seen approaching with his army. Meanwhile an Achaean force under Timoxenus, the general of the preceding year, had come from Sicyon and given substantial aid to the rebels. On this basis Polybius gave the Achaeans credit for the successful action which was the turning point of the campaign.[2] To be sure, it was a bold act. There can have been no general mobilization of the Achaeans and, since Sicyon was cut off from the rest of the Confederacy, if there had been, the army would hardly have been available to Timoxenus. He must have used the garrison which had defended Sicyon, probably somewhat strengthened by hasty local mobilization. With these troops he passed through territory under hostile control.

[1] Pol. ii. 52. 7–8, iv. 67. 7 (Philip V). Cf. 'Phocis in the Social War of 220–217 B.C.', *The Phoenix*, xix (1965), 116–28.

[2] There is no wholly satisfactory ancient account of this campaign. Polybius (ii. 52. 5–53) is chiefly interested in emphasizing the importance of the Achaean contribution, but his reference to Timoxenus and his failure to mention Aratus is proof that the latter contributed little or nothing to the outcome. This agrees with the account in Plut. *Cleom.* 20. The account in *Arat.* 43–44 is the only one to report the presence of Aratus and the *damiorgoi* at Pagae and their exchange of oaths with the king. Polybius calls Timoxenus *strategos* but apparently uses the term in a broader sense and does not mean the head of the Confederacy. Cf. Tarn, *CAH* vii. 863 f.; Walbank on Pol. ii. 53. 2 and the literature cited by them.

The fall of Argos and the consequent abandonment of Corinth by Cleomenes, whatever Achaean troops may have contributed to the outcome, was the first great victory of Antigonus Doson in Greece, and it was he and not Aratus who took charge of affairs. First and foremost, he took over Acrocorinthus, which again became the centre of Macedonian power in Greece, but also at Argos he showed that his purpose was to restore Macedonian supremacy. There the statues of former tyrants which had been removed were set up again, thus clearly indicating that these tyrants had been respectable allies or agents of Macedonia. This gives a special significance to the execution of the last of the Argive tyrants, the younger Aristomachus. This must mean that he was considered guilty of having a share in betraying the city to Cleomenes. Meanwhile at Corinth the statues of the men who had liberated Acrocorinthus were overthrown except for that of Aratus himself, for these men had been the enemies of Macedonia. Only Aratus was pardoned, as it were, on account of his later co-operation with Doson. To these actions Aratus objected at length, but to no avail. His earlier anti-Macedonian policy could not have been condemned more clearly.[1]

The next move of the king after he had secured Argos indicates that he felt that he had special ties with or obligations to Megalopolis. He by-passed the major Arcadian cities held by Cleomenes and proceeded to expel Spartan garrisons from small forts in the district in dispute between Megalopolis and Sparta. This ended the campaign, which probably had been continued well into the winter of 224–223. Thereupon Doson went to a regular meeting of the Achaean assembly at Aegium at which he was elected *hegemon* of all the allies. This must refer to the formation of the Hellenic League so that the meeting or meetings at Aegium included both a meeting of the Achaean assembly and something in the nature of a constitutional convention. This meeting has commonly been placed late in 224 but may have been held early in 223. After it Doson placed his troops in winter quarters for a short time at Sicyon and Corinth.[2]

The campaigning season of 223 was devoted to the expulsion of the Spartans from the cities of Arcadia and to the restoration of Macedonian power in the Peloponnesus by the planting of garrisons in a number of key cities. The cities listed by Polybius as recovered during the year are Tegea, Orchomenus, Mantinea, Heraea, and Telphusa.

---

[1] Affair of the statues: Plut. *Arat.* 45. 5; execution of Aristomachus: Pol. ii. 59. 1 and 60.7; Plut. *Arat.* 44.6.

[2] Pol. ii. 54. 2–5. Beloch, *GrG*² iv. i. 712 and Walbank on Pol. ii. 54. 3 place the Aegium meeting in the autumn of 224; Aymard, *ACA* 268, n. 3 considers the autumn probable but February 223 possible.

21

Of these Doson garrisoned at least Orchomenus and Heraea.[1] At Mantinea, on the other hand, the city was plundered and the entire citizen body sold into slavery, except for some who may have been executed or deported. The site was then given to the Achaeans, who refounded the city and named it Antigonea. Feeling undoubtedly ran high for the reason that when Mantinea two years earlier went over to Cleomenes, the Achaeans who had been settled there had been massacred,[2] but even so these incidents hardly show that warfare was becoming more humane. Also the other cities recovered and not garrisoned by the Macedonians must have been turned over to the Achaeans. Thus the latter were somewhat strengthened, but Doson himself, by means of the garrisons in Corinth, Orchomenus, and Heraea extended effective Macedonian control across Arcadia to the border of Elis. When he returned to Macedonia he left in charge of the Macedonian province in the Peloponnesus, Taurion,[3] who was to remain there for years and is frequently mentioned in connexion with events during the early years of Philip V.

In the autumn of 223 Antigonus sent his Macedonian troops home for the winter while he himself remained with his mercenaries at Aegium. He clearly knew that his task in the Peloponnesus was not completed, but he may have thought that the Achaean Confederacy could fend for itself during the winter. If so, he miscalculated. Cleomenes was well aware that Doson and his mercenaries were fully three days' march away from Megalopolis and so was able to prepare the seizure of the city without any fear of interference from that quarter. Since a considerable part of the wall was found unguarded, the capture was relatively easy. Yet most of the population escaped to Messene and

[1] Pol. ii. 54. 5–13. Garrison at Orchomenus: Pol. iv. 6. 5–6; Plut. *Arat.* 45. 1. The garrison at Heraea is attested more indirectly. Livy xxviii. 8. 6 and xxxii. 5. 4 shows the city under Macedonian control, but the dates are so late that it cannot be absolutely certain that this means that the occupation was due to Doson; cf. Aymard, *Premiers rapports*, 25, n. 5 (pp. 25–28); Walbank, *Philip V*, 17, n. 2. If, however, Pol. iv. 77. 5, 80. 15–16 is correctly interpreted to mean Macedonian control in 218 when Philip V used the city as his headquarters in that part of the peninsula, it becomes virtually certain that the city had been garrisoned by Doson.

[2] Pol. ii. 58. 12 states that the free population was sold into slavery; Plut. *Arat.* 45. 6 states that the leading men were executed and that of the rest some were sold and some were sent in chains to Macedonia, while the women and the children were enslaved. This more detailed statement is probably correct. The statement of Polybius is from a chapter in which he is defending Aratus against charges brought by Phylarchus. Hence he tends to minimize his guilt. In 58. 4 he states that the Mantineans had massacred the Achaeans living among them, while Plut. *Cleom.* 14. 1 states that they expelled the garrison of the Achaeans, a statement undoubtedly derived from Phylarchus. Probably both authors are right in their positive statements, but both omit details unfavourable to the point of view adopted by them. The Mantineans probably massacred the Achaean residents and dismissed the garrison of mercenaries.

[3] Pol. iv. 6. 4–6; Walbank, *Philip V*, 20 calls him 'High Commissioner for the Peloponnese'.

afterwards refused the offer to receive back their city in return for breaking away from the Achaeans and becoming the allies of Sparta. In retaliation Cleomenes plundered the city, carried off statues and paintings, and withdrew his troops. Thus he had no hope of holding the city permanently. Later he similarly raided Argive territory and withdrew. Aside from the destruction of property, the only result of these raids was discontent on the part of the Greeks with Doson for not protecting them more effectively.[1]

With the spring of 222 came the Macedonian army to be followed by the Sellasia campaign and the total defeat of Cleomenes. According to the detailed statistics of Polybius the army of Doson at this battle contained 27,600 infantry of all kinds and 1,200 cavalry. Of these, 9,600 infantry, including 1,600 Illyrians, and 600 cavalry were furnished by the allies; 18,000 infantry and 600 cavalry were Macedonians and mercenaries. Of the allied contingents 4,000 infantry, including 1,000 Megalopolitans equipped by Doson with Macedonian weapons and armour, and 300 cavalry were furnished by the Achaeans; 2,000 infantry and 200 cavalry, by the Boeotians, 1,000 and 50, by the Epirotes; the same numbers, by the Acarnanians.[2] These are round numbers but probably approximately correct. The composition of the army indicates that the new Hellenic League was functioning well, though even so its contributions to the combined force were small in comparison with those of the Macedonians.

The battle of Sellasia can almost be considered a decisive battle. A victory for Cleomenes on the field of battle did not seem impossible. His army was not much more than two thirds as large as that of Antigonus, but he occupied a very strong position, two hills and the valley between them, a position which could not readily be turned. The details of the battle will have to be left to others,[3] but an effort will be made to assess the contributions of the Greek allies. Though Antigonus with his Macedonian phalanx on his own left wing faced and ultimately defeated the Spartan phalanx on Cleomene's right, yet it is clear that the really decisive action took place on the other wing, where

---

[1] Pol. ii. 55. 1–7; Plut. *Cleom.* 23–25 (undoubtedly derived from Phylarchus).

[2] Pol. ii. 65. 1–5 and iv. 69. 5 for the equipping of the Megalopolitans by Doson. There is relatively little trouble in interpretating these statistics, though Polybius gives the total of the infantry in round numbers as 28,000. For some groups of soldiers it is also difficult to know whether they are counted as parts of the Macedonian contingent or as mercenaries. The Cretans, first mentioned in the description of the line of battle, certainly are to be counted with the mercenaries and should not be dismissed from the text as they have been in the Büttner-Wobst edition.

[3] The fullest account is that of Pol. ii. 65–69; cf. also Plut. *Cleom.* 27–28, *Arat.* 46 (bare mention), *Philop.* 6 for Philopoemen's alleged brilliant performance. For the various problems involved and for further literature see Walbank's *Commentary*, which also contains an excellent plan of the battle field (based on Kromayer).

the troops were partly those of the Greek allies. Here the most decisive blow was struck by the extreme right consisting of alternate units of Illyrians and Macedonian *chalkaspides*, probably a type of soldier somewhat more mobile than the troops of the line in the phalanx. To the left of these, however, were contingents of Greek allies. While the extreme right remained concealed from the enemy, the rest of the wing had the unenviable task of charging uphill against an enemy in a very strong position. No wonder that the situation seemed desperate when they were attacked in the rear by the light-armed troops of their opponents. This pressure was removed when these troops in turn were attacked from the rear. For this action the Achaeans gave credit to the young Philopoemen of Megalopolis, the future general of the Confederacy. Probably more important was the surprise attack of the Illyrians and the Macedonians grouped with them who had advanced unobserved.[1] After the defeat of his left wing, came the failure of Cleomenes himself to defeat the Macedonian phalanx.

After Sellasia the Macedonians and their allies had control of the entire eastern part of the Greek peninsula from Macedonia to Sparta. On the north, with Epirus and the Illyrians, their sphere of influence also reached the Adriatic. The Aetolians still held Thermopylae. Otherwise only Athens stood aloof. All the regular members of the Hellenic League were federal states. Putting together the information from the none too systematic lists given by Polybius, the following states are seen to have been members: the Achaeans, Boeotians, Epirotes, Acarnanians, Phocians, Locrians, Thessalians, and Euboeans. Also the Macedonians are included in one list, but they probably were not regular members but were united with the League only through their king, who was the *hegemon* of the League.[2] Outside the League were Aetolia, Elis, and Messene, and of these Aetolia and Elis were soon hostile to it. The position of Sparta is not too clear. A chance reference indicates that Antigonus left the Boeotians Brachylles behind as governor. This in turn implies a garrison. It may well at first have been the intention to make this permanent. On the other hand, the Spartans

---

[1] The statement of Plut. *Cleom*. 28, derived from Phylarchus, that the Illyrians and others —he says the Acarnanians—managed to bypass their opponents unobserved and so to stage a surprise attack, must be correct. The position of the Spartan left wing was so strong that otherwise it is hard to understand how it could have been defeated by infantry charging uphill against it.

[2] Pol. iv. 9. 4, 15. 1, xi. 5. 4. The Macedonians are listed among the members in iv. 9. 4, but in the dedication at Delos of spoils from Sellasia (*SIG*³ 518) the Macedonians and the allies appear as separate units; cf. Walbank on ii. 54. 4. Note also that in 198 the five Achaean *damiorgoi* who opposed putting to vote a motion for an alliance with the Romans stated that it was illegal to take up anything against the alliance with Philip (Livy xxxii. 22. 3); their obligations were to the king, not to the Macedonians. The Illyrians are mentioned in none of these lists, and it seems safe to conclude that they were not members of the League.

were also set free by Doson, and that must mean that the kingship was abolished so that the ephors became the undisputed heads of the state. The garrison and governor were soon withdrawn and Sparta made a member of the Hellenic League.[1] Most of the cities which had belonged to the Achaean Confederacy but had been taken over by Cleomenes were restored to it.

How viable the Hellenic League would have proved given favourable conditions, it is difficult to say. As it was, Antigonus himself died before the League had had a chance to become well established, and it was not many years after his death that everything was further upset by the Roman intervention. There is much to be said for the belief that the very looseness of the organization caused less ill feeling than the firmer organization of the earlier Hellenic League. The members were bound by treaties with the king who was the *hegemon*, and these treaties were confirmed by oaths renewed every year. These oaths pledged them to take no step hostile to the king.[2] The relation of the members to each other must be deduced from the course of events. Certainly the later relations of the Achaeans to the Aetolians indicate that one of the constituent states could carry on war by itself against a non-member. To have a claim to help from the other members of the League, it was necessary to secure a vote for war in the *synedrion* of the League, but this did not automatically involve all members in the hostilities. The members were free to confirm the vote and go to war, or refrain from confirming it and remain neutral. This can be seen clearly from the events connected with the outbreak of the Social War of 220–217. Here it may be enough to mention that the Achaeans, when they desired action by the League, sent ambassadors not only to Philip, but also to the Epirotes, Boeotians, Phocians, and Acarnanians.[3] At the subsequent meeting of the *synedrion* all these states and the Achaeans themselves brought complaints against the Aetolians, and, as a result, the delegates voted unanimously for war, but this decision was not binding on the states they represented. Instead the decree of the *synedrion* was submitted to all the member states for separate confirmation.[4]

---

[1] Brachylles governor: Pol. xx. 5. 12; Sparta set free by Antigonus: iv. 22. 4; membership in the League: iv. 23. 6, 24. 4–8, cf. Walbank on iv. 9. 6 and 24. 4. The withdrawal of the governor and garrison is deduced from the account of the anti-Macedonian movement in 220 in Pol. iv. 22–24, where there is no mention of them.

[2] Obligations to the king: Pol. iv. 16. 5, Livy xxxii. 5.4; annual renewal of oaths: Livy xxxii. 5. 4.

[3] Pol. iv. 15. 1. The list may not be complete. Yet it is possible that a special embassy to the Thessalians was omitted for the reason that the king was also head of the Thessalian Confederacy.

[4] The meeting: Pol. iv. 25; the submission of the decree to the member states: iv. 26. 2. The statement in iv. 16. 1 that the Epirotes and Philip 'were for receiving the Messenians into the Symmachy' (Walbank's translation) reports the reaction to the appeal of the Achaeans and does not presuppose an earlier meeting of the *synedrion*.

The decree passed called for offensive war against the Aetolians, and each state made its own decision before it took the offensive. There may not have been any clause in the treaties stipulating that the members had the choice between such action and neutrality, but this is the way it worked in practice.

Antigonus Doson must be regarded as the prime and almost sole architect of the entire structure, and he erected it as an adjunct to Macedonian power politics and not as a defence of Greek freedom except incidentally. The evidence is so strong that the conclusion is unavoidable. First there was the insistence on the return of Corinth to Macedonian control and the readiness to act as soon as this was guaranteed. Next came some symbolic acts. The statues of the liberators of Acrocorinthus, except that of Aratus, were overthrown. In other words, the enemies of Macedonia were not to be honoured. At Argos, the statutes of the tyrants were re-erected, that is, the honours of the loyal friends of Macedonia were to be restored. More substantial evidence were the garrisons at Corinth, Orchomenus, and Heraea. It was only a logical extension of this line when Philip V in 218 garrisoned Triphylia, that disputed district between Elis and Messenia.[1] Orchomenus and Heraea, therefore, at this time were not members of the Achaean Confederacy, but, as it were, Macedonian enclaves surrounded by its territory,[2] and later, apparently, Triphylia became a little Macedonian province on the coast of the Peloponnesus. Some concessions undoubtedly were made to the Achaeans, and in this connexion the chief statesman with whom Doson dealt was Aratus. But if concessions were made, Orchomenus and Heraea are proof enough that everything was not arranged as Aratus and the Achaeans would have liked. On the other hand, Doson must have considered it important to secure the co-operation of Achaean leaders and specifically Aratus. This must have been his reason for sending Philip as a teenager to Greece to become acquainted with Aratus. During his visit the young man is reported to have come strongly under the influence of the elder statesman.[3]

2. THE SOCIAL WAR

The real test of the Hellenic League came in the war of 220 to 217 which, through translation from Greek to Latin and from Latin to English, has acquired the rather unfortunate name of the Social War.

---

[1] Pol. iv. 80. 15–16. A garrison was stationed at least at Lepreum. The governor put in charge was an Acarnanian.

[2] Pol. iv. 6. 6 makes this particularly clear for Orchomenus.

[3] Plut. Arat. 46 states that Antigonus sent Philip to Aratus to be instructed. Though the attitude of Antigonus may be misrepresented, the stay of Philip in the household of Aratus certainly is historical.

This name will be used, since it has become traditional, and since there seems to be no better short name available. The preliminaries to the war will require almost as much space as the war itself. The general situation seems to have been that the Aetolians were trying to gain restitution for areas detached from their influence by the Achaeans. Naturally the latter resisted. Aratus of Sicyon, the dominant leader of the Achaean Confederacy at the time, apparently at first hoped to settle the issue as a purely local affair but later changed his policy and requested the intervention of the Hellenic League. After various vicissitudes the resulting war ended in 217 with a peace that might seem to prepare the way for Panhellenic co-operation as expressed in the speech of the Aetolian Agelaus. Nevertheless, when the Romans a few years later wanted allies in their war against Macedonia and the League, the Aetolians willingly assumed this role.

In the Social War the Peloponnesus was the scene of three rival imperialisms—maybe that is too pretentious a term—those of Macedonia, of the Aetolians, and of the Achaeans. The Macedonian imperialism needs no demonstration, while the Aetolians clearly had not given up their attempt to control the west and south coast of Greece all the way to Cape Malea, as shown in their earlier expedition into Laconia. Less well known and frequently overlooked is the Achaean attempt to cut this line and to secure the southwestern part of the Peloponnesus for themselves as part of their Confederacy or as allied states. Thus Pylos and probably also Cyparissia were induced to join the Confederacy.[1] This annexation cannot have occurred before Megalopolis joined the Confederacy in 235 and almost certainly preceded the outbreak of the Cleomenic War in 229. In other words, it occurred at a time when the Achaeans and Aetolians were allies. It may not have violated any existing treaties, but the Aetolians must have considered it an aggressive intervention in their sphere of influence. Our pro-Achaean sources, that is, chiefly Polybius and his sources, are so silent on the subject that this can almost be called suppression of evidence.

At the conclusion of the Cleomenic War, one old domineering power, Sparta, could be counted out for the time being. Macedonia had recovered its hold on the Peloponnesus, and probably seemed

---

[1] See particularly Niese, *Geschichte*, ii. 411, n. 1. The case is perfectly clear for Pylos. At the meeting of the assembly of the Hellenic league in 220 the Achaeans complained of encroachment on Pylos as though a part of the Confederacy (Pol. iv. 25. 4). Later demands that the Achaeans release the place are recorded in Livy xxvii. 30. 13; Pol. xviii. 42. 7. For Cyparissia there is little except the reference to a Cyparissian aid of Philopoemen at Mantinea in 207 (Pol. xi. 18. 2), though also the independent action of the Cyparissians in the campaign of 218 fits better a city belonging to the Achaean Confederacy than a community forming a part of the Messenian state (Pol. v. 92. 5). Probably the strongest argument is that the membership of Pylos is almost unthinkable unless also some intervening territory was Achaean.

fully as well entrenched as it ever had been in the days of Antigonus Gonatas. For the tyrants of Gonatas, Doson had substituted garrisons and direct control of key positions and had most of the rest of the peninsula tied to himself through the Hellenic League. Except for the Ptolemaic garrison at Methana, only Elis and Messene were not included in this arrangement. The Achaeans had recovered their strength and felt relatively secure in their alliance with Macedonia and their membership in the Hellenic League. This was probably the reason why, when hostilities began in 220, the Achaean military machine was found neglected and in disorder.[1] The Aetolians, on the contrary, felt hemmed in and frustrated and set out to improve the situation. In so doing some of their leaders indulged in an unusual amount of aggression before war was declared and while the Aetolians and Achaeans nominally not only were at peace with each other but still actually were allied. In so doing, however, they may have felt that their action was no more contrary to international law than the earlier aggression of their opponents.

Our sources, it is well to remember, are very one-sided and anti-Aetolian. Yet even so it is possible to draw two conclusions. In the first place, not all Aetolians favoured the policy of aggression. This, of course, cuts both ways. While it shows that there was a more moderate party among the Aetolians, it can also be argued that the policy was so extreme that even fellow-citizens disapproved. In the second place, a glance at the further career of the leaders suggests that they were not completely irresponsible criminals. Dorimachus and Scopas at a later date tried to introduce reforms in the interest of the lower classes. This was enough to blacken their reputation with the more conservative and make it difficult for them to secure an impartial hearing. Thus it is impossible to say whether they were sincere reformers or whether they played on the prejudices of the discontented for political purposes. Probably more significant is the fact that Agelaus of Naupactus took part in the ventures. Since he was the statesman who in 217 delivered the famous speech advocating Panhellenic co-operation, it is hard to believe that the policy he supported was one of irresponsible lawlessness. It must have been a policy which some of the saner Aetolian statesmen considered justified.[2]

The war appears to be a war of Aetolian making, or more specifically of the making of their more aggressive leaders. Their objective was to extend Aetolian influence in the Peloponnesus. Owing to the mistakes of Aratus, the Achaean general of 220–219, the war was

[1] Pol. iv. 7. 6–7.
[2] This in spite of the fact that the same Agelaus probably once was accused of violating the asylia which had been granted to Mytilene (IG ix². 1. 190).

almost won by the Aetolians before it was declared. In 219, under the younger Aratus, the Achaeans did little better. The Aetolians, with the co-operation not only of Elis but also of Sparta, prepared to attack Achaea from several directions while they tried to divert Philip by a raid on Macedonia. The Spartans attacked the territory of Megalopolis, while one Aetolian expedition attacked Aegira on the middle of the Achaean coast and another attacked the westernmost of the territory of the original Achaea. It was on this front that the Achaean defences were so badly handled that the three cities of Dyme, Pharae, and Tritaea withheld their taxes to the federal government and themselves engaged mercenaries. Meanwhile Philip was operating rather successfully in western Greece from Epirus south to the entrance of the Gulf of Corinth. From there he was called home by an invasion of the Dardanians, a people north of Macedonia that was an almost constant threat to the country. A winter campaign by Philip more than redressed the balance in the Peloponnesus and added territory both to the Macedonian holdings and to the Achaean Confederacy. In the summer of 218 came Philip's raid on the Aetolian capital or religious centre, Thermum, followed later by a raid on Laconia. Even so confusion and inefficiency almost ruined the situation for the Achaeans during the winter or in the early spring of 217. Things looked up when Aratus once more was elected general and reorganized the defences. Philip too made considerable advances but suddenly lost his enthusiasm for the war in Greece when at the Nemean Games he received the news of Hannibal's victory at Trasimene. The Aetolians too were ready for peace, which soon thereafter was negotiated at Naupactus.

Such was the war in outline. It is not an easy war to understand. The account of Polybius is full enough, but it is so centered around the Achaeans and especially Aratus that it is hard to do justice to the Aetolians and even to Philip. One feature of the account which arouses suspicion but cannot be refuted in detail is the tendency to make the central theme at times a conflict between Aratus and certain Macedonian advisers of the king. Almost all that can be done now is to say that much of this involves the inner thoughts and sentiments of the actors of a kind which no outsider can know. In one case Polybius himself practically admits that he is only guessing, namely, when he attributes Philip's lenient treatment of Sparta in 220 to Aratus.[1] On the other hand, it is obvious that there was a clash between Aratus and certain Macedonian leaders, but, whether Aratus loomed as large as Polybius indicates is another question. In contrast to the favourable treatment of Aratus, the account of the events of 220 is so strong in its condemnation of his inefficiency—not to say stupidity—that it is hard

[1] Pol. iv. 24. 1–3.

to believe that it was written by the author who so often has praised Aratus. An explanation which may well be correct is that Polybius here has drawn on a Megalopolitan source.[1] This, to be sure, suggests that he sometimes followed his sources more slavishly than he would like to have his readers believe. In this case, the fact that he was himself a Megalopolitan may be something of an extenuating circumstance.

The preliminary clashes between the Aetolians and Achaeans which ultimately led to the Social War grew out of the rival interests of the two confederacies in southwestern Peloponnesus. The chief centre of the Aetolian interests remained Phigalea, which they kept garrisoned, but they also had ties with Messéne. To their other grievances against the Achaeans there had been added the charge that they were trying to seduce the Messenians. In fact, the Aetolians claimed that the Messenians had promised the Achaeans and Macedonians that they would join their *symmachia*, that is, the Hellenic League. Thus the Achaeans seemed about to detach another important state from the Aetolian sphere of influence, and yet the alliance between the Achaeans and Aetolians had not been abrogated. Under the circumstances it was perfectly natural that Dorimachus, the Aetolian commander at Phigalea, was sent there not so much to protect the city as to keep a watchful eye on developments in the Peloponnesus.[2]

Dorimachus did more than keep his eye on the Peloponnesus. 'Pirates' assembled at Phigalea, and he turned them loose on Messenia. After turning a deaf ear to the complaints of the Messenians and, so the story goes, having been grossly insulted by them, he returned to Aetolia resolved to intervene against the Messenians but without declaring war. The general of the year (221–220), Ariston, was unable to take active part in any warfare and is said to have left the management of affairs to Dorimachus and his associate, Scopas. They proceeded, without submitting the proposals either to the Aetolian assembly or to the board of *apokletoi*, to send out pirates to operate along the coast from Epirus south, while they prepared to transport an Aetolian army across the narrows opposite Cape Rhium and thus disembark in the territory of Patrae and march south to Messenia through Achaean territory. Before this expedition got under way, Clarium, a fort in the territory of Megalopolis, was seized through a surprise attack—the first overt act of the year against the Achaeans—but was recovered by the Achaean general, Timoxenus, and Taurion, the Macedonian commander in the Peloponnesus. Thereafter the Aetolian

---

[1] See Walbank on Pol. iv. 7–13 citing also Ferrabino.

[2] Pol. iv. 3. 5 (cf. Walbank, *Philip V*, 24) shows clearly that Dorimachus was in Phigalea 'on public business'. Pol. iv. 15. 10 lists both Achaeans and Messenians as allies of the Aetolians; on the Messenians, cf. also iv. 6. 11. The accusation against the Messenians that they had promised to join the *symmachia*; Pol. iv. 5. 8.

army under Dorimachus and Scopas—how large is not known—arrived and crossed through the territories of Patrae, Pherae, and Tritaea to Phigalea, professing to molest no one but, says Polybius, not living up to their profession. Apparently no effort was made to interfere with the passage. All this happened in the spring of 220 while Timoxenus, the general elected the preceding spring, still was in office. After this, probably in May, came a regular meeting of the Achaean assembly at Aegium, still the old-fashioned mass meeting open to all citizens over thirty. At this meeting the cities whose territory had been crossed by the Aetolians entered their complaints, and the Messenians appealed for help. The assembly voted to help, instructed the general to mobilize the army, and delegated further decisions to the men at arms. Thereupon Timoxenus turned over the state seal to his successor, Aratus, and laid down his office five days before time. The army quite naturally was mobilized at Megalopolis. At the meeting held there, the Messenians added a request to be admitted into the Hellenic League. They were told that this could not be done without the approval of Philip and the allies, but that the Achaeans would aid. Also the Spartans mobilized and occupied a post near the border of the territory of Megalopolis. Thereupon Aratus sent an ultimatum to the Aetolians to leave Messenia and to withdraw without entering Achaean territory. If they did, they would be treated as enemies. Since the troops mobilized undoubtedly greatly outnumbered the Aetolian force, it is not surprising that Scopas and Dorimachus pretended to yield and actually sent messengers to request that transports be sent to meet them at Phea, the port in southern Elis. Had they actually withdrawn their troops by sea at this time, war might have been averted in spite of all the bad feeling so far stirred up.[1]

The Aetolian troops, instead of returning home on the transports, shipped their loot home and themselves proceeded to march right through the centre of Arcadia crossing the northern part of the territory of Megalopolis and continuing across the Arcadian plain between Caphyae and Orchomenus and finally returning home via the Isthmus of Corinth and Boeotia. On their way, as they were advancing into the hills beyond Caphyae, they were attacked by the Achaeans under Aratus and inflicted a serious defeat upon them. In following these events it becomes increasingly difficult to disentangle facts from the statements of Polybius concerning the motives of the Aetolians and

[1] For the events see Pol. iv. 4–9. Total mobilization seems implied in iv. 6. 8, but this must be a case in which Polybius uses πανδημεί without meaning literally a total mobilization. The movements of the expedition were such as to imply a smaller force. The Aetolians could not have pretended to be ready to transport the entire military force of the Confederacy by sea from Phea back to Aetolia.

even from misrepresentations.[1] It is possible, though not certain, that Scopas returned home with some of the troops on the transports and left Dorimachus with a reduced force to make his way by land.[2] The force that remained, in any case, was not so large that Aratus feared to face it with 3,000 Achaean infantry and 300 cavalry in addition to Taurion's garrison troops or army of occupation. A larger force had been mobilized, but the rest was dismissed when Aratus thought that the Aetolians were returning home. Concerning Dorimachus, Polybius states that he wished to provoke war but wished to avoid combat with Taurion, who was at Cleitor, but sought one with Aratus. This must be discounted as merely a conjecture—not to say in part at least a deliberate falsehood. A few sentences farther on, Polybius shows that also Aratus and the Achaeans were at Cleitor by reporting that they turned back from there to Caphyae.[3] Moreover, his narrative shows that the Aetolians sought to avoid battle but were attacked by the Achaeans. It is possible that the Aetolians, in spite of the ultimatum of Aratus, would have justified their crossing of Achaean territory on the basis of the right of passage. At any rate, at the later meeting of the assembly of the Hellenic League, the complaints of the Achaeans against the Aetolians contained no mention of the battle of Caphyae. Probably the rights and wrongs of the incident were not clear. The Aetolians, judging by their actions up to this point, were primarily interested in extension of their power in Messenia. From the Achaeans they demanded the right to have their troops pass through Achaean territory, and, if this could be secured without war, so much the better. After Caphyae, the leaders responsible for the intervention in Messenia apparently considered war inevitable.

It was only after the defeat at Caphyae that the Achaeans appealed to Philip and the allies. This must mean that Aratus and his associates at first had hoped to handle the case locally in co-operation with the Messenians and Spartans. This obviously would have enhanced the prestige of the Achaeans more than being rescued by the Macedonians. They might actually have succeeded in this except for the mismanagement of the Caphyae campaign and the resulting defeat. As for the Macedonians, to judge from the conduct of Taurion, they had no desire for war. When Clarium on Achaean territory was occupied, he had helped the Achaeans dislodge the marauders. That was a clear case. It was as much against Macedonian as Achaean

---

[1] Pol. iv. 9–13; cf. Walbank particularly on 10. 5.

[2] In Pol. iv. 9. 8, in the statement about the Aetolians pretending to yield to the ultimatum, both Scopas and Dorimachus are mentioned, but in 10. 3 Dorimachus alone is mentioned in connexion with the change of plan. This admittedly is little to go by, since the account of the fighting contains neither name.

[3] Pol. iv. 10. 6–7, 11. 2.

interests to allow aggression of that kind. He also seems to have been willing to help keep an eye on the Aetolians when they passed through Achaean territory, but he apparently did not wish to attack them. There is no hint that Taurion or his soldiers had anything to do with the battle of Caphyae.

Soon after the battle, the third regular meeting that year of the Achaean assembly took place. At this Aratus was violently criticized but nevertheless succeeded in regaining his hold on the Achaean voters and so dictated the policy adopted. It was voted to send ambassadors to the states belonging to the Hellenic League and to Philip to report that the Aetolians, in violation of their treaty, had twice invaded Achaean territory in arms, to ask for help, and to recommend the admission of the Messenians into the League. The general was further instructed to raise a force of 5,000 infantry and 500 cavalry, to go to the aid of the Messenians if they again were attacked by the Aetolians, and to negotiate with the Messenians and the Spartans about their contributions to the common cause. Each of the two states promised a contingent half the size of the Achaean, thus making a total of 10,000 infantry and 1,000 cavalry.[1] This force seems to have been planned as a defensive force for operations on the Peloponnesus. As such it might have proved adequate. However, at the time, by means of their appeal to Philip and the Hellenic League, the Achaeans were trying to stir up a general Hellenic war.

Some time in the summer of 220 the Aetolians held an extraordinary meeting of their assembly.[2] The meeting showed the peace party in the majority, but it is impossible to tell whether the calling of the meeting was due to the war party, which sought more general support for their policy, or to the peace party, which sought to stop the irregularities and aggression before it was too late. The assembly actually voted to maintain peace with the Spartans, the Messenians, and the rest, thus treating the raids on Messenia as though they never had happened. Concerning the Achaeans, they voted to maintain peace with them too if they would drop their alliance with the Messenians. Polybius criticizes this as most illogical, since the Aetolians were allies of both states. This criticism may be technically valid and still somewhat unfair. If, as it seems, the alliance between the Aetolians and Messenians was of old standing, and if the Achaeans were trying to wean the Messenians away from Aetolia, the act was definitely hostile. However, though professedly preferring peace, by raising this point the Aetolians were issuing a challenge which might easily provoke war. But, if

---

[1] Pol. iv. 14–15.

[2] Pol. iv. 15. 8–11; cf. the commentary of Walbank and see his *Philip V*, 27 for an account of the meeting.

the position of the Aetolians was ambiguous, that of Philip and the members of the Hellenic League was perfectly clear, though in this connexion only the Epirotes and Philip are mentioned by name. When they received the appeal of the Achaeans, they, and probably the other allies, felt that the transgressions of the Aetolians were not much worse than usual, and so they preferred to maintain peace. They favoured admitting the Messenians into the Hellenic League, but it seems that no meeting of the assembly was called and consequently no action taken.[1] Their admission seems to have come at the meeting held at Corinth later in the year.

Further developments soon embittered the situation. To these Aetolian aggressors and Illyrian adventurers contributed. Two Illyrian leaders, Demetrius of Pharos and Scerdilaïdas, in violation of the treaty of the Illyrian kingdom with Rome, sailed south along the coast of Greece with 90 *lemboi*, the light vessels used by Illyrian pirates and others, each with a crew of about 50 men. The only place along this coast mentioned as attacked by them is Pylos, and it is probable but not quite certain that they had reached an agreement with some of the Aetolian leaders to attack this town and detach it from the Achaean Confederacy. The Achaeans, at any rate, blamed the Aetolians for the raid.[2] After this the two leaders divided their force, and Demetrius with fifty *lemboi* continued on into the Aegean, while Scerdilaïdas with forty turned back and put in at Naupactus, obviously looking for further employment. There he entered into an agreement with Agelaus of Naupactus concerning the division of spoils and agreed to join the Aetolians in an attack on Achaea. This plan must have been adopted, or at least outlined in advance, for it certainly was not natural for Illyrian pirates on their way home from a raid to turn in to Naupactus. Though the Aetolian general, Ariston, maintained that the Aetolians were at peace with the Achaeans, nevertheless, Agelaus, Dorimachus, and Scopas were able to muster a considerable force for an attack on Cynaetha, an Arcadian city just south of the mountain ridge along the boundary between Achaea and Arcadia, and approached with difficulty from the coast by means of the valley of the Erasinus. The city, which had suffered considerably from civil strife and only recently had received back a group of exiles—probably members of the lower classes—was betrayed to the Aetolians by some of the returned exiles. From there the Aetolians went on to Cleitor, which they failed to take, not on account of help from the rest of the Con-

---

[1] Pol. iv. 16. 1–3; the key words usually interpreted to mean that the Messenians were admitted are rendered more correctly by Walbank on 16. 1 'were for receiving the Messenians into the Symmachy'. The Messenians were probably admitted at the meeting reported in iv. 25.   [2] Pol. iv. 25. 4.

federacy but exclusively on account of the resistance of the townsmen themselves. Had the Aetolians succeeded here, and had they retained the two cities, they would have controlled the shortest route inland from the centre of the Achaean coast and, especially if Sparta too had struck, would have been well on the way with the dissolution of the Achaean Confederacy. This seems to have been their aim, but they failed largely on account of the resistance of Cleitor. As it was, they offered Cynaetha to Elis and, when the offer was refused, destroyed the city and returned to Aetolia.[1] Their withdrawal is said to have been due to the news that the Macedonians were about to intervene,[2] and they did succeed in getting away before the arrival of Philip. This implies in turn that the second Achacan appeal, the one which led to action by Philip, was sent after the Aetolian attack on Cynaetha.

The first steps taken by Aratus was to appeal to Philip to come to the aid of the Achaeans, to mobilize the troops of the Confederacy, and to ask also the Spartans and the Messenians to mobilize in accordance with their agreement. This last move was not too successful, for the Spartans failed to raise their full quota, but this does not seem to be the chief reason for the inactivity of Aratus. Whatever the reason, he showed no desire to attack the Aetolians either when they besieged Cleitor or when they passed through the mountains on their way to the coast. At that time, according to Polybius, they passed over terrain so difficult that all that was needed to defeat them was a trumpet blast. He attributes the hesitation to excessive caution induced by the defeat earlier in the year. This may have been a factor, but probably more important, as some scholars have conjectured, was the desire to have the Aetolian aggression accepted by the entire Hellenic League as an act of war calling for its intervention. The one person to take action was not Aratus but Taurion. He cannot have had enough troops to undertake an independent campaign, but he made use of the fact that Demetrius of Pharos with his *lemboi* had put in at Cenchreae, the port of Corinth on the Saronic Gulf. After a profitable raid in the Aegean, Demetrius had been driven off by the Rhodians. Taurion now arranged with him to have his ships taken across the Isthmus. After that the Illyrians were to attack the Aetolians while crossing the strait at Rhium. The Illyrians, however, arrived two days late and so, after some raids on the Aetolian coast, returned to Corinth.[3]

---

[1] Pol. iv. 16–19. Again readers are likely to see in the text a reference to total mobilization, which it obviously was not. For the crews of *lemboi* see Pol. ii. 3. 1 and cf. Holleaux, 176, n. 1. The account of Polybius is very hostile to the Cynaethans. Apparently there was some element of social revolution in the programme of the party which betrayed the city to the Aetolians.

[2] Pol. iv. 19. 6.

[3] Pol. iv. 19; on the policy of Aratus cf. Walbank on 19. 11.

Philip this time acted promptly in response to the appeal of the Achaeans and came to Corinth with a sizable contingent of troops. From there he sent out summons for a meeting of the assembly of the Hellenic League and meanwhile himself proceeded to Tegea to deal with the Spartan problem. The Spartans theoretically had double ties with the allies. They were members of the Hellenic League and, in addition, had recently entered into the special agreement with the Achaeans and Messenians for defence against the Aetolians. In opposition to the party supporting this policy, there was also a party looking to the Aetolians for help against the Macedonians. The intrigues had been going on for some time and apparently had some connexion with the attacks on Cynaetha and Cleitor. The sudden approach of Philip is said to have precipitated matters. Three of the ephors had been intriguing with the Aetolians. For fear that he should reveal their plotting to Philip, they arranged to have one of their colleagues, as well as a number of other opponents, assassinated and then immediately sent representatives to Philip to lodge accusations against those murdered. Philip then arranged a hearing at Tegea. His ruling was that, since there had been no overt violation of the rules of the alliance, there should be no action taken against the Spartans. He did, however, arrange to have the oath of allegiance renewed.[1] This seemingly humane ruling was in accordance with the rule that internal affairs of a state should be left to the local authorities.

From Tegea Philip returned to Corinth, where he presided over the meeting of the assembly of the Hellenic League. After the various members had presented their charges against the Aetolians, it was voted unanimously to declare offensive war upon the Aetolians, adding clauses pledging the members to help the allies recover any land taken from them by the Aetolians after the death of Demetrius II, to set free communities which had been forced against their will to join the Confederacy, and to liberate the Amphictionic League from Aetolian control. Since the Achaeans were the prime movers in bringing on the war, it may be well to glance at their complaints. They were the seizure of Clarium, the excesses committed by the Aetolian troops passing through the territories of Patrae and Pharae, the ravaging of Cynaetha, the plundering of the temple of Artemis at Lusi near Cynaetha, the besieging of Cleitor, and the plans for attacks together with the Illyrians on Pylos by sea and Megalopolis by land.[2] Only violations of Achaean territory are mentioned, and, in the case of Patrae and Pherae, it is not the mere crossing of the territory which

---

[1] Pol. iv. 22–24; earlier reference to Spartan negotiations with the Aetolians: iv. 16. 5.
[2] Pol. iv. 25. 4. The one puzzle here is the plan for an attack on Megalopolis. Walbank on iv. 25. 3–4 is inclined to connect it with the raid on Cynaetha and Cleitor.

is mentioned but the alleged excesses of the Aetolian troops. Thus the guilt involved in the crossing of foreign territory is not too clear. This may be the reason why the march which led to the battle at Caphyae is not mentioned.

The states belonging to the Hellenic League were not bound by the votes of their delegates in the assembly. After the meeting ambassadors were sent to the states to secure their action on the decree proclaiming war. Meanwhile Philip, who obviously did not desire war, tried to negotiate with the Aetolians. The latter at first agreed to meet him at Rhium but afterwards countermanded their acceptance. Instead at the autumn election they chose Scopas as their general, thus indicating that they were preparing for war. The Achaeans, for their part, immediately ratified the declaration of war and authorized privateering against the Aetolians. This was done, it seems, at the regular autumn meeting of their assembly, the fourth and last of the year. Thus the two Greek protagonists both prepared for war, and Philip came from Corinth to Aegium, where he addressed the council of the Achaeans. From there he hurried back to Macedonia with his troops to prepare for war. The preparations included a visit to Illyria to negotiate with Scerdilaïdas, who felt that he had been cheated out of his promised share of the booty by the Aetolians. Consequently he was won over to Philip's side by a promise of a subsidy of twenty talents a year in return for which he was to operate against the Aetolians with thirty *lemboi*.[1]

The reactions of the members of the Hellenic League to the war decree varied. The Acarnanians immediately ratified the decree. The Epirotes in a sense ratified it but voted to go to war only when Philip did so, that is, they would not take the field unsupported. To Aetolian ambassadors they actually declared that they were maintaining peace. The Messenians told the ambassadors of the League that they could not go to war before the Aetolians were expelled from Phigalea. Finally, the Spartans dismissed the envoys without an answer, but before spring were aligned with the Aetolians. After the election of new ephors in the autumn of 220 the group which had been responsible earlier in the year for the murder of the pro-Macedonian leaders began negotiating with the Aetolians and arranged for the visit of an envoy, Machatas. This was all done irregularly and did not have the approval of the ephors. The latter, however, agreed to allow Machatas to appear before the popular assembly. After he had presented his case and withdrawn, the Spartans proceeded to debate the issue themselves. The

---

[1] Pol. iv. 26–27, 29. Holleaux, 131, n. 3 and Walbank on iv. 29. 7 think that Scerdilaïdas became a member of the 'Symmachy'. Though a literal translation justifies this conclusion, it is unlikely that it is correct. Is it possible that the Macedonian king could admit a new member—and one who was not Greek—without the approval of the other members? Moreover, members were not subsidized by Macedonia.

party favouring the alliance with Philip and the Macedonians carried the day, and Machatas was dismissed from Sparta. The victory in the assembly proved short-lived. The anti-Macedonian leaders arranged to have the ephors assassinated and to have other opponents put out of the way by death or exile. Thereupon new ephors were elected, an alliance with the Aetolians arranged, and the Spartan kingship restored, the new kings being Agesipolis and Lycurgus. The latter was quickly induced to attack Argive holdings along the coast. The Spartans further authorized privateering—this means raids by land as well as by sea—against the Achaeans. Machatas also persuaded—ordered would probably have been more correct—the Eleans to attack the Achaeans. Thus, says Polybius, in the spring of 219 the Aetolians were in an excellent position; the Achaeans, the opposite, and here he definitely writes as though it was a war of the Achaeans against Aetolians. Philip, on whom the Achaeans chiefly relied, was still making preparations, the Epirotes were holding back, and the Messenians were keeping quiet. The Aetolians, on the other hand, with the aid of Sparta and Elis, were ringing the Achaeans around with war on all sides.[1]

The events of 220 leading up to the declaration of war have been discussed in some detail in an effort to understand the positions and claims of the Aetolian and Achaean confederacies and the laws and usages of interstate relations to which their conduct should have conformed. The results have not been very satisfactory, amounting to very little more than a demonstration that the two confederacies made charges against each other. An effort will be made not to allow the accounts of the campaigns to get out of hand, but the campaigns are so complicated that the task will not be easy. One of the difficulties encountered are the repeated condemnations in our pro-Achaean source of Philip for not adopting the policy which the Achaeans considered most favourable to their own interests. However, since the war had been brought on by the selfish intrigues of the Aetolians and Achaeans, while Philip seems to have wished to avoid war, he can hardly be blamed because, when the war came, he placed Macedonian interests above those of the Achaeans.

The campaigns during the regular campaigning season of 219 took the forms of an effort of the Aetolians to break up the Achaean Confederacy while diverting Philip by means of a raid through Thessaly on Macedonia, of an insufficient defence on the part of the Achaeans, and of an effort on the part of Philip to strengthen his position on the west coast of Greece and extend his influence there southward. The con-

[1] Pol. iv. 30–31, 34–36. For the campaign of Lycurgus against the Argives see Walbank on iv. 36. 5.

tribution of the Spartans under Lycurgus was the occupation of the Athenaeum on the territory of Megalopolis. This had become the normal first step in Spartan expansion. The Aetolians themselves made a surprise night attack with a force of 1,200 men on the Achaean city of Aegira and entered the city but were driven out again by the townsmen with considerable losses. The Aetolian Euripidas, operating from Elis, met with more success when he raided the territories of Dyme, Pharae, and Tritaea. The Achaean *hypostrategos* in charge of the district proceeded to drive him off with the local levies of the three cities but was ambushed and defeated, whereupon Euripidas returned and captured a frontier fort belonging to Dyme. The three cities applied in vain to the Achaean general of the year, the younger Aratus, and, when that did no good, sent ambassadors to the central government but with no better results. At the time Aratus was unable to engage mercenary soldiers for the simple reason that the Achaeans had fallen behind in their payments. Mercenaries, however, clearly were available if money was available. On the present occasion the three cities decided to withhold their contributions to the federal government and to engage mercenaries of their own. The 300 infantry and fifty horsemen hired proved adequate. Clearly the Achaean failures this year were due to their own mismanagement. They, of course, sent the inevitable appeal to Philip to come to their aid. Whether he intended to do so that summer or not, cannot be determined, for he was called home by an invasion of Macedonia by the Dardanians.

Philip meanwhile had been campaigning in northwest Greece. He had started from Macedonia with about 16,000 men. In his first venture, the siege of Ambracus, he was joined by the Epirotes as well as by 300 Cretan mercenaries and 300 Achaean slingers. The latter, too, highly prized specialists, probably were mercenaries. With these troops after a siege of forty days, Philip captured the city, which was duly turned over to the Epirotes. By the terms of surrender about 500 Aetolians, who had been garrisoning the city, were allowed to leave unharmed, though the Aetolians during the siege had been raiding Pieria in southern Macedonia, where they had devastated the city of Dium and had overthrown the statues of the Macedonian kings. Philip, however, did not allow himself to be diverted but persisted in the siege. Next he had his troops ferried across to Acarnania, where he was joined by 2,000 Acarnanians. The purpose of the operations from now on seems to have been to recover for Acarnania districts which had been detached by the Aetolians. One city, Phoetiae, surrendered without resistance, and the Aetolians were again allowed to withdraw. Philip now moved on to Stratus, the former Acarnanian capital. This time he did not capture the city but merely laid waste the fields. At this point he received the appeal from the Achaeans, but it is doubtful whether that caused him to change his plans. He seems to have been determined from the outset to work his way south to the entrance of the Gulf of Corinth. His objective was or became Oeneadae, which he was preparing to fortify on a grand scale and equip as a stronghold and a naval station. Undoubtedly he also had planned to station a garrison there, but the work was left unfinished on account of the report that the Dardanians were planning a large scale invasion of Macedonia. Philip hurried home, apparently taking all his troops with him and leaving Oeniadae to the Acarnanians. Thus it did not become the important base for future operations which Philip seems to have planned. In Macedonia the mere return of Philip and his army was enough. The Dardanians gave up their invasion, and Philip was able to dismiss his troops in time for the harvest.[1]

The campaigns so far had not proved conclusive. Most successful was the campaign of Philip, but he had been called home too soon. The campaigns of the Aetolians had been more aggravating than anything else, but they were effective enough to demoralize the Achaeans, how completely is shown by the fact that a force of only a little over 2,000 could start from the borders of Elis to march right across Arcadia with the intention of raiding the territory of Sicyon and were only prevented from doing so by the unexpected arrival of Philip and his Macedonians. These conditions were completely changed by Philip's campaign in the winter of 219–218. But first came a raid of the Aetolians on Dodona. At the Aetolian elections in the autumn of 219 Dorimachus, the man who let loose raiders from Phigalea early in 220, was elected general and began his term of office with a raid on this Epirote centre. Somewhat later Philip moved with a force of some 5,000 and moved so fast and unexpectedly that no one in the Peloponnesus knew that he was coming till he was upon them. Since the Aetolians controlled Thermopylae, he came south by Euboea, Cynus in Opuntian Locris, the pass of Hyampolis into Phocis, and Boeotia. From Corinth he sent letters to the Achaean general, the younger Aratus and the officials in the cities instructing them to mobilize and assemble at Caphyae, the Arcadian city just a little north of Orchomenus. In a mountain pass near Stymphalus he encountered Euripidas. The latter rode off post haste leaving his leaderless troops, Eleans, 'pirates', and mercenaries, to take a terrific beating. Polybius gives the number of those captured

---

[1] Pol. iv. 37 and 57–66. For the number of Cretans, 300 as in the manuscript reading and not 500 as in recent editions, see Walbank on 61. 2. Concerning Oeniadae, Polybius does not explicitly say that it was turned over to the Acarnanians, but this can be taken for granted. The city was Acarnanian when it fell as one of the first victims of the alliance of the Aetolians with the Romans (Pol. ix. 39. 2; Livy xxvi. 24. 15).

as about 1,200 and of those that escaped as not over 100. The rest perished.[1]

At Caphyae the Macedonians were joined by enough Achaeans to swell the army to 10,000. This now proceeded westward to Psophis, a city in western Arcadia at the time held by the Eleans. Here Euripidas, the Aetolian officer whose forces had been defeated a few days earlier, had taken refuge and presumably was in command. The city had strong natural defences, having ravines with streams on three sides and being difficult to approach also on the fourth side. Nevertheless it was taken by storm by the Macedonians, though the inhabitants and the few Aetolians present were able to withdraw to the acropolis. A factor in the collapse of the defence was that the supply of missiles gave out. Since the citadel lacked supplies, the city officials, and with them Euripidas, arranged to surrender on terms of safety for all. When the invading army withdrew, the local citizens moved back into their homes, while Euripidas returned to Aetolia by way of the Isthmus. The city was duly turned over to the Achaeans. The value placed upon the city by them is indicated by the fact that they placed a considerable garrison in the citadel and a separate garrison in the city, the commanders being one from Sicyon and one from Pellene.[2] The garrisons undoubtedly consisted of mercenaries. Nevertheless, Psophis was in all likelihood admitted into the Confederacy as a regular member.

The capture of Psophis was soon followed by that of Lasion a short distance to the southwest. This former perioecic or subject city of Elis had been claimed also by the Arcadians. At this time it was garrisoned by the Eleans but, on the approach of the hostile army, the garrison withdrew, and the city was taken without any difficulty and was turned over to the Achaeans. A smaller place, Stratus, was given to Telphusa, a city belonging to the Confederacy. From Lasion, Philip continued on to Olympia apparently by the route almost straight west from Telphusa and not by the Alpheus Valley. There he gave his army a few days' rest before proceeding to plunder the country. According to the account of Polybius, Elis at the time was densely populated with a rich and highly developed agriculture, but it clearly was in no position to defend itself against the invading army. The defeat near Stymphalus and the fall of Psophis had broken the resistance of the Eleans, who did not have an army of any size since the land was controlled by a narrow oligarchy and the fields worked by dependent labour, at the time with which we are now dealing, apparently

---

[1] Pol. iv. 67–69. In this account 67. 7 contains the only statement known to the effect that the route taken by a Macedonian army coming south via Euboea involved landing at Cynus in Opuntian Locris. This route must have been used earlier by Antigonus Doson as well as by Philip himself; cf. above, p. 319.　　　　[2] Pol. iv. 70–72.

largely slaves. Hence, when the hostile army approached, the citizens took refuge in fortified places but sent masses of slaves and live stock and other movable property to a place called Thalamae, which apparently was not fortified but was so inaccessible that it was considered safe. The approach was through some narrows which could have been blockaded rather easily. Philip solved the problem by sending ahead mercenary soldiers to occupy the strategic positions and then marching through the narrows with his peltasts and light-armed troops without meeting any opposition. At Thalamae he found the Elean general Amphidamus with 200 mercenaries, but no other combatants are mentioned. On the approach of Philip, the entire establishment surrendered. As a result, Philip brought back, besides live stock and other booty, over 5,000 prisoners, probably mostly slaves, though there were also Amphidamus and his mercenaries and undoubtedly a few other free men. This booty, as well as that which had been taken earlier, so encumbered the army that it turned back to Olympia and proceeded from there to Heraea taking the route via Telphusa. At Heraea a sale of booty was conducted and preparations made for the invasion of Triphylia.[1]

Yet in the midst of all this activity, Philip was prepared to make peace with Elis. Amphidamus, the general captured at Thalamae, approached Philip and stated that he would be able to induce the Eleans to become Philip's friends and allies. Philip, in return for their alliance, offered to return prisoners without ransom, to guarantee the country against attack from the outside, and to leave it free and without garrisons and payment of tribute. This probably meant that the Eleans were to enter the Hellenic League on the same terms as the other members. Obviously the places already detached from Elis and given to the Achaeans would have remained in Achaean hands, but other-wise the state of Elis would have remained intact. This statesman-like plan probably originated with Amphidamus and was accepted by Philip. To be applied, it would have to be accepted by the Eleans and the Aetolians, and there was the obstacle, for the Aetolians could not well accept it without eliminating themselves from the Peloponnesus. Yet Amphidamus must have thought that there was some hope of

---

[1] Pol. iv. 73–75 and 77. 5. In the account of the events in Elis the greatest difficulty is the problem of the 5,000 *somata* captured (75. 7). The word occurs also in 73. 6 in the statement about the wealth of Elis and in 75. 2 in the statement concerning the depositing of property, slaves, and flocks at Thalamae, and in both these passages the word apparently refers to slaves. In any case, it is clear that Elis was controlled by a narrow oligarchy with large estates cultivated by dependents (cf. Beloch, *GrG*² iii. i. 281 f.), and in the late third century this labour may well have consisted largely of slaves. Polybius, however, uses the word about others than slaves, e.g. in v. 17. 2 and v. 94. 7, and so the *somata* captured probably refer to all prisoners, free and slave.

success. As it turned out, the Eleans tried to arrest him and send him to Aetolia to stand trial, and he only saved himself by fleeing to Philip at Dyme. Probably the majority of the Eleans favoured his plan but could do nothing since they virtually were subject to the Aetolians.[1]

Triphylia, the district along the west coast of the Peloponnesus, between the Alpheus and Neda rivers, was a part of the perioecic or subject territory of Elis. It had been secured in the fifth century, the last point to be conquered being Lepreum in the southern part of the district. By the peace of 399 Elis had been compelled to give up all her perioecic territory, which then naturally came under the influence of Sparta. When the Arcadian Confederacy had been organized in 371 it speedily tried to absorb not only Triphylia but also, other parts of the former Elean perioecic territory. This Elis tried to recover when the Confederacy collapsed, but does not seem to have succeeded in establishing firm control before well into the third century. This is probably to be connected with the Aetolian advance some time before 240 B.C. To Triphylia was added Aliphera, a town in western Arcadia which had been subject to or a part of the territory of Megalopolis.[2] Triphylia was a fertile, densely populated district and attractive for these qualities,[3] but it is likely that Philip and the Achaeans were more interested in the strategic value. By securing control of Triphylia, they would sever the line of communications from Aetolia through Elis to Phigalea, Messene, and Sparta.

Triphylia was bisected by a mountain range extending east and west from the borders of Arcadia to the sea. Between the western extremity and the sea lay the fort of Samicum, while near the eastern end of the range lay the very strongly fortified town of Typaneae. Some distance east of this lay Aliphera. These two forts were clearly intended to bar the advance of an enemy from Arcadia towards Lepreum, and this was the route by which Philip was bound to advance.[4] This time the Eleans and Aetolians were able to make some preparations. In response to an appeal for help, the Aetolians had sent

[1] Pol. iv. 84. 2–6, 86. 3–4. In 84. 8 it is clearly indicated that Philip sent Amphidamas back to Elis from Olympia, thus showing that the peace offer was made before the Triphylian campaign and even before the sale of booty at Heraea. It is typical of the way Polybius concentrates on Aratus that this incident is not told in its proper connexion and that, when it is brought in, this is done not for its own sake but only as one of the incidents in the quarrel between Aratus and Apelles.

[2] On the perioeci of Elis see Larsen, *RE* xix. 825 ff.; Gschnitzer, *Abhängige Orte*, 7–17. On the conflict between the Arcadians and Eleans, cf. pp. 189 f. under 'The Arcadian Confederacy'. For the recovery in the third century note that Pol. iv. 77. 9–10 places it shortly before the conquest by Philip; cf. Beloch, *GrG*² iv. i. 619 f.

[3] Ernst Meyer, *Neue peloponnesische Wanderungen* (1957), especially 70 f. This book hereafter will be cited by the name of the author alone.

[4] For the topography see Walbank on the pertinent passages and Meyer, especially the important account of Typaneae in ch. ii.

a new commander, Phillidas, with 600 Aetolians. In Elis he found at his disposal 1,000 Elean troops, 500 mercenaries, and a little light cavalry of the kind called Tarentines.[1] This force obviously was too small for a pitched battle. The hope lay in catching the hostile army in a trap or holding it up by means of fortifications or defences of some kind. Phillidas chose simply to strengthen the garrisons in the key cities. He sent the 1,000 Eleans to Lepreum, the mercenaries to Ali- phera, and himself with the Aetolians went to Typaneae to watch developments. Lepreum obviously was the key to the whole campaign, but by concentrating his troops there immediately after Philip's first success, Phillidas threw away whatever chance he had of holding up the invaders before they reached that city. Philip, in spite of its strength, had captured the city proper of Aliphera in one day. Thereupon the defenders, who had withdrawn to the citadel, surrendered on con- dition that their lives be spared. The next obstacle was Typaneae, but this was so located that an invading army probably could have bypassed it, though it would seem to be well located to serve as a base for a force planning a flank attack. Phillidas, however, withdrew with his Aeto- lians to Lepreum. Thereupon Typaneae went over to Philip. To Lep- reum came also the Aetolian 'pirates' who had been asked to leave Phigalea before that city went over to Philip. Their arrival swelled the number of Aetolians at Lepreum to 1,000. This concentration of troops accomplished nothing. The townsmen established themselves in one section of the city and demanded that the Aetolians, Eleans, and Spartans—there were 200 of them present—withdraw. It is unlikely that the townsmen could have held their own in actual combat against these troops, but the approach of Philip was enough to induce Phillidas to withdraw with the Aetolians, Eleans, and Spartans. He managed to get to Samicum before Philip, though the latter hurried thither with his peltasts and light-armed troops. However, since he lacked supplies, Phillidas gave up the place in return for free withdrawal of his troops under arms. Thus he did get away without suffering any great losses but having to his credit a remarkable ineffectual campaign. It may not be due to mere chance that his name is never mentioned again in the preserved parts of Polybius. After his withdrawal, the towns of northern Triphylia surrendered to Philip, and the entire conquest was completed in six days.[2]

Concerning the disposal of the conquered territory, Polybius merely tells that Philip placed a garrison at Lepreum and left Ladicus, an Acarnanian, behind as governor (*epimeletes*) of Triphylia, thus treating

[1] The Tarentines remain a mystery. G. T. Griffith, *The Mercenaries of the Hellenistic World*, 248 suggests that in the present case they may have been the citizen cavalry of Elis.
[2] Pol. iv. 77. 6–80.

it as a province of Macedonia. This is enough to warrant the conclusion that Philip and his advisers were following the same policy as Antigonus Doson, namely, that of strengthening the Achaean Confederacy at the same time as he tried to assure Macedonian supremacy. Consequently, while he allowed the Achaeans to absorb the earlier conquests, by garrisoning Lepreum he added one more to the string of garrisons established by Doson. By doing this and by taking control of Triphylia, he clearly hoped to cut the connexions between the Aetolians and the parts of the Peloponnesus beyond.

The last exploit of Philip's winter campaign was an attack on Elis from the north. After the detaching of Psophis and Lasion to the east of Elis and Triphylia and adjoining cities to the south, this must have seemed the natural next step. The other enemy in the Peloponnesus, Sparta, seemed harmless for the moment. From Lepreum Philip proceeded to Megalopolis and thence to Argos, where he may have spent some time before advancing on Elis through Achaean territory. On the way he was able to be present at Aegium at the time the assembly met and elected the general for the coming year. On this occasion the intrigues of the Macedonian Apelles are said to have led to the defeat of Timoxenus, the candidate of Aratus, and the election of Eperatus.[1] The campaign in Elis was of no great importance except for reasserting Achaean supremacy in this part of the peninsula. Teichos, a small but strong frontier fort which had been taken away from Dyme a few months earlier was evacuated by the Eleans and so recovered and returned to Dyme. It was while Philip was there that Amphidamus, the Aetolian general who was trying to negotiate peace, had to flee and seek refuge with Philip, and thus all hopes of a separate peace had to be abandoned. From Dyme Philip returned to Argos, where he settled down for the rest of the winter and sent his Macedonian troops home.[2] After two or three months rest, activities were resumed in the summer of 218.

Probably about June a force of 6,000 Macedonians and 1,200 mercenaries arrived on the scene. This time the Macedonians demanded that the Achaeans bear a part of the expenses. At the request of Philip an extraordinary meeting of the Achaean assembly was called at Aegium. Here Aratus succeeded in obstructing the proceedings,

[1] Pol. iv. 82; Plut. *Arat.* 48. 1. In Pol. iv. 82. 1 the statement that Philip spent the rest of the winter at Argos must be a mistaken anticipation of the similar statement in iv. 87. 13. The first statement implies that the stay preceded the elections. Instead the following chapters show that he returned to Argos after the election and the operations against Elis early enough to go into winter quarters and to send his army home. The time of the election is placed by Aymard, *ACA* 251 in late February or early March.

[2] Pol. iv. 83, 86. 3–4, 87. 13. Possibly *SIG*³ 529 records a grant of citizenship by Dyme to mercenaries who had taken part in the war; cf. Walbank on iv. 83. 5.

whereupon the meeting was transferred to Sicyon, the home of Aratus. There, with the aid of Aratus, Philip secured a grant of fifty talents as pay for his army for three months and 10,000 medimni of grain and a promise of seventeen talents a month if he campaigned in the Peloponnesus more than three months.[1] If the soldiers were paid three obols a day, seventeen talents would be almost enough for a month's pay for 7,000 soldiers—that is, pay without allowance for rations.[2]

Achaean affairs for the year of Eperatus (218–217) remain something of a mystery. Eperatus is said to have been completely incompetent, but most of the year Achaean affairs did not fare too badly, and it seems legitimate to wonder whether this worst defect was not that he was an opponent of Aratus and, except for the victory at the election, could not hold his own against him politically. The course of events is most plausibly reconstructed as follows. Soon after Eperatus took office, Philip, in order to secure supplies and pay for his troops, induced him to call an extraordinary meeting of the assembly. At the meeting, Aratus, whether present in person or not, succeeded in blocking action. Thereupon Philip secured the transfer of the meeting to Sicyon and made overtures to the Arati, father and son, placing the blame for what had happened at the elections on others. Then, with the help of Aratus, he secured the desired subsidies. Note, however, that all of this, including the transfer of the meeting, could hardly have been arranged without the co-operation of Eperatus, who also was in command during the summer of the sizeable forces mobilized. If anything he seems to have been better able than Aratus to forget personal grievances and work in the interest of the state. On the other hand, it is likely that the wilful obstruction on the part of Aratus this time did not go farther than to delay action until he had regained his standing with Philip. Confusion and disorganization are, however, reported for the last part of the year of Eperatus, and Polybius places the blame squarely on his incompetence and unpopularity. This may be correct but is far from certain. To Polybius, Eperatus was first and foremost an opponent of Aratus. Probably the real cause was the inevitable confusion resulting from the practice of holding elections and changing generals in the spring.[3]

---

[1] Pol. v. 1. 6– 2. 11. On the Achaean meetings of the year see *Rep. Govt.* 168 f. The question whether the fifty talents for three months was meant as pay for the winter campaign or for the coming campaign has been much debated. Aymard, *ACA* 252, n. 4 and Walbank, *Philip V*, 50, n. 3 doubtless are right in taking them to be intended for the coming campaign.

[2] Cf. Griffith, *Mercenaries*, 305 f.

[3] Pol. v. 1. 6–12. Eperatus is not specifically said to be in command of the troops stationed at Dyme, but, in the absence of information to the contrary, his command can be taken for granted. Later in the year Philip sent instructions concerning operations to him (v. 5. 11).

For the summer campaign Philip decided to take to the sea and so gathered Macedonian and Achaean ships at Lechaeum and trained his troops to row. Thus clearly his ships were to serve as transports to take his troops where he wished to go. He sailed first to Patrae, but his objective was Cephallenia, where he had instructed his allies, Messenians, Epirotes, Acarnanians, and the Illyrian prince Scerdilaïdas, to meet him. The Eleans not unnaturally feared an attack on their port, Cyllene, and their fear evidently was shared by the Aetolians. The general Dorimachus sent to their aid 500 Cretan mercenaries under Agelaus and Scopas, while the Eleans themselves engaged mercenaries and trained their own citizens. To counter this, Philip detached from his own troops a few Cretans and some Gallic horsemen, while the Achaeans themselves mobilized 2,000 of their citizen troops and also engaged mercenaries. These troops were stationed at Dyme, undoubtedly under the command of Eperatus. On approaching Cephallenia, Philip sailed first to Pronni near the southeast extremity of the island. Finding this city too difficult to besiege, he continued along the south of the island farther west to Palus. This city he failed to capture in spite of effecting a breach in the wall by undermining a section of it, propping it up, and afterwards burning the props. Whatever the reason, this was a serious setback. Polybius explains it as due to the treason of Macedonian officers who deliberately played the coward during the operations. This is most unlikely. Cephallenia was an important base of operations for the Aetolians, and would have been equally important in the hands of their enemies. Hence all in Philip's entourage, even if they disagreed on other questions, would be eager to reduce the island. Moreover, it is difficult to believe that Macedonian officers could play the coward in battle and face their soldiers afterwards.[1]

While Philip was operating on Cephallenia, Dorimachus started for Thessaly with half the available forces of the Aetolian Confederacy. At the same time Lycurgus of Sparta attacked Messenia. Thus there came requests for aid both from the north and from the south. The Messenians urged that Philip sail south and surprise the Spartans. The Acarnanians, on the other hand, urged an invasion of Aetolia in order to lay waste the land and draw Dorimachus away from Macedonia. This was the plan adopted by Philip, though it is doubtful whether, as Polybius implies, he adopted it primarily because Aratus recommended it. Nevertheless, it may be true that Aratus supported it,

For the last part of his year of office see v. 30 and 91. 4. For the verb ἐθελοκακεῖν applied to Aratus in v. 1. 7 see CP liii (1958), 250 f. The translation 'little disposed to help' (Paton) is a bit too gentle.

[1] Preparation of fleet: Pol. v. 2. 1–4. Distribution of forces and operations: v. 3–4.

strange as this may seem so soon after arrangements had been made to subsidize Philip's operations in the Peloponnesus. Possibly Aratus feared the growth there of the power of Macedonia.[1]

The plan to go north once adopted, Philip acted promptly. He sent instructions to Eperatus and the Achaeans to support the Messenians, while he himself sailed for Leucas. From there he continued through the canal separating the island from the mainland and into the Gulf of Ambracia. One morning, just before daybreak, he reached Limnaea in Acarnania at the inmost southeasterly inlet of the Gulf. There he was joined by the levy of the Acarnanians, no doubt rejoicing in the opportunity to raid Aetolia and get some revenge for past sufferings. There he stayed just long enough to feed his troops and arrange to leave behind, with adequate guards, most of the baggage and heavy equipment and thus disencumbered his troops in preparation for a rapid forced march. The afternoon of the same day he set out with guides to march to Thermum, the religious centre and, in a sense, the capital of the Aetolian Confederacy, but an isolated place, almost deserted this time of year. After a pause for the evening meal and a little rest, the march was continued, and the river Achelous was reached at daybreak somewhere above Stratus. Again Philip pressed on, advancing south of Lake Trichonis, leaving guards behind at a couple of strategic points, and reaching Thermum late in the evening.[2] He remained there only long enough to plunder and devastate the place thoroughly, destroying or carrying off movable property and masses of armour, demolishing buildings, and overturning statues, sparing only those of the gods. To the Macedonians this was only legitimate retaliation for what the Aetolians had done at Dium and Dodona, but Polybius condemned the excesses in very strong terms. In this he apparently went beyond the standards of warfare of the time. The almost friendly manner in which Philip and the Aetolians conducted peace negotiations the following year suggests that the Aetolians and Philip did not condemn each others' conduct as severely as Polybius did. Philip seems to have met with no opposition on his way to Thermum. As he withdrew, his rear was attacked, but the attackers were repelled with some losses, but this and the other fighting reported amounted to little more than skirmishes. With Dorimachus and his troops absent in Thessaly—they returned only to find Philip already gone—the Aetolians did not have a sufficient force to challenge the Macedonians and Acarnanians

---

[1] Pol. v. 5. 1–10. The promise in v. 1. 12 of an additional subsidy if the Macedonian army remained in the Peloponnesus more than three months shows that the operations to be subsidized were to be conducted there.

[2] Pol. v. 5. 11–8. 4. For further details and the route of march see Walbank, *Philip V*, 53 ff. and Commentary on v. 7. 7–8. 4 with map.

to battle. Hence Philip returned to his ships at Limnaea without difficulty and sailed from there to Leucas and from Leucas to Lechaeum.[1]

For the second time in one year Philip had succeeded, with apparent ease, in reaching a place so isolated and difficult to approach that it seemed impregnable even without special fortifications—set aside by nature to be an acropolis for all Aetolia, as Polybius remarks about Thermum.[2] This must have meant an excellent intelligence department, superb organization, and complete secrecy concerning the future movements of his troops. Much of this must have been due to the machine and staff assembled by Doson. In the present case, intelligence may have been relatively easy, for many Acarnanians must have known the lay of the land. In other cases, information may have come from political exiles. Concerning future movements, it is clear that the preparation of large expeditions, especially by sea, could not easily be kept secret. When Philip gathered ships at Lechaeum, the Aetolians and Eleans prepared the defences of Cyllene in Elis. However, when an army was in the field, only the commander and those close to him needed to know in what direction it would move next. Yet a glance at the map will suggest that a hostile army landing at Limnaea was almost certain to strike at the Achelous valley and the plains near Lake Trichonis, even if it did not strike at Thermum, and there were positions along the route where a smaller force would seem able to block the advance of a larger army. The failure of the Aetolians to do so, seems due not exclusively to the rapidity of the advance of Philip but also to the conviction that no enemy would dare to try to approach Thermum. Their general, Dorimachus, clearly had misjudged the situation badly. When he started for Thessaly, he left half of the Aetolian levy at home, but much of it must have been in places remote from Limnaea and even the Achelous valley. Moreover, he had sent his closest associates, Agelaus and Scopas to Elis, evidently thinking that this would be the most critical theatre of operations. Hence the Aetolian home forces may have lacked imaginative leadership. There were Aetolian troops at Metapa near 'the narrows' at the eastern end of Lake Trichonis, but they withdrew without fighting.[3]

Philip and his army were in the suburbs of Sparta a week after they left Leucas. They sailed from Leucas to Lechaeum, left the ships there, and sent word to their allies, the Achaeans and Messenians, to meet

[1] Pol. v. 8–13 and 17, much of this being devoted to unfavourable comment on Philip's conduct. Scholars often echo this, and Tarn (CAH vii. 767) goes so far as to say that 'at one stroke he now made reconciliation [with the Aetolians] impossible'. Walbank, Philip V, 55 notes that this is disproved by the speech of Agelaus the following year.

[2] Pol. v. 8. 6.

[3] Arrangements of Dorimachus in Aetolia: Pol. v. 6. 4; dispatch of Agelaus and Scopas to Elis: v. 3. 1; the affair of Metapa: v. 7. 8–9.

them at Tegea at evening of a day two or three days ahead. After at most one day in Corinth, Philip started for Tegea and arrived there the evening of the second day. There he picked up the Achaean levies as planned. Since the messengers sent to summon the allies did not have more than one day's start on the rapidly moving army, this is a remarkable proof that the federal system of communications and mobilization was in order and functioning well. The Messenians, on the other hand, were not able to arrive on schedule, and that is not surprising, since it was almost as far from Messene to Tegea as from Corinth to Tegea. Philip did not await their arrival, but marched the next day reaching Amyclae near Sparta on the second evening, thus having covered the distance from Corinth to the Menelaum near Amyclae in four days.[1] Failure to make the necessary arrangements for the arrival and future movements of the Messenians seems to have been the one major mistake in planning the campaign. As it was, Philip merely pressed on with his Macedonians and Achaeans—a force adequate for what he was to undertake. Judging by the route later taken by the Messenians, he did not take the direct route from Tegea to Sparta but went south in Argive, that is, Achaean, territory and then approached Sparta from the east by a pass across the Parnon mountains and encamped at the Menelaum on the left bank of the Eurotas slightly below Sparta. From there he set out to devastate the countryside, first going south as far as Cape Taenarum and then rounding the Laconian Gulf and going south again as far as to Cape Malea. Meanwhile 2,000 Messenian infantry and 200 cavalry, making all the speed they could, arrived at Tegea and decided to try the impossible, to catch up with the rapidly moving Philip, who had a considerable head start. The route they took, indicated above, was particularly unfortunate, for, when they reached Glympeis, a fortified town east of Sparta and near the boundary of the Spartan territory, Philip had already moved beyond Sparta, and the city and the Spartan army were between him and the Messenians. The latter encamped alongside the town without taking any precautions. This enabled Lycurgus to come out from Sparta and stage a surprise attack. The casualties were few, as most of the Messenians escaped within the walls, but they lost their horses and baggage. Thereupon they naturally returned home. The initial trouble apparently was that the date for the appearance of the Messenians at Tegea was impossibly early. After that their chief mistakes were over-eagerness and carelessness, though it must have

---

[1] Pol. v. 17. 8–18. 10. The journey from Leucas to Lechaeum had taken two days (18. 9) and the march from Corinth to Amyclae four days (18. 2–3). Since 18. 10 implies seven days from Leucas to Amyclae, Philip had probably stopped a day in Corinth in spite of the statement in 18. 1 that he did not delay there; cf. Holleaux, 157, n. 8 and Walbank on v. 17. 8.

been natural to take for granted that the Macedonians and Achaeans were between them and any Spartan army.[1]

When Philip returned from his raid on the southern peninsulas, Lycurgus was back in Sparta and prepared to obstruct his march northward, though he was not able to challenge him to a pitched battle. The plan was to force him to march along a narrow road exposed to flank attacks. Philip came north along the west bank of the Eurotas. Below the city the hills on the east bank rose almost directly from the river. Here, at the Menelaum, Lycurgus himself took up his position with about 2,000 troops with the intention of swooping down upon the right flank of the army on the march. To the troops left behind in the city, he gave orders to come out on a given signal and draw up their lines facing the river and the river road. To counter these preparations, Philip crossed the river with his light-armed mercenary troops, peltasts, and Illyrians and dislodged Lycurgus. Leaving the Illyrians behind to hold the hills, he recrossed the river with the other troops, undoubtedly somewhere above the city so that he could attack the Spartans in the flank or rear if they tried to attack the phalangites as they marched by. An attack by the Spartans, not on the phalangites but on Philip's detachment which as it were, stood guard, was repelled. Then, when the heavy-armed troops had passed and proceeded to cross the Eurotas above the city—their first crossing that day—Philip and the troops with him fell in as a rearguard, thus themselves crossing the river for the third time.[2] After this, Philip encamped the first night near Sparta, the next on the site of the battle of Sellasia, and the following day reached Tegea. From there, after conducting a sale of spoils, he proceeded to Corinth. The year's campaigning was over except for some obscure machinations in Phocis.

In Phocis, it seems that an effort was made to secure through treason or trickery some city or cities still held by the Aetolians. If so, the effort failed, but certainly the hold of the Macedonians and their allies on eastern Phocis was not loosened. It has been noted that the route taken by Macedonian troops going and coming passed through Phocis. When Philip came there in the autumn of 218, the country was apparently already garrisoned by Macedonian troops. In all likelihood, they had been planted there when Philip came south in 219 or, at the very latest,

---

[1] Pol. v. 19–20; cf. Walbank for the location of the places mentioned. Polybius (20. 1–2) is emphatic that the Messenians hurried and came to Tegea as fast as possible, but he blames them for going beyond Tegea with inadequate numbers and without expert guides (20. 7), not to speak of their foolish carelessness at Glympeis.

[2] Pol. v. 20–23. In 21. 4–9 he holds forth about the need of accurate geographic information. His own topographical information is clear enough except that he fails to tell where Philip crossed the Eurotas after dislodging Lycurgus. The conclusion that it must have been above the city is based merely on the account concerning his later actions.

early in 218. It will be recalled that the Aetolians that year found Thessaly so well guarded that they did not dare to descend into the Thessalian plain. The placing of garrisons in Phocis would be a part of the same policy, namely, to station troops at vulnerable spots where attacks could be anticipated. The commander in Phocis undoubtedly was the same Alexander who was in charge the following year, while the troops in Thessaly were under the command of Chrysogonus and Petraeus. These were all officers trusted by Philip and loyal to him.[1] This meant that, from the Peloponnesus under Taurion through Phocis and Thessaly, there was a solid block of districts held by troops and officers loyal to the king. Thus, even if Chalcis was in disloyal hands, Philip in the Peloponnesus was not cut off from communications with Macedonia. Undoubtedly this contributed to the failure of the plots headed by Apelles.

This is not the place to go into these plots in detail. It must be enough to note that they came to a head this summer. Already before Philip left Corinth for Cephallenia, Apelles had gone to Chalcis to cut off supplies. Whatever damage he succeeded in doing, he did not prevent Philip from completing his campaigns successfully, and, before the summer was over, all the plotters had been put out of the way. Nevertheless, according to Polybius, the plotters indirectly did contribute to the failure of overtures for peace. Ambassadors from Rhodes and Chios had tried to negotiate peace. They were well received by Philip, and the Aetolians at first agreed but later, on hearing reports of restlessness in the Macedonian army, became less eager, and so Philip, though he sent his Macedonians home for the winter, clearly anticipated further campaigning.[2]

To take stock of the summer campaigns of 218, they were not the sort of campaigns which resulted in decisive victories. There was no major battle with heavy casualties. Probably most crucial was the attack on Cephallenia. If successful, it might have changed completely the balance of power in western Greece. In Aetolia and Laconia, Philip did great damage, but he did not annihilate or even inflict a severe defeat on any hostile army. When he withdrew, the Aetolians and Spartans were about as ready to fight as they ever had been. The raids staged in the meantime from Sparta and Elis seem to have been even less effective. More damaging perhaps were the raids made by the Aetolians and Eleans in the winter of 218–217 on the territories of Dyme and Patrae and later other cities in the western part of old

---

[1] Philip in Phocis: Pol. v. 24. 12, 26. 1 and 16; Alexander in Phocis in 217; v. 96. 4–8: Chrysogonus and Petraeus in Thessaly: v. 17. 6; cf. *The Phoenix*, xix (1965), 124 ff.

[2] Pol. v. 2. 8–10, 15–16, 24–29. The efforts of the Rhodians and Chians to restore peace are reported in v. 24. 11, 28. 1–2; change of heart of the Aetolians: 29. 1–3. For the fate of the conspirators, cf. Walbank on v. 15. 9 ff.

Achaea. The invaders established themselves for some time on the Panachaean Mountain south of Patrae. The situation, according to Polybius, became so bad that cities tended to hold back their quotas of money for the federal treasury, and that the force of mercenaries maintained by the federal government fell apart.[1] Yet there was no great loss of manpower. With efficient organization and leadership, the Achaeans could quickly recover their former strength and prestige.

The Achaean arrangements for 217 and their success seem enough to show that the difficulties of the preceding years were due to lack of organization, and that the most crucial problem commonly was the raising of money to engage mercenaries. The elder Aratus was again elected general and immediately prepared to organize the defences against raids by the enemy and to provide for some plundering of enemy territory by the Achaeans themselves. At a special meeting of the Achaean assembly it was voted to engage 8,000 mercenary foot soldiers and 500 horsemen, and to mobilize 3,000 Achaean footsoldiers and 300 horsemen. These were to constitute a sort of standing army, at least for the duration of the war. In addition, there were local levies that could be mobilized when needed. Provision was made also for two small squadrons, each containing three ships, to operate, one off the coast of Argolis and one off the Achaean coast by Patrae and Dyme.[2]

These preparations proved adequate even without help from the Macedonians except those stationed in the Peloponnesus. The first operations reported were synchronized attacks on Messenia by the Aetolian Pyrrhias from the north and Lycurgus from Sparta by a Taygetus pass. The plan failed chiefly because Pyrrhias was turned back by the local levies of Cyparissia. Otherwise the Achaeans took no part in the fighting. Aratus had brought the mercenaries and a few citizen soldiers to Megalopolis. He now proceeded to arrange for the future defence of the various frontiers.[3] The test of these defences came when the *synteleia* of Patrae was raided from Elis. The Eleans, dissatisfied with Pyrrhias, had asked the Aetolians for another commander and had received Euripidas. His first attack was made with 2,000 infantry and sixty horsemen at a time when Aratus had gone to a meeting of the assembly of the Achaeans but had left the mercenaries in charge of Lycus, the *hypostrategos* of the district. The invaders penetrated quite deeply into Achaean territory before Lycus could act, but were defeated with a loss of 400 killed and 200 captured. A little later Euripidas tried again, this time invading the territory of Tritaea.

[1] Pol. v. 30. 1–7.   [2] Pol. v. 91.
[3] Pol. v. 92–93. 1. There are several problems involved. How did Pyrrhias' force, described as weak, manage to pass through Triphylia and get as far as Cyparissia? And what pass did Lycurgus take? The only clue is that he captured Calamae, which apparently lay at the Messenian end of the pass. For its location see Walbank on v. 92. 4.

23

Thereupon Lycus and the Achaean hipparch made use of the absence of the Aetolian troops from Elis to invade that unhappy country with the Achaean mercenaries and the local levies of Dyme, Patrae, and Pharae, the three more northerly cities of the district. In Elis, Lycus succeeded in drawing the Eleans into battle, ambushing, and defeating them again, but not with as great casualties as in the earlier battle. Concerning Euripidas and Tritaea nothing further is reported. Meanwhile the Achaean ships raided the Aetolian coast and brought home enough booty to make the soldiers hope that their pay would be safe and the Achaean citizens that their taxes would be reduced. One prisoner brought back was Cleonicus of Naupactus, who was a *proxenos* of the Achaeans, probably acting much like an Achaean consul in that port. Instead of being sold into slavery, he was set free and later employed in the peace negotiations between Philip and the Aetolians.[1]

One apparently minor incident deserves a little special attention, namely, the hoax perpetrated by the Macedonian commander of the garrison at Phanoteus who pretended to be ready to betray the city to the Aetolians. Instead he laid a trap and captured 100 Aetolian troops who were sent ahead to occupy the acropolis. Involved in the affair was also Alexander, who was in general charge of the troops of occupation in Phocis. On the other side, the Aetolian general, Agetas, was sufficiently interested to take charge himself, though he naturally did not join the advance guard that walked into the trap. Equally important is the fact that this all happened while Philip was still in Macedonia. This must mean that the Macedonian garrisons had remained in Phocis during the winter, and that the safeguarding of this line of communication was taken very seriously. Thessaly too undoubtedly was well taken care of, whether there were Macedonian troops there during the winter or not. The chief weakness in frontier defences was now the northern front towards the Dardanians. This Philip took care of early in 217 before he started south by capturing and occupying Bylazora and thus blocking the pass by which they were in the habit of invading Macedonia.[2]

The Macedonian defences were thus in better condition than they had been for long, but from the point of view of a Macedonia aiming to dominate Greece, there remained the aggravation that not only Thermopylae but also Phthiotic Achaea were in Aetolian hands. Apparently a main objective of Philip in 217 was to rectify this somewhat by capturing Phthiotic Thebes, the most important port in this part of Greece controlled by the Aetolians and aggravatingly close to

[1] Pol. v. 94–96. For the *synteleia* of Patrae see p. 221 above.
[2] Phanoteus incident; Pol. v. 96. 4–8; Bylazora: v. 97. 1–2; for its approximate location see *CAH* vii, map 10 opposite p. 768.

Pagasae and Demetrias, and also located conveniently for Aetolian raids into Thessaly. For use against it, siege engines were prepared during the winter. While the equipment was being gathered, Philip tried to seize Melitaea by a surprise attack. Success here would have brought him near to Thermopylae, but something went wrong, and Philip obviously had no intention of besieging or blockading the city. Instead he fell back a short distance north into the Enipeus valley and prepared for the siege of Thebes.[1] The siege itself was an elaborate affair involving circumvallation, catapults, stone-throwing engines, and the undermining and underpinning of a section of the wall, but not the final step of burning the underpinning to cause the collapse of the wall. As it turned out, the underpinning was not strong enough to uphold the heavy wall, which collapsed without the use of fire. At this stage the inhabitants surrendered but were, nevertheless, sold into slavery and replaced by Macedonian settlers. This harsh treatment may have been due in part to a desire to have this important site in safe hands.[2]

Concerning his plans for the rest of the year little is known except that they involved the use of a fleet consisting of twelve decked ships, eight ships without decks, and thirty of the type of small ships known as *hemioliai*. Of these the twelve decked ships were ordered to sail around the Peloponnesus in the direction of Dyme and Patrae; the rest were taken across the Isthmus and instructed to moor at Lechaeum. How formidable these ships were is not known, but they probably were a match for the Illyrian *lemboi*. They undoubtedly were to be added to the fleet used the preceding year. What could have been accomplished by this fleet will never be known. While Philip was attending the Nemean Games, a letter arrived from Macedonia reporting Hannibal's victory at Lake Trasimene. This caused him to become willing to make peace with the Aetolians and concentrate on the west.[3]

Negotiations were already under way, though it looks as if Philip did not really desire peace before the news about Hannibal's victory reached him. Rhodes and Chios had renewed their efforts· of the preceding year. Just after the capture of Phthiotic Thebes ambassadors came from the two islands, this time supported also by ambassadors from Byzantium and King Ptolemy. Again Philip gave the ambassadors

[1] Polybius indicates clearly that the attack on Melitaea was a side-issue, and that all there depended on a quick coup. He gives two accounts, v. 97. 5–6 and ix. 18. 5–9, which differ in detail; cf. Walbank on v. 97. 5. The one point on which the two accounts agree is that the scaling ladders proved much too short—a perfect text for a lecture by Polybius.

[2] Pol. v. 99–100. Polybius remarks that Philip's success here proved that his failure at Palus the preceding year was due to treason on the part of Leontius—a beautiful *non sequitur*.

[3] Pol. v. 101. It is interesting to note that the news about Trasimene came to Philip at Argos from Macedonia. Apparently the intelligence agents abroad sent their reports to the home offices.

a friendly reception and sent them on to the Aetolians, but this time, after receiving the news about Trasimene, he did not wait for their return but sent Cleonicus of Naupactus, the Achaean *proxenos* captured earlier that year by the Achaeans, as his agent to open negotiations with the Aetolians.[1]

At the time that Cleonicus was sent to approach the Aetolians, Philip moved his forces, both military and naval, to Aegium and proceeded to Lasion near the border of Arcadia and Elis, where a small fort at an unknown location was captured. Apparently this was a demonstration rather than a major operation. Then, when Cleonicus brought back the report that the Aetolians wished to confer with him, he immediately prepared to make peace and sent messengers to the allies urging them to send representatives to take part in the negotiations. Thereupon he moved his forces to Panormus, just across the strait from Naupactus, to await the representatives. Meanwhile he sailed to Zacyhthus and arranged affairs on the island, which doubtlessly meant that he annexed it.[2] Thus at the very last moment he acquired an island which could compensate to some extent for the failure to secure Cephallenia. In fact, with Cephallenia in Aetolian hands and Corcyra already a Roman protectorate, it was about the only important island available on the west coast of Greece.

When the representatives of the allies had come to Panormus, Aratus and Taurion, symbolizing the double leadership of the alliance, were sent across to Naupactus to negotiate with the Aetolians. Thereupon the Aetolians invited Philip to bring his forces over to their territory. He did so and established a camp with a palisade around it very near to Naupactus. The Aetolians, unarmed, took up their position just outside the camp, and the negotiations began. There seems to have been no untoward incidents and no difficulty in negotiating peace on the terms that all parties retain what they were holding at the time—a rather remarkable illustration of how belligerents who desired peace could conduct negotiations in an orderly manner.[3] What is more, the absence of any special bitter hatred tends to show that the depradations of the Aetolians at Dium and Dodona and of Philip at Thermum were not so bitterly condemned by the victims as by Polybius. In other words, the conduct of the war had not been excessively cruel by the standards of the time, and the parties to the

---

[1] Pol. v. 100. 9–11, 102. 4. It is the dispatch of Cleonicus, without waiting for the return of the ambassadors, which lends credence to the report that the news about Trasimene caused Philip to change his policy.

[2] So Freeman, *Fed. Govt.* 434; Walbank, *Philip V*, 66 and *Commentary* on Pol. v. 102. 10.

[3] Pol. v. 102–5. It is safe to conclude that there were no untoward incidents for the simple reason that Polybius would have loved to find something to criticize in the conduct of either Philip or the Aetolians or both.

negotiations acted as though they considered peace and future under-standing perfectly possible. The most remarkable evidence of this is found in the speech delivered by the Aetolian, Agelaus of Naupactus, urging peace and co-operation between Greeks and particularly urging Philip to take a sort of paternalistic interest in the good of all Greeks. If there must be war, it was better to reserve one's energies for the west. Neither the Carthaginians nor the Romans, if victorious in the war then in progress, would be content with Italy and Sicily. If he must fight, Philip would do well to keep his eye on their conflict. If he inter-vened at the right time, this might even give him a chance to contend for world supremacy. These are some of the chief points in this remark-able document which scholars generally regard as a summary of what Agelaus actually said.[1] This verdict is based on the general treatment of speeches by Polybius but may also be influenced by the feeling that he would not ascribe to an Aetolian anything so creditable unless it was genuine. As to contents, the plea for Hellenic peace and co-operation was something of a commonplace, and the appeal to the king to serve as a benevolent leader of the Greeks was at least as old as Isocrates. Nor was even the prophecy that the victor in the war in the west would prove a menace to Greece too surprising. After the Roman inter-vention in Illyria and the establishment of a protectorate there, re-emphasized, as it were, by the Second Illyrian War of 219, many Greeks must have been aware of what might come of this. With their interest in western Greece, the Aetolians may have been more con-scious of the situation than the Achaeans. This may explain in part that the speaker was an Aetolian.

The outcome of the war was essentially a stalemate, though it may have looked like a Macedonian victory,[2] for Macedonia had acquired Triphylia, Phthiotic Thebes, and Zacynthus—the latter two picked up in 217—and had maintained her communications north and south via Euboea, Cynus, and eastern Phocis. At the same time gains were registered also for members of the Hellenic League. The Achaeans had acquired Psophis and Lasion; the Epirotes, Ambracus; and the Acarnanians the inland city of Phoetiae and the important port of Oeniadae. Philip's campaign of 219 gives the impression that he had planned to open a way to the Peloponnesus through western Greece and to make Oeniadae a stronghold and naval base. After his return home and the winter campaign of 219–218 he relied upon the route through Thessaly and Phocis, but still tried to secure a stronghold in western Greece, first on Cephallenia and then on Zacynthus. Yet, in

---

[1] Most recent, Walbank in 'Polybius and Rome's Foreign Policy', *JRS* liii (1963), 1–13 at 9 and 11; Pédech, *La Méthode*, 264.

[2] Walbank, *Philip V*, 66 f.

spite of the gains of the Macedonians and their allies, Aetolia had not been greatly weakened. Above all, it still retained its contacts with Elis, while Sparta and Messene were, to put it mildly, pretty much in the doubtful column. The only hope for peace within Greece and for solidarity in the face of outsiders lay in the co-operation of the Aetolians with their former enemies, or, in other words, in the union of all Greek states in a friendly alliance—the old dream of the Hellenic Leagues from 480 to the time of the Roman intervention in Greece.

CHAPTER III
THE FEDERAL STATES BETWEEN
MACEDONIA AND ROME

THE Peace of Naupactus marks the end of an era. So far Macedonia and the Greek states had conducted their intrigues and wars almost as though there were no powers beyond the Adriatic. After this, whatever happened, Rome was always in the background, but Rome's ultimate success and supremacy was not as clear to contemporaries as it has been to modern historians looking back upon the events or even as it seemed to Polybius. At first, even as Macedonia prepared for intervention in the west, Macedonia and the Greek states continued their intriguing within Greece. This is illustrated by the visit of Philip and Aratus to Mount Ithome in 215 and the resulting controversy. This will be discussed below. Concerning the Romans, it is difficult to determine whether their intervention in Illyria and Greece was due to a conscious policy or whether they were merely the victims of circumstances which involved them in one complication after another.[1] My own conviction that the Romans were more sophisticated and had a more conscious foreign policy even before the Second Punic War than most historians believe, has grown stronger year by year. A statement on the subject can best be made in connexion with the Illyrian wars.

1. TO THE END OF THE FIRST MACEDONIAN WAR

Before taking up the First Macedonian War it is necessary to consider Rome's policy at the time of the First Illyrian War (229–228). This war resulted in a protectorate over cities that were considered free but tied to Rome through *amicitia* and served as listening posts for Roman intelligence agents and ports of debarkation and naval stations for Roman armed forces. This protectorate, it seems, was not due to accident but was based on a programme prepared in advance. This is proved by the fact that the various cities and tribes taken under the Roman protection were urged or invited to surrender and entrust themselves to the *fides* of the Roman people and then afterwards were declared free. Now when it is known that the Romans often entered into relations of friendship (*amicitia*) without

[1] Note the striking sentence of Eduard Meyer, *Kleine Schriften*, ii. 394: 'Freilich liesz die Weltpolitik Rom, nachdem es einmal in sie eingetreten war, nicht wieder los.'

treaties and that this status often resulted when a state had surrendered and was set free, and, when it is further known that Rome in the third century commonly was generous in the treatment of those who surrendered,[1] then a careful reading of the account of the war given by Polybius should make it clear that the Roman consul had this plan in mind when he invited first Corcyra and then other cities to surrender.[2] Furthermore, the treaty of peace contained the surprisingly advanced clause that the Illyrians were not to sail beyond Lissus, a town just outside the northern extremity of the Roman protectorate, with more than two ships, and those unarmed.[3] When this is taken in conjunction with the Ebro Treaty negotiated two years later, it becomes clear that Roman statesmen of the time understood something very much like the principle of spheres of influence. Moreover, they not only applied this principle, but the consul who negotiated the treaty sent ambassadors to the Aetolians and Achaeans explaining the causes of the intervention and giving an account of the conduct of the war and the terms of the peace treaty.[4] Thus, at least the chief magistrates of the two states which had suffered defeat at the hands of the Illyrian fleet, were informed of the Roman victory and the steps taken to check Illyrian piracy. Clearly, at least the consul who had sent the ambassadors wanted the two leading Greek states to be aware of the new situation in Illyria. The senate too, which later sent another embassy, this time to Corinth and Athens, must have shared this desire.[5]

[1] See particularly A. Piganiol, 'Venire in fidem', *Mélanges Fernand de Visscher*, iv (1950), 339–47.

[2] See especially αὐτοί τε σφᾶς ὁμοθυμαδὸν ἔδωκαν παρακληθέντες εἰς τὴν τῶν 'Ρωμαίων πίστιν (Pol. ii. 11. 5), in which παρακληθέντες must mean 'invited (by the Romans)' (Walbank, ad loc.). The statement is made specifically about the Corcyraeans, but the same procedure must have been followed in the treatment of the other cities. This is a piece of information which can be pretty well trusted, since it is incidental and there can have been no motive for distortion.

[3] For the treaty see Pol. ii. 12. 3 and Appian, *Illyr.* 7, quoted and discussed *Econ. Surv. Rome*, iv. 261 f. Some later discussions: E. Badian, *Studies*, ch. i; S. I. Oost, *Roman Policy in Epirus and Acarnania*, 12; Walbank on Pol. ii. 12. 3. Badian takes the prohibition against sailing south of Lissus as applying only to the government and not binding on subjects in their private capacity, so that the later raid of Demetrius of Pharos and Scerdelaïdas was not a violation of the treaty. It is possible to argue thus on the basis of the very brief accounts of the treaty itself, but this is contradicted by the very positive statements of Polybius (iii. 16. 3; iv. 16. 6) that the raid was a violation of the treaty. Moreover, it seems unthinkable that the Romans should give in to the defeated on the very point which had started all the trouble. Verily the defeated would have been the real victors. Except for this point Badian's chapter is very valuable.

[4] Pol. ii. 12. 4. The ambassadors probably appeared before a group of the chief magistrates of each of the two confederacies. It is very unlikely that in either confederacy a special meeting of the primary assembly was called.

[5] Pol. ii. 12. 8. An embassy sent by 'the Romans' in this period was undoubtedly sent by the senate; cf. Holleaux, 113 ff.

The conclusion that Rome, or rather certain Roman leaders, in 229 meant to establish a protectorate in Illyria and in the treaty of peace at the end of the war even established a boundary between the Roman sphere of influence and the Illyrian kingdom, is based as supporting evidence not only on the Ebro Treaty but on the entire Roman foreign policy of the period. As pertinent evidence indicating a positive expansionist policy and interest in places outside of Italy, there is the annexation of Sardinia, the embassy to Hamilcar Barca in Spain in 231,[1] and the *entente* with Saguntum. Also the number of years between the two first Punic wars in which both consuls took the field,[2] indicates a very active government. When to the Illyrian and Ebro treaties is added the fact that in 227 praetors were sent for the first time to Sicily and Sardinia, it looks as if Roman statesmen at this time were organizing the Roman holdings and fixing the boundaries of their spheres of interest. This does not solve the problem of Roman imperialism, but it does indicate an active government with a conscious policy.

Nevertheless, for some years the intervention of the Romans did not noticeably affect Greek politics, but this was all changed with the coming of the First Macedonian War, after which there was no return to the conditions under which it was possible for the Greeks 'to go to war against each other and be reconciled again whenever they wished and in general to control themselves the settlement of controversies with each other'.[3] Thereafter, to draw on the titles of two chapters by Maurice Holleaux in the *Cambridge Ancient History*, the war of Philip against the Romans was followed by that of the Romans against Philip. The First Macedonian War was brought on by Philip V through his alliance with Hannibal, and the chief objective of the Romans during the war seems to have been to keep Philip occupied in the Balkans and so out of Italy. In 208 there seems to have been a more aggressive effort to break the power of Macedonia in Greece, but that appears to have been, as it were, a temporary aberration and to have been due to Attalus of Pergamum and Sulpicius Galba, the Roman commander at the time. The Second Macedonian War was definitely begun by the Romans, but that does not settle the questions of war guilt and of Roman foreign policy. The wars have commonly been discussed with emphasis on whether Rome was or was not imperialistic.[4] This discussion will not be continued here.

---

[1] This is attested only in Dio Cassius xii. 48 but is commonly accepted as historical. So E. Meyer, *Kleine Schriften*, ii. 393; E. Groag, *Hannibal als Politiker* (1929), 29.

[2] See the summary of the evidence in *MRR*.

[3] Paraphrased from the last sentence of the speech of Agelaus in Pol. v. 104. 11.

[4] Some important accounts are: G. Colin, *Rome et la Grèce de 200 à 146 avant Jésus Christ* (1905), which also contains a brief summary of earlier events; Tenney Frank, *Roman*

Nor will any effort be made to settle the question whether the Macedonian kings had so many interests in Illyria that they considered the
Roman protectorate an encroachment on what was legitimately a
Macedonian sphere of influence. The present account will try to avoid
also too many details which can be found in any account of the war.
In general, it will seek to approach the events from the point of view
of the Greeks.

The plan for a loose protectorate based on *amicitia*, which the
Romans seem to have had ready made when they intervened in
Illyria, was later adopted for use in Greece, but this does not mean
that a protectorate over Greece was planned as early as the intervention in Illyria. If it was, the plan was rudely interrupted by Hannibal.
All that it is safe to say is that the Romans cared enough about the
protectorate in Illyria to intervene there again in 219. Later, when
further wars developed in the Balkans and beyond, geographic
determinism caused the cities of this protectorate to become
Roman ports of debarkation and bases of operations. Probably they
also were one of the objectives of Philip's first offensive against the
Romans.

Already in 217 Philip had campaigned against the Illyrian prince,
Scerdilaïdas, who had broken with him the preceding year. Then,
during the winter he built 100 *lemboi* and early in the spring of 216
set out with a force of at least 5,000 men, taking the course through
the Euripus and around the Peloponnesus and continuing on in the
direction of Apollonia in the Roman protectorate and the principality
of Scerdilaïdas. The latter, however, had forewarned the Romans,
who, in response to his appeal had detached and sent a squadron
consisting of ten quinqueremes. The mere report that Roman
quinqueremes on their way to Apollonia had been sighted was
enough to cause Philip to retreat and return to Macedonia. Since
he turned back so abruptly, it is impossible to know for certain
whether it was Philip's purpose merely to subdue Scerdilaïdas, or
whether, as it has frequently been maintained, he had hoped to
secure cities in the Roman protectorate. This may well have been
the case. Roman preoccupation elsewhere seemed to offer an
opportunity for such action, and, since the cities theoretically were

Imperialism (1914), chs. vii–xi inclusive; G. De Sanctis, *Storia dei Romani*, iii. ii (1917), ch. viii
and iv. i (1923), chs. i–iii inclusive; Larsen, 'Roman Greece', in T. Frank (ed.), *Economic
Survey of Ancient Rome*, iv (1938), 259–498 at 261–325. Certain aspects of Roman policy are
analysed acutely in E. Badian, *Foreign Clientelae (264–70 B.C.)* (1958). Also H. H. Scullard's
discussion of family rivalries and the like in *Roman Politics 220–150 B.C.* (1951) has a bearing
on foreign policy. All these works approach the subject chiefly from the Roman point of view.
An outstanding work which approaches the subject more from the Macedonian point of
view is F. W. Walbank's *Philip V of Macedon* (1940).

free, an attack upon them need not be considered an act of war against Rome.[1]

The following year saw the negotiation of the treaty of alliance between Philip and Hannibal. This need not be discussed here except to note that it was binding not only on the Macedonians but also on 'the other Greeks' who were their allies, and that a special clause insisted that the Romans must be ousted from the protectorate in Illyria.[2] Thus it is clear that Philip desired to eliminate all Roman influence in Illyria, and that he wished to negotiate and act as the head of the Hellenic League, which, in turn, was to represent a united Greece. Actually, he was far from doing so. In fact, though the Achaean Confederacy was his leading ally and the largest state in the League, not even the entire Peloponnesus was united. To strengthen his position there, Philip intervened that same year at Messene, obviously intending to place a Macedonian garrison on Mount Ithome, the acropolis of the city, and siding with the lower classes and the more nearly democratic elements in the local political strife. This angered Aratus and other Achaean leaders on two counts. In the first place, they undoubtedly thought that, if any garrison of outsiders should occupy Ithome, this should be an Achaean garrison. In the second place, they were opposed to social revolution in any form. Philip, on the other hand, tended to appeal to the lower classes, as he was doing about the same time in urging Larisa in Thessaly to broaden the basis of its citizenship. Of course, according to the accounts of Polybius and Plutarch, both wholly favourable to Aratus, nothing could be said for the attitude or action of Philip at the time. In fact, though Philip yielded to Aratus, this incident is regarded as marking the beginning of a complete change in the conduct of Philip symbolized by his alienation from Aratus and his dependence upon the advice of the despicable Demetrius of Pharos.

As background for what happened it is necessary to remember that Philip and Aratus were working in different ways for the greater unity of the Peloponnesus, and that they had failed in two respects. Elis was Aetolian for all practical purposes, and Sparta had broken with the Hellenic League during the Social War and had co-operated with Aetolia. In addition, Messene, though a member of the Hellenic League, was not too whole-heartedly devoted to either the Achaeans or the Macedonians. If Messene could be securely held, Aetolian

[1] The only account is Pol. v. 108–10. The estimate of 5,000 as the minimum size of the force is based on the 100 *lemboi* and 5,000 men of Pol. ii. 3. 1. Holleaux in *CAH* viii. 118 estimates the force carried as 6,000 or 7,000. He is positive that Philip was aiming at the Roman protectorate; Walbank on Pol. v. 109 is much less positive; Badian, *Studies*, 19 is inclined to think that the expedition was aimed exclusively at Scerdelaïdas.

[2] Pol. vii. 9. 5 and 13.

communications with Sparta would be severed, and Aetolian interests in the Peloponnesus limited to Elis. At the time civil strife in the city went so far that almost two hundred of the wealthiest citizens were put to death and many had to go into exile. When both Philip and Aratus rushed to the city to settle the strife, Philip won the race by a day with the inevitable result that he was accused by his enemies of having stirred up the strife with ulterior motives. This is probably nothing but gossip, but it does seem clear that the revolution led to a more liberal if not democratic government in the city and that Philip favoured the change. When Aratus arrived, Philip took him along with himself and Demetrius of Pharos to sacrifice on Mount Ithome. Apparently he had a sufficient escort so that he could have planted a garrison in the citadel then and there if he had wished to do so. Then came the exchange of remarks when Philip asked the others whether he should hold the fort or withdraw. Demetrius advised holding the fort; Aratus, withdrawing, and it seems, coupled with his advice an indirect threat of secession from the Hellenic League. Philip yielded and withdrew.[1] Thus he was prevented from adding Messene to the string of fortified cities which had been garrisoned by Doson, and to which he himself had added Lepreum, and thus cutting off Sparta from contact with Aetolia. Later efforts to secure Messene only made matters worse, and the city was soon to be lined up with the Aetolians and the Romans. Two years earlier, as a symbol of a unity of purpose, Philip had used Taurion, the Macedonian viceroy in the Peloponnesus, and Aratus as a team of agents in negotiating with the Aetolians. Now the break between Philip and Aratus was fully as great as if Philip had disregarded the advice of the other and had garrisoned Ithome. When Aratus died after a lingering illness, he believed that he was poisoned on orders from Philip and that Taurion acted as the king's agent.[2] Two men with much the same aim had failed because the one had placed too much emphasis on Macedonian supremacy; the other, on Achaean independence and leadership. Viewed thus, the fault of Aratus probably was the greater, for Achaean supremacy in the Peloponnesus without Macedonian support had proved impossible.

Late in the summer of 214 Philip assumed the offensive again with a fleet of 120 *lemboi* and so a force of at least 6,000 men, aiming at Oricus and Apollonia on the coast of Illyria. Again the cities appealed

---

[1] The only continuous account is Plut. *Arat.* 49–50. Only fragments have been preserved of the fuller account of Polybius (vii. 12–14) on which Plutarch has drawn. Concerning the 'democracy' of the Messenians in Pol. vii. 10. 1, cf. Roebuck, *A History of Messenia*, 81, n. 73. Concerning the advice of Aratus, Walbank, *Aratos*, 156 remarks: 'It was half a plea and half a threat, and Philip understood and yielded.'

[2] Pol. viii. 12. 2–5; Plut. *Arat.* 52.

to the Romans, and Valerius Laevinus crossed from Brundisium, recovered Oricus, which had been captured by Philip, and defeated the Macedonians before Apollonia. This may not have been a major engagement, but it was the first direct clash between Macedonian and Roman troops, and it was sufficiently decisive to cause Philip to burn his ships and return to Macedonia by land. Moreover, the Roman squadron entrusted with keeping a watchful eye on the Macedonians, transferred its base of operations from Brundisium to Oricus, where Laevinus and his fleet wintered.[1] Thereafter Philip confined himself to attacks on Illyria by land. Apparently in 213 he actually won access to the Adriatic by the capture of Lissus, just north of the Roman protectorate.[2] The Romans, though they kept watch on the coastal cities of their protectorate, apparently did nothing to check this advance. What they finally did was to look for a Greek ally to keep Philip occupied in Greece. The result was the famous treaty of alliance with the Aetolian Confederacy. The common view that the purpose of the Romans was to make absolutely certain that Philip would not be able to invade Italy is probably correct. Nevertheless the treaty increased the involvement of Rome beyond the Adriatic and so inevitably began or continued the process by which the Romans were drawn farther and farther into wars and conquests, and this in spite of the fact that the treaty practically pledged them not to acquire holdings in Greece.

The situation in Greece at the time, with the Hellenic League allied to Macedonia, was such that the Aetolian Confederacy was the only possible candidate for the position of the chief Greek ally of Rome. Elis was a satellite of Aetolia, and Sparta was too remote and, even if still dangerous, not to be compared to Aetolia. There the policy of reconciliation adopted at Naupactus had been abandoned, and by this time the majority of Aetolian leaders seem to have been looking for immediate gain—gains to themselves from booty and gains to the Confederacy from annexations. Since the treaty with Rome provided for alliances with other states, it is possible that the Aetolians, that is, some of their leaders, hoped to build an alliance which should be more powerful than the Hellenic League and might replace it, but, since the sources are uniformly hostile to the Aetolians, they give no statement of their policy.

Of the treaty between the Romans and the Aetolians there are two copies extant, neither complete, the version of Livy and parts of a Greek translation contained in an inscription from Thyrrheum in

---

[1] Livy xxiv. 40 is the only account of value but seems to exaggerate grossly the Roman accomplishments; cf. Holleaux, 188–93; Walbank, *Philip V*, 75–77.

[2] Pol. viii. 13–14. Apparently Livy passes over this brilliant performance.

Acarnania first published in 1954.[1] The two may not even be derived from the same text. Judging by its position in his narrative, the version of Livy should contain the text of the preliminary treaty, though not in its complete form, while that of the inscription may be based on the version finally ratified, which may have been modified in details.[2] This version is an Aetolian translation of the Latin original. Whether Polybius used this or made his own translation is not known. Since the account of the negotiations in Livy is derived from Polybius, it is likely that his version is a Latin retranslation of a Greek version.

The Romans, when the treaty between Philip and Hannibal became known to them, at first merely instructed the commander of a fleet stationed in southern Italy to watch the situation. From the beginning this commander was M. Valerius Laevinus, first as praetor and then as propraetor, stationed first at Tarentum and then at Brundisium. As already noted, he crossed from Brundisium to Oricus in 214 and remained there the following winter and probably thereafter retained headquarters in Illyria year after year.[3] Practically nothing is reported about his activities these years except that some time in 211 he negotiated with the Aetolians a preliminary treaty of alliance, which, according to the usual translation of *biennio post*, was ratified two years later. The date of the final ratification is of no importance, since the terms of the treaty were observed by the two parties as soon as the preliminary negotiations were completed. This was early enough for some military operations to follow that same year.[4]

---

[1] Livy xxvi. 24. 8–14. The *editio princeps* of the inscription, now *IG* ix². 1. 241 and Suppl., p. 77, was by G. Klaffenbach, *Sitzungsberichte Berlin*, 1954, no. 1. See also discussions by A. Momigliano, *Rivista storica italiana*, LXVII (1955), 93 f.; A. H. McDonald, *JRS* xlvi (1956), 153–7; Ida Calabi, *Riv. fil.* lxxxiv (1956), 389–97; E. Badian, *Latomus*, xvii (1958), 197–211. Cf. also *Bull. ép.* 1955, no. 132; 1958, no. 276. The text as first published: *SEG* xiii. 382; cf. also xvi. 370 and xvii. 280.

[2] So McDonald, 156.

[3] For 213 his province is given as *Graecia Macedoniaque cum legione et classe* (Livy xxiv. 44. 5) and for 212 as *Graecia* (xxv. 3. 6).

[4] The negotiations, placed by Livy late in 211, have often been dated 212; so recently by Klaffenbach (p. 4) and Bengtson, *GrG*² 413 and n. 1, who both treat the subject very briefly depending largely on Niese, *Geschichte*, ii. 476 and n. 4. Three fuller discussions are Walbank, *Philip V*,301–4; McDonald, 157; Badian, 198–203, all three coming out for some time in 211. According to Livy xxvi. 24. 7 the treaty was negotiated while Scopas was the general of the Aetolian Confederacy, and he is usually taken to have been general still the following spring (xxvi. 26. 1). Now the generalship of Scopas is commonly placed in 212–211, and the general for 211–210 given as Dorimachus. This is the chief argument for placing the treaty in the autumn of 212. The chief argument for 211 is that this date is so firmly fixed in the Roman chronology. There are two ways of disposing of the difficulties involved in the Aetolian chronology. It can be argued that the negotiations came in 211 towards the end of the term of Scopas, and that in the operations of the following spring he was not *the* general of the Confederacy but merely the commanding officer of the troops in the field (Walbank, 302 f.). Alternatively it has been argued that there is no real evidence for the generalship of

The two versions of the treaty, with the aid of a passage in Polybius, provide lists of the belligerents on the two sides. The part of the treaty preserved in the inscription begins with a clause to the effect that the leaders of the Aetolians are to conduct war 'against all these', indicating that just before this there must have been a list of states joined in war against the Aetolians and the Romans. It seems certain that this list is reproduced in a passage in Polybius listing as allies of Philip 'most of the Peloponnesians, Boeotians, Euboeans, Phocians, Locrians, Thessalians, Epirotes'.[1] Here 'most of the Peloponnesians' is, of course, a grandiloquent substitute for the Achaeans or the Achaean Confederacy. The parts of the Peloponnesus not included are indicated in the list, preserved in Livy, of states with which the Romans were willing to enter into alliance on the same terms as with the Aetolians. Those listed are 'Eleans, Lacedaemonians, and Attalus and Pleuratus and Scerdelaïdas'.[2] Thus, in the Peloponnesus, Elis and Sparta were counted among the enemies of Philip and potential allies of Rome. Noticeable by its absence from both lists is Messene. If listed anywhere it would have been among the potential allies of Rome, and some scholars have taken its omission to be a slip on the part of Livy.[3] At any rate, before the war was over, treaties of alliance with Rome were contracted by Sparta, Messene, and, most likely, Elis.[4] Thus, whoever was the architect, there was here a plan for the construction of a coalition of Greek states supported by Rome to counterbalance the Hellenic League. The various members of the group apparently were in it only for the profits to be derived from it. In 196, after the Second Macedonian War, the Eleans as Roman allies were still claiming Triphylia; the Messenians, Pylos and the Messenian Asine; and the Aetolians, the Arcadian city of Heraea.[5]

An important clause in the treaty was the one providing for the division of war gains. According to the text in Livy, the land and

Dorimachus in 211–210 except Pol. ix. 42. 1, which may mean not that he was the general but rather that he was the commander. Thus the '*strategia* of Dorimachus ... should disappear from our lists'. This, an old theory revived by Badian (202), makes it possible to place the *strategia* of Scopas in 211–210. Pol. ix. 42. 1 is difficult, but Walbank seems right in interpreting it as evidence for the *strategia* of Dorimachus. McDonald apparently is right in attributing the difficulties largely to the infelicities of Livy's combining of annalistic material with that taken from Polybius. In spite of criticism of details, Badian's view does not seem too far removed from this.

[1] Pol. xi. 5. 4. On this point cf. Klaffenbach, 10 f.; McDonald, 154.
[2] Livy xxvi. 24. 9 incorrectly makes Pleuratus a Thracian king. He was an Illyrian, son of Scerdilaïdas (xxxi. 28. 1).
[3] Holleaux, 211, n. 1; Walbank, *Philip V*, 84, n. 2; Badian, *Foreign Clientelae*, 57.
[4] See now especially Badian, *Foreign Clientelae*, 57 f.; cf. *CP* xxx (1935), 210–15. Even if Pol. xviii. 42. 7 is not considered convincing proof for treaties with Elis and Messene (Walbank, *Philip V*, 101, n. 3), Livy xxxiv. 32. 16 is conclusive for Sparta and Messene, and for Sparta also 31. 5.
[5] Pol. xviii. 42.

buildings of captured cities were to go to the Aetolians and all other gains—the movable objects and the prisoners—to the Romans. Such a proviso for the division of the profits from war, contrary to what was once believed, has been shown to be not specifically Greek or Roman but universal in antiquity.[1] The application of this rule, involving the carrying off of all valuables in town and country and the sale of the entire population into slavery, was not contrary to the rules of war, but the wholesale and systematic application of it was condemned in antiquity, and the condemnation has been echoed by modern historians.[2]

The clause concerning the division of gains just discussed has been shown by the Thyrrheum inscription to apply in the form stated only to places captured by the Romans unaided. In case of joint capture, the real property was to go to the Aetolians and the movable property to be divided. In addition, there was a clause to the effect that, when cities came over voluntarily, whether they approached the Romans or the Aetolians, the Romans were not to stand in the way of their admission into the Aetolian Confederacy. This clause may seem puzzling. There certainly is no reason to believe that the alliance with Rome should prevent the Aetolians from admitting new members into their Confederacy. If, on the other hand, the clause is interpreted as a self-denying clause on the part of the Romans and taken in conjunction with the clause in which the Romans denied the Aetolians the right to annex Corcyra or anything beyond it,[3] that is, to trespass on the Roman protectorate in Illyria, then the clause is seen to provide a sort of counterweight to the restrictions imposed on the Aetolians. The Romans promised in their turn that they would prevent no state outside the restricted area from joining the Aetolian Confederacy, even if it voluntarily came over to the Romans. This probably refers to *deditio in fidem*. After this the rest of the inscription becomes hopelessly fragmentary. A special clause, at least in the preliminary version given by Livy, provided that the Romans were to aid the Aetolians to secure Acarnania. Another clause provided that the Romans were to support their allies with a fleet of not less than twenty-five quinqueremes.

Laevinius, after negotiating the treaty, that same year conquered

---

[1] See the important and convincing article of A. Aymard, 'Le partage des profits de la guerre dans les traités d'alliance antiques', *Revue historique*, ccxvii (1957), 233–49. Aymard uses 'profits de la guerre' instead of 'butin' on the grounds that *butin* is not applied to human beings or to land and that it has a pejorative connotation.

[2] See, for instance, J. Carcopino, *Points de vue sur l'impérialisme Romain* (1934), 37 ff.; M. Rostovtzeff, *Social and Economic History of the Hellenistic World* (1941), 606 f.

[3] In spite of difficulties, this is certainly the meaning of the *Corcyra tenus* clause in Livy xxvi. 24. 11; for a recent discussion see Klaffenbach, 7, n. 1.

the island of Zacynthus, all but the citadel of the city, and the Acarn-anian port of Oeniadae and another unknown place. At least the Acarnanian cities were turned over to the Aetolians. With this accomplished he withdrew to Corcyra and went into winter quarters there. Apparently the Aetolians that same autumn had planned a concerted attack on Acarnania but gave it up, though they may have secured Thyrrheum. All that is known is that a copy of the Roman-Aetolian treaty was inscribed there and, when this was done, the city must have been in Aetolian hands. Meanwhile Philip had been busy on the Illyrian and northern fronts.[1] In the spring of the next year, Laevinius turned his attention to the Macedonian communications with the Peloponnesus. From Corcyra he proceeded to Naupactus and from there to Anticyra in Phocis, which the Romans and the Aetolians under their general, Scopas, besieged. After a few days the city surrendered to the Romans, who turned it over to the Aetolians but themselves kept the booty and sold the population into slavery. This was replaced by the Aetolians with new settlers, who drew lots for the houses.[2] Clearly in such joint operations the Roman com-mander looked upon himself as having the supreme command.

Early the same year the system of alliances was developed in the Peloponnesus. When the Aetolians sent an ambassador to Sparta to urge the Spartans to join them, the Acarnanians also sent an ambas-sador to plead the other side of the case. At the time the Aetolian could speak of the Eleans and Messenians as already allied with the Aetolians.[3] Of these the Eleans had probably been under the influence of the Aetolians all the time, but the alliance with the Messenians may have been new. The Spartans too joined the Aetolians, but whether they did so immediately is not known. Judging by the debate at Sparta, the negotiations were conducted by the Aetolians and the new allies are spoken of as allies of the Aetolians, but this does not exclude treaties with Rome.

So far so good from the Roman point of view. After the capture of Anticyra, Laevinius, who though absent had been elected consul, returned to Rome. He reported to the senate that the war was going well, that the legion in Greece could be recalled, and that the fleet would suffice to keep Philip out of Italy. His successor, Sulpicius

[1] Livy xxvi. 24. 15–25. 17. On the chronology see Walbank, *Philip V*, 84 and 302 ff. As for Thyrrheum, Klaffenbach, 22 thinks that the treaty was negotiated there and that the city had been acquired by the Aetolians at an earlier date.

[2] Livy xxvi. 26. 1–3 gives the city as Anticyra in Locris, but certainly the city involved was the much more important Anticyra in Phocis. Some details are derived from the speech delivered at Sparta by the Acarnanian Lyciscus only a short time after the event (Pol. ix. 39. 2–3).

[3] The speeches: Pol. ix. 28–39; Eleans and Messenians allies: ix. 30. 6. The report of the Spartan action at the time has not been preserved.

24

Galba, one of the consuls of the preceding year, was told to send home all his men except the *socii navales*. Just when this was done is uncertain, for there is mention of a legion in connexion with the renewal of his imperium for 209.[1] In any case there seems to have come a falling off in the efforts of the Romans, who thereafter probably operated in Greece exclusively with a fleet manned by *socii navales*, probably chiefly Greeks from southern Italy. The other operations of 210 involved Phthiotic Achaea and Aegina, involving the first appearance of a Roman fleet in the Aegean. In Phthiotic Achaea Philip apparently was advancing west along the coast of the Malian Gulf and had constructed elaborate siege works before Echinus. The Roman fleet under Sulpicius and Aetolian troops under Dorimachus tried to come to the relief of the city but failed. It was probably the same season that Philip acquired Phalara, the port of Lamia, thus establishing control of practically the entire coast of Phthiotic Achaea.[2] The same year the Romans captured Aegina and enslaved those inhabitants who were captured, though an arrangement was made to ransom prisoners, and turned the island over to the Aetolians. The latter, instead of keeping it, sold it to Attalus of Pergamum for thirty talents.[3] Since the Aetolians in this period definitely were interested in the Aegean, it is surprising that they gave up the island. They undoubtedly did so in order to curry favour with Attalus and give him a base of operations in Greece.[4] With the Macedonians ensconced at Corinth, a Ptolemaic garrison at Methana, and an Attalid one at Aegina, the three kingdoms had, as it were, armed legations in Greece only a few miles apart.

Apparently at the regular autumn meeting in 210 the Aetolians elected Attalus to be their supreme commander with the title of *strategos autokrator*, while Pyrrhias was elected as the regular general who took direct command of the Aetolian forces during the campaigning season of 209.[5] The campaigns of this year are complicated and confusing, marked by no great activity by the Romans or Attalus—

[1] Livy xxvi. 26. 4, 28. 1–2, 28. 9; xxvii. 7. 15.

[2] Operations at Echinus: Pol. ix. 41–42; Phalara in the hands of Philip the following season: Livy xxvii. 30. 3.

[3] Pol. ix. 42. 5–8; xxii. 8. 9–10; cf. especially Flacelière, *Les Aitoliens à Delphes*, 300 and n. 2.

[4] On the basis of the *aparche* from Aegina in *OGI* 281, Niese, *Geschichte*, ii. 484 and n. 5 and Esther V. Hansen, *The Attalids of Pergamum* (1947), 46 f. argue for the participation of Attalid troops in the capture of Aegina. This is very doubtful. R. B. McShane, *The Foreign Policy of the Attalids of Pergamum* (1964), 107 is noncommittal and mentions the problem only in n. 50.

[5] The title of Attalus is given as *strategos autokrator* by Holleaux, 209, n. 1 and *CAH* viii. 128 and by Flacelière, *Les Aitoliens à Delphes*, 300 without any direct evidence but almost certainly correctly, for this is the most likely Greek title for a commander of unusual dignity.

just enough to block peace negotiations between Philip and the Aetolians—but feverish activity on the part of Philip. Early in the season he was campaigning near Lamia, where he twice defeated the Aetolians under Pyrrhias, though they were strengthened by 1,000 men from the Roman fleet. When ambassadors from Rhodes, Athens, Chios, and king Ptolemy arrived and urged peace, an armistice of a month was arranged to allow for peace negotiations to be conducted at Aegium. On his way to the meeting, Philip proceeded through Boeotia to Chalcis to strengthen its defences and to garrison it against a possible attack by Attalus. At Aegium peace negotiations were conducted with the Aetolians 'in order that neither the Romans nor Attalus should have any reason for invading Greece'. Thus the purpose was a separate peace with the Aetolians. At first they seemed willing, though this would be a violation of the treaty with Rome, but, when they learned that Attalus had reached Aegina and that the Roman fleet was off Naupactus, they submitted such extreme terms that the negotiations were dropped. Of the later operations of the season, it may be enough to mention that Sulpicius sailed around Greece to Aegina, where he joined Attalus and both fleets established winter quarters.[1] There they must have had ample time to plan the ambitious offensive of the following year.

The plan for the 208 campaign which emerges from the accounts available—mostly Livy drawn from Polybius—was nothing less than to cut off the contacts of Macedonia with central and southern Greece and thus to end its day as a great power once and for all. To accomplish this, the Aetolians garrisoned and fortified Thermopylae more strongly, while the Roman and Pergamene fleets prepared to capture the cities which controlled the sea route from Macedonia south as well as the route across northern Euboea, Phocis, and Boeotia. At the same time diversions in the shape of attacks on such allies as the Achaeans and Acarnanians and on Macedonia itself could be expected. The plan was not entirely new. The attack on the lines of communication had begun in the spring of 210 with the capture of Anticyra, and in 209 Philip had been prepared for further attacks. The chief difference in 208 was that there was greater activity. Philip promised help wherever it was needed and sent reinforcements to the island of Peparethus, to Chalcis, to Phocis, and to Boeotia and then himself made a dash for Heraclea in the hope of breaking up a conference there of the Aetolians and Attalus, but arrived too late. Thereupon he took his army back to Scotussa in Thessaly and arranged to have movements of the enemy reported by fire signals from

---

[1] Livy xxvii. 29. 9–33. 5. Just enough of the account of Polybius (x. 26) is preserved to show that the account of Livy is derived from it.

Peparethus, Phocis, and Euboea to Mount Tisaeum near the southern tip of the Magnesian peninsula.[1]

The Romans are said to have operated with 25 quinqueremes; Attalus, with 35. These were enough to give them decided superiority at sea and enable them to choose their fields of operation. They were not, however, as events were to show, strong enough to enable them to capture fortified and well defended cities, the chief successes being due to treason or hasty surrender. The Aetolians proved noticeably ineffective. The fleets of the Romans and Attalus began the season with a raid on the island of Lemnos. Since nothing more is reported, the raid cannot have been successful. Next they made for Peparethus, an island near the north point of Euboea and the southern point of the Magnesian peninsula. There they overran the countryside but failed to capture the city, to which Philip sent reinforcements. Not knowing where the enemy would strike, he sent troops also to a number of other places. Meanwhile the Roman-Pergamene fleet proceeded to Nicaea on the south coast of the Malian Gulf. From there Attalus, and probably also Sulpicius, went to Heraclea for a conference with Aetolian leaders. It was this conference which Philip sought in vain to surprise. Though he failed in that respect, he did considerable damage to the crops. Thus the raid is probably to be dated in May.[2] After the conference, the combined fleet made for Oreus (Histiaea), which was betrayed by the commander of the garrison. By holding this city the allies could hope to interfere both with the route across northern Euboea and with the approaches from the Aegean to the Gulf of Pagasae and the Malian Gulf. Next an attempt was made on Chalcis, but this city was too strong, and there was no traitor there. Consequently the fleet crossed to Cynus, the port of Opus, which was a key position on the route of communication between Macedonia and central and southern Greece. This, apparently, was the chief objective and, when Cynus had been captured, Sulpicius took the Roman fleet back to Oreus and left Attalus to capture and plunder Opus. In this he was interrupted by Philip and his Macedonians, who had forced Thermopylae and, so it was said, covered over sixty miles from Scotussa to Elatea in a single day.[3] It

---

[1] The only continuous account of the campaigns of 208 is Livy xxviii. 5–8. Only a part of the account of Polybius is found in x. 41–42.

[2] Livy xxviii. 5. 13–15 calls the meeting a *concilium* and implies a meeting of the Aetolian assembly, but Pol. x. 42. 4 shows that the gathering was smaller, rather a council of war or a staff meeting. On this meeting see *TAPA* lxxxiii (1952), 19–22. Livy mentions only the presence of Attalus and says nothing about Sulpicius, but it is unlikely that he would stay away from a consultation concerning plans of campaign.

[3] Livy xxviii. 7. 3. If this is correct, he must have taken the short cut from Thronium to Elatea instead of the much longer route by Hyampolis, but he did so with troops unencumbered by heavy baggage.

must have been the next day that Cretan mercenaries out foraging saw the approaching Macedonians and warned Attalus, who barely got away from Cynus with his life. He sailed from there to Oreus, from where he was called home by the news that Prusias of Bithynia had attacked his domains. Thus Opus and Cynus were lost almost as soon as they had been captured. Philip next campaigned in Locris and Phocis capturing Thronium in Locris and some minor towns in the upper Cephissus valley. It must have been during these operations that he captured Lilaea, which, however, later expelled the Macedonian garrison.[1] While Philip was in Phocis, ambassadors from Ptolemy and the Rhodians conferred with the Romans and Aetolians at Heraclea and then by prearrangement with Philip at Elatea.[2] This conference was interrupted by the report that Machanidas, the guardian of the Spartan king, Pelops, threatened to attack the Achaeans.[3] Thereupon Philip hurried to the Peloponnesus via the Isthmus. His arrival at Heraea was enough to cause Machanidas to give up his plan.

The remaining operations of that season largely centered around the Gulf of Corinth. This was the year in which Philip looked in vain for the arrival of a Carthaginian fleet. This advanced as far as to the Acarnanian coast but turned back for fear that it be caught in the Gulf of Corinth by the squadron of Sulpicius, which was reported to have started back from Oreus. As a matter of fact, the squadron did leave Oreus some time after Attalus thus giving up the last gain made that year by the combined fleets. Disappointed as he was, Philip made the best he could out of the situation. With a few Achaean ships he sailed across to Anticyra in Phocis, where he picked up seven Macedonian quinqueremes and twenty *lemboi*. Thus this important port had been recovered some time earlier and was again serving as a Macedonian naval station.[4] So completely had the efforts to interrupt the Macedonian lines of communication failed. With the ships thus gathered Philip staged a raid on the coast of Aetolia. After that he returned to Corinth. From there he sent his army home overland while he himself took ship at Cenchreae for Chalcis and from there again to Oreus. At Oreus he restored the city to those who were left of its earlier

[1] Paus. x. 33. 3. It is difficult to fit into the picture the soldiers sent to the defence of the city by Attalus as known from decrees of Lilaea published at Delphi (*Fouilles de Delphes*, iii. iv, nos. 132–5). It is natural to think of the time when the fleet of Attalus lay off Nicaea, but, if they had been sent at the time and been present when the city was captured, would there have been these records?

[2] Livy xxviii. 7. 13–14.

[3] When Livy xxviii. 7. 14 states that he had decided to attack the Eleans, this clearly is an error; cf. Walbank, *Philip V*, 304, n. 5.

[4] Livy xxviii. 8. 7–8. The fact that a Macedonian squadron was awaiting Philip at Anticyra implies that the port had been recovered some time earlier.

population. It must have been after Philip had left that Sulpicius, on his way back to Italy, sacked Dyme. The last act of Sulpicius reported by Livy in his account of the season's campaigns was the return from Oreus to Aegina. If it is true that Philip on his way to Chalcis sailed almost through the midst of the enemy's fleet, Sulpicius must still have been in the Aegean and must have returned west later. His sack of Dyme is known only from indirect evidence.[1] In this case too the population was sold into slavery but was later redeemed by Philip. Thus there was good reason for the attitude of the Dymaeans when, ten years later, they refused to vote for breaking with Philip and joining the Romans. If the Aetolians tried to take over the city and hold it, either directly themselves or through their allies, the Eleans, nothing has been heard of it. Thus except for what they got for the booty and the prisoners, all the Romans gained from this exploit was ill will.

Looking back over the year, the conduct of the campaigns by the Romans, Pergamenes, and Aetolians seems markedly ineffectual. The united fleet had struck at key positions but had gained no lasting results. At Oreus treason at first brought success. At Chalcis it is hard to avoid the impression that the besiegers were not very persistent. Yet, if they had held Oreus, Cynus, Opus, and Anticyra, and if the Aetolians had held their own at Thermopylae, it would have been difficult for the Macedonians to bring help to their southern allies. From this point of view, the recovery of Cynus and Opus by Philip was fatal to their plans, and it seems to have been due largely to the carelessness of Attalus. The latter undoubtedly blamed the Aetolians. The impossible had happened. Philip was securely blockaded in Thessaly, but the Aetolians let him slip through Thermopylae. Thus Cynus and Opus were recovered so quickly by Philip that it is impossible to tell how his opponents intended to dispose of the places. Were they to go to Aetolia as the treaty would seem to suggest? Or were they to be treated as Pergamene conquests and taken over by Attalus as lord of the naval stations and forts detached from Macedonian control? Certainly this seems to have been the plan for Oreus. With Attalus called home, the Romans soon returned to Aegina, and Aegina became the only Greek port retained by Attalus. When the Romans withdrew from the Aegean, the war was lost as far as their offensive was concerned, and the sack of Dyme was only a parting shot.

[1] Livy xxxii. 22. 10; Paus. vii. 17. 5. Only Pausanias mentions Sulpicius by name. The capture cannot well have been earlier than late in 208, and, since the Romans are said to have been inactive in 207 and 206 (Livy xxix. 12. 1), this becomes the most likely date. So Walbank, *Philip V*, 98, n. 1.

The Roman-Aetolian cause received another setback in the autumn of 208 in the election of Philopoemen as general of the Achaean Confederacy. This famous soldier by this time had garnered experience as a commander of mercenary forces in Crete. After his return home he had already served as hipparch of the Confederacy and as such had reformed the cavalry.[1] The reform seems to have involved the restoration of discipline, training, pride in service, and the acquisition of better horses but otherwise no radical changes. Not so with the infantry. The Achaeans hitherto had been lightly armed and very mobile. Philopoemen introduced heavier armament and placed emphasis on a more stable phalanx. Hitherto the infantry had carried an oblong or rectangular shield (*thyreos*) which was too light and too narrow to protect the body adequately. For this there was substituted another type of shield, the *aspis*, clearly the Macedonian shield, which, though not huge, was more effective. Likewise the shorter spear was replaced by the long Macedonian pike (*sarissa*).[2] These reforms by no means deprived the light-armed troops of their importance, but they gave to the phalanx a firmness and stability it had lacked and enabled the Achaeans not only to raid but to fight pitched battles. That this was the phase that Philopoemen himself emphasized is shown by the fact that in 205, during this second generalship, he brought his troops to the Nemean Games and gave an exhibition of hoplite drill.[3]

Philopoemen's reforms bore fruit almost immediately. In 209, when he served as hipparch, he distinguished himself at the battle of Larisus on a campaign of Philip in Elis and is reported to have killed the Elean cavalry commander with his own hand.[4] Two years later Philopoemen led the Achaeans to victory over the Spartans under their 'tyrant' Machanidas at Mantinea in the greatest pitched battle fought in Greece since Sellasia. In this battle the centre of the Achaean

---

[1] Pol. x. 22–24; Plut. *Philop.* 7.

[2] Pol. xi. 9–10; Plut. *Philop.* 9; Polyaen. vi. 4. 3. Most of the statement of Polybius concerning the details of the reforms has been lost. Moreover, some confusion has been caused by the fact that Pol. vi. 23. 1–2 applies *thyreos* to the large and heavy Roman shield 2½ by 4 feet. This is probably the reason why Feyel, *Polybe et Béotie*, 194 and n. 3 states that the abandonment of the *thyreos* in Boeotia meant a change to a lighter shield and implies that this was the case also in Achaea. Whether this was the case in Boeotia or not, it definitely was not the case in Achaea. *Thyreos* was a term defining a shield not by size or weight but by shape. Polybius himself applies the name to a small Gallic shield (ii. 30. 3). For *thyreos* applied to Gallic shields see also the dedication by Pyrrhus cited by Plut. *Pyrrh.* 26. Notice further that Livy i. 43 and Dion. Hal. *Ant. rom.* iv. 16. 2–3 associate *thyreos-scutum* with lighter armament than *aspis-clipeus*. As Launey, *Armées hellénistiques*, i. 140 f. remarks, the Achaeans before the reforms of Philopoemen were light-armed. For this lighter equipment, Philopoemen substituted the Macedonian. Cf. also G. T. Griffith, *Mercenaries*, 103.

[3] Plut. *Philop.* 11.

[4] Plut. *Philop.* 7 (fullest account); Paus. viii. 49. 7; Livy xxvii. 31. 11.

line was occupied by the phalanx of citizen soldiers and the right wing by the citizen cavalry, while the left wing was made up wholly or primarily of mercenaries.[1] The number of mercenaries may have been proportionally larger than this suggests. There are no ancient statistics for the number of troops involved except for the Spartan casualties, and any other statistics given in modern accounts are pure estimates. The battle fell into two parts, a battle between the mercenaries on the Achaean left and the mercenary soldiers of Machanidas and a second action involving the two phalanxes, followed by the pursuit and slaughter of the defeated. Philopoemen opened the first action hurriedly because he observed that Machanidas had brought up catapults to use as field artillery, and he did not wish to allow them to take effect. When, after heavy fighting, the light-armed mercenaries of the Achaeans gave way, Machanidas pursued too enthusiastically and too far. It seems that even the phalanx of the Spartans was drawn along in the pursuit and advanced breaking ranks, while Philopoemen kept the Achaean phalanx immobile and allowed those fleeing and those pursuing to pass by. Then, at the psychological moment, he ordered it to lower pikes and charge. The result was a complete defeat of the Spartans with a loss, according to Polybius, of not less than 4,000 dead and even more captured.[2] It seems that the casualties were unusually high because Philopoemen ordered his troops to spare none of the mercenary troops of the enemy. This he did in order to disrupt completely the mercenary forces of the tyrant.[3] In this he was largely successful. Thus ended the battle which definitely shifted the balance in the Peloponnesus and transferred the predominance, for the time being, from the Aetolians and Spartans to the Achaeans. Nevertheless, it was to have little effect on the course of history, for the real issue at stake was Roman or Macedonian supremacy in the Balkans, and on this issue the battle of Mantinea had little effect. Hence the historians of Rome from Livy to Mommsen, seldom if ever, deign to mention the battle.[4] It is significant that the Achaeans, who had won the victory for the cause of themselves and the Macedonians, a few years later were to be allies of the Romans against the Macedonians.

At the moment, the battle must have had considerable effect. It

---

[1] There are two problems involved. First, were the Illyrians (Pol. xi. 11. 4, 14. 1) mercenaries or auxiliaries? Holleaux, 254, n. 2 takes them to be auxiliary troops sent by the Macedonians; Griffith, *Mercenaries*, 104 takes them to be mercenaries and thinks the entire left wing consisted of mercenaries. There is also the question whether lower-class citizens served as light-armed troops or whether all light-armed troops were mercenaries.

[2] Pol. xi. 11–18; Plut. *Philop.* 10.

[3] Pol. xi. 18. 1; cf. Griffith, *Mercenaries*, 96.

[4] De Sanctis, *Storia*, iii. ii. 426 ff. has an account.

must have helped to discourage the Aetolians so that, when the Romans quit sending a fleet to Greece, they were ready to make a separate peace with Philip and his allies. A separate peace, of course, was a violation of the treaty with Rome, but the Aetolians could argue that the Romans, by their failure to send the promised help to their allies, had been the first to break the treaty. The treaty negotiated in 206 is given only brief notices in our sources.[1] The next year the Romans changed their policy and sent P. Sempronius Tuditanus to Greece, as proconsul, though he had not yet served as consul, with a force, it is reported, of 10,000 infantry, 1,000 cavalry, and thirty-five beaked ships—a force considerably larger than the one stipulated in the treaty with the Aetolians. The Roman leaders responsible for this expedition were planning on major operations against Macedonia but were not ready to carry on the war by themselves. Tuditanus landed at Dyrrhachium and later withdrew to Apollonia. There he refused Philip's challenge to battle. When the Aetolians could not be induced to re-enter the war, the Romans too became ready for peace, which was negotiated at Phoenice in Epirus. The terms were favourable to Philip, for while the Romans resumed the protectorate of the Illyrian tribe of Parthini and certain towns, probably near Dyrrhachium, Philip retained control of Atintania, a district which had once gone over to the Romans and which was strategically important because it contained the Aous valley and thus controlled the communications from Macedonia and Greece to the district of Illyria near Apollonia. Yet it was not completely one-sided. Tuditanus had besieged Dimale but failed to capture it. Nevertheless it was included in the treaty in the sphere of Roman influence.[2]

The entire venture shows that the Romans were planning to retain their foot-hold east of the Adriatic and, if anything, strengthen it. Yet, though it almost looks as if the controlling element in the senate was more willing to support Tuditanus in his venture in Illyria than Scipio in his plans for the invasion of Africa, the force sent was not large enough to carry on without some Greek support. This does not mean that the Romans did not take the matter seriously. They had long ago begun to learn to make use of allies. In the treaty of peace, they showed their continued interest not only by the clauses concerning Illyria but also by including a list of other allies who were entitled to the benefits of the treaty. Both sides listed such states as *foederi adscripti*. The lists given by Livy are not entirely trustworthy, but it

[1] Livy xxix. 12. 1; Appian, *Mac.* 3; Dio, frag. 59. For the Roman withdrawal from the war see also Livy xxxi. 31. 19.

[2] Livy xxix. 12; Atintania goes over to the Romans in 229: Pol. ii. 11. 11; Appian, *Illyr.* 7. On the negotiations in 205 see particularly Holleaux, 276 ff.; De Sanctis, *Storia*, iii. ii. 432–9; Oost, *Roman Policy in Epirus and Acarnania*, 36 f.

is reasonably certain that those listed by the Romans included the Spartans, the Eleans, and the Messenians. The Athenians included in Livy's list, certainly do not belong there, but probably the clearest proof that the list has been tampered with, is the inclusion of *Nabis, Lacedaemoniorum tyrannus*. The title of tyrant could not possibly be applied to him in an official document. Instead the Spartan state must have been mentioned in some other way. These allies or associates listed here, were not unconditionally guaranteed protection, but the protection of their interests could be used as a pretext for intervention.[1]

2. THE SECOND MACEDONIAN WAR AND THE ROMAN OCCUPATION OF GREECE TO 194 B.C.

The Second Macedonian War clearly was begun by Rome, but why was it begun? Was it an imperialistic war? Or was it, as it has been called, a 'preventive offensive' undertaken for fear lest the Hellenistic powers should wax too strong and thus become dangerous? For the present it is enough to note that Rome, when once involved abroad, seldom or never drew back. The protectorate in Illyria, once established, was not relinquished, and the ties established in Greece during the First Macedonian War were likewise maintained. It is well to remember that there are other ways to direct and control than by outright annexation, and so the failure to annex in the period 200–150 B.C. does not prove lack of imperialistic aims. Instead of annexation and provincial governors, there was a succession of embassies and communications from the senate.[2] In the period in question, the policy adopted by the Romans was the maintainance of a loose protectorate over states connected with Rome by *amicitia* alone but becoming increasingly dependent and subservient—or occasionally recalcitrant. In Greece circumstances led to the negotiation of a number of formal alliances during the First Macedonian War. To these, the Second Macedonian War and its aftermath added treaties of alliance with the Achaean Confederacy and Macedonia itself. Yet this did not seriously alter the general policy and, when freedom for the Greeks was proclaimed in 196, this remained almost permanently the official version of the status of the Greeks.[3]

[1] On the *foederi adscripti* see *Econ. Surv. Rome*, iv. 265 f.; Walbank, *Philip V*, 103 and n. 6; Badian, *Foreign Clientelae*, 58–60 and the literature cited in these works.

[2] For this kind of control see 'Roman Supervision of Greece between Wars', *Econ. Surv. Rome*, iv. 286–90; for an example more fully studied, A. Aymard, *Les Premiers Rapports de Rome et de la confédération Achaienne* (1938); for an observation of how little change the creation of a province might involve, M. Rostovtzeff, *Hellenistic World*, 1016 f.

[3] Cf. 'The Policy of Augustus in Greece', *Acta Classica, Proceedings of the Classical Association of South Africa*, i (1958), 123–30.

If it is difficult to determine the point of view of the Roman leaders of the time, it is even more difficult to determine the attitude of the various other powers involved. Philip obviously did not want a war with Rome at the time and apparently did not anticipate further trouble from that quarter. With his recently rebuilt Macedonian navy he was engaged in aggression in Asia Minor and around the Hellespont. To this period belongs the real or alleged secret treaty of Philip and Antiochus III for the division of the Ptolemaic holdings outside of Egypt. It was a period of aggression and conquest, in which Philip by no means confined himself to attacks on Ptolemaic possessions. His aggression in Asia Minor quite naturally aroused Rhodes and Pergamum, and Philip found himself at war with these two states. This led to heavy fighting. An account of these events, which are adequately covered in several works,[1] will not be included here. As an indication of the seriousness of the fighting, it may be enough to mention that at the battle of Chios in 201 the casualties on the Macedonian side are reported to have included 3,000 Macedonians and 6,000 crew members killed and upwards of 3,000 captured.[2] Even if, as most scholars believe, these statistics are derived from patriotic Rhodian sources greatly exaggerating the losses of their enemy, it is clear from the account of the battle that the losses were very great. Thus, though the outcome was not all in favour of his enemies, it is a wonder that, after such losses, Philip could boldly face war on several fronts and that his soldiers, both Macedonians and mercenaries, continued to serve him faithfully. He must have possessed real qualities of leadership. And yet it seems that these same eastern adventures brought out his ruthless qualities to an extent to which they had not so far been revealed, and that his passions thereafter sometimes interfered with his better judgement.[3]

The great Hellenistic monarchies of the time seem to have thought that they could continue their struggles for supremacy in the Near East without worrying about the future advance of Rome. Meanwhile Pergamum and Rhodes, which both normally adopted a balance of power policy in an attempt to keep any single power from completely overshadowing the others and thus endangering their own freedom, probably regarded the Romans as exceedingly convenient auxiliaries who could be used to help break the power of an over-aggressive Macedonian king. Even the Achaeans and Spartans seem to have thought that they could resume their local squabbles unhindered. If

[1] See, for instance, Walbank, Philip V, ch. iv.
[2] Pol. xvi. 7. 5–6. The numbers are considered exaggerated by Holleaux, CAH viii. 154; De Sanctis, Storia, iv. i. 13 f.; Walbank, Philip V, 124. On the text of xvi. 7. 6, which has been altered by the editors so as to change the meaning, cf. De Sanctis, 8, n. 22.
[3] See particularly Walbank, Philip V, 135 ff.

these were the points of view of the various states, future events were to show them completely mistaken.[1]

At Sparta, Machanidas, after his death at Mantinea in 207, had been succeeded by Nabis, first as guardian of the young king Pelops and then as king in his own name.[2] His social reforms and tyrannical excesses—probably much exaggerated by his enemies—need not be discussed here. It is enough to note that he was soon at war with the Achaeans. A frontier incident, which according to Polybius led to the outbreak of hostilities, may deserve to be noticed as an example of what could and did happen. Some Boeotians induced a groom to come with them and bring along an exceptionally fine horse from the stable of Nabis. The agents of the latter pursued them and caught up with them at Megalopolis. They succeeded in bringing back the horse and the groom, but the Boeotians, when they called for help, were rescued by the bystanders, who did not allow them to be carried off. Using this as a pretext Nabis began to rustle cattle from Megalopolitan territory. This apparently led to a series of raids but no declaration of war.[3] More serious was a surprise attack by Nabis on Messene in 201, though at the time Messene was the ally both of Sparta and of Aetolia, and so in the opposite camp from that of the Achaeans. Nevertheless, the occupation of Messene by the Spartans would be a decided menace to the Achaeans, and so Philopoemen, a private citizen at the time, urged the Achaean general to intervene. When the latter refused, Philopoemen himself with volunteers from Megalopolis rushed to Messene. On the news of his approach Nabis withdrew.[4]

It is possible that Philopoemen's intervention could have been construed as aid in the defence of the attacked party against an aggressor and thus not be considered an act of war against the Spartans. Philopoemen, however, seems to have regarded his country as at war. In the autumn of the same year he was elected general. During his term of office he staged an important action against Nabis, probably in the spring or summer of 200. Orders were issued to the

[1] The best general introduction to these problems remains Holleaux's chapters in *CAH* viii. Among the many studies and controversial articles, J. P. V. D. Balsdon, 'Rome and Macedon, 205–200 B.C.', *JRS* xliv (1954), 30–42, which on many points challenges Holleaux, is important. All details are not convincing but the conclusion that 'the Roman government, now that it was free of Hannibal, was very determined indeed on war with Philip' (p. 41) seems inescapable. For the view that Rome was imperialistic at the time, cf. also Bengtson, *GrG*[2] 465.

[2] For Nabis and his relations with the Achaeans see especially Aymard, *Premiers Rapports*, 33–49.

[3] Pol. xiii. 8.

[4] The fact that Sparta and Messene were allies at the time is emphasized by Pol. xvi 13. 3; Livy xxxiv. 32. 16. For the campaign see Pol. xvi. 16–17; Plut. *Philop.* 12; Paus. iv. 29. 10–11, viii. 50. 5. The notices of Pausanias add the unlikely detail that an agreement was negotiated before Nabis left Messene.

Achaean militia to assemble on a certain day, but were so manipulated that neither the assembling troops nor the people of Tegea knew of the plan before the entire army gathered there. Orders were sent first to the more distant cities to mobilize and march to the next city on the route and deliver the letter of summons there. This again specified only the next city on the route, and so it went till all gathered at Tegea. In this way it was possible to keep Nabis from getting wind of the matter. Meanwhile the troops of the standing army (*epilektoi*) had been sent to raid Spartan territory near Sellasia and draw out the mercenary soldiers of Nabis. When they had succeeded in doing this, they fell back, according to the pre-arranged plan, to a place where the militia lay in ambush. The result was a decisive victory for the Achaeans. The defeat inflicted on the enemy was not as devastating as that at Mantinea, but seemed decisive enough. That is probably the reason why Philopoemen, thinking the war was over, went to Crete for further military experience.[1] However, any belief that the war against Nabis was finished proved false. Consequently, Cycliades, Philopoemen's successor as general, soon after his election, found it expedient to call an extraordinary meeting of the Achaean assembly to take up the question of the war against Nabis.[2] This war, rather than the threat of Roman intervention was the burning question for the Achaeans at the time.

To return to Philip, it is clear that he was aware of the threat from Rome but did not give exclusive attention to it. He had no intentions of giving up his interests either in Asia Minor or in Greece. As late as 197 he had troops both in the Peloponnesus and in Caria. In the Peloponnesus his chief effort at first seems to have been directed at securing the co-operation of the Achaean Confederacy in the war and, failing that, at least its neutrality. His problems were further complicated by the fact that the nature of his empire made it necessary to garrison cities in Greece, in Thrace, and in Asia Minor. The estimates of the number of troops in these garrisons vary, but apparently the lowest estimate of the number of mercenary soldiers involved is 15,000. To these, in some places at least, a certain number of Macedonians were added.[3] But it is his operations in Greece which concern this study most intimately. Late in 200 he attended the meeting of the Achaeans called to consider the war against Nabis and offered to take over the war. In return he asked the Achaeans to supply troops to garrison Corinth, Chalcis, and Oreus and thus protect

[1] Pol. xvi. 36–37. On Philopoemen's departure for Crete (Plut. *Philop.* 13; Paus. viii. 50. 6) see Aymard, *Premiers Rapports*, 45 and n. 79.

[2] Livy xxxi. 25. 2–10. On the Achaean meeting cf. *Rep. Govt.* 171.

[3] See Walbank, *Philip V*, 142, n. 2 and the literature cited there. Note, however, that so few statistics are available that an exact estimate is impossible, but 15,000 is hardly too high.

his rear while he advanced into Laconia. This clearly was a scheme to get Achaean troops so placed that the Confederacy could not avoid taking part in the war against Rome. Cycliades, the Achaean general of the time, who presided, tended to be pro-Macedonian and was later exiled for that reason and became practically a member of Philip's staff.[1] Nevertheless, he avoided putting Philip's proposal to a vote by ruling that it was illegal to act on any subject except the one for which the meeting had been called and so, after passing a decree to mobilize troops to fight Nabis, dismissed the meeting.

Next, probably in the autumn of 199, Philip tried to woo the Achaeans by turning over to them the cities in the Peloponnesus other than Corinth which the Macedonians had kept garrisoned since the Cleomenic and Social wars. This too failed. Hence in 198, after the Romans had entered Greece, all he asked was that they remain neutral. In the autumn of that year, while Titus Flamininus was beseiging Elatea and his brother Lucius with the Roman fleet stood off Cenchreae, pressure was brought on the Achaeans to go over to the side of the Romans. In opposition to this, the Macedonians merely requested their neutrality. The story of the three day meeting of the primary assembly called at Sicyon to consider the question is well known. This was the meeting at which feeling ran so high that, paradoxically, after the Roman, Pergamene, Rhodian, Macedonian and Athenian envoys had been heard, no Achaean at first was willing to speak. When the general, Aristaenus, almost bullied them into action, the ten *damiorgoi* proved divided equally, five being willing to put the alliance with the Romans to a vote, five saying that it was illegal for the magistrates to put to vote and for the assembly to pass any decree in violation of the alliance with Philip. The latter undoubtedly were right, but expediency, or what the Achaeans thought was expediency, carried the day. The deadlock was broken when the father of one of the *damiorgoi* opposed to putting the question to vote threatened his son and induced him to change his verdict. When the question was to be put to vote, the citizens of Megalopolis and Dyme and many of those of Argos—the vote was taken by cities—withdrew. Even at this date there were Achaeans who thought of Philip and the Macedonians as benefactors.[2] Since a treaty of alliance with the

---

[1] Cycliades exiled: Livy xxxii. 19. 2; later with Philip: Pol. xviii. 1. 2, 34. 4; Livy xxxii. 32. 10.

[2] Livy xxxii. 19–23, derived from Polybius. The accounts of this meeting and the one at Argos in 200 (Livy xxxi. 25) constitute the most important evidence available for the procedure at such meetings after the Achaeans had passed the law that the *ekklesia* was to be summoned only on special occasions to deal with a single major problem of foreign affairs announced in advance. Polybius (xviii. 13. 8–11) defended Aristaenus for transferring the Achaeans from the alliance with Philip to that with the Romans, but did so in words which imply that some considered the action treason.

Romans required the approval of the *comitia* at Rome, the contracting of a formal alliance with them had to be postponed, but alliances were arranged immediately with Attalus and the Rhodians. This arrangement made, the Achaeans had to take part in the war. What fell to them was co-operation in the siege of Corinth, participation in the later fighting near Corinth, and the sending of troops to aid the Rhodians in Caria. More of this later.

Immediately after the meeting the Achaeans joined the Romans and their allies in the siege of Corinth. This failed, in part because Philocles, who was practically the Macedonian viceroy with head-quarters at Chalcis, brought fifteen hundred additional troops who were ferried across the Gulf of Corinth in *lemboi*. When the siege was raised and the Achaeans dismissed, it was time to go into winter quarters, and Attalus withdrew to Piraeus and the Roman fleet to Corcyra. Meanwhile Philocles stayed on and, profiting from the pro-Macedonian sentiment in Argos, brought that city over.[1] But the advantage was soon lost, in part on account of a mistake by Philip himself, who early in 197 instructed Philocles to turn Argos over to Nabis as a sort of guarantee of his friendship to himself. Instead of remaining loyal to Philip, Nabis got in touch with Flamininus and Attalus, and a conference was arranged at or near Mycenae. As a result the alliance of Sparta with Rome dating from the First Mace-donian War was revived, or probably rather was recognized as still valid. Nabis thereupon contributed 600 Cretan auxiliaries to the Roman army and agreed to an armistice with the Achaeans, who, as will be seen later, were thus free to fight the Macedonians. Flamin-inus, apparently, was so elated by this success that he even tried to induce Philocles to surrender Corinth, but to no avail. Thereupon he himself took ship to Anticyra to join his army in Phocis and start north on the campaign which was to lead to the victory at Cynoscephalae.[2]

Before turning to a brief account of the Macedonian and Roman campaigns, the contributions of the other Greek states will be con-sidered, and first those of the Aetolians, who, except for the Athenians and Attalus of Pergamum were the first Greeks to enter the war on the side of the Romans.[3] Of all Greek states, the Aetolians certainly were the most desirable allies with the possible exception of the

[1] Livy xxxii. 23. 4–13. For the position of Philocles see below in connexion with the naval warfare.

[2] Livy xxxii. 38–40. The length of the armistice is given as four months. Aymard, *Premiers Rapports*, 148, n. 54 has shown that there is something wrong here. Hostilities were not resumed before 195. Cf. Walbank, *Philip V*, 166 and n. 2.

[3] Apart from the envoys of Attalus, those who approached the Roman consul encamped in Illyria in the winter of 200–199 were not Greeks (Livy xxxi. 28. 1–4). The Athenian ambas-sadors were already on hand at the time of his arrival (xxxi. 14. 1–3).

Achaeans. They would also seem to be natural allies on account of their hatred of the Macedonians and their earlier co-operation with the Romans. Yet they were not among those who hastened to align themselves with the Romans as soon as they landed in Illyria, probably on account of pique over the treatment they had received in the earlier war. Therefore in the spring of 199 Sulpicius Galba, the Roman commander, sent an envoy to the *Panaitolika*, the regular spring meeting of the Aetolian assembly. The assembly was addressed by Macedonian, Athenian, and Roman envoys. The majority at the meeting favoured acting in accordance with the Roman appeal, but the general of the Confederacy, Damocritus, secured postponement of the decision to an extraordinary meeting later in the year. Before the meeting a delegation of Aetolians headed by Pyrrhias had a conference at Heraclea near Thermopylae with Apustius, the commander of the Roman fleet operating in the Aegean and Attalus, who came by ship into the Malian Gulf from somewhere on northern Euboea. For Attalus, who had been there in 208, the conference was not a unique experience. The Romans 'promised everything', but obviously no treaty was drawn up and no precise agreement reached. Yet the success both of the Roman army in Illyria and of the allied fleet in the Aegean impressed the Aetolians sufficiently so that at the special meeting they voted to enter the war. Before that was done, however, Scopas, who had been so prominent in earlier wars and intrigues but now was acting as a recruiting officer for Ptolemy, carried off to Egypt 6,000 Aetolians of military age as infantry and 500 as cavalry men and would have recruited even more had not the general of the Confederacy checked his activities. Nevertheless, the Aetolians entered the war that very year, but their big contribution to the war effort was to come in the Cynoscephalae campaign.

This year Flamininus started north from Elatea in Phocis just in time to get to Thermopylae at the time that the Aetolians were conducting their spring meeting, the *Panaitolika*, at Heraclea. This year, as in some other cases, the meeting was called near the scene of operations and combined, as it were, a mass meeting and a general levy of the army. As a result, only a couple of days later, Flamininus was joined at Xyniae by about 6,000 Aetolian infantry and 40 cavalry. With this addition, his army outnumbered that of Philip. In order to realize that the Aetolians made important contributions to the campaign which followed, all that is needed is to read the accounts of Polybius and Livy or any moderately full modern account. The general impression gained thus is that the Roman and Aetolian officers trusted each other and co-operated and that the jealousy and ill feeling between them developed later. Thus, at one point in the preliminary skirmishes, when a Roman contingent was in trouble, Flamininus sent to its aid 500 cavalry and 2,000 infantry, mostly Aetolians, Livy says, under the command of two Aetolian officers and two military tribunes.[1]

The Boeotian Confederacy at the outbreak of the war was probably as loyal to Macedonia as any member of the Hellenic League, and Boeotian troops continued to serve under Philip even after the Confederacy early in 197 was tricked and pressured into going over to the Romans. This is shown by the presence of Boeotian troops in the operations near Corinth later in the year. Boeotia was important strategically. It was the control of Boeotia which enabled the Macedonians and Acarnanians to raid Attica in 200 and Philocles to bring troops from Chalcis to Corinth in 198. The chief task of the Confederacy at this time must have been to guard against any advance of the Romans beyond Phocis. Yet, in addition to the troops at Corinth, there seems to have been another little contingent serving under Philip. The commander of this and the leader of the pro-Macedonian faction among the Boeotians was Brachylles, who once had served for Antigonus Doson as governor of Sparta. During the reign of Philip, he and other pro-Macedonian leaders had probably turned to demagoguery and legislation in the interest of the lower classes. Under the circumstances the more conservative opposition was or became pro-Roman. Arrangements were made to have Flamininus and Attalus come to Thebes to address the assembly of the Boeotians. The Roman proconsul and the king appeared with a small escort but, when they were met by Boeotian dignitaries, slowed their pace so that 2,000 legionaries following at a distance could come up and be smuggled into the city. This was attributed to treason on the part of Antiphilus, the head of the Confederacy. Thus there probably was no need for the expenditure of eloquence at the meeting next day by Attalus, by the Achaean Aristaenus, and by Flamininus himself. All the cities of Boeotia—the vote in the assembly at that time was taken by cities—

[1] *Panaitolika* of 199: Livy xxxi. 29–32; conference at Heraclea: xxxi. 46. 1–5; later decision by Aetolians: 40. 9–10; Scopas recruits Aetolians: 43. 5–7; Aetolian meeting and mobilization in 197: xxxiii. 3. 7–9. On the order of events in 199, cf. *TAPA* lxxxiii (1952), 23, n. 40; on the *Panaitolika* of 199 and 197, ibid. 24 f. Though in Livy xxxiii. 3. 8 *tertio die* applies strictly to the advance of Flamininus from Heraclea to Xynia, the implied promptness of the arrival of the Aetolians is enough to show that messengers with mobilization orders were not sent home from Heraclea but that the Aetolians went directly from the meeting into camp. Concerning the numbers, the manuscript reading in Livy xxxiii. 3. 9 gives the infantry as 600, a number obviously too low and commonly considered corrupt. In his edition (1965) McDonald, following a conjecture of Drakenborch, corrects this to *sex milia peditum* to agree with Plut. *Flam.* 7, while in xxxiii. 4. 6 he restores the manuscript reading indicating that the Aetolian contingents gave the Romans numerical superiority not only in the cavalry but in the total numbers. The incident at Cynoscephalae: Pol. xviii. 21.5; Livy xxxiii. 7.7.

25

voted to accept the alliance with Rome. However, there was no formal treaty drawn up and recorded.[1] After Cynoscephalae, Brachylles and other exiles returned, and he was elected head of the Confederacy but was murdered by his political opponents. Thus began a protracted and bloody civil strife which led to the waylaying and murdering of Roman soldiers and ultimately to Roman intervention.[2]

Of the members of the Hellenic League, the Acarnanians were peculiarly involved through the incident of the two Acarnanian youths who had violated the Eleusinian mysteries and had been put to death by the Athenians. In retaliation, the Acarnanians, with Philip's approval and Macedonian help, raided Attica and carried off considerable booty. Such self-help to secure restitution for wrongs suffered apparently was considered legitimate if the two states involved were not bound by a treaty of *asylia*, but this did not make the act any more popular with the sufferers. The anger of the Athenians seems to have been directed mostly against the Macedonians, who not only supported the Acarnanians on land but also seized some Athenian ships, which later were set free again by the Rhodians.[3] The declaration of war which the raid provoked was directed against Macedonia and not Acarnania. During the war little is heard of Acarnania before the last year. Apparently the pro-Roman party was not strong enough to bring it over earlier even though the Confederacy, after the Romans had taken over Epirus, was pretty well separated from the other allies of Philip.

The Thessalian Confederacy was especially closely knit to Macedonia for the reason that the king of Macedonia was also the head of the Confederacy. This, however, did not give it any preferential treatment during the war but rather the opposite. Yet its sufferings were due chiefly to its location and the fact that it served as the main theatre of operations during large parts of two campaigning seasons. Raided and plundered by the Aetolians, Athamanians, and Romans and in part devastated by Philip himself when he laid waste the country ahead of the advancing Romans, Thessaly probably saw more of the horrors of war than any other part of Greece. The special emphasis placed on the capture of Gomphi, captured by Amynander of Athamania with the aid of Roman troops, was due to its importance as terminal of the overland route from Ambracia to Thessaly. Yet,

---

[1] Boeotians at Corinth: Livy xxxiii. 14. 5; Brachylles at Sparta: Pol. xx. 5. 12; commander of Boeotians with Philip: Livy xxxiii. 27. 8; with Philip at Nicaea: Pol. xviii. 1. 2. Boeotia brought over by the Romans: Livy xxxiii. 1–2; no formal treaty: Livy xlii. 12. 5. On Brachylles as a demagogue cf. Feyel, *Polybe et Béotie*, 284 f., 304.

[2] Pol. xviii. 43; Livy xxxiii. 27–29.

[3] The incident of the Acarnanians: Livy xxxi. 14. 7–10; ships captured: Pol. xvi. 26. 9; Livy xxxi. 15. 5.

in spite of all their troubles nearer home, Thessalian troops, as well as Acarnanian and Boeotian, were stationed at Corinth.[1]

The course of the campaigns of the Romans will be discussed only in so far as they affected various Greek states. The less well known naval campaign will be treated somewhat more fully than the campaigns on land. The latter were by all odds the more important from the Roman point of view, partly because the Romans adopted the practice of never transporting an army any distance by sea if a route over land was available. Therefore, the ports taken under Roman protection in the Illyrian wars remained crucial for the operations beyond the Adriatic. After the initial try in 199 the route from these bases east across the mountains to Macedonia was abandoned. Clearly it was found too difficult in the face of opposition. The one exception, its use in 191 in the campaign against Antiochus III in Greece, proves the rule, for at that time the Romans had the co-operation of Philip and his Macedonians. Later, when Rome had established the province of Macedonia, this became the route of the Egnatian Way. Meanwhile the route south through Epirus and across the mountains to the plains of western Thessaly was adopted in 198 and was used regularly thereafter. Thus Epirus became crucial for the Roman communications. This may explain both the favourable treatment given Epirus at first and the terrible punishment inflicted on the Epirotes in 167 by Aemilius Paulus. The Epirotes had committed the unpardonable sin of threatening the Roman line of communications.

In 198, after having secured supplies through Gomphi, Flamininus struck out across Thessaly in the direction of the pass of Tempe. Some distance west of Larisa he was held up at the city of Atrax, which he proved unable to capture. Even when a breach in the wall had been effected, the massed Macedonian phalangites with their long pikes effectively kept the Romans at bay. The defence thus seems to have been shared by natives and a Macedonian garrison. After this check, Flamininus decided to go into winter quarters. Wintering in devastated Thessaly, far from the sea, was impossible. What was needed was a port with moorings for transports and quarters for troops. For this Anticyra in Phocis was chosen, doubtless because it meant a significant advance into enemy territory, the detaching of Phocis from the coalition of his enemies, and serious interference with the Macedonian communications with Greece. The coast of Acarnania and Aetolia, that is, Ambracia and Leucas, suggested as an alternative, can hardly have been considered. To have withdrawn to these ports would have seemed like a retreat similar to the withdrawal of Sulpicius

[1] Capture of Gomphi: Livy xxxii. 14. 1–3; forts retained by Amynander: Pol. xviii. 47. 13, Livy xxxiii. 34. 11; Thessalians at Corinth: Livy xxxiii. 14. 5.

Galba from Macedonia the preceding year. The advance to Anticyra, on the contrary, represented an important gain. The list of Phocian cities first captured, Phanoteus, Ambrysus, Hyampolis, and Anticyra, shows that beyond Thermopylae he followed the route through the Pass of Hyampolis. After the capture of these cities he turned to Daulis and Elatea, which both caused trouble, especially Elatea.[1] After a long resistance Elatea surrendered on the terms of freedom for the city and free departure for the troops of the royal garrison stationed there. This happened after the defection of the Achaeans to the Romans and may in part have been influenced by that event. This ended the campaigning season for the Roman army. For the Macedonians and their allies, it meant not only the loss of Phocis but serious interference with their communications. Yet, as long as they controlled Boeotia and Chalcis, communications were not entirely cut, but had to depend much more than formerly on the sea. The presence of a Macedonian garrison at Elatea when the Romans arrived, suggests that Phocis had been garrisoned continuously from the time of the Social War.

The naval warfare actually got under way earlier than the campaigns on land. In a sense it was a continuation of the earlier conflicts of Rhodes and Pergamum with the Macedonians. The surprising feature is that with the Roman fleet added to the others, the naval warfare as a whole proved rather ineffective. Ports were captured, but soon afterwards appear once more to be in Macedonian hands. An important factor undoubtedly was the Macedonian control of Corinth, which deprived the Romans of the use of its harbours and of the *diolkos* by which at least smaller ships could be hauled across the Isthmus. Instead ships going to the Aegean, where most of the fighting took place, had to round the Peloponnesus.

The operations began already in the autumn of 200. When Sulpicius Galba arrived in Illyria, he found there Athenian ambassadors with an appeal for help and in response to it immediately sent C. Claudius Cento with twenty ships. These are once called triremes by Livy and, if they were triremes, they were not intended to be used for major naval operations. Apparently Sulpicius sent what was on hand, and that was not very much. It seems, however, to have been enough, in co-operation with a few Rhodian and Athenian ships, to bring some sort of protection to Attica against raids by sea by the Macedonian forces stationed at Chalcis. The story that the Romans and their allies captured and completely destroyed Chalcis, massacred its garrison, and even overthrew the statues of Macedonian kings, is at best a gross exaggeration. Chalcis and the adjoining parts of Euboea

[1] Atrax: Livy xxxii. 15. 8, 17. 4–17; Anticyra and Phocis: xxxii. 18 and 24.

were at the time under the command of the Macedonian officer, Philocles, who had raided Attica earlier in the year and who, a few weeks after the supposed destruction of his headquarters on the Euripus brought 2,000 troops from Euboea—obviously across the Euripus—and then through Boeotia and across Cithaeron to raid Attica. Livy mentions the strategic importance of Chalcis, which was as important for communications by sea as Thermopylae for those by land. It would have been a great advantage to the Romans to have been able to hold it, but they lacked the man-power and so withdrew as soon as they had finished the work of destruction. Even this report of a quick withdrawal cannot save the story. As will be seen below, Chalcis was to continue to serve as Macedonian headquarters and there is no indication that it had suffered extensively. Clearly some innocuous raid is the most that can be accepted. The Roman ships undoubtedly helped to defend Attica but won no major victory that year.[1] Since next year's naval expedition set out from Corcyra, it is clear that the Roman squadron at the end of the operations withdrew to that port, which served as the headquarters for the Roman fleet operating beyond the Adriatic.

The operations next year (199) were on a larger scale. The Roman squadron was sent out early in the spring under the command of L. Apustius, an officer who had served under Sulpicius the preceding year. Apparently preparations had been made during the winter for an expedition on a larger scale. There was also more help from the allies than the preceding year. Naturally, a large naval expedition would attempt to interrupt the Macedonian naval communications by attacking Chalcis from the south or by going around Euboea and striking at the line of communications at its northern end. Moreover, the route north of Euboea was the only one by which ships could approach the Malian Gulf when Chalcis was in hostile hands. Apparently they at times managed to do so even when the Macedonians held ports both on northern Euboea and in Phthiotic Achaea.[2] The greatest feat that the fleet could hope to accomplish was to capture Chalcis, and its commander seems to have played with the idea but hardly more. When the Roman contingent entered the Aegean, it effected a junction with Attalus off the coast of northeastern Peloponnesus, and they, after a visit to Piraeus, continued on to Andros and

---

[1] Operations of the Roman ships: Livy xxxi. 14. 3, 22. 4–23. 12; Philocles brings troops from Euboea: Livy xxxi. 26. 1. He undoubtedly had been in command on Euboea since the raid on Attica in the spring (Livy xxxi. 16. 2). De Sanctis, Storia, iv. i. 47, n. 85 remarks that Livy's account of the Chalcis incident is exaggerated.

[2] In 199 the visit of Apustius and Attalus to Heraclea for a conference preceded the capture of Oreus (Livy xxxi. 46. 1–6). Similarly in 208 the conference at Heraclea preceded that year's attack on Oreus.

secured its surrender. Operations against this island off the south point of Euboea might be the prelude to operations in either direction. The fleet first turned southwest. After an unsuccessful attack on the island of Cythnos, some other minor operations, and the addition of twenty *lemboi* arriving from Illyrian Issa, it turned and rounded Euboea and made for Mende and Cassandrea on the Chalcidic peninsula of Pallene. Here the attackers suffered losses both from a storm and at the hands of the defenders. After this setback, they sailed south again along the west coast of Pallene and, rounding the cape at its extremity, continued past also the extremity of the peninsula of Sithonia and across the Singitic Gulf to Acanthus situated at the head of the Gulf. There they laid waste the fields and sacked the city, where-upon they returned to Euboea with their ships loaded with booty. The dash to Cassandrea and Acanthus seems to have been nothing but a raid to gather booty. The attackers may have hoped to capture Cassandrea but can hardly have thought of retaining it.[1] When the fleet returned to Euboea, it established some sort of headquarters—where is not known—and from there Apustius and Attalus entered the Malian Gulf with ten light ships in order to go to Heraclea for the conference with Aetolian leaders which already has been mentioned. On their return to the fleet, the siege of Oreus was begun. While the Roman and Pergamene forces attacked the city, a Rhodian squadron is reported to have stood guard against the Macedonian fleet stationed at Demetrias. After the capture of Oreus, the united fleet returned to Piraeus. There Apustius left thirty ships, while he himself with the rest of the Roman fleet continued on to Corcyra. Later the Pergamene forces returned home. Thus, since the Rhodians had started home earlier, the Romans took upon themselves to guard Athens during the coming winter.[2]

The one lasting gain of the campaign seems to have been the occupation of Andros by the Pergamenes. When the city surrendered on the terms that the citizens and the garrison be transferred to Delium in Boeotia, the Romans took the booty but left the city to Attalus. The latter thereupon persuaded both some of the natives and some of the members of the Macedonian garrison to stay and even brought back a certain number of the Andrians who had been trans-

---

[1] The geography of Livy's account is not too easy to follow. However, when he states that the fleet, returning from Cassandrea, after passing Cape Canaestrum also passed *Toronae promuntorium*, he must mean Cape Derrhis at the tip of Sithonia just a short distance from Torone. When he further has the fleet proceed from there directly to Acanthus, he must mean that it sailed across the Singitic Gulf; cf. map in *CAH* v, opposite p. 173. Note also that while this and other maps place Acanthus on the north side of the isthmus, Strabo vii, frag. 33 (Jones, Loeb ed.) definitely places it on the Singitic Gulf and even gives the distance around the peninsula from Acanthus to Stagirus. Arrival of Rhodian ships: Livy xxxi. 46. 6.

[2] Livy xxxi. 46. 1–47. 3.

ferred to Delium. In addition, he must also have stationed a garrison in the city. Since the Pergamene and Rhodian squadrons met there the next spring, it is clear that the city was retained. Oreus too had been given to Attalus, but it is doubtful whether he made any effort to hold the city. Probably there were too many Macedonian strongholds nearby. Or, if he did take possession, the city was soon lost and was in Macedonian hands at the end of the war.[1] Two cities turned over to Attalus and one retained, does not sound like much, but undoubtedly more had been planned. The directors of Roman policy at the time obviously were determined that if any naval power was to be built up in opposition to Macedonia, it was to be that of Pergamum.

The year 198 brought a considerable change in the conduct of the war. Titus Flamininus, a consul of the year, to whom Macedonia was assigned as a province, went out early and took charge of the greater part of the campaign on land. The command of the fleet was assigned by the senate to his brother Lucius, who had served as praetor the preceding year. The nature of his command is not clear, but he may have held a propraetorian imperium.[2] The appointment by the senate was an innovation; the two preceding years the ships sent to operate in the Aegean had been in charge of *legati* appointed by the commander of the army. Thus the senate had given thought to the conduct of the war by sea as well as by land. Further evidence of advance planning is to be seen in the early rendezvous with the Pergamene and Rhodian squadrons. The forces mobilized were considerable. Later in the year, during the meeting at which the Achaeans decided to go over to the Romans, the Achaean general Aristaenus stated that the hostile fleet, aside from lighter vessels, numbered 100 decked ships. The Pergamene squadron which came to Andros that spring consisted of twenty-four quinqueremes; the Rhodian, of twenty decked ships, probably quadriremes. This suggests that the Romans themselves furnished some fifty decked ships, probably mostly quinqueremes.[3] The united fleet was a force large enough to undertake major operations, though apparently not strong enough to capture Chalcis. As it turned out, the fleet operated more in concert with the army than it had done the preceding years. When the two brothers left Italy, the plan of striking with the army through Epirus into northern Greece must already have been adopted. The task of the fleet was to strike at the centre of Macedonian power farther south.

---

[1] Attalus and Andros: Livy xxxi. 45. 6–8; squadrons meet there in 198: Livy xxxii. 16. 6–7; Oreus, Eretria, and other cities at the end of the war to be handed over to the Romans: Pol. xviii. 45. 5; Livy xxxiii. 31. 3. For what it may be worth, note that Andros is not included in the list.

[2] On his command see *MRR* i. 332, n. 6.

[3] The fleets at Andros: Livy xxxii. 16. 6; the statement of Aristaenus: 21. 27.

Here the first ultimate objective seems to have been Chalcis. When the Roman army entered Phocis, this was changed to Corinth.

Lucius Flamininus left Italy with two quinqueremes rather early in the season, but found that the ships at Corcyra already were under way. He caught up with them at Same on Cephallenia.[1] After rounding Cape Malea, since the fleet was slowed by towing supply ships, he himself hurried to Piraeus to pick up the ships that had wintered there. By this time the Pergamene and Rhodian ships had already raided the territory of Carystus but had been prevented from capturing the city by a garrison sent there from Chalcis and had moved on to Eretria, where they were joined by the Romans. The united forces now settled down to besiege the city. Philocles, who still was in command at Chalcis, tried to come to its relief but was driven back, and Eretria ultimately surrendered. Thereupon the fleet returned to Carystus, which now immediately surrendered on the terms that the citizens should go free and that the Macedonian troops in the garrison could be ransomed. From Carystus the fleet then proceeded to Cenchreae. This looks like an admission that Chalcis, if not impregnable, was too difficult for the forces available. Even so, Eretria and Carystus might have given the allies control of Euboea south of Chalcis, but there is no indication that any attempt was made to hold the two cities. Like Oreus, Eretria was soon again in Macedonian hands, and the same is undoubtedly true also of Carystus, unless the city was left ungarrisoned.[2] Without Chalcis, the rest counted for little. Thus the real gain so far amounted to little more than a moderate amount of loot.

More was accomplished when the fleet moved to Cenchreae and prepared to besiege Corinth, though this was accomplished by diplomacy rather than by force of arms. While the Romans were besieging Elatea, Titus Flamininus suggested to his brother that he, Attalus, the Rhodians, and the Athenians send ambassadors to the Achaeans. To hear the ambassadors the Achaeans called an extraordinary meeting of their primary assembly at Sicyon. The result was that the Achaeans decided to abandon their alliance with Macedonia and join the enemy. At the same time they voted that their entire army was to take part in the siege of Corinth. This must have meant the standing army, certainly not a general mobilization. Corinth was now besieged by the joint forces of the Romans, Attalus, and the Achaeans. Nevertheless, Philocles was able to bring 1,500 troops from Chalcis

---

[1] There is some textual difficulty in Livy xxxii. 16. 3, but *ad Samen insulam* seems correct and must refer to Same on Cephallenia. Also in xxxvi. 42. 5 Same seems used as the name of the island.

[2] Livy xxxii. 16. 1–17. 3. For Macedonian control of Oreus and Eretria, see p. 391, n. 1 above.

through Boeotia and the Megarid to the shore of the Gulf of Corinth, whence they were transported in *lemboi* to Lechaeum. Obviously there was no Roman fleet of any size in the Gulf at the time. The arrival of the reinforcements was enough to turn the tables against the besiegers, who burned their seige engines and returned to their ships at Cenchreae. Thence Attalus proceeded to Piraeus, while the Romans returned to Corcyra.[1] Thus again the fleet had failed to gain its chief objective, though the occupation of Cenchreae was of considerable importance. It seems to have been garrisoned by the Pergamenes for the duration of the war.[2] After the war it must have been given to the Achaeans together with Corinth.

Looking back over the three years' naval campaigns, that of 200 may be classed as a hurried minor expedition undertaken in the defence of Athens. The other two seem based on a realization that the Macedonian power in Greece depended largely on the control of Chalcis and Corinth. The expedition of 199 quickly gave up the thought of reaching Chalcis from the south, turned to plundering, and then captured Oreus but apparently made no real effort to hold it. The expedition of 198 again failed before Chalcis, though Livy, our chief source, avoids telling us so. It then turned against Cenchreae and Corinth, and, though the seaport was captured, failed before Corinth, even though also the Achaeans joined in the attack. The war of Rome against Philip certainly was not won by these expeditions. On the other hand, the position of Pergamum was somewhat strengthened by the addition of Andros to its former holding, the island of Aegina. Yet the greatest gain, undoubtedly in large part due to the presence of the fleet, was the detaching of the Achaean Confederacy from the alliance with Philip. Its aid next spring was to keep the Roman operations around Corinth from being a total loss. Even so, the successful detaching of Argos by Philocles, already mentioned, must have seemed to counteract to some extent the gain resulting from the transfer of allegiance on the part of the Achaeans. Yet this particular gain was soon lost by the Macedonians on account of Philip's mistake in entrusting Argos to Nabis.

The year 197, the year of Cynoscephalae, was to prove decisive, though it would not have been easy to foretell this at the beginning of the campaigns. Philip certainly did not act like a leader gambling everything on one venture and the last desperate stand by a single

---

[1] Livy xxxii. 19. 1–6, 23. 4–13. The order of events is not always easily determined. The most charitable explanation of the fact that Philocles could slip through with his relieving force is that the Romans had no naval force to speak of in the Gulf. Their fleet was off Cenchreae.

[2] After the conference with Nabis early next year Attalus returned to his ships at Cenchreae (Livy xxxii. 40. 9).

army. Instead, he was prepared to carry on the war on more than one front, though not on the same scale. Macedonian troops were serving both in Caria and at Corinth, and the forces gathered at Corinth were so large that they clearly were intended not only to defend Acrocorinthus but also to conduct an offensive, as they actually did, at least by raids on the surrounding territory. However, if he hoped thereby to distract the Romans and force them to go to the aid of their allies, he was guilty of a miscalculation. As it was, the Achaeans proved surprisingly efficient in the exercise of self-help. There was resistance to the Romans also in Acarnania, though there were no Macedonian troops on hand. Instead Acarnanian troops were actually serving at Corinth. The operations in the three fields cannot be dated exactly. They are represented as approximately contemporary with each other and with Cynoscephalae.

The operations in Acarnania were a continuation of those of the Roman fleet, which this year did not operate in the Aegean. At the end of the campaign of the previous season, it had returned to Corcyra. From there, early in the spring, Lucius Flamininus sailed to Anticyra with ten quinqueremes. With these he escorted his brother to Sicyon and went with him to the conference with Nabis. Afterwards he took Titus back to Anticyra and then returned to Corcyra to deal with Acarnania. The procedure adopted was one used on other occasions, namely, not to attack if a state could be won by diplomacy or intrigue. Therefore Lucius began by inviting leading Acarnanians to Corcyra and plotting with them. They, in turn, called a meeting of the assembly of the Confederacy at the capital, Leucas. There, though members from some cities failed to show up, and those from other cities opposed the measure, an irregular decree (*privatum decretum*) was passed favouring alliance with the Romans. In the assembly votes were taken by cities, and the abstention of some cities and the negative votes of others apparently were enough to make the decree invalid. Nevertheless, the pro-Roman leaders were prepared to carry it out, but their opponents managed to call another meeting, cancel the offending decree, depose the general of the Confederacy, and condemn the authors of the measure. Yet, with a moderation rare in Greek civil strife, they apparently did not inflict any harsh punishment upon them. As soon as the revocation of the decree of alliance was reported to him at Corcyra, Lucius Flamininus brought his fleet across and laid siege to Leucas. The city resisted desperately but finally fell through treason. Soon afterwards, when the report of Cynoscephalae reached Acarnania, all the other cities of the Confederacy surrendered.[1] After

---

[1] Livy xxxii. 39. 4–7, 40. 7, xxxiii. 16–17. For a fuller discussion see Oost, *Roman Policy in Epirus and Acarnania*, 49 ff.

its capture, the Romans apparently held Leucas until they evacuated Greece and transferred their naval headquarters to it from Corcyra.[1] The campaign in Caria is of interest as much for the soldiers employed as for the outcome. Philip's governor, besides Carians, had under his command 500 Macedonians and a corps of Agrianians, some 400 strong, no doubt also from Macedonia. On the other side, the Rhodian general had in his original force 800 Achaeans. During the campaign he was joined by an additional 1,000 Achaean infantry and 100 cavalry. Thus the Achaean Confederacy, at a time when it had war on its own doorstep, was called upon to send troops overseas to serve at Rhodes. The 800 Achaeans who were there at the outset probably were mercenaries. In the battle fought near Alabanda, rather far north in Caria, the Rhodians and their Achaean allies were victorious.[2] Yet, though this was a defeat for the Macedonians, it did not end their control over cities in Asia Minor. At least four Carian cities were still held at the end of the war and were included among the cities from which Philip was ordered to withdraw his garrisons.[3] Thus Philip's holdings in Caria were not lost as a result of this campaign but were given up after the defeat at Cynoscephalae.

From the point of view of Macedonian interests and participation the most important of the secondary campaigns of the season was the Peloponnesian campaign in the neighbourhood of Corinth. The amount of reinforcements sent by Philip to Corinth is astonishing, showing that he dared detach troops from his main army. The regular garrison at Corinth consisted of 500 Macedonians and 800 mercenaries of various origins. To this there were added 1,000 Macedonians, 1,200 Illyrians and Thracians, 800 Cretans, and a corps of 1,000 light-armed troops from Boeotia, Thessaly, and Acarnania. In addition 700 young Corinthians were mobilized raising the total from 1,300 to 6,000. Of these the Macedonians, Illyrians, and Thracians, and probably also the Cretans, were troops who, had they not been sent south, might have served in the main Macedonian army or somewhere on the home front. This may have been the case also with the Boeotians. They and other allied troops undoubtedly served also as hostages.[4] With these troops Androsthenes, the commander at Corinth, began to raid the surrounding countryside. The Achaean

---

[1] It was from Leucas that Lucius sailed in 195 to take part in the campaign against Nabis.

[2] Livy xxxiii. 18. In this relatively difficult chapter one detail is clear, namely, the arrival of Achaean reinforcements after the campaign had got under way. It is not stated in so many words that they were sent by the government of the Confederacy, but the words *Theoxenus iis praeerat* seem to imply a commander commissioned by the government.

[3] For Euromus, Pedasa, Bargylia, and Iasus see Pol. xviii. 44. 4 and Livy xxxiii. 30. 3 from the Roman *senatus consultum* concerning the arrangements to be made after the peace with Philip; cf. *CP* xxxi (1936), 342–8.

[4] Livy xxxiii. 14. 1–5; cf. Griffith, *Mercenaries*, 71 f.

general of the year, Nicostratus, was stationed at Sicyon with 2,000 infantry and 100 cavalry, a force too small to take the field against the enemy. So, unbeknown to his opponents, Nicostratus called together the militia of the nearby cities and brought them by night to Cleonae. From there he succeeded in falling upon the enemies when they were scattered and defeating them with a loss of 1,500 killed and 300 captured. For mobilizing his troops he must have used a system similar to that used by Philopoemen a few years earlier, with the difference that Nicostratus mobilized not the militia of the entire Confederacy but only a section. Moreover, the efficiency of the mobilization, as well as the subsequent conduct of the troops, indicate that the reforms of Philipoemen were still bearing fruit, though he himself had gone abroad. There were also mercenaries in the Achaean army, no doubt, trained, mobile, light-armed troops. Nicostratus sent a divisign of these ahead to seize a key position. The rest of the infantry followed in two divisions, one consisting of heavy-armed troops or phalangites and one of light-armed troops and mercenaries. In the account of the battle also peltasts (*caetrati*) are mentioned and are grouped with the more heavily armed infantry.[1] For losses in proportion to the numbers engaged, this defeat was disastrous, but even so Corinth was not captured but was retained by the Macedonians to the end of the war.

Thus, in spite of victories of the allies of the Romans in these secondary campaigns, the outcome depended entirely on the Cynoscephalae campaign. This cannot be discussed here except to notice the extent of the casualties. The army of Philip at the time of the battle numbered about 25,000. Of these about 8,000 are said to have fallen and not less than 5,000 to have been captured.[2] All such round numbers can be only approximate. The numbers for the army are probably as correct as any such statistics can be. The numbers for the casualties have probably been exaggerated by the enemies of the Macedonians, but, even so, the losses must have been very heavy. Yet, in some ways, the situation was not entirely desperate for Philip. The Romans had not entered Macedonia, and he still retained the 'fetters of Greece', Demetrias, Chalcis, and Corinth. Hence his readiness to make peace may have been due to the conviction that it might prove more advantageous to co-operate with the Romans in the future than to continue to fight them. Soon after the battle, he sent a herald to Flamininus asking for a truce to bury the dead and for permission to send ambassadors, that is, to open peace negotiations. Both requests

---

[1] Livy xxxiii. 14–15.

[2] Plut. *Flam.* 7 gives the Roman army as over 26,000 and the Macedonian as about the same; the numbers given for the latter by Livy xxxiii. 4. 4–5 add up to 25,500. For the casualties Pol. xviii. 27. 6, Livy xxxiii. 10. 7, and Plut. *Flam.* 8 all give the same numbers. Those of the later authors must be derived from Polybius.

were granted, and in a manner sufficiently friendly and encouraging to offend the Aetolians. When next year one of the Roman commissioners advised Philip to send ambassadors to Rome to negotiate a treaty of alliance, he followed the advice. Though there is no further information, it is safe to conclude that the treaty actually was negotiated.[1] The new ally was to render valuable service to the Romans in their war against Antiochus and the Aetolians, but the acquisition of Macedonia as an ally was to complicate the situation by adding one more to a group of allies with conflicting interests.

The treaty of peace between the Romans and Philip, as far as can be judged from indirect evidence, mostly specified what Philip and the Macedonians had to give up, which included practically everything they held outside Macedonia. The title to all of this passed to the Romans. It was in the settlement that followed that the principle of the freedom of the Greeks was applied,[2] but it was applied in such a way that it was clear that the Roman authorities were decidedly interested in the organization and governments of the states involved. The *senatus consultum* regulating the settlement was brought to Greece by the ten commissioners sent out to co-operate with Flamininus, and it was given wide publicity. It contained a general statement that the Greeks of Asia and Europe, with certain exceptions, were to be free. The exceptions were those subject to Philip and the cities garrisoned by him. These were to be turned over to the Romans before the Isthmian Games of 196. This was followed by a list of cities, mostly in Asia Minor and Thrace, from which Philip was to withdraw his garrisons and set them free immediately. This meant that all former Macedonian holdings became Roman, but that the senate already had decided that those more remote were to be set free at once. The Aetolians were quick to notice that the list of garrisoned cities to be set free in this manner included none in Greece and so charged that at Oreus, Eretria, Chalcis, Demetrias, and Corinth the Macedonian would be succeeded by Roman garrisons. So they actually were, and they continued to be occupied by the Romans to the withdrawal of all troops from Greece in 194.[3] So far the question whether or not the Romans were to retain garrisons in Greece remained an open question. Actually this was a point delegated by the senate to the commissioners to be decided on the spot.

The form in which this is reported is that the commissioners had been given definite instructions on all other points, but that they were

---

[1] Herald sent by Philip: Livy xxxiii. 11. 3–4; advice to Philip concerning treaty: Pol. xviii. 48. 3–5; Livy xxxiii. 35. 5–7. For the attitude of Philip at the time cf. Walbank, *Philip V*, 172 f.

[2] Most of the pertinent passages in the sources are quoted and discussed *Econ. Surv. Rome*, iv. 271–80; cf. *CP* xxxi (1936), 342–8.

[3] The accusation of the Aetolians: Pol. xviii. 45. 3–6; Livy xxxiii. 31. 1–4.

authorized to settle the problem of Chalcis, Corinth, and Demetrias themselves. What caused hesitation was the fear of Antiochus.[1] The debate on this subject shows clearly that the Roman authorities, whatever their motives, considered Greece their future protectorate. It was merely a question whether it was more expedient to hold or give up these forts. The decision to give them up was announced to the Greeks at the Isthmian Games, though the cities were not mentioned by name. The decision to turn the city of Corinth over to the Achaeans immediately, though the Acrocorinthus continued to be held, may have had some value for propaganda purposes. But the proclamation concerned more than these forts. During the period from 198 to 194 the Romans occupied large parts of Greece and created something very much like a provincial organization with Elatea as its capital. The extent to which this was done, though well attested, is seldom noticed. It is generally known that Flamininus occupied Elatea late in 198 and wintered there. It does not seem to be equally well known that he returned there in the autumn of 197 and again wintered there.[2] During the winter troops were sent from there to operate in Boeotia, and, in the spring, when the ten commissioners arrived, they and Flamininus went from Elatea to Anticyra and crossed from there to Corinth for the Isthmian Games and the conference that preceded them.[3] Next year again, the Roman troops that operated against Nabis were brought from Elatea and sent back there in the autumn, while the general evacuation of Greece in 194 began officially when the troops started to march from Elatea through Thessaly and Epirus to Oricus in Illyria.[4] Only the recall of the Roman army prevented the development of a permanent province. Probably the army had been somewhat reduced in 195, but what remained was an army of two legions, a normal consular army.[5]

Though Elatea was the Roman headquarters in Greece, the entire army, aside from the garrisons on Acrocorinthus and in the Euboean cities and Demetrias, cannot have been quartered in the city. The most natural places to quarter the rest of an army which had come to Elatea via Thermopylae, was Phocis itself and Eastern Locris. Troops were also quartered in Boeotia, as is shown by the waylaying there of Romans in 197–196. Moreover, the Romans undoubtedly wished to keep control of the route by which they had come. Hence there must

---

[1] Pol. xviii. 45. 10–12; Livy xxxiii. 31. 4–11.

[2] Pol. xviii. 43. 1 and 7; Livy xxxiii. 27. 5.

[3] Pol. xviii. 45. 7; Livy xxxiii. 31. 7.

[4] Livy xxxiv. 25. 1–3, 41. 7, 48. 2, 50. 9–10.

[5] In connexion with the assignment of provinces for 195 the imperium of Flamininus was prorogued for a year and two legions assigned to him (Livy xxxiii. 43. 6). Next year he was ordered to bring back his army and discharge it (xxxiv. 43. 8).

have been Roman troops stationed in Thessaly and most likely also in Phthiotic Achaea. Now the peoples mentioned in the proclamation at the Isthmian Games were the Corinthians, Phocians, Locrians, Euboeans, Phthiotic Achaeans, Magnesians, Thessalians, and Perrhaebians, with one or two exceptions precisely those whose cities or land had been occupied by the Romans.[1] The correspondence is so close that it is clear that the purpose of the famous proclamation was nothing more or less than to let it be known that the parts of Greece occupied by the Romans were to be set free, with the Roman troops withdrawn, free to govern themselves by their ancestral laws, and exempt from tribute. This promise was eventually kept, but it did not prevent the Romans before withdrawing from adjusting boundaries and forms of government. This, in turn, meant that some sort of conformity to Roman wishes and interests was expected even after the withdrawal of the troops. Such a plan might have worked if there had been some sort of agency for supervising Balkan affairs and maintaining peace in the peninsula. This was precisely what was lacking. There was no single state strong enough to guide and restrain the others, and no league or union of states to secure peace and order through the co-operation of the states.

Trouble began in Boeotia even before the ten commissioners came out from Rome in 196. This Confederacy, which had been brought over by a show of force, and which had had troops serving with the Macedonians even after the home government had chosen the Roman side, asked Flamininus to allow the return of those Boeotians who had served with Philip. This request was granted in the hope, it was said, of winning over the Boeotians by kindness. They responded by electing the chief pro-Macedonian leader, Brachylles, Boeotarch and in general favouring his party so much that the pro-Roman leaders believed or pretended to believe that their lives would not be safe when the Roman troops were withdrawn. They finally suggested to Flamininus that Brachylles be put out of the way. Flamininus answered that he would have no share in the deed, but advised the Boeotians to speak to Alexamenus, the general of the Aetolian Confederacy. The latter thereupon arranged to have Brachylles murdered by three Aetolian and three Italian soldiers. This, at least, is the story reported by Polybius, and it may well be correct that Flamininus more or less encouraged the plotters but avoided being directly involved. The plot succeeded. Brachylles was murdered on his way home from a public dinner, and the murderers escaped in the

---

[1] Pol. xviii. 46. 5; Livy xxxiii. 32. 5 (same names but in different order). Whether Perrhaebia had been occupied by Roman troops is not known. Its inclusion in the proclamation suggests that it had been.

excitement. At first some of those who had been with Brachylles that evening were brought to trial, but suspicion soon fell on leaders of the pro-Roman party, and the Romans themselves were suspected of not being without blame. The result was that Roman soldiers began to be waylaid and killed, to the number of 500, it is said. Surely this number is an exaggeration. Flamininus thereupon demanded that the guilty be surrendered and an indemnity of 500 talents paid. When neither demand was met, he sent ambassadors to the Athenians and the Achaeans to inform them that he was about to wage a just war against the Boeotians and proceeded to invade Boeotia. The Boeotians immediately tried to send ambassadors, but these were not received before the Achaeans and Athenians interceded for them. Thus they secured peace in return for an indemnity of thirty talents.[1] Thus the Romans were given a foretaste of the kind of problems that were to face them in the future.

Even more troublesome was the problem of Nabis of Sparta and especially his control of Argos, a city which had been a member of the Achaean Confederacy and only recently had been acquired by him. In fact, the control of Argos was one of the chief issues in the war between the Achaeans and Nabis which had been cut short by the armistice arranged by Flamininus.[2] This made it inevitable that some sort of action concerning him be taken when the war with Philip had been brought to an end. Moreover, to leave Nabis unchecked would seem to mean giving too much rein to social revolution and thus endanger the control of society by the wealthier people, normally favoured by Rome.[3]

The chief account of the action against Nabis that has been preserved is that of Livy, and it is, strange to say, one of the fullest accounts of any event in the history of the times. It obviously is based on the lost account of Polybius, but it is impossible to say to what extent Livy may have altered it, as in the case of the plot to murder Brachylles, so as to represent the Romans in a more favourable light. There is reason to believe, however, that already the account of Polybius was highly coloured, for a tyrant was involved, and a tyrant was beyond the pale.

[1] The account of Pol. xviii. 43 is preserved only to the formation of the plot to assassinate Brachylles. For the rest, there is only the revamped version of Livy xxxiii. 27–29. That Livy has altered the account somewhat is shown by his omission of any mention of Flamininus and Alexamenus in connexion with the plot, thus placing all blame on the Boeotians themselves.

[2] Livy xxxii. 39. 10.

[3] The execution of helots by Nabis (Livy xxxiv. 27. 9) has been cited as proof that all helots were not liberated by him, but there still is evidence enough that he was regarded as a social revolutionist. Former helots enrolled as citizens (Livy xxxviii. 34. 6) certainly owed their freedom to him. See particularly Aymard, *Premiers Rapports*, 35 and nn. 24 and 25; cf. now also B. Shimron, 'Nabis of Sparta and the Helots', *CP* lxi (1966), 1–7.

There is the additional consideration that Polybius and other ancient historians held that in biographies and monographs the same standard of veracity was not required as in histories with a broader scope. Such works, obviously were now and then drawn on as sources and so affected more serious history. It is perfectly possible that someone had written an account of Nabis as a typical tyrant attributing to him all the vices and excesses associated with tyranny. If so, Polybius may have been influenced by this work, or he may himself have overdrawn the picture.[1] There are actually indications that such an overdrawn account existed and was used by Polybius, namely the accounts of the excessive cruelty of Nabis and especially the story of the instrument of torture in the shape of an image of his wife.[2] This all means that it is impossible to know the truth about Nabis, and yet the main lines of the operations in 195 seem clear enough.

The decision to go to war against Nabis was taken at a sort of Panhellenic congress at Corinth at which Flamininus pretended that the entire decision rested with the Greeks themselves but clearly implied that he took for granted that they would wish to liberate Argos. In the debate that followed, Alexander, the Aetolian general, not only aired all Aetolia's grievances over the settlements so far made but stated plainly that the Romans should withdraw their troops from Greece. In that case the Aetolians would either induce Nabis peacefully to withdraw his garrison from Argos or compel him by force of arms to do so and thus yield to the will of Greece.[3] The Aetolian proposal naturally aroused the ire of the Achaean general, Aristaenus, and the rest of the Greeks agreed with him and voted to go to war unless Nabis surrendered Argos to the Achaeans. This was equivalent to a declaration of war, and consequently the allies were urged to send contingents of troops. This was clearly what Flamininus wanted, though it was in form a resolution of the Greek allies. Yet the decision covered only the disposal of Argos and not the more important question of how to dispose of Nabis himself. Thus the most vital question was reserved for a future decision.

[1] On the attitude of Polybius towards particular histories or monographs see B. L. Ullman, 'History and Tragedy', *TAPA* lxxiii (1942), 25–53 at 42 ff. For a different treatment of the larger question and references to other later literature, see Walbank, 'History and Tragedy', *Historia*, ix (1960), 216–34. For the point that Polybius himself was less strict about veracity in monographs and the like and permitted, for instance, exaggerated praise of a hero in a biography, see his statement about his own life of Philopoemen in x. 21. 8.

[2] Pol. xiii. 7. Niese, *Geschichte*, ii. 565, n. 1 remarks: 'Es klingt wie ein Mythos'; see also Aymard, *Premiers Rapports*, 36, n. 33, who questions not only this story but other implausible details about his persecution of his enemies.

[3] Livy xxxiv. 23.

26

The forces mobilized were surprisingly large. Their composition showed that the war was primarily a war of the Romans and the Achaeans against Nabis. The Roman army was brought by the military tribunes from Elatea to Cleonae near Argos, in all likelihood through Boeotia, and the Megarid and across the Isthmus of Corinth. At Cleonae the Romans were joined by the Achaean general Aristaenus with 10,000 infantry and 1,000 cavalry. Other smaller contingents included Macedonians and Thessalians. Meanwhile Lucius Flamininus brought forty ships from Leucas to the Aegean to operate together with Rhodian and Pergamene squadrons.[1] The Aetolians obviously sent no troops thus indicating their opposition to the project. The total size of the army proper mobilized cannot be fixed, chiefly because there is no information concerning the number of Roman troops involved. The Roman army in Greece probably was a consular army of two legions with the usual number of auxiliaries, but half of this force, more or less, must have been stationed in the many garrisons throughout Greece. This will suggest that the Roman troops operating against Nabis numbered about 10,000. For the final operations against Sparta, when also all available troops from the Roman and allied fleets had been added, the total number is said to have been upwards of 50,000.[2] The Roman-Achaean army first made a demonstration before Argos. When this did not cause a successful revolt within the city, it was decided to pass it by and advance on Sparta itself. The army then crossed the mountains into Arcadia and moved south past Tegea. Since Nabis apparently was not strong enough to risk a pitched battle, the army of the allies was able to proceed past Sparta to Amyclae with only minor skirmishes on the way. Meanwhile the allied fleet had captured the Laconian coastal towns including the important Gytheum.

The terms finally granted Nabis meant that he would have to give up his fleet—he was to be allowed only two sixteen-oared *lemboi*—and any and all possessions outside of Laconia and to renounce making any alliances or waging war together with such allies. A clause pledging Nabis not to interfere with cities which he had given up or which had surrendered to the Romans, meant that he had to give up the Laconian maritime towns which had been captured by the allied fleet.[3] Though this fleet was anything but exclusively Roman, the sur-

---

[1] Livy xxxiv. 26. 10–11.

[2] Livy xxxiv. 38. 3. This number is accepted by such careful scholars as Niese, *Geschichte*, ii. 662; De Sanctis, *Storia*, iv. i. 109; Holleaux, *CAH* viii. 191.

[3] Livy xxxiv. 35. From later events it is clear that these towns were placed under the protection of the Achaean Confederacy.

render of cities was considered a surrender to the Romans giving them the right to dispose of these communities as they wished. These terms would seem to circumscribe the power of Nabis enough to render him relatively harmless, but they were not satisfactory from the point of view of the Greek allies, undoubtedly primarily the Achaeans, who wished to have Nabis completely eliminated.[1] Nabis, on the other hand, found them so severe that he did not give in without further fighting. When he finally decided to give up, he first wished to surrender but was not permitted to do so. Instead an armistice and a preliminary peace on the terms already submitted were arranged. This is a case in which it appears that the Roman commander felt that, if he had accepted the surrender, he would have been under obligation to treat the defeated enemy more mercifully than the terms of the treaty indicated.[2] Soon after the cessation of hostilities, Flamininus appeared at the Nemean Games at Argos and proclaimed the freedom of the city but apparently in such a way that the city had to join the Achaean Confederacy. Nevertheless the Argives celebrated the recovery of their freedom by establishing in honour of Flamininus games known as Titeia, which continued to be celebrated for a considerable time.[3] From Argos Flamininus returned to Elatea with his army, which meant that, except for the garrison of Acrocorinthus, the Romans evacuated the Peloponnesus.[4] This garrison could not be expected to supervise the Roman peace on the Peloponnesus. This unenviable task fell to the Achaean Confederacy.

That the Confederacy actually was assigned this task by implication if not in so many words is shown by the fact that the Laconian towns detached from Sparta were placed by Flamininus under the protection of the Achaeans.[5] This can mean only that the Achaeans were to see to it that Nabis did not regain control of them. The task was complicated by the fact that the towns were not incorporated into the Confederacy. They probably constituted a number of tiny independent communities. At least there seems to be no evidence that they now as later formed a little federal state. It is possible that Flamininus really regarded the solution adopted as the best possible and thought that the incorporation of Sparta into the Achaean Confederacy would

[1] Livy xxxiv. 33. 5–8, reporting the discussion preceding the formulation of the terms offered Nabis.

[2] Livy xxxiv. 40. 3, where *Prima oratio fuit omnia permittentis arbitrio Romanorum* implies *deditio in fidem*.

[3] An inscription from Argos published by G. Daux, *BCH* lxxxviii (1964), 569–76 refers to expenditures for the *Titeia*. Daux dates the inscription about 100 B.C.

[4] Livy xxxiv. 41. 1–4 and 7, 49. 5; 50. 8.

[5] Livy xxxv. 13. 2; xxxviii. 31. 2.

have resulted in even worse difficulties.[1] Who, after observing what happened when Sparta later was annexed, can say that this conclusion was not correct? Yet it was a solution which did not work and could not work. Nabis naturally would seize any opportunity to aggrandize himself, and he had not been so completely shorn of power as to be negligible. The Achaeans, for their part, resented the presence of Nabis and were not likely to be too reasonable in dealing with him. The situation was further complicated by the fact that Elis and Messene, the old allies of Rome and Aetolia, were not members of the Confederacy and were conveniently available for intrigues. Whether the settlement could have worked if the Achaeans had continued to be led by men completely subservient to Rome is now a purely academic question. It was sure to fail when the guidance of Achaean policies was assumed by Philopoemen, who, though ready to perform all duties of a Roman ally, claimed for the Achaeans the right to an independent policy in the Peloponnesus.

In 194 Flamininus, in accordance with orders from the senate,[2] withdrew the Roman army from Greece, but he did more than that. He put the finishing touches on the Roman organization of Greece. After having spent the winter at Elatea 'administering justice' (*iure dicundo*), he summoned a congress of representatives of all states at Corinth early in the spring. The meeting may not have been as inclusive as Livy's language seems to imply. The meeting seems to have been more an assembly called to listen to pronouncements of Flamininus than a real congress. In his address he defended his policy in leaving Nabis in power in Sparta. As for Demetrias and Chalcis, the garrisons would be withdrawn within ten days while those present would themselves see Acrocorinthus turned over to the Achaeans, 'that all might know whether to lie was a habit of the Romans or of the Aetolians'. Then followed admonitions to the Greeks to use their freedom with moderation, the leading men and the members of the upper classes within the various states and all the states, working in harmony and thus showing that they were worthy of the gift the Roman people had bestowed upon them.[3] Finally Flamininus requested that any Roman citizens in slavery in Greece be set free. These were mostly prisoners captured by Hannibal. The Achaean Confederacy alone was said by Polybius to have set free 1,200. At

[1] For an analysis of the arrangements as a whole favourable to Flamininus, see Aymard, *Premiers Rapports*, 229–47.

[2] Livy xxxiv. 43. 8.

[3] In the statement above it is taken for granted that the account in Livy xxxiv. 48–49 is derived from Polybius and is approximately correct. In the admonition concerning harmony, *ordines* is taken to refer to the upper classes.

500 drachmas a head, this cost the state 100 talents. This was undoubtedly the largest single contingent.[1]

Before the assembly was dismissed, the garrison of Acrocorinthus
was seen descending. Flamininus followed it and returned to Elatea.
From there he sent Appius Claudius with the main army through
Thessaly and Epirus to Oricus in Illyria. There he also ordered his
brother Lucius to gather the transports scattered along the coast of
Greece. Meanwhile he himself went to Chalcis, where he had called
a meeting of representatives from the cities of Euboea. Next he withdrew the garrisons not only from Chalcis but also from Eretria and
Oreus and continued on to Demetrias, where there was another
garrison to be withdrawn, and from there on to Thessaly and ultimately through Epirus to Oricus.[2] Clearly the garrisons of Chalcis
and Eretria were evacuated via Demetrias, going north by sea. Had
they taken the route of the rest of the army, they would have been
withdrawn before the army set out from Elatea. It was on this tour that
Flamininus organized the Thessalian and Magnesian confederacies.
This makes it likely that the meeting of the Euboeans at Chalcis meant
a revival or reorganization of the elusive Euboean Confederacy. For
the period after 194 there is evidence in an inscription for a *koinon*
of Euboeans headed by a *hegemon* and possessing also a secretary, a
treasurer, a *boule* and an *ekklesia*.[3] There is not enough evidence to
describe further the functioning of the federal government. Thus the
strongest arguments for a revival in 194 are the manner in which this
fits with the other activities of Flamininus and, above all, the co-
operation of Euboean cities a few years later in opposing Antiochus.

There was a peculiar sequel to the story of Elatea during the war
and the Roman occupation, a sequel known only from an inscription
first published a couple of decades ago. Elatea had been captured in
198 only after Flamininus had opened to the Romans the land route
from Thermopylae to Anticyra and negotiated through his brother
with the Achaeans for the transfer of their allegiance from Macedonia
to Rome. Elatea had resisted stubbornly, but the resistance was due
largely to Philip's garrison in the city. When it finally surrendered, it
was on the terms that the citizens be promised freedom and the
mercenaries of the king allowed to leave unharmed. Thus when the
Elateans soon after were banished, this cannot have been due to

---

[1] Livy xxxiv. 50. 3–7, this time citing Polybius by name; Plut. *Flam.* 13; Diod. xxviii. 13;
Val. Max. v. 2. 6, who states that 2,000 Roman citizens set free in this manner marched in
his triumphal procession.

[2] Livy xxxiv. 50. 8–52. 1.

[3] There is one fragmentary federal proxenic decree for this period, *IG* xii. 9. 898 (899 is a
decree of the city of Chalcis); for federal officials see also *IG* xii. 9. 916. 1–4; cf. the account
of the Euboean Confederacy pp. 97 ff.

Flamininus. It would not only have been contrary to his general policy but also to the special pledge given the city. Moreover, the exiles were given a temporary refuge at Stymphalus in Arcadia, then a member of the Achaean Confederacy. At this moment the Achaeans, who just then had decided to go over to the Romans, would hardly have dared to give refuge to exiles banished by them. The banishment must have been due to the Aetolians, who had received Phocis in the settlement of Greek affairs in 196. The banishment of the Elateans probably followed immediately on the withdrawal of the Romans in 194 and was a natural expression of Aetolian resentment. This too would explain the readiness of Glabrio, called merely *Manios* in the inscription, to restore Elatea to its former inhabitants after the Romans had regained control of central Greece.[1] Glabrio's ruling must have been issued in 191 or early in 190 before the Scipios came to Greece and assumed command.

3. THE AETOLIANS, ANTIOCHUS III, AND THE AFTERMATH

When the Romans went to war beyond the Adriatic, anything the enemy gave up was surrendered to them no matter what allies co-operated with them. This was clearly demonstrated by the Second Macedonian War and the settlement following it. If Pergamum was permitted to keep a city in Greece, it was because Rome so willed. Similarly, when the Greeks were free, they were free by the grace of Rome, but some of them had their boundaries fixed and even the form of government to some extent dictated by the Romans. These detailed arrangements were enough to indicate that the Romans would continue to take an interest and were likely to regard any change as an offence. This must have been realized by the Aetolians, who set out to liberate Greece from the Romans. They apparently thought that this was possible, and that Hellenistic states by uniting could defeat the Romans if necessary. In this effort they even hoped for the aid of Macedonia. Considering the rapidity with which Greek states could change sides if it seemed to suit their interests, this is not too surprising. Hence the success of the Romans in securing the friendship of Philip in 197 or 196 and later an alliance with him, was of the greatest importance.

The plots and intrigues and minor hostilities of the period between the evacuation of Greece by the Romans and the return of major Roman forces in 191 are unusually complicated and certainly not lacking in puzzles. Even so the policies and actions of most Greek states were not too surprising. The greatest surprises came from the Romans themselves. They obviously expected to continue to direct

---

[1] *SEG* xi. 1107; terms of surrender of Elatea; Livy xxxii. 24. 7.

the affairs of Greek states or, better still, have these states automatically function exactly as the Romans would prefer. On the other hand, they do not seem to have been too anxious to go to war. Their difficulties in mobilizing fleets, indicate that they already had begun to neglect naval affairs. Most surprising of all, the distribution of commands in 192 suggests that they actually feared an attack by Antiochus.

Plans for a coalition of Philip, Antiochus, Nabis, and themselves against the Romans were formulated by Aetolian leaders the year after the Roman army had withdrawn from Greece. It is likely that envoys of Antiochus to Rome conferred with the Aetolians on their return journey in 193,[1] but there is no reason to attribute the plans adopted by the Aetolians to these ambassadors or to Antiochus and his advisers, though they probably did nothing to cool the anger of the Aetolians towards Rome. This was the embassy that brought back the virtual ultimatum that the Romans would not meddle in Asia if Antiochus would stay out of Europe—terms not only communicated to the ambassadors of Antiochus but announced also to all ambassadors of Greek cities in Europe and Asia present in Rome.[2] The Aetolians may well have thought that Antiochus would never accede to this and that war was inevitable. However, instead of awaiting developments, they decided to hasten its approach.

Thoas, the general for the year 194–193, was a firebrand and apparently the leader of the war party. Probably rather late in the summer of 193 he called an extraordinary meeting of the Aetolian assembly at Naupactus. There it was decided to send ambassadors to Nabis, Philip, and Antiochus in order to stir them up for war against Rome. Nabis was urged to recover the maritime cities of Laconia; the Romans certainly would not send legions back to Greece merely for their sake. Philip was reminded how strong a stand he had made against Rome when alone, and how much stronger an alliance of the Aetolians and Antiochus with Macedonia would be than Macedonia alone. Antiochus probably was given an overdrawn picture of the support he would find if he intervened. Both Philip and Nabis, he was told, were ready to renew the war. These embassies aroused Nabis to immediate action but only Nabis. From Philip, the Aetolian envoys may have come away with the impression that he would be on their side. Their advice to him is said to have been to

---

[1] Walbank, *Philip V*, 192 deduces that the envoys broke their journey in Aetolia from the fact that one of them, Hegesianax, was made a *proxenos* at Delphi in 193 (*SIG*³ 585, 43); according to the chronology of Daux, *Delphes*, 21 and 188, this belongs in the second half of the year 194–193. For the ambassadors at Rome see Livy xxxiv. 57. 6, 58. 4.

[2] Livy xxxiv. 57–59; Diod. xxviii. 15; Appian, *Syr.* 6.

act only after the army of Antiochus had entered Greece. In spite of the difficulty of knowing what ambassadors actually said, this is probably correct. Certainly no one could expect Philip to reopen the war suddenly by himself. Under the circumstances, Philip undoubtedly failed to tell the Aetolians that, in case of war, he would function as an ally of the Romans. Even if he had fully made up his mind on this point, why should he lay bare his soul to the Aetolians, his enemies for over twenty years?[1]

The developments that followed are complicated and difficult to trace. It is clear that Nabis already in 193 began to plot to secure control of the Laconian maritime towns. He relied largely on intrigue, but found it necessary to besiege Gytheum. The Achaeans, to whom the protection of these places had been assigned by Flamininus, sent an embassy to Nabis to protest, sent troops to Gytheum, and sent an embassy also to Rome to report. The Achaean general for 194–193 is not known but almost certainly belonged to the party which favoured deferring to Rome and avoiding independent action.[2] To send troops to defend a state against attack was not an act of war according to Greek international law. The next year it was still an open question whether war was to be declared or not. Thus the autumn of 193 saw the attack of Nabis on Gytheum, but none of the major powers was involved in war. Yet the course of events was such that the Roman senate in assigning provinces for 192 made preparations for eventual war wherever it might strike, in Greece, in Sicily, or even in Italy. Yet the measures adopted show that the preference was still for settlement by diplomacy. At the same time, the dictatorial and uncompromising attitude towards Antiochus made war inevitable or nearly so, for it still seems to have required the aggressiveness of the Aetolians to get it under way.

Thus was brought on a war that was desired by neither of the two major participants. Antiochus clearly would not have gone to war if the Romans had not interfered in what he considered places that by right belonged to his empire. The Romans, for their part, tried to gain their objectives by threats rather than by fighting.[3] In 196 ambassadors of Antiochus present at Corinth at the time of the proclamation of freedom were told that the king must keep his hands off free cities, must withdraw from those that had belonged to

---

[1] Livy xxxv. 12. The reason for placing the meeting rather late in the summer is that Nabis seems to have acted promptly after the embassy, but, even so, the normal campaigning season was about over.

[2] Livy xxxv. 13. 1–3. For the leadership and policy of the Achaeans at the time cf. Aymard, *Premiers Rapports*, 292 and n. 15, 294–302.

[3] Cf. E. Badian, 'Rome and Antiochus the Great', *Studies in Greek and Roman History* (1964), 112–39.

Ptolemy or Philip, and must not cross into Europe. Later in the year, Roman envoys confronted the king himself at Lysimachea in Thrace.[1] When ambassadors from Antiochus came to Rome in 194 after the return of Flamininus, he and the ten commissioners who had worked with him two years earlier were entrusted by the senate with the negotiations. It was they who formulated the offer that the Romans would not meddle in Asia, if Antiochus would stay out of Europe— proof enough by itself that the Romans were not idealistic champions of Greek freedom. Since the result of the negotiations in Rome naturally was a deadlock, three of the commissioners were sent on an embassy to Antiochus.[2] The composition of the embassy suggests that it was considered very important and that the situation was regarded as critical. One of the three was P. Sulpicius Galba, who had been consul in 211, had served as commander several years during the First Macedonian War, had been consul again in 200 and had been the first Roman commander in the Second Macedonian War. A second member was P. Villius Tappulus, who had served as consul in 199 and had succeeded Galba in the command and had been prominent in the negotiations with Antiochus.[3] The activity of such men in 193 suggests continuity in Roman policy.

At Rome, in the assignment of provinces for 192, the senate at first made no provision for war in Greece except to instruct one consul to be ready to go abroad if the necessity should arise. The six praetors were at first assigned the normal provinces, Sicily, Sardinia, the two Spains, and the two jurisdictions. Later by a *senatus consultum* and a plebiscite, A. Atilius Serranus, who at first had been assigned to Further Spain, was put in charge of the fleet and 'Macedonia', while M. Baebius Tamphilus, first assigned to Hither Spain, was put in charge of two legions and auxiliary troops in Bruttium. The two provinces of Spain were then taken care of by proroguing the imperium of each of the two governors on the ground.[4] This arrangement must mean that the plan of sending one consul abroad was abandoned for that year, but it hardly means that the situation was regarded less seriously. Most surprising was the state of the navy as revealed by the measures taken. Atilius was ordered to build thirty quinqueremes and to launch any old ship that still was usable. Apparently it was not anticipated that many ships would be found seaworthy, for the two

---

[1] Pol. xviii. 47–50; Livy xxxiii. 34. 1–4, 39–40.

[2] Livy xxxiv. 57–59; Diod. xxviii. 15; Appian, *Syr.* 6.

[3] On all such statements concerning the careers of Roman officials see the appropriate entries in *MRR*.

[4] Livy xxxv. 20, where in one passage the names of the two praetors are reversed, but the future operations make it clear that the assignment of commands was the one indicated above.

praetors who were to remain in Rome were ordered to prepare 100 additional quinqueremes.[1] The consuls were also instructed to turn over to Atilius 2,000 allied and 1,000 Roman troops, an indication that the plan to handle affairs in Greece, if necessary, by means of a small fleet and a tiny detachment of soldiers already had been adopted. Meanwhile the return of Roman ambassadors sent to Antiochus was awaited. When they came, Atilius was ordered to proceed to Greece with his fleet. Yet the implementation of Roman policy in Greece was to fall more to a commission headed by Flamininus than to Atilius. With Flamininus were Villius, the consul of 199, Cn. Servilius, consul in 203, and Cn. Octavius, a former praetor. At the same time Baebius was ordered to move his troops from Bruttium to Tarentum and Brundisium, while a contingent of twenty ships was assigned to guard the coast of Sicily and a warning sent to the praetor in charge of the island that Antiochus might attempt to invade it and that he should raise troops and prepare accordingly.[2] These precautions suggest that the senate actually considered an invasion of Italy or Sicily a possibility. The movement of troops to Tarentum and Brundisium served the double purpose of protecting these ports and having the troops in readiness for a transfer across the waters at any moment. Yet the fact that only the fleet of Atilius was ordered to Greece shows that there still was hope that any problems could be settled by diplomacy and a minimum display of force. In the account in Livy the dispatch of the fleet is mentioned before that of the commission, but the course of events shows that Flamininus and his associates arrived in Greece considerably before the fleet.

The early spring of 192 saw Nabis again besieging Gytheum. In retaliation for the aid sent to that city the preceding year, he also raided some of the fields of members of the Achaean Confederacy. This was an act of the kind which was regarded by the perpetrators as self-help to gain restitution for wrongs suffered rather than as an act of war. Whether it would result in war or not depended entirely on the attitude of the other party. Though Philopoemen, probably the most bellicose Achaean leader of the time, was general, the Achaeans did not act immediately but held back until the ambassadors they had sent to Rome the preceding autumn should return. Meanwhile the Achaeans assembled in an extraordinary meeting and decided to send ambassadors to Flamininus to ask his advice. His advice was to the effect that the Achaeans should await the arrival of

---

[1] Livy xxxv. 21. 1. This is a case, and not the only one, in which the praetors to whom the two jurisdictions fell had other tasks to perform than merely to supervise the administration of justice.

[2] Livy xxxv. 22. 1; 23. 5–10.

Atilius with the Roman fleet. The Achaeans, however, voted war but left the time for starting hostilities and the method of conducting the war to Philopoemen. The latter immediately launched some unseaworthy ships and approached Gytheum by sea. The result was a disastrous defeat. The loss was soon recouped in other actions, but this brought no relief to Gytheum. Consequently he decided on a major campaign, but almost before it got under way, Gytheum fell. Philopoemen and the Achaeans nevertheless advanced and inflicted a major defeat on Nabis. At that point it appears that Flamininus imposed a truce upon the belligerents.[1] This all happened in the spring, much of it, and probably all of it, before the *Panaitolika*, the regular spring meeting of the Aetolians, that is, before the normal opening of the campaigning season. This is deduced from the course of events in other parts of Greece.

While the fighting between the Achaeans and Nabis was in progress, the Roman commissioners were making the rounds of Greek states including Athens, Chalcis, Thessaly, and Demetrias, the capital of the Magnesian Confederacy. In the other places it appears that they encountered no trouble, though measures adopted later show that they did not quite trust the Athenians and the Chalcidians. By contrast, at Demetrias there was real trouble. Many of the leaders, including Eurylochus, that year's Magnetarch or head of the Confederacy, were anti-Roman. The situation was rendered more acute by the rumour that the Romans were about to return Demetrias to Philip. At the meeting of the assembly of the Confederacy called to receive the Roman ambassadors, Eurylochus spoke out openly against the Romans. Nevertheless, the pro-Roman group prevailed that day, and Eurylochus fled to Aetolia. There feelings had been brought to a fever pitch by the return from Asia of Thoas, the Aetolian general of 194–193. With him came Menippus, an ambassador from Antiochus who painted rosy pictures of the strength and wealth of the king. It is clear that Antiochus by now was determined on war or considered war inevitable and was doing his best to keep the determination of the Aetolians from weakening. Thoas and Menippus arrived early enough to circulate their propaganda so long before the *Panaitolika* of the year that its nature was reported to Flamininus. To counteract it, he induced the Athenians to send ambassadors to the meeting, and the Athenians in turn secured a hearing for Flamininus personally.

---

[1] Livy xxxv. 25–30, based on Polybius, is the chief account; see also Plut. *Philop.* 14–15; Zonaras ix. 19; Paus. viii. 50. 6–10. On the meeting at Sicyon cf. *Rep. Govt.* 172. The negotiation of a truce by Flamininus is omitted by Livy but is reported by Plut. *Philop.* 15 and placed before the assassination of Nabis; so also Paus. viii. 50. 10, who, however, does not mention Flamininus by name. The course of events is enough in itself to show that there must have been a peace or armistice of some kind at this time.

Nevertheless, in his presence, the Aetolians passed a resolution to invite Antiochus to free Greece and to arbitrate between the Aetolians and the Romans. Livy's account of the Magnesian and Aetolian meetings is unusually vivid. Undoubtedly it is derived from Polybius, who was old enough at the time to preserve a memory of contemporary reports concerning the meetings. Thus the account of Livy is likely to be correct as a whole, though it may be somewhat overdrawn.[1] Consequently no one hesitates to believe that the Aetolian decree was actually passed while Flamininus was present, but the story that, when the latter asked for a copy, the Aetolian general, Damocritus, answered that he would soon deliver it in Italy on the banks of the Tiber, has been suspected. And yet, if the Romans themselves feared an invasion, why should not the Aetolians too believe that such a movement was in the offing?[2] The clause in the Aetolian decree concerning arbitration made it possible for the members of the peace party to make one last effort to avert the inevitable even after Antiochus had entered Greece. Needless to say, both friends and enemies took the decree to mean war and acted accordingly.

The critical decision for some Greek states came before there were Roman forces of any size in Greece. Even Atilius with his little fleet and small detachment of troops did not arrive before very late in the season.[3] Baebius may have crossed to Apollonia on the Illyrian coast somewhat earlier, but he was too remote from the theatres of operation in Greece to intervene before Philip V opened the route through Macedonia to him. Moreover, his troops may not have been very numerous. According to Livy's account, he took along his entire army, which should have consisted of two legions and auxiliary troops, but it is clear that the force he actually brought across was much smaller.[4] Yet his force cannot have been so small as to be negligible. It was big enough for him to send Appius Claudius with 2,000 men to relieve Larisa and still to begin campaigning with the rest of his

[1] Cf. Pédech, La méthode, 266 f.

[2] Livy xxxv. 31–33. The reply of Damocritus is referred to also by Appian, Syr. 21; Zonaras ix. 19. Niese, Geschichte ii. 687 accepts the story and takes it as proof that Damocritus expected soon to accompany Antiochus to Italy; De Sanctis, Storia, iv. i. 137 f. is sceptical; Badian, Studies, 131 and Pédech, La méthode, 267 accept the story.

[3] His appearance off Gytheum after the death of Nabis (Livy xxxv. 37. 1–3) must mean that Atilius had just arrived in Greece. The expedition of Alexamenus to Sparta, his stay there, and the murder of Nabis presuppose that Sparta was at peace at the time but was preparing for the renewal of hostilities and certainly do not suggest that Roman forces were near. The late departure of Atilius for Greece was probably caused by neglect of the navy in the immediate past. This is suggested by the great amount of new construction reported; cf. J. H. Thiel, Studies on the History of Roman Sea-Power in Republican Times (1946), 258–76.

[4] His forces: Livy xxxv. 20. 11; ordered to cross cum omnibus copiis: xxxv. 24. 7. For discussion with references to the literature, see Aymard, Premiers Rapports, 327, n. 14. Walbank, Philip V, 199 estimates his force at 'perhaps 2000 men'.

troops in 191 before the arrival of Glabrio and his army. Thus, when Polybius speaks of the Achaeans as voting to go to war four months before the crossing of the Romans into Greece, this must mean that the troops of Atilius were so few as to be discounted and the army of Baebius so far away as not to be really in Greece.[1]

To return to the Aetolians, after they had voted early in 192 to invite Antiochus, the *apokletoi* took over and definitely acted on the supposition that war was coming. Their plan seems to have been to secure at the outset complete control of the eastern coast of Greece except the territory of the Achaean Confederacy. To this end they planned to secure Demetrias, Chalcis, and Sparta.[2] At Demetrias they were successful in a sense. A certain Diocles was sent with the Aetolian cavalry ostensibly to bring back Eurylochus from exile, but the troops infiltrated the city and put to death the leaders of the opposing party. It is doubtless correct that this action spoiled any chance of securing Philip as an ally.[3] To Sparta was sent Alexamenus, who as general a few years earlier was suspected of having plotted the murder of the Boeotarch Brachylles. Now he was given the task of doing away with Nabis by treachery and taking over Sparta. The plot failed completely. With him were 1,000 infantry and thirty picked cavalry men. The latter had been ordered to obey any order of Alexamenus no matter how strange. This force doubtlessly reached Sparta via Elis and Messene. The Aetolians were able to pose as allies, and their plot worked well up to the point when Nabis was murdered. However, when they tried to take over the city, the Spartans refused to greet them as liberators and put up such a stubborn resistance that Alexamenus and many of his troops were killed. Others who fled to Tegea and Megalopolis were sold into slavery. To make matters worse from the Aetolian point of view, Philopoemen soon appeared on the scene and brought Sparta over to the Achaeans. The Aetolians failed also at Chalcis, where Thoas, a former general of the Confederacy, approached the city with 2,000 infantry and 200 cavalry hoping for the co-operation of traitors but, when the Chalcidians entrusted the defence of their city to the men of Eretria and Carystus and themselves took up a position at Salganeus across the Euripus, the Aetolians withdrew. Thus, of their three projects, two had ended in miserable failures, and these failures were due to local resistance. So far the Romans had contributed little or nothing. After the Aetolian failure before Chalcis, Flamininus

---

[1] Pol. xxxix. 3. 8. It seems that even Atilius had not arrived at the time of the meeting but came soon afterwards.

[2] Livy xxxv. 34–38.

[3] Walbank, *Philip V*, 196.

arranged with Eumenes to station 500 troops in the city. After that came an unsuccessful attempt to win back Demetrias, in connexion with which Flamininus actually had ordered the general of the Thessalian Confederacy to mobilize.[1]

Soon after these events Antiochus arrived with his army of some 10,000 infantry, 500 cavalry and six elephants and occupied Demetrias as his first headquarters in Greece. This was already late in the autumn, for the special meeting of the Aetolian assembly before which Antiochus appeared took place at Lamia in the generalship of Phaeneas (192–191). This means that it took place after the *Thermika* of that autumn and thus after the end of the normal campaigning season. At this meeting Phaeneas made a last effort to avoid a major war by proposing that Antiochus be asked merely to arbitrate between the Aetolians and the Romans, but the more warlike policy of Thoas carried, and Antiochus was elected *strategos autokrator*. Thirty of the Aetolian *apokletoi* were assigned to consult with him. On their advice, his first step was to secure Chalcis. The method first used was again to advance in company with Aetolian leaders and a moderate number of troops and to cross over to Euboea for a conference with Chalcidic leaders, but all this was in vain.[2] To secure Chalcis, stronger action was needed, but before that could be applied, there were other developments of which the most remarkable was an extraordinary meeting of the Achaean assembly at which the Achaeans voted to declare war on both Antiochus and the Aetolians, though the Romans were not yet formally at war with them, and though there were no Roman troops near.

The meeting in question took place at Aegium in the autumn of 192. It was addressed by an ambassador of Antiochus, by at least one Aetolian, and by Flamininus himself. As the Aetolian spokesman is listed a certain Archedamus, who had rendered important services at Cynoscephalae at the request of Flamininus himself. If Livy's account can be trusted, he was very outspoken in his criticism of the ingratitude of Flamininus and went so far as to say that the latter owed the safety of himself and his army to the Aetolians. The ambassadors of Antiochus and the Aetolians did not ask the Achaeans for aid but only requested them to remain neutral. The Achaeans nevertheless voted to have the same friends and enemies as the Romans and to declare war on Antiochus and the Aetolians, and this though the Romans themselves were not officially at war. This decision to

---

[1] Livy xxxv. 39.

[2] Livy xxxv. 43–46. On the Aetolian meetings of the year, cf. *TAPA* lxxxiii (1952), 26. For the title of Antiochus Livy has *imperator*; the Greek title is found in Appian, *Syr.* 12.

subordinate the Achaean policy on the larger issues to that of Rome is said to have had the support of Philopoemen. This must be correct. It was the sort of bold, decisive policy that harmonized with his personality. Later events were to show that he was equally positive in claiming a right to an independent policy in Peloponnesian affairs, but that obviously was not to prove acceptable to the Romans. The assembly decided further, on the request of Flamininus, to send 500 troops to Athens and 500 to Chalcis. Obviously there were still no Roman troops available.[1]

Soon after this Atilius must have reached Greece with his fleet and troops. Antiochus is reported to have hastened to move against Chalcis after he learned that both Eumenes and the Achaeans had sent troops there. These troops garrisoned Salganeus on the Euripus opposite Chalcis. Also 500 troops were sent by Flamininus. These troops who suddenly appear on the scene must have come from the fleet of Atilius. When they drew near, they found their way blocked by a detachment of the army of Antiochus under the command of Menippus. Thereupon they withdrew to Delium, where it is said they wandered around unarmed trusting to the inviolability of the sanctuary and the fact that war had not been declared. Nevertheless, Menippus staged an attack with the result that most of the Roman soldiers were massacred. After that the city of Chalcis surrendered and members of the pro-Roman party went into exile. Somewhat later the Pergamene and Achaean troops at Salganeus surrendered the fort and were allowed to leave under a safe-conduct. The other cities of Euboea followed the example of Chalcis and Antiochus thus secured control of the island.[2]

The task of winning the war was made easier for the Romans by the mistakes of the Aetolians. By securing Demetrias, and probably also by exaggerated statements concerning the readiness of Greece to co-operate, the Aetolians caused Antiochus to hasten to Greece with a relatively small army. Yet the inadequacy of the army should not be exaggerated. If Greece had been ready to fight, 10,000 trained soldiers would have been a valuable addition, but judging by their later conduct, the Greeks seemed to expect the king to scatter garrisons broadcast over the country and in addition maintain an army adequate for battle. The Aetolian failure at Sparta had had far-reaching effects. Sparta itself, instead of being an Aetolian stronghold,

---

[1] Livy xxxv. 48–50. 4. For Archedamus at Cynoscephalae, Pol. xviii. 21. 5–6; Philopoemen's support of the decree: Pol. xxxix. 3. 8. De Sanctis, *Storia*, iv. i. 149 f. characterizes the Achaean policy as treason to the Greek cause.

[2] Livy xxxv. 50. 6–51. The story that a small group of Romans held a fort on the Euripus and defended it stubbornly even after the Pergamene and Chalcidic troops had withdrawn is obviously apocryphal.

had been taken over by the Achaeans, and the Peloponnesian states siding with Aetolia and Antiochus felt in need of help. The request came from Elis to Antiochus, and he felt obliged to send a thousand men who remained in Elis until after the defeat of Antiochus at Thermopylae. Nothing is heard of Messene at this time, but it is likely that the troops stationed in Elis served indirectly also to protect Messenia.[1] Troops stationed in Messenia would have been more isolated; stationed in Elis, they were in closer touch with Aetolia if not with the army of Antiochus himself. Yet there was nothing Antiochus could afford less than to decrease his main force in this manner.

The autumn of 192 also saw important operations in Thessaly which seemed on the way to bring great gains to Antiochus and his allies but were frustrated by Roman troops sent from Illyria through Macedonia on the invitation of Philip. A conference, including Aetolian leaders and Amynander of Athamania, was summoned to Demetrias. The plan adopted called for immediate action against Thessaly, though winter was approaching. While troops were mobilizing near Pherae, Antiochus sent Philip of Megalopolis with 2,000 men to bury the bones of the Macedonians fallen at Cynocephalae, thereby gravely offending Philip, who immediately got in touch with Baebius the Roman commander in Illyria and proposed a conference. This was to have serious effects for the allies, but meanwhile their combined armies went into action. They began by besieging and capturing Pherae. From there they did not move by the direct route against Larisa but advanced south of the ridge which cuts across the plains of Thessaly and secured much of western Thessaly before moving against Larisa. At this juncture, the camp fires of what appeared to be a huge army were seen above Gonni at the exit of the Vale of Tempe. After a conference with Philip, Baebius had sent a force of 2,000 men under Appius Claudius through Macedonia. By means of the simple stratagem of laying out an unnecessarily large camp and lighting extra camp fires, Appius had induced Antiochus to give up the attack on Larisa.[2] Antiochus, however, does not seem to have realized the significance of the co-operation of Philip with the Romans and, though Roman troops had come to Thessaly through Macedonia, he seems to have thought that the main Roman army would, as before, advance from Illyria through Epirus. That this was the expectancy also in Epirus is shown by the Epirote embassy which appeared before Antiochus late in 192.

---

[1] Pol. xx. 3; Livy xxxvi. 5. 1–3, 31. 3; cf. Roebuck, *History of Messenia*, 91 f.

[2] Livy xxxvi. 6–10; Appian, *Syr.* 16. On Philip's aid to the Romans cf. *CP* xxxviii (1943), 57 in a review of Walbank, *Philip V.*

Among the first embassies to appear before Antiochus at Chalcis was this embassy from Epirus headed by Charops, who in 198 had aided Flamininus in turning the position of Philip. The plea of the Epirotes was that Antiochus should not involve them in war and then leave them exposed to fight the Romans by themselves. If he could take up a position on the frontier of Epirus and defend the country, they would receive him in their cities and ports. If not, they must be forgiven for fearing to go to war against the Romans. Thus they indicated clearly that, if no help was sent, they would not resist the advance of the Romans. The king answered that he would send ambassadors to discuss their common interests.[1] The projected embassy probably was never sent, for the Romans did not choose to advance through Epirus. Before he was aware of this, Antiochus undertook operations in Acarnania early in 191. As far as can be judged from the one confused account transmitted to us, Antiochus ordered a general mobilization and sought to secure control of Acarnania before moving north into Epirus. Troops advancing from Illyria through Epirus into Thessaly need not—and normally did not—pass through Acarnania, but it would have been decidedly uncomfortable for an army operating in Epirus to have the enemy establishing himself in Acarnania in its rear. Since Acarnania was of special interest to the Aetolians, it is surprising that he did not meet with better success even though he was aided by Acarnanian traitors or super-patriots. He secured Medeon and a number of other cities but obviously not the important seaport of Leucas, and he failed before Thyrrheum. The failure was in part due to the rumour spread by Roman ships at Leucas to the effect that the consul, Acilius Glabrio, already was in Thessaly with his army. Thereupon Antiochus returned to his winter quarters at Chalcis, leaving behind garrisons at Medeon and certain other towns, thus again weakening his army.[2]

While Antiochus was in Acarnania, Philip and Baebius began an attack from the north on the parts of Thessaly controlled by their opponents. After the two had got together in the autumn at the time Appius Claudius was sent to Larisa, they had gone into winter quarters. For Baebius this must have meant returning to the Illyrian coast, but early in the spring he was back with whatever troops were available—how many is not known. It may well have been in connexion with these operations that Philip first was promised that he could keep certain cities which he captured. When it came to the actual invasion of Thessaly, the two advanced by different routes. Philip advanced down the valley of the Europus river, where he was held up by the resistance

---

[1] Pol. xx. 3; Livy xxxvi. 5; cf. Oost, *Roman Policy in Epirus and Acarnania*, 59 f.
[2] Livy xxxvi. 11. 5–12. 11; Appian, *Syr.* 16 (too brief to be of much help).

27

of Malloea in Perrhaebia. Baebius probably entered Thessaly by the Vale of Tempe and, operating out of Atrax west of Larisa captured Phaestus and Phacium, thus opening the door to western Thessaly. Then he turned back to Atrax and moved up the Europus valley to Malloea. After the surrender of this city, the combined forces moved into western Thessaly, most of which was reduced before the main Roman army under Acilius Glabrio arrived on the scene.[1]

One point about the advance of Glabrio that seems clear but is seldom mentioned, is the fact that he must have advanced from his port of debarkation through Illyria and Macedonia by approximately the same route as Baebius had taken and so approached Thessaly from the north. The infantry was sent directly to Larisa, where the army was given a few days of rest chiefly for the sake of the army mules (*iumenta*), which were tired by the sea voyage and the marches after debarkation. Thus, this time at least, the Romans brought baggage animals with them and started on the march immediately after debarkation.[2] The use of this route was due to the friendship and co-operation of Philip, a fact which our sources apparently deliberately pass over when they merely report that the consul crossed the ocean and appeared in Thessaly. Of course, the mere fact that he first appeared near Larisa is proof enough that he entered Thessaly from the north, that is, that he came through Macedonia.

The Thermopylae campaign of 191 will not be taken up at any length. The reinforcements coming from Asia to Antiochus were disappointingly small. According to the reports preserved, they were just sufficient to make up for the troops placed in garrisons and those lost by capture or desertion as Philip and the Romans advanced through Thessaly. Thus, with only 10,000 infantry and 500 cavalry and the Aetolians mobilizing 4,000, there was nothing to do but to stand on the defensive and wait for reinforcements. The combined forces of Antiochus and the Aetolians were smaller than the Roman army alone, not counting the Macedonians. Nevertheless, with Antiochus holding Thermopylae and having garrisons at Chalcis and Demetrias, the situation need not be hopeless as long as the position at Thermopylae was not turned. The task of guarding the paths over the mountains naturally fell to the Aetolians. When Cato succeeded in dislodging one of the Aetolian detachments and bore down upon

---

[1] Livy xxxvi. 13. What little is said above about the movements of troops is deduced from the order in which cities were captured. That Baebius operated out of Atrax is shown by the statement that he later 'returned' there (13. 4). The agreement permitting Philip to retain certain cities captured by him (Livy xxxix. 23. 10, 25.5) must have been made before these operations. Thus the agreement was first negotiated by Baebius and probably renewed later by Acilius Glabrio.

[2] The approach of the army: Livy xxxvi. 14. 1; rest at Larisa: 14. 10.

the army of Antiochus, it took to flight. Antiochus himself escaped to Chalcis with 500 men. The rest were killed, captured, or scattered, probably largely scattered.[1] The elephants brought up the rear of the army of Antiochus and delayed the pursuers. Moreover, they pursued that day only to Scarphea, a few miles beyond the battlefield, returned to camp, and resumed the pursuit next day. From Chalcis Antiochus sailed to Ephesus thus enabling the enemy to take over Euboea without opposition. Some of his ships which were in the Malian Gulf sailed to Demetrias and remained there till Philip took over the city.[2] Even after Thermopylae, Antiochus continued to control the sea in the Aegean. The fleet starting from Ostia or thereabouts had not yet arrived, and the squadron of Atilius was not strong enough to interfere. Yet the flight was sufficiently headlong so that the Romans not only were able to lay their hands on royal silverware to grace the triumph of Glabrio but also a considerable number of *cistophoroi*, coins which must have been brought along from Asia.[3] In the accounts of the Thermopylae campaign there is no mention of Philip. Though he had been prominent in the operations in Thessaly, he did not take part in the battle. Later he alleged illness as an excuse, but it has been suspected that the real reason was dissatisfaction with the way he had been treated.[4]

After Thermopylae the Aetolians probably were given a chance to make peace on favourable terms, but, if so, the negotiations failed. If terms were offered, this need not mean that Glabrio personally favoured the move. Clearly the Roman leaders in Greece were not always in agreement, and the consul may often have had differences with the men that surrounded him. Flamininus was still in Greece and did not mind giving Glabrio the benefit of his own superior knowledge and understanding. Moreover, the consul had on his staff or in his army in some capacity or other two former consuls, Cato and Valerius Flaccus, the consuls of 195. After Thermopylae Glabrio sent Cato home to report. Was this to get rid of a troublesome critic? Flaccus, it will be noted later, favoured more lenient treatment of the Aetolians than Glabrio did. With Flamininus Glabrio clashed over the treatment of the Chalcidians, and Flamininus carried the day and was honoured by the Chalcidians by deification with a typical Greek

---

[1] Many made their way to Demetrias (Livy xxxvi. 33. 4).

[2] The chief source accounts are Livy xxxvi. 14–21; Appian, *Syr.* 17–20; and for Cato's role, Plut. *Cato* 13–14, who also emphasizes the panic in the army of Antiochus. Livy too mentions the panic but states that the elephants and the fortifications delayed the pursuers. He also mentions their return to camp. The ships which had sailed from the Malian Gulf to Demetrias (20. 5–6) were still there when Philip approached (33. 7).

[3] Livy xxxvii. 46. 3; cf. *Econ. Surv. Rome*, iv. 318 f.

[4] Philip alleges illness: Livy xxxvi. 25. 1. Walbank, *Philip V*, 204 thinks that Philip felt that he had been humiliated by the Romans.

cult expressing gratitude to a benefactor. This cult was still maintained in the days of Plutarch. The hymn still used emphasized the *pistis* (*fides*) of the Romans.[1] This must mean that the Chalcidians threw themselves on the mercy of the Romans by a *deditio in fidem* and were leniently treated. A communication from Glabrio to the Aetolians implied that other Greek states which had joined the war but had repented had been given the same lenient treatment, and that the Aetolians themselves, though they had started the war and had invited the king, if they would repent, would receive the same treatment and go unpunished.[2] This offer means that even in 191, before the rejection of the Roman offer by the Aetolians, the Romans were still treating those who surrendered in this manner with leniency. The change came with the negotiations with the Aetolians later in the year.

The result of the Aetolian rebuff of the peace overtures was that the war in Greece was continued as a war of the Romans and the Macedonians against the Aetolians and took the form of a series of sieges. In the first stage the Romans besieged Heraclea while Philip besieged Lamia. During this period the Aetolians maintained almost a temporary capital at the nearby Aenian city of Hypata. This apparently lay far enough off any main line of communication so that the Romans did not try to capture it even when they moved on to Naupactus. Of the two cities besieged, Heraclea fell first. The city was taken by storm and the soldiers were allowed to plunder in order that they who had 'so often been restrained when cities had been recovered from the enemy', might enjoy the fruits of victory. This was perfectly in accord with the usages of the time but seems to mark a definite change in policy. Immediately after the capture of Heraclea, the consul ordered Philip to withdraw from Lamia, and this city was for the time being left to itself.[3]

Shortly after the fall of Heraclea came another effort to negotiate peace, the initiative this time coming from the Aetolian peace party led by their general Phaeneas. Shortly before the fall of Heraclea, his opponents had been strong enough to secure the dispatch of ambassadors to Antiochus to ask him to intervene again in Greece or at least send money. For the present the king sent money but promised armed intervention by land and sea for the future. As luck would have it, Nicander, the Aetolian ambassador entrusted with the money, landed at the Malian port of Phalara after Philip had raised the siege

---

[1] The exact status of Cato and Flaccus is debated but matters little. Livy xxxvi. 17. 1 calls them *legati*; Pol. xx. 10.10 calls Flaccus a *chiliarchos*, i.e. a military tribune. Glabrio sends Cato to Rome: Livy xxxvi. 21. 4; Plut. *Cato* 14. Flamininus and the Chalcidians: Plut. *Flam.* 16.

[2] Livy xxxvi. 22. 1–3.   [3] Livy xxxvi. 22–25.

of Lamia and was able to bring it safely that far. When he tried to make his way from there to Hypata, he fell in with a Macedonian outpost and was captured but was given a friendly reception by Philip and released. His report concerning the promises of the king may have contributed to the decision of the Aetolians to continue the war. Before his return they had sent three ambassadors to Glabrio to try to negotiate an armistice and peace. These were informed by Glabrio that he was too busy disposing of the booty taken at Heraclea to confer with them, but he did grant an armistice of ten days and sent Valerius Flaccus to negotiate with the Aetolians. Though the reference to the booty does not sound tactful, the refusal to negotiate personally may not have been meant as an affront. The man assigned to the negotiations was, after all, a former consul and senior to Glabrio and thus seemed an excellent choice for the task.

What followed seems to show that Flaccus was more inclined to leniency than Glabrio. Flaccus returned to Hypata with the Aetolian ambassadors and there consulted, apparently, with the *apokletoi* and chief magistrates. It is easy to believe that the Aetolians talked too much about their past services to the Romans and sought to justify themselves, though it is well to remember that Polybius, from whom most of our information ultimately is derived, was far from friendly to the Aetolians. Flaccus, at any rate, seems to have advised the Aetolians not to argue but to surrender and throw themselves on the mercy of the Romans. This is exactly what they proposed to do expecting that a *deditio in fidem* would be followed by lenient treatment, as it had been in other cases that very year. They certainly were not aware how completely, according to Roman ideas, those who surrendered were at the mercy of the victors. What followed was most unfortunate, unless Glabrio deliberately set out to make reconciliation impossible. The Roman officers must have known that Phaeneas was the leader of the peace party among the Aetolians and that their best chance of negotiating a peace came through co-operation with him. Yet, because he spoke up about what, in his opinion, was and was not proper, Glabrio, to demonstrate the meaning of *deditio*, caused chains to be put on the ambassadors. Thereupon Flaccus and 'other military tribunes' urged him not to treat them harshly, since they were ambassadors. When Glabrio gave in, Phaeneas stated that he and the *apokletoi* would do as ordered but that the peace required the approval of the assembly of the Aetolians. To enable such a decision to be made, an additional ten days armistice was granted. The explanation of this strange situation is probably that after *deditio* the victors could have executed or carried off in chains any number of citizens or officials of the surrendering state, but, nevertheless, public opinion would condemn the abuse of ambassadors while functioning as such. Moreover, the treaty or act of surrender had not been ratified by the Aetolian assembly and so was not yet valid. Phaeneas, all the same, felt that he and the *apokletoi*, who had offered to surrender, were in honour bound by their word. In this incident, the despised Aetolian comes off better than the Roman consul. Stragetically too the consul was foolish. His insult to their general so angered the Aetolians that they rejected the proposed act of surrender, apparently by boycotting the meeting at which it was to be considered. The arrival about this time of Nicander with encouraging and, therefore, deceptive messages from Antiochus also helped to confirm the Aetolians—so often optimistic at the wrong time—in their resolution to continue to resist. When the armistice lapsed, the war was again resumed.[1]

When the hostilities were resumed, the Romans made their way across the mountains from Heraclea to Naupactus without meeting with opposition from the Aetolians and then proceeded to besiege the latter city. That was another story. The Aetolians defended themselves energetically and the siege dragged on. Meanwhile the Achaeans were taking steps to secure the adhesion of Elis and Messene to their Confederacy. They began with diplomatic representations. The Achaeans, no more than the Romans, cared to fight for what they could have for the asking. The Eleans, who earlier had requested and received a garrison from Antiochus, replied that they would dismiss the garrison and take their future course of action up for consideration. This took time but led to the Eleans joining the Confederacy. The Messenians, on the other hand, dismissed the Achaean ambassadors without reply and prepared for hostilities. When the result was that their country was overrun by the Achaeans, the Messenians sent to Flamininus, then at Chalcis, and offered to surrender the city to the Romans. There is no indication that the surrender was accepted, though Flamininus took upon himself to set matters right. He ordered Diophanes, the Achaean general, to withdraw the Achaean troops from Messenia and the Messenians to join the Confederacy. If any disputes should arise, they could appeal to himself at Corinth. At the same time he directed Diophanes to summon an extraordinary meeting of the Achaean assembly. From this he secured the cession to the Romans of the island of Zacynthus, which by a complicated series of incidents had recently come under Achaean control. The fact that a special *synkletos* was summoned shows that Flamininus wished to drive

---

[1] Pol. xx. 9–11; Livy xxxvi. 26–29, differing from Polybius in a number of details. Thus he states (27. 7) that Flaccus actually promised the Aetolians to support them both before the consul and before the senate at Rome. For a discussion of the Aetolian meetings involved in the negotiations, cf. *TAPA* lxxxiii (1952), 26–28.

home a lesson, which must have been that, while the Achaeans might expand within the Peloponnesus, they would not be allowed to extend their control to any island west of the peninsula. Certainly, in spite of his simile comparing the Achaean Confederacy to a turtle which is safe as long as it does not expose any part of its anatomy outside its shell, he did not have the good of the Achaeans in mind. Nor is it likely that the cession to Rome meant that he intended to establish any more direct control over the island than over other parts of Greece.[1]

Meanwhile, Philip, after reaching an agreement with Glabrio allowing him to conquer cities which had deserted the Roman alliance, proceeded against Demetrias, reducing cities along the Malian Gulf on the way. Demetrias surrendered without resistance, and it probably is the truth when Livy states that its citizens were less afraid of Philip than of the Romans. Even so some of the anti-Macedonian leaders went into exile and one committed suicide. The troops of Antiochus within the city, by the terms of the surrender, not only were permitted to leave but, for their safety's sake, were escorted through Macedonia and Thrace to Lysimachea by a Macedonian guard, much as the Roman army was escorted and protected the next year. Also the few ships of Antiochus present at Demetrias were allowed to leave. When Philip earlier had aided the Romans in Greece, this had been done in order to gain advantages for himself and his Macedonians. The total elimination of the power of Antiochus was not a part of his programme.[2]

While this was going on, Glabrio continued the siege of Naupactus without success. This was too much for Flamininus, whose activities often must have irked Glabrio. On this occasion he is represented as scolding Glabrio for wasting time on the siege while Philip was aggrandizing himself. The incidental remark that Glabrio's year of command was almost over, sounds like an advance warning that his imperium was not going to be prorogued. Glabrio, hesitating to admit that the siege had failed, turned the matter completely over to Flamininus. This must mean simply that he decided to follow the latter's advice, for he took charge himself of the negotiations which followed. Before this Flamininus had already shown himself to the besieged and now repeated the performance, advising the Aetolians to ask the consul for an armistice to send ambassadors to Rome to entrust their affairs to the senate. He himself would plead their case before the consul. This sounds much like deditio. There were no

---

[1] Livy xxxvi. 30–32, 35. 7; Plut. Flam. 17.

[2] Livy xxxvi. 33. Clearly Philip had not yet established his control of the coast of the Malian Gulf at the time when Nicander could land at Phalara and proceed from there to Lamia.

conditions stipulated in advance, but everything was left to the senate. The one difference was that the Aetolians were free to accept or reject the terms to be offered. When an armistice had been granted on these conditions, the siege was lifted and the Roman army went into winter quarters in Phocis, where it had been stationed a few years earlier under Flamininus.[1]

Details in the incident just discussed remain obscure, but it at least seems clear that Flamininus had asserted his ascendancy over the Roman commander-in-chief. Undoubtedly he would have liked to impose on Greece a peace dictated by himself. Furthermore, he undoubtedly viewed with alarm the extension of the power of Philip, though he himself had taken the first steps towards bringing about the reconciliation of Philip with the Romans. He also must have realized that the reduction of Greek cities by Philip was a violation of the freedom of the Greeks, which had been his pet policy. Apparently there was nothing he could do about this problem at the moment, and so he turned in another direction.

Flamininus, having settled the Aetolian question for the time being, took Glabrio along and crossed to Aegium to deal with the Achaeans, whom he apparently found harder to dominate than the Roman consul. Earlier in the year the Achaeans had accepted the virtual arbitration of Flamininus in the matter of the Messenians, and had lost nothing by so doing. They had also given way on the question of Zacynthus. But there had been an incident which showed that they would not yield on all points. The situation probably was aggravated by the personal hostility of Flamininus and Philopoemen. The incorporation of Sparta into the Achaean Confederacy had been arranged by Philopoemen without Roman advice or permission. When, after the murder of Nabis, Sparta had been hurriedly admitted into the Confederacy, the city was taken as it had been left by Nabis without the restoration of the wealthy men exiled by him. This is proved by their later restoration by the Achaeans. The situation must have been unsatisfactory to many. Hence it is not surprising that soon there was unrest of some sort at Sparta. When the Achaean general, Diophanes, prepared to intervene, Philopoemen advised against it, but Diophanes insisted and marched on Sparta accompanied by Flamininus. At that point Philopoemen hurried to Sparta, closed the gates of the city on Diophanes and Flamininus, and brought about a peaceful settlement. This brought him great popularity among the Achaeans and, for the time being, also in Sparta.[2] Yet, whatever was settled at the time, the

---

[1] Livy xxxvi. 34–35. 6, an account completely centred on Flamininus.

[2] Plut. *Philop.* 16; Paus. viii. 51. 1–2; cf. De Sanctis, *Storia*, iv. i. 169 f.; Aymard, *Premiers Rapports*, 330–8; Walbank, *Philip V*, 208, n. 3.

problem of the exiles, obviously largely members of the upper classes, remained. This problem was brought to the front by Flamininus in the fall of 191 when he and Glabrio were present at a meeting of the Achaeans at Aegium, apparently a regular meeting of the Achaean council (*synodos*) and probably the one at which Philopoemen was elected general for the year 191–190. At the time Flamininus broached two subjects, the admission of the Eleans into the Achaean Confederacy and the problem of the Spartan exiles, but was rebuffed on both issues. The Eleans preferred to do their own negotiating with the Achaeans, and the Achaeans wished to reserve the credit for restoring the exiles to themselves.[1] Thus it seemed that Philopoemen, in spite of the intervention of the Romans in the case of Messene, had been able to carry through fairly successfully his claim to an independent Achaean foreign policy in the Peloponnesus, but his victory, if it was a victory, was to prove very short-lived.

The naval campaign of 191 is significant largely as a foretaste of what was to come the next year and as an illustration of the extent to which Rome already was beginning to depend for her naval power on Greek or Hellenistic allies. The extensive use of Greek *socii navales* from southern Italy was of long standing. In addition, in the wars in the east, the allies of Rome, particularly the Rhodians and the Pergamenes, contributed a great deal. This year the Roman fleet was relatively late to get under way and did not arrive in the Aegean in time to interfere with the retreat of Antiochus. C. Livius Salinator, the praetor assigned to the fleet, sailed 'from Rome', which probably means Ostia, to Naples with fifty quinqueremes.[2] These were supplemented by undecked ships which allied cities, according to the terms of their treaties, had been ordered to send to Naples. Others were later picked up at Rhegium and Locri. On the way Livius was also joined by six Carthaginian ships, which, to judge by the count of ships later given, were decked ships. After he had effected a junction with the squadron of Atilius, he is credited with eighty-one decked ships, counting the ones he had brought from Rome, the twenty-five he had found waiting for him in the Aegean, and the six Carthaginian ships, probably all quinqueremes. In addition, he had a number of lighter ships which had been furnished by the Greek allied cities in Italy. With this force he sailed across the Aegean to the neighbourhood of Erythrae. By this time Antiochus was back in Asia mustering his forces. His fleet, under the command of Polyxenidas, a Rhodian exile,

---

[1] Livy xxxvi. 35. 7–8. For the Achaean meetings of the year cf. *Rep. Govt.* 173.

[2] Livy xxxvi. 42. 1 has *cum quinquaginta navibus tectis*, but had reported for the previous year the plan to prepare 100 quinqueremes (xxxv. 21.1). The ships of Livius must have been those of this number that were ready and available.

with headquarters at Ephesus, contained seventy decked ships. Thus, in this department his fleet was outnumbered by the Romans. In addition, though faster, these ships were smaller, apparently largely quadriremes.[1] It is possible that the fleet of Polyxenidas made up for its deficiency in decked ships by a great number of lighter vessels, possibly even as many as 130.[2] He hastened to try to fight the Romans before they were joined by the Pergamene and Rhodian fleets. Eumenes, however, managed to join the Romans with twenty-four decked ships and a slightly larger number of lighter vessels. Polyxenidas, nevertheless, prepared for battle but was defeated at the battle of Corycus with the loss of thirteen ships captured and ten sunk. Further losses were prevented by the greater speed of the ships of Antiochus. The Roman victory seems to have been due to the use of grappling hooks. The defeated fleet withdrew to Ephesus. The day after the battle a Rhodian squadron of twenty-five decked ships joined the Romans. Soon after this the Romans sent the Pergamene and Rhodian fleets home and established their own winter quarters at Canae near the Pergamene port of Elaea.[3] This in itself indicates that they were determined to carry the war into Asia.

News of the victory at Corycus reached Rome at about the time the consuls for 190 assumed office on November 18.[4] After the proper religious rites, the first business taken up by the senate, even before the assigning of provinces, was the negotiation with the Aetolian ambassadors. The reason given by Livy is that the truce was about to expire. Probably equally important was the fact that the assignment of provinces and the allocation of troops might be affected by the outcome of the negotiations. The debate in the senate probably represented a contest between the policy of Flamininus, who gave some support to the Aetolians, and the harsher policy of Glabrio, and it was

[1] The largest ships in the fleet of Antiochus are classed as triremes by Thiel, *Roman Sea-Power*, 274 on the basis of Livy xxxvi. 43. 8, where they are spoken of as *minoris formae* in comparison with the Roman quinqueremes. But quadriremes were used extensively by the Rhodians and it would be natural for the navy of Antiochus to use this type. As an example of the use of quadriremes, note the squadron of Roman quinqueremes and Rhodian quadriremes sent to attack Patara in 190 (Livy xxxvii. 16. 1–3).

[2] Livy xxxvi. 43. 8 gives the total number of his fleet as 100, of which seventy were decked ships; Appian, *Syr.* 22 gives the total as 200. Thiel, 273 f. argues that the latter number is correct and that Livy's text too should have this number, which, if written CC, could easily be corrupted in the transmission of the text.

[3] Our knowledge of the campaign and battle depends largely on Livy xxxvi. 42–45. On the many problems involved, cf. Thiel, *Roman Sea-Power*, 293–310.

[4] It is well known that the Roman calendar in this period was maladjusted in such a manner that the consuls, who assumed office on the Ides of March, actually did so months before March 15. For this year the extent of the maladjustment is known. The eclipse which Livy xxxvii. 4. 4 reports for *a.d. quintum idus Quinctiles* (July 11) has been fixed at March 14. Thus when the Roman soldiers were ordered to appear at Brundisium on the Ides of Quinctilis, the date was actually March 18; cf. Walbank, *Philip V*, 332.

the latter policy which prevailed. The Aetolians were given the choice between two alternatives, either to entrust everything to the Romans, that is, to surrender unconditionally, or to pay an immediate indemnity of 1,000 talents and accept a treaty pledging them to have the same friends and enemies as the Romans, that is, to give up an independent foreign policy and instead subordinate their policy completely to that of the Romans. The reaction of the Aetolians was to ask the extent of control resulting from surrender. When no definite answer was given, the ambassadors went home without making peace, and so the war was renewed. When their treatment by Glabrio earlier in the year is remembered, it is easy to understand the attitude of the Aetolians. On the other hand, the Romans, who were intent on defeating Antiochus, gained nothing by the resumption of war against the Aetolians, and it would seem that it should not have taken too much diplomacy to have secured the peace which all parties directly concerned desired.[1]

The assignment of provinces for 190 was made as if the war with Antiochus and with the Aetolians would require only one army. After Africanus had announced that, if his brother was sent to Greece, he would go along as a legate, Greece was assigned to Lucius Scipio as his province with the proviso that he might take his army into Asia if this was judged to serve the best interests of the state. This would seem to imply that the advancing army would leave a peaceful and untroubled Greece in its rear. If there were plans to send an army to Greece to replace the one that moved on into Asia, the plan was abandoned. The command of the fleet was assigned to the praetor L. Aemilius Regillus. Both Scipio and Aemilius set out for their respective provinces already in March.[2]

The chief achievement of the Scipios in Greece was to arrange an armistice with the Aetolians so that they could get on their way to Asia. The additional troops they brought with them were transported from Brundisium to Apollonia and advanced by the usual route

[1] Pol. xxi. 2; Livy xxxvii. 1. 1–5; very little is to be got from Diod. xxix. 4 and Zonaras ix. 19. Polybius indicates that the 1,000 talents were to be paid immediately in a single payment. The statement about the disagreement in the senate is derived from Livy. Scullard, *Roman Politics*, 128 clearly is right that 'no dissentient voice is heard' on the question of following Antiochus into Asia, but there clearly was disagreement concerning the policy to be adopted in Greece.

[2] Livy xxxvii. 1. 7–10, 2. 1, 2. 10, 4. 1–5; on the time cf. n. 4 on p. 426. According to Livy 2. 7–8 and 4. 1 A. Cornelius Mammula, a praetor of the preceding year who had commanded troops in Bruttium, was ordered to transport these troops to Aetolia 'if the consul so desired'. Whatever this means, Mammula and his troops did not cross to Greece. When the Scipios crossed to Asia, Greece was denuded of Roman troops. At least there is no indication that Fulvius Nobilior next year found any Roman troops in Greece. The story of a false rumour transmitted from Greece by Mammula (Livy xxxvii. 48. 1–5) is derived from Valerius Antias.

through Epirus and Thessaly. After a fruitless exchange of messages with the Aetolians at Hypata, who refused to surrender the city, they bypassed it and encamped a few miles from Amphissa, which was being besieged by Glabrio.[1] The Aetolians that year had concentrated on the defence of the approaches to Naupactus. Glabrio, however, who had his headquarters at Elatea, had begun the year's campaign by sacking Lamia and had moved on to besiege Amphissa, which by the time the Scipios arrived was so battered that all had taken refuge on the acropolis.[2] With the Scipios present, it did not take long to arrange another six months armistice. Africanus clearly had in mind transferring operations to Asia as soon as possible, and it is difficult not to feel that he used his prestige and reputation for arousing false hopes among the Aetolians. As soon as the arrival of the Scipios was reported, the Athenians sent an embassy headed by Echedemus to try to secure peace. He was given a friendly reception by Africanus, who asked him to approach the Aetolians. Thereupon he first sent a herald to prepare the way and then himself proceeded to Hypata, where the Aetolians still maintained their headquarters. He found them ready to negotiate and send ambassadors. These first had an interview with Africanus, who urged them to entrust themselves to him. This aroused hope among the ambassadors, but, when they met Lucius Scipio, they were told that they had the choice of the same two alternatives as before. These terms the ambassadors, accompanied by Echedemus, carried back to Hypata, where they consulted with the *apokletoi*. The terms seemed impossible. The Aetolians could not raise the 1,000 talents required for immediate delivery on the one alternative, and their experience with Glabrio made them afraid to surrender. When all efforts to secure modifications or explanations failed, the Aetolians took the advice of Echedemus and once more asked for a truce of six months so that they could appeal to the senate. Since that would bring the campaigning in Greece to an end for that year, the request was readily granted. Glabrio thereupon abandoned the siege of Amphissa, turned over his army and equipment to his successor, and departed for Rome with his military tribunes.[3]

For the advance into Asia, there were two preliminary requirements, passage through Macedonia and Thrace for the army on its way to the Hellespont and control of the sea. The passage by land was secured through the co-operation of Philip, who not only granted free

[1] Livy xxxvii. 6. 1–4. Also Pol. xxi. 4. 9 reports that the Scipios encamped within sixty stades of Amphissa.

[2] Livy xxxvii. 4. 6–6. 4.

[3] Pol. xxi. 4–5; Livy xxxvii. 6. 1–7. 7. When Polybius states that Echedemus sent a message in advance before going to Hypata, this must mean that a herald was sent to learn whether his visit would be acceptable.

passage through Macedonia but also aided the Romans in their passage through Thrace. He even allowed them to enrol volunteers (mercenaries?) in Macedonia. As a sort of reward, the Scipios announced the cancellation of the remaining indemnity payments due from Macedonia, the sum involved apparently being 200 talents.[1] It was unusual to have such an announcement made by a general in the field, but the grant probably had been authorized, in case of good behaviour, by a previous promise of the senate.

Livius, the commander of the Roman fleet wintering at Canae, and Eumenes acted in the spring as if the battle of Corycus had decided the issue at sea. The first act of Livius reported for 190 was to sail with thirty Roman ships and seven quadriremes belonging to Eumenes to the Hellespont to prepare for the arrival of the army. There he had secured Sestus and was besieging Abydus when his operations were interrupted by the news of a decisive victory of Polyxenidas, the admiral of Antiochus, over the Rhodians.[2] Early in the spring a Rhodian fleet under the command of Pausistratus was trapped by Polyxenidas. The latter, a Rhodian exile, pretended to betray his fleet to Pausistratus on the condition that the latter help him to return home from exile. Though Pausistratus tried to take all sorts of precautions, he was completely outwitted with the result that almost his entire fleet was lost, about thirty ships. Only seven, five Rhodian and two Coan, escaped by holding off hostile ships by means of fire dumped from containers on long poles on any enemy ship that came too close.[3] The repercussions of this defeat were extensive. The Romans gave up the siege of Abydus, and though the Rhodians soon sent out more ships so that the united fleet was not outnumbered, it was for some time unable to involve the enemy in a decisive battle. The most surprising detail reported is that it was found necessary to send the Rhodian Epicrates with two Rhodian triremes and two allied ships from Italy to clear the strait between Cephallenia and Leucas, where pirates were interfering with the transportation of supplies from Italy. It looks as if the Romans had left the safeguarding of the lines of transportation entirely to the fleet which had been sent east and now was off the coast of Asia Minor.[4] Epicrates got no farther than to Piraeus, where he was met by L. Aemilius Regillus, the Roman

---

[1] Livy xxxvii. 7. 8–16; Appian, *Syr.* 23, *Mac.* 9. 5; Zonaras ix. 20. Only Appian states that the Scipios announced the cancellation, but the statement can safely be accepted, since hopes of cancellation had been held out to Macedonian ambassadors at Rome (Pol. xxi. 3).

[2] Livy xxxvii. 8. 6–9. 11; Appian, *Syr.* 23.

[3] Livy xxxvii. 10–11; Appian, *Syr.* 24. There is some difficulty with the numbers so that the exact number of ships lost is not known.

[4] Livy xxxvii. 13. 11–12. On Roman neglect of the sea at this time cf. Thiel, *Roman Sea-Power*, 310 f.

praetor who was assigned to the naval command and arrived with two quinqueremes. Most likely he had set out with a larger squadron but had left the rest behind, possibly at Corcyra, to operate against pirates and safeguard communications, but, on account of lack of evidence, this cannot be known for certain.[1] Epicrates, at any rate, turned back with Aemilius, who proceeded to Samos, where the allied fleet was stationed. In a council of war, Epicrates advocated an attack on Patara, the Lycian capital, which had been garrisoned by Antiochus and was used by his fleet as the one important naval station between Cilicia and the Aegean. Control of this port by the allies would have made it difficult if not impossible for the Seleucid squadron being prepared in Cilicia to proceed to the Aegean. The proposal of Epicrates is reported to have made a very favourable impression. Nevertheless it was decided that the main fleet was to approach Ephesus to challenge Polyxenidas. Only a small squadron, consisting largely of Rhodian ships, was sent against Patara. This proved insufficient and had to withdraw. Later Aemilius proceeded towards Patara with his entire fleet but turned back.[2]

The chief theatre of naval operations now became the waters between Samos, Ephesus, and Erythrae with the fleet of Antiochus stationed at Ephesus and that of his opponents at Samos. The Roman base of supplies, however, was Chios. Thus the two fleets faced each other in nearby ports without joining battle. The impression is that the Seleucid fleet, if anything, had the upper hand. Just before the battle of Myonessus the Roman admiral tried in vain to catch a group of about fifteen 'pirate' ships which had raided the coast of Chios. In these closed waters there cannot have been any pirate headquarters for so large a group. The pirates must have been privateers in the service of the Seleucids raiding the island on which the Romans had their supply depot at which all the transports from Italy put in. During 190 the arrival of a large shipment of grain from Italy is reported, while the ships bringing wine were being held up by inclement weather.[3] Probably most of the grain from 'Italy' came from Sicily and Sardinia, where as early as 191 the Romans began to raise a second tithe, which meant that the government purchased an amount of grain equal to that collected as the regular tithe. Such

---

[1] Livy had reported that in 191 the praetor M. Iunius Brutus had been ordered to repair and equip old ships (xxxvi. 2. 15) and that Aemilius had been ordered to take over twenty of these (xxxvii. 2. 10). No number is given when his departure is reported (xxxvii. 4. 5), but it is stated that he reached Piraeus with two quinqueremes (xxxvii. 14. 2). If it can be taken for granted that he had started out with twenty, then eighteen had been left behind; cf. Thiel, *Roman Sea-Power*, 311, 326.

[2] Livy xxxvii. 14–17. For the expeditions against Patara cf. *Mélanges A. Piganiol.*, 1638 f.

[3] Chios as supply centre and the pirates: Livy xxxvii. 27.

transactions were ordered in 191, 190, 189, and 171 in connexion with the assignment of provinces. The navy is not mentioned in these statements, but that does not preclude assigning some of the grain to it.[1] At one stage the Roman and Rhodian fleet went north to Elaea to support Eumenes, whose territory had been invaded by Seleucid troops. At this point Antiochus felt strong enough to try to negotiate peace but was told by Aemilius that he could not negotiate before the arrival of the consul.[2]

During this period of approximate stalemate, a detachment of 1,000 Achaean infantry and 100 cavalry, under the command of Diophanes, who had been general of the Confederacy in 192–191, is reported to have distinguished itself. An embassy from Eumenes had appeared before an extraordinary meeting of the Achaean assembly and arranged for the renewal of the alliance between the two states and the dispatch of the troops. This was arranged between the two states, which, to this extent at least, tried to have an independent foreign policy instead of merely taking orders from the Romans. These troops, of course, were transported across the Aegean in ships. They were all experienced troops led by a brilliant officer. By their bold sorties, they caused the siege of Pergamum to be abandoned.[3] These or other Achaean troops were also to fight at Magnesia.

The allied fleet was soon back at Samos, with the difference that now Eumenes had taken his ships north to prepare to receive the Scipios when they should arrive, and that a number of Rhodian ships returned home to help keep watch on the squadron under Hannibal that was expected to sail westward from Cilicia. With them went a Coan and a Cnidian quinquereme. To these were added more Rhodian ships making a total of thirty-two quadriremes and four triremes, the two quinqueremes probably being counted with the quadriremes. This fleet faced a larger fleet consisting of larger ships, thirty-seven being quinqueremes or larger. The two fleets met near Side in Pamphylia, and the Rhodians, through their superior seamanship and the superior manoeuvrability of their ships, won a decisive victory, though the crews were too exhausted from recent illness to pursue as vigorously as they normally would have done. Yet they did enough so that Hannibal did not try to advance again. After their victory, the Rhodians stationed twenty ships to stand guard at Megiste, an island just off Patara. This kept much of the Rhodian

[1] Second tithes in Sicily and Sardinia: Livy xxxvi. 2. 12–13; xxxvii. 2. 12, 50. 9–10; xlii. 31. 8; cf. especially V. Scramuzza, *Econ. Surv. Rome*, iii. 240, 255 f. On supplying the fleet see Thiel, *Roman Sea-Power*, 310 f.

[2] Livy xxxvii. 18–19; Pol. xxi. 10.

[3] The embassy from Eumenes: Pol. xxi. 3b; the operations: Livy xxxvii. 20–21; Appian, *Syr.* 26.

fleet busy, so that they sent only seven ships back to join the allied forces at Samos.[1]

The absence from Samos of the Rhodian squadron keeping watch at Megiste and of the Pergamene fleet at the Hellespont, gave the Seleucid fleet a numerical superiority and determined Antiochus and Polyxenidas to challenge the Roman fleet to battle. This was done by an attack on Notium, the port of Colophon, while the Seleucid army moved up to join in the attack. Before proceeding to the relief of Notium, the Roman fleet found it necessary to start for Chios to get supplies. On the way they learned that Teos had been furnishing supplies to the Seleucid fleet and had just promised 5,000 amphoras of wine. Since there would have been a shortage of wine at Chios on account of delay in a shipment, this seems to have determined the Romans to proceed to Teos to demand supplies for themselves. At Teos they began by plundering the countryside near the city, though as late as 193 the senate had recognized the inviolability of the city— an indication that there was no certainty that such a decision by the senate would be respected by a commander in the field. While the Romans were thus occupied, Polyxenidas brought up his fleet to an island near Myonessus very near to Teos. When this was reported to the Roman praetor by a local farmer, it caused a panic, the crews were hurriedly summoned, and the fleet put to sea. Aemilius led the way and put out to form the right wing of the battle line leaving it to the Rhodians under Eudamus to bring up the rear and form the left wing. Fortunately for the Romans, Eudamus took matters into his own hands. When he observed that the enemy was about to outflank the right wing of the Romans, he hurriedly transferred the Rhodian ships to the right. Again the superior seamanship of the Rhodians and their use of fire which could be poured upon the hostile ships carried the day and defeated the left half of the Seleucid fleet so disastrously that this fleet no longer was a menace to the Romans and their allies.[2]

The battle of Myonessus opened the way for the Scipios to Asia Minor. Antiochus had gathered supplies at Lysimachea near the isthmus of the Thracian Chersonesus and had prepared to resist their advance at this point. When he learned of the naval defeat, he immediately ordered the troops withdrawn and even the civilian population evacuated and, even more than that, he made no effort to try to prevent the crossing of the Hellespont. Livy and other ancient writers criticized him severely for this. These criticisms seem to go

---

[1] Livy xxxvii. 22–24, 45. 2 (indicating the Megiste was occupied by the Rhodians).

[2] Livy xxxvii. 26–30. For the Roman recognition of the inviolability of Teos, see *SIG*[3] 601. Menippus, one of the ambassadors sent to Rome by Antiochus late in 194 (Livy xxxiv. 57. 6–59. 6), had acted also for the Teans. The action of the senate was reported to the Teans by the *praetor peregrinus* of 193, M. Valerius Messala.

back to a single source, perhaps Polybius. Modern historians tend to be more sympathetic. They may criticize Antiochus for letting his supplies fall intact into the hands of the Romans, but they argue that Lysimachea could not have been held after the loss of the supremacy at sea and approve of his policy of drawing the Roman army into the interior of Asia Minor and accepting battle in a plain near Magnesia-under-Sipylus advantageous for his large division of cavalry.[1] Before the battle, Antiochus had offered peace on what seemed liberal terms, but the Romans countered by demanding that he pay their entire cost of the war and withdraw beyond the Taurus, that is, give up all possessions in Asia Minor except along the south coast. These terms naturally were rejected and the war continued.[2]

In the campaign which followed upon the arrival of the Roman army in Asia Minor, except for Eumenes and his Pergamene troops, few Greeks were involved. There were Achaean troops at the battle of Magnesia, but they were there more as allies of Pergamum rather than of Rome. There do not seem to have been contingents from any Greek city in Asia Minor. There were Cretans, but these were certainly mercenaries. In fact, there were Cretans in both armies.[3] But if Greek cities did not send contingents to the Roman army, there were cities enough that suffered simply on account of their location. The evacuation of Lysimachea and the disregard of the inviolability of Teos have already been noted, and these cities certainly were not the only sufferers. Probably no city suffered worse than Phocaea, but that would be a complicated story.

The role of Eumenes and Pergamum in the war is so well known that it hardly calls for comment. His ships had been active in the naval operations, though they had not done as much fighting or contributed as much as the Rhodians. On the other hand, he must have contributed heavily to the support of the Roman forces, both of the fleet, which wintered 191–190 in a Pergamene port, and of the army of the Scipios. His contingent in the army at Magnesia was not overly large, probably not over 4,000 including the Achaeans who served with him.[4]

[1] Criticisms: Livy xxxvii. 31. 1; Appian, *Syr.* 28; Diod. xxix. 5. Contrast De Sanctis, *Storia*, iv. i. 192; Holleaux, *CAH* viii. 222.

[2] Pol. xxi. 13–14; Livy xxxvii. 34–36; Appian, *Syr.* 29.

[3] Livy xxxvii. 39. 10, 40. 8. There were also Trallians in both armies and in both cases mentioned as though linked with the Cretans. In this period Cretan mercenaries were almost omnipresent; Trallians are more scarce and harder to explain.

[4] Livy xxxvii. 39. 9 gives 3,000 foot including Achaean *caetrati* (peltasts) and Eumenes' *auxiliares* and 800 horse; Appian, *Syr.* 31 gives about 3,000 Achaean peltasts in the army of Eumenes and otherwise mentions only the cavalry. His 3,000 peltasts undoubtedly should include not only the Achaeans but also the others. The Achaeans must be the 1,000 and 100 who arrived earlier in the year. Their dedication honouring Attalus, the brother of Eumenes, shows clearly that they regarded themselves as allies of Eumenes rather than of the Romans (*SIG*³ 606).

28

It is clear that Eumenes distinguished himself also in the conduct of the battle. Antiochus had a detachment of scythe-bearing chariots. Eumenes instructed archers and slingers to aim their missiles at the horses thus stampeding them and causing them to throw other divisions, particularly of the cavalry, into confusion. Next he ordered a cavalry charge against some of Antiochus' cavalry which already was in an uproar, thus starting a rout which ultimately involved the entire army.[1] Soon after the battle also the remnants of the Seleucid fleet withdrew, going to Patara, where it disbanded. A brief account of this has been given above in connexion with the Lycian Confederacy.

Peace negotiations began during the winter early in 189. The terms were again formulated by Africanus and were much the same as those he had proposed earlier, except that the amount of the indemnities was fixed at 15,000 Euboeic talents. Of these 500 were to be paid immediately, 2,500 as soon as the Roman people ratified the treaty, and the rest in twelve annual instalments of 1,000 talents each. Otherwise the terms included as before the withdrawal from Europe and from Asia up to the Taurus mountains and, of course, other restraints. These terms were accepted by the ambassadors of Antiochus, and it was agreed that ambassadors were to be sent to Rome to appear before the senate. As it turned out, ambassadors were sent to Rome not only by Antiochus but also by numerous Greek states in Asia Minor, while Eumenes went in person.[2] They did not reach Rome, it seems, until after both consuls had left for their provinces in the summer. There followed a lengthy hearing and debates in the senate. In the end, the treaty was accepted by the senate and ratified by the people, whereupon oaths were exchanged with the ambassadors of Antiochus.[3] Thus, the treaty commonly known as the Peace of Apamea was really ratified at Rome in 189. That this was the case is shown by the fact that the Rhodian ambassadors, before they left Rome, put in a claim to Soli in Cilicia but had to back down because this claim was contrary to the treaty which already had been ratified.[4] What later took place at Apamea was just an additional ceremony of ratification. There remained, of course, many details to be settled by Manlius Vulso, who by this time was commander in Asia, and the ten commissioners sent out in 188 to work with him.

---

[1] The chief accounts of the battle are Livy xxxvii. 38–43; Appian, *Syr.* 30–36.

[2] Pol. xxi. 16–17; Livy xxxvii. 45. 4–21; Diod. xxix. 10; Appian, *Syr.* 38, all giving indemnities in Euboeic talents. The text of the treaty itself has Attic silver, each talent to contain eighty Roman pounds (Pol. xxi. 43. 19; Livy xxxviii. 38. 13).

[3] Debate etc.: Pol. xxi. 18–23; Livy xxxvii. 52–54. Ratification: Pol. xxi. 24. 1–4; Livy xxxvii. 55. 1–3.

[4] Pol. xxi. 24. 10–15; Livy xxxvii. 56. 7–10; cf. *CP* xxxi (1936), 347 f.

The settlement of the affairs of Asia Minor followed much the same pattern as that in Greece after the Second Macedonian War. What Antiochus gave up was ceded directly to the Romans and was theirs to do with as they pleased and in the treaty actually was spoken of as subject to Rome.[1] Again, too, the Romans clearly did not intend to annex anything or to establish direct control but relied on their informal protectorate over friends, who were expected to take directions from them. Hence the question became, which ones of their friends were to receive the territory surrendered by Antiochus to the Romans, in other words, what was to go to Eumenes of Pergamum and what to Rhodes? And, since Rome pretended to be the protector of the freedom of the Greeks, which cities were actually to be left free instead of being subjected to one of the larger states? The general lines of the settlement were laid down in the instructions given by the senate to the commissioners[2] and only the details left to be arranged on the grounds. After the completion of the settlement, Manlius Vulso with the ten commissioners and the army started homeward via the Hellespont, Thrace, Macedonia, Thessaly, and Epirus to Apollonia in Illyria, where they wintered. While crossing Thrace they suffered considerably at the hands of the natives. The suspicion voiced by Livy that Philip was behind these attacks may not be warranted, but his agents were not on hand as they had been in 190 to make straight the pathway of the Romans.[3] By this time much had happened to make the relations of Philip to the Romans less cordial than they had been when the Scipios were at the head of the army.

The events in Greece in this period were marked by the extreme bellicose energy of the Aetolians and their efforts to secure more favourable terms from Rome than those first offered. In this they were finally successful but only after the expenditure of a good deal of energy and the loss of many lives. They also caused the Romans considerable trouble, but, even so, the hostility towards the Aetolians on the part of the Romans in 188, when peace was finally concluded, appears to have been less than at any time since 196.

The Aetolian ambassadors sent to Rome after the armistice negotiated with the Scipios were given a hearing before the senate only after the consuls for the following year had been elected. The Aetolians are reported to have been so insistent on the services once rendered to the

[1] Cession of land up to the Taurua and Halys and prohibition against engaging mercenaries from land subject to Rome: Pol. xxi. 43. 5 and 15; Livy xxxviii. 38. 4 and 10. In the Polybius passage the references to the boundaries have been lost but can be supplied from Livy; cf. also the preliminary treaty.

[2] Pol. xxi. 24. 5–9; Livy xxxvii. 55. 4–56. 6.

[3] Livy xxxviii. 39. 2–3, 40–41. Livy (41. 15) states that Manlius led his army *per Macedoniam in Thessaliam . . . inde per Epirum.*

Romans and so stiff-necked in refusing the harsh terms offered that they were expelled from Italy. The *senatus consultum* to this effect is reported to have been proposed by Glabrio. Thus the party favouring harsh treatment of the Aetolians prevailed. A contributing factor was the report that had just reached Rome to the effect that the Aetolians were carrying on aggressive war in Athamania and other regions north of Aetolia.[1] The little kingdom of Athamania in the mountains west of Thessaly, consisting largely of the upper valley of the Achelous river, enters into the history of the period partly on account of its location and partly on account of the warlike character of its inhabitants. The Roman ambassadors, going the rounds of Greek states in 200 B.C., had called on its king, Amynander, and the Athamanians in 197 contributed 1,200 men to the army of Flamininus, a contingent certainly as large in proportion to the population of their country as the Aetolian contingent.[2] Of the larger states in their neighbourhood, the one with which the interests of the Athamanians clashed most frequently was Macedonia, while their country was separated from Aetolia by Dolopia and Amphilochia. Consequently the Athamanians were usually aligned against Macedonia and, more often than not, were on the side of the Aetolians. Thus it was not unnatural for them to line up with the Aetolians and Antiochus in 192. This made Athamania fair game for Philip, who in 191 expelled Amynander from his kingdom.[3] The following year, with the aid of the Aetolians, he recovered his kingdom, and Philip, though he is reported to have intervened with an army of 6,000, was unable to dislodge him and suffered considerable losses himself. The Aetolians, not unnaturally, made use of the situation to reduce districts between Aetolia and Athamania. After the recovery of his kingdom, Amynander, anxious to align himself on the side of Rome, sent ambassadors to the Scipios at Ephesus and to Rome. The Roman interests in Greece clearly were still regarded as a part of the province of Lucius Scipio. These hostilities tended to prejudice the Romans against the Aetolians. Consequently repeated sending of ambassadors and repeated efforts to appeal to the Romans, ended in failure.[4] The action of the Romans in this case is rather startling, for it meant that they would have to send an army to Greece and assume the offensive there. They cannot possibly have considered the Aetolians a menace to themselves and Italy; they were a menace only to the Roman arrangements in Greece.

[1] Livy xxxvii. 49; Diod. xxix. 9.
[2] Roman embassy: Pol. xvi. 27. 4; troops in 197: Livy xxxiii. 3. 10. Beloch, *GrG*² iii. i. 293 estimates the population at 30,000.
[3] Livy xxxvi. 14. 7–9, 32. 1.
[4] Pol. xxi. 25; Livy xxxviii. 1–3.

In reopening the war with Aetolia, the Romans would seem to have had a choice between waiting till they could bring back to Greece the army in Asia Minor or sending out another army from Italy. The latter course was the one chosen. The consul, M. Fulvius Nobilior, crossed with an army, probably a regular consular army of two legions and auxiliaries, to Apollonia in Illyria.[1] After landing there, Fulvius really had no choice. There was only one course open to him, to go south and attack Aetolia from the north or west. To have taken the old route through Thessaly and by Thermopylae would not only have been farther but also more difficult. Since the Roman troops had been withdrawn, it is possible and even likely that the Aetolians had reoccupied Heracles and would have been ready to challenge the Roman advance at Thermopylae. At Apollonia Fulvius had a conference with Epirote ambassadors, who advised him to attack Ambracia. It is likely that this advice was unnecessary. By this time there were many Romans who knew the lay of the land in Greece.

The defence of Ambracia was largely conducted by the citizens themselves except for 1,500 troops sent to their aid by the Aetolians, who meanwhile were able to conduct operations on other fronts. The campaign is also interesting as another example of the manner in which Aetolians established headquarters in a city near the scene of the most important operations. Now, naturally, the city chosen was not Hypata but Stratus, the former Acarnanian capital, located some forty miles south of Ambracia. To this city, the general of the year, Nicander, summoned a combined meeting of the assembly of the Aetolians and a mobilization of the army and afterwards used it as headquarters during the campaign. The first step taken was the dispatch of 1,000 light-armed troops to Ambracia. With the rest of the army, Nicander does not seem at first to have done more than raid Acarnania. Later he managed to send 500 more troops to Ambracia and this time arranged with the commander in the city to make a sortie on a predetermined night. The sortie was made, but for some reason Nicander failed to support it as promised. Livy (Polybius) suggests that he may have considered it more important to repel an invasion of Dolopia and Amphilochia by Philip's son, Perseus. Even so the defenders of Ambracia did a good deal of damage with their sortie. What finally caused the Aetolians to give up was that Illyrian and Achaean ships began raiding their coast, thus adding a new front.[2]

[1] According to Livy xxxvii. 50. 1–4 the consul who was assigned to Aetolia was to take over the army in Aetolia and enrol additional troops, but it is clear that there was no army 'in' Aetolia and that he brought all his troops from Italy. On the various problems involved see De Sanctis, *Storia*, iv. i. 211, n. 154.

[2] Pol. xxi. 27–28; Livy xxxviii. 4–7. Livy mentions Stratus in connexion with the meeting summoned there (4. 6) and states that the Aetolians returned there after their raids on

The peace negotiated with the Aetolians in 189 means somewhat of a retreat on the part of the Romans from the harsh demands of the past few years to a more liberal treatment. The divergent policies involved were connected with factional strife at Rome, and this may also colour the accounts in our sources. Thus, when negotiations were resumed during the siege, Fulvius is reported by Livy to have made demands if anything harsher than those made during the earlier negotiations. Now Fulvius was later accused of unreasonable cruelty towards the Ambraciotes by political opponents, who had suborned ambassadors from Ambracia to act as witnesses to support their accusations. It is possible that some of the details about his negotiations are derived from these accusations.[1] The negotiations also supply an early example of the intervention in the interest of a foreign state on the part of a son of the man who first arranged a settlement with that state, while the story of the accusations against Fulvius gives an early example of the use of suborned witnesses from a subject or allied state in Roman political warfare.

The Aetolian embassy which negotiated with Fulvius was headed by Damoteles, who earlier had served as an ambassador to Rome, and Phaeneas, the old leader of the peace party. These, after their first meeting with Fulvius, returned 'home', undoubtedly to Stratus, to consult with the Aetolian government. On their way back to the Roman headquarters, they were waylaid and captured by the Acarnanians, who, however, were ordered by Fulvius to bring them to his camp. This time they were supported by Athenian and Rhodian ambassadors, who pleaded their cause and advised them to cultivate C. Valerius Laevinus, son of the M. Valerius Laevinus who had negotiated the early treaty of alliance between the Romans and the Aetolians, and a half brother of the consul. While he pleaded the cause of the Aetolians, Amynander of Athamania pleaded for the city of Ambracia. As a result there were separate settlements so that Ambracia was detached from the Confederacy by the peace negotiations themselves. The Ambraciotes surrendered on the condition that the Aetolian troops in the city be allowed to leave unharmed—a pledge which Fulvius duly observed. Since this came before he had received confirmation of the preliminary peace from the Aetolian government, it is indicative of the new spirit of understanding and decency which was animating the negotiations. Fulvius received the confirmation from the Aetolian government only after he had advanced to Amphilochian Argos, half way between Stratus and

Acarnania (5. 6). It also seems evident that the later negotiations with the Romans were initiated from there. On the role of Stratus cf. *TAPA* lxxxiii (1952), 29.

[1] Livy xxxviii. 8, 43 (accusations against Fulvius).

Ambracia. The securing of confirmation of the treaty at Rome still remained. For this purpose he sent his half brother, Valerius Laevinus, and the Aetolians, Phaeneas and Nicander, the general of 190–189.[1]

The treaty now granted the Aetolians meant a considerable mollification of the terms offered earlier. Of the two old alternatives, *deditio* or indemnity and a treaty pledging the Aetolians to have the same friends and enemies as the Romans, it was the second alternative that was chosen, but the indemnity was greatly reduced. Instead of 1,000 talents payable immediately, the sum was set at 500 talents, 200 payable immediately and the rest in six annual installments. One clause in the preliminary treaty is surprising. It stated that the Aetolians could not retain in their Confederacy or admit into it in the future any city which had been captured by the Romans or had gone over to them after the crossing of Lucius Cornelius (Scipio) into Greece.[2] This would have given the Aetolians permission to recover places captured by Glabrio, but this permission was withdrawn, when, in the treaty as validated at Rome this clause was altered and the time limit moved up two years to 192.[3] Nevertheless, after the war, Heraclea continued to be held by the Aetolians. This may not be as surprising as it sometimes has been considered. The signing of a document does not automatically evacuate garrisons or transfer cities from one government to another. If no Roman official insisted on the evacuation of Heraclea by the Aetolians, they may well have continued to hold it. The Romans apparently no longer took any special interest in Thermopylae. On the other hand, the exclusion of Cephallenia from the treaty, specifically indicated already in the preliminary treaty, and its later conquest by Fulvius, shows the interest of Rome at the time in the western approaches to Greece.

The treaty is interesting from several points of view. It is the earliest treaty in which a Greek state in so many words was deprived of an independent foreign policy. At the same time it is the oldest extant treaty of the kind that has been classed as a *foedus iniquum*, a term obviously not used in the body of any treaty but used as a descriptive term as early as by Livy and probably much earlier.[4] In Livy's

---

[1] Pol. xxi. 29–30; Livy xxxviii. 8–10. 2. On C. Valerius as patron of the Aetolians cf. Badian, *Clientelae*, 158.

[2] Polybius xxi. 30. 4 is followed instead of Livy xxxviii. 9. 10, who has T. Quinctius, which would have to refer to the arrival of Flamininus in 198, and which clearly is wrong.

[3] Again following Polybius xxi. 32. 13, who gives the year as that of the consulate of Lucius Quintius (Flamininus) and Gnaeus Domitius (Ahenobarbus). Undoubtedly Livy's *T. Quinctio* (xxxviii. 11. 9) is due to confusing the names of the two brothers.

[4] Livy xxxv. 46. 10, in a speech said to have been delivered in 192 by a leading citizen of Chalcis. The speech given in indirect discourse may well be derived from Polybius and reproduce approximately what was said at the time, but, if so, it is impossible to know what terms were used.

version of the treaty with the Aetolians the dependence is indicated by the *maiestas* clause pledging the Aetolians to preserve without malice the rule and majesty of the Roman people, which later is followed by the Greek formula for a subordinating alliance, stating that the Aetolians are to have the same enemies as the Roman people and go to war against them.[1] The *maiestas* clause, in a slightly different form, is cited by Proculus, a jurist of the first century after Christ, as characteristic of the form of treaty, obviously the *foedus iniquum*, though the term is not used, which is contrasted with the *foedus aequum*. Thus during the Republic this had become the formula used in treaties of alliance involving subordination, and the inclusion of the citation in the *Digest* shows that it had become the official form.[2] This is not the place to deal with the impossibly difficult question of the origin of this formula. It must suffice to note that in the preliminary negotiations the old Greek formula about having the same enemies and friends was used throughout.[3] This clause certainly was clear enough, and the *maiestas* clause cannot have elucidated the matter in any sense. It looks as if it were included and put at the head of the treaty because it already was the recognized Roman formula. To this the Greek formula was added for the sake of clarity, but in between was inserted a clause no doubt derived from Greek usage, the promise not to give right of passage or aid to anyone attacking the friends or allies of the Romans. This clause had been developed on account of the old Greek habit of belligerents to expect right of passage through neutral territory.

Territorially, the settlement was not too severe. Besides Delphi, detached before the peace negotiations, Ambracia detached by the manner in which the negotiations were conducted, and Cephallenia mentioned already in the preliminary peace, only Oeniadae was transferred from Aetolia to Acarnania. The detaching of Delphi, not mentioned in the literary sources, had already been arranged by Glabrio, who during the winter of 191–190 had restored to 'the god and the city' lands and houses in the city and its territory which had been acquired by Aetolian citizens. In a letter to the city he promised

[1] The fullest text is that of Pol. xxi. 32, which, however, suffers from several lacunae in the opening clauses, though enough has been preserved to show that he also included the formulas mentioned. The version of Livy xxxviii. 11 is somewhat shorter but has the opening formulas preserved. Cf. *Econ. Surv. Rome*, iv. 282–4.

[2] *Digest* xlix. 15. 7. 1. While Livy has *imperium maiestatemque*, the *Digest* and Cic. *Pro Balbo* 35 omit *imperium*. It is possible that *maiestas* seemed so vague that *imperium* was added in the Aetolian treaty for the sake of clarity. Badian, *Clientelae*, 26 and 84 f. considers the use of the *maiestas* clause in the Aetolian treaty as its earliest use.

[3] To the Aetolian embassy of 191–190: Pol. xxi. 2. 4; Livy xxxvii. 1. 5. In negotiations with the Scipios in Greece: Pol. xxi. 4. 13: Livy xxxvii. 6. 7. The accounts of occurrences in the senate when Aetolian ambassadors later came to Rome by Livy xxxvii. 49. 4 and by Diod. xxix. 9 imply that the same terms were maintained.

further to champion the ancient freedom of the city and the sanctuary.[1] This meant that he was already treating Delphi as no longer subject to the Aetolians. Naturally this required the approval of the government at Rome. Consequently Delphi sent three ambassadors who secured a *senatus consultum* to the effect that the temple of Pythian Apollo and the city of the Delphians and their land were to be inviolate, autonomous, and free. This settled the status of Delphi, and was reported in letters to the city and to the Amphictionic League from Sp. Postumius Albinus, one of the praetors of 189. But if this settled the status of the city, it did not end its troubles. The three ambassadors were murdered on their way home, and it appears that the Aetolians too caused some trouble. When these matters came to the attention of the senate, C. Livius Salinator, one of the consuls of 188, reported in a letter to Delphi that the senate had decided to write to Marcus Fulvius to search out and punish the murderers after he had reduced Same. The senate had likewise decided to write to the Aetolians concerning their offences against Delphi, ordering them to restore what they had carried off.[2]

The preliminary settlement with Ambracia, though the city was set free, was conducted with great severity and greed by Fulvius, who not only received as a 'gift' (*stephanos*, one of the many ancestors of the notorious *aurum coronarium* of imperial times) a sum of 150 talents but, in addition, carried off paintings and statues.[3] The question of Ambracia does not seem to have been taken up when the senate agreed to the ratification of the treaty with Aetolia. It was brought up early in 187 in connexion with charges lodged against Fulvius, who still was absent, by M. Aemilius Lepidus, who secured the passage of a *senatus consultum* to the effect that the Ambraciotes were to recover all their property, to be free, to employ their own laws, and to be allowed to collect what import and export duties they wished, provided only that Romans and their Latin allies be exempt. A special decree ruled that Ambracia had not been captured by force of arms (*vi*), which undoubtedly meant to imply that the captor had no right to plunder it.[4] As far as securing the return of property to the Ambraciotes

---

[1] For the letter and donations see the edition of P. Roussel in *BCH* lvi (1932), 1 ff.; cf. Daux, *Delphes*, 225–33.

[2] For the letters of Postumius and Livius see Holleaux, *BCH* liv (1930), 38–41, now *Études*, v. 282–6; cf. Daux, *Delphes*, 259–68.

[3] Pol. xxi. 30. 9–10; Livy xxxviii. 9. 13. The *stephanos* was not a crown or wreath but a sum of money. Livy has taken it to be a real wreath of gold, but, since a wreath weighing 150 talents is impossible, has made it a wreath weighing 150 pounds—only slightly less nonsensical.

[4] Livy xxxviii. 43. 1–44. 6. It is practically certain that the clause concerning the restoration of property—obviously directed against Fulvius—was not carried out. Livy xxxix. 5. 14–17 shows that the value of the booty carried in his triumph was very high; cf. *Econ. Surv. Rome*, iv. 319 f., 323.

is concerned, these decrees apparently had no effect, and Fulvius deserves the verdict that large scale despoiling began with him.

After the conclusion of the negotiations with the Aetolians, Fulvius crossed to Cephallenia, where he found it necessary to besiege Same for four months before the city was finally captured. During the siege he himself returned to Rome to conduct the consular elections and to have his own imperium prorogued. From Rome he again returned to Cephallenia to finish the stubborn siege, in which the Romans seem to have suffered more casualties than the besieged until they secured the aid of 100 Achaean slingers from Aegium, Patrae, and Dyme, who are said to have been more effective than the famous slingers from the Balearic Islands. In this case, there was no consideration shown the brave defenders. The city was plundered and the survivors sold into slavery.[1] Thus the special protectorate along the Adriatic coast established in the Illyrian wars was extended south along the west coast of Greece. Zacynthus had been claimed from the Achaeans by Flamininus, and now the campaigns of Fulvius had added Ambracia and Cephallenia. These were undoubtedly declared free, and continued so under the Principate. Delphi, also free, was somewhat in a class by itself, and Phocis was in yet another category. The effect of the withdrawal of troops by the Scipios and the later operations against Aetolia and Cephallenia was that Phocis was left unoccupied and that the Roman army, which remained in Greece from 189 to 187, was stationed in western Greece, in all likelihood with headquarters on Cephallenia. The only information on this point is that when Fulvius left for the Peloponnesus, he stationed a garrison at Same.[2] Since he obviously did not take the bulk of his army along with himself, it probably remained on Cephallenia, and much of it must have remained there until it returned to Italy. How much Cephallenia meant to the Roman plans, is shown by the pains taken to detach it from Aetolia and to capture Same. It certainly was not the intention of the Romans that, when their army returned to Italy, the island was once more to become the headquarters for pirates or enemies, and it did not become so. How was this managed? Historians have sometimes used the word annexation in connexion with the protectorate in Illyria and also for Zacynthus and Cephallenia, but there is no evidence for Roman officials stationed permanently in these places. Yet somehow the cities seem to have understood from the very beginning that, though they were called free, they were not entirely so.

[1] Livy xxxviii. 28.5–29.11 (siege of Same), 35 (consular elections etc.) ; for the chronology, see Walbank, *Philip V*, 333.
[2] Livy xxxviii. 30. 1–2.

After the settlement at Cephallenia, Fulvius crossed to the Peloponnesus to intervene in the affairs of the Achaean Confederacy and Sparta. This was not an armed intervention but was much like that of Roman ambassadors in the periods between wars, the chief difference being that he came from the Roman headquarters on Cephallenia instead of from Rome. The closest earlier parallel is the intervention at various times of Flamininus after his return to Greece in 192. The merits of the issues are difficult to determine. The chief source is Livy, who drew on Polybius, and Polybius was anything but unprejudiced when the Achaeans were involved. In addition, the chief actor on the Achaean side was Philopoemen, and Lycortas, the father of Polybius, had been the right hand man of Philipoemen. In 189 and 188 Philopoemen should have found the situation very complicated—'should have found', for it is possible that he acted so impulsively and dictatorially that he ignored the complications. In spite of all danger signals, he persisted in claiming for the Achaeans the right to be masters in the Peloponnesus and settle issues themselves. This policy had seemed logical enough in 192, but even then Flamininus had indicated that greater subservience was desired. Now the issue was raised again when the group at Sparta hostile to the Achaeans appealed to Fulvius and he intervened in their interest. In the events which followed the special antagonism of Sparta and Megalopolis came to the fore. At the same time, Philopoemen secured the passage of a law or rule that the regular meetings of the Achaean council were no longer to be held exclusively at Aegium but were to rotate between various cities. This definitely marked an advance but the settlement seems to have caused some bad feeling between the original Achaeans of the northern coastal district, or at least Aegium, and the rest of the Confederacy.

The break with Sparta was precipitated by the actions of the Spartans themselves but was due to antagonism between the radical group controlling Sparta and the conservative element—oligarchic in spite of its professed democracy—which controlled the Achaean Confederacy. When Sparta had been brought into the Confederacy in 192 by Philopoemen, it had been taken over as it was with organization given it by Nabis and with its territory reduced as it had been by the settlement of 195. In the coastal cities, at that time placed under the protection of the Achaeans, were harboured exiles sent into exile by Nabis. These exiles must constantly have been on the lookout for an opportunity to return and recover their property and the control of the city, and in this they had the sympathy of Philopoemen and other Achaean leaders. As a result of this situation, the Spartans, who felt cooped up and shut off from the sea, staged a night attack on Las, a town a short distance south of Gytheum. The attackers, at first successful, were expelled without too much difficulty when daylight came, but the incident aroused the other towns and the exiles in them, who all sent ambassadors to the Achaeans. Philopoemen, who had just been elected general for 189–188 called an extraordinary meeting of the Achaean primary assembly and sent an ultimatum to the Spartans to surrender those responsible for the attack. The Spartans instead executed thirty of their citizens who favoured the exiles and the policy of Philopoemen. They also renounced their membership in the Achaean Confederacy and sent ambassadors to Fulvius on Cephallenia offering to surrender their city to Rome and asking him to come to the Peloponnesus to accept their surrender. The Achaeans, when informed of this, assembled in another extraordinary meeting and declared war on Sparta, but it was so late in the autumn that hostilities that season were confined to minor raids.[1]

Before he proceeded to the Peloponnesus, Fulvius received an appeal also from Aegium, the old capital of the Confederacy, where for long all regular meetings of the council of the Confederacy had been held by custom rather than by law. Thus, Philopoemen may have acted arbitrarily but not illegally when he summoned what must have been the first regular meeting of the year to meet at Argos and, at the same time, proposed the passing of a law to make it compulsory to rotate the meetings between various cities. This became known early enough for the citizens of Aegium to send their appeal to Fulvius. This appeal in a purely domestic controversy is a startling example of the tendency of any Greeks who felt aggrieved to appeal to the Romans. Fulvius, as it turned out, came to Aegium too late. Though the *damiorgoi*, the federal cabinet, so to speak, held out for Aegium, everybody else had gone to Argos. Apparently public opinion was strongly on the side of Philopoemen. Fulvius too now went to Argos but again came too late to influence the decision.[2] Hence all he did was to arrange to have another extraordinary meeting summoned at Elis, a meeting which also the Spartans were asked to attend. Fulvius now found himself in an impossible position. In 191 the Romans had urged the return of the exiles. To do so now, would have meant supporting the policy of Philopoemen, while to support the Spartans would have meant co-operating with a state transformed by social revolution. Hence he could think of nothing better than to ask that

[1] Livy xxxviii. 30. 6–32. 2. The order of events is somewhat confused, but the Spartan communication sent to Fulvius on Cephallenia and the declaration of war late in the autumn help fix the time. On the two Achaean meetings, which both must have been *synkletoi*, see *Rep. Govt.* 174 and Aymard, *ACA* 236 f.

[2] Livy xxxviii. 30. 1–5; cf. *Rep. Govt.* 174 f. On the change in the place of meetings see above under 'The Achaean Confederacy' at p. 235 and n. 1.

hostilities be postponed until the Roman senate could be consulted. The senate was to do no better than Fulvius, nor can one say too much for the way the Achaeans handled the situation. Their ambassadors were Lycortas, who represented the point of view of Philopoemen demanding a free hand in Peloponnesian affairs, and Diophanes, who was willing to leave everything to the senate.

The senate apparently wished to avoid offending either the Achaeans or the Spartans and sent both parties away feeling that the reply of the senate was favourable to themselves. The explanation must again be that the two embassies were heard separately and did not confront each other. That made it possible to give both ambiguous but friendly answers. Philopoemen, acting on the supposition that the Achaeans had been given a free hand, mobilized the Achaean army on the Spartan frontier. From there he sent ambassadors with a list of men considered responsible for the revolt, demanding their surrender and promising that those surrendered would not be punished without a trial, and that the city itself then be left in peace. When these demands were announced, the men named and a certain number of others volunteered to go. The situation looked promising for as reasonable a settlement of a difficult problem as was possible. Though war had been declared, Philopoemen had chosen to negotiate, and those Spartans who had most at stake had shown confidence in the pledge given by the Achaean ambassadors. Unfortunately everything was spoiled by the failure of the Achaeans to keep their promises, and it looks as if a great deal of blame must fall on Philopoemen personally. There was a considerable number of Spartan exiles with the army of Philopoemen. These exiles fell upon the Spartans who were giving themselves up as they approached the gate of the camp and incited some of the Achaeans to join them. The result was that seventeen were killed on the spot. It would seem that a man with Philopoemen's ability as a commander should have been able to prevent such an occurrence. What is worse, there seems to have been a certain hypocrisy in his pledge to give the surrendered Spartans a fair trial. Sixty-three were rescued from the mob only to be put to death next day after a perfunctory trial. If the blame on Philopoemen implied in Livy's account is derived from Polybius, it shows that even he could not acquit Philopoemen of all responsibility.[1]

[1] Livy xxxviii. 32–33 gives the fullest continuous narrative. Plut. *Philop.* 16 gives the number put to death by Philopoemen as eighty according to Polybius and 350 according to a certain Aristocrates otherwise unknown but clearly hostile to the Achaeans. A great deal of difficulty has been caused by the last words in Livy xxxviii. 32. 10 *Philopoemeni continuatur magistratus*, which have caused scholars to conclude that Philopoemen was elected general two years in succession and so also to divide events given above as belonging to the year 189–188 between the two terms. So Niese, *Geschichte*, iii. 44 f.; De Sanctis, *Storia*, iv. i. 230

The Achaeans now gave orders to the Spartans as to a conquered community. The walls of the city were to be demolished, the former mercenaries of the tyrant and the helots liberated by him were to leave the country, subject to the right of seizure and sale into slavery if they remained behind, old Spartan laws and customs were to be replaced by Achaean laws, and exiles were to be restored. Many of the former mercenaries and helots, instead of leaving, tried to hide in rural districts. These were hunted down, and the number sold into slavery has been put at 3,000. In addition, according to one account, 300 leaders were exiled, so that the Achaeans, when they restored one group of exiles, themselves created another group.[1] The best that can be said for Philopoemen is that he may have hoped to settle the question once and for all by vigorous and decisive action. If so, he failed miserably and helped prepare the way for long years of bitter controversy. To what extent the Romans were to blame is difficult to say. Certainly their intervention this time did more harm than good. Possibly if it had not been for their hope of support from Rome, the Spartans would not have attacked Las and thus started a long sequence of troubles for themselves and the Achaeans.

The intervention of Flamininus, Glabrio, and Fulvius in Achaean affairs shows the extent to which the Romans expected the Greeks to follow their instructions. The extent of subservience expected is shown even more strikingly in an incident involving Boeotia which occurred in 187–186. Flamininus interested himself in the case of Zeuxippus, the pro-Roman leader held responsible for instigating the murder of Brachylles. Since then he had been in exile. Flamininus now induced the senate to write to the Boeotians to recall Zeuxippus and members of his party. The answer of the Boeotians was that he had been condemned for the murder of Brachylles and also had been found guilty of sacrilege and that these verdicts could not be invalidated. Thereupon the senate, before which Zeuxippus had appeared in person, wrote to the Aetolians and Achaeans to restore him. What the Aetolians did, if anything, is not known. The Achaeans sent ambassadors urging compliance with the Roman demands and at the same time seeking settlement of outstanding grievances of their own. The Boeotians promised compliance, but failed to keep their promises.

and 404; Holleaux, *CAH* viii. 236. But see Aymard, 'Les stratèges de la Confédération achéene, de 202 à 172 av. J.-C.', *REA* xxx (1928) 1–62 at 14–23. Granting that *continuatur magistratus* normally would refer to re-election, need it mean more than that Philopoemen was still in office? If taken in this meaning many difficulties disappear.

[1] Livy xxxviii 34 is the fullest account. The number of those sold into slavery is given as 3,000 by Plut. *Philop.* 16 and Paus. viii. 51. 3; the latter also adds that 300 leaders were banished. Undoubtedly there were some banished at this time; cf. the reference in Pol. xxiii. 4. 5 to Spartans banished by the Achaeans.

Thereupon Philopoemen, who again was general, authorized those with grievances—clearly Achaean rather than Roman grievances—to use self-help. This was much like privateering against a state with which one was not at war. This time war almost followed, but the Roman senate dropped the case, and the Megarians succeeded in reconciling the Boeotians and Achaeans and putting an end to the raids.[1] Zeuxippus apparently still remained in exile. The action of the Boeotians shows that the Greeks were not always weak-kneed and subservient, while Philopoemen was his own independent self. They must have realized that Rome would not go to war for every minor offence. At the same time, it was already becoming clear that the Romans could assert themselves by using Greeks against Greeks.

4. MACEDONIAN AND ACHAEAN AMBITIONS AND FRUSTRATIONS TO 146 B.C.

The period between the defeat of the Aetolians and the creation of the province of Macedonia in 148, soon followed by the Achaean War and the destruction of Corinth, in some ways is the most difficult in Greek history. It is not made any more easy by being regarded as only an aspect of Roman history. From the point of view of the ultimate establishment of Roman power, this has a tendency to cause all opposition to Rome to be regarded as the height of absurdity. It is realized that after the Second Macedonian War Philip V had rebuilt the Macedonian war machine sufficiently to be a real menace, but the effort of the Achaeans to be independent meets with little appreciation. Yet surveying the period in detail almost leads to the opposite conclusion. The statesmen and politicians who were constantly deferring to a distant power without any military force on the ground look like the ones who should be called stupid and naïve, and, when they combined with this attitude plots against their political opponents, they deserve a stronger characterization. This statement must not be taken too seriously, though it remains true that, when the events of the period are observed, the efforts of Greek leaders to be independent were not as unrealistic as they have been judged after their failure. These leaders knew that at the time the Romans had no troops in Greece, were not anxious to send an army there, and so would be likely to overlook even certain acts of which they did not approve.

What follows will largely be a discussion of Achaean and Peloponnesian affairs. The settlement of 196 had left three major states in the Balkans, Macedonia, Aetolia, and Achaea. Of these, Aetolia had now lost its former importance. On the other hand, the wars against

[1] Pol. xxii. 4.

Antiochus and the Aetolians had strengthened the other two. Clashes with Roman authorities soon caused hostility between the Macedonian and Roman governments, which finally led to the Third Macedonian War. The Achaean situation was different, as the Confederacy developed statesmen with opposite points of view, one group, ready to follow directions from Rome unquestioningly; the other, trying to assume a more independent attitude. The second group was in the ascendancy most of the time and scored some successes, but it was also the group which finally led the Confederacy into the ill-fated Achaean War.

The Achaean Confederacy had two primary trouble spots, Sparta and Messene. The citizens of both states felt themselves wronged by the Achaeans, both appealed to Rome, and in both cases Roman interference did more harm than good. At the same time Roman ambassadors and letters from the senate dealt also with the affairs of other Greek states and of Macedonia. All this produced a situation of such a kind that Rome either had to intervene again by force of arms or declare herself bankrupt as the director of the affairs of the eastern Mediterranean world. That Rome had assumed such a role, consciously or unconsciously, is clear to anyone who surveys the activities of Roman ambassadors and the many rulings by the senate on eastern questions.[1]

In the controversy with the Achaeans, the Spartans continued to act as citizens of a city independent of the Achaean Confederacy and one of which the relations to that Confederacy were still open to negotiations. The Achaeans seem to have admitted this, no doubt much against their will, to the extent that they did not interfere with the sending of ambassadors from Sparta to Rome. At least such ambassadors appeared in Rome year after year, and there seems to be no report about any of them being arrested on the way, though much of their journey must have been by a route or routes easily supervised by the Achaeans. Since the Achaeans regarded foreign affairs as the domain of the federal government, this absence of interference must have been due to consideration for the disapproval of Rome. Certainly the attitude of the Romans was far from correct. It seems that their treaty with the Achaeans actually specified that only ambassadors from the federal government were to have access to the senate; the individual cities were forbidden to send ambassadors.[2] After several years of bickering, the issue came to a head in 183, when the senate

---

[1] Aymard, *Premiers Rapports* demonstrates the early adoption of such an attitude in relations with the Achaeans.

[2] Paus. vii. 9. 4 apparently derived from an excellent source; cf. Wachsmuth, 'Über eine Hauptquelle für die Geschichte des achäischen Bundes', *Leipziger Studien*, x (1887), 269–98.

appointed a commission of three experts who attempted to draw up a general and permanent settlement.

Philopoemen and the Achaeans undoubtedly wished to consider the settlement they had imposed on Sparta in 188 as permanent. Not so the Spartans, who already that year sent ambassadors to Rome. These secured a letter from Aemilius Lepidus, one of the consuls of 187, criticizing the handling of the situation by the Achaeans. To answer the criticisms involved, Philopoemen, who had been elected general for 187–186 sent to Rome an embassy headed by Nicodemus of Elis. The embassy probably set out late in 187 but seems to have been held over in Rome so that it did not return to Greece before the spring of 185. That year, at a meeting of the Achaean council at Megalopolis, at which a great deal of miscellaneous business was transacted, Nicodemus reported that the senate had criticized several features of the Achaean settlement of the Spartan affairs but had invalidated nothing.[1] Thus the senate seems to have adopted the policy for the time being of merely expressing disapproval and hoping that the Achaeans would act in accordance with its hints without further intervention.

The same desire to direct the affairs of Greece was shown the same year also by the embassy headed by Q. Caecilius Metellus which was to mean so much to the future of the Achaeans. This embassy went into great detail in conferences with Philip at Tempe and Thessalonica on questions concerning Macedonia and Thrace. On the way back, the ambassadors, according to instructions, visited the Peloponnesus. There Aristaenus, the general of the year 186–185, the same who had been general and presided over the meeting at Sicyon in 198 at which the Achaeans decided to break with the Macedonians and the Hellenic League and join the Romans, now summoned a meeting of federal officials at Argos. It seems that an attempt was made to settle the Spartan dilemma in this manner, and the chances for a settlement were as good as they well could be with the Achaeans led by a general considered pro-Roman and the Roman embassy headed by a senior statesman, who had been consul in 206. That the conference failed and even led to an unfortunate impasse between the Achaean officials and the ambassadors, shows the utter impossibility of reconciling Rome's demand for domination with the demand of Philopoemen and his supporters for a free hand in the Peloponnesus. The account of the conference shows further that Philopoemen carried more weight with

---

[1] Pol. xxii. 3. 1–4, 7. 5–7. Lacunas in the latter passage make it difficult to determine what special features were criticized except the destruction of the walls, on which cf. Diod. xxix. 17, where, however, the report is said to have been presented by Roman ambassadors. The version of Polybius is to be accepted.

29

the Achaean officials than the general of the year, but it also shows that there were dissident voices among the Achaeans and that they did not hesitate to speak up even if by so doing they seriously embarrassed their government. The Achaeans never learned to present a united front to the outside world. When Metellus criticized the Achaean treatment of the Spartans, Aristaenus made no reply, thus, according to Polybius, indicating agreement with the criticism. Diophanes, whom Polybius terms a better soldier than statesman, even suggested that not only the affairs of Sparta but also those of Messene had been mishandled. It was left to Philopoemen, Lycortas the father of Polybius, and Archon to defend the Achaean policy and induce their fellow magistrates to answer that the Achaeans would retain the arrangements made. At this point Metallus demanded the summoning of an extraordinary meeting of the Achaean *ekklesia* or primary assembly. The Achaean officials countered by asking for the written statement of the senate on the subject and, when Metallus did not submit any such statement, refused to summon the assembly. The laws did not permit such an action without a written statement from the senate concerning the subject to be submitted. Metellus, angered by this, refused to accept the answer offered and thus officially went off without an answer. The story as told by Polybius implies that the instructions to the ambassadors called for an effort to settle the Spartan question by a conference, and that the request for a meeting of the *ekklesia* was not included but was due to the decision of Metellus made on the spur of the moment.[1]

In refusing to call the meeting requested by Metellus, the Achaean officials undoubtedly had the law on their side, but they may have applied the letter of the law more strictly than necessary. Yet there was a real problem involved. The Achaean officials were not permitted to summon the *ekklesia* except to deal with a question of alliance or war or a subject specified in a written communication from the Roman senate—this latter proviso most likely an amendment added to an earlier law. Moreover, the meeting was to deal with only one item announced in advance. Yet, had the Achaean officials been accommodating, they could themselves have concocted a statement concerning the subject to be submitted and worded it in such a way as to satisfy the requirements. As it was, the incident served only to embitter the relations, already none too good, between the Achaeans and the Romans. Polybius[2] states that the Achaeans at the time

---

[1] Conference with Philip: Livy xxxix. 24–29; meeting with Achaean officials: Pol. xxii. 10; Paus. vii. 8. 6, 9. 1; cf. *Rep. Govt.* 89 f. The meeting requested by Metellus clearly was one of the kind called *synkletos* by scholars, but Polybius here does not use this term but speaks of the *ekklesia*.

[2] Pol. xxii. 10. 14.

attributed the intervention of Metellus and the earlier intervention of Fulvius Nobilior to the machinations of Aristaenus and Diophanes. If the Achaeans really thought that the Roman representatives intervened only because certain Achaeans had induced them to do so, they may have thought that the Romans took little real interest in the issues involved. Otherwise it is hard to understand their defiance of a man as prominent as Metellus.

The Achaean treatment of Sparta and the rebuff of Metellus were taken up in the Roman senate during the winter of 185–184. By special arrangement the Achaean and Spartan ambassadors were brought before the senate at the same time to argue their cases. The Spartan ambassadors were Areus and Alcibiades, who had been among the exiles restored by Philopoemen and the Achaeans. To the Achaeans, this seemed a case of flagrant ingratitude, though it is also possible to argue that their action shows that the Achaean settlement was so bad that even those who owed them a debt of gratitude turned against them. As will be noted below, Areus and Alcibiades did not belong to the extremists but to the more moderate element among the 'old exiles'. After listening to the arguments of both sides, the senate merely turned the matter over to another embassy which had already been appointed to go to Macedonia. This embassy was headed by Appius Claudius, the consul of the preceding year, who earlier had served under Flamininus in Greece and at the time of the evacuation in 194 had led the main division of Roman troops from Elatea in Phocis to Oricus in Illyria. After this, the senate took up the question of the Achaean treatment of Metellus, now apparently with only Achaean and no Spartan ambassadors present. The Achaeans defended their treatment of Metellus. The report of this defence, incidentally, contains the best statement we have concerning the Achaean law forbidding the summoning of the *ekklesia* except for special questions. In his reply, Metellus accused Philopoemen and Lycortas by name. The senate thereupon told the Achaean ambassadors that it would send representatives to look into the Spartan question—undoubtedly meaning the embassy headed by Appius Claudius. They further advised the Achaeans for the future to pay courteous and proper attention to Roman ambassadors visiting them.[1] The senate, it seems, was still trying to avoid being excessively harsh. The Achaeans, however, did nothing to further an understanding. Before the arrival of the Roman ambassadors, Lycortas, the general for the year 185–184,

---

[1] Pol. xxii. 11–12; Livy xxxix. 33; Paus. vii. 9. 1–3. In this case the report of proceedings in the senate undoubtedly is derived by Polybius, directly or indirectly, from the Achaean ambassadors. Livy's report is very brief but contains the statement that the senate instructed the Achaeans to allow Roman ambassadors free access to their assembly. The less specific statement reported by Polybius is probably more correct.

at a meeting of the Achaeans, apparently one of the regular meetings of their representative council, presented the case of Areus and Alcibiades with the result that they were condemned to death *in absentia*. Legally and technically the condemnation may have been justified, but it was hardly good politics. A few days later the Roman ambassadors arrived with Areus and Alcibiades in their party. This time an extraordinary meeting of the Achaean primary assembly was called. In spite of the warnings of Appius Claudius, the Achaeans still refused to make any changes in their former arrangements, but they did cancel the death sentence of the two Spartans. Livy reports further that the Achaeans requested the Romans to make those changes which they themselves could not actually make without violating their oath.[1] It is doubtful that the Achaeans actually made such a request, and yet the next year a Roman commission did proceed to draw up a plan for settlement. On the other hand, it appears that Appius actually invited the Spartans to come to Rome with their complaints.[2] This must be the reason for the spate of Spartan ambassadors appearing in Rome the following year.

The procedure next adopted by the senate was to appoint a committee of experts, namely, Titus Flamininus, Metellus, and Appius Claudius,[3] to draw up a plan of settlement. They did so on the basis of conferences exclusively with the ambassadors of the Spartans and the Spartan exiles. Appius Claudius probably already had this procedure in mind when he issued his invitation to the Spartans to bring their complaints to Rome. When the plan formulated in this manner had been drawn up, it was presented to the Achaean ambassadors then in Rome and they were induced to accept it.[4] There actually were four groups of Spartan ambassadors present. Of these two represented the old exiles restored by the Achaeans. Of these the extremists demanded the return of their former landed estates in their entirety; the more moderate group represented by Areus and Alcibiades asked that each returning exile should recover his estate up to a value of a talent and that the rest should be distributed to men deserving citizenship. A third group of ambassadors, headed by Serippus, asked

---

[1] Livy xxxix. 35. 5–37. 21; Paus. vii. 9. 3–4. On the two Achaean meetings cf. *Rep. Govt.* 177 f.

[2] This seems to be the meaning of Paus. vii. 9. 4.

[3] Pol. xxiii. 4. 7 gives the number of members as three, but the manuscripts give the names of only two. That the third was Appius Claudius is made almost certain by a mistake in Paus. vii. 9. 5, where it is stated that the senate sent back to Greece Appius and those who had been there with him. It is clear from Polybius that the commission did its work in Rome.

[4] The chief account is that of Pol. xxiii. 4. Next in importance is Paus. vii. 9. 5, which contains the information concerning the use of foreign judges for the trials of Spartans on capital charges; cf. *CP* xliii (1948), 189. The account of Livy xxxix. 48. 2–4 is excessively brief.

for the retention of the organization they had had while members of the Confederacy; in other words, they represented the pro-Achaean group. A fourth set, headed by a certain Chaeron, represented those who had been condemned to death or exiled by the decrees of the Achaeans. These naturally wished to be restored and to have the government of the city modified, apparently so as to give more rights to the lower classes. The three commissioners seem to have made an honest attempt to evolve a workable arrangement. They began by deciding that those exiled or condemned to death were to be restored and the sentences against them cancelled, and that Sparta was to remain a member of the Confederacy. The Spartans were to be subject to the jurisdiction of the Achaean federal courts, but capital charges were to be brought before foreign judges. It is this detail which most clearly indicates something of an effort to produce a working compromise. Achaean pride was to be salvaged by the retention of Sparta in the Confederacy, subject to the jurisdiction of Achaean courts, while the use of foreign judges in capital cases was to safeguard the lives of the Spartans against the vindictiveness of the Achaeans. Unfortunately there are so many lacunae in the text of Polybius that it is impossible to know for certain the terms concerning the control of property, but it looks as if the old exiles were not permitted to recover all of their former property but were each allowed a sizeable estate.[1] Whatever the merits of this settlement, its chance of success was small for the simple reason that it had been drawn up without consulting the Achaeans and had been presented to their ambassadors only after it had been completed. Under pressure, the Achaean ambassadors affixed their seal to the document. Whether or not this was regarded as binding by the home authorities, it seems that the plan submitted was adopted at least to the extent that the group of exiles represented by Chaeron were allowed to return,[2] but their return led to confusion rather than peace. Nevertheless, even if they yielded in this one case, the party of Philopoemen and Lycortas otherwise continued to be as stubborn as ever in upholding the rights of the Achaeans.

The restoration of the group of exiles just mentioned should have meant that there no longer were any Spartan exiles. Instead, already in the summer of 183 the problem of exiles was back to vex all concerned. What had happened seems to be that the band of exiles headed by Chaeron on their return had immediately formed a sort

[1] Pol. xxxiii. 4. 9 indicates that there was disagreement about the question of retaining estates to the value of one talent, thus implying that the more extreme claims were disallowed.

[2] This is deduced from the facts that Chaeron later appeared as an ambassador from Sparta to Rome, and that he was very active in Spartan politics (Pol. xxiii. 18. 4, xxiv. 7).

of coalition with the party headed by Serippus—an alliance of the lower and middle classes—and had driven into exile once more many, if not all, of the old exiles. Instead of allowing them to recover parts of their former estates, the authorities now actually confiscated the land which the 'tyrants' (Cleomenes and Nabis) had allowed sisters, wives, mothers, and children of those exiled to retain.[1] Since this happened at a time when Sparta belonged to the Achaean Confederacy and in part as the result of a settlement by Roman commissioners, it is startling evidence of the extent of discontent among members of the lower classes and of the tendency towards social revolution. The same year an embassy headed by Q. Marcius Philippus, the consul of 186, was sent to Macedonia and told also to look in on the Peloponnesus.[2] There is no report of its activities there, but there is a report that Flamininus, who was on his way to Bithynia, wrote from Naupactus to the Achaean general and *damiorgoi* demanding that they summon a *synkletos*, an extraordinary meeting of the Achaean primary assembly. When they asked for a written statement concerning the subject to be submitted and he failed to send one, the Achaeans refused to call the meeting.[3] In this case the Achaeans obviously were in the right. To expect them to call a meeting for a Roman dignitary who was merely passing by, even if that dignitary was Flamininus, was going rather far. This rebuff of Flamininus is said by Polybius to have been a great disappointment to the so-called old exiles who had recently been exiled from Sparta. Thus this group had been exiled already in the summer of 183. Thus the failure of the settlement drawn up by the Roman commissioners was immediate and complete. The Roman government, however, with its usual tendency to uphold a ruling once made, seems to have regarded it as valid to the end. This will be seen in connexion with the negotiations preceding the Corinthian War of 146.

The year 182, in which also troubles with Messene came to a head, was decisive for the history of the Achaean Confederacy and its relations with Rome. The Achaeans were still determined to direct their own policy in the Peloponnesus and even to call on Rome as an ally to aid them against the Messenians. The embassy sent to Rome in the autumn of 183 apparently made no mention of Sparta, acting on the supposition that the question was settled. Instead it requested aid against Messene, or, failing that, at least an embargo on the ship-

---

[1] In this activity Chaeron was most prominent (Pol. xxiv. 7). That the party of Serippus was active can be deduced from his embassy to Rome in 183–182 (Pol. xxiii. 9. 11). It is clear that the new exiles were the old exiles, as is stated in Pol. xxiii. 5. 18.

[2] Pol. xxiii. 4. 16; Livy xxxix. 48. 5.

[3] Pol. xxiii. 5. 14–18.

ment of weapons and supplies from Italy to Messenia. In spite of the refusal of the Romans to grant aid, the Achaeans succeeded in reducing Messene. During the winter 183–182 there probably were as many embassies as ever in Rome, but the senate saved itself a lot of time by paying little attention to the embassies from the Achaeans, Spartans, and Spartan exiles and instead basing its decision on the report of Marcius Philippus. He suggested that if the senate expressed its disapproval but otherwise ignored the Achaeans, then Sparta and Messene would soon get together and the Achaeans would be in such difficulties that they would appeal to Rome. In accordance with this advice, the Spartan ambassadors were told that the Romans had done all for them that they could do, while the Achaeans were told that they need not be surprised if the Romans did not consider it any concern of theirs if Lacedaemon, Corinth, or Argos should secede from the Confederacy. This reply was publicized, but the ambassadors detained in Rome to await the outcome of events in Messenia.[1] When the news of the reduction of Messene reached Rome, the senate reversed its policy and told the Achaean ambassadors that measures would be taken to prevent the shipment of arms or grain to Messene.[2] The Achaeans may well have considered this a real triumph for their cause and concluded that the Romans would rather let things go their own way than intervene with force of arms.

The summer of 182 saw strange developments in Achaean affairs. Sparta was admitted into the Achaean Confederacy and the terms of admission properly recorded on a stele. It is difficult to determine just what happened. The Achaeans apparently treated the Roman settlement as non-existent and so proceeded to draw up their own. They may have been emboldened to do so by the statement of the senate to the effect that the Romans would not consider that it concerned them if Lacedaemon seceded from the Confederacy. The admission was voted at an extraordinary meeting of the Achaean assembly, at which Lycortas, the general of the year, argued that the Romans had dropped their championship of Sparta—a conclusion justified by the statement of the senate to the Spartan ambassadors that Rome had done all that she could for Sparta. Probably the chief difference between the Achaean and the Roman plan was that the Achaeans claimed complete jurisdiction over the Spartans for their normal courts and did not consider it necessary to refer capital charges to foreign judges. The settlement apparently was not reported to the Roman authorities by the Achaeans, but it was called to their attention both by an embassy from Sparta headed by Chaeron and by an embassy sent by the exiles. The latter were told that the senate would write to the

---

[1] Pol. xxiii. 9; Livy xl. 2. 6–8.   [2] Pol. xxiii. 17. 3.

Achaeans and recommend their restoration. The exiles presented this letter to the Achaeans, but the latter decided to await the return of their own ambassadors from Rome. These reported that the senate had sent the letter about the exiles, not on account of any real interest in their cause but merely to please them. As a consequence the Achaeans voted to make no change in their earlier arrangements. In other words, the exiles remained exiles.[1]

All at first seems to have gone well. Trouble began after Chaeron returned from his embassy to Rome some time in 181. He proceeded to turn demagogue and squandered public funds illegally and irresponsibly. When auditors were appointed, clearly by the Spartans themselves, Chaeron had the most prominent member of the board assassinated. This was too much for the general of the Achaeans, no doubt Lycortas, who intervened, brought Chaeron to trial, and had him imprisoned. Steps were also taken to restore to the relatives of exiles property which had been taken away from them by Chaeron. These actions seem to have been salutary, even if the general may have stretched somewhat the right of federal officials to intervene in local affairs. So far the party of Philopoemen and Lycortas was clearly in the ascendancy. In the autumn of 181 Lycortas was succeeded as general by Hyperbatus, a member of the opposite group. After his election he summoned an extraordinary meeting of the Achaean assembly and submitted once more the letter from the Roman senate concerning the restoration of exiles at Sparta, thus trying to use his influence as general to get the earlier action of the Achaeans overruled. In this he was disappointed. At the meeting Lycortas once more defended the arrangements already made, while Hyperbatus and Callicrates urged the Achaeans to follow the advice of the Romans. Lycortas won on this issue, but an embassy was sent to Rome, and among the ambassadors was Callicrates, who advised the senate to be more firm with the Achaeans. To the praise given him by the Romans is attributed the election of Callicrates as general for 180–179. During his term of office, he secured the restoration of exiles both at Sparta and at Messene.[2] Before considering further the significance of this it is necessary to glance at the situation at Messene.

The first admission of Messene into the Achaean Confederacy had been arranged by Flamininus in 191 after he had called off the Achaean army under the command of Diophanes. At the time the Messenians were told to bring home their exiles. The restoration led

---

[1] Pol. xxiii. 17–18; xxiv. 1–2; Livy xl. 20. 2. On the Achaean meetings, cf. *Rep. Govt.* 179 f.

[2] Pol. xxiv. 7–10. The summoning of a *synkletos* by Hyperbatus was probably irregular; cf. *Rep. Govt.* 180. Callicrates honoured for the restoration of Spartan exiles: *SIG*[3] 634.

to disputes and difficulties, in which Philopoemen intervened later as general but obviously without too much success. Yet the dispute does not seem to have been brought to the attention of the Romans before in 185, when Metellus visited the Peloponnesus. In his conference with Achaean dignitaries concerning Sparta, Diophanes injected the statement that this was not the only affair that had been mishandled. There was also the case of Messene, where there was trouble arising from the decree of Flamininus concerning the exiles and the efforts of Philopoemen to adjust matters.[1] To contrast the Messenians with the ever cantankerous Spartans, it is interesting to note that the complaint was not lodged by a Messenian but by an Achaean politician. Next year the Messenians seem to have decided to appeal to Rome. At any rate, Deinocrates of Messene was in Rome as an ambassador during the winter 184–183 or early in 183. On his arrival he found out about the appointment of Flamininus to go to Bithynia. Thereupon Deinocrates centred all his attention on Flamininus hoping through his intervention, while on his way to Bithynia, to secure the settlement of Messenian affairs to suit himself. Apparently his plans involved secession and war if necessary. All this he is said to have undertaken rather thoughtlessly. Flamininus, though he rebuked him for his levity, promised to do his best for the cause.[2] Though Flamininus had no instructions to intervene in Greece, the appeal to him was not unnatural. Yet, as already noted, he accomplished nothing. The same year Quintus Marcius Philippus, on his way back from Macedonia at least had the opportunity to urge the Achaeans to do nothing about the Messenians without the approval of Rome. The Achaeans disregarded this advice and late in 183 voted to go to war. The advice of Marcius suggests that Deinocrates and his supporters already had proclaimed the secession of Messene and trusted to the Romans to support their action.[3]

Hostilities probably began in the autumn of 183, but the only operations about which much information is preserved belong to the following year. Meanwhile Achaean ambassadors sent to Rome called on the Romans as allies for military aid, or, failing that, for the prevention of the shipment of arms or food from Italy to Messene. The answer was the famous warning that the Romans would not consider it any

---

[1] Livy xxxvi. 31; Pol. xxii. 10. 4–6; cf. Roebuck, *History of Messenia*, 91 ff.

[2] Pol. xxiii. 5. 1–12; Plut. *Flam.* 17. The latter states that Deinocrates planned to detach Messene from the Confederacy; this receives a certain amount of verification from the statement of Flamininus as reported by Polybius concerning the serious nature of his plans.

[3] Flamininus and Achaeans: Pol. xxiii. 5. 14–18. The report of the advice of Marcius is contained in a speech delivered later by the Achaean Callicrates before the senate (Pol. xxiv. 9. 12–13).

concern of theirs if Sparta, Corinth, or Argos were to secede. This must mean that the bonds between the Achaeans and the Messenians were considered severed and that others were encouraged to follow their example. The senate apparently thought that Marcius was right when he prophesied that the Achaeans, if left to themselves, would have more trouble with the Spartans and Messenians than they could handle.[1] As it turned out, after the capture and execution of Philopoemen the Messenians were quickly brought to terms by Lycortas, who was elected to complete the unexpired term of Philopoemen and further elected to serve for 182–181.[2] When Deinocrates found it necessary to negotiate, Lycortas demanded that the Messenians surrender those responsible for the revolt and the death of Philopoemen, receive a garrison in their acropolis, and allow all other questions to be settled by the Achaean nation (*ethnos*). This settlement was arranged at the second regular *synodos* of the year, probably in the late spring or early summer. In the settlement so made a number of towns were detached and admitted into the Confederacy as separate communities so that Messene no longer should be too large.[3] When the news of the Achaean success reached Rome, the senate informed the Achaeans that it had placed the embargo on the shipment of weapons and food to Messene which they had requested, but which the senate had refused earlier. What is more, when Achaean ambassadors in Rome reported the victory over the Messenians and their subsequent arrangements, they were given a friendly reception by the senate.[4] It could hardly have indicated more clearly that the Achaeans had won. Hence, though the senate sent the letter about the Spartan exiles already mentioned, it is no wonder that the Achaeans felt free to disregard it. The fact that, when they came to the final settlement of the Messenian question, they granted the city three years exemption from federal taxes,[5] indicates that whatever their attitude towards those responsible for the death of Philopoemen, they meant to carry no grudge against the average citizen of Messene. The dividing of an

[1] Pol. xxiii. 9. 8–14.

[2] The chief accounts are Livy xxxix. 49–50; Plut. *Philop.* 18–21; Paus. iv. 29. 11–12, viii. 51. 5–8; Justin xxxii. 1. 4–10. Livy places the outbreak of the war in 183 and then relates immediately the story of the death of Philopoemen, but that only means that, having taken up the story, he finishes it. The presence of Achaean ambassadors in Rome early in 182 shows that the problem had become acute before their dispatch in 183, and that the hostilities were not yet over. For the puzzling problems of the succession on the death of Philopoemen and the assemblies of the year, cf. *Rep. Govt.* 178 f.

[3] Pol. xxiii. 16, 17. 1–2. For a discussion of the cities probably detached in 191 see Roebuck, *History of Messenia*, 93 f. and n. 124.

[4] Pol. xxiii. 17. 3, xxiv. 1. 6–7; Livy xl. 20. 2. At this point, Benecke, *CAH* viii. 299, though critical of the policy of Philopoemen, remarks: 'An independent policy had so far proved successful'.

[5] Pol. xxiv. 2.

over-large community into several smaller units was a natural policy for a federal state to adopt and was not a sign of special hostility.

Serious difficulties for the party of Philopoemen, of which, after his death, Lycortas was the leader, began at home with the meeting in the autumn of 181 at which the newly elected general Hyperbatus asked the Achaeans to reconsider a decision made earlier in the year under the presidency of Lycortas. At the meeting, Hyperbatus apparently was defeated, for it was decided to send an embassy to Rome to defend the policy of Lycortas. Yet, even if it was not realized at the time, the decision to send an embassy was contrary to the interests of Lycortas, for what was to be gained by sending an embassy to inform the senate that its advice was being disregarded? Thus the very dispatch of the embassy was in a sense a victory for Hyperbatus, but an even greater victory was the inclusion in the embassy of Callicrates, who was at least as strong an opponent of Lycortas as Hyperbatus himself. At Rome, Callicrates seems to have taken over and disregarded his colleagues, a Lydiades of Megalopolis and an Aratus of Sicyon. Instead of defending the policy of Lycortas, he proceeded to condemn it and to advise the senate to be more firm in support of its partisans. Influenced by his advice, the senate not only wrote to the Achaeans about the restoration of the Spartan exiles but also sent statements to the Aetolians, Epirotes, Athenians, Boeotians, and Acarnanians. In its reply to the Achaeans, it added further that it would be well if they had more statesmen like Callicrates. On the strength of this recommendation, Callicrates was elected general for 180–179, and during his term of office effected the restoration of exiles both at Sparta and Messene. It is difficult to appraise his work. Polybius considers him the author of great evils for Greece. At the time it would still have been possible for a state which had been a faithful ally to deal with the Romans almost on terms of equality. The Romans had a laudable weakness for supporting people who appealed to them but, when the claims of justice were pointed out, usually gave in.[1] This statement by the son of Lycortas may be rather strong. Yet it is noticeable that, except for the generalship of Callicrates and his temporary control of the policy of the Confederacy, there was no sudden change in the Achaean attitude and policy or in the Roman treatment of them. The great change came only with the Third Macedonian War and

[1] Pol. xxiv. 8–10. Judgements on Callicrates vary. Freeman, *History of Federal Government*[2], 513 f. is strong in his condemnation of 'this wretch'; Niese, *Geschichte*, iii. 59 represents him as an ambitious politician lacking a conscience; Cary, *The Greek World from 323 to 146 B.C.* (1932), 197 f. considers the transfer of leadership from Philopoemen to Callicrates fortunate; Badian, *Foreign Clientelae*, 90 f., in an interesting account written from the Roman point of view, almost makes Callicrates the saviour of the Roman policy and states that 'there is no doubt that he was right'.

specifically with the victory at Pydna. Before that victory there were, even during the war, some surprising concessions to public opinion in Greek states.

The two Achaean political parties differed also in their attitude towards relations with the Hellenistic monarchies and in particular Ptolemaic Egypt. The party of Philopoemen and Lycortas seemed to feel that negotiating treaties of alliance with this kingdom and going on embassies to Alexandria, even if the Ptolemies were interested in Greece chiefly as a source of mercenary soldiers, gave them some standing in international affairs. Hyperbatus, on the other hand, tried to prevent the renewing of an alliance, obviously because he wished the Achaeans to be closely involved only with the Romans. At the same time there were negotiations also with Seleucus IV of the Seleucid monarchy and Eumenes of Pergamum. All of this and more came up at a *synodos* or regular meeting of the Achaean council at Megalopolis in 185. Both the Pergamene and Seleucid ambassadors received a less friendly reception than those of Ptolemy. It was at this meeting that the Achaeans received and rejected the offer of Eumenes of a gift of 120 talents to be invested and the proceeds used for paying members of the Achaean *boule* when attending the meetings. Whatever the real reason for the refusal, the debate revealed considerable hostility towards Eumenes, thus showing a marked reversal from the close association of 190. The reversal was due to resentment against him for his control of Aegina and probably further meddling in Greek affairs. There is no indication of a similar resentment against Seleucus IV, whose ambassadors wished to renew friendship and offered a gift of a squadron of ten 'long ships'. The Achaeans decided to renew the friendship but to refuse the gift. The significance of this is not clear, but the Seleucid embassy does not seem to have attracted much attention. The embassy from Ptolemy Epiphanes was quite another matter. In 186, while Philopoemen was general, an Athenian, Demetrius, had come as ambassador from Ptolemy to renew the existing treaty between Ptolemy and the Achaean nation (*ethnos*). The renewal was gladly accepted, and an embassy headed by Lycortas sent to Egypt for the exchange of oaths connected with the ratification. In 185 Lycortas was back, but now Aristaenus, a member of the opposition party, was general. By merely asking which treaty was being renewed and pointing out the differences between the various old treaties, he managed to block proceedings. A treaty was, however, renewed later when Lycortas became general.[1] The story of the confusion caused by the conflict between the various older treaties gives

---

[1] Meeting of 185: Pol. xxii. 7–9 and, very brief, Diod. xxix. 17; the 186 dispatch of ambassadors: Pol. xxii. 3. 5–6; renewal under Lycortas: xxiv. 6. 4.

a clue to the significance of the transaction. The Peloponnesus was one of the great sources of mercenary soldiers, and the many treaties of alliance between the Ptolemies and the Achaeans must mean that the kings found that such treaties facilitated the raising of mercenaries. All this time the Ptolemies held Methana as what must have been something like a permanent armed legation and recruiting station, nor is there any sign that the Achaeans raised the same objection to the control of Methana by the Ptolemies as they did to that of Aegina by Eumenes. For about this time there is also a report of a Ptolemaic recruiting officer busy in Greece.[1] Meanwhile it seems to have tickled the vanity of the Achaeans to say that they were allies of the Ptolemies, while leading Achaeans took pleasure in visiting the court at Alexandria as ambassadors.

In 181, in the case of an embassy to Alexandria that was planned but did not materialize, it is clear that at least one ambassador was appointed to give the young man a treat. In that year a Ptolemaic embassy offered a gift of ten penteconters, probably actually fifty oared *lemboi*. To receive this gift and bring the ships to Greece, Lycortas and his son Polybius, though under age, and Aratus, the son of Aratus of Sicyon were selected. The latter was probably a grandson of the famous Aratus. Since Lycortas was general in 182–181 it must have been the intention to leave in the autumn after the election of his successor. This embassy was cancelled on the news of the death of Ptolemy Epiphanes. Later in the autumn Aratus was chosen to go to Rome with Callicrates and Lydiades of Megalopolis, probably a descendant of the tyrant who later served as general of the Achaean Confederacy.[2] Thus members of great families tended to be favoured in the selection of ambassadors, at least in the period of the ascendancy of Lycortas. The Ptolemaic drive for mercenaries and the Achaean game of diplomatic relations with the Ptolemies continued even during the Third Macedonian War.

The Third Macedonian War, as is generally realized, marked a turning point in Rome's relations with Greek and eastern states. At the outbreak of the war, the Romans called on their Greek allies—allies in the broadest sense—for help, but they also showed the same desire to direct the affairs of these states as they had done in the earlier period. Yet, when any of them failed to comply, the Romans at first yielded, and it was only after Pydna that they became oppressive and dictatorial. Before that they even adopted measures to protect their allies against the excesses of Roman commanders. Some were brought

[1] Pol. xxii. 17. 6.
[2] Pol. xxiv. 6 and 8. 8. With reference to the penteconters, though smaller *lemboi* are known, Pol. ii. 3. 1 implies fifty men for each of the Illyrian *lemboi*.

to trial, and in 170 a *senatus consultum* stating that nothing was to be furnished commanders beyond what the senate had decreed was passed and given wide publicity. The continued co-operation, or at least friendship, of the various states, was of prime importance. The Macedonian kingdom had recovered to such an extent that the outcome of the war was not a foregone conclusion. Some of the Boeotian cities sided with Macedonia, and the Epirotes started a rebellion that implied some hope of defeating the Romans.

To take up in detail the question of the causes of the war and the diplomatic sparring preceding it, would serve no good purpose. Most of the information about all of this comes from Livy, but his sources are largely annalistic, and it is not always easy to know how much of what is reported is reliable. For the war itself, no general account will be given. Only some special subjects will be considered, namely, the participation of Greeks in the early operations, the attitudes and contributions of some of the federal states, and finally the change in Roman methods following the victory at Pydna.

For several Greek states the first test in connexion with the Third Macedonian War came in 172, whether war actually had been declared by that time or not. The beginning of the war is usually placed in 171, though in 172 the Romans sent a commission headed by Marcius Philippus to Macedonia and Greece to prepare for the war to come. The commissioners divided the tasks between themselves and set out to visit various Greek states to induce them to send troops to occupy strategic positions and in other ways to prepare for the war that was expected. Marcius is reported to have granted Perseus a truce to enable him to send ambassadors to Rome.[1] This means that war already had been declared but that Perseus was deceived into believing that the chances for peace and the avoiding of the conflict were good. This is said to have been nothing but a deception practiced in order to gain more time for preparations. The commissioners brought 1,000 infantry with them to Corcyra. Even before their arrival Cn. Sicinius, the *praetor peregrinus* of the year, had landed at Apollonia in Illyria with at least 5,000 infantry and 300 cavalry. There he was to remain in control until a consular army should arrive next spring.[2]

---

[1] The commission and its work; Livy xlii. 37–44; the armistice: 47. 1–4. The existence of the armistice, sometimes doubted, is confirmed by the later reply of Perseus to certain Boeotian cities that his armistice with the Romans made it impossible for him to send them a garrison (Livy xlii. 46. 9–10). Pédech, *La méthode*, 123 states that the most original and carefully elaborated study of the causes of a war by Polybius is that of the Third Macedonian War. He considers the unfavourable sketch of Perseus to be due not to hatred but to conviction and to be correct (138 f.).

[2] In Livy xlii. 27, reporting instructions to C. Licinius, the urban praetor, and Sicinius to enrol sailors and soldiers, the number of troops to be raised is given as 8,000 and 400; in 36. 8 the number taken to Apollonia is given as 5,000 and 300.

These arrangements must mean that the Roman leaders were determined on war, but, since there were no forces available for an immediate offensive on a large scale, the war was postponed to the following year.[1] Hence it was desirable to induce Perseus to remain inactive and also to see to it that as many as possible of the key positions should be controlled by the Romans and their allies when the war did break out. To accomplish this use was made of the few Roman soldiers available and of detachments of Greek allies. While asking for help the Roman officials also intervened in local affairs as much as they dared. Already in 172 they managed to dissolve the Boeotian Confederacy and encourage particularism in the Achaean Confederacy.

Now to touch on some particulars, Sicinius, soon after he landed in Illyria sent 2,000 men to occupy Illyrian forts near the frontier of Macedonia. When the five commissioners had reached Corcyra, two of them, Marcius himself and A. Atilius, went first to Gitana in Epirus, where they appeared before the assembly of the Epirote Confederacy at what probably was an extraordinary meeting called to receive them. There they induced the Confederacy to send 400 men to help defend Orestis, a district between Epirus and Macedonia.[2] Next they went to Aetolia and then to Thessaly, where, at Larisa they received all the assurances they desired from the Thessalians. While there they were approached by ambassadors from Acarnania and Boeotia. The Acarnanians were given a lecture and advised to be on their good behaviour. Since there were signs of dissension between pro-Macedonian and pro-Roman parties in Boeotia, the Boeotians were advised to express themselves city by city, that is, to dissolve the Confederacy. Most important, however, was the arrival of ambassadors from Perseus asking for an interview. It was arranged that this was to take place on the banks of the Peneus, probably just beyond the Vale of Tempe.[3]

After the conference at which the armistice between Perseus and the Romans was arranged, the envoys now set out for Boeotia with the purpose of severing the alliance of the Boeotians with Perseus and at the same time dissolving the Confederacy. They successfully realized both objectives. When they approached Boeotia, they were met first by ambassadors from the frontier city of Chaeronea and then by ambassadors from Thebes claiming that they had not voted for the alliance. These ambassadors were told to follow the Romans to Chalcis, where Marcius and his associates established themselves for

---

[1] *Cum Macedonicum bellum in annum dilatum esset* . . . (Livy xlii. 18. 6).

[2] Livy xlii. 38. 1.

[3] Livy xlii. 38. Here Boeotian exiles are mentioned, but the brief account of the conference implies that more than one point of view was represented.

the time being.[1] While there the Roman commissioners accepted expressions of allegiance from most of the cities of Boeotia, and the Boeotian Confederacy was thus effectively dissolved. The work of Marcius and Atilius at Chalcis was now finished, but the place was not to be left unwatched and unguarded. Ser. Cornelius Lentulus, one of two Lentuli who had been sent to Cephallenia and the Peloponnesus, was summoned and put in charge. Marcius and Atilius themselves went to Argos, where they had a conference with the general and chief magistrates of the Achaeans and arranged to have 1,000 Achaeans sent to garrison Chalcis.[2] Thereupon the two, mission completed, returned to Rome at the beginning of the winter.

So far the general chronology is clear enough, though some of the events related as belonging in 172 are placed by Livy in the following year, but, since the work of the commission headed by Marcius was completed before the beginning of the winter and before the consuls for 171 took over, it is clear that all its activities belong to 172. Where to place the events that followed is less clear, though it is certain that there was considerable activity before P. Licinius Crassus, the consul for 171 to whom Greece was assigned as his province, arrived on the scene. Probably some or much of this belongs to the autumn of 172.

In Boeotia, the settlement arranged by Marcius Philippus did not quite put an end to the unrest. Some time later Perseus sent an ambassador to three cities which still were loyal to Macedonia, Coronea Thisbe, and Haliartus. Thereupon the cities appealed to Perseus for help, particularly against Thebes, but received the reply that, on account of the armistice, he was unable to send any aid.[3] Whether this was known to the Roman authorities or not, they did not consider Thessaly and Boeotia sufficiently well guarded. After Marcius, Atilius, and P. Cornelius Lentulus had reported to the senate, it is said that they were all sent back to Greece. Marcius was sent with a number of quinqueremes into the Aegean, Atilius was to occupy Larisa in Thessaly with 2,000 men secured from the force with Sicinius in Illyria, and Lentulus was sent to Thebes with 300 Italian

---

[1] Livy xlii. 43. 4–6. The ambassadors of the two Boeotian cities stated *non interfuisse se, quo societas ea decreta esset, concilio*. This should mean that their citizens were not present at the meeting at which the decision was made. This is almost unthinkable, at least for Thebes. It must rather mean that they abstained from voting for the measure. In the Boeotian assembly at this time the vote was taken by cities (Livy xxxiii. 2. 6).

[2] Pol. xxvii. 1–2; Livy xlii. 43. 4–44. 8. The part of the account of Polybius preserved is much fuller than that of Livy but begins only after the arrival of the Roman ambassadors at Chalcis.

[3] Pol. xxvii. 5; Livy xlii. 46. 7–10. The manuscript reading of Polybius gives Thebes as one of the three pro-Macedonian cities, but this is an obvious mistake which has been corrected by Buettner-Wobst following Mommsen. The mistake was already in the text of Polybius used by Livy. That Thisbe had opposed Rome is confirmed by the *senatus consultum de Thisbensibus* (*SIG*[3] 646).

soldiers.[1] The sending of troops to Larisa may seem the most surprising item in this list, but that they were sent is proved by the fact that next spring Roman and Thessalian troops were able to hold not only Larisa but also nearby Gyrton when Perseus invaded Thessaly.[2] The Roman troops involved must have been sent out in the autumn of 172, and if troops were sent to Thessaly, it was natural to plant a small garrison also at Thebes.

At Thebes, Cornelius Lentulus was not satisfied merely to hold the city. He also organized an attack on Haliartus, drawing on Boeotian troops for the purpose. This was probably early in 171, for the siege was still in progress when the Roman fleet under the command of the praetor, C. Lucretius Gallus, arrived on the scene. The latter had gathered a considerable fleet of Roman and allied ships at Cephallenia. From there he sent his brother Marcus Lucretius with the greater part of the fleet around the Peloponnesus to Chalcis, while he himself entered the Corinthian Gulf on a trireme making for Boeotia. He was somewhat delayed by illness and, on his arrival, found that Marcus had already transmitted the praetor's orders to Lentulus that he should withdraw from Haliartus and was himself making preparations to begin a new siege with 10,000 troops from the Roman fleet and 2,000 furnished by Eumenes of Pergamum. Meanwhile there arrived contingents of ships from as far away as Heraclea Pontica, Rhodes, and Carthage. These were dismissed because there was no naval war in progress. Clearly this mobilization, obviously planned well in advance, had had as its purpose naval operations in the Aegean. If the original objective had been Boeotia, the approach by the Gulf of Corinth would have been much more convenient. The Lucretii, however, chose to operate in Boeotia, probably in the hope of profiting from the booty. Unfortunately, from the point of view of the attackers, Haliartus, aided by some volunteers from Coronea, defended itself stubbornly. When the besiegers finally made their way into the city, they slaughtered young and old. The armed garrison made its way to the citadel, surrendered next day, and was sold into slavery to the number of almost 2,500. *Objets d'art* were carried off, and the city destroyed. This was certainly one of the least creditable of all Roman military adventures. Next Lucretius turned against Thisbe, which surrendered without resistance. The city was turned over to the exiles and other pro-Romans, while the members of the pro-Macedonian faction were sold into slavery. Coronea, the third of the openly

[1] In Livy xlii. 47. 9–12 there is a lacuna in what must have been the instructions to Marcius, but their character can be deduced from the fact that he appeared at Chalcis with a squadron of ships early in 171 after having operated on the coast of Phthiotic Achaea (56. 7).

[2] Livy xlii. 54. 7.

30

pro-Macedonian cities apparently held out until it was captured when the consul, P. Licinnius Crassus brought his army to Boeotia to go into winter quarters there at the end of the 171 campaign. Next year the senate regulated the affairs of Thisbe in favour of the former exiles and other pro-Romans in great detail.[1]

These incidents illustrate the Roman attitude and claims. The friends and allies of the Romans were expected to give military aid when required and were always expected to follow direction from the Roman authorities. The latter also showed a definite desire to deal with many small rather than a few large states. This is seen clearly in the dissolution of the Boeotian Confederacy. The Roman envoys were less successful with the Achaeans. Yet, when the two Cornelii Lentuli in 172 visited the Peloponnesus, they directed their pleas not only to the Achaean federal authorities, but also went the rounds of various cities, among them Elis and Messene, thus repeating the old hint that Rome would appreciate secession and dissolution of the Confederacy.[2] Yet, as already noted, the Roman envoys requested from the Confederacy and received a detachment of 1,000 men to be sent to Chalcis. It is not known how long they remained there. They may have been sent home when the Roman fleet arrived, but the Achaean contributions to the armed forces did not end with this. In 171 there were 1,500 Achaeans with the consular army, probably some of the expert light-armed Achaean troops.[3] Another aspect of the Roman conduct was the tendency to look for loot and profits. The capture of Haliartus suggests looting and, even if unusually cruel, it probably was not an isolated case. The *senatus consultum* concerning Thisbe contains a clause about gold which had been gathered for a 'crown' to be presented to Iupiter Capitolinus. Apparently this had been confiscated, and it was now decreed that it be returned to the Thisbeans to be used for the crown in question. This supplies an example of the many 'voluntary' gifts which found their way to Rome.

The exactions of money and supplies and other arbitrary acts by Roman officials in Greece and other provinces became so extreme that the home authorities found that they had to take measures to restrain their governors and commanders abroad. At the same time the treatment of various Greek states shows that the Roman authorities in no

---

[1] The Roman fleet: Livy xlii. 48. 5–10; operations; 56. 1–6, 63. 3–12; *senatus consultum*: *SIG*³ 646. Livy's text (63. 11) reports that the army moved from Haliartus against Thebes, but here again there is confusion between Thebes and Thisbe. The SC reports that Lucretius brought the army against Thisbe. The capture of Coronea is not reported but is implied in the SC and Livy xliii. 4. 11. In xlii. 67. 11–12 it is reported that when Licinius considered using Boeotia for winter quarters, he was asked to intervene by the Thebans, who claimed to be harassed by the Coroneans. This suggests that it was he who captured Coronea.

[2] Livy xlii. 37. 3 and 7–9.   [3] Livy xlii. 55. 10.

way renounced their desire to dominate and direct, but it was only after Pydna that they dropped all consideration and became utterly ruthless. Thus it is not clear whether there was any real sympathy for the victims behind the efforts to restrain Roman commanders or whether it all was a matter of policy. These measures were of two kinds, prosecutions for past offences and restraint on future activities. To begin with the prosecutions, of the numerous prosecutions of 170 or thereabouts only those connected with Greece and the Macedonian war will be noticed. The information comes chiefly from Livy, who under 170 tells that both the consul commanding the army and the praetor commanding the fleet in 171 were accused of having conducted the war cruelly and avariciously—a charge which in the case of the praetor Lucretius seems amply justified by his operations against Haliartus. It was also charged by the Athenians that Licinius, the commander of the army, and Lucretius had refused the ships and soldiers offered but demanded a large quantity of grain, something naturally considered unreasonable in the case of a city which had to import much of its own food. Complaints were lodged also against Hortensius, the commander of the fleet in 170, while he was still in charge. From Abdera in Thrace came ambassadors reporting that Hortensius had demanded not only a large quantity of wheat but also 100,000 denarii from the city. When the city asked to appeal to Hostilius, the consul in command of the army, Hortensius, without waiting for his verdict, captured the city, executed a number of leading men and sold others into slavery. Ambassadors from Chalcis, used as headquarters for the Roman fleet, complained of the exactions of both Lucretius and Hortensius and of their practice of quartering sailors in private homes. For his various offences, Lucretius was first attacked by tribunes in public addresses (*contiones*) while still in the service. Later he was brought before the senate and after that accused by tribunes before the *comitia tributa* and fined 1,000,000 asses by the unanimous vote of the thirty-five tribes. Hortensius, who still was in Greece, was let off at the time with rebukes, but precise rulings were issued concerning both Abdera and Chalcis. To Abdera ambassadors were sent to restore the liberty of the city and to inform Hostilius and Hortensius that they had waged an unjust war against Abdera and that it was up to them to search out and set free those who had been sold into slavery. The ambassadors from Chalcis were told that the conduct of Lucretius and Hortensius did not have the approval of the senate. Hortensius was further instructed that of the *socii navales* only high officers (*magistri*) should be quartered in private homes.[1] There must have been other decrees of the senate concerning other cases.

[1] Livy xliii. 4, 6. 1–3, 7–8.

One example is the decree concerning Thisbe; another, a decree concerning Coronea referred to in connexion with Abdera. Thus it is not surprising that the senate was ready to issue a general ordinance imposing restrictions upon commanders.

A *senatus consultum* of this nature was adopted that same year according to our calendar, but during the next consular year according to the Roman calendar of the time. A decree was passed and published in Greece and other parts of the Mediterranean world—at least there is information about news of the decree reaching Rhodes—to the effect that no one was to furnish supplies for the conduct of war beyond what was determined by the senate.[1] In spite of the wording, this decree certainly was not intended to serve as a restraint on voluntary efforts on the part of friendly states but as a check on excessive demands on the part of Roman commanders.[2] In the autumn of 170, A. Hostilius Mancinus sent C. Popilius Laenas and Cn. Octavius to various Greek states, to Thebes, the Peloponnesus, Aetolia, and Acarnania to announce the decree and conduct other negotiations. Mancinus, one of the consuls for 170, was already a proconsul at the time, that is, the term of his consulate had expired. At the time the Roman calendar was out of kelter to such an extent that the consuls who took office on the Ides of March actually did so in the autumn. The maladjustment was not always the same, and usually it is impossible to determine the exact date on which the consuls assumed office. In the present case, it seems to have been exceptionally early. Popilius returned from his embassy to Larisa in Thessaly early enough to be sent into winter quarters at Ambracia.[3]

Popilius Laenas, notorious for his treatment of Antiochus Epiphanes, was a strange ambassador to go the rounds to announce a Roman self-denying ordinance. Following him around by no means removes the feeling of strangeness. It is clear that neither he nor the

---

[1] Best statement, Livy xliii. 17. 2; references to the decree, Pol. xxviii. 3. 3, 13. 4; report reaches Rhodes, Pol. xxviii. 16. 2. This decree may be the model for the regulations of 27 B.C. reported in Dio Cassius liii. 15. 6.

[2] Freeman, *History of Federal Government*[2], 524 f. considers the decree 'a monstrous insult when it was addressed to an equal ally like the Achaian League.' The Achaeans, offering their help in 169, clearly showed that they did not consider the decree as one limiting their initiative.

[3] Pol. xxviii. 3–5; Livy xliii. 17; cf. also *SEG* xvi. 255, a decree of the city of Argos honouring Octavius, first published by P. Charneux, *BCH* lxxxi (1957), 182–202. For the chronology see Charneux and especially S. I. Oost. 'The Roman Calendar in the Year of Pydna', *CP* xlviii (1953), 217–30. On the calendar in 191–190 cf. p. 426, n. 4 of this chapter. Livy places the embassy in the consular year 169, but the events recorded show that it belongs in 170. There seems no reason to doubt the statement of Pol. xxviii. 3. 1 that Mancinus already was a proconsul when he dispatched the embassy, and yet it returned early enough for Popilius to go from Larisa to Ambracia to go into winter quarters. On the embassy, cf. *TAPA* lxxxiii (1952), 6 f.; *Rep. Govt.* 93 f.

Roman administration in Greece had any regard for the feelings of the Greeks. Yet again and again, for the sake of expediency, they made concessions to public opinion. They clearly did not feel strong enough or safe enough to be too dictatorial. Still, if their activities have been correctly reported, it should have been clear to all observers that the attitude of the Romans would change completely when they felt safely in control of the situation. Thus the Greek leaders ought to have anticipated to some extent what happened after Pydna. A difficulty in studying these developments is that all the information comes directly or indirectly from Polybius, who himself was one of the Achaean leaders suspected of anti-Roman activities. With his strange combination of pro-Roman and pro-Achaean points of view, he must have been in real difficulties in his exposition. He undoubtedly wished that he and his father Lycortas should appear as important as possible but to have done nothing dishonourable and nothing for which his Roman friends could blame them. Yet he did belong to the party which had inherited the policy of Philopoemen, and which by those who curried favour with the Romans was dubbed anti-Roman.

Popilius and his colleague, after a stop at Thebes, proceeded to the Peloponnesus, where they made a round of the cities. This might conceivably be explained as due to a desire to give the greatest publicity possible to the liberal policy of the senate, but it is undoubtedly more correctly explained as due to the desire to treat the cities as independent states and not as mere members of the Confederacy. Moreover, wherever they went, the ambassadors are said to have let it be understood that they knew who were the ones who had withdrawn from active participation in politics, the implication being that such men were enemies of Rome who by their inactivity were trying to avoid showing their hostility. Probably no one was mentioned by name. To have mentioned names would have been less effective. Finally it was reported that the ambassadors were going to call for a special meeting of the Achaean *ekklesia*, that is a *synkletos*, with the intention of accusing Lycortas, his son Polybius, and Archon of being hostile to the Romans but remaining inactive waiting for developments. Just what happened is not clear. Apparently the suggested meeting never took place. Instead the ambassadors appeared before the Achaean *boule* at Aegium, probably at an extraordinary meeting of that body, and addressed words of greeting and exhortation to it. Since it appears that the meeting of the *ekklesia* did not take place and so was not addressed by the ambassadors, the statement that they had planned to accuse the three Achaean leaders may be pure guess work, but a plausible guess based on the conduct of the ambassadors in other places.[1] In Aetolia, they appeared before an extraordinary meeting of the assembly summoned to Thermum. There Popilius actually let drop his original demand for hostages and thus again gave way before local public opinion. Finally he appeared before the assembly of the Acarnanian Confederacy. Here one group of leaders requested that Acarnania be garrisoned; a second group opposed it. Popilius pretended to agree with the latter. The decision is said to have been due to regard for the feelings of the majority of the Acarnanians and to a desire to comply with the purpose of the senate. It looks as if the Roman officials in Greece had been instructed not to antagonize local authorities.

The same year the leaders of the former party of Philopoemen called a conference to decide what strategy to adopt. They had been aroused not only by the visit of Popilius and Octavius but also by the Roman attitude after their defeat at Callicinus in 171. They placed the blame for the defeat on the Aetolian cavalry and had arrested and sent to Rome at least five Aetolian leaders, among them Nicander, who had been prominent as ambassador to Antiochus and later had served as a general of the Confederacy.[2] The group gathered at the conference consisted of Lycortas, Archon, Polybius, and five others. In the debate which followed, Lycortas, undoubtedly the senior statesman present, argued against helping either side in the war, since the victor would be oppressively strong. On the other hand, it would be dangerous to oppose the Romans. Two other speakers supported him and stated that it would be unwise to oppose the Romans but still favoured action against those Achaeans who went too far in currying favour with the Romans. It looks very much as if these men would have opposed the Romans if they had dared to do so. The policy advocated by Archon differed from that of Lycortas only in being more careful in avoiding offending the Romans. He advocated being out and out time-servers and avoiding any offence to the Romans lest they suffer the fate of Nicander. This point of view was supported by Polybius and three others and so won over that of Lycortas by a vote of five to three. The group decided further to support the candidacy of Archon as general and Polybius as hipparch. The two were duly elected to serve for the year 170–169.[3] They and their supporters at this time apparently were in complete control of the Confederacy, and Callicrates and his followers had suffered an eclipse.

---

[1] Cf. *Rep. Govt.* 93 f. and 216, nn. 18 and 19.
[2] Livy xlii. 60. 8–9, mentioning no names; references to Nicander, Pol. xxvii. 15. 14, xxviii. 4. 6, 6. 7.
[3] Pol. xxviii. 6.

Archon was soon to show that his policy of avoiding offence, in practice meant taking positive steps to please the Romans. The first opportunity came in the strange affair of the restoration of the honours once voted to Eumenes of Pergamum but later cancelled. The Confederacy had once voted to abolish the excessive honours. The decision concerning which honours were excessive was left to a court and, since the Achaeans made some use of foreign judges, the particular judges to whom the decision was left chanced to be Rhodians. As good Rhodians they were hostile enough to Eumenes to cancel all honours. It was this wrong which was now to be set right. Ambassadors from Attalus, the brother of Eumenes, appeared before the first *synodos* or meeting of the Achaean council in 169. Though there was some opposition, the ambassadors were supported by Archon, the general of the Confederacy, but the most telling speech in their support was delivered by the hipparch or vice president, Polybius, or so at least he reports.[1] At a meeting later in the year Archon secured the passage of a decree that the Achaeans should send their entire military force to Thessaly to support the Romans. It was voted further that Archon was to take charge of the mobilization and preparation of the force, while Polybius was to head an embassy to report the Achaean decision to the Roman consul and to make arrangements for supplies along the line of march. That the Achaeans were trying to assume the role of an independent state of some importance is shown also by two other acts of the same meeting. An embassy was sent to Attalus to report the restoration of the honours of Eumenes and another to Egypt to congratulate Ptolemy VI on coming of age.[2]

When the Achaean embassy reached Thessaly, Quintus Marcius Philippus, the consul in command of the Roman army, had already started on the march which was to take him through Perrhaebia and past Mount Olympus to the coast of southern Macedonia. Polybius caught up with the Roman army in Perrhaebia and followed it on its difficult march but postponed communicating his message to Marcius until the army reached Heracleum on the coast. Marcius refused the help offered, remarking, it is said, that he did not need the help now that he had gained control of the approaches to Macedonia. This may seem to lend some credence to the accusation that Polybius had avoided reporting to Marcius until the latter had completed successfully the dangerous march across the mountains. However, if it is true that Polybius did not catch up with the Roman army before it

---

[1] Pol. xxviii. 7. Here, as normally, Polybius writes about himself in the third person and gives his speech in indirect discourse. Pédech, *La méthode*, 283 calls it his *chef-d'oeuvre*. On the use of foreign judges, cf. *CP* xliii (1948), 189; on Achaean meetings, *Rep. Govt.* 183 f.

[2] Pol. xxviii. 12.

was encamped between Azorus and Doliche far north in Perrhaebia, it would have been impossible to bring up the Achaeans in time to have been of any help on this particular march.[1]

Another difficult question faced the Achaeans that same year. The Roman campaigns in Illyria and Epirus had been none too successful. Some time in 169 Appius Claudius Cento, at that time in command in Illyria, requested the Achaean Confederacy to send 5,000 men to Epirus. Somehow Marcius got wind of this and, according to Polybius, sent the latter home with instructions to prevent the sending of the troops. The question was submitted to an Achaean *synkletos* at Sicyon. Polybius, according to his own report, did not feel that he could reveal the secret instructions he had received from Marcius. Therefore he fell back on the *senatus consultum* instructing states not to honour requests from commanders except when they were based on decrees of the senate. He succeeded further in getting the decision transferred to the consul, and Marcius, of course, vetoed the proposal.[2] If the first action was proper and valid, it should have been unnecessary to refer the question to Marcius. The situation was saved for the moment, but it did not augur well for the future.

The next year, the year of Pydna, saw one more attempted flirtation of the Achaeans with the Ptolemies. Ambassadors from the two Ptolemies ruling as joint rulers appeared before what was probably the first *synodos* of 168 meeting at Corinth. They brought the request that the Achaeans send a contingent of 1,000 foot and 200 horse with Lycortas as commander-in-chief and Polybius as commander of the cavalry. The majority favoured sending the help requested, while Callicrates argued that the Achaeans should avoid all other entanglements and be ready to render any aid that the Romans might wish, pointing out that the Romans were wintering in Macedonia and that the decisive action could soon be expected. When he failed to convince the majority, he succeeded in having the decision postponed to a *synkletos* to be called at Sicyon. On the second day of the meeting, the day for formulating motions, Lycortas moved that the troops requested be sent; Callicrates, that ambassadors be sent to reconcile the Ptolemies with Antiochus Epiphanes. When the party of Lycortas and Polybius still seemed to have the majority, Callicrates brought on a messenger with a letter from Marcius Philippus urging the Achaeans to join the Romans in trying to reconcile the kings. Undoubtedly the opportune appearance of the messenger had been arranged in ad-

---

[1] The Achaean embassy; Pol. xxviii. 13. 1–8; the march of Marcius: Livy xliv. 3–5; cf. De Sanctis, *Storia*, iv. i. 300–3.

[2] Pol. xxviii. 13. 7–14. Livy does not mention the incident. On the command of Appius Claudius, see below in connexion with the Illyrian and Epirote campaigns.

vance, but it was enough to induce Polybius to give in, and the Achaeans decided to send not troops but ambassadors. Thus ended what was probably the last effort of Achaean leaders to gain glory from relations with the Ptolemies. The troops, if sent, undoubtedly would have been, at best, glorified mercenaries. It is unlikely that the Achaean leaders really thought that they could get any effective aid against Rome from Egypt as De Sanctis suggests.[1]

The one other confederacy whose role in the war requires consideration is that of the Epirotes, the state that brought the Romans close to disaster and suffered the most terrible punishment. The events in Epirus are closely linked with those in Illyria, and for them the account of Livy is confused and contradictory. Nevertheless a few points must be noted. From the outset, the Romans used Illyrian ports for debarkation and then, as in earlier wars, advanced through or near Epirus. In 170 the consul A. Hostilius Mancinus, the new commander for that year, was at Phanote in north-western Epirus when it was learned that there was a plot on foot to capture him and turn him over to Perseus. The latter actually was on the way but was held up by the Molossians. Hostilius escaped by night, gave up the plan of passing through Epirus, and took ship for the Phocian port of Anticyra.[2] This must be considered the beginning of the revolt of Epirus, which was very largely a Molossian undertaking, though it was Molossians who delayed Perseus and thus enabled Hostilius to escape. Yet, though Perseus came too late, it was probably at this time that he planted the garrison at Phanote which later was active under the command of a certain Cleuas who seems to have been an energetic and effective officer. Next winter (170–169) Perseus conducted a successful campaign in Illyria north of Lake Lychnidus where he captured the important city of Uscana in spite of the presence of a Roman garrison. The Romans apparently suffered other reverses too. Soon after this, L. Coelius, an otherwise unknown officer, who is described as a Roman legate in command in Illyria, tried to recapture Uscana but was repulsed with heavy losses, while the commander-in-chief, Appius Claudius Cento, was besieging Phanote in Epirus with the aid of Chaonian and Thesprotian troops but made no progress against the defence conducted by Cleuas.[3] While Appius Claudius

---

[1] Pol. xxix. 23–25; De Sanctis, *Storia*, iv. i. 348. For the meetings at Corinth and Sicyon cf. *Rep. Govt.* 87 f., 184.

[2] Pol. xxvii. 16; Diod. xxx. 5a.

[3] Perseus' Illyrian campaign: Livy xliii. 18–20; the Roman attacks on Uscana and Phanote: 21. 1–5. The earlier attack of Appius Claudius on Uscana, in Livy xliii. 10 actually placed before the Macedonian capture of the city, is recognized as a doublet of the later attack attributed to Caelius; so De Sanctis, *Storia*, iv. i. 296, n. 160; Scullard, *Roman Politics*, 201, n. 2; *MRR* i. 422. In Livy xliii. 9. 6–7 Appius Claudius is said to have been sent by

was still besieging Phanote, Perseus, in response to an appeal from the Epirotes, made a dash for Stratus, the former Acarnanian capital which was now an Aetolian stronghold. The fact that he crossed the Arachthus river early on this march shows that he entered eastern Epirus so far south as to avoid the Roman troops operating around Phanote and, even more, those at Uscana and Lychnidus. Having once struck the Arachthus he must have followed the valley of this river south and thus passed near Ambracia. Thus it was almost inevitable that Popilius Laenas, the Roman officer in command at Ambracia, should learn about his advance and hasten to send troops to Stratus, especially since he was asked to do so by some of the Aetolians. Perseus too had been invited, but when he arrived he found Popilius at Stratus with 1,000 troops. At the same time a detachment of 600 Aetolian infantry and 100 cavalry, said to have been raised to co-operate with Perseus, entered the city and joined the Romans. Though opinions within the city were divided, these troops were enough to keep the city from falling into the hands of Perseus, who, against the advice of Aetolian and Epirote supporters, decided not to commence a siege but to withdraw. Meanwhile Appius Claudius had been led by the report of the advance on Stratus to raise the siege of Phanote, only to be pursued and harried by Cleuas. Finally he dismissed his Epirote allies and returned to Illyria.[1] It must have been from there that he next spring called for troops from Achaea. Phanote was finally reduced by L. Anicius late in 168.[2]

The campaigns just discussed involved a series of setbacks for the Romans relieved by only one success, the fact that Stratus was saved, but, from the point of view of effects, this counted for more than all the setbacks. If Stratus had fallen to Perseus, Epirus would have been completely under his control. Acarnania, no doubt, would have followed and much, if not all, of Aetolia. The Aetolian statesman who invited Perseus was an older man who had distinguished himself at Cynoscephalae and does not seem to have been a hasty and hot-headed anti-Roman. He undoubtedly had a strong following. If all these regions had been gained for Perseus, he would have been able to interfere with the route of communication from Ambracia to Thessaly. In that case the Roman army would be almost exclusively dependent on the sea route to Anticyra, not to mention that success

Hostilius Mancinus to Illyria with 4,000 soldiers, which would mean that these troops had been detached from the none too adequate army in Thessaly. This does not sound very plausible, but yet he may have been considered a subordinate of the consul.

[1] Livy xliii. 21. 6–23. 8.
[2] Livy xlv. 26. The campaign is related under the consular year 167, but the fact that the troops went into winter quarters at the conclusion of the campaign indicates that it took place the preceding autumn.

in the northwest would be likely to inspire unrest among other Greeks. No wonder that in 168 Illyria was treated by the Romans as a theatre of warfare almost as important as Macedonia itself. To Illyria was sent L. Anicius Gallus, who at the time of the first assigning of provinces was appointed *praetor peregrinus* but subject to a further assignment by the senate. Later he was assigned to Illyria and given two legions and a corresponding number of auxiliary troops.[1] When to these were added the few troops already with Appius Claudius and troops from friendly cities in Illyria, his force became so large that the defeat of the Illyrian king Genthius became relatively easy. This was followed later in the year by the reduction of Epirus.

Except for the subjugation of the rebelling parts of Epirus, the Greek federal states were not involved to any extent in the campaign of 168, the year of Pydna, and yet the outcome of the battle affected the states of Greece fully as disastrously as it did the defeated states, Macedonia and Illyria. There was no longer fear of any armed opposition in the Balkans and now, with Roman armies both in Macedonia and Illyria, the Romans could give free rein to their pent up resentment against all those who were not sufficiently subservient or were even suspected of being anti-Roman. The terms imposed on Macedonia and Illyria showed elements of statesmanship, but the action against sinners and suspects was arbitrary and brutal. Nevertheless, the principle of freedom adopted earlier was maintained and theoretically no state involved was deprived of its freedom. They might be subject to taxation, they might have territory detached, they might have their leaders carried off to Italy, but free they remained and free they were, for so the Romans said they were. It is tempting to say that the ancient definition of freedom—and not only that of the Romans—for practical purposes was: 'They are free who take orders from no one but us'.

The settlement of 167 is very important also for the light it throws on the development of the Roman system of provincial government, though Illyria and Macedonia were not themselves made into permanent provinces at the time. They supply the earliest documented examples of the combination of freedom with the payment of taxes to Rome. This should be enough to serve as a warning that it never can be certain that *civitates liberae* were also *immunes* unless there is specific evidence to that effect. The Illyrian settlement involves additional difficulties since it is an early example of a case in which certain communities within a larger free area were granted the additional privilege of immunity. The ruling that Macedonians and Illyrians were to be

---

[1] Livy xliv. 17. 10, 21. 4–10. When Livy, after giving the commands of the consuls, continues *additus est his tertius*, he emphasizes that this is a third major command.

free is contained both in the preliminary *senatus consultum* and in the plans later reported drawn up for the two countries. The *senatus consultum* as reported states that the purpose is that it may become clear to all nations that the armies of Rome did not impose subjection on the free but, on the contrary, brought freedom to those in subjection, and so that the free nations would believe that under the protection of the Roman people their freedom would be safe forever, while the nations living under kings would believe that these kings would be gentler and more just on account of the influence of the Roman people, and further that, if war came, the outcome would be victory for the Romans and freedom for themselves.[1] If this statement was broadcast, it clearly was intended to serve as pro-Roman propaganda. It is also interesting for its identification of subjection with the rule of kings and freedom with the absence of kings, and for the implication that both free nations and kings would do well to be guided by Rome.

A description of the organization imposed on Macedonia has already been given.[2] Less is known about the organization of Illyria, but it is likely that it followed the same pattern as that of Macedonia. In Macedonia there were four parts; in Illyria, three. This probably means three small federal states. As in Macedonia, so in Illyria the tribute (*vectigal*) imposed was one half of that formerly paid to the king. Here the immune communities constitute a problem. They can hardly have been exempted from their share in the expenses of the new federal governments. A solution will be suggested, but it is frankly a guess. In most federal states taxes were collected by the local authorities who sent their share in a lump sum to the federal treasury. For the Macedonian republics it was suggested that the member communities probably paid the same as before and that their federal government kept one half and transmitted the other half to Rome. In Illyria, probably the same system was used, the difference being that the immune cities were exempt from payment of the share intended for Rome and contributed only to the expenses of their own federal government.

The spirit of the times is illustrated by the account of Polybius of the efforts of the Rhodian, Polyaratus, to avoid being sent to Rome. He had fled to Egypt before the arrival there of the embassy of Popilius Laenas. The latter ordered him to be sent to Rome. Instead a *lembos* was sent to take him to Rhodes. On the way he managed to

---

[1] A somewhat free and shortened version of Livy xlv. 18. 1–2.

[2] Above, Part II, ch. i, section 10, 'The Four Macedonian Republics'. Most of the source material is cited, *Econ. Surv. Rome*, iv. 294–300. Oost, *CP* xlviii. 219 suggests that the Roman commissioners may have come out already in the autumn of 168. For the five commissioners to Illyria this is indicated by Livy xlv. 26. 11–12. So probably also the commissioners for Macedonia, but it is likely that the complicated settlement was left over to the spring.

escape and seek sanctuary first at Phaselis. When the Phaselites did not dare to keep him, he tried Caunus and Cibyra with no better success. The Cibyrates reported his presence both to Rhodes and to the Roman consul in Macedonia. The latter instructed him to be sent from Cibyra to Rhodes and from Rhodes to Rome, and so it was done.[1] The instructions concerning Polyaratus were most likely issued by Aemilius Paulus late in 168 before the arrival of the ten commissioners. Probably to the same period belongs the sacking of Aeginium in Thessaly, Agassae probably in Macedonia, and Aenia not far from Thessalonica. Against Agassae there was the charge that, after coming over to the Romans, the city had again gone back to Perseus; against Aeginium, that the inhabitants had assaulted Roman soldiers; against Aenia, merely that the city had defended itself more stubbornly than its neighbours. It has been suggested that the Roman commander was looking for a chance to allow his soldiers to gather loot.[2] At any rate, this action indicated that anyone out of favour with the Romans need not look for mercy or consideration.

When the ten commissioners arrived and established themselves at Amphipolis, they and Aemilius Paulus, in addition to planning the future organization of Macedonia, proceeded to act as a supreme court and supreme arbiters of the Greek world. While Aemilius Paulus was returning from a tour of Greece and was near Demetrias, he was met by a group of Aetolians who reported that the pro-Roman leaders, Lyciscus and Tisippus, with the aid of Roman soldiers, had surrounded the Aetolian council, had killed 550 members and had driven others into exile and had appropriated the property of all of them. Thereupon Aemilius ordered those accused to appear at Amphipolis.[3] Thus the plan to use Amphipolis as headquarters not only for arranging the affairs of Macedonia but also for hearing cases concerning controversies in Greece had already been adopted. At Amphipolis ambassadors from numerous Greek states met to congratulate the Romans on their victory.[4] According to Livy, after the first meeting of the commissioners with the Macedonians, the Aetolians were summoned and their case heard. He is undoubtedly right in stating that their case was judged more on the basis of what party had favoured Rome and what Perseus rather than on the basis of who had committed a crime and who had suffered wrong. The Aetolians who had massacred their fellow citizens were acquitted, and the exile

[1] Pol. xxx. 8–9.

[2] Livy xlv. 27. 1–4; on Aeginium, xliv. 46. 3; cf. De Sanctis, *Storia*, iv. i. 334.

[3] Livy xlv. 28. 6–8.

[4] Pol. xxx. 13, merely stating that the ambassadors gathered in Macedonia. The account of Livy shows that the commissioners did their work at Amphipolis.

of those exiled confirmed. The only person to be condemned was A. Baebius, the Roman officer who had lent Roman soldiers to the Aetolians for the occasion. Probably at the time a considerable amount of territory was detached from Aetolia. This included Amphilochia and undoubtedly some of the territories of the minor *koina* of central Greece known to have come into being at this time.[1] Thus the Aetolians, who had supplied troops to their Roman allies in 171 and had committed no openly hostile act, were treated more harshly than they had been in 188.

A number of other decisions were made at Amphipolis. Leucas was detached from Acarnania. This was a part of the policy of allowing none of the important island ports along the west coast of Greece to remain attached to a mainland state. A squadron was sent to Lesbos to destroy the town of Antissa, which had had dealings with some Macedonian *lemboi*, and transplant its population to Methymna. Also what appears to be two trials of individuals is reported. A certain Aetolian named Andronicus was executed. So also Neon of Thebes, held responsible for the alliance of Boeotia with Perseus.[2] This latter act was a sort of sequel to the earlier settlement of the affairs of Boeotia. Undoubtedly there were also decisions made at Amphipolis that have not been reported, for instance, the decision to detach the Magnesian peninsula from Macedonia and reconstitute the Magnesian Confederacy but to demolish the fortifications of Demetrias.[3]

Another task performed at Amphipolis was the drawing up of lists of suspects to be sent to Rome for trial. These lists were based on the accusations lodged by the ambassadors that came to Amphipolis and information gleaned from the Macedonian archives. Missives sent in the name of Aemilius Paulus went to Aetolia, Acarnania, Epirus, and Boeotia, and it is implied that this was not all. Polybius lists Perrhaebians and Thessalians with Achaeans as peoples against whom charges were made even though they had remained inactive, and it is possible that also some of their leaders went to Rome. At least there is enough information to show that something like a mass extradition of suspects had been adopted as part of the Roman programme. Macedonians too were included. In their case the names of leading men, former old royal officials and the like, who were to go to Italy were announced at a meeting. They apparently were left to their own devices to get to

[1] Livy xlv. 31. 1–3; Diod. xxxi. 8. 6 (Amphilochia). *SIG*[3] 653 lists the *koina* of the Dorians, Aenians, Oetaeans, and Eastern Locrians. To these can be added Western Locris, known from inscriptions (Busolt, *Staatskunde*, 1460 and n. 3). Very little is known about the governments of these states.

[2] Livy xlv. 31. 12–15.

[3] The Magnesian Confederacy is merely seen to have resumed its functioning. The decision to dismantle the walls of Demetrias is reported in Diod. xxxi. 8. 6.

Italy, but were threatened with death if they did not obey.[1] For Epirus and Acarnania the last act came later when Anicius announced the names of leaders whom he wished to go to Italy to be judged by the senate.[2]

The Achaeans were given special treatment. Instead of sending a written communication, two of the commissioners went in person to present their demands. One of the two, C. Claudius Pulcher, had served as consul in 177, while the second, Cn. Domitius Ahenobarbus was a younger man. Thus it was an embassy which would carry weight, though it is not quite true, as Polybius says, that the most distinguished men among the ten were sent.[3] One difficulty facing the commissioners was that the Macedonian archives had furnished no incriminating evidence against any Achaeans. All they had to go by was their own suspicion and the evidence of Callicrates and others who sought to win favour with the Romans. The Achaeans called a special meeting to meet the Roman envoys. The latter, most likely, demanded that the Achaeans vote to send all those suspected by the Romans to stand trial at Rome and that they do this without knowing the names of the men involved. When the Achaeans objected to voting thus blindly, they were told that all the generals of the period were guilty. This aroused one former general, Xenon, who at the caucus of Achaean leaders in 170 had sided with Archon and Polybius. He got up and stated that he had served as general, had done nothing against the Romans, had held no good will for Perseus, and was ready to stand trial before the Achaeans and even before the Romans. He, so to speak, was taken up on this, with the result that over a thousand Achaeans were taken to Italy and there sent into a sort of exile or private imprisonment in the cities of Etruria, probably the part of Italy where Achaeans would feel least at home.[4]

The last acts of Aemilius Paulus and his army exhibit the tendency to use warfare as a source of enrichment both for the state and the

---

[1] Summons sent to cities and confederacies; Pol. xxx. 13. 6; Livy xlv. 31. 9; charges against Achaeans, Thessalians, and Perrhaebians: Pol. xxx. 7. 5.

[2] Livy xlv. 34. 9.

[3] Pol. xxx. 13. 8. His inaccuracy here is probably due to a desire to magnify the Achaeans. The commission (*MRR* i. 435) contained four or five former consuls, some of them senior to Claudius.

[4] Pol. xxx. 13. 6–11, cf. 7. 5–6; Livy xlv. 31. 9–11; Paus. vii. 10. 7–11. Only Pausanias gives an account of the meeting with the Achaeans; he states that the Roman spokesman demanded that the Achaeans condemn to death the so far unnamed enemies of the Romans, and this statement is commonly accepted by historians. Against it is really the evidence of Polybius and Livy, who imply that the purpose of the envoys was the same as that of the written communications to other states, namely, to indicate what suspects were to go to Rome. Thus the envoys must have asked for *carte blanche* to draw up a list of Achaeans to be sent to Rome for trial. This interpretation also makes sense of the answer of Xenon, who indicated that he was ready to stand trial.

individual soldiers. The early commanders in the war had acted on this principle until a check was imposed on them, but after Pydna the spirit of aggrandizement was given free rein. The accumulated treasures of the Macedonian government was reserved for the Roman state. The treasures thus brought to Rome were several times larger than those secured in any of the earlier wars in Greece and Macedonia. In fact, they were so large that their transfer can be considered an important step in the transfer to Italy of the accumulated capital of the ancient world. The treasures transferred at this time have been estimated at 210,000,000 sesterces or 52,500,000 denarii.[1] But even if this indirectly benefited the soldiers as Roman citizens, it did not satisfy their desire for personal gain, and so far, apparently, they had been allowed to loot only a few not very large towns. To rectify this situation, if this is the term for it, the soldiers of the army in Macedonia were allowed to help themselves in Illyria and Epirus, and this was done after Anicius had reduced Epirus and he and the five commissioners had organized Illyria. The actions of Aemilius and his army thus seem gratuitous acts of cruelty inflicted after a peaceful settlement had been completed. It is difficult to know where to place the blame for this outrage, but it seems clear that Aemilius was not personally as guiltless as the ancient sources usually depict him. Here there enters the suspicion that the defence of Aemilius may be due in part to the gratitude of Polybius for the kindness shown him in Rome in the Scipionic circle. Aemilius, even if he did not enrich himself personally in other ways, did at least help himself to the library of Perseus, the reason being that his sons were fond of reading.[2] After completing the session at Amphipolis, Aemilius marched his army to Pella and from there sent part of it to Illyria to plunder those Illyrians who had supported Perseus, while he himself continued with the rest of the army to Passaron in northern Epirus, where Anicius already had his headquarters.[3] Nothing more is known of the conduct of the troops in Illyria while relatively elaborate reports have been preserved concerning the plundering of Epirus. It may be enough to recall that 150,000 were sold into slavery and about seventy settlements, mostly Molossian, destroyed. It appears that the prisoners and other spoils were sold and the proceeds used for soldiers' bonuses. There is disagreement about the size of these. Livy says that each cavalry man received 400 denarii; each footsoldier, 200, while Plutarch states that

---

[1] For the booty from the Third Macedonian War see *Econ. Surv. Rome*, iv. 320–3; for the economic and political significance, cf. Aymard in A. Aymard and J. Auboyer, *Rome et son empire* (1954), 146. f.

[2] Plut. *Aem.* 28. Pédech, *La Méthode*, 221 *et passim* apparently thinks that the historian had a genuine high regard for Aemilius.

[3] Livy xlv. 33. 8.

there were only 11 drachmas for each individual, which supplies him with a text to bring home how small the profits from war are.[1] The larger sums are certainly more nearly correct. Even so the soldiers remained dissatisfied. After Aemilius Paulus and his soldiers had done their worst, there remained for Anicius only to summon the 'remaining Epirotes' and the Acarnanians to a meeting and announce the names of those expected to go to Rome to stand trial.

What can have been the reasons for this harsh treatment of Epirus? What has already been said indicates that a desire for booty entered in. The soldiers of Aemilius, when they returned to Italy, are said to have been dissatisfied with their share of the loot from the royal treasures.[2] They may well have felt that these treasures should have enriched themselves rather than the state treasury, and certainly the spoils from Illyria and Epirus were small in comparison. When action was decided on, the soldiers were allowed to profit, but it is hard to believe that any statesman with any pretence of insight and judgement, would have ordered anything as cruel as the sacking of Epirus simply for the sake of the profits. It has been suggested that a large part of the blame should be placed on the machinations of the pro-Roman Epirote Charops in co-operation with ruthless Roman statesmen of the kind whose actions had been repressed and in part punished a few years earlier, but this explanation has been submitted even by its author as an unproved hypothesis.[3] Certainly pro-Roman Epirotes were used as informers, but it is unlikely that a Roman commander would go this far to please partisans, and it is equally unlikely that Charops would desire to have his country devastated to such an extent. What happened in Epirus is best explained by the attitude assumed by Aemilius Paulus and the commissioners ever since the first arrival of the latter at Amphipolis, namely, that they had authority to judge any enemy of Rome. The Epirotes were informed in advance that the Roman garrisons in their cities were to be withdrawn so that they could be free. What followed must have been considered judgement passed and punishment inflicted on enemies of Rome. The responsibility for the verdict must be placed on Aemilius and the commissioners who passed judgement and supervised the execution of the judgement.

The explanation of the severity of the Romans apparently is to be

---

[1] Pol. xxx. 15; Livy xlv. 34; Plut. *Aem.* 29. Concerning the sums realized by the soldiers, Niese, *Geschichte*, iii. 187, n. 2 argues that Plutarch is right; De Sanctis, *Storia*, iv. i. 350, n. 300 argues cogently that the sum given by Plutarch is much too low.

[2] Livy xlv. 35. 6.

[3] H. H. Scullard, 'Charops and Roman Policy in Epirus', *JRS* xxxv (1945), 58–64; but cf. Oost, *Roman Policy in Epirus and Acarnania*, 85 with nn. 106 and 112 on pp. 133 ff. Badian, *Clientelae*, 98, n. 2 agrees with Oost.

31

found in the fact that the Epirotes had interfered with the chief line of military communication between Italy and not only the Balkans but the entire Near East. To appreciate this it is necessary to bear in mind the Roman preference for communications by land. In the eastern wars, beginning with the Second Macedonian War, Roman troops were normally landed on the coast of Illyria. After the failure to invade Macedonia from the west in 199, the route thence went regularly through Epirus, or just alongside of it, to Thessaly. The one exception was in 192 and 191 when the Romans with the co-operation of Philip V were able to go east from the coast to Macedonia and approach Thessaly from the north. Some change must have come with the building of the Egnatian Way, but even so, Sulla used the old route in 88,[1] as did Caesar in his campaign against Pompey in 48. Now the Epirotes had so far been treated well and minor peccadillos had been forgiven, apparently in the hope that they would prove friendly and accommodating. When instead an Epirote revolt almost resulted in the capture of a consul and the following winter almost enabled Perseus to get control of northwest Greece and at the same time interfered with Roman communications, it is easy to understand the anger of the Romans. Unfortunately for the Epirotes, this happened at a time when a new spirit of ruthlessness inspired Roman policy.

Questions continued to be referred to the Roman senate for settlement in spite of all the activities of the commissioners sent to Illyria and Macedonia. At the beginning of the consular year 166—most likely in the autumn of 167—there must have been masses of ambassadors in Rome. Unfortunately this is where the extant part of Livy's history comes to an end, so that there is little information preserved about the activities of the senate in this and subsequent years. One item reported is the appearance of an embassy from Athens. This at first pleaded for Haliartus in Boeotia. When this plea proved ineffective, the embassy changed its tune and asked that the territory of Haliartus, as well as the islands of Delos and Lemnos, be granted to Athens. The request was approved but with the stipulation that Delos become a free port.[2] Earlier in 167 the senate had made a decision of some importance. The victory in Illyria had left the Romans with 220 captured *lemboi*. These the senate ordered to be given to Corcyra, Apollonia, and Dyrrhachium.[3] Was this a gentle hint that these three

---

[1] The details are not given, but the fact that he began requisitioning in Aetolia and Thessaly and approached Athens through Boeotia indicates that he must have come via Illyria and Epirus (Appian, *Mithr.* 30); cf. G. F. Hertzberg, *Die Geschichte Griechenlands unter der Herrschaft der Römer*, i (1866), 360.

[2] Pol. xxx. 20, 31. 10; Strabo ix. 411 (Haliartus), x. 486 (*ateleia* of Delos).

[3] Livy xlv. 43. 10. Q. Cassius, the official instructed to transfer the ships, was the *praetor urbanus* of 167.

sea ports should police the seas and keep down piracy? If so, they could at most police the Adriatic and Ionic seas. Certainly there is no hint that the Roman government itself intended to patrol the seas.

After the Third Macedonian War the Roman government largely directed the affairs not only of Greece and Macedonia but also of Asia Minor and much of the Near East. In this it was greatly aided by the habit of states with grievances of appealing to Rome against their enemies. Thus Rome could always appear as the champion of some friend or ally. The will of the Romans was made known through responses to these appeals, by decrees and letters of the senate, and by means of embassies and commissions. Two embassies can be mentioned as examples. In 164 a pair of ambassadors were sent to check on Greek affairs in general, to arbitrate a territorial dispute between Sparta and Megalopolis, and especially to check on the plans of Antiochus Epiphanes and Eumenes of Pergamum. Two years later three ambassadors, including Tiberius Sempronius Gracchus, the father of the tribunes, were sent to check on affairs in Greece and then cross to Asia Minor to observe the Seleucid and other kings as well as the Galatians.[1] Such embassies suggest broad interests and close observation. To be sure, as long as there were no Roman governors or soldiers permanently on hand, it was still possible for leaders of Greek states to imagine that they could act independently. The outbreak of wars in Macedonia and Greece in 150 and the years following tends to give the impression that the period from 167 down to that date was one of confusion and disorder. This is hardly borne out by a check of the few events known. The system set up at first worked well from the Roman point of view. The explanation seems to be that all the Greek leaders taken to Rome in 167 served as hostages. The story of their treatment, in so far as it can be traced in the case of the Achaeans, indicates that the Romans had no intention either of giving them a regular trial or of allowing them to return. Even when the survivors did return in 151 or thereabouts, it is doubtful that it affected the situation to any extent. Of the two returning Achaeans known by name, Stratius strove to prevent a break with the Romans, and Polybius certainly did nothing to bring on the break.

Conditions in Greece in this period can best be observed in connexion with the Achaean Confederacy. Here two points may be noted at the outset. In the first place, it does not seem that Callicrates and the extreme pro-Roman faction were in complete control. This is particularly significant since all the leaders who had shown any independence had been carried off. It can hardly have been Callicrates who inspired the repeated sending of embassies to Rome concerning the Achaeans

[1] Pol. xxxi. 1. 6–8, 15. 9–10.

detained in Italy, or, if it was, then Callicrates was not as extreme as he has been represented but co-operated in this matter with the opposition. In the second place, the Spartan case had been settled sufficiently well for a Spartan to be elected general of the Confederacy. There was a connexion between the Spartan question and the outbreak of the Achaean War in 146, but the question did not become acute before the last part of the period. This conclusion, of course, is based on the information which chance has preserved. The activities that can be observed are the string of embassies sent to Rome in the interest of the Achaeans detained in Italy, trouble with Athens caused by the championing of the Delian refugees exiled by Athens, intervention in the affairs of Athens and Oropus, and the final outbreak of trouble with Sparta.

The first embassy to Rome concerning those detained must have been sent in 166. There is no account of its dispatch or of its appearance in Rome but only a mention of its return, but, from the account of the next embassy it is clear that it was told that the senate was surprised that they appealed in the interest of men whom they themselves had judged. The Achaeans in return next year sent to protest that their state had not judged the men and, therefore, requested that the senate do so or, if pressure of business made this impossible, that it turn the men over to the Achaeans for judgement. The justice of the Achaean plea was obvious. Their fellow citizens had been taken to Italy to stand trial and had already been kept there two years. Yet the senate did not wish them returned to Greece and so answered that it was in the interest neither of Rome nor of the Greek states that these men should return home. This reply, given to the Achaeans, apparently was interpreted as applying to all Greeks. Polybius, in reporting this, indicates that the senate was uncomfortable, since it was proved wrong on every point, but still places his emphasis on the despair of most Greeks and the elation of Charops, Callicrates, and men of their kind.[1] Some years later, at a time when many of the prominent exiles had already died, two further embassies are reported. In both the ambassadors were Xenon of Aegium and Telecles of Aegira, both thus from old Achaean cities. The second of these embassies occured in 155. At that time, according to Polybius, the release would have been secured had it not been for the manner in which the praetor, Aulus Postumius, who presided at the session, handled the case. There were three motions proposed, one favouring release, a second favouring detention, and a third favouring release but retention for the time being. The majority, it is implied, favoured this third alternative, but, when the praetor put to vote the question of release or detention, those favouring this

[1] Pol. xxx. 29. 1, 30. 1, 32.

alternative voted with those favouring detention.[1] The statement of Polybius is thus somewhat misleading. The most favourable action possible would have been a vote for release but temporary detention, and no one can say how long that might have lasted. The Achaeans, however, were encouraged enough to send an embassy the following year. Telecles served again and had as colleague Anaxidamus of Megalopolis, who had served in 165. Whether they were foolish or not, there is something touching about the persistence of these men. The result was merely that the senate voted to retain existing arrangements.[2] When the return finally was voted in 151, there still was a lively debate on the subject. According to an anecdote, the tables were turned by Cato, who rebuked the senate for wasting time debating whether a few old men were to be buried by Roman or Greek undertakers. The ruling of the senate at the time seems to have applied to all Greeks still being held in Italy.[3]

After the Third Macedonian War Roman influences made themselves felt both in Greek inter-state and domestic relations. An example of intervention of the latter kind is to be found in the intervention in the dispute between Sparta and Megalopolis concerning the possession of Sciritis. As already noted, the embassy of 164 was directed to arbitrate the dispute. The action of the Romans is also referred to in a fragmentary inscription which contains the report of a commission chosen at a later date to pass judgement on the case.[4] Though both Sparta and Megalopolis at the time were members of the Achaean Confederacy, the Roman ambassadors had proceeded to arbitrate between them as between independent states. Their verdict favouring Megalopolis probably was due to a tendency to uphold existing affiliations except when they conflicted with Roman interests. Later the whole case was brought up for review before a special court of some kind, the two parties involved being now the Spartan and the Achaean governments. Again the verdict went against Sparta.

In inter-state politics, the Achaeans, in spite of the restraining influence of the Romans, actually became involved in hostilities, though not at first on a large scale. When war broke out between the Rhodians and the Cretans in 155, both sides appealed to the Achaeans for help. The Achaeans were inclined to send help to the Rhodians but dropped the matter when Callicrates warned them that they must

[1] Pol. xxxii. 3. 14–17, xxxiii. 1. 3–8. A. Postumius Albinus was urban praetor in 155.
[2] Pol. xxxiii. 3 and 14.
[3] Pol. xxxv. 6, quoted by Plut. *Cato* 9; Paus. vii. 10. 12 places the release of the Achaeans in the seventeenth year after their detention. This was probably 151 rather than 150. So Benecke, *CAH* viii. 302. Both Pol. iii. 5. 4 and Zonaras ix. 31 imply the release of Greeks in general and not merely of Achaeans.
[4] Pol. xxxi. 1. 7; *SIG*³ 665, a very fragmentary inscription difficult to interpret.

neither go to war nor send aid to anyone without the approval of the Romans.[1] In this case, as far as the Achaeans were concerned, hostilities were averted. Probably not so in the case of the former Delians who had become Achaean citizens. When the Athenians had taken over the island, they had ordered the former inhabitants to leave. The latter protested and appealed to Rome but were told that they must leave but could take along their movable property. Obviously complications prevented some from taking along all to which they felt entitled. The departing Delians went to the Peloponnesus (*Achaia*) and were enrolled as Achaean citizens, whereupon they tried to sue the Athenians under the commercial treaty regulating the relations of Athenians and Achaeans. Not unnaturally the Athenians denied that this was a proper procedure in the case of the former Delians. The latter thereupon requested that the Achaean government grant them the right of reprisal and thus authorize the use of self-help. The request was granted, and raids and counter-raids must have followed. How extensive they were and how long they continued, is not known. The result was that both the Athenians and the Achaeans sent ambassadors to Rome, where the senate ruled that the arrangements made for the Delians by the Achaeans were valid. This seems to mean that the Delians had a right to approach the Athenians as Achaean citizens. It is not known whether this actually settled the dispute.[2]

Another case involving Athens and Achaea was that of Oropus, the little town on the border between Attica and Boeotia. This actually led to the armed intervention of the Achaean Confederacy against Athens though probably not to actual fighting. The situation was so complicated, and our sources of information are so fragmentary and contradictory, that it may be impossible ever to get at the exact truth. Some time, at the latest a few years after 160, the Athenians exacted from the Oropians what they claimed to be legitimate taxes or tribute. To this the Oropians objected and appealed to the Roman senate, which condemned the action of the Athenians and entrusted the assessment of the proper amount of damages to the city of Sicyon. The choice—not the Achaean Confederacy but a city belonging to it—is significant of the attitude of Rome. The Sicyonians assessed the damages at 500 talents, an unreasonably large sum. To appeal against this verdict the Athenians sent to Rome the famous embassy of the three philosophers, Carneades the head of the Academy, Critolaus

---

[1] Pol. xxxiii. 16. The chief interest of this passage is incidental. The wording implies that a state can send help to a beligerent without itself becoming involved in war, but it would be unwise to base too positive a conclusion on the evidence of a single passage.

[2] Pol. xxxii. 7. Since Pol. xxx. 20. 8–9 implies that the acquisition of Delos involved the Athenians in many unpleasant consequences, it has been taken for granted that the situation led to protracted raids. Cf. Niese, *Geschichte*, iii. 191; Ferguson, *Hellenistic Athens*, 323 f.

the Peripatetic, and Diogenes the Cynic. These appeared before the senate in 155, the one sure date in this affair, and secured the reduction of the sum to 100 talents. Apparently the Athenians failed to pay even this sum but instead imposed some sort of settlement involving planting a cleruchy on Oropian soil. There is no indication that this brought the Athenians into trouble with Rome. The Oropians eventually appealed to the Achaean Confederacy; apparently there seemed to be more hope of help from a nearby power than from distant Rome. The appeal was supported particularly by Hiero of Aegira, the son of that Telecles who repeatedly had gone to Rome as Achaean ambassador. He acted as patron of the Oropians, first at a *synodos* at Corinth and then at a *synkletos* at Argos. In a honorific decree he is honoured by the Oropians for bringing about their return to their fatherland. In this case the drawback connected with the Achaean law that an act of war required action at an extraordinary meeting of the Achaean *ekklesia*, is clear. When action was planned against a neighbour, it must have been impossible to keep it secret. Therefore, the account of Pausanias is probably correct in reporting that the Achaean decision became known to the Athenians who, before the Achaeans arrived, had time to devastate the Oropian territory so thoroughly that it amounted to an expulsion of the population. Since there is no battle reported, the Athenians in turn must have withdrawn on the approach of the Achaean army under the command of Menalcidas of Sparta, the general of that year. The restoration of the Oropians must have followed on the withdrawal of the Athenians. The role of Menalcidas, who was prominent in the events leading to the outbreak of the Achaean War, indicates that the Achaean intervention can hardly have been earlier than 150.[1]

The way in which the affairs of the Delians and Oropians were handled shows that the policy of trying to direct the affairs of Greece without armed intervention still had strong support in the senate. What is more, the advocates of this policy still carried the day when news of the successes of Andriscus, the Pseudo-Philip, reached Rome. This may have been due in part to underestimating the danger involved.[2] Nevertheless events were soon finally to convince the Roman authorities that the attempt to control Greece and Macedonia merely by diplomacy and dictation had ended in failure. The result was the creation of the province of Macedonia in 148 by the simple process of sending out successors to the commander who had finally ended the

---

[1] The chief sources are Paus. vii. 11. 4–8; *SIG³* 675. In addition Cic. *Acad.* ii. 137 gives the date of the visit of the philosophers to Rome; Aulus Gellius, *NA* vi. 14. 8–10 (Pol. xxxiii. 2) is important as suggesting that Polybius too gave the original fine assessed as 500 talents.

[2] Pol. xxxvi. 10. 4 emphasizes the incredulity with which the first news of the success of Andriscus were received.

war in that year. After that the process of learning how to administer the subject provinces was to be long and painful. In 150 the senate had sent not an army against the pretender but an embassy headed by Scipio Nasica, undoubtedly the great opponent of Cato, who had served as consul in 162 and 155.[1] The Romans commonly sent senior statesmen on such missions, and it would be perfectly in character for the man who had tried to prevent a break with Carthage to try to heal the wounds of Macedonia and Thessaly, and, as far as can be judged by what little information there is, he did remarkably well, at least as compared with the utter failure of his successor. Before his arrival on the scene, the Thessalians, fearing trouble, had appealed to the Achaeans for help. When Scipio arrived, he took command of the Achaean and undoubtedly other Greek troops, inflicted a defeat on Andriscus, and drove him out of Thessaly.[2] This was as it should be according to one school of thought. Rome's allies—using the term in its most inclusive sense—under Roman leadership were themselves taking action against the disturber of the peace. But the task was not completed. Andriscus had not been expelled from Macedonia. Consequently in 149 a praetor, Publius Iuventius, was sent out with one legion.[3] With the auxiliaries, this probably was an army of about 10,000. It was totally annihilated and the commander killed. What happened can hardly be deduced from the meagre accounts preserved. Did Iuventius try to fight without the aid of Greek allies? Or had disturbances in other parts of Greece gone so far that Greek allies failed to support him? The Achaeans were probably already pretty well immersed in the Spartan and other problems. Or had Andriscus simply grown so strong on account of his earlier success that he was too much for the opposing army? In any case, after the defeat of Iuventius, the troops of Andriscus again entered Thessaly. In 148 the praetor Q. Caecilius Metellus Macedonicus was sent out with a larger army and made his way by the old route from Illyria by Epirus to Thessaly. Here only two points concerning his advance need be noted. The only ally mentioned as co-operating with him seems to be the Pergamene fleet,[4] but others too may have aided. In the second place, the successful campaign brought to Greece and Macedonia Roman troops and a Roman commander available for other emergencies.

[1] The name is given only in Zonaras ix. 28 and merely as Scipio Nasica. In *MRR* he is identified as P. Cornelius Scipio Nasica (Corculum).

[2] The Thessalian appeal to the Achaeans: Pol. xxxvi. 10. 5. Livy, *Per.* 50 reports *Thessalia . . . per legatos Romanorum auxiliis Achaeorum defensa est; Oxyr. Per.* has *per socios popu[li R.*

[3] Florus i. 30. 5 refers to this army as a legion. With it there must have been the usual complement of auxiliaries.

[4] Zonaras ix. 28; cf. Strabo xiii. 624.

The Achaean War of 146, which led to the destruction of Corinth and the temporary dissolution of the Achaean Confederacy, with its causes and complicated background remains one of the most difficult problems in ancient history. It is clear that Polybius wrote a very full account, but only parts of it have been preserved. These are some of the most vivid passages in all of his work and cause the loss of the rest to be regretted. Almost equally regrettable is the loss of Livy's account, no doubt based on Polybius but supplemented with information from annalistic sources. The only fairly full narrative is that of Pausanias, which as a whole seems good. To this are added briefer statements in epitomies. The events involved are frequently referred to, and yet a satisfactory interpretation is very difficult, not to say impossible.

The war came so soon after the return of the Greeks detained in Italy that it is natural to think of their return as a cause. Rome no longer had hostages for the good behaviour of the Greeks. Instead a group of embittered old men had returned home. Yet, as already noted, this was not the way it worked. Stratius, the one Achaean known to have been active in politics after his return, on the contrary worked to prevent the war. One account does state that the return of the survivors led to disputes about property.[1] Such disputes must have been inevitable on the return of exiles, and it is known that something in the nature of social revolution was connected with the war. Yet it is unlikely that so much of the property of those taken to Italy had fallen into the hands of members of the lower classes that the return of the survivors aggravated seriously the social unrest. It is well to remember that there were signs of social unrest in many parts of Greece in this period, and that the Romans were generally on the side of property and the upper classes. Yet, it is unlikely that this unrest by itself was strong enough to cause the Achaeans to try to fight Rome. It seems rather that the demagogues who led the Achaeans stirred up unrest in order to secure their hold on the masses. In fact, it seems necessary to agree with Polybius that the blame must largely be placed on the leaders of the Achaeans and especially on Critolaus and Diaeus.[2] There is some excuse for the mistakes both of these leaders and of the people they led in the impression that the Romans had no desire to indulge in armed intervention. As late as 147 the Roman government sent two embassies in an effort to reach a peaceful settlement of the Spartan controversy. Each of these embassies was headed by a man who had been consul ten years before, and, though the first had been abused at Corinth, the second still assumed a conciliatory attitude. When armed intervention finally was adopted, it looks at first glance

[1] Zonaras ix. 31.
[2] Cf. Pédech, La méthode, 244 f.

as if an element of comic opera was injected into the tragedy. Two armies raced, as it were, for the privilege of defeating the Achaeans. Metellus came south from Macedonia and almost completed the war only to withdraw and leave the completion to the consul Mummius. The real explanation probably is that the authorities at Rome did not know at the beginning of the consular year that the army of Metellus would be available. In addition they foresaw that the advance from the north might be blocked at Thermopylae. To make sure of completing the war that year, Mummius was sent by the sea route. The determination to finish the job was so great that even the commissioners who were to arrange the settlement after the victory were sent out in 146 before the campaign was completed.

It was stated above that occupation with local problems may have kept the Achaeans from sending troops to Iuventius in 149. The campaign of the Achaeans against Sparta took place in 148, but it seems that the Spartan and Oropian incidents were so closely connected that the year or two preceding this action were filled with intrigues. The Achaean general at the time of the intervention at Oropus was Menalcidas of Sparta, general in 151–150. He must have been something of an adventurer and intriguer. When Popilius Laenas was in Alexandria in 168, he secured the release from prison of Menalcidas, who had served in Egypt but had intrigued so much in his own interest that he had been imprisoned. This release through the influence of a Roman ambassador was probably enough to make him something of a pro-Roman. Yet he was popular enough to be elected Achaean general.[1] Apparently at the end of his term of office the old quarrel between Sparta and the Achaean federal government broke out again. There seems to be no adequate cause for this, except that a latent dispute needs little stimulus to cause an active outburst. Otherwise only antagonism between intriguing leaders is reported. Even if much of the scandal involving Menalcidas and his successor as general, Diaeus, is discounted, it appears that the latter was largely to blame for the outbreak of the war and the calamities to which it led.

The story that Callicrates brought capital charges against Menalcidas as a traitor may be true, since the question of the jurisdiction of the Achaean government over Spartans was raised again. Once more the senate is said to have ruled that the Achaean authorities had jurisdiction except in capital cases. Once more the action of the senate is said to have been misrepresented, Diaeus claiming that complete jurisdiction had been granted the Achaeans, the Spartans denying

---

[1] Menalcidas general at the time of the Oropus incident: Paus. vii. 11. 7; in Egypt: Pol. xxx. 16. 2.

this and wishing to appeal to Rome. The Achaeans thereupon denied the right of cities to send ambassadors to Rome. If a new ruling on these disputes was issued by the senate, it must have been done late in 150 or early in 149. Diaeus, the Achaean general for 150–149 had brought the quarrel to an issue. He presented to the Spartans a list of twenty-four who were considered disturbers of the peace. These went into voluntary exile and left for Rome, obviously hoping for Roman intervention in their favour. At the end of his term of office, Diaeus and Callicrates went to Rome as ambassadors. Callicrates died on the way. The purpose of the embassy was to counteract the Spartan exiles, whose spokesman is said to have been Menalcidas, the former Achaean general. The only result was a promise that the senate would send ambassadors to judge between the Achaeans and Spartans.[1]

This action of the senate should normally have brought a Roman embassy to Greece in 148, but no embassy arrived before 147. It is true that in 148 an embassy on its way to Asia is said to have been induced by Metellus to turn aside to visit the Achaeans and urge them not to attack Sparta but to await the ambassadors from Rome. The message was delivered but came too late. Damocritus, the general for 149–148, had already invaded Spartan territory and defeated the Spartans with heavy losses but, instead of capturing the city, had called off his army. For this he was condemned to pay a fine of fifty talents and, being unable to pay, went into exile. As successor, Diaeus had been elected. When Metellus again sent ambassadors to the Achaeans, apparently in the autumn of 148, Diaeus promised not to attack but to await the arrival of the Roman arbitrators. He did, however, proceed to garrison perioecic cities. The one untoward incident before the arrival of the ambassadors from Rome, was the capture and sacking of one of these by Menalcidas, now acting as a Spartan general. Since this brought him nothing but unpopularity even with the Spartans, he committed suicide.[2] Strange as it seems this story may be true. Public opinion may have felt that Damocritus should have eliminated the Spartan problem once and for all and faced the Roman ambassadors with a *fait accompli*. Diaeus, even if he shared this opinion, may have felt that once the opportunity had been lost, further aggression would have been unwise. At this stage of his career he had shown some restraint. In his previous term as general he had sought action only against individual Spartan leaders. The action of

[1] Paus. vii. 12.
[2] Paus. vii. 13. There seems to be no other evidence for the intervention of Metellus or for the Roman embassy that year to Asia. The story of the exile of Damocritus gains some confirmation from the reference in Pol. xxxviii. 17. 9 to his return from exile.

Menalcidas may have won general condemnation on the grounds that it accomplished little except aggravating a bad situation.

When the Roman embassy headed by L. Aurelius Orestes arrived in 147, an extraordinary meeting of the Achaean assembly had been summoned to meet the ambassadors at Corinth. For this meeting Spartans had turned up in considerable numbers. The solution submitted by the ambassadors was more than acceptable to them but was such as to kindle the anger of the Achaeans. The partial dissolution of the Confederacy, which the senate as early as 182 had hinted would be desirable, was now demanded outright. This came as a surprise to the Achaeans. This action must have been decided on after the embassy of Diaeus had left Rome, and it naturally was not published in Greece before the arrival of Orestes. In that sense it was 'secret', as one of the sources puts it. If, as reported, the senate had recently ruled a second time that Spartans should be subject to Achaean jurisdiction except for capital charges, it also represented a sudden reversal of policy, at the same time as it was a return to an old policy. Orestes apparently thought that, by reasoning with the leaders, he could prepare the way for his pronouncement to the mass meeting of the Achaeans and so invited Diaeus and other high officials to his quarters. To them he announced that the senate wished not only Sparta but also Corinth, Argos, the Arcadian Orchomenus, and the Herclea near Thermopylae to be detached from the Confederacy. The announcement had the opposite effect from that desired. The Achaean officials rushed out and incited the assembled Achaeans to seize all Spartans and all suspected of being Spartans. Later the real Spartans were retained in prison and the others released. Orestes, who had been unable to restrain the Achaeans, could only call to their attention the insolence they had exhibited against the Romans and depart.[1] The ambassadors were later reported to have been driven out of Corinth and themselves to have been in danger.[2] The Achaeans, not unnaturally, sent to Rome an embassy headed by Thearidas, the brother of Polybius, to explain and apologize.[3]

The Romans reacted surprisingly rapidly to the developments at Corinth. Orestes returned to Rome and reported to the senate, which sent out a second embassy that very summer. It was led by Sextus

[1] Paus. vii. 14. 1–3; Livy, *Per.* 51 and Dio xxi. 72. 1 state that cities which had been subject to Philip were to be detached; Justin xxxiv. 1. 7 implies a general dissolution; it is Justin too who speaks of secret instructions to the ambassadors. Pol. xxxviii. 9. 6 refers to the demands of Orestes. On the Achaean meetings cf. *Rep. Govt.* 185–7.

[2] Livy, *Per.* 51; Justin xxxiv. 1. 9; Dio xxi. 72. 1–2. Pol. xxxviii. 9. 1–2 states that the ambassadors, when reporting at Rome, exaggerated their danger.

[3] Pol. xxxviii. 10. 1; Paus. vii. 14.3. Polybius does not identify Thearidas as his brother in any extant part of his work; for the identification see *SIG*³ 626, n. 2.

Iulius Caesar, who had been the colleague of Orestes as consul ten years earlier. On the way he met the embassy of Thearidas and induced it to return to the Peloponnesus with himself. Sextus apparently reached Aegium just before the autumn *synodos* at which the federal officials were elected and addressed the meeting. He had been instructed to deal leniently with the Achaeans and acted accordingly, condemning their abuse of the Roman ambassadors less severely, it was said, than the Achaeans themselves had done, but there was no indication that the terms offered by Orestes were being relaxed. Nevertheless, the courteous manner of the ambassador is said to have deceived Diaeus and Critolaus, who was just being elected general as the successor of the former. They and their circle thought that the Romans were so preoccupied with troubles in Africa and Spain that they would avoid war with the Achaeans. Critolaus, in any case, replied courteously to the Roman ambassadors and promised a meeting at Tegea for negotiations with the Spartans.[1] In so doing he acted in bad faith.

The meeting announced for Tegea must have been an extraordinary meeting of the Achaean *ekklesia* called in this Arcadian city conveniently located for negotiations with Sparta. The general in office at the time was Critolaus. He and his circle agreed that Critolaus should go to the meeting alone and that the rest of the Achaeans were to stay away. The story goes that the officials announced the meeting but sent secret instructions to the members to stay away. The Romans and the Spartans arrived at Tegea in due time and consulted about the attitude to adopt towards the Achaeans. Meanwhile the latter failed to show up, and Critolaus at last came alone and announced that he could do nothing by himself. The Romans might present their case before the next *synodos*, which was scheduled to meet in six months. Sextus thereupon naturally dismissed the Spartans and himself returned to Italy.[2] This incident made war inevitable. The deliberately planned insult and frustration must have seemed more offensive to the Romans than the outbreak of mob spirit at the time of the visit of Orestes. Moreover, the conference of Sextus with the Spartans should have suggested to the Achaeans that the Romans now were definitely on the side of the Spartans. Yet Critolaus does not seem to have realized the seriousness of the situation, probably still thinking that the Romans would not expend any serious effort on reducing the Achaeans. Hence he spent the winter going the rounds of Achaean cities and stirring them up against the Romans and declaring a moratorium on debts for the duration of the war. The latter measure

[1] Pol. xxxviii. 9–10; Paus. vii. 14. 3–4.
[2] Pol. xxxviii. 11. 1–6; Paus. vii. 14. 4–5.

seems to have been an executive order. Then in the spring of 146 at a wild meeting at Corinth, which seems to have combined a regular *synodos*, which could handle a variety of subjects, and a *synkletos*, a special mass meeting competent to rule on a question of war and peace, he secured a vote of war against Sparta—an act which inevitably involved war with Rome. During the meeting he inveighed against his political opponents, stating that he feared Lacedaemonians and Romans less than traitors within the state. So at least is the report of Polybius, who was contemporary though not present at the meeting. The war vote was followed by a decree giving dictatorial powers to the general in office.[1]

If Critolaus and other Achaeans misjudged the intentions of the Romans, it was not because they had not been warned. They may have been misled by the fact that the senate decidedly took its time about sending out the embassy of Orestes. They may also have been misled by the courtesy shown especially by Sextus and, when they later received warnings from Metellus, they may have felt that these embassies did not carry as much weight as those coming directly from Rome. Looking back at what happened, it seems clear that the senate, before it sent Orestes to Greece, had decided on intervention in case its instructions were disregarded. Sending out Sextus meant giving the Achaeans another chance. After all, it was too late to send an army from Italy to Greece that year, and, as for the other alternative, Metellus probably was not yet free to move south. In all likelihood, Mummius was assigned Achaea as his province at the beginning of the consular year, and was instructed to prepare an army and a fleet. Meanwhile Metellus was able to act and probably was instructed to do so. The story that he hurried hoping to complete the war before Mummius should arrive may be correct, though there seems to have been somewhat of a definite break between the two campaigns or two parts of the campaign of 146. Possibly Metellus had been told not to go beyond the Isthmus of Corinth.[2] Before he commenced hostilities, he sent four ambassadors to the Achaeans to urge them to avoid a break. These ambassadors were present and addressed the meeting of the Achaeans at Corinth which voted war against Sparta. When they left Corinth, one of the four went to Athens first and from there to Sparta, two remained in Athens until Metellus himself arrived, while a fourth went to Naupactus, probably to deal with the Aetolians and

[1] Pol. xxxviii. 11. 7–13. 7; Diod. xxxii. 26. 4–5; Paus. vii. 14. 5–6. On the meeting at Corinth cf. *Rep. Govt.* 187 f.

[2] Paus. vii. 15. 1 reports that Mummius was instructed to prepare ships and an army and mentions the rivalry of Metellus; Zonaras ix. 31 places the commissioning of Mummius after the death of Critolaus (this seems impossible); Florus i. 32. 3 mentions instructions to Metellus (*Metello . . . mandata est ultio*), but his account is too confused to carry much weight.

to assure that this port would be available when Mummius arrived.[1] Apparently it was planned from the outset that Mummius was to transport his army by sea to the Gulf of Corinth.[2]

It may be worth while to try to reconstruct the plan of campaign of Critolaus and the Achaeans, though it must be remembered that information is scarce and that all conclusions must be tentative. So far Roman advances into Greece had normally been by the land route through Illyria, Epirus, and Thessaly. This meant that in case of such an advance, Phocis, Locris, Boeotia, and a fortiori the Peloponnesus itself were safe as long as Thermopylae could be held. This seems the basis for the Achaean plan of campaign. At this time the Achaeans claimed Heraclea below Mount Oeta as their own. This must mean that they were trying to hold the gateway to central Greece. In this they were supported by the Boeotians, Locrians, and Euboeans. Phocis was probably a land of passage and a scene of battle rather than an active participant. Thus most of central Greece, except Attica and Phocis, was united with the Achaeans in defence of Thermopylae. The leader of the coalition outside of the Confederacy appears to have been Pytheas of Thebes.[3] The plan was not in itself hopeless. If they had had first class military leadership, the Greeks should have had a good chance of holding Thermopylae. This seems to have been the opinion also of the Romans, who must have anticipated the plan. Hence Mummius was sent by sea so that he could land in the rear of the forces defending Thermopylae or effect a landing on the Peloponnesus, whatever should prove most advantageous.

Hostilities began with the siege of Heraclea, which wished to break away from the Achaeans, by Critolaus and the Boeotians. On the approach of Metellus they fell back to Scarphea in Eastern Locris just beyond Thermopylae. It may be that the best spot for defence had been bypassed, but the situation still did not seem hopeless. However, at Scarphea the Romans caught up with Critolaus and his force and defeated it decisively with heavy losses. Critolaus himself disappeared, fallen in battle or a suicide. To make matters worse, two divisions

[1] Pol. xxxviii. 12. 1–4, 13. 8–9; Paus. vii. 15. 2.

[2] Direct information is almost non-existent except on the two points that Mummius arrived suddenly one morning at the camp of Metellus (Paus. vii. 16. 1) and that the original instructions to him provided for ships. He must have used these for transporting his troops. Had he come by the normal route from the north, Metellus would have had advance information about his approach.

[3] Concerning the Thebans, Paus. vii. 15. 9 states that they had taken part in the siege of Heraclea and the battle of Scarphea. Since the Thebans were accused of having invaded Phocis, it looks as though the Phocians were unwilling to take part in the fighting (Paus. vii. 14. 7). References to calamities overtaking Boeotians, Phocians, Locrians, and others; Pol. xxxviii. 3. 8; Thebans and Euboeans: Paus. vii. 14.7. Pytheas active at Thebes: Paus. vii. 14. 6; cf. Pol. xxxviii. 14. 1–2.

coming too late for the battle were annihilated, both apparently advancing through Phocis to join Critolaus. A division of 1,000 picked Arcadian troops had got as far as Elatea, where they were admitted into the city. While they were there, news of Scarphea reached the city, whereupon the Elateans asked the Arcadians to leave. The latter started homeward by the land route down the Cephissus valley but were caught at Chaeronea. The conduct of the Phocians suggests that they allowed the belligerents the right of passage through their territory but themselves wished to remain neutral.[1] From Chaeronea Metellus continued on to Thebes, which had been deserted by its population.[2] While there he learned that the troops of the Achaean *synteleia* of Patrae were in Phocis. They obviously had been transported across the Gulf of Corinth and knew nothing about the defeat at Scarphea. When Metellus learned of the presence of this division in Phocis, he turned back to fight it. There are no reliable statistics concerning the troops involved in this action, but Polybius connects with this battle the demoralization and despair which overtook not only the defeated contingent but also much of Greece and seems to imply that the defeat in Phocis rather than Scarphea was the great disaster of the campaign. In fact, he implies that a senior Roman statesman anticipated so rough a battle that he preferred to stay away and remain in Thebes.[3] This, as it were, ended the campaign of Critolaus, though he himself had died before it was completed. It would seem that the plan of the Achaeans and Boeotians was not without merit, but that it failed in part because they allowed themselves to become engaged in a major battle before their army was at full strength. This had the disastrous sequel that the contingents that came too late were waylaid separately and destroyed. The second such contingent, that from Patrae, seems to have been so large that its defeat involved a real battle.

After these defeats, strange to say, the Achaeans were allowed a breathing spell in which they made preparations for the continuation of the war. Diaeus took over as the successor of Critolaus in accordance with the Achaean law that, in case of the death of the general of the Confederacy, his predecessor was to serve until the next regular

[1] Paus. vii. 15. 1–6. Concerning Critolaus, Pausanias merely tells that he was never seen again. Livy, *Per*. 52 states that he took poison; is this an independent story or merely a transfer to Critolaus of the suicide of Diaeus? The statement of Florus i. 32. 3 that Metellus defeated Critolaus in Elis along the Alpheus is, of course, pure nonsense.

[2] Paus. vii. 15. 9–10; Pol. xxxviii. 16. 10.

[3] Polybius' account of Scarphea has not been preserved. For the battle in Phocis see xxxviii. 16. 4–9, xxxix. 1. 11. The anecdote concerning Aulus Postumius told in the last passage indicates that Thebes was in the hands of the Romans and thus in turn suggests the sequence of events given above.

synodos or meeting of the council of the Confederacy. When the meeting occurred, Diaeus was duly elected and served to the end of the war, or rather his own suicide.[1] Diaeus apparently practically had to make a new start and chose to do so by depending on slaves suddenly liberated. His orders were that 12,000 household slaves were to be set free, armed, and sent to Corinth, where also all citizens of military age were to gather. At the same time compulsory war contributions were extracted from men of property. It must have been a sorry lot mobilized in this way. The men of Elis and Messene were kept at home to guard against possible attacks by the Roman fleet. This was probably a part of the original plan of campaign. Then the troops of the *synteleia* of Patrae had apparently suffered such losses that there now were no troops to send. From the rest of the Confederacy a force of 14,000 infantry and 600 cavalry is said to have been gathered. These troops were stationed at Corinth except that 4,000 were detached and sent to Megara. The latter withdrew as soon as the Roman army approached, and the citizens surrendered the city without resistance. Corinth and the Isthmus thus became the line of defence.[2]

Up to this point the determination not to yield to the Roman demands but to fight if necessary can be understood. Until Thermopylae was passed, the Achaeans may even have thought that there was some hope of success, but the determination to carry on after the defeat and death of Critolaus, though a chance to make peace was offered, must be judged a sort of desperate madness. At its worst it brooked no opposition. At first the more reasonable group of leaders was able to secure the dispatch of an embassy headed by Andronidas, an old associate of Callicrates, to Metellus to open negotiations. He returned with the offers of Metellus and was supported by the Thessalian, Philo. These negotiations appear to have been opened by the Achaeans. A prime mover among them, unless he was falsely accused by Diaeus, was Sosicrates, the *hypostrategos*, one of the highest officers in the army.[3] Among those who urged the acceptance of the terms offered was Stratius, one of the Achaeans taken to Rome in 167, who now as an old man humiliated himself enough to embrace Diaeus and implore him to yield. It was all to no avail. By this time Diaeus had secured such control over the men surrounding him that he was able to bring charges against his opponents. The *hypostrategos* Sosicrates was tortured to death but revealed no secrets. Others were acquitted

---

[1] Pol. xxxviii. 15. 1, 17. 1; Paus. vii. 15. 7.

[2] Pol. xxxviii. 15–16; Paus. vii. 15. 7–11.

[3] At the time of the Social War a *hypostrategos* was in command of the *synteleia* of Patrae, but this is the only such district attested. In the present case the definite article suggests a single *hypostrategos* for the army, though other interpretations are possible.

32

because, even under the conditions of the time, the populace considered the cruel treatment of Sosicrates excessive. Polybius also charges that some secured their acquittal by bribing Diaeus, and he is specific in his charges.[1]

When the hostilities opened again, the Roman commander was the consul Mummius, who had arrived with a force, it is said, of 3,500 horse and 23,000 foot. To this were added contingents of Cretan archers and Pergamene troops. His army had been brought by sea from Italy into the Gulf of Corinth. On its arrival Metellus and his army were dismissed and the newly arrived forces took over. Some success against a Roman detachment made the Achaeans over bold, so that they offered the Romans a pitched battle, which resulted in a disastrous defeat. The Achaean leaders now turned from over confidence to excessive despair. Diaeus made no attempt to hold Corinth or to delay the advance of the Roman army. Instead he fled to his home city, Megalopolis, put his wife to death with his own hand, and then took poison. Under the circumstances, it is not surprising that both the 'defenders' of Corinth and most of the inhabitants left the city. Nevertheless, Mummius, fearing a trap, waited two days before he entered the city, sacked, and burned it. The war was now over.[2] Some impression of the Achaean losses in the battle of the Isthmus can be derived from the list of 156 citizens and residents of Epidaurus fallen in the battle.[3] This implies losses of thousands in this battle alone, not to mention the battles of the campaign of Critolaus.

5. AFTER 146 B.C.

The organization of Greece and its vicissitudes after 146 cannot be discussed here in any detail.[4] Only a very brief statement will be given followed by a somewhat fuller treatment of certain points involving federal states. It is now clear that Greece as a whole was not at the time made tributary. In those parts which had taken part in the war

[1] Pol. xxxviii. 17–18, where there is no account of the dispatch of the Achaean embassy but only of its return. Paus. vii. 15. 11 reports that Metellus, when he arrived at the Isthmus, sent a herald inviting the Achaeans to negotiate peace. As between Polybius and Pausanias it is necessary to side with Polybius, but it is possible that Pausanias reports another act—a last effort to arrange a negotiated peace before the arrival of Mummius.

[2] Paus. vii. 16. 1–8 is the only fairly full account of these events; see also Zonaras ix. 31; Florus i. 32. 4–7; Justin xxxiv. 2. 1–6, who has some impossible details about the excessive confidence of the Achaeans.

[3] IG iv². 1. 28.

[4] Econ. Surv. Rome, iv. 306–11; Rostovtzeff, Hellenistic World, 745 ff., especially 748. On the question of taxation see also H. Hill, 'The Roman Revenues from Greece after 146 B.C.', CP xli (1946), 35–42. A very full and careful treatment is that of Silvio Accame, Il dominio romano in Grecia dalla Guerra Acaica ad Augusto (1946). This work will be cited by the name of the author alone.

considerable land was confiscated and made *ager publicus*. Probably also some districts were made tributary. Nor was Greece made into a province. Instead it was placed under the watchful eye of the governor of Macedonia. It has been suggested that parts of Greece were definitely subjected and put under the control of that governor.[1] There seems to be some basis for this distinction. True, the general freedom going back to 196 was not cancelled. A letter of about 115 B.C. of the governor of Macedonia, Quintus Fabius Maximus, to the city of Dyme in Achaea, though dictatorial in tone, refers to the freedom granted the Greeks in general.[2] From a certain point of view it was later possible to speak of all subjects of the Roman Empire as free,[3] but there was a great deal of difference between this general freedom and that of the *civitates liberae*, which were less under the control of the provincial governor than the province proper. So, in the period after 146, there may have been a distinction between cities more directly under the control of the governor of Macedonia and those exempt from his direct supervision, corresponding somewhat to the later *civitates liberae*, with the difference that the latter were enclaves within the province, while in the period after 146 the 'subjected cities' were enclaves between the more numerous free communities. Yet all, both subject and free, were expected to take direction from Rome, and the nearest high Roman authority was the governor of Macedonia. In that sense, all Greece was a part of the province of Macedonia.

The terms imposed on the defeated states were, as usual, drawn up by a commission of ten in co-operation with the victorious commander. The commissioners came out to Greece in 146, probably some of them before the arrival of the army of Mummius, worked through

---

[1] Accame, 6 ff. and *passim*. The argument is based on Cic. *ii in Verrem* i. **55**: *quid de L. Mummio, qui . . . urbisque Achaiae Boiotiaeque multas sub imperium populi Romani dicionemque subiunxit?* and on an inscription which seems to refer to the province of Macedonia and the part of Greece under the control of the Romans. This is *IG* vii. 2413 as re-edited by Klaffenbach in his Berlin dissertation (1914), quoted by Accame, 2 f. Coupled with it is 2414, a fragment of a letter of a *strategos hypatos*. Klaffenbach supplied Lucius Mummius; Accame argues that it rather must be Marcus Livius Drusus, consul 112.

[2] *SIG*³ 684. 15 f. The governor in question is identified by Accame, 149 f. as Q. Fabius Maximus Eburnus, consul in 116, chiefly because every other Q. Fabius Maximus known to have served as consul was so occupied in other parts of the empire that he cannot have served as governor of Macedonia; cf. *MRR* ii. 644, addition to i. 532. The passage in Zonaras ix. 31 which has been interpreted by Colin, *Rome et la Grèce*, 640 and n. 4 and myself, *Econ. Surv. Rome*, iv. 310 as reporting a ruling that all states except Corinth were to be free actually applies only to the prisoners rounded up in the city. The Corinthians were to be enslaved; the others, set free. The letter of Fabius, however, is evidence enough. C. B. Welles, in his interesting article 'Greek Liberty', *Jn. Juristic Pap.* xv (1965), 29–47, treats the Roman intervention in Greece too briefly to help much in solving the problem of the status of Greece after 146.

[3] Dio Cassius lii. 5. 4; cf. *CP* xl (1945), 89.

the winter, and returned to Italy in the spring.[1] No list of the members has been preserved, but among them there seem to have been at least two former consuls. Thus the senate continued its old practice of including senior statesmen in such commissions. In this case it is clear that the destruction of Corinth and other harsh measures were not due to Mummius but were acts of deliberate policy due, most likely, to the senate itself. Apparently, Mummius personally was responsible for some harsh acts, including the execution of prominent citizens at Chalcis, but this Polybius blamed on his friends.[2] The starting point of the settlement was undoubtedly the demand which had been to the fore since 147, namely, the dissolution of the Achaean Confederacy. Probably also other confederacies involved in the war were dissolved, and, like the Achaean, refounded a short time afterwards. The parts of Greece which had not taken part in the war were left to themselves without having changes imposed upon them. In the case of the Achaeans, it was no longer a question of detaching a few cities. It was rather a total dissolution, which meant that the federal government disappeared and that the cities thereafter functioned as independent states. That this continued to be the status of a number of former members is clear from the examples of Sparta and Messene. Very likely, when the war was over, Messene and Elis felt that they had profited from it. Their troops had not gone to the front but had remained at home to guard against an eventual attack from the sea. This did not materialize, while the defeat of the Achaeans meant the restoration of freedom to these states.

The Achaean Confederacy was soon reconstituted, and, if the letter of Fabius Maximus is to be taken literally, this was done by the Romans themselves. The revived Confederacy was much smaller than the one dissolved in 146, and it naturally was believed that it included only old Achaea proper.[3] This has been proved a mistake by the publication a few years ago of an inscription from Olympia from the base of an equestrian statue in which soldiers from nineteen Achaean cities who had served under the consul Gnaeus Domitius in Transalpine Gaul in 122 B.C. or thereabouts honoured their commanding officer, Damon of Patrae. Of the cities listed at least the following were Arcadian: Heraea, Thelphusa, Psophis, Cleitor, Cynaetha, and

---

[1] This information is derived from Polybius. An anecdote indicates that Aulus Postumius, undoubtedly one of the ten, was in Greece at the time of the battle in Phocis (xxxix. 1. 11). After completing their work in six months the ten returned to Italy in the spring (xxxix. 5. 1). No list of members has been preserved. MRR i. 467 under 146 lists five including two ex-consuls, A. Postumius Albinus and Orestes. The latter, according to Paus. vii. 16. 1, came out with Mummius. In MRR he is listed with a query, but, if he was in Greece, his participation in the settlement can almost be taken for granted.

[2] Pol. xxxix. 6. Livy, Per. 52 and probably other later accounts are derived from this.

[3] Niese, Geschichte, iii. 355; Accame, 17 and 149.

Pheneus.[1] This document is important both for conditions in Greece and for Roman policy. It shows that the Achaean Confederacy at the time included not so little of northern and northwestern Arcadia. This membership must have been voluntary, for it is hard to believe that the Romans compelled them to join or allowed the Achaeans to use compulsion. It was probably in this period that some referred to the old Achaean city of Tritaea as Arcadian. It may well have felt itself more closely tied to Psophis, Cleitor, and Cynaetha than to the Achaean coastal cities and thus could count itself as belonging to the Arcadian part of the Achaean Confederacy.[2] The document is important further as showing that the federal government was not entirely negligible. When the Romans called for a contingent of Achaean troops, it was organized by the federal government and the troops from all cities placed under a single commander. From the point of view of Roman policy, it adds one more to the meagre list of examples of the use of Greek troops in wars in the west.[3] This new evidence suggests that such a practice may have been more common than has been suspected, but the evidence, like most of the evidence for this period, has disappeared. It may seem surprising that troops should be transported from Greece to Gaul, but this is hardly more startling than the use of Numidian troops in Greece in the Third Macedonian War. Yet services such as these must have amounted to very little compared with the services resulting from the Mithradatic wars and the Roman civil wars.

There were also frequent financial contributions required for the various wars including the wars against the pirates. Thus, being

[1] *Bericht über die Ausgrabungen in Olympia*, v (1956), 160–4; *L'année épigraphique*, 1960, no. 76; *SEG* xv. 254; commentary and references to literature, J. and L. Robert, *Bull. ép.* 1959, no. 170. Of the Arcadian cities mentioned, Strabo viii. 388 lists Heraea, Cleitor, Pheneus, and Cynaetha as cities which had disappeared by his time. For evidence that Strabo exaggerated the devastation of Greece, see *Econ. Surv. Rome*, iv. 473. Cn. Domitius Ahenobarbus, the consul of the document, served in 122 and operated against the Allobroges and Arverni (*MRR* i. 516). Thus the Galatians against whom the Achaeans served must have been some of the Gauls of Transalpine Gaul.—After the account given above was written, there came to hand L. Moretti, 'Per la storia della lega achea', *Riv. fil.* xciii (1965), 278–83. Moretti takes the Gnaeus Domitius of the inscription to be the consul of 192 and the operations against the Galatians to be those of the consul against the Boii. But it is most unlikely that Achaean troops were brought to Italy in 192 for minor local operations. Moreover, Moretti seems to hold almost as an axiom requiring no proof that the revived Achaean Confederacy can have contained only Achaeans of old Achaea. Against this it is enough to recall the way in which Achaea became the name of the Roman province and later of the Peloponnesus. The interpretation of Moretti is to be rejected.

[2] Paus. vi. 12. 8–9; cf. Accame, 148.

[3] Thessalians and Acarnanians are reported to have served in the slave war in Sicily in 103 (Diod. xxxvi. 8. 1); a citizen of Carystus, one of Clazomenae, and one of Miletus were voted privileges by the senate for their services in the fleet during the Social War in Italy (*IGR* i. 118); Sulla is reported to have brought Peloponnesian and Macedonian troops to Italy in 83 (Appian, *BC* i. 79).

immune and exempt from paying tribute did not mean immunity from financial burdens. Probably the best known illustration is that of the collection of a contribution of eight obols for every mina (Aeginetan standard) of assessed property at Messene, that is, a tax of a little less than 2 %.[1] Other evidence shows that requisitions could be frequent and oppressive. It is known that cities, when in great financial difficulties, borrowed money at 48% compound interest. The one completely sure example of this recorded in an inscription is a loan made to Gythium in connexion with requisitions, apparently about 71 B.C., for the war against the pirates.[2] In this case the money-lenders, the brothers Cloatii, afterwards reduced the interest to 24% simple interest. Nor was this the only favour shown the city by the brothers. The inscription gives a vivid impression of conditions in a city subject to frequent requisitions, once including soldiers, and also liable frequently to have to entertain visiting dignitaries. Once in connexion with the requisitioning of grain and clothing, a reference to the share that fell to the city indicates that such demands were not limited to Gythium. At the same time the number of instances in which the Cloatii interceded to have Gythium exempted from payments suggests that cities with good connexions with influential Romans some-times could secure exemptions—a fact which must have made the situation more difficult for cities without such patrons. The situation must have become more difficult during the civil wars from 49 to 30 B.C.[3]

In the period after 146 the federal states that continued in existence developed into what they were under the Empire, instruments for local government of more or less importance. Some had an active political life with considerable local patriotism. From this point of view, probably the most important were the Lycian and Thessalian confederacies. The first, though its institutions were closely related to those of the confederacies of Greece, was geographically isolated from them, and so consideration of its history under the Empire, has been included in the section on the Confederacy. Thessaly too had some-thing of a history of its own, especially during the civil wars, and again consideration of this is included in the account of the Confederacy. Other confederacies might be equally interesting if more information

---

[1] *IG* v. 1433. All later scholars who have studied this and the documents closely connected with it owe a great deal to A. Wilhelm, 'Urkunden aus Messene', *Jahreshefte*, xvii (1914), 1–120. Cf. *Econ. Surv. Rome*, iv. 429 f.; Rostovtzeff, *Hellenistic World*, 750–3; Accame, 136 f.

[2] *SIG*³ 748; cf. *Econ. Surv. Rome*, iv. 373 f. For Roman Asia, Broughton, ibid. 561 f. under 'Rates of Interest', lists no example of this rate except the loan of Brutus to Salamis on Cyprus.

[3] Cf. 'The Effects of Wars between 146 and 30 B.C.', *Econ. Surv. Rome*, iv. 422–35.

were available. The restored Achaean Confederacy, as noted above, was larger than sometimes supposed, but it must not be confused with the Panachaean (sometimes called Achaean) League probably first organized during the civil wars and retained under the Empire.[1] It is also interesting for the reason that there is a record of a leftist revolution in the Achaean city of Dyme about 120 B.C. This resulted in the death sentence being imposed on two ringleaders by the governor of Macedonia while a third was ordered to be sent to Rome.[2] The laws proposed by the revolutionists were condemned on the ground that they violated the constitution of the Confederacy. Nevertheless, the communications seem to have passed directly from the city to the governor and vice versa without passing through federal intermediaries. Note, however, that the appeal to the governor can hardly have been sent before a counter-revolutionary government had gained the upper hand in the city. It is not known whether the local conservatives regained control unaided, or whether they were helped by their neighbours, or whether federal authorities had intervened. In this connexion it may be appropriate to recall that social revolution seems to have been an important factor in bringing about the loss of freedom of the Lycian Confederacy. Finally, it may be noted that the one of the old federal states for which there is evidence that it remained alive almost to the rise of Diocletian, is the little Magnesian Confederacy of which Demetrias was the capital.[3]

That the Roman government under the Republic was not opposed to the continued existence of federal states is indicated clearly enough by the revival of the Achaean Confederacy. That the policy was continued under the Empire is shown by the practice of emperors of occasionally allowing themselves to be listed as the general or head of a confederacy. Examples of this are known for the Thessalian and Magnesian confederacies. The service of Augustus in the Thessalian Confederacy appears to have been more than a routine matter. It seems to have symbolized his recognition of the Confederacy at the outset of his reign and was a part of his policy to pose in Greece almost as a Greek rather than as an outsider. He, and still more Hadrian, seem to have tried to remake the Amphictionic League on the model of the true federal states by an adjustment of representation. Unfortunately the details of Hadrian's reorganization are not known. His Panhellenion was rather inspired by amphictionies and symmachies, though an inscription published a few years ago has shown that it too must have employed representation somewhat in proportion to the

---

[1] *Rep. Govt.* 110 and 112 f.
[2] *SIG*[3] 684; for the date see p. 499, n. 2 above.
[3] *SIG*[3] 896, an inscription honouring the emperor Carinus.

size and importance of the community represented.[1] The Hellenistic federal states also furnished the model for the system of representation in proportion to population in the assembly of the Three Gauls and doubtless other western 'provincial' assemblies.[2]

[1] On Augustus cf. 'The Policy of Augustus in Greece', *Acta Classica*, i (1958), 123–30; on the Panhellenion of Hadrian see P. M. Fraser, 'Hadrian and Cyrene', *JRS* xl (1950), 77–87; Larsen, 'Cyrene and the Panhellenion', *CP* xlvii (1952), 7–16, where references to earlier literature can be found. The inscription published by Fraser is very fragmentary and I do not think it has been reproduced in any collection, not even in *SEG*. For discussion see J. and L. Robert, *Bull. ép.* 1951, no. 243; 1953, no. 255.

[2] Rep. Govt. 138. On the provincial assemblies, see now J. Deininger, *Die Provinzial-landtage der Römischen Kaiserzeit* (1965), reviewed *JRS* xlvi (1966), 240–1.

SELECT BIBLIOGRAPHY

(For more detailed information see the footnotes.)

GREEK FEDERALISM

Freeman, Edward A., *History of Federal Government in Greece and Italy*, 2 ed. by
J. B. Bury, 1893.

Moretti, Luigi, *Ricerche sulle leghe greche*, 1962.

Gschnitzer, Fritz, 'Stammes und Ortsgemeinden im alten Griechenland',
Wiener Studien, lxviii (1955), 120–44.

Larsen, J. A. O., *Representative Government in Greek and Roman History*, 1955
(paperback, 1966).

GREEK POLITICAL INSTITUTIONS

Kuhn, Emil, *Ueber die Entstehung der Staedte der alten*, 1878.

Szanto, Emil, *Das griechische Bürgerrecht*, 1892.

Francotte, Henri, *La Polis grecque*, 1907.

Swoboda, Heinrich, *Lehrbuch der griechischen Staatsaltertümer*, 1913 (vol. i part
iii of K. F. Herrman's *Lehrbuch der griechischen Antiquitäten*, 6 ed.).

Busolt, Georg, *Griechische Staatskunde*, vol. i, 1920, vol. ii (ed. Swoboda),
1926.

Ehrenberg, Victor, *The Greek State*, 1960.

Ehrenberg, Victor, *Der Staat der griechen*, 2 ed., 1965.

HISTORIES OF GREECE ETC.

Grote, George, *A History of Greece*, 1846–56.

Meyer, Eduard, *Geschichte des Altertums* (*GdA*), iii–v, 1900–02.

Busolt, Georg, *Griechische Geschichte bis zur Schlacht bei Chaeroneia* (*GrG*),
i–iii (all published), 1885–1906, vols. i and ii cited from ed. 2, 1893 and
1895.

Beloch, Karl Julius, *Griechische Geschichte*, 2 ed. (*GrG²*), 1912–27.

Cambridge Ancient History, 1924–39.

Glotz, Gustave and Cohen, Robert, *Histoire grecque*, 1925 ff., part of
Histoire générale planned by Glotz.

Bury, J. B., *A History of Greece to the Death of Alexander the Great*, 3 ed. by
Russel Meiggs, 1952.

Hammond, N. G. L., *A History of Greece to 322 B.C.*, 1959.

Bengtson, Hermann, *Griechische Geschichte von den Anfängen bis in die römische
Kaiserzeit*, 2 ed. (*GrG²*), 1960.

Cary, M., *The Geographic Background of Greek and Roman History*, 1949.

Buck, Carl Darling, *The Greek Dialects*, 1959.

Gschnitzer, Fritz, *Abhängige Orte im griechischen Altertum*, 1958.

Hampl, Franz, *Die griechischen Staatsverträge des 4. Jahrhunderts v. Christi
Geburt*, 1938.

Roebuck, Carl, *Ionian Trade and Colonization*, 1959.
Ryder, T. T. B., *Koine Eirene: General Peace and Local Independence in Ancient Greece*, 1965.
Accame, Silvio, *La lega ateniese del secolo IV a. C.*, 1941.
Head, B. V., *Historia Numorum*, 2 ed. (*HN²*), 1911.
Gardner, Percy, *A History of Greek Coinage 700–300 B.C.*, 1918.
Seltman, Charles, *Greek Coins*, 2 ed., 1955.
Noe, S. P., *Greek Coin Hoards*, 2 ed., 1937.

HELLENISTIC HISTORY

Niese, Benedictus, *Geschichte der griechischen und makedonischen Staaten seit der Schlacht bei Chaeronea*, 1893–1903.
Cary, M., *A History of the Greek World from 323 to 146 B.C.*, 1932.
Tarn, W. W., *Hellenistic Civilization*, 1927; 3 ed. by Tarn and G. T. Griffith, 1952.
Meyer, Ernst, *Neue peloponnesische Wanderungen*, 1957.
Griffith, G. T., *The Mercenaries of the Hellenistic World*, 1953.
Daux, Georges, *Delphes au IIᵉ et Iᵉʳ siècle depuis l'abaisement de l'Étolie jusqu' à la paix romaine, 191–31 av. J.C.*, 1936.
Walbank, F. W., *Aratos of Sicyon*, 1933.
Walbank, F. W., *Philip V of Macedonia*, 1940.
Walbank, F. W., *A Historical Commentary on Polybius*, vol. i, 1957; vol ii, 1967.
Porter, W. H., *Plutarch's Life of Aratus*, 1937.
Pédech, Paul, *La Méthode historique de Polybe*, 1964.
Lévêque, Pierre, *Pyrrhos*, 1957.
Rostovtzeff, M., *The Social and Economic History of the Hellenistic World*, 1941.

SECTIONAL AND LOCAL HISTORY

Sordi, Marta, *La lega tessala fino ad Alessandro Magno*, 1958.
Kazarow, Gawril, *De foederis Phocensium institutis*, 1899.
Meyer, Eduard, *Theopomps Hellenika*, 1909.
Cloché, Paul, *Thébes de Béotie des origines à la conquète romaine, c.* 1952.
Feyel, Michel, *Polybe et l'histoire de Béotie de IIIᵉ siècle avant notre ère*, 1942.
Roesch, Paul, *Thespies et la confédération béotienne*, 1965.
West, A. B., *The History of the Chalcidic League*, 1918.
Oberhummer, E., *Akarnanien, Ambrakia, Amphilochien, Leukas im Altertum*, 1887.
Woodhouse, W. J., *Aetolia*, 1897.
Flacelière, R., *Les Aitoliens à Delphes*, 1937.
Aymard, André, *Les Assemblées de la confédération achaienne, (ACA)*, 1938.
Aymard, André, *Les Premiers rapports de Rome et de la confédération achaienne*, 1938.
Roebuck, Carl, *The History of Messenia from 369 to 146 B.C.*, 1941.
Nilsson, M. P., *Studien zur Geschichte des alten Epeiros*, from 'Lunds Universitets Årsskrift', 1909.

Klotzsch, Carl, *Epirotische Geschichte bis zum Jahre 280 v. Chr.*, 1911.

Cross, Geoffrey Neale, *Epirus: A Study in Greek Constitutional Development*, 1932.

Franke, P. R., *Alt-Epirus und das Königtum der Molosser*, 1955.

Wallace, W. P., *The Euboean League and its Coinage*, 'Numismatic Notes and Monographs', no. 134, 1956.

Fougères, Gustavus, *De Lyciorum communi*, 1898.

Robert, L., *Études anatoliennes*, 1937.

Hansen, Esther, V., *The Attalids of Pergamum*, 1947.

ROMAN HISTORY AND EXPANSION

De Sanctis, Gaetano, *Storia dei Romani*, vols. iii–iv. i, 1910–23.

Broughton, T. R. S., *The Magistrates of the Roman Republic*, 1951–52, Supplement, 1960.

Frank, Tenney (editor), *An Economic Survey of Ancient Rome*, 1933–40.

Colin, G., *Rome et la Grèce de 200 à 146 avant Jésus Christ*, 1905.

Frank, Tenney, *Roman Imperialism*, 1914.

Holleaux, Maurice, *Rome, la Grèce et les monarchies hellenistiques au IIIe siècle avant J.-C.*, 1921.

Badian, E., *Foreign Clientelae* (264–70 B.C.), 1958.

Badian, E., *Studies in Greek and Roman History*, 1964.

Accame, Silvio, *Il dominio romano in Grecia*, 1946.

Jones, A. H. M., *The Cities of the Eastern Roman Provinces*, 1937.

Magie, David, *Roman Rule in Asia Minor*, 1950.

Oost, S. I., *Roman Policy in Epirus and Acarnania in the Age of the Roman Conquest of Greece*, 1954.

Thiel, J. H., *Studies on the History of Roman Sea Power in Republican Times*, 1946.

Deininger, Jürgen, *Die Provinziallandtage der römischen Kaiserzeit von Augustus bis zum Ende des dritten Jahrhunderts n. Chr.*, 1965.

INSCRIPTIONS

Tod, M. N., *A Selection of Greek Historical Inscriptions*, i (nos. 1–96), 2 ed. 1946; ii (nos. 97–205), 1948.

Pouilloux, Jean, *Choix d' inscriptions grecques, textes, traductions et notes*, 1960.

Michel, Charles, *Recueil d'inscriptions grecques*, 1900.

See also the collections entered in the list of abbreviations under *IGR*, *IG*, *SIG³*, *SEG*, *SGDI*, *TAM*.

For keeping in touch with new discoveries and developments see besides *Supplementum Epigraphicum Graecum* (*SEG*) especially the *Bulletin épigraphique* of the *Revue des études grecques* prepared by J. and L. Robert. The last report of M. N. Tod on 'The Progress of Greek Epigraphy', was that for 1952–53 in *JHS*, lxxv (1955), 122–52.

GENERAL INDEX

(The name Philip without a numeral refers to Philip V. Roman names are listed under the name most frequently used, as T. Quinctius Flamininus under Flamininus. In names of confederacies, Confederacy is abbreviated C.)

Abdera, captured in 170 by Roman fleet, 467.

Acanthus (Andrian colony) located on Singitic Gulf, 390 n. 1; secured by Brasidas, 65 f.; not member of Chalcidic C., 66; appeals to Sparta, 74; in 199 raided by Romans and allies, 390.

Acarnania, Acarnanian C., 89–95, 264–73; geography, 89; dialect, 90; seven generals in early treaty, 93 f.; later single general, 270; federal *synedrion*, 94, 271; primary assembly, 94, with votes counted by cities, 270; special federal law court, 91, 95, 272; customs duties collected by cities, 271; coinage, 269 n. 2, 272; capital Stratus, 91; later successively Leucas and Thyrrheum, 269; involved in rivalry of Athens and Corinth, 121; secures Amphilochia, 129; alliance with Athens, 129; the 426 campaign, 134–8; treaty with Ambracia, 138 f.; secures Leucas, 266 f.; attack on Calydon, 86, 93, 167; alliance with Sparta, 93, 168; not dissolved after King's Peace, 171; 264; member Second Athenian League, 93, 264; joins coalition against Philip II, 265; partial synoecism in 314 by Cassander, 265; treaty of *isopoliteia* with Aetolia, 205, 266 f., 304 f.; divided between Aetolia and Epirus, 267; Confederacy takes over sanctuary at Actium, 269; in 218 join in raid on Thermum, 348; in 200 raid Attica, 386; in 197 have troops at Corinth, 394; campaign of 197 in Acarnania, 394; Leucas detached, 478; leaders summoned to Rome (167), 481.

Achaea, Achaean C., 80–9, 215–40; dialect and mixture of population, 5, 81; expands beyond ethnic boundary, 10, 80; roles and procedure of the council (*boule*) and assembly (*ekklesia*), 223–31; number of meetings of *ekklesia* limited, 224, cf. 450 and 451; *boule* also 86; *gerousia*, 231; two and later one general, 217, 220; *hipparch*, second highest official, 220; *nauarch* (admiral), 220; change in time of election, 220; succession to dead general, 496;

secretary, 86, 217, 221; *damiorgoi*, 86, 221–3, 230, 320, 382; federal courts and foreign judges, 236; jurisdiction of assemblies, 237; lawmaking, 234; *nomographoi*, 231; periodic revision of laws, 235; federal citizenship, 85, 239; cities send 'ambassadors' to federal government, 222, 238; capital Aegium, 84, 87, 239 f., at first Helice, 87; federal finances, 232–4; coinage, 234; foreign affairs, 227–9; Achaeans and colonization of the west, 83; institutions copied by Italiotes, 84, 96; unified the Peloponnesus, 218–20; Achaeans as mercenaries, 144; help Athens control Gulf of Corinth, 126 f.; not ally of Sparta after Thirty Years' Peace, 128; nor after Peace of Nicias, 153; Spartan intervention in Achaea (417), 87, 155; oligarchy established, 88 f.; member of Peloponnesian League, 86, 155; controls Calydon, 86, 156, 167 f.; not dissolved by King's Peace, 171; revival of Confederacy, 216; continuity with old confederacy, 84, 216, expansion, 218 f.; c. 250 shift in political orientation, 218, 306; face Aetolians and Antigonus Gonatas, 307; help from Agis of Sparta, 308; allied with Aetolians against Demetrius II, 305; alliance lasted to 220, 313, 330; peace time intervention at Argos (c. 240), 310; defeat at Phylacia (233?), 312; Arcadian cities turned over to Aetolians, 313; naval defeat by Illyrians, 313; embassy from Rome, 360; declare war on Cleomenes, 315; negotiations with Antigonus Doson, 316 f.; in 225 with Cleomenes, 318; surrender Acrocorinthus to Doson and join Hellenic League (224), 319, 321; efforts to expand in southwest Peloponnesus, 327; meetings, intrigues, and clashes with the Aetolians in 220, 330–35; in 219 mismanage campaign, 339; join Philip in 219–218 winter campaign, 341; election of 218, 345; subsidies voted Philip, 346; summer 218 mobilize rapidly and effectively, 350; in 207 defeat Spartans at Mantinea, 375 f.;

33*

troops sent to Pergamum, 431; in 188 sent to Rome, 445; in 185 accuses Achaeans before Roman ambassadors, 450, 457.

Dium, Chalcidic town on Acte, resists Brasidas, 66; later absorbs Thyssus and joins Chalcidic C., 72.

Dium in Macedonia, raided by Aetolians, 339, cf. 348.

Domitius Ahenobarbus, Cn., in 167 envoy to Achaeans, 479.

Dorimachus, Aetolian leader, 328; plots and operations in 220 before declaration of war, 330–35; elected general for 219–218, 340; raids Dodona, 340; sends Cretan mercenaries to Elis, 347; campaigns of 218 in Thessaly and Aetolia, 347, 349; in 210 commands Aetolian troops at siege of Echinus, 370.

Doris, controlled the upper Cephissus valley, 42; Phocian attack and Spartan intervention (457), 122 f.

Dyme, helps revive Achaean C., 84, 216; member of *synteleia* of Patrae, 221; complains to federal government, 222; withholds contributions to federal treasury, 233, 339; in 217 local levies go into action, 354; sacked in 208 by Sulpicius Galba, 374; in 198 avoided anti-Macedonian vote in Achaean assembly, 230, 382; *c.* 120 leftist revolution suppressed, 503.

Dyrrhachium, in 167 given Illyrian *lemboi* by Romans, 482.

Ebro Treaty, 360.

Ecdelus, philosophic tyrannicide, 309.

Echedemus, Athenian ambassador negotiating Roman-Aetolian armistice, 428.

Echinus in Phthiotic Achaea, occupied by Spartans *c.* 411, 156; in 210 captured by Philip, 370.

Eïon, Chalcidic city attacked by Athenians, 64.

Elatea in Phocis, surrenders to Flamininus, 388; Roman headquarters, (198–194), 398; evacuated by Romans, 405; Elateans banished by Aetolians, 405; given refuge by Stymphalians, 238 f., 406; restored by Glabrio, 406; in 146 Arcadians received into city but dismissed, 496.

Elis, alliance with Argives and others, 150; in 418 withdraw from allied campaign 154; opposes the rise of the Arcadian C., 189 f.; under Aetolian control, 307; rejects offer of Cynaetha, 335; in 220–219 induced by Aetolians to attack

Achaeans, 338, 340; invaded by Philip from the southeast, 341; social conditions at the time, 341 f.; peace negotiations with Philip, 342 f., cf. 345; attacked by Philip from the north, 345; later preparation of defences, 347, 349; in campaigns of 217, 353 f.; listed in treaty as potential ally of Rome, 367; ally of Aetolians, 369; in 209 attacked by Philip and Achaeans, 375; in 192 receives 1,000 troops from Antiochus III, 416; next year enters Achaean C., 422.

Epaminondas, naval policy, 177; brings over Achaeans for a short time, 87; not founder of Megalopolis, 186 n. 1; founder of Messene, 186; attitude towards Arcadians, 192; not to be credited with advance of federalism in Aetolia, 196; gave Boeotia unnatural prominence, 304.

Eperatus, Achaean general 218–217, election, 227, 345; finances confused the last part of his term, 233; his record as general, 346; in command at Dyme, 347; rapid mobilization suggests efficient government, 350.

Ephesus, member fourth-century federation, 101; in 191 base of Seleucid fleet, 426.

Epicrates, Rhodian officer serving with Romans, 429 f.

Epirus, Epirote C., 273–81; tribal subdivisions, 274; for early period see Molossians; *c.* 300 new name (Epirote) adopted, 277; *symmachia* applied to C. is misleading, 277 f.; *c.* 235 kingship abolished, 278; *prostatas* alongside of king, 278; continued under the republic, 279; also official of smaller units, 280; republican head a *stratagos* (or three), 279; primary assembly, 278 f.; law of citizenship, 281; customs duties collected for federal government, 281; importance of country for Roman communications, 387; embassy to Antiochus III at Chalcis, 417; in 188 Epirotes advise Nobilior to attack Ambracia, 437; in 172 induced to station troops in Orestis, 463; revolt of 170–169, 473 f.; punishment, 480; thereafter names of those to go to Rome announced, 481.

Eretria, one of four cities of Euboean C., 98; from 506 to 490 supreme on island, 98; leads revolt against Athens, 99; treaties with Athens and Histiaea, 102; treaty of *isopoliteia* with Ceos, 203; captured by Romans in 198 but soon lost, 392; 196–194 garrisoned by Romans, 397; in 192

TECHNICAL TERMS

(Not all occurrences of the words indexed are listed. For the sake of eventual Greekless readers, all Greek words are transliterated.)

agora, used in Locris for assembly, 51.

aphedriateuontes, Boeotian college of officials, 179.

amicitia (friendship), in Roman foreign policy, 359 f.

apoklesia, city council in Western Locris, 54.

apokletoi, members of Aetolian inner council, 200 f.

apoteleios, commander of local contingent in federal army in Achaea and Lycia, 241, 252.

archairesiake ekklesia, electoral council in Lycian C., 248 f.

archiphylax, head of Lycian federal police, 254.

archon, title for head of federal state, 24, 177, 301.

archos, East Locrian federal official, 52.

archostatai, members of *archairesiake ekklesia*, 248.

asylia, guarantee against arbitrary seizure, 20.

atagia, in Thessaly a period without a *tagos*, 15.

ateleia, exemption from taxation, 20, 277.

boularch, chairman of *boule*, 91, 197.

boule, council both of cities and federal states, *passim*.

chalkaspides, a type of Macedonian infantry, 324.

concilium, for Greek states means primary assembly, 296 f.

consilium, for Greek states means bodies smaller than primary assemblies, 296 f.

damiorgoi, group of magistrates, 86, 187.

dechemeroi spondai, truce terminable on ten days notice, 73 and n. 1; cf. 148, n. 3.

deditio (surrender) used as a form of appeal to Rome, 246, 420.

demokratia, change in meaning so as to cover governments not very democratic, 87, 175.

diodos, right of passage, 144, n. 2.

diolkos, contrivance for taking ships across Isthmus of Corinth, 388.

eisphorai, payments of cities to federal treasury, 233.

ekecheiria dechemeros, truce terminable on ten days notice, 148 n. 3, cf. 73, n. 1.

ekklesia, for Achaean C. as for cities means primary assembly, 223.

enktesis, right granted non-citizens to acquire real property, 56, 75.

eneteria, fee for admission to citizenship, 56.

eparitoi, troops of Arcadian standing army, 188.

epigamia, right of intermarriage, 56, 256.

epimachia, defensive alliance, 141 f.

epistates, Lycian official in charge of foreign judges, 255.

ethnos, tribe, nation, 4, 8.

foedus iniquum, treaty involving the inferiority of one of the two parties, 439 f.

foederi adscripti, peoples included in a treaty contracted by others, 377.

gerousia, in Achaean C. probably the *damiorgoi*, 231; in Lycia under Empire, a club of mature citizens, 262.

hegemon, head of Euboean C., 100; of Hellenic League, 325; Cleomenes demands title from Achaeans, 318.

Hellenotamiai, treasurers of Delian League, xvii.

hierapolos, high priest of temple at Actium, 269.

hieromnemones, members of Amphictionic council, 205.

hipparch, commander of cavalry and at times second highest official in a federal state, 220, 270.

hippeis, not always cavalry, sometimes mounted infantry, 106 f.

hyloros, magistrate in a Thessalian city, warden of forests, 20.

hypogrammateus, undersecretary, 253.

hypophylax, subordinate Lycian police official, 254.

hypostrategos ('subordinate general') high ranking officer, 220 f., 497.

imperator, Livy's rendering of *strategos autokrator*, 201, n. 2.

isopoliteia, exchange of potential citizenship, 202 ff.

kleroi, units in Thessalian military organization, 17.

koine eirene, common or general peace, 169.

koinoboulion, federal *boule* or its quarters, 250.

koinon, corporation, etc., but also federal state or government, 8.

koinopoliteia, federal citizenship, 204.

kyria ekklesia, important session of assembly, 249.

lemboi, light Illyrian ships with crews of some 50 men, 363 and n. 1.

Meris (part), used in names of four Macedonian republics, 297.

metapempta dikasteria (summoned courts), courts manned by foreign judges, 255, n. 2.

mora, unit of Spartan army, 166.

Myrioi (Ten Thousand), Arcadian assembly, 186, 194 f.

nauarch, admiral, 252.

nomia, in Locris existing body of laws, 55.

nomographoi, officials for writing and/or recording laws, 209, 235.

nomothesia, making or revision of laws, 272.

Panaitolika, spring meeting of Aetolian assembly, 199.

pandemei, does not always mean complete total mobilization, 228, n. 1, 331, n. 1.

panegyris, at Actium involved market as well as religious festival, 271.

paraphylax, police official in a Lycian city, 254.

patris, in the Lycian C. means one's ancestral city, 257.

penestai, Thessalian serfs, 14, 105 f.

pentekoste, 2% customs duty, 271.

polis, state, city-state; a term once about to be applied also to a federal state, 280, n. 3.

polites, used for a citizen of a federal state as well as of a city-state, 8 f., 85.

praetor, used by Livy to translate *strategos*, 286.

preiga, council in a city-state of Western Locris, 54.

presbeutai (ambassadors), used also for envoys sent by cities to the federal government of their confederacy, 222, 244.

privatum decretum, irregular decree of the Acarnanian C., 394.

promnamon, in Acarnania chairman of federal council, 270.

prostatas, highest elected official of Epirote tribes, 274 ff.

proxenos, in West Locrian cities official in charge of interests of foreigners, 58.

psephos, voting token, vote; used in indications of representation, 242, 248.

socii navales, allies serving on Roman ships, 370, 425.

somata (bodies), sometimes, but not always, means slaves, 342 and n. 1.

stephanos, wreath or crown, actually donation of money, 441.

strategos, general, often used as title of the head of a confederacy, 188 *et passim*.

strategos autokrator, general with extraordinary authority, 44, 201.

symbola, commercial treaties, 212.

symmachia, alliance, xvii f.; misleading when applied to Epirote C., 277 f.

sympoliteia, federal state or citizenship, xv; also merging of cities, 199; use of term by Polybius, 203.

sympromnamones, colleagues or assistants of the *promnamon*, 270.

synarchia, body of officials in Achaean C., 222.

synedrion, council, frequently of federal states, 198, 297.

synedroi, members of a *synedrion;* Livy equates them with senators, 297.

synkletos, in Achaean C. an extraordinary meeting of council, or assembly, or both, 223 f.

synodos, in Achaean C. meeting of council, or assembly, or both, 223 f.

synteleia, subdivision of Archaean C., 221 and n. 1.

tagos, head of Thessalian C., 14 f., 19; later *tagoi* city officials, 285.

Tarentines, type of cavalry, 344 and n. 1.

telos, subdivision of Aetolian C., 197.

tethmos, statute law in Locris, 55.
tetrads, four subdivisions of Thessaly, 16, 289.
tetrarchs, commanders of the military contingents of the *tetrads*, 16.
thearoi, city officials in Arcadia, 183.
thethmios, the same as *tethmos*.
xenodikai, judges handling cases involving aliens, 55, 57.

PROBLEMS IN LITERARY SOURCES

SOME INSCRIPTIONS DISCUSSED